CONTENTS

VOLUME TWO

184 95

PRINTED IN THE UNITED STATES OF AMERICA

THE SUPREME COURT

IN

UNITED STATES HISTORY

BY

CHARLES WARREN

FORMERLY ASSISTANT ATTORNEY-GENERAL OF THE UNITED STATES
AUTHOR OF "A HISTORY OF THE AMERICAN BAR"

IN THREE VOLUMES

VOLUME TWO

1821–1855

BOSTON

LITTLE, BROWN, AND COMPANY

1924

JOHN MARSHALL
From the portrait by Robert M. Sully.

THE SUPREME COURT
IN UNITED STATES HISTORY

VOLUME TWO

ILLUSTRATIONS

Volume Two

ABBREVIATIONS OF TITLES OF BOOKS FREQUENTLY CITED

[For the purpose of conciseness in the citation of books most frequently quoted, the following abbreviations have been used in the notes.]

J. Q. Adams, Memoirs of John Quincy Adams (1874–1877), edited by Charles Francis Adams, 12 vols.

J. Q. Adams' Writings, The Writings of John Quincy Adams (1913–1915), edited by Worthington Chauncey Ford, 7 vols.

Clay, The Works of Henry Clay (1904), edited by Calvin Colton, Federal edition, 10 vols.

Curtis, The Life and Writings of Benjamin Robbins Curtis, LL.D. (1879), edited by Benjamin R. Curtis, 2 vols.

Hamilton, The Works of Alexander Hamilton (1904), edited by Henry Cabot Lodge, 12 vols.

Hamilton (Lodge's ed.), *The Works of Alexander Hamilton* (1885–1886), edited by Henry Cabot Lodge, 9 vols.

Hamilton (J. C. Hamilton's ed.), *The Works of Alexander Hamilton* (1850–1851), edited by John Church Hamilton, 7 vols.

Iredell, Life and Correspondence of James Iredell (1858), edited by Griffith John McRee, 2 vols.

Jay, The Correspondence and Public Papers of John Jay (1890–1893), edited by Henry Phelps Johnston, 4 vols.

Jefferson, The Works of Thomas Jefferson (1904–1908), edited by Paul Leicester Ford, 12 vols.

Jefferson (A. C. Lipscomb ed.), *The Writings of Thomas Jefferson* (1903–1904), edited by Andrew C. Lipscomb, 20 vols.

Jefferson (H. A. Washington ed.), *The Writings of Thomas Jefferson* (1853–1854), edited by Henry Augustine Washington, 9 vols.

King, The Life and Correspondence of Rufus King (1894–1900), edited by Charles Ray King, 6 vols.

Madison, The Writings of James Madison (1906–1910), edited by Gaillard Hunt, 9 vols.

Madison (1865), *Letters and Other Writings of James Madison* (1865), published by order of Congress, 4 vols.

Marshall, Life of John Marshall (1916–1919), by Albert Jeremiah Beveridge, 4 vols.

Mason, Memoir and Correspondence of Jeremiah Mason (1873), edited by George S. Hillard.

Monroe, The Writings of James Monroe (1898–1903), edited by Stanislaus Murray Hamilton, 7 vols.

Story, Life and Letters of Joseph Story (1851), by William Waldo Story, 2 vols.

Sumner, Memoir and Letters of Charles Sumner (1877–1893), by Edward Lillie Pierce, 4 vols.

Taney, Memoir of Roger Brooke Taney (1872), by Samuel Tyler

Ticknor, Life, Letters and Journals of George Ticknor (1876), 2 vols.

Washington, Writings of George Washington (1834–1837), edited by Jared Sparks, 11 vols.

Washington (Ford's ed.), *Writings of George Washington* (1886–1893), edited by Worthington Chauncey Ford, 14 vols.

Webster, The Writings and Speeches of Daniel Webster (1903), 18 vols.

Wirt, Memoirs of the Life of William Wirt (1849), by John Pendleton Kennedy, 2 vols.

permanency, its *esprit de corps,* its unbounded latitude, its power, all combine to excite apprehension not only for the rights of individuals but for the rights of the States. The infringement of the rights of the States by the Judiciary is more likely to effect a consolidation of the Union than any other excuse or causes which exist." [1]

Especially did the Southern States fear the effect of the judicial doctrine of widely extended Congressional power upon the settlement of two great political issues — slavery and internal improvements. The opinion in the *McCulloch Case* had been delivered at a time when the slavery question had just become a source of vital and violent dissension in the political field. Missouri was seeking to enter the Union as a new State. The North and the East were endeavoring to make its admission conditional upon its agreement to exclude slavery from its borders. The right of Congress to impose such a condition was hotly denied by the representatives of the South. At the very time when Ohio was contesting the power of Congress to charter a bank, the great debate as to the extent of Congressional power over slavery, which finally resulted in the Missouri Compromise, was taking place during the months of January, February and March, 1820. In this hot debate, constant fears were expressed by Southern statesmen lest Marshall's broad views of the "necessary and proper" clause of the Constitution might support Congressional interference with the States on the subject

[1] *National Intelligencer,* Feb. 24, 1820; *Washington Gazette,* Feb. 20, 1821; *Independent Chronicle,* March 3, 1819. For the contrary view, however, see *Columbian Centinel,* Feb. 10, 1819, and an article on *Constitutional Law* by Warren Dutton, in *North Amer. Rev.* (Jan., 1820), X, 115: "This part of the law of the land is daily becoming more interesting, and exerting a wider influence upon the affairs of our country, from the respect that is generally felt for judicial decisions, from the intelligible form in which principles are exhibited, and from the gradual formation of a body of constitutional exposition, which will furnish precedents and analogies to future times."

THE SUPREME COURT
IN UNITED STATES HISTORY

VOLUME TWO

CHAPTER THIRTEEN

VIRGINIA AGAINST THE COURT

1821

DURING the year 1820, while the State of Ohio was pressing the question of State Sovereignty in connection with the Bank issue, Republicans (or Democrats as they were about to be known) both in the North and the South were becoming apprehensive as to the effect of the attitude of the Court upon the powers of the States over other subjects of State concern. The important part which it was likely to play in determining the course of vital political and economic questions was now apparent to all who realized the full scope of the doctrines announced by Marshall in the three great cases in 1819. "The encroachment already made by Judicial legislation on our State-Rights is . . . the first movement in the mighty contest between the States and the Confederacy . . . in which the States must prevail or give up their liberties forever" was the comment of one paper in 1820, referring to the decision in the *Bankruptcy Case*. Another said: "We confess that we look with infinitely more apprehension to the Judiciary than to any other department of the government. Its

THE SUPREME COURT
IN UNITED STATES HISTORY

of slavery. "If there is any one point on which the people of America universally agree," said Senator Barbour, of Virginia, "it is that necessity of restraining the Federal Government within the prescribed limits, to guard against encroachments on the authority of the States and thereby prevent a consolidation which has been universally considered as a synonym with monarchy." Senator Roberts of Pennsylvania said that our political salvation depended on a strict construction of the Constitution, and that "a consolidation of their extended empire must end in the worst kind of despotism." Congressman Holmes of Massachusetts said that the power claimed by Congress to restrict slavery in the new States "is not express, and if given at all it must be constructive. This amplifying power by construction is dangerous, and will, not improbably, effect the eventual destruction of the Constitution. . . . All powers not granted are prohibited, is a maxim to which we cannot too religiously adhere." "This principle of broad construction, this sweeping clause, this strong constitutional interpretation," said Congressman Johnson of Virginia, "has a strong squinting not only at monarchy but at despotism." "Every principle of policy forbids the interference on the part of Congress with the internal policy of the States," said Senator Walker of Georgia. "Collisions between the State and the Federal Government might be productive of the most unhappy consequence, such as no patriot would be willing to see. . . . If Congress persist in the determination to impose the restriction contemplated, I fear there is too much cause to apprehend that consequences fatal to the peace and harmony of this Union will be the inevitable result." [1]

On the other hand, the Federalists of the North were

[1] *16th Cong., 1st Sess.*, Jan. 19, 20, 27, Feb. 1, 4, 9, 1820.

fearful of a narrow construction of the Constitution, restricting the power of Congress over slavery in the Territories; for they considered that the prevalence of such a doctrine would place the future control of the United States in the hands of the Slave States of the South. "I feel much concern for the issue," wrote Rufus King, "which, if decided against us, settles forever the dominion of the Union. Not only the Presidency, but the Supreme Judiciary, at least a majority of its members, will forever hereafter come from the Slave region. This is as fully understood, and almost avowed, as any future purpose." [1] Another subject was also prominently to the fore in Congress at this period, which was productive of sectional division almost equal to that caused by the slavery question, and the settlement of which might also depend upon judicial decision. This was the much mooted question as to the power of Congress to appropriate money for internal improvements — canals and roads. On few subjects had there been more bitter discussion, and the division between its opponents and its advocates followed the lines of the strict or the broad construction of the Constitution. Thus the final settlement of three absorbing and important questions — the existence and powers of the Bank of the United States, the extension of slavery in the new States and the development of National internal improvements — all were felt to depend largely upon the future trend of the Supreme Court of the United States. The antagonism, therefore, to that Court was not based on dogmatic grounds or on any abstract adherence to a particular theory of constitutional law, but on a present fear of the effect of the application of a broad construction of the Constitution to the absorbing problems of the day.

[1] *King*, VI, letter to J. A. King, Feb. 6, 1820.

Three statesmen of Virginia led the attempt to awaken the people to the crisis which impended. In 1820, John Taylor of Virginia issued his famous *Construction Construed and Constitution Vindicated*, which with his *New Views of the Constitution* published in 1823, constituted for many years the political Bible of the extreme State-Rights school. "The Missouri question is probably not yet closed; the principle on which it turns is certainly not settled. Further attempts are to be made to wrest from the new States about to enter into the American Confederacy the power of regulating their own concerns. The tariff question is again to be agitated. . . . The usurpation of a Federal power over roads and canals is again to be attempted and again to be reprobated. . . . That charter (of the Bank) . . . has been justified by the Supreme Court, on principles so bold and alarming, that no man who loves the Constitution can fold his arms in apathy . . . principles calculated to give the tone to an acquiescent people, to change the whole face of our Government, and to generate a thousand measures which the framers of the Constitution never anticipated. . . . The period borrows new gloom from the apathy which seems to reign over so many of our sister States. The very sound of State-Rights is scarcely ever heard among them." In his *Tyranny Unmasked*, in 1822, Taylor denounced the judicial power, and set forth the doctrine that "whenever the Constitution operates upon collisions between individuals, it is to be construed by the Court; but when it operates upon collision between political departments, it is not to be construed by the Court."

Jefferson, from 1819 to 1823, issued constant warnings against the consolidating tendency of the Court and of Congress, which had long been to him a source of apprehension.[1] He had termed the Missouri question "the most portentous one which ever yet threatened the Union"; and had said: "This momentous question, like a firebell in the night, awakened and filled me with terror. I considered it at once as the knell of our Union." "The Judiciary of the United States," he wrote, in 1820, "is the subtle corps of sappers and miners constantly working underground to undermine the foundations of our confederated fabric. They are construing our Constitution from a coördination of a general and special government to a general and supreme one alone." "The steady tenor of the Courts of the United States," he wrote again, "is to break down the constitutional barriers between the coördinate powers of the States and the Union." "I am sensible of the inroads daily making by the Federal into the jurisdiction of its coördinate associates, the State governments," he wrote early in 1821. "The Legislative and Executive branches may sometimes err, but elections and dependence will bring them to rights. The Judiciary branch is the instrument which, working like gravity, without intermission, is to press us at last into one consolidated mass. Against this, I know no one who, equally with Judge Roane himself, possesses the power and the courage to make resistance; and to him I look, and have long looked, as our strongest bulwark. If Congress fails to shield the States from dangers so palpable and imminent, the States must shield themselves, and meet the invader foot to foot." To Roane himself, he wrote, March 9, 1821: "The great object of my fear is the Federal Judiciary. That body like gravity, ever acting, with noiseless foot, and unalarming advance, gaining ground step by step, and holding what

---

[1] *Jefferson*, XII, letters to Nelson Feb. 7, 1820, to Holmes April 22, 1820, to Ritchie, Dec. 25, 1820, to Gallatin, Dec. 26, 1820; to Thweat, Jan. 19, 1821.

it gains, is ingulphing insidiously the special governments into the jaws of that which feeds them. . . .
Let the eye of vigilance never be closed." And typical
of the fears of the State-Rights advocates was an article, just at this time in the *Washington Gazette*, which
said: "We have too often had occasion to regret the
undefined power of the Judiciary of the United States
and the disposition manifested by the Judges to extend
their jurisdiction, not only to clashing and conflicting
with the Judiciary of the States, but to legislating over
the Legislatures of the various States." [1]

It was amid apprehensions so expressed by Jefferson
and by many other statesmen, politicians and newspapers of the South and West that the great case of
Cohens v. *Virginia*, 6 Wheat. 264, came before the Court
at the 1821 Term, involving what was claimed by the
State of Virginia to be an immense extension of Federal power and an infraction of the State sovereignty.
Cohens had been prosecuted and found guilty in a Virginia State Court for selling a lottery ticket in Virginia,
in violation of the State law forbidding such sale.
The lottery was organized by the City of Washington
in the District of Columbia, under a statute of Congress authorizing the city to institute lotteries. On appealing to the Supreme Court of the United States by
writ of error to the Virginia Court, Cohens was met by
the contentions on the part of the State — first, that the
Court had no jurisdiction on a writ of error to a State
Court in a State criminal prosecution; second, that
Congress had no power to authorize a lottery to sell
tickets in a State whose law forbade such sale. The
attempted exercise of appellate jurisdiction by the
Court in this case had aroused high indignation in Virginia; and the Legislature had passed resolves denying

[1] *Washington Gazette*, Feb. 20, 1821.

the existence of any such jurisdiction, and saying that the Court had "no rightful authority under the Constitution to examine and correct the judgment for which the Commonwealth has been 'cited and admonished to be and appear at the Supreme Court of the United States', and that the General Assembly do hereby enter their most solemn protest against the jurisdiction of that Court over the matter." [1] It further resolved that the counsel who were to represent the State before the Court "be limited (in sustaining the rights of the State and in the discharge of the duties required of them) alone to the question of jurisdiction; and if the jurisdiction of the Court should be sustained, that they will consider their duties at an end." [2] The *Richmond Enquirer* had vigorously indorsed this resolution, saying that it presented "one of the most important questions in the whole range of the Judiciary Department. The principle which it asserts seems to be essential to the existence and preservation of State-Rights, and the true foundation of our political system."

In accordance with instructions, the counsel for the State, Philip P. Barbour (who later became a Judge of the Court), and Alexander Smythe, on February 19, 20, 1821, when the case came before the Court on a motion to dismiss the writ of error, confined their arguments solely to the question of the right of the Court to entertain jurisdiction. "The power to revise decisions of the State Courts was not expressly given by the Constitution," said Smythe, "and can it be believed that it was meant that the greatest, the most consolidating of all the powers of the Government should pass by an unnecessary implication?" And in closing his argument, Smythe rather truculently warned the Court

---

[1] *Niles Register*, XX, 118, 129; *State Documents on Federal Relations* (1911), by Herman V. Ames.

[2] *Niles Register*, XIX, 211, 340, 417, Dec. 2, 1820, Jan. 20, Feb. 24, 1821.

of the desirability of preventing "clashing of Federal and State powers." "Let each operate within their respective spheres," he said, "and let each be confined to their assigned limits. We are all bound to support the Constitution. How will that be best effected? Not by claiming and exercising unacknowledged power. The strength thus obtained will prove pernicious. The confidence of the people constitutes the real strength of this government. Nothing can so much endanger it as exciting the hostility of the State governments. With them it is, to determine how long this government shall endure." For the plaintiff in error, the full power of the Court was splendidly upheld by David B. Ogden and in a masterful argument by William Pinkney: "This particular portion of the judicial power of the Union is indispensably necessary to the existence of the Union. The judicial control of the Union over State encroachments and usurpations was indispensable to the sovereignty of the Constitution — to its integrity — to its very existence. Take it away, and the Union becomes again a false and foolish confidence — a delusion and a mockery!" Supervisory power of the Federal Supreme Court, he said, was especially necessary in criminal cases in the State Courts, for it is in such cases "the sovereignty of the State — State pride — State interests — are here in paramount vigor, as inducements to error; and judicial usurpation is countenanced by legislative support and popular prejudice." [1]

Two weeks after the argument, on March 3, 1821,

---

[1] While the case was pending the *Washington Gazette*, Feb. 20, 1821, a strong Republican paper, printed an article on State-Rights, commenting on the *Cohens Case* and resolutions in Congress relating to it; and evidently fearing prosecution for contempt, the editor added at the end the following note: "We had the above in type before we recollected that the case alluded to was actually before the Supreme Court. Its insertion, therefore, is intended, not as a hint to that Tribunal, on which the press has no influence, but solely as an article worthy of attention from the American public at large."

Chief Justice Marshall gave the opinion of the Court.[1] "The questions presented," he said, "are of great magnitude, and may be truly said vitally to affect the Union." The counsel for the State contend, he continued, that the Court is excluded from inquiry whether the laws and Constitution of the United States have been violated by the judgment of a State Court. "They maintain that the Nation does not possess a department capable of restraining peaceably, and by authority of law, any attempts which may be made, by a part, against the legitimate powers of the whole; and that the Government is reduced to the alternative of submitting to such attempts, or of resisting them by force." "If such be the Constitution," the Chief Justice determinedly said, "it is the duty of the Court to bow with respectful submission to its provisions. If such be not the Constitution, it is equally the duty of this Court to say so, and to perform that task which the American people have assigned to the Judicial Department." Thereupon, in an opinion which became one of the chief bulwarks of American unity, the Court held that its jurisdiction under the Constitution, in all criminal cases arising in State Courts in which a Federal question was involved, was undeniable and supreme. This decision, supplementing that in *Martin* v. *Hunter*, five years before, forever settled, so far as the Court was concerned, the validity of its appellate jurisdiction over State Courts under the provisions of the Judiciary Act. Having thus denied Virginia's contention that it had no jurisdiction on the writ of error, the Court proceeded to determine the merits of the decision made by the Virginia Court. The points involved were twofold; first, whether the Act of Congress, properly con-

[1] Judge Story wrote, Feb. 28, 1821: "We have had some very interesting constitutional questions argued at this Term. The only one which has yet excited much attention is one from Virginia — it is not yet decided." *Story*, I, 397.

strued, authorized the sale of lottery tickets in States where such sale was forbidden by State law; second, whether Congress had any constitutional power to authorize such sale. Counsel for Virginia declining to take part in the argument on the merits, and it appearing that a decision of the questions would affect various other cases already arisen or about to occur in other States, the Court "deemed it necessary to hear an argument, before it pronounced judgment on the merits." On March 2, Daniel Webster argued in denial of the power of Congress and against the interpretation of the statute contended for by Cohens, arguing not as counsel employed by Virginia "but in consequence of his being counsel for the State of New York in a similar case." [1] Cohens' side was argued by David B. Ogden and William Wirt. On Monday, March 5, three days after the argument, the Court decided the case on the merits in favor of the State of Virginia, holding that Congress did not intend to authorize sale of tickets in Virginia, even if it had the power so to do.[2] The Court found it unnecessary to decide as to the power of Congress, though Marshall uttered several *dicta* which implied the existence of such a power in cases involving functions of a National nature. Thus, Virginia, though losing the case on the jurisdictional question, won it on the merits — "a singular result of their assuming an unexampled latitude

[1] See *National Intelligencer*, March 23, 1821.

[2] It is interesting to note that lotteries were involved in several cases about this time. In *Brent* v. *Davis*, 10 Wheat. 395, in 1825, involving another City of Washington lottery, the Court intimated its views of the general subject saying: "However questionable may be the policy of tolerating lotteries, there can be no question respecting the policy of removing, as far as possible, from those who are concerned in them, all temptation to fraud." In *Clarke* v. *City of Washington*, 12 Wheat. 40, in 1827, argued by Webster, Wirt and Walter Jones against Thomas Swann, the city was held liable to pay $150,000 in prizes — a decision which practically put an end to this method of paying for public improvements in Washington. See *National Intelligencer*, Jan. 31, Feb. 8, 1827; *United States Telegraph*, Feb. 5, 1827; *Niles Register*, XXVIII, 148. See also other lottery cases, *Corporation of Washington* v. *Young*, 10 Wheat. 406; *Shankland* v. *Washington*, 5 Pet. 390.

of jurisdiction," said the *Washington Gazette*. "This course, which we do not ascribe to artifice, seems the more dangerous, as it tends to lull the States into acquiescence with their assumptions."[1]

To the Republicans, the decision as to jurisdiction and the language of Marshall's opinion came now as a climax to the continual march of encroachment by the Court on the sovereignty of the States, and they seriously believed that the fundamental doctrines on which the Union was based were in grave peril of destruction.[2] "We had no manner of doubt as to the result," said *Niles Register*, "that the State sovereignty would be taught to bow to the Judiciary of the United States. So we go. It seems as if almost everything that occurs had for its tendency that which every reflecting man deprecates." The *Richmond Enquirer* spoke of the opinion, "so important in its consequences and so obnoxious in its doctrines", and said that "the very title of the case is enough to stir one's blood." It feared that "the Judiciary power, with a foot as noiseless as time and a spirit as greedy as the grave, is sweeping to their destruction the rights of the States. . . . These encroachments have increased, are increasing and ought to be diminished"; and it advocated a repeal of the fatal Section of the Judiciary Act as "the most advisable and constitutional remedy for the evil." A leading Ohio paper spoke of

[1] *Washington Gazette*, March 22, 23, 24, 1821; *National Intelligencer*, March 15, 1821; *Liberty Hall and Cincinnati Gazette*, March 21, 1821. The *Norfolk* (Va.) *Herald* said, March 31, 1821: "The high importance of the decision . . . makes it our duty to publish it in full. . . . We can assure our readers, however, that we could give them nothing better." The decision in Virginia's favor was lamented by those who favored lotteries, and the following singular criticism appeared in a letter in the *National Intelligencer*, March 14, 1821, deploring the decision: "However much this opinion of the learned Judge may accord with justice, it cannot but be regretted by every liberal and unprejudiced man. A great check is thus given to the improvement of the city," which, it was said, depended on its lotteries.

[2] *Niles Register*, XX, March 17, 1821; *Richmond Enquirer*, March 23, April 6, 1821.

"the alarming progress of the Supreme Court in subverting the Federalist principles of the Constitution and
introducing on their ruins a mighty consolidated empire
fitted for the sceptre of a great monarch"; and it continued: "That the whole tenor of their decisions, when
State-Rights have been involved, have had a direct
tendency to reduce our governors to the condition of
mere provincial satraps, and that a silent acquiescence
in these decisions will bring us to this lamentable result, is to us as clear as mathematical demonstration."
Letters in many papers said that: " The Judges are pro-
gressively widening the sphere of their duties so as to
swallow up almost every other influence in the Nation
in that of the General Government.   The cases of the
*Town of Pawlett, Dartmouth College, Maryland and Mc-
Culloch*, and *Cohens and Virginia*, have each developed
some new principle of Federal jurisdiction, not before
supposed to exist.   The principle of each of these cases,
it may be said, sprung upon the States, without an opportunity afforded them to consider and combat the
doctrines involved.   They have not originated in public legislative provisions, publicly enacted, upon a
theatre where public opinion can be felt, but have
started up as from a lurking place, concealed under
enactments made, it is conceived, for very different purposes.   Among the most serious objections that I feel
to the principles of these cases is that each asserts a
power in the government of the Union to cherish and
protect a different species of corporation.   I do not
believe that the framers of the Constitution intended to
commit to the National Government the protection of
corporate towns, colleges, banks or lottery offices.   It
is, nevertheless, very evident that, by attaching to the
General Government all these establishments, its power
and influence is greatly strengthened."   "Well indeed

may our wisest and best men deprecate the strides that are made, and have been making, towards cleaving down the State Sovereignties, and erecting upon their ruins a consolidated oligarchy." [1]

The most effective and vigorous attacks upon the Cohens decision again came naturally from Virginia, and particularly from Judge Spencer Roane of the Court of Appeals. Roane had first tried to persuade James Madison to write a public criticism of the case; but the latter declined to undertake the task of "unravelling the argument applied by the Court." [2] Though concurring with Roane in his fear of the consolidating tendency of the Court, Madison disagreed with his advocacy of a repeal of the appellate power of that Court from State Courts. While the latitude of jurisdiction assumed was to be regretted, he wrote to Roane, nevertheless it was "less formidable to the reserved sovereignty of the States than the latitude of power which it has assigned to the National Legislature." But that the Supreme Court must be the final arbiter of questions arising in the States under the Federal Constitution and laws, Madison felt almost as strongly as Marshall himself. "The Gordian knot of the Constitution seems to be in the problem of collision between the Federal and State powers, especially as eventually exercised by their respective tribunals. If the knot cannot be untied by the text of the Constitution, it ought not certainly to be cut by any political Alexander," he wrote, and while the Constitution should be

---

[1] *Liberty Hall and Cincinnati Gazette*, April 16, 1821; later June 18, 1821, in a six-column article on the case, it said that the decisions of the Court had "given alarm. . . . Consolidation of these States is the signal of the loss of their liberties." Letters from "Hampden" in *Western Herald*, Oct. 6 to Nov. 24, 1821.

[2] *Madison*, IX, letters to Spencer Roane, May 6, June 29, 1821. For effective criticism of the doctrines of the *Cohens Case*, see *New Views of the Constitution* (1823), by John Taylor; see also *Construction Construed* (1820), by John Taylor; and John Taylor correspondence in *John P. Branch Historical Papers* (June, 1908).

construed as far as possible so as "to obviate the
dilemma of a judicial rencounter or a mutual paralysis",
nevertheless, "on the abstract question whether the
Federal or the State decision ought to prevail, the
sounder policy would yield to the claims of the former." [1] Roane, himself, accordingly, undertook the
onslaught on the *Cohens Case* by two series of letters
published in the *Washington Gazette* under the name of
"Hampden", and in the *Richmond Enquirer* under the
name of "Algernon Sidney", in April, May and June,
1821.[2] "A most monstrous and unexampled decision",
he termed it.   "It can only be accounted for from that

[1] Writing to Joseph G. Cabell, eight years later, Sept. 7, 1829, Madison referred
to his correspondence with Roane, and said: "A political system that does not
provide for a peaceable and effectual decision of all controversies arising among the
parties is not a Government, but a mere Treaty between independent nations,
without any resort for terminating disputes but negotiations, and that failing, the
sword. . . . In the years 1819 and 1821, I had a very cordial correspondence with
the author of Hampden and Algernon Sidney. . . . I was induced in my last
letter to touch on the necessity of a definitive power on questions between the U. S.
and the individual States, and the necessity of its being lodged in the former, where
alone it could preserve the essential uniformity."

Writing to Thomas Jefferson, June 27, 1823, Madison said: "Believing as I
do, that the General Convention regarded a provision within the Constitution for
deciding in a peaceable and regular mode all cases arising in the course of its operation, as essential to an adequate system of government; that it intended the authority vested in the Judicial Department as a final resort in relation to the States
for cases resulting to it in the exercise of its functions . . . and that this intention
is expressed by the Articles declaring that the Federal Constitution and laws shall
be the supreme law of the land and that the Judicial Power of the United States
shall extend to all cases arising under them; believing, moreover, that this was the
prevailing view of the subject when the Constitution was adopted, and put into
execution; that it has so continued through the long period which has elapsed, and
that even at this time an appeal to a National decision would prove that no general
change has taken place: thus, believing, I have never yielded my original opinion
indicated in the *Federalist*, No. 39, to the ingenious reasonings of Col. Taylor against
this construction of the Constitution." *Madison*, IX.

[2] See letters of Algernon Sidney in *Richmond Enquirer*, May 25, 29, June 1, 5,
8, 18, 21, republished in many newspapers of the day, and recently in *John P. Branch
Historical Papers* (June, 1906).   *Niles Register* said July 7, 1821 :) "The decision
. . . still claims the attention of some of our ablest writers, and the correctness of
it is contested with a fine display of talents and profound reasoning by 'Algernon
Sidney' in the *Richmond Enquirer* and 'Hampden' in the *Washington City Gazette* —
to which we refer those who are not already satisfied on the subject.   For ourselves,
though not exactly prepared to submit, it seems as if it were required that all who
do not subscribe to their belief in the infallibility of that Court are in danger of
political excommunication."

love of power which all history informs us infects and
corrupts all who possess it, and from which even the
upright and eminent Judges are not exempt"; and he
referred to the Court's extravagant pretensions" and
"zenith of despotic power." He advocated a repeal of
the Twenty-Fifth Section, which, he said, showed an
"unwarrantable jealousy of the State Judiciaries and
finds nothing to warrant it in the Constitution." These
series of articles were republished in full in many Southern and Western newspapers and produced a profound
effect upon the community.[1] Another virulent set of
letters appeared in the *Richmond Enquirer* in May, June
and July, 1821, by a writer under the pen name of
"Somers", attacking the Court and its alleged political
prejudice and bias and the ascendancy of the Chief
Justice.[2] "The opinion must excite alarm in the mind
of every man who feels any attachment to the independence of the States," he declared. "There never was
an opinion which contained as many principles of
vital importance to the chartered rights of a free people.
The fears of some of our wisest statesmen, so loudly
expressed at the adoption of the Constitution, are more
fully realized; and consolidation with all its terrors
comes forth under the high sanction of the Supreme
Judiciary. . . . A death blow has been aimed at the
very existence of the States. . . . If the independence
of the States is anything but a name, a revolution has
been effected in our country, and we no longer enjoy
that Constitution which our fathers have given us, — a
revolution not the less to be dreaded because it is accomplished without the noise of arms, or because it

---

[1] See the "Hampden" series from the *Washington Gazette*, republished in full
by the *Western Herald* in Ohio, Oct. 6, 13, 20, 27, Nov. 3, 9, 17, 24, 1821 (the
editor stating erroneously that the letters were written "by a plain and practical
Republican farmer residing in the State of Ohio").

[2] See *Richmond Enquirer*, May 15, 22, June 1, 12, 19, 29, July 13, 1821.

approaches us in the insidious shape of a construction, and not in the avowed forms of usurpation. Let us consider this as a salutary warning of what they are to expect from the *impartial* tribunal of a Federal Court. . . . The Supreme Court, by the latitude of construction in which they have indulged, have rendered the Constitution the sport of legal ingenuity. No one measure has made so alarming a breach in our political institutions as this opinion." [1] Jefferson wrote to Roane, suggesting the publication of his letters in pamphlet form, and stating that he would then send them to friends in the different States, "in the hope of exciting others to attend to this case, whose stepping forward in opposition would be more auspicious than for Virginia to do it. I should expect that New York, Ohio, and perhaps Maryland might agree to bring it forward, and the two former being Anti-Missourians might recommend it to that party." [2] Writing to Nathaniel Macon, October 20, 1821, Jefferson continued to impress his views of the dangerous tendency of the Court: "Our Government is now taking so steady a course as to show by what road it will pass to destruction, to wit, by consolidation first, and then corruption, its necessary consequence. The engine of consolidation will be the Federal Judiciary, the two other branches the corrupted and corrupting instruments." To James Pleasants, he wrote, December 26, as to the "difficult task in curbing the Judiciary in their enterprises on the Constitution." After considering various other remedies, he said that a more immediate effect could be produced by a "joint protestation of both Houses of Congress that the doc-

[1] Echoes of these attacks were also heard in a few places in the Northern States, more especially in New York, where DeWitt Clinton supported the view taken by Virginia; see *Chief Justice Marshall and Virginia*, by William W. Dodd, *Amer. Hist. Rev.* (1906), XII.

[2] *Roane Correspondence*, in *John P. Branch Historical Papers* (June, 1905), letter of Jefferson to Roane, June 25, 1821.

trines of the Judges in the case of Cohens, adjudging a
State amenable to their tribunal, and that Congress can
authorize a corporation of the District of Columbia to
pass any Act which shall have the force of law within
a State, are contrary to the provisions of the Constitution of the United States.   This would be effectual; as
with such an avowal of Congress, no State would permit
such a sentence to be carried into execution within its
limits." [1]   Of the methods suggested by Jefferson for
the reform of the Court and its conduct, a description
will be given in a subsequent chapter.   Neither Jefferson's pronounced views nor his proposed remedies
seemed, however, sufficiently drastic to Roane, the
more radical.   "The career of the High Court must be
stopped or the liberties of our country are annihilated,"
he wrote in December, but "Jefferson and Madison
hang back too much in this great crisis.   Jefferson at
least ought to do, in regard to republicanism and
republicans, what one of the French literati did in regard
to the French language.   Being on his deathbed and
surrounded by friends, one of them sinned against the
purity of that language, whereupon the sick man cor-
rected him with great energy.   One of his friends seeming surprised that he should do this, under his extreme
situation, he replied with increased energy, that he
would defend the purity of the French language with
his last gasp, and instantly expired." [2]   In Roane's

[1] To Archibald Thweat, he wrote, Dec. 24, 1821, referring to his previous letter
to William C. Jarvis, of Sept. 28, 1820, "in which letter I formally combatted his
heretical doctrine that the Judiciary is the ultimate expounder and arbiter of all
constitutional questions."   See also letter of Jarvis to Jefferson, Oct. 16, 1820,
Jefferson Papers, Mass. Hist. Soc. Coll.   And letter of Jefferson to John Taylor,
Feb. 14, 1821, *ibid.*, stating that Taylor's book on the Constitution "pulverizes
the Judges on bank taxation and of the 5 lawyers on lotteries.   This last act of ve-
nality (for it cannot be of judgment) makes me ashamed that I was ever a lawyer."

[2] *Roane Correspondence*, in *John P. Branch Historical Papers* (June, 1905), letters
to Archibald Thweat, Dec. 11, 24, 1821.   Roane wrote previously to Thweat,
Dec. 11, 1821: "The Governor's patriotic message on the subject of the Supreme
Court has been very well received by the republicans here, in consequence of the

view, the State of Virginia itself should act and should advocate Constitutional Amendments to curb, if not abolish, the Court. This, however, was farther than Virginia was willing to go; and though resolutions were introduced advocating these radical measures, the Virginia Legislature finally decided to take no action in the matter.[1]

Meanwhile, the Court found many defenders in the press at the North, amongst the ablest of whom was Henry Wheaton of New York, who wrote: "Very able and professional men are satisfied that the whole argument against the jurisdiction of the Supreme Court has been completely demolished in the opinion delivered by Chief Justice Marshall . . . and certainly it bears the strongest marks of his acute and enlarged mind, which when it applies itself to the interpretation of the fundamental law, soars above the ordinary element of a Judge and technical lawyer and displays the wisdom and skill of a great law-giver."[2] In the South as well, the

public mind having been somewhat prepared on the subject. But such is the apathy of the times, and the dearth of talents in the Legislature, that I doubt whether anything will be done by that body. Certainly not, I expect, unless they should be aided by some of our veteran statesmen.

[1] There was a difference of opinion "as to the expediency of a remonstrance at that time, the general mind of the State being then under extraordinary excitement by the Missouri question." . . . "But this case is not dead, it only sleepeth," wrote Jefferson to Judge William Johnson, June 12, 1823; and he further said that Roane's Algernon Sidney letters "appeared to me to pulverize every word which had been delivered by Judge Marshall of the extra-judicial part of his opinion; and all was extra-judicial except the decision that the Act of Congress had not purported to give to the corporation of Washington the authority claimed by their lottery law of controlling the laws of the States within the States themselves. The practice of Judge Marshall of travelling out of his case to prescribe what the law would be in a moot case not before the Court is very irregular and very censurable. . . . The States supposed by their Tenth Amendment, they had secured themselves against constructive powers. They were not lessoned yet by *Cohens Case,* nor aware of the slipperiness of the eels of the law." The *New York Evening Post,* Feb. 14, 1822, quoted the *New York American* as to resolutions pending in the Virginia Legislature on the *Cohens Case:* "They amount to nothing less than a serious proposition to dissolve the Republic, to introduce anarchy in the place of the beautiful order that is now established."

[2] *New York American,* May 8, 1821; *Southern Patriot,* March 31, 1821. A series of letters under the name of "Fletcher of Saltoun", in the *Richmond Enquirer,*

opinion was eloquently supported, notably by the
Southern Patriot in Charleston, which said that : "Such
illustrations of the true theory and intention of the
Constitution are of the highest public utility. They
reconcile the people to the exercise of a power which
they are apt to view with a spirit of jealousy. . . .
That branch of the opinion of the Court which regards
the question of jurisdiction presents one of the best
connected and most vigorous constitutional arguments
that we have seen ;" and a week later, it commented on
the jealousy of the Court by Virginia as, "not a little
remarkable", and said that that State seemed unnecessarily more sensitive on her rights than the rest of the
States, that "consolidation was a chimera that haunted
the imagination of those unfriendly to the Constitution
at the period of its adoption", that no part of State
sovereignty had ever yet been lost and that only pretensions destructive of the integrity of Federal authority
had been repressed. Very wisely, it pointed out that
the practice of disputing repeatedly the decisions of the
Court had the effect to diminish respect for it.

The criticisms launched against his opinion were
hotly resented by Chief Justice Marshall, who wrote
to Judge Story that : "The opinion of the Supreme
Court in the *Lottery Case* has been assaulted with a
degree of virulence transcending what has appeared
on any former occasion . . . but I think for coarseness and malignity of invention, Algernon Sidney surpasses all party writers who have ever made pretensions to any decency of character. There is on this
subject no such thing as a free press in Virginia, and
of consequence the calumnies and misrepresentations

June 22, 26, July 3, 6, 1821, assailed this *New York American* article, stating : "It
is not the least alarming symptom of these tranquil times that a judicial decision
which has struck a vital blow at the independence of the States has, by some, been
received with adulation, and by others submitted to as oracular."

of this gentleman will remain uncontradicted and will by many be believed to be true. He will be supposed to be the champion of State-Rights, instead of being what he really is, the champion of dismemberment." Later, Marshall wrote to Story, saying: "I send you the papers containing the essays of Algernon Sidney. Their coarseness and malignity would designate the author if he was not avowed. The argument, if it may be called one, is, I think, as weak as its language is violent and prolix. . . . In support of the sound principles of the Constitution and of the Union of the States, not a pen is drawn. In Virginia, the tendency of things verges rapidly to the destruction of the government, and the reëstablishment of a league of sovereign States. I look elsewhere for safety." [1] The situation, Marshall rightly attributed largely to the influence of Thomas Jefferson, and he expressed his personal views of the latter with some acerbity: "For Mr. Jefferson's opinion as respects this department, it is not difficult to assign the cause. He is among the most ambitious, and I suspect among the most unforgiving of men. His great power is over the mass of the people, and this power is chiefly acquired by professions of democracy. Every check on the wild impulse of the moment is a check on his own power, and he is unfriendly to the source from which it flows. He looks, of course, with ill will at an independent Judiciary. That in a free country with a written Constitution any intelligent man should wish a dependent Judiciary, or should think that the Constitution is not a law for the Court as well as the Legislature, would astonish me if I had not learnt from observation

[1] See letters of June 15, July 13, Sept. 18, 1821, in *Mass. Hist. Soc. Proc., 2d Series,* XIV.

that with many men the judgment is completely con-
trouled by the passions. The case of the mandamus
may be the cloak, but the batture is recollected with
still more resentment." On September 18, having
heard that Hall, the editor of the *American Law Journal*, had been requested to publish the "Sidney"
letters, Marshall wrote to Story, inferring that Jefferson was the instigator of such republication, and
stating that Jefferson's "settled hostility to the Judicial Department will show itself in that and in every
other form which he believes will conduce to its object", [1] and after giving his views as to the course
the editor should pursue, Marshall concluded by
prophesying that an attempt would be made in Congress to repeal the obnoxious Twenty-Fifth Section:
"A deep design to convert our government into a
mere league of States has taken strong hold of a powerful and violent party in Virginia. The attack upon
the Judiciary is in fact an attack upon the Union.
The Judicial Department is well understood to be
that through which the government may be attacked
most successfully, because it is without patronage,
and of course without power. And it is equally well
understood that every subtraction from its jurisdiction is a vital wound to the government itself. The
attack upon it, therefore, is a masked battery aimed
at the government itself. The whole attack, if not
originating with Mr. Jefferson, is obviously approved
and guided by him. It is therefore formidable in

[1] This gentleman "has several motives; and it is not among the weakest that
the department would never lend itself as a tool to work for his political power.
The Batture will never be forgotten. Indeed, there is some reason to believe that
the essays written against the Supreme Court were, in a degree at least, stimulated
by this gentleman, and that although the coarseness of the language belongs
exclusively to the author, its acerbity has been increased by his communications
with the great Lama of the mountains. He may therefore feel himself in some
measure required to obtain its republication in some place of distinction."

other States as well as in this, and it behooves the friends of the Union to be more on the alert than they have been. An effort will certainly be made to repeal the 25th Sec. of the Judicial Act."

That Marshall's apprehensions of a move in Congress against the Court were amply justified was seen, when, in the following winter session of 1821–1822, there began a series of Congressional attacks upon the Court's powers and jurisdiction which continued for ten years (a full description of which is given in a later chapter). The Court itself, however, was not deterred from adhering to its determined stand in behalf of the supremacy of the National law, in spite of the increasing evidence of State opposition to the Judiciary; and it gave another example of its Nationalistic policy, when, in *McClung* v. *Silliman*, 6 Wheat. 598, decided only eleven days after the *Cohens Case*, it denied the right of a State Court to issue a writ of mandamus to a Federal official (the Register of the Government Land Office). This case again evoked criticism, due to the language of Judge Johnson (himself a Republican) in the opening words of his opinion: "This case presents no ordinary group of legal questions. They present a striking specimen of the involutions which ingenuity may cast about legal rights, and an instance of the growing pretensions of some of the State Courts over the exercise of the powers of the General Government." Referring to this comment, a writer in the *Richmond Enquirer* sarcastically asked a few months later: "After the Supreme Court of the United States had asserted through the lips of the Chief Justice its right of jurisdiction over a State in the case of *Cohens* v. *The State of Virginia* — which of the Judges was it who, on *another* occasion, spoke with a sort of sneer of *that* case

being a new evidence of the growing pretensions of
these State Governments? Was this Judge one of
those who formerly passed for a Republican? Was he
raised to the Bench by Thomas Jefferson on account
of his reputed attachment to the principles of '98
and '99? Was it for him to venture this contemp-
tuous kick at the 'sick lion'?"[1]

An echo of the Cohens decision was heard in Congress, the next year, when a seemingly harmless bill
to incorporate the United States Naval Fraternal
Association, for relief of families of deceased naval
officers, was defeated, through fear that the Supreme
Court would construe too broadly the power of Congress to authorize such a corporation to operate within the States.[2] Archer of Virginia stated that: "It
was not the arbitrary or even despotical authority
asserted over the District which was contested, but
the competency to pervert it to a coextensive authority over the Union." The State-Rights advocates had heard the right of Congress to incorporate
a bank upheld by the Court, and had listened to remarks of Chief Justice Marshall in the *Cohens Case*
as to the possible power of Congress to authorize
other corporations to extend their functions, if of a
National nature, into the States, and they were unwilling to run any further risk by giving a National
charter, even to a philanthropic relief association.

[1] For editorials and quotations from numerous other newspapers, continuing
the attack upon the Court for its decision in the *Cohens Case*, see *Richmond Enquirer*, July 27, Aug. 7, 14, 17, 31, Sept. 4, 25, 1821.

[2] *17th Cong., 2d Sess.*, Dec. 20, 1822, Jan. 6, 7, 8, 1823. The bill was defeated
in the House by a vote of 65 to 91.

CHAPTER FOURTEEN

INTERNATIONAL LAW

1816–1822

WHILE during these seven years, from 1816 to 1822, the Court was laying deep the foundations of American constitutional law, it was at the same time becoming a potent factor in the history of the foreign relations of the country, by reason of the firmness with which it insisted on the strictest fidelity of the United States to the provisions of treaties, and on the honest observance by neutrals of their international duties.[1] And the large number of cases involving international and prize law, which were decided at the 1822 Term, afforded striking proof of the importance of this phase of the Court's work. At the very outset of the Term, the development of international law, however, sustained a severe loss in the sudden death of the most eminent advocate in that branch of law — William Pinkney.[2] "We all lament the death of Mr. Pinkney as a loss to the profession generally, and most especially to that part of it which is assembled in this room. We lament it too as a loss to our country," said Chief Justice Mar-

---

[1] Marshall wrote to Rufus King, May 5, 1802: "The National tribunal, I hope, will continue to manifest in the exposition of the treaty of peace that share of prudence which is required by justice and which can alone preserve the reputation of the Nation." *King*, III; see *The Part taken by Courts of Justice in the Development of International Law*, by Simeon E. Baldwin, *Yale Law Journ.* (1900), X.

[2] Pinkney died, Feb. 25, 1822, from apoplexy brought on by overwork in the argument of *Ricard* v. *Williams*, 7 Wheat. 59. Rufus Choate wrote: "I heard his last great argument, when, by his overwork, he snapped the cord of his life. His diction was splendidly rich, copious, and flowing. Webster followed him, but I could not help thinking he was infinitely dry, barren and jejune." *Reminiscences of Rufus Choate* (1860), by Edward G. Parker.

shall, when the Court paid the very unusual tribute of adjourning on the news of Pinkney's death;[1] and his contemporaries at the Bar did not stint their recognition of Pinkney's supreme leadership. "He died literally in harness. . . . The void will never be filled that he has left," wrote John Randolph.[2] "It seems undisputed that he was deservedly the head of the Bar," wrote Rufus King. "Some days ago, speaking of himself, he said that he found he was obliged to give more time and labour to his profession than formerly, that he considered himself at the head of the Bar, and being resolved to continue so, he found it necessary to be most diligent and laborious, in preparing himself to appear before the Court."[3] William Wirt wrote: "Poor Pinkney, he died opportunely for his fame. It could not have risen higher. . . . He was a great man. On a set occasion, the greatest, I think, at our Bar. . . . He was an excellent lawyer; had very great force of mind, great compass, nice discrimination; strong and accurate judgment; and for copiousness and beauty of diction was unrivalled. He is a real loss to the Bar."[4] And Pinkney's devoted admirer, Judge Story, wrote: "His genius and eloquence were so lofty, I might almost

[1] The following entry was ordered to be made on the minutes of the Court (7 Wheaton, v): "The Court being informed that Mr. Pinkney, a gentleman of the Bar, highly distinguished for his learning and his talents, departed this life last night in this city, the Judges have determined, as a mark of their profound respect for his character, and sincere grief for his loss, to wear crape on the left arm for the residue of the Term; and to adjourn for the purpose of paying the last tribute to his remains, by attending them from the place of his death." While the Court was at this time accustomed to wear crape in memory of its deceased Judges, this was the first time, so far as it appears, when they did so in honor of a member of the Bar.

[2] *Life of John Randolph* (1851), by Hugh A. Garland, II, 170.

[3] *King*, VI, letter of Feb. 26, 1822. In 8 Cranch (1812–1813), of the forty-six cases in which names of counsel are given, Pinkney argued in exactly one half. For most striking instances of the reliance placed on Pinkney by other counsel at the Bar, see interesting unpublished letters of Wirt to L. E. Stanboch, March 16, April 7, 1820, regarding the arguments of *The Amiable Isabella*, 6 Wheat. 1, in *Wirt Papers MSS.*

[4] *Wirt*, II, letters of Oct. 13, 1818, May 9, 1822.

say so unrivalled, his learning so extensive, his ambition so elevated, his political and constitutional principles so truly just and pure, his weight in the public councils so decisive, his character at the Bar so peerless and commanding, that there seems now left a dismal and perplexing vacancy. His foibles and faults were so trifling or excusable in comparison with his greatness, that they are at once forgotten and forgiven with his deposit in the grave. His great talents are now universally acknowledged." [1] "The lamented demise of Mr. Pinkney," said the *National Intelligencer*, "has left so large a space at the Bar of the Supreme Court that it will probably induce many distant gentlemen of the profession to attend the Terms of the Court regularly, who have heretofore attended only occasionally." [2]

While Pinkney's fame had been enhanced by his great constitutional arguments, it was on the development of international law that he had left his deepest impress. For this branch of practice was little known to the profession in general,[3] and it was largely by the aid of arguments of great counsel like Pinkney, Wirt, Webster, Joseph Hopkinson, Samuel Dexter, John Sergeant, David B. Ogden, Henry Wheaton and William H. Winder that Marshall and Story were enabled to create and embody in a masterly series of opinions that distinctively American conception of international, prize and admiralty law, which developed during these years

[1] *Story*, I, 415, Feb. 28, 1822. A contemporary wrote in the *North American Review*, XXIV: "To the time of his last appearance in Washington, the Court-room was always thronged with the wise, the learned, and the fashionable, when it was known that he was to speak; and he uniformly riveted the attention of his auditors through the technical details of his longest and dryest arguments."

[2] *National Intelligencer*, March 23, 1822.

[3] In 1817, in *The Dos Hermanos*, 2 Wheat. 77: "The Court cannot but watch with considerable solicitude irregularities which so seriously impair the simplicity of prize proceedings and the rights and duties of the parties. Some apology for them may be found in the fact that from our having been long at peace, no opportunity was afforded to learn the correct practice in prize causes. But that apology no longer exists."

between 1815 and 1822.[1] Since European treatises
on this branch of the law were mostly antiquated, and
since Lord Stowell's famous decisions in England were
so tinged by the illegal attitude of the English Government in the Napoleonic wars that they failed to represent the true state of the law and could not be consistently followed in this country, it became necessary for
the American Courts to formulate doctrines of international law which should more fairly express the rights
and duties of neutrals and of belligerents.[2] As long
ago as 1807, Marshall had written to District Judge
Peters, congratulating him on publishing his admiralty
decisions.[3] "If a great system of public law is ever
to prevail on the ocean," he said, "it must, in analogy
to the municipal system, result from decisions and reasonings, appealing through the press to the common
judgment of the civilized world. Heretofore, admiralty
proceedings have been concluded with too little pub-
licity, and without disclosing the privileges on which
they were founded. Naturally, they have been sub-

---

[1] It is interesting to note how many of the great lawyers made their first appearance in the Court in prize cases. Thus, Pinkney's first appearance was in 1806 in
a case involving capture of a cargo, *Manella* v. *Barry*, 3 Cranch, 415; Hopkinson
appeared first in 1807 in a prize case, *Rhinelander* v. *Insurance Company of Pennsylvania*, 4 Cranch, 29; Sergeant in 1816 in *The Aurora*, 1 Wheat. 96; Wheaton in
1816, in *The Antonia Johanna*, 1 Wheat. 159; Wirt (after one case in 1816) appeared
in 1817 in *The Fortuna*, 2 Wheat. 161; Webster made his first appearance in 1814
in *The St. Lawrence*, and *The Grotius*, 8 Cranch, 434, 456.

[2] John Jay wrote to Trumbull, as to the English Admiralty at an earlier date,
Oct. 27, 1797: "The delays of the Court of Admiralty do not surprise me. I have
no faith in any British Court of Admiralty, though I have the greatest respect for
and confidence in their Courts of *justice*, in the number of which those Courts do
not deserve to be ranked (I do not extend this stricture to the Lords of Appeal)."
Life of John Jay (1833), by William Jay, II, 283. John Quincy Adams wrote to
Rufus King, Oct. 3, 1796: "The maritime law of nations recognized in Great Britain
is all comprised in one line of a popular song, 'Rule, Britannia! Britannia rule
the waves!' I never could find that their Admiralty Courts were governed by
any other code." *J. Q. Adams Writings*, II, 33; and in his *Memoirs*, Adams wrote
Dec. 19, 1827: "Cannon law is the law of Great Britain. . . . Belligerent, she
tramples upon neutral rights; neutral, she maintains them at the cannon's
mouth."

[3] *Peters Papers MSS*, letter to Peters, Sept. 5, 1807.

stituting for principles the capricious mandates of power and of belligerent policy. . . . It seems to be peculiarly necessary, therefore, that neutral tribunals should be heard on subjects in which neutral nations are equally concerned. . . . A general practice pursuing your example will not be without a beneficial influence on the conduct of nations on the high seas." [1] And twelve years later, Judge Story, writing to Lord Stowell in 1819, described the difficulties under which the Court labored: "The admiralty law was in a great measure a new system to us; and we had to grope our way as well as we could by the feeble and indistinct lights which glimmered through allusions incidentally made to the known rules and proceedings of an ancient Court. . . . I hope that a foundation has now been laid, upon which my successors in America may be able to build with more ease and security than fell to my lot." [2]

The conflicting rights of belligerents and of neutrals presented, during this period in the Court's history, a peculiarly difficult problem. So far as the Court dealt with cases involving the protection of the *rights* of neutrals, it cannot be said to have solved the questions with entire satisfaction (nor indeed have Courts of the present day) ; for as was tersely stated by Judge Johnson in the *Atalanta*, 3 Wheat. 409: "We find the law of nations embarrassed with the principle that it is lawful

[1] In 1815, in *Thirty Hogshead of Sugar* v. *Boyle*, 9 Cranch, 191, argued by Harper against Pinkney, Marshall laid down the American principle as to the authority of legal decisions on international law.

[2] *Story*, I, 318, letter of Jan. 14, 1819. The two long notes on the principles and practice in prize causes inserted (anonymously) at the end of the first and second volumes of *Wheaton's Reports* were written by Story, and remain today the basis of prize law in the United States. Story had written to N. Williams, Aug. 24, 1812: "I have been industriously reading Prize Law and have digested into my commonplace books everything I could find. . . . I hope the Supreme Court will have an opportunity to enter largely into its jurisdiction both as an Instance and a Prize Court." *Ibid.*, 228.

to impose a direct restraint upon the industry and enterprise of a neutral, in order to produce an incidental embarrassment to an enemy. In its original restricted application, this principle was of undoubted correctness and did little injury; but in the modern extended use which has been made of it, we see an exemplification of the difficulty of restraining a belligerent in the application of a convenient principle." On the other hand, the enforcement of the *obligations* of neutrals was a problem with which the Court dealt masterfully and effectively, and in such a way as to affect materially the foreign relations of the country. For many years, it became one of the most potent factors in preserving peaceful relations between the United States and Spain and Portugal, amid the serious complications which had arisen out of the revolutions of the Spanish and Portuguese colonies in Central and South America. From the outset of these revolutions, constant violations of neutrality had taken place with reference to the revolting South American States; and it is unquestionably true that conditions in this respect were intolerable.[1] As has been vividly said: "Ship after ship, armed and equipped for fighting, cleared from the customhouses at Baltimore and New Orleans as merchantmen, and after touching at some port specified in the papers, would hoist the flag of New Granada or the United States of Mexico and begin to rob, plunder and destroy the commerce of Spain. Some, without going through the form of entering the port for which they had cleared, would throw off their merchant character, the moment they were on the high seas, would mount their guns, raise their flag and prey on the commerce of a nation at amity with the United States. In other instances,

[1] *Amer. State Papers, For. Rel.*, IV, 422, letter of De Onis, Minister of Spain, to Secretary of State, Dec. 30, 1815; *History of the People of the United States*, by John Bach McMaster, IV, 372 *et seq.*

ships from the revolted provinces, with the flags of their governments at their mast-heads, would enter our ports and buy guns, powder and food, enlist men for the armies, and even take on board as passengers citizens of the United States who were to serve in the army of the insurgents. In other cases, blank commissions to act as privateers were sent to vessels in American ports, which were then equipped and manned, the blanks filled in, and the ships set sail to attack Spanish commerce, without ever having been near a port of the Colony issuing the commission." From 1808 to 1815, diplomatic intercourse between the United States and Spain had been broken off (for reasons disconnected with South American conditions); but as soon as it was resumed, Spain, with much reason on its side, demanded that the United States should put an end to the constant violations of neutrality. Congress and the President recognized the National duty to comply with the obligations imposed by international law; and a statute enacted in 1817 strengthened the old Neutrality Law of 1794, especially by amending it so as to prevent the fitting out of vessels in our ports with intent to be employed in the service of "any colony, district or people" (the former Law referring only to service of a "foreign prince or state"). This legislation, however, was not enacted without difficulty; for the South and West were hotly opposed, being mindful of the antagonistic attitude held by Spain in earlier days with reference to the opening of the Mississippi River and the disputes over the boundary of the Louisiana Territory. Spanish spoliations on our own commerce also had not been forgotten. Moreover, owing to the widespread sympathy for the South American Colonies in their effort to achieve independence, laws like the Neutrality Act, which might impede their success, were felt to be unAmerican; and even after the Act passed there was a strong pressure for its repeal.[1] The opportunities for great financial profits in the sending out of these privateers also proved such an inducement to merchants and adventurers to violate the law that the most determined efforts by the President and by the Judiciary to enforce international obligations of the United States became imperative. As Judge Washington well said, in a charge to the Grand Jury in 1817: "It is to be hoped that the strength of the Executive arm (for the President is vested with very extensive powers to prevent the perpetration of the offences above described) and the vigilance of the customhouse officers, with the coöperation of the judicial authorities, aided by the patriotism of all well-disposed citizens, will release our country from the unmerited stigma of secretly taking part in a war which our Government is unwilling to countenance. I know that plausible pretexts are not wanting to palliate these lawless acts, and even to render them popular, with those who regard rather the avowed, than the real motive of the perpetrators of them. The emancipation of an oppressed people is urged as an excuse for these military expeditions. . . . A wilful violation of these laws can never find an excuse in the motive which induced it, however we might approve the motive, were the laws silent on the subject. I must, nevertheless, be permitted to suspect the sincerity of the motive which is professed in these cases. Search to the bottom, and it will be found to originate in self-interest, in a cupidity for that wealth which is torn by power from the hands of its defenceless owners." [2] Since the coun-

[1] John Quincy Adams in his *Memoirs*, IV, records, March 17, 1818: "Mr. Clay pushes for repeal of the laws which trammel the means of giving aid to the South American revolutionists."

[2] *Niles Register*, XIII, Nov. 8, 1817. See also *Monroe*, VI, letters of Aug. 3, and Sept. 4, 1820, as to neutrality and the duty to enforce the laws.

try at large was not in sympathy with the enforcement of its international duty, it became peculiarly incumbent upon the Courts, and especially the Supreme Court, to enforce the law with strictness; for both the honor of the United States and the preservation of its peace with Spain were at stake. Accordingly, in a long series of cases extending from 1816 to 1825, and presenting the greatest variety of facts, the Supreme Court reaffirmed its well-established doctrine that the taking of a prize by a ship fitted out or acting in violation of the neutrality of the United States would be held invalid by our Courts, and restitution of the prize so taken decreed. By its decisions, ship after ship belonging to Spanish or Portuguese owners was ordered restored, when captured by privateers from Venezuela, or the Argentine Republic, or Carthagena, which had been fitted out or unlawfully manned or equipped in American ports, or which brought their prizes into American ports in violation of law.[1]

Of this series of cases, the most famous was that of *The Santissima Trinidad*, 7 Wheat. 283, argued at great length by David B. Ogden and William H. Winder, against Daniel Webster and Littleton Waller Tazewell, and decided at the 1822 Term. Four questions were presented: first, whether the captor ship was a public ship of the United Provinces of Rio de la Plata, and the Court, through Judge Story, found that she was such a public ship; second, whether the dispatch of a vessel equipped for war but sent to Buenos Ayres as a commercial adventure was a violation of our neutrality.

[1] See *Divina Pastora*, 4 Wheat. 52; *Estrella*, 4 Wheat. 298; *Nuestra Signora de la Caridad*, 4 Wheat. 497; *Amistad de la Rues*, 5 Wheat. 385; *Josefa Segunda*, 5 Wheat. 338; *Bello Corunnes*, 6 Wheat. 152; *Nueva Anna*, 6 Wheat. 193; *La Concepcion*, 6 Wheat. 235; *Gran Para*, 7 Wheat. 471; *Santa Maria*, 7 Wheat. 490; *Arrogante Barcelona*, 7 Wheat. 496; *Monte Allegre*, 7 Wheat. 520, s.c., 9 Wheat. 616; s.c., 11 Wheat. 429, see *Writings of James Monroe* (1898), VI, letter of June 26, 1820; *La Nereyda*, 8 Wheat. 108; *The Fanny*, 9 Wheat. 658.

Judge Story held that: "There is nothing in our laws, or in the law of nations, that forbids our citizens from sending armed vessels, as well as munitions of war, to foreign ports for sale. It is a commercial venture which no nation is bound to prohibit, and which only exposes the persons engaged in it to the penalty of confiscation." The third point was whether, in case of a capture made by a public ship whose crew had been augmented in our ports, in violation of our neutrality, goods so captured and brought into our ports should be restored to their former owner. It was held that such augmentation, being a violation of our neutrality, "infects the captures subsequently made, with the character of torts, and justifies and requires a restitution to the parties who have been injured by such misconduct. It does not lie in the mouth of wrong-doers, to set up a title derived from a violation of our neutrality." The doctrine was held to apply as well to captures by public ships as by private ships, and it was further held that, though the property had been condemned in prize proceedings in Buenos Ayres, nevertheless, being in custody of our Courts and litigated here, a foreign Prize Court could not by its adjudication take away jurisdiction, or forestall and defeat the judgment of the Courts of this country. The final decision was in favor of Webster's clients; and his argument had done much to convince the Bar that international law had found in him as its advocate the fit successor to Pinkney.[1] "Tazewell and Webster have been reaping laurels in the Supreme Court, and I have been — sighing," wrote William Wirt. "North of the Potomac, I believe

[1] Hugh B. Grigsby in his *Discourse on the Life and Character of Littleton Weller Tazewell* (1860), 43–45, says that it was Tazewell who had suggested that Webster be engaged as his associate counsel. "He ever held the abilities of Mr. Webster in the highest respect, and when asked on reaching Norfolk after the argument what he thought of Webster he said . . . he ' was excessively clever but a lazy dog.'

to a man, they yield the palm to Webster; South to Tazewell." [1]

Upon the strained relations existing between Spain and Portugal and the United States at this time, the Court further poured judicial balm, by a series of decisions clarifying and enforcing the law as to piracy. While the problems as to rights and obligations of neutrality could arise only where Governments were involved whose independence or belligerency had been recognized by the United States, and while such recognition had been given by the United States to many of the Spanish revolting Colonies, there were other revolutionary movements in Mexico and South America which had not attained such a status as to warrant recognition.[2] Moreover, owing to the general disturbed conditions in the Western Hemisphere and to the temptations for pecuniary gain, marauding on the sea conducted by persons sailing under no recognized flag, by mutineers, and by private adventurers from ports of the United States, had become deplorably common during the years 1817 to 1822. Such acts constituted nothing but piracy; and again Spain made violent protests to the United States Government against the toleration shown here towards such illegal acts. The conditions were described by Judge Story in an address to the Grand Jury in 1820: "This offense (piracy) has in former times crimsoned the ocean with much innocent blood, and in its present alarming progress threatens the most serious mischiefs to our peaceful commerce. It cannot be disguised, that at the present time there are hordes of needy adventurers prowling upon the

---

[1] John Randolph wrote: "Tazewell is second to no other man that ever breathed; but he has taken almost as much pains to hide this light under a bushel as Pinkney did to set his on a hill. He and the Great Lord Chief are in that, *par-nobile;* but Tazewell in point of reputation is far beyond Pinkney and Marshall." *Wirt,* II, 137.

[2] See *Moore's International Law Digest,* I, 67–96.

ocean, who, under the specious pretext of being in the
service of the Patriot Governments of South America
commit the foulest outrages. Being united together
by no common tie but the love of plunder, they assume
from time to time the flag of any nation, which may
best favor their immediate projects; and depredate,
with indiscriminate ferocity, upon the commerce of
the neutral world, regardless of the principles of law
and dictates of justice." "The practice is so obvious
and dishonorable to the United States, as well as pernicious in its consequences, that it must be suppressed,"
wrote President Monroe to John Quincy Adams, then
Secretary of State.[1] *Niles Register* asked: "When is
this miserable business — this wretched privateering
piracy, which so much corrupts the morals of sea-faring
men and leads them into every excess, terminating so
often in murder and punishment by the executioner, to
end? The 'patriot' service as of late fitted for in some
ports of the United States is a disgrace to the country,
but unhappily it has been so managed in general as to
elude our laws intended for its suppression." Thomas
Jefferson wrote to the Portuguese Minister: "The late
piratical depredations which your commerce has suffered, as well as ours, and that of other nations,
seems to have been committed by renegado rovers of
several nations, French, English, Americans, which
they, as well as we, have not been careful enough to

---

[1] *Monroe*, letters of June 26, July 24, 1820; *Jefferson*, XII, letter to Correa, Oct.
24, 1820; *Niles Register*, XVI, XVII, XVIII, *passim* in 1819–20. See also letter
from George McNeill, in Baltimore, to Thomas Ruffin, July 8, 1819; *Papers of
Thomas Ruffin* (1918). "There is much distress here, but it is confined chiefly to
adventuring and not to the regular merchants, but the whole community is more
or less affected by them — they are of three classes — 1st, speculators in U. S.
Banks; 2d, pirates, called South American or patriot privateers; 3d, traders in
the African Slave trade in connection with the privateers. That infamous trafick-
ing and plundering has been carried on to a great extent — most of the parties are
now, however, reaping part of their reward, infamy and ruin stares them in the
face; they disgrace the whole country and the laws should be so amended as not
to be evaded with impunity."

suppress. I hope our Congress . . . will strengthen the measures of suppression. Of their disposition to do it, there can be no doubt; for all men of moral principle must be shocked at these atrocities."

At first, the lower Courts were inclined to rule the law in favor of the pirates; and an illuminating description of the situation is given by Adams in his diary (though allowance must be made for his well-known bitter personal prejudices) :

March 29, 1819: The misfortune is not only that this abomination has spread over a large portion of the merchants and of the population of Baltimore, but that it has infected almost every officer of the United States in the place. They are fanatics for the South American cause. The District Judge, Houston, and the Circuit Judge, Duval, are both feeble, inefficient men, over whom William Pinkney, employed by all the pirates as their counsel, domineers like a slave driver over his negroes.

May 26, 1819: I spoke to Wirt about the acquittal at Baltimore of the pirate Daniels. The case went off upon a legal quibble. Wirt says it is because the judges are two weak, though very good, old men who suffer themselves to be bullied and browbeaten by Pinkney.

August 21, 1819: Pinkney is the standing counsel for all the pirates who, by browbeating and domineering over the Courts, and by paltry pettifogging law-quibbles, has saved all their necks from the richly merited halter. . . . Baltimore, upon privateering and banking, is rotten to the heart.

Violent attacks were made against the United States District Judges in Baltimore and Charleston by diplomatic representatives of Spain and Portugal, which, though possibly justifiable, were resented by President Monroe, who wrote to Adams: "I do not recollect any previous example of an attack on the integrity, as this seems to be, of the Judiciary of any power, by a foreign minister." [1] Fortunately, the Supreme Court now again played a great part in allaying the heated feelings of Spain and Portugal, by a series of decisions, in 1820, laying down the law as to piracy with great rigidity. The question had come before the Supreme Court for the first time in 1818, in *United States* v. *Palmer*, 3 Wheat. 610, in which case, the acts alleged to be piracy had been committed by persons who were not American citizens and who were in service of one of the acknowledged revolutionary governments and while on a ship of that government.   The Court held that the Piracy Act of 1790 punishing robbery committed by "any person or persons on the high seas", was not intended to apply to other than American citizens; and it said that: "These questions which respect the rights of a part of a foreign empire which asserts and is contending for its independence, and the conduct which must be observed by the Courts of the Union towards the subjects of such section of an empire who may be brought before the tribunals of this country are equally delicate and difficult. . . . Such questions are generally rather political than legal in their character.[2]   To cure this decision, Congress passed an Act, March 3, 1819, punishing piracy committed by "any person or persons whatsoever ", if such persons were afterwards found in the United States.   But the Court, the next year, 1820, made it clear in *United States* v. *Klintock*, 5 Wheat.

[1] *J. Q. Adams Writings*, VII, letters of Adams to Monroe, Aug. 21, 1820, Monroe to Adams, Sept. 4, 11, 1820, Adams to Correa, Sept. 30, 1820.

[2] The decision was savagely attacked by Adams, who recorded his opinion of it in his *Memoirs*, May 11, 1819: "The Supreme Court of the United States by a decision founded upon captious subtleties, in *Palmer's Case*, cast away the jurisdiction which a law of Congress had given . . . construing the words 'any person or persons' to mean only citizens of the United States.   Their reasoning is a sample of judicial logic, disingenuous, false, and hollow — a logic so abhorrent to my nature, that it gave me an early disgust to the practice of the law, and led me to the inalterable determination never to accept a judicial office.   In this case, if human language means anything, Congress had made general piracy by whomsoever and wheresoever committed upon the high seas, cognizable by the Circuit Courts."

144, that the scope of its previous decision had been misunderstood, and that a citizen of the United States, sailing in a ship under the flag of an unacknowledged revolutionary government (in this case under the flag of the "Brigadier of the Mexican Republic, a republic of whose existence we know nothing, or as Generalissimo of the Floridas, a province in the possession of Spain"), and attacking a Spanish vessel, could be properly convicted as a pirate under the settled doctrines of international law.[1]   At the same time, the convictions of about fifty men, sentenced to death for piracy, at Boston, Baltimore, Richmond, Charleston and New Orleans, came before the Court; and in a series of nine cases, *United States* v. *Smith,* 5 Wheat. 153; *United States* v. *The Pirates,* 5 Wheat. 184, there were laid down principles of law which dealt a death blow to this form of crime in the United States.   The cases were presented on certificates from the Judges of the Circuit Courts on a division of opinion.   As the defendants had no counsel, the Court initiated a somewhat novel practice, by directing Daniel Webster to appear in their behalf.   The Attorney-General, Wirt, opened the case, February 14, 1820, for the United States, and as stated by the *National Intelligencer:* "Mr. Webster, having been directed by the Court to argue for the prisoners, took notes for the purpose of replying on some future day to the Attorney-General."   Webster made his argument a week later, February 21; and within a few days afterwards (February 25 and March 1) the Court, in opinions by Judge Story and Judge Johnson, affirmed all the convictions.   Following these decisions, many of the defendants were later executed, and piracy became a rare crime.[2]

[1] See *Moore's International Law Digest,* II, 454–464.

[2] John Quincy Adams in his *Memoirs* March 13, 1820, notes that at a Cabinet Meeting called to consider the question of the fate of the convicted pirates, "it

In the maintenance of the foreign relations of the United States on a high and honorable level, and in the preservation of peace, no decisions of the Court have played a more important part than have those in which, from the outset of its history, it has upheld with the utmost scrupulousness the sanctity of treaties and their strict construction, regardless of the contentions of the Administration which happened to be in power. In no case was its attitude in this respect more vividly illustrated than in *The Amiable Isabella*, 6 Wheat. 1, which was decided in 1820, and which again involved the extremely strained relations then existing between Spain and the United States. The claimant in this case had urged that the facts brought it within the provisions of the Spanish Treaty of 1795 embodying the doctrine of "free ships, free goods." Pinkney had argued for the Government, on the other hand, that though the treaty did not specifically except cases of fraud, the Court must so construe it, and he eloquently urged the serious consequence which might flow from the adoption of the opposite construction. "The only mode of preserving amicable relations between the two powers," he said, "is by judicial interposition, preventing the effect of such violations of the spirit of the treaty, before they grow too mighty to be controlled by diplomatic remonstrances." To this plea, however, Judge Story (while construing the treaty on another ground in favor of the Government) replied that the case embraced "the interpretation of a treaty which we are bound to observe with the most scrupulous good faith, and which our Government could not violate without disgrace, and

was agreed that Mr. Wirt, the Attorney-General, should see Chief Justice Marshall and enquire of him where the severity of the law and where the beneficence of humanity may best be dispensed"; and that, on March 31, 1820, the President decided to have two persons executed at each place where convictions had been obtained — Boston, Baltimore, Richmond, Charleston and New Orleans.

which this Court could not disregard without betraying its duty." And the Court, he continued, could "look to consequences no further than the sound principles of interpretation and international justice require." And Judge Johnson (though construing the treaty differently) was equally vigorous in upholding the scrupulous execution of the treaty provisions, uninfluenced by "the pressure or allurement of present circumstances", and in expressing the view that "considerations of policy or the views of the Administration are wholly out of the question in this Court. What is the just construction of the treaty, is the only question here. And whether it chimes in with the views of the Government or not, this individual is entitled to the benefit of that construction." And in the following noble words, he set forth the doctrine by which the Court has always been guided in regard to treaties: "Where no coercive power exists for compelling the observance of contracts but the force of arms, honor and liberality are the only bonds of union between the contracting parties, and all minor considerations are to be sacrificed to the great interests of mankind. . . . The execution of one treaty in a spirit of liberality and good faith is a higher interest than all the predatory claims of a fleet of privateers."

Four years later, the Court aided in the maintenance of friendly relations with another foreign nation, through a decision against the Government in the case of *The Apollon*, 9 Wheat. 362, in 1824. Much friction had arisen between France and the United States during President Monroe's term, and a tonnage duty had been imposed by Congress in 1820 on all French vessels entering our ports. The French ship involved in this case, having sailed up the St. Mary's River to land goods in Spanish territory across our boundary, as a convenient depot for illicit trade with the United States, had been seized in Spanish waters by our custom authorities. The case was argued warmly by Attorney-General Wirt, against Henry Clay and Harper. The Court, through Judge Story, held the seizure "wholly without justification under our laws"; and it again refused to pay heed to the political considerations advanced in arguments in behalf of the United States, saying:

The questions arising upon the record have been argued with great zeal and ability, and embrace some considerations which belong more properly to another department of the government. It cannot, however, escape observation, that this Court has a plain path of duty marked out for it, and that is, to administer the law as it finds it. We cannot enter into political considerations, or the authority of the Government to defend its rights against the frauds meditated by foreigners against our revenue system, through the instrumentality and protection of a foreign sovereignty. . . . We must administer the laws as they exist, without straining them to reach public mischiefs which they were never designed to remedy. It may be fit and proper for the government, in the exercise of the high discretion confided to the Executive for great public purposes, to act on a sudden emergency, or to prevent an irreparable mischief, by summary measures, which are not found in the text of the laws. . . . But this Court can only look to the questions, whether the laws have been violated; and if they were, justice demands that the injured party should receive a suitable redress.

The political situation relative to the approaching nomination of Presidential candidates was clearly reflected in the argument, as Henry Clay took occasion to animadvert severely on the conduct of his rival for the Presidency, John Quincy Adams, who was then Secretary of State. "The Supreme Court seems for a time to have borrowed from the legislative bodies some of the peculiarities of their debates," wrote a New York correspondent, "and the case of *The Apollon,*

the argument of which was concluded yesterday, has
afforded a wide field for the copious display of them.
We happened to stop in yesterday whilst Mr. Wirt was
concluding the case for the United States in reply to
Mr. Clay, and heard enough of the 'tart reply' to
make us wish we had heard the 'grand debate' which
preceded it. The argument was not exactly limited to
the question *coram judice*, but covered other ground.
The occupation of Amelia Island, some years ago, by
order of the President was introduced into the discussion, its constitutionality questioned on the one hand
and defended on the other." [1] And Adams made a
characteristic comment on the case, in his diary:

I attended this evening alone the drawing room at the
President's. Less company than usual. Bad weather.
Heard of Mr. Wirt's reply this day before the Supreme Court
to Clay's attack upon the Administration and upon me on
Monday in the case of the *Apollon*. G. Hay was in raptures
at the scourging Clay received. Clay spoke of it to me
himself, but in a very humble tone compared to that of
Monday. Clay said he had wanted a half an hour for reply.
I said he should have thought of that when he attacked me,
where he knew I could not reply. He said Wirt had made
my letter to De Neuville a part of his argument. I told
him he had fine scope for assailing me where I was not
present to defend myself, but in this instance, I had been
gratified to learn that my defence had fallen into better
hands than my own.

One further decision on international law, rendered a
few years later than the period of the Court's greatest
activity on this subject, may be noted, because of its
intimate connection with the great subject of slavery
which was, in the next twenty years, to produce such a
profound effect upon the Court's history. It is a singu-

[1] *New York Statesman*, March 30, 1824. See also *Georgia Journal*, March 30,
1824; *J. Q. Adams*, VI, March 15, 17, 1824.

lar fact that the first decision rendered on this delicate
and long-debated question should have involved a question of international rather than of domestic law. For
several years prior to 1825, cases of violations of the
Federal criminal laws against the African slave-trade
had crowded the inferior Federal Courts; and the
question of the proper disposition of slaves unlawfully
introduced into the United States had occasioned to
Congress much perplexity.[1] In 1825, the Court was
confronted for the first time with the question whether
the slave trade was illegal under international law, and
if so, what disposition should be made of slaves brought
into the country by an American warship from a vessel
captured on the high seas. Three years previously,
Judge Story, in *La Jeune Eugenie*, 2 Mason, 90, in the
First Circuit, had held the slave trade to be contrary
to the law of nations, on the ground that it carried with
it "a breach of all moral duties, of all the maxims of
justice, mercy and humanity, and of the admitted rights
which Christian nations now hold sacred, in their intercourse with each other." "I rejoice that you have
been able to come to the result you have, so suitable to
the character of a Court of Justice and to the nature of
our system of government and so congenial to all our
best feelings," wrote Jeremiah Mason to Story.[2] "I
take it you must necessarily come into conflict with
the opinion of Lord Stowell. It will be highly honorable
to our country to take the lead and give the law on this
subject, and I trust you will be supported by the
Supreme Court, and not impeded by any interference

---

[1] See *Sundry African Slaves* v. *Madrazo; Governor of Georgia* v. *Sundry African
Slaves* (1828), 1 Pet. 110; *United States* v. *Attorney-General of Louisiana* (1830),
3 Pet. 57.

[2] *Mason*, letter of Jan. 8, 1822; in the *Josefa Segunda*, 5 Wheat. 338, in 1820,
Judge Livingston had referred to "this inhuman traffic for the abolition of which
the United States have manifested an early and honorable anxiety."

of the Executive Government." [1] While the decision did credit to Judge Story's moral fervor, it was, nevertheless, altogether in advance of the morals of the times, and in direct conflict with established international law, and with several decisions of the English Courts. The Supreme Court, therefore, when the question was presented in *The Antelope*, 10 Wheat. 66, in 1825, was practically called upon to decide whether it would adhere to international law as then existing, or whether it would decide the question upon moral grounds. Elaborate arguments were made by William Wirt and Francis Scott Key against John M. Berrien of Georgia and Charles J. Ingersoll of Pennsylvania. "I never heard a more interesting case," wrote a newspaper correspondent. "Mr. Wirt's argument was worthy of all praise; his talents are an honor not only to the profession of which he is a member, but to our country and to its Executive." [2] The Court decided that it must adhere to international law as then formulated, which did not regard the slave trade as piracy. Such a decision much relieved the minds of the slavery men of the South, who viewed with apprehension any attempt on the part of the Judiciary to deal with the slavery question in any phase. That the Court, however, was not impervious to the moral issue (which nevertheless was a question for the Legislature rather than for the Court) was seen from the opening words of Marshall's

[1] Story replied, Feb. 21, 1822: "The opinion has been read by several of the Judges here, and in general, I think it not unsatisfactory to them in its results. The Chief Justice, with his characteristic modesty, says he thinks I am right, but the questions are new to his mind."

R. F. Stockton wrote to Daniel Webster, Nov. 5, 1821, referring to the question involved in *La Jeune Eugenie:* "I shall rejoice to hear that you maintain the great point even in the Circuit Court. I should think its fate at Washington would be doubtful, especially if it be true, as Judge Story in one of the papers is made to say, that the Court is called upon to establish a new principle of public law." *Van Tyne Copies of Webster Papers* in Library of Congress; see also *Life of Daniel Webster* (1870), by George T. Curtis, I, 196.

[2] *Boston Patriot,* quoted in *Niles Register,* XXVIII, March 26, 1825.

opinion: "In examining claims of this momentous importance; claims in which the sacred rights of liberty and of property come in conflict with each other; which have drawn from the Bar a degree of talent and of eloquence worthy of the questions which have been discussed; this Court must not yield to feelings which might seduce it from the path of duty, but must obey the mandates of the law. . . . It is not wonderful that public feeling should march somewhat in advance of strict law. . . . Whatever might be the answer of a moralist to this question, a jurist must search for its legal solution in those principles of action which are sanctioned by the usages, the national acts, and the general assent of that portion of the world of which he considers himself as a part, and to whose law the appeal is made." [1]

[1] See *United States* v. *Morris* (1840), 14 Pet. 464, as to the intent of Congress to abolish the slave trade by legislatior

CHAPTER FIFTEEN

THE STEAMBOAT MONOPOLY CASE

1822–1824

WITH the end of the 1823 Term, questions of international and admiralty law ceased to occupy the Court's attention; and questions of National concern again came to the front. When, on March 18, 1823, Judge Henry Brockholst Livingston died at the age of sixty-six and after seventeen years' service on the Bench, the vacancy thus caused arose at a critical juncture in the Court's history; for three cases of immense importance in the field of constitutional law were then pending and awaiting argument — *Gibbons* v. *Ogden* involving the New York steamboat monopoly, *Ogden* v. *Saunders* involving the validity of State bankrupt laws, and *Osborn* v. *Bank of the United States* involving the struggle against the Bank in Ohio. Considerable concern was displayed in the newspapers as to the character of the man whom President Monroe might appoint to fill the vacancy, and there seemed to be slight confidence in his discretion in selection.[1] Many names were mentioned as possible candidates from New York, chief of which were Smith Thompson (then Secretary of War and a brother-in-law of Robert R. Living-

---

[1] *National Gazette*, April, 1823. See also *New York Evening Post*, March 22, 24, 27, 28. A singular pessimistic expression of Chief Justice Marshall regarding Monroe's possible appointments to the Bench is found in a letter to Judge Story of July 2, 1823: "You alarm me respecting the successor of our much lamented friend. I too had heard a rumor which I hoped was impossible. Our Presidents, I fear, will never again seek to make our department respectable." *Mass. Hist. Soc. Proc., 2d Series*, XIV, July 2, 1823.

ston), Ex-Chancellor James Kent, Chief Justice Ambrose Spencer and Henry Wheaton.[1] Thompson had been offered the position within a week after Livingston's death, but he was doubtful as to accepting, partly because of poor health, and partly because of the fact that (as he wrote) his work when on the New York Supreme Court had led him principally to the sway of the common law, whereas "the questions which arose in the Supreme Court of the United States are mostly other branches of legal science and would therefore be in some measure a new field for me." The salary, he felt, was inadequate "to the expense of living here where you are unavoidably exposed to much company . . . . undoubtedly, the most expensive place in the United States." The chief reason, however, for his reluctance was his belief that he would be nominated by the Republicans as their candidate for President in 1824. "Thompson can undoubtedly have the appointment but is hesitating, having his eyes on the Presidency," wrote Webster to Story. "When a man finds himself in a situation he hardly ever dreamed of, he is apt to take it for granted that he is a favorite of fortune, and to presume that his blind patroness may have yet greater things in reserve for him. In the event of his finally declining, those now talked of as prominent candidates are, J. Kent and Ambrose Spencer. If a nomination were now to be made, I think it would be the former of these two

---

[1] William H. Crawford, writing to Van Buren, May 9, 1823, said: "Exertions are making to place Mr. Wheaton on it (the Court). . . . In a conversation upon the subject introduced by the President, I said that I believed that the appointment of Mr. Sanford would be as acceptable to the State as that of any other person unless you were disposed to accept it." *Van Buren Papers MSS.*

John C. Calhoun writing July 20, 1823, said: "You say nothing of the vacant place on the Bench. Who ought to fill it? Spencer, Kent, Van Ness, Wheaton, Edwards and Sanford are named. What could be the effect of making the selection of either of these gentlemen? The subject is an important one in any point of view. I consider the officer as the highest, except the Chief Magistrate, under our system." *Amer. Hist. Ass. Rep.* (1899), II.

names, altho' there are some who wish to give a decided rebuke to the Bucktails of N. York by appointing Mr. Spencer. What time may produce no one can say. Mr. Tazewell and some others have mentioned Mr. Macon's name to the Executive. *If he lived in the Circuit, I verily believe he would at this peculiar moment be appointed.* There are *two* of the President's advisers who would I think, give him a decided preference, if locality could be safely disregarded. On the whole, my expectation is that the appointment will be delayed, and that in the end, Mr. Thompson will take it." [1]   While Thompson was still hesitating, Adams and Wirt, as members of Monroe's Cabinet, were urging upon the President the tremendous importance of the appointment of a man of the highest character, and acceptable to the whole Nation rather than to local State interests, especially at this particular period when the jurisdiction of the Court was subject to so frequent attack. The lofty status of the Court, and the philosophy by which appointments upon it should be guided, have never been more adequately set forth than in a letter written by Wirt, recommending the appointment of a man whose political faith differed from that of the President — that of the strong old Federalist, Chancellor Kent: [2]

I sincerely wish Judge Thompson could see his interest in relieving you from this embarrassment by accepting the appointment. If he will not, can you make an appointment more acceptable to the Nation than that of Judge Kent? I know that one of the factions in New York would take it in high dudgeon at first. Probably, too, some of the most heated republicans and interested radicals who seize every topic for cavil, might, in every quarter of the Union, harp a

[1] *Van Buren Papers MSS*, letter of Thompson to Van Buren, March 25, 1823; *Story*, I, letter of Webster to Story, April 6, 1823.
[2] *Wirt*, II, 133, letter of Wirt to Monroe, May 5, 1823.

little for a time on the same string. But Kent holds so
lofty a stand everywhere for almost matchless intellect and
learning, as well as for spotless purity and high-minded honor
and patriotism, that I firmly believe the Nation at large
would approve and applaud the appointment. It would
sustain itself and soon put down the petty cavils which
might at first assail it. The appointment of a Judge of the
Supreme Court is a National and not a local concern. The
importance of that Court in the administration of the Federal Government, begins to be generally understood and
acknowledged. The local irritations at some of their
decisions in particular quarters (as in Virginia and Kentucky
for instance) are greatly overbalanced by the general approbation with which those same decisions have been received
throughout the Union. If there are a few exasperated portions of our people who would be for narrowing the sphere
of action of that Court and subduing its energies to gratify
popular clamor, there is a far greater number of our countrymen who would wish to see it in the free and independent
exercise of its constitutional powers, as the best means
of preserving the Constitution itself. The Constitution
is the public property of the United States. The people
have a right to expect that the best means will be adopted
to preserve it entire; which can be no otherwise ensured
than by organizing each department under it, in such a
manner as to enable it to perform its functions with the
fullest effect. It is now seen on every hand, that the
functions to be performed by the Supreme Court of the
United States are among the most difficult and perilous
which are to be performed under the Constitution. They
demand the loftiest range of talents and learning and a
soul of Roman purity and firmness. The questions which
come before them frequently involve the fate of the Constitution, the happiness of the whole Nation, and even its
peace as it concerns other nations. . . . It is in this view
of the subject, I have said, that the appointment of a Judge
of the Supreme Court is a *National* and not a *local* concern;
and therefore, in making the appointment, I think that
instead of consulting the feelings of local factions (whose
heat, as Dean Swift says, is always in proportion to their
want of light), and instead of consulting the little and narrow

views of exasperated parties, the President of the United States should look to the good of the whole country, to their great and permanent interests, and not to the ephemeral whims and exacerbations of the day. A mediocre appointment would be regarded as a sacrifice to the local factions in New York, or as a sacrifice to the contracted prejudices of the most contracted of our own party there and elsewhere. And I do verily believe that such an appointment to the bench of the Supreme Court would occasion more mortification and disgust, and draw down on the President far more censure than could result from the appointment of Judge Kent. . . .   That Bench should be set apart and consecrated to talent and virtue, without regard to the shades of political opinion by which its members may have been or may still be distinguished.   If, indeed, a man were a violent, bitter and persecuting federal partisan, intolerant of opposite opinions, I would not place him there; for that is a cast of character which, whether he belonged to the one side or the other, would disqualify him for a seat, there or anywhere else, where judgment was to be coolly and impartially exercised. This, however, is not the character of Judge Kent. . . . With regard to the great subject of State-Rights, which has produced so much excitement in Virginia and Kentucky, it happens that, if he (Kent) has any leaning, it is rather in favor of State-Rights.   This has been shown by his decisions in the steamboat cases, where he has uniformly upheld the State laws of New York against all the objections which could be raised of their repugnance to the Constitution and laws of the United States. . . .   I expressed these opinions to Mr. Calhoun, two months ago, and he concurred in them.

While Wirt was recommending the Federalist, Kent,[1] it is a singular fact that the Federalist Senator from New York, Rufus King, was strongly urging upon Secretary of State Adams and upon President Monroe

[1] Kent was supported by another strong Democrat, the veteran Col. Marinus Willett of New York, who wrote an urgent letter in his behalf to President Monroe, praising Kent's "candor, integrity and purity" and recommending his nomination despite his Federalist views. *Kent Papers MSS.*

the appointment of his Republican colleague, Martin Van Buren, than whom, he said, no man was "better qualified for a high and difficult judicial station." King also emphasized the especial need of placing upon the Bench a man possessing the rare qualification of "prudence." "Prudence is eminently possessed by the Chief Justice," King wrote, "who, while he reflects honor upon his native State, likewise adorns and imparts strength and harmony to the Constitution of the Nation. It cannot be concealed that the Chief Justice is unfortunately without an Associate who, in this respect, is competent to supply his loss." He furthermore pointed out that, possessing such qualities, Van Buren "might become invaluable in reconciling and adjusting the powers of the General and the State Governments; a reconciliation that, from year to year, becomes more critical and which can be effected by no other means than by the prudent exercise of the powers of the National Judiciary. Upon a subject, the right understanding of which is so essential to the preservation of the public liberties, I cannot forbear to press upon your mind the necessity of the utmost caution (perhaps not always heretofore observed) in the selection of the members of the Supreme Court; a tribunal which not only decides civil and criminal cases affecting individuals, but all questions arising under the Constitution, which by restricting or enlarging the power of the States or of the Union may disturb the nice and complicated balance of our political system. No other nation has established a tribunal so powerful, conclusive and independent. We must not forget that the wisdom of the other departments is inadequate to supply a defect of the Judiciary. We are, therefore, all responsible, and President and Senate above others, that the Supreme Court be so composed that the Master Spirit of the Chief Justice may not die, but, by the appointment from time to time, of able and prudent men, may be rendered perpetual." [1] To Van Buren himself, King had already expressed his indorsement of his nomination, though he had frankly warned him that "the office was very important, and in our system, of great authority, dignity and independence; but that it does not admit of any expectations of ulterior advancement, nor could it tolerate the interference of the Judge in party or personal politics; that he, Van Buren, had been deeply engaged in the party politics of the times. . . . To be a member of the Supreme Court, he must be wholly and forever withdrawn and separated from these connections. The dissolution must be absolute; and entering the Judicial Department, like taking the vow and veil in the Catholic Church, must forever divorce him from the political world. Unless he was confident of his strength to do this, he should not think of the Supreme Court for a moment." And he counseled Van Buren to model himself on Marshall, "who harmonized the powers of the Constitution by strengthening them, while another distinguished man of the same State taught the paradox that these powers could and should be harmonized by weakening of them. This is not only political heresy, but absurdity." To this advice, Van Buren responded, as he wrote to Thompson himself, that: "If I should accept the appointment of Judge, I should consider a total abstinence from interference in party politics as a duty of the most imperious nature, and I feel entire confidence in my ability to withdraw entirely and forever from the scenes in which for many

[1] *King*, VI, letters of April 1, 2, 1823, to Adams and Monroe; memoranda by King, April 7, 1823, of his talk with Van Buren; *Van Buren Papers MSS*, letter of King to Van Buren, April 6, 1823.

years I have taken part." [1]   Thompson himself had already asked Van Buren whether he would accept the appointment. John Quincy Adams also concurred with King as to Van Buren's qualifications, and he later said that, he believed that, had Van Buren been appointed, "he would have followed in the tracks of Marshall and proved himself a sound interpreter of National principles." [2]   Thompson, however, after considerable vacillation, and apparently after satisfying himself that he stood no chance to be nominated for President as against John Quincy Adams and William H. Crawford, finally accepted the position; and he was nominated to the Senate by President Monroe on December 8, 1823, and confirmed the next day.[3] Curious surmise may be made as to what would have been the history of the law laid down by the Court had Van Buren been on the Bench and in a position to succeed Marshall, twelve years later, as President Jackson's choice for Chief Justice, instead of Taney.

At the Term following this new appointment, the Court was confronted, for the first time in its thirty-five years' existence, with the question of the construction and scope of that great clause in the Constitution granting to Congress the power to regulate commerce between the States. That Marshall and his Associates would give a broad construction to this clause had been long anticipated and feared by the

[1] *Van Buren Papers MSS*, letters of King to Van Buren, April 6, 1823, Van Buren to Thompson, March 30, 1823.

[2] *Life and Letters of George Bancroft* (1908), by M. A. DeW. Howe.

[3] As to Thompson's various attitudes towards the nomination, and towards Van Buren, see letters of Thompson to Van Buren, April 25, June 26, July 11, 1823, letter of Crawford to Van Buren, May 29, Aug. 1, 1823, letter of Van Buren to Thompson, June 4, 1823, *Van Buren Papers MSS*. Van Buren himself in his *Autobiography* in *Amer. Hist. Ass. Rep.* (1918), II, 141, states his belief that King's object was to withdraw Van Buren from politics and from advocacy of Crawford's nomination for the Presidency.

Republicans in Congress, for the question had been actively debated in that body in connection with the subject of the Federal power over internal improvements. "The plan of the Federal Courts seems to be to keep pace with Congress," wrote Nathaniel Macon to Jefferson in 1822. "As Congress attempts to get power by stretching the Constitution to fit its views, it is to be expected, if other departments do not check the attempt, that each of them will use the same means to obtain power, and thus destroy any check that was intended, by the division of power into three distinct and separate bodies." [1] Within six months after this letter was written, the Court expressed to President Monroe an unofficial opinion on the subject of the power of Congress over internal improvements, which would have caused even greater anxiety among the adherents of a limited construction of the Constitution, had the opinion been generally made public. On May 4, 1822, Monroe had vetoed a Cumberland Road bill which sought to extend Federal power over turnpikes within the boundaries of the States. He had embodied his general views as to the proper limitations of such power in a lengthy pamphlet which he caused to be sent to each of the Judges. In acknowledging its receipt, Chief Justice Marshall wrote that, while the question "very much divides the opinions of intelligent men ", Monroe's views appeared to him to be "profound" and "most generally just." "A general power over internal improvement, if to be exercised by the Union, would certainly be cumbersome to the Government, and of no utility to the people. But to the extent you recommend, it would be productive of no mischief, and of great good. I despair, however, of the adop-

---

[1] *John P. Branch Historical Studies* (1909), III, letter of Feb. 2, 1822.

tion of such a measure."[1]   Judge Story replied that:
"Upon the constitutional question, I do not feel at
liberty to express any opinion as it may hereafter
perhaps come for discussion before the Supreme Court;
but I rejoice that the wisdom and patriotism of the
statesmen of our country are engaged in developing
the materials for a sound judgment on this highly interesting subject."   After these letters were sent,
however, it appears that Judge Johnson obtained
the views of his Associates and communicated them
to the President in the following interesting letter,
which showed to what a far-reaching extent the Court
was inclined to carry the doctrines enunciated by it
in *McCulloch* v. *Maryland*:

Judge Johnson has had the Honour to submit the President's argument on the subject of internal improvement
to his Brother Judges and is instructed to make the following Report.   The Judges are deeply sensible of the mark of
confidence bestowed on them in this instance and should
be unworthy of that confidence did they attempt to conceal their real opinion.   Indeed, to conceal or disavow it
would be now impossible as they are all of opinion that
the decision on the Bank question completely commits
them on the subject of internal improvement, as applied
to Postroads and Military Roads.   On the other points,
it is impossible to resist the lucid and conclusive reasoning contained in the argument.   The principle assumed
in the case of the Bank is that the granting of the principal power carries with it the grant of all adequate and
appropriate means of executing it.   That the selection of
these means must rest with the General Government, and
as to that power and those means the Constitution makes
the Government of the U. S. supreme.   Judge Johnson
would take the liberty of suggesting to the President that

---

[1] *James Monroe Papers MSS*, letters of Marshall to Monroe, June 13, 1822,
Story to Monroe, June 24, 1822, Johnson to Monroe, undated. See also *Judicial
Interpretation of Political Theory* (1914), by William Bennett Bizzell, 115 *et seq.*
"The incident is one of the most interesting and unusual in our political his-
tory."

it would not be unproductive of good, if the Secretary of
State were to have the opinion of this Court on the Bank
question, printed and dispersed through the Union.

To what extent Monroe ever made public these unofficial views of the Judges does not appear in any contemporary document.

When the Court convened in 1824, however, it found
on the docket for argument the noted case of *Gibbons* v.
Ogden, 9 Wheat. 1, in which it was destined to express,
in immortal terms, its views as to the broad extent
of Federal power over internal commerce. The issues
presented by this case brought the Court once more
into the political contest between the upholders of
State-Rights and the believers in a strong Federal
Government; for it was urged, not only to adopt a
construction of the Constitution enhancing the power
of Congress over commerce, but also to hold invalid
New York statutes which had been warmly fostered
by the leaders of the Republican Party. The Liv-
ingston-Fulton steamboat monopoly, whose fate was
involved in the case, had been created by Republican
legislators, owned by Republican statesmen and defended largely by Republican lawyers — all connected
with the faction in New York politics, headed by the
Livingstons, Judge Ambrose Spenser and Cadwallader
D. Colden. And while the Republicans had long inveighed against the "monster monopoly" of the Bank of
the United States chartered by the Federal Government,
and had attacked the Court for upholding it in the
McCulloch Case, they were now engaged in vigorously
supporting an even more stringent monopoly chartered
by a State. For twenty-four years, Ex-Chancellor
Robert R. Livingston and Robert Fulton and their
heirs and assigns had enjoyed, under grant from the
New York Legislature, an exclusive right to run steam-

boats in the waters of New York. Efforts in the Courts
to break this Monopoly had been frequent but unavailing. A case in the United States Circuit Court,
in 1811, had been dismissed for want of jurisdiction.
A case in the State Court of Errors between the same
parties had resulted in a decree upholding the power
of the State to grant such exclusive rights. Pending
this case, the State had passed a further statute authorizing the seizure of any steam vessel found in
New York waters in violation of the Livingston grant,
thus practically making it impossible for any person
to try his rights in Court, without first forfeiting his
vessel. Retaliatory statutes had been passed in New
Jersey, Connecticut and Ohio in 1818 and 1822, forbidding boats "operated by fire or steam" under the
license granted by the New York Legislature from
plying in the waters of those States; and so bitter
were the feelings aroused by the Monopoly that, as
William Wirt said in his final argument in the Supreme
Court, the four States "were almost on the eve of civil
war." Meanwhile, exclusive rights of steam navigation had been granted to the Monopoly in 1811 in
Louisiana.[1] Similar exclusive rights had also been
granted in Massachusetts, New Hampshire, Vermont
and Georgia to various persons. Finally, a test case
was brought in New York by Ex-Governor Aaron
Ogden, of New Jersey, who, having established a steamboat line between New York and Elizabethport in
defiance of the Monopoly, had been enjoined by John
R. Livingston and had accepted a license from the
latter. The defendant was Thomas Gibbons of Georgia,

[1] A suit was brought by Livingston in 1817 in the United States District Court
for the Territory of Orleans to enforce his rights under this grant, no printed record
of which has ever been published — *Heirs of Livingston and Fulton* v. *Reuben
Nichols and Steamboat Constitution*, filed Nov. 21, 1817 (see files of U. S. District
Court for Eastern District of Louisiana) — and in which, a year after the decision
in *Gibbons* v. *Ogden*, verdict was found for the defendant, Dec. 16, 1825.

a former partner of Ogden, who had refused to act under the Livingston license, and who had started an opposition line in 1818. A motion to dissolve the injunction issued had been heard by Chancellor Kent and denied in 1819; and the Court of Errors had sustained Kent in 1820. The case was finally docketed in the United States Supreme Court in January, 1822, Daniel Webster and William Pinkney appearing as counsel against each other.[1] Before it was reached for argument in 1824, both Pinkney and John Wells, the leading counsel for Gibbons, had died; but a galaxy of great lawyers had been retained — Daniel Webster, William Wirt and David B. Ogden for Gibbons, and Thomas Addis Emmet and Thomas J. Oakley for the Monopoly. Of these, Emmet was the senior, fifty-nine years old, a strong Republican in politics, and noted for eloquence, passion and force. Oakley was forty-one, a former State Attorney-General of brilliant talents. Ogden was fifty-five and had one of the largest practices at the Federal Bar. Webster was forty-two, and had been recognized, since Pinkney's death, as sharing with Wirt and Littleton Waller Tazewell the leadership of the Bar. "We in the South have not his superior and you in the North have not his equal," said William Lowndes of South Carolina. "In point of genius and rare

[1] A previous appeal to the United States Supreme Court in 1821 had been dismissed owing to the fact that the decree appealed from was held not to be a final decree. *Gibbons* v. *Ogden*, 6 Wheat. 448. See also *Livingston* v. *Van Ingen* (1811), 1 Paine, 45; *Livingston* v. *Van Ingen* (1812), 9 John. 807; *Livingston* v. *Ogden and Gibbons* (1819), 4 John. Ch. 48; *Livingston* v. *Gibbons* (1819), 4 John. Ch. 94; *In Re Vanderbilt* (1819), 4 John. Ch. 57; *Ogden* v. *Gibbons* (1819), 4 John. Ch. 176; *Livingston* v. *Tompkins* (1820), 4 John. Ch. 415; *Livingston* v. *Gibbons* (1820), 4 John. Ch. 570; *Livingston* v. *Gibbons* (1821), 5 John. Ch. 250; *North River Steamboat Co.* v. *Hoffman* (1821), 5 John. Ch. 300; *Gibbons* v. *Ogden* (1820), 17 John. 488; *Steamboat Co.* v. *Livingston*, 3 Cowen, 741; s.c. (1824), 1 Wend. 560; *Gibbons* v. *Livingston* (1822), 6 N. J. Law, 236; *Gibbons* v. *Ogden* (1822), 6 N. J. Law, 285; *Gibbons* v. *Ogden* (1822), 6 N. J. Law, 582; *Gibbons* v. *Ogden* (1825), 8 N. J. Law, 288.

endowment inferior to no man among us," wrote Rufus King; and Charles J. Ingersoll termed him "the most eminent practitioner in this Court."[1] Wirt was fifty-two; he had been for six years Attorney-General of the United States and was at the height of his fame as an orator and lawyer. "His presence is peculiarly imposing and all his manners graceful," wrote a New York correspondent at this time. "His voice is powerful, his tones harmonious, and his enunciation clear and distinct. He never speaks without evincing ardor and feeling, and his fluency is peculiar and never interrupted. He delights and convinces, and no man hears him without understanding his arguments — a sure indication of a clear head and a logical mind. His arguments are constantly enlivened by classical allusions and flashes of wit. Many a dry cause, calculated to fatigue and weary, is thus rendered interesting to the spectator as well as to the Court. . . . There is no man of the Bar but esteems and respects Mr. Wirt. His gentlemanly deportment, his affable and conciliating manners, his disposition to serve his professional brethren, his exemption from everything like envy, his equanimity of temper, his admiration of genius and success when displayed by his rivals, — these traits of character are well calculated to secure the admiration and regard of his professional brethren. No ill-natured, no illiberal, no irritating language ever escapes his lips, even in the ardor of argument and reply."[2] Of

---

[1] *King*, VI, letter to Christopher Gore, Nov. 3, 1822; *Life of Charles J. Ingersoll* (1897), by William A. Meigs, diary entry, Feb. 6, 1823; and for an unusual contemporary picture of Webster, see *Charleston Courier* (S. C.), Jan. 29, 1824. Jefferson wrote to Monroe, Dec. 15, 1824, describing a visit from George Ticknor and Daniel Webster: "I am much gratified by the acquaintance made with the latter. He is likely to become of great weight in our Government." *James Monroe Papers MSS.*

[2] *New York Statesman*, Feb. 24, 1824.

THE COURT-ROOM FROM 1809 TO 1859, NOW THE LAW
LIBRARY OF THE COURT

this great galaxy of lawyers, Wirt wrote to his brother-in-law, shortly after the Court convened in 1824: "Tomorrow week will come on the great steamboat question from New York. . . . Come on and hear it. Emmet's whole soul is in the case and he will stretch all his powers. Oakley is said to be one of the first logicians of the age, as much a Phocion as Emmet is a Themistocles, and Webster is as ambitious as Caesar. He will not be outdone by any man, if it is within the compass of his power to avoid it. It will be a combat worth witnessing. I have the last speech, and have yet to study the cause; but I know the facts and have only to weave the argument." [1] Five questions were to be presented for argument in the case. Did the New York statute, granting an exclusive right, conflict with the patents issued by the United States? Was it a regulation of commerce at all? If it was, did the State possess the concurrent right to regulate commerce in this manner? Did Congress possess exclusive power to regulate? Did the New York statute conflict with any Act of Congress? The counsel opposed to the Monopoly differed as to the method to be adopted in the argument. Wirt favored laying stress on the first and last questions; but Webster insisted on the broader ground that the State statute was void, irrespective of its conflict with Federal legislation. As stated by himself, later, he declined to argue this cause "on any other ground than that of the great commercial question presented by it — the then novel question of the constitutional authority of Congress exclusively to regulate commerce in all its forms on all navigable waters of the United States . . . without any monopoly, restraint, or interference created by States' legisla-

[1] *Wirt*, II, 164, letter of Feb. 1, 1824.

tion." [1] It was finally agreed that each counsel should argue on his own lines.

On Tuesday, February 3, the great steamboat case was called, "but as the counsel did not expect to answer so soon and were not prepared, it was postponed till tomorrow," so wrote a Washington correspondent. "Judge Story and Mr. Ogden of New York arrived last evening. They had a narrow escape on their way from Baltimore to this city. The stage was upset by a wagon running against it. None of the passengers were materially injured." [2] On Wednesday, February 4, at eleven o'clock, Webster opened the case. "It was one of the most powerful arguments we ever remember to have heard. The Court-room was excessively crowded," said the *Washington Republican*.[3] He devoted almost his full time, two and a half hours, to developing his broad thesis as to the plenary and exclusive power of Congress over the commerce in question, paying slight attention to the question of the interference of the State statute with the Federal coasting license, and leaving entirely to Wirt the question of the relation of the State statute to the Federal patent laws. Webster himself has described the

[1] *Reminiscences and Anecdotes of Webster* (1877), by Peter Harvey.

[2] *New York Statesman*, Feb. 7, 1824; *Washington Republican*, Feb. 4, 1824 The *National Intelligencer* said, Feb. 6, 1824: "The Hall of the Supreme Court is the center of considerable attraction just now on account of the interesting case which first came up to be argued in it, which is commonly known as the Steam Boat cause."

[3] George Ticknor Curtis in his *Life of Daniel Webster* (1870), I, 216, 217, states that Webster sat up all night to prepare his argument. "To use his own phrase 'the tapes had not been off the papers for more than a year!' He worked all night and, as he has told me more than once, he thought he never on any occasion had so completely the free use of his faculties. . . . At nine A.M., after eleven hours of continuous intellectual effort, his brief was completed. He sent for the barber and was shaved; he took a very slight breakfast of tea and crackers; he looked over his papers to see if they were all in order, and tied them up; he read the morning journals to amuse and change his thoughts, and then he went into Court and made that grand argument which, as Judge Wayne said about twenty years afterward 'released every creek and river, every lake and harbor in our country from the interference of monopolies.'"

moment when he opened out to the Court the scope
of the great principle urged by him: "I can see the
Chief Justice as he looked at that moment. Chief
Justice Marshall always wrote with a quill.   He
never adopted the barbarous invention of steel pens.
That abomination had not been introduced.   And
always, before counsel began to argue, the Chief Justice would nib his pen; and then, when everything
was ready, pulling up the sleeves of his gown, he would
nod to the counsel who was to address him, as much
as to say, 'I am ready; now you may go on.'   I think
I never experienced more intellectual pleasure than
in arguing that novel question to a great man who
could appreciate it, and take it in; and he did take
it in, as a baby takes in its mother's milk."   Judge
Story later described Webster's argument as follows:
"Of Mr. Webster's argument in the opening of this
cause (for it was closed by Mr. Wirt in a speech of
great splendor and force) it may be said to furnish
as good a specimen of the characteristics of his mind,
as any which could be named.   We have here, in as
favorable light as we could desire, his clearness and
downright simplicity of statement, his vast comprehensiveness of topics, his fertility in illustrations drawn
from practical sources; his keen analysis, and suggestion of difficulties; his power of disentangling a complicated proposition, and resolving it in elements so
plain as to reach the most common minds; his vigor in
generalizations, planting his own argument behind the
whole battery of his opponents; his wariness and caution not to betray himself by heat into untenable positions, or to spread his forces over useless ground. . . .
Whoever, with a view to the real difficulties of the case
and the known ability of his opponents, shall sit down
to the task of perusing this argument, will find that it

is equally remarkable for profoundness and sagacity, for the choice and comprehensiveness of the topics, and for the delicacy and tact with which they were handled." [1]

Thomas J. Oakley, counsel for Ogden, followed Webster and delivered a powerful and eloquent argument, occupying an hour on February 4, and the whole day on February 5. At the close of the first day, a Washington correspondent wrote that: "Mr. Oakley did not, however, appear to be at all intimidated by the able argument of his antagonist, but set about attacking the ramparts of the law which had been erected, with his usual coolness and deliberation. He broke ground at a great distance from the immediate question, and commenced a system of mining. His argument thus far has been chiefly confined to a description of the powers of the General and State governments, contending that in many cases they are concurrent, which Mr. Webster denied *in toto*. The argument excites a very lively interest here. The Court-room was crowded with ladies and gentlemen." [2] Of Oakley's argument on the second day, he wrote: "It may probably without any exaggeration be pronounced one of the most ingenious and able arguments ever made in this Court. . . . Upon the Attorney-General will devolve the task of dissecting, analyzing, and refuting, if he can, his reasoning; and I have a curiosity to see how he will manage this ingenious and powerful argument. . . . You can form no idea what interest this decision excites at Washington." The veteran Thomas Addis Emmet occupied the whole of the third day, February 6, and two hours on February 7, with a vehement and brilliantly eloquent oration, described as follows: "It is hardly credible

[1] See MSS discovered in the Congressional Library and quoted by Everett P. Wheeler in his *Daniel Webster, the Expounder of the Constitution* (1905).
[2] *New York Statesman*, Feb. 7, 9, 10, 13, 1824.

that this veteran at the Bar, who is now advanced in years, could endure for so long a time without the least intermission, the *laborem strepitumque fori*. But the cause of which he was the zealous advocate seemed to have absorbed all thought of himself and of time; and he manifested no disposition to pause in his argument. . . . Mr. Emmet's argument drew together an unusual number of spectators. In short, the Court-room was full to overflowing. So great was the assemblage of ladies that many of them were obliged to find seats within the bar. . . . Several gentlemen of distinction were present, among whom was the Secretary of State and many members of both Houses of Congress." Wirt closed the case with a " classical and eloquent" argument, absorbing two hours on February 7 and four hours on February 9 ; and it is evident that his brilliant effort made upon his auditors a greater impression than Webster's cogently and profoundly reasoned argument. "The great contest seemed to be reserved for Mr. Emmet and the Attorney-General," wrote a correspondent of the *Richmond Enquirer*.[1] Wirt's peroration was " the finest effort of human genius ever exhibited in a Court of Justice . . . a powerful and splendid effusion, grand, tender, picturesque, and pathetic. The manner was lofty and touching; the fall of his voice towards the conclusion was truly thrilling and affecting, and I never witnessed such an effect from any burst of eloquence; every face was filled with the fine transport and prophetic fury of the orator, and all united in applauding the peroration, as affording for matter, diction, manner, happy application and striking effect the most powerful display of real oratory that they ever witnessed." Chancellor George M. Bibb of Kentucky wrote to John

[1] *Richmond Enquirer*, March 2, 1824. See also *Georgia Journal*, March 23, 1824.

J. Crittenden: "I heard from Wirt the greatest display that I have ever heard at the Bar since the days of Patrick Henry. His legal argument was very strong; his peroration was beautiful and grand. I did not hear Webster, nor Oakley, nor Emmet in this case, but all are said to have exhibited great talents. I have heard Webster, Sergeant, and White of Tennessee. Wirt, Webster, White and Ogden are the ablest lawyers, and Walter Jones should also be ranked among the first. Emmet I have not heard, but his reputation is high. After all, I have not been convinced that the Bar of Kentucky does not contain as much talent and force as any other Bar in the Union." [1]

Though Webster, a week after the close of the argument, wrote to his brother, "our steamboat case is not yet decided, but it can go but one way," [2] his

[1] *Life of John J. Crittenden* (1871), 61, letter of March 8, 1824. To Thomas Ruffin, later Chief Justice of North Carolina, his friend Henry Seawell wrote, Feb. 12, 1824, describing the argument as follows, *Papers of Thomas Ruffin,* I, 292: "My time begins to hang heavily upon me — the novelty of scene has passed away; I have been physicked with the expression of sympathy for the Greeks; I have attended the Supreme Court and heard several interesting questions relative to State-Rights discussed; and the right of Congress to make internal improvements being common talk for the hackmen; I may say in truth I am pretty well gorged with Washington. . . . The great men in the Supreme Court almost read their speeches — they have a *book* in manuscript on each point, fastened together in the form of a bill in equity. . . . The counsel in argument begin so low as scarcely to be heard and gradually swell until they fairly rave; then they gently subside into a soft whisper; their gesticulation is menacing, both to the Court and the bystanders, and an equal portion of all they say is distributed to every part of the hall. The Constitution of the United States appears to be acquiring in the political world what was ascribed to the philosopher's stone in the physical regions. It is gathering, by its own growth, the capacity of converting everything into exclusive jurisdiction of Congress; for according to the construction now contended for, and what is more than probable will be supported by the Supreme Court, the States can do nothing, what it is not in the power of Congress to *regulate;* and there is scarcely anything they can act upon at all — the trade or commerce, being subject to the regulation of Congress, is supposed to draw after it almost all power of regulation, and according to a definition given to the word 'commerce' by the Attorney-General that it means '*intercourse.*' I shall soon expect to learn that our fornication laws are unconstitutional."

[2] *Letters of Daniel Webster* (1902), ed. by Claude H. Van Tyne, letter of March 15, 1824. Writing to Jeremiah Mason, the same day, Webster said: "We have

confidence was not entirely warranted by the theretofore known trend of the views of the various members of the Court. While Marshall and Washington
were both strongly Federal in their political doctrines,
Todd and Duval were equally firm in their State-Rights
views; Johnson in a recent case on Circuit in South
Carolina had held that the Federal power over interstate commerce was exclusive; Story's view, however,
was more problematical, for, only four years before,
in *Houston* v. *Moore*, 5 Wheat. 1, in 1820, he had expressed extremely broad views as to the concurrent
powers of the States on many subjects. If he held to
this position in the *Steamboat Case*, it was open to him
to deny Webster's doctrine that the power of Congress
in the matter was exclusive of the State, and to decide that the whole question turned on whether the
New York statute did or did not "run counter" to any
law of Congress. The newly appointed Judge, Smith
Thompson of New York, having been a brother-in-
law of the originator of the Monopoly, Robert R.
Livingston, and restrained also by family affliction
in the recent death of his daughter, did not take his
seat upon the Bench until February 10, after the close
of the argument.

The outcome of the case was awaited with intense
interest, not only in New York but throughout those
States over which the steamboat Monopoly had so
powerful a control.[1] On February 24, a New York
paper said that: "Great anxiety is manifested in this
city to learn the decision of the great steamboat ques-

no opinion yet in the Steam Boat cause; but I presume there can be no doubt how
it will go. The case of collision is, I think, unquestionably made out; and I have
no doubt the Court will decide that, as far as respects commerce, between different
States (which is this case) the law of New York is inoperative. Possibly the
navigation of the New York waters between port and port in her own territory
may be subject to a different consideration."

[1] See *New York Statesman*, Feb. 14, 1824.

tion which has lately been argued with consummate ability at Washington." [1] Meanwhile, Chief Justice Marshall sustained an accident dislocating his shoulder, which delayed the writing of the opinion. On March 1, a Washington correspondent wrote that "it is rumored that the decision will be adverse to the State of New York *in toto*"; and on March 3, another New York paper contained the following extremely interesting comment: [2] "Inquiries are hourly made respecting the anxiously-looked-for decision of the Supreme Court in this important case. The opinion of the Court has not yet been given, nor do we know when it will be. Judge Marshall, we are informed, had commenced writing the opinion when his labors were interrupted by his unfortunate fall; and it is understood that Mr. Justice Story is now engaged in completing it." The concluding sentence contained a fact which, so far as is known, no biographer or eulogist of Marshall or of Story, and no law writer, has ever mentioned, that Judge Story is possibly entitled to share in the glory of having aided in writing the opinion in *Gibbons* v. *Ogden*. Hitherto, the honor of having settled the trend of the whole American law of interstate commerce has been attributed entirely to Marshall.

The decision in the case was finally announced on March 2, 1824, only three weeks after the argument. "This morning, his Honor, Chief Justice Marshall,

---

[1] *New York Commercial Advertiser*, Feb. 24, 1824. "We regret to hear from Washington that on Thursday evening (February 19) as Chief Justice Marshall was stepping from his carriage on returning to his lodgings from the President's drawing-room, his foot slipped and he fell, by which accident his shoulder was dislocated and his head somewhat bruised. The bone was soon replaced by a surgeon, but he will be confined to his room for some time; and as there are many important causes upon the docket, the vacancy upon the Bench makes the accident a double misfortune." See also *New York American*, Feb. 25, 1824.

[2] *New York Statesman*, March 4, 1824; *New York Commercial Advertiser*, March 3, 1824.

appeared for the first time since his confinement on account of the dislocation of his shoulder, and took his seat on the bench of the Supreme Court," wrote a Washington newspaper correspondent. "His return to his elevated and important station is welcomed by every member of the Bench and the Bar, and the whole community. The Court-room was thronged at an early hour in anticipation of what has taken place — the reading of the opinion of the Court in the great *Steamboat Case*." Another correspondent wrote that the reading of the opinion took three quarters of an hour, and that "the decision excited as much interest as the argument. Many spectators were present, who in their eagerness to hear (the Chief Justice reading in a low, feeble voice) collected close around the bench." [1] In his opinion — "that opinion which has done more to knit the American people into an indivisible Nation than any other one force in our history, excepting only war," [2] — the Chief Justice gave, for the first time in the history of the Court, a full interpretation of the meaning of the Commerce Clause of the Constitution, defining in memorable terms the words "regulate" and "commerce." "Commerce undoubtedly is traffic, but it is something more, it is intercourse." It comprehends navigation. It comprehends every species of commercial intercourse among States and nations, and "is regulated by prescribing rules for carrying on that intercourse." Though this definition now seems almost a self-evident truism, so embedded has it become in our law, the rad-

[1] *New York Commercial Advertiser, New York Statesman*, March 5, 1824. On March 15, 1825, Marshall delivered the opinion of the Court (unreported) in the case of *Cornelius Vanderbilt* v. *John R. Livingston*, "the question being the same with that involved in the Steamboat cause, decided at last Term and submitted without argument by Webster against Henry Wheaton." *National Intelligencer*, March 21, 1825.

[2] *Marshall*, IV, 429.

ical departure which it made from the views popularly held in 1824 as to the limits of the Federal power
to regulate commerce may be best appreciated, by
contrasting it with the restricted scope which President Monroe had then just expressed in his veto of
the Cumberland Road Act in 1822. "Commerce between independent powers or community is universally regulated by duties and imports. It was so
regulated by the States before the adoption of this
Constitution, equally in respect to each other and to
foreign Powers. The goods and vessels employed in
the trade are the only subject of regulation. It can
act on none other. A power, then, to impose such
duties and imports in regard to foreign nations and
to prevent any on the trade between the States, was
the only power granted." [1] The further question
which had been urged, whether the States retained
the power to legislate on the subject in the absence
of Congressional legislation, or whether the power
of Congress was exclusive, Marshall found unnecessary to decide in this case, since he held that Congress,
by enacting the Federal coasting laws, had already
acted upon the subject, and hence that the State
statute, being in conflict with the Federal law, was
unconstitutional. Judge Johnson in a concurring
opinion was less cautious, and maintained the exclusiveness of the Federal power over commerce in the
fullest degree.

Of the indebtedness of the Chief Justice to Webster's great argument, there can be no question; and
Webster himself said later that: "The opinion of the
Court, as rendered by the Chief Justice, was little
else than a recital of my argument. The Chief

[1] See *Federal Control of Interstate Commerce*, by George W. Wickersham, *Harv. Law Rev.* (1910), XXIII.

Justice told me that he had little to do but to repeat that argument, as that covered the whole ground. And, which was a little curious, he never referred to the fact that Mr. Wirt had made an argument. He did not speak of it once. . . . That was very singular. It was an accident, I think. Mr. Wirt was a great lawyer, and a great man. But sometimes a man gets a kink and doesn't hit right. That was one of the occasions. But that was nothing against Mr. Wirt." [1]

In view of the pinnacle on which Marshall's opinion has ever since been placed, it is interesting to note that all his contemporaries did not concur in the general praise. John Randolph, writing soon after the delivery of the opinion, said: [2]

It is the fashion to praise the Chief Justice's opinion in the case of Ogden against Gibbons. But you know I am not a fashionable man; I think it is unworthy of him. Lord Liverpool has set him an example of caution in the last speech of the King; one that shames our gasconading message. I said it was too long before I read it. It contains a great deal that has no business there, or indeed anywhere. . . . A judicial opinion should decide nothing

[1] *Reminiscences and Anecdotes of Webster* (1877), by Peter Harvey. Writing to Edward Everett, Oct. 30, 1851, Webster said: "I presume the argument in *Gibbons* v. *Ogden* was written by me and given to Mr. Wheaton. The argument is a pretty good one and was on a new question. It has been often observed that the opinion of the Court delivered by Chief Justice Marshall follows closely the track of the argument. He adopts the idea which I remember struck him at the time — that by the Constitution the commerce of the several States has become a unit."

Judge Wayne in the *Passenger Cases* in 1849 said: "The case of *Gibbons* v. *Ogden*, in the extent and variety of learning, and in the acuteness of distinction with which it was argued by counsel, is not surpassed by any other case in the reports of Courts. In the consideration given to it by the Court, there are proofs of judicial ability, and of close and precise discrimination of most difficult points, equal to any other judgment on record. . . . The case will always be a high and honorable proof of the eminence of the American Bar of that day, and of the talents and distinguished ability of the Judges who were then in the places which we now occupy." 7 How. 283, 437.

[2] *Life of John Randolph* (1851), by Hugh A. Garland, II, 212, letter of Randolph to Dr. Brockenbrough, March 3, 1824.

and embrace nothing that is not before the Court. If he had said that "a vessel, having the legal evidence that she has conformed to the regulations which Congress has seen fit to prescribe, has the right to go from a port of any State to a port of any other with freight or in quest of it, with passengers or in quest of them, *non obstante* such a law as that of the State of New York, under which the appellee claims," I should have been satisfied. However, since the case of *Cohen* v. *Virginia*, I am done with the Supreme Court. No one admires more than I do the extraordinary powers of Marshall's mind; no one respects more his amiable deportment in private life. He is the most unpretending and unassuming of men. His abilities and his virtues render him an ornament not only to Virginia, but to our Nation. I cannot, however, help thinking that he was too long at the Bar before he ascended the Bench; and that, like our friend T——, he had injured, by the indiscriminate defense of right or wrong, the tone of his perception (if you will allow so quaint a phrase) of truth or falsehood.

Randolph's view, however, was not generally held by his contemporaries. Throughout the United States, the newspapers, regardless of political affiliation and with few exceptions, highly praised the decision and rejoiced over the destruction of the obnoxious steamboat Monopoly. The New York papers naturally hailed it with especial satisfaction.[1] "This morning, Chief Justice Marshall delivered one of the most able and solemn opinions that has ever been delivered in any Court on the *Steamboat Case*," wrote the correspondent of the *New York Evening Post*. "The Court-room was crowded with people, and during more than an hour, which was consumed in pronouncing the decision of the Court, the most unbroken silence prevailed. Chief Justice Marshall commenced by stating the importance of the case

[1] *New York Evening Post*, March 5, 8, 18, 24; *New York Commercial Advertiser*, March 12, 1824; *New York Statesman*, March 8, 1824. See also *Columbian Centinel*, March 10, 1824.

and by passing a short but dignified eulogium on
the late Judiciary of the State of New York. He
stated the regret which was felt by the highest tribunal in the Nation in differing from the opinion
which the Courts of New York had given to the world
on a great constitutional question. The Chief Justice then proceeded in his long and luminous view of
the *Steamboat Case*. This opinion . . . presents one of
the most powerful efforts of the human mind that
has ever been displayed from the bench of any Court.
Many passages indicated a profoundness and a fore-
cast, in relation to the destinies of our confederacy,
peculiar to the great man who acted as the organ of
the Court. The steamboat grant is at an end."
Many other New York papers published the opinion
in full, and said editorially that it would "command
the assent of every impartial mind competent to embrace such a subject"; that it was "written with great
clearness, perspicuity and, considering the importance
of the subject, with great conciseness"; and that it
was "probably the strongest document in support
of the powers of the Federal Government that has
ever issued from the same authority." In other parts
of the country, the papers greeted the decision with
equal approval.[1] "The constitutional law which is
so thoroughly expounded in this masterpiece of judicial reasoning concerns every citizen. . . . It is matter
for general complacency that unlimited scope is now
afforded to enterprise and capital in steam naviga-

---

[1] *National Gazette*, March 9, 1824; *New Brunswick Fredonian*, March 11, 1824;
Louisville Public Advertiser, March 28, 1824; *Charleston Courier*, March 17, 1824;
Augusta Chronicle and Georgia Advertiser, March 17, 1824; *Missouri Republican*
(St. Louis), April 26, 1824. See also *The Federal Power over Carriers and Corporations* (1907), by E. Parmalee Prentice, and the following newspapers mentioned
therein: *New York National Union*, March 13, 1824; *Connecticut Courant*, March
9, 1824; *Albany Argus*, March 9, 1824; *Delaware Gazette* (Wilmington), March
19, 1824.

tion," said a Philadelphia paper. "The unprincipled steamboat monopoly of New York is at length broken up. . . . The waters are now free, and those who heretofore held with an iron grasp, and exercised with unfeeling perverseness, their precarious power will now perhaps lament, when it is too late, the rashness and severity which has involved them in embarrassment, if not ruin," said a New Jersey paper. "We not only believe the opinion of the Court to be correct, but we feel confident that, had the same case been tried by any competent tribunal not within the State of New York, the result would have been the same," said a Kentucky paper. "This decision will have an important bearing upon the navigation companies of New York, which have been brought into existence and pampered by the unnatural and unconstitutional measures adopted by the Legislature of that State," said a South Carolina paper. A Georgia paper said: "The principle settled in the great Steam Boat Question recently before the Supreme Court of the United States is one of such vast interest and importance to our country that we deem it a duty to lay the entire opinion of the Court, long as it is, before our readers. . . . The ability displayed in it will amply compensate for . . . its perusal. We cannot suppose that the decision which has conclusively determined that the navigable waters of every State are the common passway of all the citizens of the United States, so that all boats or vessels however propelled, sailing under coasting licenses have a right to traverse them, will be unacceptable to any portion of the American population, who have not an *interest* in wishing that a question of this magnitude had been brought to a different result." A Missouri paper said: "Some of the New Yorkers show themselves a little restive under the late decision of the U. S. Supreme Court on the subject of the steam boat monopoly. They may rest assured that it is a decision approved of in their sister States, who can see no propriety in the claim of New York to domineer over the waters which form the means of intercourse between that State and others, and over that intercourse itself."

The effects of the decision were at once felt in the waters of New York and the other States. Shortly after the fourteenth of March, the newspapers of the North carried this item: "Yesterday the Steamboat *United States*, Capt. Bunker, from New Haven, entered New York in triumph, with streamers flying, and a large company of passengers exulting in the decision of the United States Supreme Court against the New York monopoly. She fired a salute which was loudly returned by huzzas from the wharves." A representative Southern paper spoke of "the immense public advantages that flow from the decision. The fare in the steamboats that ply between New York and New Haven has been reduced from five to three dollars. The boats that heretofore went from Charleston to Hamburg now touch at Savannah and come directly to the wharves of Augusta. On Monday, the 29th, two steamboats from Charleston arrived at Augusta. Their arrival was greeted by the citizens who fired a *feu de joie*, accompanied by a band of music, which was returned by one of the boats, amidst repeated huzzas and cries of 'down with all monopolies of commerce and manufactories— one is as great an evil as the other. Give us *free trade* and sailor's rights!'" [1] Shortly over a year after the decision, *Niles Register* reported that the number of steamboats plying from New York had increased from six to forty-three.[2]

[1] *Georgia Journal*, April 6, 1824.   [2] *Niles Register*, XXIX, Nov. 12, 1825.

As revealed in the above comments, the chief importance of the case in the eyes of the public of that day was its effect in shattering the great monopoly against which they had been struggling for fifteen years. It was the first great "trust" decision in this country, and quite naturally met with popular approval on this account. But economic results of more far-reaching importance than the mere demolition of the monopoly were involved, which were not appreciated until later years. The opening of the Hudson River and Long Island Sound to the free passage of steamboats was the most potent factor in the building up of New York as a commercial center. The removal of danger of similar grants of railroad monopolies in other States promoted immensely the development of interstate communication by steam throughout the country; for the first railroad was built only five years later. The coal industry, then but an experiment, was developed through the growth of New England's manufacturing industries, made possible by cheap transportation of coal by water. In short, Marshall's opinion was the emancipation proclamation of American commerce.[1]

It was not, however, the economic results of the Court's decision in the *Steamboat Case* which signalized its leading place in the history of American law. The political effect of Marshall's opinion was equally potent; for it marked another step in the broad construction of the Constitution, and became at once a mighty weapon in the hands of those statesmen who favored projects requiring the extension of Federal authority. As has been pointed out, before and during and immediately after the argument of *Gibbons* v. *Ogden*, Congress was engaged in a vigorous debate

[1] *History of the American Bar* (1911), by Charles Warren.

on two subjects which for ten years had sharply divided the two political parties — the power of the National Government over internal improvements and its power to enact protective tariffs in aid of favored interests.[1] While the actual decision of the case was based on the conflict between the New York and the Federal statutes, the language used by the Chief Justice in his opinion as to the extent of the power of Congress was directly contrary to the contentions of the Republican Party, and could be used in support of every political measure favored by its opponents. Republican Congressmen were not slow in perceiving the aid which the opinion gave to the advocates of the obnoxious measures of Federal expansion. "More danger is now to be apprehended from tyranny in the head than from anarchy in the extremities," said Stevenson of Virginia. "We are now sweeping down at one blow the independence and power of the State Governments." "Not one or two but many States in the Union see with great concern and alarm the encroachments of the General Government on their authority," said John Randolph, and denouncing the tariff bill, as based on a broad construction of the commerce clause of the Constitution, he added: "There are firebrands enough in the land, without this apple of discord being cast into the assembly."

Some of the newspapers of the country were also greatly concerned over the political effects of Marshall's views. A South Carolina paper said that: "The exercise of the power of the United States Courts in matters of this kind cannot but be interesting to the individual States in its bearing on the independence of their

---

[1] *Marshall*, IV, chap. 8; see also *18th Cong.*, *1st Sess.*, Jan. 12, 14, 16, 27, 28, 29, 30, Feb. 3, 4, 5, 6, 9, 10, April 21, 23, 1824, for debates on the Roads and Canals Survey Bill; *ibid.*, Feb. 11, to April 16, 1824, for debate on the Tariff Bill.

legislation. . . . By this decision, it would appear that
the sovereignty of a State under the Federal Constitution is not unlimited. A principle of the greatest magnitude is thus settled in the United States,
and consequences of material interest in every part of
the Republic will flow from its decision." [1] The *Richmond Enquirer* considered the opinion as "too elaborate, too long", and as traveling beyond the record;
and it sounded this note of warning to its readers:
"The last paragraph of the opinion states what would
be the consequence of contracting 'by construction
into the narrowest possible compass' 'the powers expressly granted to the Government of the Union.'
It 'would explain away the Constitution of our country,
and leave it (says the opinion) a magnificent structure,
indeed, to look at, but totally unfit to use.' And
suppose we fly to the opposite extreme, suppose we
stretch the power of the Government by a most liberal
construction, suppose we consider 'necessary' to be
synonymous with 'convenient', what would be then
the state of the case? The State Governments would
moulder into ruins, upon which would rise up one
powerful, gigantic and threatening edifice. To which
of these extremes the stream of decisions from the
Supreme Court is sweeping, we refer to the case of
McCulloch and the case of the Cohens." Similar views
were vigorously expressed by Thomas Addis Emmet,
arguing in May, 1824, before the New York Court of
Chancery.[2] He viewed "the progress of the Union
towards consolidation, with a fearful solicitude." " If
some of the principles of *Gibbons* v. *Ogden* are not overruled within twenty years, the Constitution will before

[1] *Charleston City Gazette* (S. C.), March 10, 24, 1824; *Georgia Journal*, April
6, 1824; *Richmond Enquirer*, March 16, 1824.
[2] *North River Steamboat Co.* v. *Livingston* (June, 1824), 1 Hopkins, Ch. 170;
s.c. 3 Cowen 741.

then have verged towards a form of government which
many good men dread, and which assuredly the people
never chose"; and he concluded with the following
pessimistic prediction: "There is a pretty general
impression that the decisions of that Court on constitutional law tend to such a result. It is the avowed
opinion of Mr. Jefferson and of many who now labor
to check it. If that impression be correct, the consequences are much to be lamented; for such a course
pursued by that Court (the value and importance of
which ought to be estimated most highly) may well
aid in its own destruction, and possibly in that of the
fabric of our government. . . . It is upon State-
Rights we stand and State-Rights are State liberty.
They are more; they are in this land the bulwarks of
individual and personal liberty; they are the outposts
of the Constitution. While they are preserved entire,
our federative Union will stand against the shocks
of time and the approaches of despotism. But let
them be broken down or suffered to moulder away,
and a consolidated power must succeed in governing
this mighty empire. Consolidation will be the eutha-
nasia of our Constitution. Make that consolidated
government as democratic and free as you please,
make its base as broad and its principles as liberal as
philanthropy and philosophy can devise; it will still be
a single government over a vast extent of territory;
it will follow — it will surely and speedily follow —
the course of all the governments of ancient times and
modern Europe, which began with elective rights and
free institutions but have silently sunk into despotisms."

On the other hand, the newspapers which favored
the views of the opponents of the Republican Party
applauded the breadth of the opinion, the *Connecticut*

Courant saying: "It was natural that the Courts of New York should insensibly receive a bias in support of the legislative proceedings of that State; and it was wisely provided by the Constitution of the United States that questions of this nature should be finally settled by a tribunal removed from the influence of those State and private interests which give rise to them. Thus every year unfolds new relations growing out of our Federative and republican government. It will take many years to settle the boundary line between State and Federative rights. These will be adjudged peaceably as they arise, so long as the decisions of the Supreme Court of the United States shall continue to be respected. It is the duty of every citizen to cherish a spirit of respect and acquiescence in the decisions of this Court. If the States should once embrace a feeling of hostility or even jealousy toward the National councils, it is to be feared those ties which bind us together will be dissolved, and we shall again be made to experience all the evils of the old Confederation, or, what is worse, of separate and independent States." [1]

The doctrine thus proclaimed by the Court in the *Steamboat Case* filled Jefferson with horror. He was an old man of eighty-two years; he had been out of office for sixteen years; yet his frequent letters to his personal friends in the years since 1818, frequently printed in the newspapers, had become the fountainhead of Democratic dogma. Accordingly, one of the last of these letters, written to William B. Giles, December 26, 1825 (in the year before his death), represented the general attitude of his party: "I see, as you do, and with the deepest affliction, the rapid strides with which the Federal branch of our Government

---

[1] *Connecticut Courant*, March 9, 1824.

is advancing towards the usurpation of all the rights reserved to the States, and the consolidation in itself of all powers, foreign and domestic; and that too by constructions which, if legitimate, leave no limits to their power. Take together the decisions of the Federal Court, the doctrines of the President and the misconstructions of the Constitutional Compact acted on by the Legislature of the Federal branch, and it is but too evident that the three ruling branches of that department are in combination to strip their colleagues, the State authorities, of the powers reserved by them, and to exercise themselves all functions foreign and domestic. Under the power to regulate commerce, they assume indefinitely that also over agriculture and manufactures, and call it regulation to take the earnings of one of these branches of industry — and that, too, the most depressed — and put them into the pockets of the other — the most flourishing of all. Under the authority to establish postroads, they claim that of cutting down mountains for the construction of roads, of digging canals, and, aided by a little sophistry on the words 'general welfare', a right to do, not only the acts to effect that which are sufficiently enumerated and permitted, but whatsoever they shall think or pretend will be for the general welfare."

There was one question in connection with the Court's trend of decision to which Jefferson made no reference, and on which in all his correspondence he ever preserved a discreet silence — the slavery issue. While the wide scope of Marshall's opinion gave concern to the South with reference to the political issues of internal improvements and tariffs, the effect of the Court's constitutional doctrines as to Congressional power was viewed with even greater alarm in its relation to commerce in slaves. Not without reason did a Representative from Virginia rise on the floor of Congress, a month after the decision, and say with solemnity: "Sir, we must look very little to consequences, if we do not perceive in the spirit of this construction, combined with the political fanaticism of the period, reason to anticipate, at no distant day, the usurpation on the part of Congress of the right to legislate on a subject, which, if you once touch, will inevitably throw this country into revolution — I mean that of slavery." [1] For the slavery issue had been presented during the argument of the *Gibbons Case*, in connection with the discussion of the respective powers of the States and of Congress. Emmet had pointed out that the power to legislate in prohibition of the importation of slaves had been exercised by many States; that by the Constitution slaves were treated as articles of commerce; that, in 1803, Congress passed an Act imposing penalties on the importing or landing of any person of color in any States which by law had prohibited or should prohibit their admission or importation, and he asked: "How could Congress do this, if the power of prohibiting the trade were not unquestionably possessed by the States in their sovereign capacity?" From this, he argued that the States had concurrent power with Congress in the regulation of commerce. Webster in his argument referred to the question, but declined to discuss the constitutionality of the State laws, until their particular provisions should be more clearly set forth. Neither Oakley nor Wirt appear to have adverted to the subject of slavery. The Chief Justice, however, in his opinion disposed of the whole argument in a single paragraph, by pointing

[1] Speech of Robert S. Garnett of Virginia, April 2, 1824. *18th Cong., 1st Sess.*, 2098.

out that, by the express provision of the Constitution, the power of the States to prohibit the importation of slaves previous to the year 1808 "constitutes an exception to the power of Congress to regulate commerce, and the exception is expressed in such words as to manifest clearly the intention to continue the pre-existing right of the States to admit or exclude, for a limited period", but for a limited period only ; and "the possession of this particular power, then, during the time limited in the Constitution, cannot be admitted to prove the possession of any other similar power." Marshall thus clearly intimated that the power of the States over the importation of slaves did not extend beyond the year 1808, and that State laws passed later with reference to the subject would be invalid. It was this phase of his opinion which caused great alarm in the South, for the specific question had already arisen in two cases in the United States Circuit Courts. Virginia and South Carolina had enacted statutes directed against the entrance of free negroes into the State, and providing for their detention in custody until the vessel in which they arrived should leave port. By these statutes, thus interfering with the right of transit between the States, the South attempted to protect itself against the possibility of insurrectionary movements being stirred up amongst the slave population by the presence of free negroes from Northern States.[1] The validity of the Virginia law had been contested before Chief Justice Marshall in the Circuit Court, in the case of *The Brig Wilson*, in 1820 ;

[1] See debate in the House, Jan. 31, 1849, for an interesting discussion by Congressmen Robert B. Rhett and Isaac F. Holmes of South Carolina, as to the origin and necessity of these laws. Holmes said : "The whole thing was done with a view to self-protection after the experience of the year 1823, in consequence of Denmark Vesey and other blacks coming from the North for the purpose of creating an insurrection, which was prevented, only by timely discovery, from bursting with all its horrors upon the city of Charleston." *30th Cong., 2d Sess.*

but he had evaded the dangerous issue by construing one of the statutes involved as inapplicable to the facts in the case.[1] In the fall of 1823, however, eight months before the decision in *Gibbons* v. *Ogden*, Judge Johnson had met the issue squarely in a case in the Circuit Court for the District of South Carolina, and, though a Republican appointed by Jefferson, he had held the South Carolina statute clearly unconstitutional, stating that the right of the Federal Government to regulate commerce between sister States and with foreign nations was "a paramount and exclusive right." "The plea of necessity is urged," he said "and of the existence of that necessity, we are told, the State alone is to judge. Where is this to land us? Is it not asserting the right in each State to throw off the Federal Constitution at its will and pleasure? If it can be done as to any particular article, it may be done as to all, and, like the old Confederation, the Union becomes a mere rope of sand."[2] This decision had been bitterly resented by South Carolina, and her officials had proceeded to enforce the statute, in flat disregard of the decision, and in sympathy with the threat made by one of the counsel at the argument that "if South Carolina was deprived of the right of regulating her colored population, it required not the spirit of prophecy to foretell the result; and rather than submit to the destruction of the State I would prefer the dissolution of the Union." *Niles Register* regarded the issue involved as more dangerous to the existence of the Union than even the Missouri question, and said that while Johnson's decision was "such as everyone must have expected that it would be . . . the decision

---

[1] *The Brig Wilson*, 1 Brock, 423; *Elkinson* v. *Deliesseline*, Federal Cases No. 4366.
[2] See especially *John C. Calhoun and the Labor Question*, by E. Parmalee Prentice, *Harv. Law Rev.* (1900), XIV.

is said to have created much excitement at Charleston, and no wonder; for self-preservation is said to be the first principle of law." [1] Judge Johnson, himself, was much perturbed over the recalcitrant attitude of the State and wrote to John Quincy Adams (then Secretary of State): "I am daily made sensible that the eyes of the community are turned most particularly to the Judges of the Supreme Court for protection of their constitutional rights, while I feel myself destitute of the power necessary to realize that expectation. Hence, altho obliged to look on and see the Constitution of the United States trampled on by a set of men, who, I sincerely believe, are as much influenced by the pleasure of bringing its functionaries into contempt, by exposing their impotence, as by any other consideration whatever, I feel it my duty to call the attention of the President to the subject as one which may not be unworthy of an official remonstrance of the Executive of the States." [2] And Marshall wrote to Judge Story:

[1] See *Niles Register*, XVII, XXIV, XXV. On Dec. 25, 1819, it said in reference to the South Carolina laws when first proposed: "If a free black, who is a 'citizen', pleases to locate himself in South Carolina, he may undoubtedly do so, any law of the State to the contrary notwithstanding." On Aug. 23, 1823, it said that Judge Johnson's decision was "such as every one must have expected that it would be. . . . The decision is said to have created much excitement at Charleston — and no wonder, for self preservation is said to be the first principle of law. We trust, however, that no possible injury can result from the proceeding." On Sept. 6, 1823, it printed the opinion in full; and on Sept. 20, after saying that "the Charleston papers have teemed with essays on the subject," it printed a long letter from one of the counsel in the case. See also *ibid.*, XXVII, Dec. 18, 24, 1824, Jan. 8, 1825. The *Washington Union* edited by the veteran, Thomas Ritchie of Richmond, said, March 13, 1851: "This law of South Carolina was enacted at a moment when Charleston was threatened with insurrection. Colored sailors were suspected of having ministered to the fuel. To repress such danger, the law was passed. We well recollect when Judge Johnson leaned in his decision against the execution of the law. It threw Charleston into a flame which extended into Virginia. Mr. Jefferson and his political associates took the other side and vindicated the right of South Carolina to pass such a moral quarantine law."

[2] Quoted in *31st Cong., 1st Sess., App.*, 1661, Sept. 12, 1850, letter of Johnson to Adams, July 3, 1824; *Story Papers MSS*, letter of Marshall to Story, Sept. 26, 1823.

Our brother Johnson, I perceive, has hung himself on a democratic snag in a hedge composed entirely of thorny State-Rights in South Carolina, and will find some difficulty, I fear, in getting off into smooth, open ground. You have, I presume, seen his opinion in the *National Intelligencer*, and could scarcely have supposed that it would have excited so much irritation as it seems to have produced. The subject is one of much feeling in the South. Of this I was apprised, but did not think it would have shown itself in such strength as it has. The decision has been considered as another act of judicial usurpation; but the sentiment has been avowed that, if this be the Constitution, it is better to break that instrument than submit to the principle. Reference has been made to the massacres of St. Domingo, and the people have been reminded that those massacres also originated " in the theories of a distant government, insensible of and not participating in the dangers their systems produced." It is suggested that the point will be brought before the Supreme Court, but the writer seems to despair of a more favorable decision from that tribunal, since they are deserted by the friend in whom their confidence was placed. Thus you see fuel is continually added to the fire at which *exaltées* are about to roast the Judicial Department. You have, it is said, some laws in Massachusetts, not very unlike in principles to that which our brother has declared unconstitutional. We have its twin brother in Virginia; a case has been brought before me in which I might have considered its constitutionality, had I chosen to do so; but it was not absolutely necessary, and as I am not fond of butting against a wall in sport, I escaped on the construction of the act.

Two months after the decision in *Gibbons* v. *Ogden*, Attorney-General William Wirt rendered an opinion to President Monroe, holding the South Carolina statute unconstitutional; and the President, to whom the British Government had complained of the application of the statute to its citizens, wrote to the Governor of the State urging a repeal of the law.[1] No atten-

[1] See opinion of Wirt, May 8, 1824, *Ops. Attys.-Gen.*, I, 659. Seven years later, March 25, 1831, Attorney.- General Berrien gave an opinion directly to the contrary,

tion, however, was paid to this request; but on the contrary, the Governor sent a message to the Legislature, December 1, 1824, urging a reaffirmance of its policy and containing the following truculent sentiments of Nullification: "The evils of slavery have been visited upon us by the cupidity of those who are now the champions of universal emancipation. A firm determination to resist, at the threshold, every invasion of our domestic tranquillity and to preserve our sovereignty and independence as a State is earnestly recommended; and if an appeal to the first principles of the right of self-government be disregarded, and reason be successfully combated by sophistry and error, there would be more glory in forming a rampart with our bodies on the confines of our territory than to be the victims of a successful rebellion or the slaves of a great consolidated government." The officials and Courts of South Carolina continued for over twenty-five years to disregard Judge Johnson's opinion and to insist that the decision in *Gibbons* v. *Ogden* was inapplicable.[1] The whole episode is a striking illustration of the fact that, throughout the long years when the question of the extent of the Federal power over commerce was being tested in numerous cases in the Court, that question was, in the minds of Southerners, simply coincident with the question of the extent of the Federal power over slavery. So the long-continued controversy as to whether Congress had exclusive or concurrent jurisdiction over commerce was not a conflict between theories of government, or between Nationalism and State-Rights, or between

holding that the law belonged strictly to the State's internal police, like a quarantine law, and that "the right of self-protection was not limited to defence against physical pestilence but that a State might protect itself against the introduction amongst its colored people of moral contagion." *Ops. Attys.-Gen.*, II, 426. See also *27th Cong., 3d Sess.*, House Doc. No. 800.

[1] See Chapter XXIV, *infra*.

differing legal construction of the Constitution, but was simply the naked issue of State or Federal control of slavery. It was little wonder, therefore, that the Judges of the Court prior to the Civil War displayed great hesitation in deciding this momentous controversy.

While the States were thus exceedingly concerned over the possible encroachment on their powers as to the subjects of monopoly, of transportation, slavery and internal improvements which lurked in the constitutional doctrines announced in the *Steamboat Case*, they were about to be confronted at this Term of Court with a still more startling invasion of their sovereignty. Exactly one month after the close of the argument in *Gibbons* v. *Ogden* on February 10, 1824, arguments were begun in the great case of *Osborn* v. *Bank of the United States*, which had been pending on the docket for three years, and which presented four questions of the highest importance : the right of the Bank to maintain suit against the officials of a State ; the right of the Bank to sue in the Federal Circuit Courts ; the power of Congress to charter the Bank ; and the power of the State of Ohio to tax the Bank. The second question was also pending in a case before the Court arising in Georgia — a case which added that State to the long list of opponents of the Federal authority. Though the Bank of the United States had no branch in Georgia and hence was not subjected to a State tax, a heated conflict had arisen between it and the State over its policy of requiring State banks to redeem their notes in specie. As a retaliatory measure, Georgia had enacted statutes, in 1819 and 1821, expressly excepting the Bank from rights given to other injured suitors in her Courts, and providing that State bank notes held by the Bank should not be redeemable in specie, unless the person presenting them would swear that the notes were not procured by the Bank "for the purpose or with any intent to demand or to draw specie from the bank issuing the notes." As a result of this unfair legislation, the effort of the Bank to collect in specie naturally met with open resistance. The largest State bank, the Planters Bank of Georgia, announced, in 1821, that it would cash no more of its notes presented by the Bank of the United States, and stated in a circular that "this mammoth came here to destroy our very substance. Ships, plantations, negroes, wharves, stores, — all the sources of wealth of the State have been devoured by this all-assuming power." In December, 1822, the principles of the Ohio resolutions opposing the *McCulloch Case* decision of the United States Supreme Court had been approved in a debate in the Georgia Legislature, and resolutions were introduced stating that the Bank of the United States "must alter its policy" or "it will encounter the utmost exertion of the power of this State." And in the latter part of 1823, the Georgia Legislature had passed a resolution calling for an Amendment of the Constitution so as to restrict the powers of the Federal Courts. Meanwhile, in a suit by the Bank against the Planters Bank of Georgia, brought in the United States Circuit Court, a defense was raised which, if sustained, might have been almost fatal to the Bank's operations. It was objected that the Circuit Court had no jurisdiction of the case, as there was no requisite diverse citizenship and the provision of the Bank's charter allowing it to sue in the Circuit Court, properly construed, did not permit such suit. Had the point been successfully maintained and the Bank excluded from the Federal Courts and obliged to trust its fate to local juries, its fortunes would have been highly insecure. In

December, 1823, the case accordingly had been certified
to the Supreme Court.[1] After the Ohio case had been
argued by Charles Hammond and John C. Wright
for the State against Henry Clay for the Bank, the
Court expressed a wish that it be reargued with
this Georgia case, upon the constitutional points raised,
as well as upon the effect of the section of the Bank's
charter authorizing suit in the Federal Courts.[2] In
this second argument, which occurred on March 10
and 11, 1824, a galaxy of counsel took part. The
State had retained Robert Goodloe Harper, the talented
Maryland lawyer, then fifty-nine years old and famed
for his knowledge of commercial law and his keen
reasoning powers; Ethan Allen Brown of Ohio, then
forty-eight years old, who had been Judge of the
Supreme Court and Governor of Ohio; and John C.
Wright. For the Bank, there appeared Daniel Webster,
then fresh from his triumph in *Gibbons* v. *Ogden* (for
this case had been decided in the *interim*, on March 2)
and from his recent powerful argument in *Ogden* v.
Saunders (argued March 3–5); and John Sergeant,
the long-time leader of the Philadelphia Bar, then
forty-five years old, and the Bank's regular counsel.[3]

[1] See *Niles Register*, XXI, Jan. 25, 1822; XXV, Jan. 10, 24, 1824.

[2] In 1823, the *Western Herald and Steubenville Gazette* (Ohio), said: March 1:
"The great cause between the State of Ohio and the United States Bank was
expected to have been decided by the Supreme Court at Washington City this
present week, Messrs. Wright and Hammond are in attendance as counsel for
State and Mr. Clay as counsel for the Bank."

Judge Story had written to Judge Todd on March 14, 1823: "Your friend Clay
has argued before us with a good deal of ability, and if he were not a candidate
for higher offices, I should think he might attain great eminence at this Bar. But
he prefers the fame of popular talents to the steady fame of the Bar." As to
Charles Hammond, Chief Justice Marshall, on a trip down the Potomac with
William Greene of Cincinnati in 1824, "spoke of his remarkable acuteness and accu-
racy of mind, and referred with emphatic admiration to his argument in the *Bank
Case*. He said that he met no judicial record of equal intellectual power since
Lord Hardwicke's time." *History of Ohio* (1912), by Emilius O. Randall and
Daniel J. Ryan, III, 329.

[3] "*Osborn* v. *The Bank* was argued with equal zeal and talent, and decided on great
deliberation," said Chief Justice Marshall in *Ex parte Madrazo* (1833), 7 Pet. 627.

Only one week later, on March 19, 1824, the decision was rendered by Chief Justice Marshall upholding the Bank in all its contentions and reaffirming *Mc-Culloch* v. *Maryland* as to the constitutionality of the Bank's charter and the invalidity of the State tax law. This action of the Court had been generally expected. But the further rulings proclaimed a new doctrine in constitutional law, when the Court held that a State officer who had committed a trespass, relying on an unconstitutional State statute, might be sued in spite of his official position; that Ohio's contention that the suit against Osborn was a case in which the State was a party and hence barred by the provisions of the Eleventh Amendment was untenable; and that the State officials must return to the Bank the tax money taken from it.[1] By this fateful decision, the narrow limits to the power of the Federal Courts so strenuously urged by the State-Rights men were overthrown and demolished. Rendered at a time when attacks in Congress upon the Court and its jurisdiction were becoming increasingly frequent, and when threats of resistance to Federal protective tariff laws and to decrees of Federal Courts in relation to State negro legislation were being heard in various States, the decision constituted another firm bulwark to the Union. That these conditions of the time were clearly in the mind of the Court was apparent from the ringing words employed by the Chief Justice in maintaining the power of the Nation to protect its agents in executing its laws and to restrain or commit State officials who sought to obstruct the authority of the National Government. Judge Johnson also, though dissenting on a technical point, pointed out that "a state of things has now

[1] See especially *Osborn* v. *The Bank*, by Daniel H. Chamberlain, *Harv. Law Rev.* (1887), I; *The State as a Defendant under the Federal Constitution*, by William C. Coleman, *ibid.* (1917), XXXI.

grown up in some of the States which renders all
the protection necessary that the General Government
can give to this Bank."

To those who favored a strong Union, the decision
was a source of great satisfaction, but to the ardent
State-Rights advocates it afforded only more fuel to
their opposition to the Court. "The opinion of the
Court goes far beyond any heretofore given, as to the
reduction of the State Sovereignty, and will, it is apprehended, give much cause of alarm to the friends of
republican principles and of the rights of the people,"
said a leading Ohio paper; and a Kentucky paper said
that the decision repealed the Eleventh Amendment,
"for if Federal Courts can punish State officers for
official acts, and take money from the State Treasurer,
their exemption from suits is a mere mockery." [1]

[1] See *New England Palladium* (Boston), March 30, 1824; *Western Herald and
Steubenville Gazette*, March 27, 1824; *Argus of Western America*, April 7, 1824.

CHAPTER SIXTEEN

KENTUCKY AGAINST THE COURT

1821-1825

IT will be noticed that during the years from 1819 to 1824, the criticisms of the Court, outside of Virginia and Ohio, had come largely from Kentucky politicians and newspapers, and (as will be described in a later chapter) the most serious attempt made in Congress to weaken the Court's power originated with Kentucky Senators and Representatives. "To the mass of democracy, it would be grateful to see the Judges rendered dependent on the will of the National Legislature and to the inhabitants of Kentucky and other new portions of the Union peculiarly acceptable," wrote Pickering to Richard Peters in 1810.[1] This attitude on the part of Kentucky was reflected in the support which it was destined to give to Jackson and the Democratic Party, as opposed to Clay, Adams and those who were supposed to favor Chief Justice Marshall's principles of constitutional construction; and thus the Court became in that State a distinct factor in political history.

There were three local causes for the intensity of feeling which Kentucky displayed on the subject of judicial power; for that power had been exercised in setting aside the assertion of State control in four vital classes of subjects. The Federal Courts had insisted on their jurisdiction in admiralty over Kentucky's inland waters;

[1] *Peters Papers MSS*, letter of Pickering, Jan. 1, 1810; "In all suits respecting lands where non-residents are parties they deprecate the intervention of an able and impartial Judiciary."

they had declared the invalidity of Kentucky's laws protecting settlers who had made improvements on disputed land patents; they had disregarded Kentucky's laws passed for the protection of judgment debtors; and they had sustained the rights of the obnoxious Bank of the United States. In all these instances, the Federal Courts had run counter to tides of intense State sentiment; and nowhere in the United States had the feeling of hostility thus aroused been so generally entertained by the whole people of the State.

Of the four "usurpations" by the Federal Courts, the one of least importance may be noted first — the extensive admiralty jurisdiction claimed by the United States District Court in inland waters, which had been feared and resented by the States bordering on the Ohio and Mississippi Rivers. Cases involving mechanics' repairs, sales of supplies and seamen's wages on riverboats had been brought in large numbers in the Federal Courts, owing to the fact that a trial by jury was thus avoided, and the Federal executions required payment in gold (the State Courts allowing payment in paper and subject to stay-laws). The assumption of jurisdiction in these cases had aroused much feeling against this increase of Federal power.[1] In 1821, the action of the District Court in Kentucky had been the subject of attack in Congress by Senator Richard M. Johnson, who said that : "It was a new era in the history of our country; for Kentucky was about to learn from the exercise of admiralty jurisdiction that she was a maritime State"; that if this jurisdiction was confirmed, the Federal Courts in Kentucky would at one step double their jurisdiction, and that "the people never can and never will submit to this extraordinary assumption of admi-

[1] See *Kentucky Gazette*, July 5, 1821. See also *Niles Register*, XVII, Sept. 11, 1819, giving an account of a case upholding admiralty jurisdiction on the United States District Court for the Western District of Pennsylvania.

ralty jurisdiction . . . the most serious encroachment upon the constitutional jurisdiction of the State tribunals and the most dangerous inroad upon State sovereignty." He urged that, though steamboat navigation had produced a new epoch in the interior navigation of the country, those who engaged in such navigation would be ruined if subjected to the processes of Federal Admiralty Courts, and that the people could not be governed by two systems of law — "one maritime, and the other the statute laws of the State — one demanding the pound of flesh, the other extending these charities of the law. . . . Such a system has the most powerful tendency to lessen confidence in the Federal Judiciary and to generate in the minds of the people the most inveterate hatred towards that essential arm of the General Government." Johnson's bill to confine admiralty jurisdiction to places within the ebb and flow of the tide and on the high seas was passed in the Senate in 1822, but failed in the House.[1] Each of the three succeeding years, however, witnessed strong criticisms in Congress on this unwarranted extension of admiralty jurisdiction, and the hostile feeling did not subside until 1825, when the Court, through Judge Story, relieved the situation by deciding, in *The Thomas Jefferson*, 10 Wheat. 428, that admiralty jurisdiction did not extend beyond the ebb and flow of the tide.[2]

[1] *17th Cong., 1st Sess.*, Dec. 28, 1821, Feb. 13, March 15, 1822; *17th Cong., 2d Sess.*, Feb. 15, 1823. In the House, the bill was opposed by J. S. Johnston of Louisiana who thought that the matter should be left to the decision of the Supreme Court. J. S. Johnson of Kentucky favored the bill, and argued that if the Courts had jurisdiction on interior rivers, they might also take jurisdiction on the Erie Canal and on the Canal systems throughout the country. "The more we reflect upon this subject, the more we will be alarmed at this mighty power. . . . Shall we sanction that doctrine which makes necessity the arbiter of constitutional law, convenience and necessity?"

[2] Judge Story had been extremely liberal hitherto in construing the extent of admiralty jurisdiction, so far as related to its subject matter. In 1815, in *De Lovio v. Boit*, 2 Gallison, 398, he had held marine insurance policies to be subject to that jurisdiction — "the broad pretension for the Admiralty set up, under which the legal

Far more dangerous opposition to the Federal Courts had meanwhile been aroused by their decisions on the subject of the Kentucky land laws. For many years, Kentucky had been the scene of complicated and troublesome controversies over the desperate condition of her land titles, as a result of the innumerable surveys and patents of land which frequently overlapped each other.[1] The State in order to mitigate this situation had enacted laws, providing that no claimant should be awarded possession of land to which he proved title, unless he should compensate the occupier for all improvements, and that, in default thereof, the title should rest in the occupier upon paying the value of the land without improvements. The validity of these laws had been at once attacked in the Courts of the State, but they had in general been upheld. Grave fears, however, were entertained by Kentuckians lest the United States District Court should hold otherwise. Senator John Breckenridge, in drafting the Circuit Court Act of 1802, was bombarded with demands from his constituents to restrict the jurisdiction of the Federal Courts, by abolishing suits based on diverse citizenship, so as to eliminate the possibility of the validity of the land laws being tested by non-residents in these Courts.[2] As early as 1804, the Legislature had passed a resolution reciting that: "The artful and wealthy land-claimant who is an inhabitant of this State, by a transfer of title to a non-resident, may give jurisdiction . . . and thereby put it out of the power

profession and this Court staggered for thirty years before being able to maintain it," as Judge Campbell said in *Jackson* v. *Steamboat Magnolia*, 20 How. 296, in 1858. See also *The General Smith*, 4 Wheat. 438, in 1819, and the dissenting opinion of Judge Johnson in *Ramsey* v. *Allegre*, 12 Wheat. 611, in 1827, and letter of Marshall to Story, June 25, 1831, *Mass. Hist. Soc. Proc.*, 2d Series, XIV.

[1] See *Kentucky's Contributions to Jurisprudence*, by Judge Henry Burnett, *Kentucky State Bar Ass.* (1909); *Land Titles in Kentucky, ibid.;* speeches of W. P. Mangum and C. A Wickliffe, *19th Cong., 1st Sess.*, 931, 946, Jan. 10, 11, 1826.

[2] See *supra*, I, 219–221.

of his indigent opponent to pursue or support his claim
with success. This is evident when we recollect the
great distance which many of our citizens live from the
District Court of the United States and their inability
to prosecute an appeal at the Federal City. . . . Serious
and alarming consequences may ensue from contradictory adjudications in the Supreme Federal Court and the
Court of Appeals of the State. The Judiciary of each
State ought to be considered best qualified to decide
upon its law." The Legislature accordingly advocated
an Amendment to the Federal Constitution, confining
judicial power to cases arising under the Constitution
and laws of the United States. Fifteen years later, in
1819, the constitutionality of its land-claimant laws
was contested in the United States Circuit Court,
on the ground that they constituted an impairment
of the obligation of a contract which had been entered
into between Virginia and Kentucky when the latter
became a State in 1791, providing that all private
rights and interests within Kentucky should "remain
valid and secure" and should be determined by the then
existing laws of Virginia. Violation of this contract
was hotly denied by Kentucky and by the innocent
occupiers of land. The case, *Green* v. *Biddle,* finally
reached the Supreme Court for argument in 1821, and
on March 8, that Court, through Judge Story, rendered
a decision holding the laws unconstitutional. Kentucky
was at once set aflame with resentment. "It is a
fact which we have noticed, and our readers must have
remarked the same of late," said a leading newspaper,
"that at almost every session of the Court, the laws of
the States are treated in a manner that does no credit,
either to the motives or understanding of our State
Legislatures. The Supreme Court of the United States
is the proper tribunal to settle *some* disputed cases,

and it must be submitted to; but the principles upon which it has recently acted are so broad, that it begins to look like the old iron bedstead that accommodated every person by stretching or lopping off a limb." "The slow encroachments and gradual usurpation of the Judiciary, facilitated by the irresponsible tenure of their office, are more dangerous to the liberties of the people and the right of the States, than Congress and the President with the army and navy at their command."[1] In October, 1821, the Legislature met and passed a resolution calling the decision "incompatible with the constitutional powers of this State", and protesting against the power of the Court, in very much the same language used by the Legislature of Ohio, in the preceding year, in the latter's attack on the decision of *McCulloch* v. *Maryland*.[2] Henry Clay, having been directed by the State to ask for a reargument, the case was argued for a second time in 1822.[3] As the Court had beeen warned by Clay in his argument that the power to pass on the validity of State statutes was one to be exercised "with the most deliberate caution", and that the success of the experiment of government by written Constitution "depends upon the prudence with which this high trust is executed", and as the Court was thoroughly alive to the seriousness of the adverse sentiments which had been aroused towards the Judiciary in Ohio, Virginia, Maryland,

---

[1] *Kentucky Gazette*, March 29, 1821, Dec. 26, 1822. See also editorial in *Argus of Western America*, March 22, 1821. It is to be noted that this decision was rendered only five days after the decision in the *Cohens Case;* see editorial in *Niles Register*, March 17, 1821.

[2] *Niles Register*, XXI, Feb. 23, 1822; *National Intelligencer*, Feb. 20, 1822; *State Documents on Federal Relations* (1911), by Herman V. Ames.

[3] *Niles Register*, XX, March 17, 1821, Clay and Bibb were requested to oppose the Court's decision, "in such manner as they may deem most respectful to the Court and consistent with the dignity of the State." The second argument by Thomas Montgomery and Benjamin Hardin against Henry Clay and George M. Bibb, occupied six days, March 7–13, 1822.

Kentucky and other States, it held the case under consideration for a full year; but on February 27, 1823, it rendered its final decision, adhering to its former view, and again holding these Kentucky statutes to be unconstitutional. How desirous it had been of upholding their validity, if it could have conscientiously done so, was seen from the remarks of Judge Bushrod Washington, who wrote the opinion: "We hold ourselves answerable to God, our consciences and our country, to decide this question according to the dictates of our best judgment, be the consequences of the decision what they may. If we have ventured to entertain a wish as to the result of the investigation which we have laboriously given to the case, it was that it might be favorable to the validity of the laws; our feeling being always on that side of the question unless the objections to them are fairly and clearly made out." And Judge Story, in a letter to Judge Todd (the Kentucky member of the Supreme Court who was ill this Term of Court), spoke of the "tough business" before the Court and of the solicitude which he had felt over the Kentucky cases: [1]

We have missed you exceedingly during this Term, and particularly in the Kentucky causes, many of which have been continued, solely on account of your absence. God grant that your health may be restored and that you may join us next year. Poor Livingston has been very ill of a peripneumony and is still very ill; whether he will ever recover is doubtful. . . . Judge Washington has also been quite sick and was absent for a fortnight. He is now recovered. The Chief Justice has been somewhat indisposed; so that we have been a crippled Court. Nevertheless, we have had a great deal of business to do; and as you will see by the Reports, tough business. We wanted your firm vote on many occasions. Your friend Clay has argued before us

[1] *Green* v. *Biddle*, 8 Wheat. 1; *Story*, I, 422, letter of March 14, 1823.

with a good deal of ability; and if he were not a candidate for higher offices, I should think he might attain great eminence at this Bar. But he prefers the fame of popular talents to the steady fame of the Bar. . . . The Occupying Claimant Law has at last been definitely settled after many struggles. I see no reason to take back our opinion, though, for one, I felt a solicitude to come to that result, if I could have done it according to my views of great principles. I could not change my opinion, and I have adhered to it.

The antagonism excited by this decision was heightened by reports as to the manner in which it was rendered, for statements were current that it had been concurred in by less than a majority of the members of the Court. "Three out of seven Judges constituting the Court declared our laws unconstitutional," so stated a Kentucky paper. "Marshall refused to sit. Johnson expressly dissented. Todd was prevented by ill health from leaving home and Livingston was sick. Thus three men, a minority of the Judges, have prostrated a system of laws which has been thought essential to their prosperity by almost half a million people constituting an independent State. *Independent*, do we say? Scarcely has Kentucky a sovereign power left!" [1] Although it became known later that the three absent Judges agreed with the decision,[2] the halls

[1] See also letter of Senator Rowan to Governor John Adair describing the efforts to secure a re-hearing, which was denied by Judges Washington, Duval and Story, in *Western Monitor*, May 6, 1823. The *Argus of Western America* said, May 12, 1824: "Kentucky has felt a shock more tremendous than the dreadful earthquake, in the destruction of her occupying claimant laws." *Works of Henry Clay* (1897), IV, letter of Clay to Francis Brooke, March 9, 1823: "The dissatisfaction which will be felt by the people of Kentucky with the decision will be aggravated, in no little degree, by the fact that the decision is that of three Judges to one, a minority therefore, of the whole Court."

[2] *19th Cong., 1st Sess.*, Jan. 6, 1826. Congressman Mercer stated as to *Green v. Biddle*, 903: "I well know and here affirm on unquestionable authority that one of the absent Judges, now in his silent but honored grave and then confined by sickness, concurred in the sentence of the Court, and another of those Judges was withheld from expression of his opinion, by its coincidence with that of the Court, and delicacy only. He had near relatives deeply interested in that judgment. Had it met his disapprobation, no moral or judicial propriety would have restrained him from

of Congress rang with assaults upon the "minority opinion." When the Kentucky Legislature met in December, 1823, resolutions were adopted, solemnly protesting the "doctrines promulgated in that decision as ruinous in their practical effects to the good people of this Commonwealth and subversive of their dearest and most valuable political rights"; the Governor in his speech to the Legislature said that the decision degraded the sovereignty of the State; and a memorial of protest was drawn up and presented to Congress urging changes in the Federal judicial system.[1] As a result of these official proceedings, bills were introduced into Congress and vigorously supported by the Kentucky Senators and Representatives, providing for radical abrogation of the powers of the Court, either through the entire repeal of the Court's appellate jurisdiction, or through a requirement of a concurrence of all, or of five, of the seven Judges, in constitutional cases.

As a curious commentary on the local nature of the doctrine of State-Rights, it may be noted that though Kentucky, in thus arraying herself against the "encroachments of the Federal Judiciary", was but following the position taken and arguments advanced by Virginia after the *Cohens Case*, in 1819, Virginia now was heartily supporting the decision of the Court in

saying so, and every principle of justice would have permitted, if it had not more earnestly prompted, the avowal of his opinion. The sentence of the Court, therefore, which has produced, I admit, much suffering, and excited, very naturally, much discontent, expressed the opinion, not of three, but of five Judges, and I believe of every Judge of that Court but one." In *Bronson* v. *Kinzie*, 1 How. 317, it is said that: "This judgment of the Court is entitled to the more weight, because the opinion is stated in the report of the case to have been unanimous, and Judge Washington, who was the only member of the Court absent at the first argument, delivered the opinion of the second."

[1] *Niles Register*, XXV, Nov. 8, 29, Dec. 27, 1823, Jan. 2, 1824.

The Kentucky State Court refused to be bound by the United States Supreme Court decision, and hence it could be enforced only in the inferior Federal Courts; see *Bodley* v. *Gaither*, 3 T. B. Monroe, 57, in 1825; *Fisher* v. *Cockrell*, 5 Peters, 248; *Niles Register*, XXI, Dec. 30, 1826; *Gaines* v. *Buford*, 1 Dana, 481, in 1833; *Shepherd* v. *McIntire*, 5 Dana, 574, in 1837.

Green v. *Biddle*. Thus again, it was made plain that
State opposition to judicial action depended, not so
much on the political theory held by the States, as on the
particular interest aided or injured. With much reason
did Henry Clay write to a friend in Virginia: "Has
not Virginia exposed herself to the imputation of selfish-
ness by the course of her conduct or of that of many of
her politicians? When, in the case of *Cohens* v. *Virginia*, her authority was alone concerned, she made
the most strenuous efforts against the exercise of that
power by the Supreme Court. But when the thunders
of that Court were directed against poor Kentucky, in
vain did she invoke Virginian aid. The Supreme
Court, it was imagined, would decide on the side of
supposed interests of Virginia. It has so decided; and,
in effect, cripples the sovereign power of the State of
Kentucky more than any other measure ever affected
the independence of any State in the Union; and not
a Virginia voice is heard against this decision." [1]

Just at this time, when hostility towards the Federal
Judiciary was at its height among the occupiers of land
in Kentucky, the Federal Courts again became a storm-
center, by reason of the decisions rendered, in 1825, in
connection with that bugbear of the South, the Bank of
the United States. "I have long entertained the
opinion," said a writer in a leading Kentucky paper in
1824, "that the Bank of the United States was the chief
cause of all the aggressions upon the sovereignty of the

[1] *Works of Henry Clay* (1897), IV, letter to Francis Brooke, Aug. 28, 1823. The
National Intelligencer, Feb. 18, 1822, said: "The people of Virginia already
feel that if the Judiciary of the United States sometimes decides against their
interests, it is, at others, the sure palladium of their rights. At this moment, they
look up to it for protection against the adjudication of the State Courts of Kentucky." The *Richmond Enquirer* said, January 22, 1822, referring to a resolution of the Kentucky Legislature, that only "the most imperious necessity should
justify such a resort" to resistance by force. Yet only the year before, the *Richmond Enquirer* had been most vigorous in counseling resistance to the Court in the
Cohens Case.

States and the rights of the people which have proceeded
from the Federal authorities. . . . I have seen the
Bank leaning on the judicial arm, which not only awards
to the corporation all she claims but seeks every occasion
to humble the States. . . . If the doctrine for which
the Bank contends in those cases prevails, not only
will Kentucky be degraded, but the sovereignty of
every State in the Union will be prostrate in the
dust." [1] The "doctrine" so savagely referred to as
contended for in the Bank cases was the simple doctrine of honesty, good faith and sanctity of contract on
the part of the State; and its reaffirmation by the
Federal Courts had been made necessary by the business
and political conditions prevailing in the Southwest.
When, in the *McCulloch Case* in 1819, and in the *Osborn
Case* in 1824, the Court had denied the power of the
States to tax the Bank of the United States, the financial situation became serious; for the States had been
relying on a policy of chartering State banks with an
almost unlimited issue of paper currency, and these
weak and numerous creations could not withstand the
competition of a strong National banking institution.
"We are in the West in a terrible condition with our
currency," wrote Henry Clay to Caesar A. Rodney,
"of which there is but little prospect of its speedy
melioration. The effect from it which I most apprehend
is collision with the Federal authority." [2] This collision so predicted was soon to be brought about in connection again with the Bank of the United States, for
it was to that institution, instead of to their own rotten
State financial policy, that the people and the newspapers attributed all their woes. In order to relieve
the distressed situation of its debtors, Kentucky

---

[1] *Argus of Western America*, May 12, 1824.
[2] *Caesar A. Rodney Papers MSS*, letter of Aug. 9, 1821.

had determined upon a radical course of action and, in 1821, it passed four remedial acts. The first abolished all imprisonment for debt (Kentucky thus being the first State in the Union to do away with the old and barbarous methods of imprisoning insolvent debtors) ; a second act provided that real estate of a debtor should not be sold on execution for less than three quarters of the appraised value ; a third incorporated the Bank of the Commonwealth with power to issue notes not required to be redeemable in specie ; and the fourth, a "stay"-law, prevented creditors to whom debtors had given bond with security from levying their executions for a period of two years, unless the creditor should indorse on his execution his willingness to accept in payment of his judgment notes on the Bank of Kentucky or the Bank of the Commonwealth. This legislation, thus enabling debtors to pay their debts in a depreciated currency, and sweeping away the creditors' rights to take property on execution, and compelling them to receive payment of less than the amount of their debts or incur the hazards of indefinite and vexatious delays, applied to all past as well as to future loans. There would seem to be no clearer instance of laws directly impairing contract rights ; and the Bank of the United States, as well as other creditors, were determined to contest their validity in both the State and Federal Courts. Though the temper of the people was such that actual threats of personal violence were made against any Judge who should dare to set this legislation aside, and vehement pressure was brought to force the State Judges to bow to the popular will, both Judges of the inferior Courts and of the Kentucky Court of Appeals, in 1822, displayed their courage, integrity and independence by holding that they were bound to follow the law as laid down by the United States Supreme

Court in *Sturges* v. *Crowninshield*, four years before, and to declare the State laws to be violative of the Constitution of the United States and therefore invalid.[1] "Although there are some decisions of the Supreme Court which I could wish were otherwise," said Judge Benjamin Miller, "yet I do not perceive the danger of encroachment and usurpation so loudly sounded; and until I do, I cannot be foremost in volunteering in opposition to a government — the most happy and just, known in the world." This decision aroused a furious outcry against the State Judges. They were denounced as usurpers, tyrants and kings, and their authority or power to destroy a legislative act by declaring it to be unconstitutional was denounced on all sides. The Legislature adopted resolutions, practically echoing the sentiments of the Ohio resolutions of two years before, and denying the power of the Judges to overrule the sovereignty of the State as expressed in the acts of the Legislature, and urging that the statutes should be enforced regardless of the opinion of the Court.[2] After making an unsuccessful attempt

[1] *Blair* v. *Williams, Lapsley* v. *Brashears*, 4 Littell, 34, 47, 64. In Tennessee, a similar decision had been rendered as early as 1821, holding a stay-law invalid, *Townsend* v. *Townsend*, 7 Tenn. 1. In Georgia, in 1815, when the Judges of the Superior Court had been sturdy enough to declare unconstitutional a stay-law, enacted in aid of the debtor class and to the delay and oppression of creditors, the Legislature passed a resolution denouncing and protesting against this action of the Judges, and asserting that the extraordinary power of determining upon the constitutionality of laws regularly passed by the Legislature was not vested in the Judiciary and would not be yielded by the Legislature. See also letter of Thomas Jefferson to W. H. Torrance, June 11, 1815, approving this resolution. *Jefferson*, IX. *Niles Register*, XXI, said, Sept. 15, 1821, that the Tennessee law was undoubtedly invalid, "together with all its kindred acts in other States, which have a tendency to violate the obligation of contracts."

[2] "Further resolved that this Legislature, as the first measure to avoid the degradation and oppression inflicted by that opinion upon the State of Kentucky, will present to the Congress of the United States a temperate but firm remonstrance against its doctrines, and thereupon call upon the Nation to guarantee to the State its Republican form of government, and its co-equal sovereignty with the States which compose this Union." "Resolved that any effort which the Legislature may find it a duty to make, for contravention of the erroneous doctrine of that decision, ought not to interfere with or obstruct the administration of justice according

to remove the Judges by impeachment, the Legislature took the further radical step of abolishing the existing Court of Appeals, in 1824, and establishing an entirely new Court to which the Governor appointed men known to be supporters of the debtor-relief laws.[1]

But while temporarily evading the force of judicial decisions which they deemed obnoxious, by this expedient of abolishing the State Court, the people of Kentucky could not so easily dispose of the questions involved when they arose in the Federal Courts. For while these stay and replevin laws, regulating as they did the manner of enforcing judgments and writs of execution, might be recognized as binding in such State Courts as chose to hold them valid, they were not necessarily binding upon the Courts of the United States, and Judge Trimble in the Circuit Court of Kentucky had already held them to be invalid.[2] Moreover, acting under the Federal Process Act of 1792, the Federal Judges in Kentucky had adopted Rules of Court regulating process in their own Courts, directing that judgments should be discharged only by payment in gold and silver, and restricting the right of debtors to reclaim their property seized on execution. It followed that whenever a plaintiff was capable of suing in the Federal Court, that is, if he were a non-resident creditor or the Bank of the United States (which by Act of Congress was entitled so to sue), he was enabled to secure

to existing laws which, whether they were or were not expedient, are believed to be constitutional and valid, and which should, when it shall be thought expedient to do so, be repealed by the Legislature and not by the appellate Court."

[1] This New Court secured possession of the records by force, and heard and decided fifty-two cases in the Spring Term of 1825 (see 2 T. B. Monroe). In 1826 an act restoring the Old Court was passed by the Legislature over the Governor's veto, and in 1829, the Court in *Hildreth's Heirs* v. *McIntire's Devisee,* 1 J. J. Marshall, 206, declared null and void all proceedings of the New Court. See also *Stark's Admr.* v. *Thompson* (1830), 3 J. J. Marshall, 299.

[2] See editorial in *Kentucky Gazette,* July 12, 1821, attacking Judge Trimble, warning him of the fate of Judge Samuel Chase, and deploring the interference of the Federal Judges with the State execution laws.

payment of his judgment debts in gold or silver.   Kentucky creditors, on the other hand, being obliged to sue in the State Courts found that under the State laws they must be content with payment in paper and extension of the debtor's rights to replevy.   It was entirely natural that the people of Kentucky should feel outraged at this situation, and that they should denounce the right of the Federal Courts to disregard the State laws or to adopt Rules of Court regulating judgments and executions, in derogation of the State authority, and that they should warmly applaud the violent speech in Congress of their Senator, who stated that these Courts had "turned Kentucky over, a prey to the Bank and the mercenary vultures that hovered round that institution." [1]   On the other hand, newspapers in the East applauded the "firmness and decision" of the Judges and were "rejoiced to find the Judiciary in various States interposing to defeat the unconstitutional and pernicious laws of their Legislatures impairing the obligations of contract. . . .   These opinions . . . must, in time, have considerable effect in correcting the wild notions and unfortunate feelings which exist in the West concerning banks and debts and the omnipotence of State Legislatures." [2]

To test the power of the inferior Federal Courts to require the levying of executions in a manner other than that prescribed by the laws of Kentucky, three cases were quickly brought before the Supreme Court from the Circuit Court of the United States in Kentucky. While the State was anxious to obtain a decision on this point, the Bank of the United States was equally anxious to obtain the opinion of the Court as to the constitutionality of the State stay and replevin laws —

[1] *20th Cong., 1st Sess.*, Feb. 21, 1828, speech by Senator Rowan.
[2] *Franklin Gazette* (Pa.), quoted in *Richmond Enquirer*, July 27, 1821.

an opinion which there had hitherto been no possible
means of obtaining by writ of error from the State Court
of Appeals, since that Court had itself held the laws
invalid. These cases of *Wayman* v. *Southard, Bank of
the United States* v. *Halstead* and *Bank of the United
States* v. *January*, 10 Wheat. 1, came before the Court
for argument first in March, 1824, John Sergeant, the
Bank's chief counsel and head of the Pennsylvania
Bar, and Langdon Cheves, its former president and a
leader of the South Carolina Bar, appearing for the Bank
against George M. Bibb and Benjamin M. Munroe, of
Kentucky.[1]   As the Court, however, at this 1824 Term
had already decided the *Osborn Case* against the contentions of Ohio and the *Steamboat Monopoly Case* against
the contentions of New York, and had heard the argument in *Ogden* v. *Saunders,* in which it had been asked
to overthrow the bankrupt laws of all the States, it was
loath to set aside these Kentucky stay-laws, and consequently it rendered no decision at this Term.   The
next year, nevertheless, on February 12 and 15, 1825,
it announced a decision which, though cleverly avoiding
a conclusion as to the constitutionality of the stay and
replevin laws, dealt quite as severe a blow to the debtor
interests of Kentucky; for it held that the Federal
Courts had the power to regulate their own processes
by their own Rules of Court, that as no State had the
power to regulate the processes of the Federal Courts,
the State laws relative to executions, replevy of property
sold to satisfy judgment, etc., were not binding upon such
Courts, and, therefore, "if the laws do not apply to the
Federal Courts, no question concerning their constitutionality can arise in those Courts."   The result of this
decision, of course, was that the Bank and any creditor

---

[1] "The question is interesting to the Western country as well as to the merchants
of the seaboard who have given credit to Western traders." *New York Statesman,*
Feb. 24, March 18, 1824.   See also *Lexington Gazette* (Ky.), April 18, 1824.

who was not a citizen of Kentucky could escape the restrictions of the State laws by suing in the Federal Courts, and thus the State laws which had been enacted chiefly for the purpose of attacking the obnoxious Bank were rendered of no avail.   As soon as this decision was rendered, the people of the State rose in wrath.[1] "Blow after blow, first by the Supreme Court, then by our Court of Appeals, then by the Supreme Court again," said a Kentucky paper, "has been aimed at the power of our Legislature — so that unless those tribunals are effectually checked, nothing will shortly be left to distinguish us from the subjects of Eastern monarchs who are not allowed to have any voice in the making of laws for their own government." "This decision," it said, "carries judicial power a step beyond any conception which we hitherto entertained of it. . . . By this principle, the people are to be subjected to two systems of execution laws, one springing from their own Legislature, and the other from the Federal Courts. . . . They assume to do what Congress never dared to do, to pass a system of execution laws independent of the States. Shall we suffer Judges to assume a power for the exercise of which we would instantly turn out our representatives? They would not dare it, were they not confident of security in life office. But they may be reached."[2] In July, 1825, a great popular meeting was held at which resolutions were passed to the effect that the Constitution did not authorize the Courts to alter the regulation of legal processes by the Court, and

---

[1] In a review of *Kent's Commentaries* by Willard Phillips in *North American Review* (1827), XXIV, it was said: "The decision in *Wayman* v. *Southard*, on one of the Kentucky 'Stop Laws' in relief of debtors, and some other decisions of the Supreme Court, have given great dissatisfaction to some of the people of Kentucky and provoked much virulent declamation against the Court itself. During the late session of Congress, some member intimated that a judicial tyranny was secretly creeping in upon us."

[2] *Argus of Western America*, June 29, July 13, 1825.

advising resistance. The Kentucky Legislature demanded changes in the Federal judicial system and in the Supreme Court; and the House of Representatives took the serious action of calling on the Governor to inform them "of the mode deemed most advisable, in the opinion of the Executive, to refuse obedience to the decisions and mandates of the Supreme Court of the United States considered erroneous and unconstitutional, and whether, in the opinion of the Executive, it may be advisable to call forth the physical power of the State to resist the execution of the decisions of the Court, or in what manner the mandates of said Court should be met by disobedience." Kentucky was thus brought to the verge of open rebellion against the Court. Other Southern States which had similar stay-laws viewed the doctrine laid down by the Federal Judiciary with grave apprehension, and (as will be seen in the next chapter), the movement for Judiciary reform grew strong in Congress.[1] Eventually, however, as financial conditions improved, and as the practical injustice produced by a false sympathy for debtors became more

---

[1] *Niles Register,* XXIX, Dec. 10, 1825, 228–229; *State Documents on Federal Relations* (1911), by Herman V. Ames; *Letters on the Condition of Kentucky in 1825* (1916), by Earl G. Swem; *Louisville Public Advertiser,* March 26, 1825; *19th Cong., 1st Sess.,* speech of Bates of Kentucky, in the House, May 12, 1826.

Congress by the Act of May 19, 1828, enacted a new Process Law making existing State process law binding upon the Federal Courts, with power to alter the same in the future; see *Ross* v. *Duval* (1839), 13 Pet. 45. The Kentucky Senators opposed this law, saying that "any measure which should directly or indirectly sustain the power of the Judges of the Federal Courts as now exercised in Kentucky, operated to sanction the principle of tyranny and oppression which caused the separation of this country from Great Britain"; and they moved the enactment of legislation to take away all such power from the Federal Courts. *20th Cong., 1st Sess.,* speeches of Senator Rowan and Senator Johnson, Jan. 20, Feb. 13, 21, 1828. See also *Argus of Western America,* June 22, July 13, 1825. On the general subject, see *Stay and Exemption Laws,* by Isaac S. Sharp, *American Law Register,* N. S. (1872), XI, 201; *Homestead and Exemption Laws of the Southern States, ibid.* (1871), X, 137; *Final Process in the Courts of the United States as Affected by State Laws, Amer. Law Rev.,* I, 23; *Stay and Appraisement Legislation,* by Harold Preston, *Washington State Bar Ass.* (1891); see also especially *Coffman* v. *Bank of Kentucky* (1866), 40 Miss. 29; *Aycock* v. *Martin* (1867), 37 Ga. 124.

evident, the public veered round to the belief that relief statutes such as had been enacted were demoralizing and impolitic. Nevertheless, the hostility to the Federal Courts remained as an active factor in political life in Kentucky for many years.[1]

[1] Webster wrote to Jeremiah Mason, March 20, 1828: "If Barry should succeed by a strong vote, I should give up Kentucky and with Kentucky all hope of Adams' re-election." *Letters of Daniel Webster* (1902), ed. by C. H. Van Tyne. Barry was a strong supporter of the Kentucky stay-laws.

CHAPTER SEVENTEEN

JUDICIARY REFORM

1821–1826

WHILE the decade since the War of 1812 had been marked by a growing antagonism against the Court in States whose commercial and financial policies and legislation had been affected by its decisions, practical expression of this sentiment had been confined to agitation in the press and to the passage of resolutions in State Legislatures. No actual move towards curtailment or abrogation of the powers and functions of the Court was made until the year 1821, when there was initiated in Congress the first of a series of Legislative attacks lasting through the next ten years. The grounds of opposition to the Court were diverse in their nature. Throughout the South, and principally in the Republican Party, there was a fear of a consolidated government by extension of Congressional power through a broad judicial interpretation of the Constitution; consequently, attacks on the Court based on such a fear were directed at its course in holding Federal legislation constitutional, and were not in any wise evoked by the possibility of judicial decisions limiting or invalidating Federal power. It was this phase of the Court's activities which had created such alarm in Jefferson's mind. The other and quite distinct source of opposition to the Court was the increasing number of instances in which it had come in conflict with alleged sovereign rights of the States and had been obliged to hold State legislation invalid. Attacks based on this latter ground were not confined to any particular section or party, but were vigorous in Northern as well as Southern States and among the Federalists as well as the Republicans. By the end of the year 1825, the Court had held unconstitutional the laws of ten States — Georgia, Virginia, New Hampshire, New Jersey, Vermont, Maryland, New York, Pennsylvania, Ohio and Kentucky; and in each instance its decision had aroused resentment in the particular community whose political tenet or whose financial or commercial or social policy had been affected.[1] The remedies proposed by those who wished to curb the powers and jurisdiction of the Court were varied. Jefferson, fearing more especially the tendency of the Court to uphold extension of Federal authority by Congress, believed that the remedy lay first in requiring every Judge to deliver a separate opinion so that he might be held responsible for his views individually. Though he believed that impeachment was "an impracticable thing", "a mere scarecrow", a "bugbear" which the Judges "fear not at all", Jefferson considered that a practice (which he erroneously claimed originated with Chief Justice Marshall) had rendered impeachment even less feasible than it otherwise might be, namely, Marshall's "habit of caucusing opinions" and "his practice of making up opinions in secret and delivering them as the orders of the Court": "an opinion huddled up in conclave, perhaps by a majority of one, delivered as if unanimous and with the silent acquiescence of lazy or timid associates, by a crafty Chief Judge, who sophisticates the

[1] See especially series of eighteen articles on the jurisdiction of the Supreme Court of the United States, written under the pseudonym of "Patrick Henry" in *Argus of Western America*, beginning May 12, 1824.

law to his mind, by the turn of his own reasoning." [1] No one had apparently claimed the abandonment by the Court of its former practice to be an evil, until the decision in *McCulloch* v. *Maryland;* but in that case, the fact that all the Judges, Federalist and Republican alike, had concurred in Marshall's broad doctrines without rendering separate opinions had caused surprise and dismay to the advocates of strict construction of the Constitution. Jefferson and Madison simultaneously resented this fact, and from that date pointed out in frequent letters that, as Jefferson said, this "cooking up of a decision and delivering it by one of their members as the opinion of the Court without the possibility of our knowing how many, who, or for what reasons each member concurred . . . completely defeats the possibility of impeachment by smothering evidence." Writing in 1823 to Judge William Johnson, who also favored *seriatim* opinions, Jefferson urged that each Judge should "prove by his reasoning that he has read the papers, that he has considered the case, that in the application of the law to it, he uses his own judgment independently and unbiased by party views and personal favor or disfavor. . . . The very idea of cooking up opinions in conclave, begets suspicions that something passes which fears the public ear, and this, spreading by degrees, must produce at some time abridgment of tenure, facility of removal, or some other modification which may promise a remedy. For, in truth, there is at this time more

---

[1] *Jefferson*, XII, letters to Thomas Ritchie, Dec. 25, 1820, to James Pleasant, Dec. 26, 1821, to William Johnson, Oct. 27, 1822, March 4, June 12, 1823. Jefferson's charge that Marshall originated the practice of having the opinions of the Court delivered by the Chief Justice was without foundation. The change in the practice of the Court had occurred before Marshall's accession to the Bench. See opinion of Chase, J., in *Bas* v. *Tingy*, 4 Dallas, 37, in which he said: "The Judges agreeing unanimously in this opinion, I presumed that the sense of the Court would have been delivered by the President, and therefore, I have not prepared a formal argument on the occasion."

hostility to the Federal Judiciary, than to any other organ of the government." [1] And to James Madison, who also agreed with him, Jefferson wrote urging him to bring his influence to bear on the Judges to secure a reversal of the present practice, saying: "I suppose your connection with Judge Todd, and your antient intimacy with Judge Duval might give you an opening to say something to them on the subject. If Johnson could be backed by them in the practice, the others would be obliged to follow suit, and this dangerous engine of consolidation would feel a proper restraint by their being compelled to explain publicly the grounds of their opinions." [2] When the Judges should at last be forced to announce their individual views, then it was Jefferson's plan that the Congress should formally denounce such judicial views as it disagreed with, and that if the Judges failed to adopt the conclusion reached by Congress, impeachment should follow. We are undone, he wrote to Nathaniel Macon, unless we "check these unconstitutional invasions of State-Rights by the Federal Judiciary. How? Not by impeachment in the first instance, but by a strong protestation of both houses of Congress that such and such doctrines, advanced by the Supreme Court are contrary to the Constitution, and if afterwards they relapse into the same heresies, impeach, and set the whole adrift." Such a remedy of course

[1] See letter of Johnson to Jefferson, Dec. 10, 1822, in which he very frankly expressed his views of his brethren; he said: "When I was on our State Bench, I was accustomed to delivering *seriatim* opinions in an Appellate Court, and was not a little surprised to find our Chief Justice in the Supreme Court delivering all the opinions. . . . But I remonstrated in vain; the answer was, he is willing to take the trouble, and it is a mark of respect to him. I soon, however, found out the real cause. Cushing was incompetent, Chase could not be got to think or write, Paterson was a slow man and willingly declined the trouble, and the other two Judges (Marshall and Bushrod Washington) you know are commonly estimated as one Judge."

[2] *Jefferson*, XII, letters to Madison, Jan. 6, June 13, 1823; *Madison*, IX, letters to S. Roane, Sept. 2, 1819, and to Jefferson, Jan. 15, 1823.

amounted to nothing more nor less than making Congress the final arbiter of the meaning of the Constitution. To the proposition to erect the Senate as the Supreme Appellate Court, however, Jefferson wrote that he doubted if such a plan "would be deemed an unexceptionable reliance." His own reliance as a last resort was in a Constitutional Amendment abolishing the present judicial tenure. "A better remedy, I think, and indeed the best I can devise," he wrote "would be to give future commissions to Judges for six years (the Senatorial term) with a reappointmentability by the President, with the approbation of both Houses." [1] The appointment of Judges for a term of years was also favored by *Niles Register*, which had a wide circulation and considerable influence and which said

[1] *Jefferson*, XII, letter to Nathaniel Macon, Aug. 19, 1821; see also letter to Lieut. Gov. Barry, July 2, 1822; letter to James Pleasant, Dec. 26, 1821.

An amusing comment on Jefferson's view is found in a letter of that staunch old Federalist statesman, Timothy Pickering of Massachusetts to James Hillhouse of Connecticut, Feb. 18, 1823: "He would have them hold their commissions only for four or six years — but renewable by the President and Senate. Thus rendering them temporizing, corrupt, and mischievous creatures and tools of the parties which may successively bear sway. How must the sage of Quincy . . . have bounced at the preposterous idea of his Monticello friend? After writing as many volumes on checks and balances, and the necessity of the independence of the several branches of the Government?" *Pickering Papers MSS*, 532. Martin Van Buren, writing in 1854 in his *Autobiography* in *Amer. Hist. Ass. Rep.* (1918), II, 183, 185, describes a visit to Jefferson in 1823, in which the latter "expressed the belief that the life tenure of their offices was calculated to turn the minds of the Judges", to the "subversion of the republican principles . . . and that the attention of our young men could not be more usefully employed than in considering the most effectual protection against the evils which threatened the country from that source. He spoke of the power of impeachment with great severity, not only as a mockery in itself, but as having exercised an influence in preventing a resort to a more thorough remedy, which he thought was only to be found in a change in the tenure of the judicial office. Annual appointments, as in the New England States, were, he thought, the best, but he would be content with four, or even six years, and trust to experience for future reductions. Fresh from the Bar, and to some extent, at least, under the influence of professional prejudices, I remember to have thought his views extremely radical, but I have lived to subscribe to their general correctness. . . . The only effectual and safe remedy will be to amend the Constitution so to make the office elective." *Ibid.*, 229: "The tide of public opinion on the subjects of the jurisdiction of the Federal Courts and the term for which their Judges should hold their offices has had floods, and it is my firm belief that the time is not far distant when these questions will be more seriously agitated."

editorially, in 1822: "There are two parties in
the United States, most decidedly opposed to each
other as to the rights, powers and province of the
Judiciary, which many people believe are equally in
the wrong. One party almost claims infallibility
for the Judges, and would hedge them round about in
such a manner that they cannot be reached by popular
opinion at all, and hardly by any other means; the
other would subject them to the vacillations of popular
prejudice and seemingly to require it of them to define
and administer the law, and interpret the Constitution
according to the real or apparent expediency of things.
It is essential that the Judges should not be subject
to discharge, except on very strong grounds, yet it
seems equally necessary that some plan should be
adopted by which the cool and deliberate opinion of
the people may be brought to act concerning them." [1]

The "disastrous" decisions of the Court in *Cohens* v.
Virginia and *Green* v. *Biddle* in 1821 gave rise to the
first concrete proposal made in Congress for the curbing
of the power of the Court, when, on December 12, 1821,
Senator Richard M. Johnson of Kentucky introduced
in the Senate a resolution for an Amendment to the
Constitution, providing that in cases where a State
shall be a party, " and in all controversies in which a
State may desire to become a party in consequence
of having the Constitution or laws of such State questioned, the Senate of the United States shall have
appellate jurisdiction." In his speech he stated that
he introduced it because of the "serious consequences
which had lately taken place between several of the
States and the Judiciary of the United States." [2]

---

[1] *Niles Register*, XXII, June 22, 1822.

[2] *17th Cong., 1st Sess.*, Dec. 12, 1821, Jan. 14, 15, 1822. Spencer Roane wrote to
Archibald Thweat, Dec. 24, 1821: "The subject of amending the Constitution
in relation to decisions of the Federal Courts has been taken up in the Senate, as

In another long speech assailing the Federal Judiciary, he employed every argument which at the present day has been used in behalf of the doctrines of recall of Judges and of judicial decisions. "At this time," he said, "there is, unfortunately, a want of confidence in the Federal Judiciary, in cases that involve political power; and this distrust may be carried to other cases. . . . There is a manifest disposition on the part of the Federal Judiciary to enlarge, to the utmost stretch of constitutional construction, the powers of the General Government. . . . Judges, like other men, have their political views. . . . Why, then should they be considered any more infallible, or their decisions any less subject to investigation and reversion? . . . Every department which exercises political power should be responsible to the people. . . . The short though splendid history of this government furnishes nothing that can induce us to look with a very favorable eye to the Federal Judiciary as a safe depository of our liberties." He attacked the decisions in *McCulloch* v. *Maryland*, the *Dartmouth College Case*, *Sturges* v. *Crowninshield*, *New Jersey* v. *Wilson, United States* v. *Peters, Cohens* v. *Virginia* and *Green* v. *Biddle*, as "subject of much animadversion and dissatisfaction, . . . prostrating the States and in effect legislating for the people and regulating the interior policy of the States." "There must be a remedy," he said, "for this serious encroachment upon the first principles of self government of the States. . . . Some interposition is necessary. The preservation of harmony requires it. The security of our liberties demands it."

you will see, on the res. of Mr. Johnson of Kentucky, supported by Barbour. With a few to aid them, or rather to lead, on this important subject, I have prepared some Amendments to the Constitution to be adopted by our Assembly. They are very mild, but go the full length of the wishes of the Republicans on this subject. . . . Jefferson and Madison hang back too much."

Though Senator Johnson's extreme views were indorsed by a few other Senators, notably John Holmes of Maine, no action was taken by Congress upon the proposal. The movement, however, was regarded with great seriousness by friends of the Court. As has been seen, Marshall himself believed that the violent criticisms of the *Cohens Case* decision in Virginia were a part of a design to attack the Union; and this move in Congress was now generally regarded as a continuation of that attack. "I learn from Washington," wrote Jeremiah Mason to Judge Story, January 8, 1822, "that the expected attack on the Judiciary will be made, but, according to my informant, with little prospect of success at this time. The Kentucky proposal for amending the Constitution will end in smoke. The objections to that project are obvious and insuperable. Besides destroying one of the leading principles of our government, a separation of the departments, it would subject judicial decision to all the intrigue and management to which a Legislative body is always exposed. What chance for justice or consistency in a factious and somewhat popular body, feeling little responsibility, a vast majority of whom if left to the influence of correct motives would be wholly incompetent to the proposed task! If this experiment could be tried without disturbing the Constitution, I should not dislike to see the attempt. The Nation would soon become sick of it, and the failure would free the Supreme Court of much undeserved odium. I do not believe there is any immediate danger to the Judiciary by any acts of the Legislature. But what may be finally effected by perseverance and reiterated attempts, it is impossible to say. . . . The Supreme Court has no choice of courses to be pursued. The straightforward course is the only one

that can be followed. It may be with as much
temperance as the Chief Justice pleases, and no man
ever excelled him in the exercise of that virtue. But
any vacillation or retracting, which might be set down
to the score of the present noisy threats would be not
only inconsistent with a due regard to personal character, but in their consequences destructive of the best
interests of the Nation." [1] To this, Story answered
with some despondency: "I am glad you write somewhat encouragingly respecting the Judiciary. My
only hope is in the discordant views of the various interested factions and philosophists. Mr. Jefferson
stands at the head of the enemies of the Judiciary,
and, I doubt not, will leave behind him a numerous
progeny bred in the same school. The truth is, and
cannot be disguised, even from vulgar observation,
that the Judiciary in our country is essentially feeble
and must always be open to attack from all quarters.
It will perpetually thwart the wishes and views of
demagogues, and it can have no places to give and
no patronage to draw around it close defenders. Its
only support is the wise and the good and the elevated in society; and these, as we all know, must
ever remain in a discouraging minority in all Governments. If, indeed, the Judiciary is to be destroyed, I should be glad to have the decisive blow
now struck, while I am young and can return to the
profession and earn an honest livelihood. If it comes
in my old age, it may find me less able to bear the
blow, though I hope not less firm to meet it. For
the Judges of the Supreme Court there is but one
course to pursue. That is, to do their duty firmly
and honestly, according to their best judgments. . . .
I believe the Court will be resolute, and will be

[1] *Mason,* Jan. 8, 1822; *Story,* I, 411, letter to Mason, Jan. 10, 1822.

driven from its course, only when driven from the seat of justice." [1]

To Rufus King, Mason wrote at this session : "From the excitement that prevailed in Virginia and several other States, a violent attack on the Supreme Court was expected in the course of the present session of Congress. I am glad to see that this . . . will probably end in smoke. I know it has often been said that lawyers are apt to attach too much importance to the Judiciary Department. I confess I have long been of opinion that the vigorous exercise of the Judiciary power, to the full extent now authorized by law, was absolutely necessary for the preservation of the Government. . . . Were it not for the extreme jealousy on the score of State-Rights felt in some sections of the Union, I should like to see provision made by law for the exercise of this power, to the utmost limits fixed by the Constitution. I cannot see how the other two departments of Government can be effective, where the Judiciary can do nothing. A restriction of the Judiciary powers necessarily involves a correspondent restriction of the other powers of government. It must be so, at least in all cases where the General Government comes in conflict with the State Government."

Although the move to constitute the Senate a supreme appellate judicial tribunal was not pressed in Congress, it continued to be advocated for several years in the press and by public men, especially in New York by Governor DeWitt Clinton and some of the Democratic papers.[2] *Niles Register*, in 1824,

[1] Story wrote to Mason, Feb. 21, 1822: "The propositions of Virginia, etc., and of Mr. Johnson of Kentucky, respecting the Judiciary are not likely to find much favor here in Congress." *Mason*, letter to Rufus King, April 12, 1822. Webster wrote to Story, Jan. 14, 1822, referring to Senator Johnson's speech which he said "has dealt, they say, pretty freely with the Supreme Court . . . so things go, but I see less reality in all this smoke than I thought I should before I came here."

[2] Richard Riker of New York wrote to Martin Van Buren, April 14, 1828, saying:

alarmed at the latest State opposition to the Court in the case of South Carolina, pointed out that "in the progress of time, the exposition of the Constitution may more depend on the opinions of the Supreme Court than on its own very carefully defined powers"; and it indorsed the plan of confiding a revisionary power in the Senate on all constitutional questions, as "essential to public harmony." On the other hand, the change was viewed with horror by the staunch Federalist papers, one of which termed it "one of the wildest and most hazardous of the innovations" which "would affect the Judiciary system and the Federal Constitution as deeply as any other change whatever"; and another said: "Whatever we do, for God's sake, let us abstain from that damnable political heresy of blending judicial with legislative powers. If we needed a warning voice on this subject, the decisions made in party times in the State of New York, as well as some other decisions connected with party, are amply sufficient to deter every considerate man from listening for a moment to a proposition so largely pregnant with momentous mischief." [1]

Reforms of the nature advocated by Jefferson required a Constitutional Amendment; but by those men who opposed the Court because of its alleged

"'The encroachments made by latitudinary construction of the Federal Constitution have always been a source of alarm to me. This political heresy ought to be constantly watched. . . . I wish, myself, that all decisions by the Judiciary of the United States which involved either the rights of the States or the construction of the Federal Constitution were reviewable by the Senate. What would have been the consequences, if the Courts of the Union had decided, as was feared at the time, that the Embargo which was recommended by Mr. Jefferson and adopted by Congress was unconstitutional! . . . I would much rather trust the Senate with constitutional questions than the Judges. The sovereignty of the States, so vitally essential to the continuance of our great democratic Confederacy, would be always safe in the hands of the Senate of the Union. Not so with the Judges." *Van Buren Papers MSS.*

[1] *Niles Register*, XXVII, Dec. 18, 25, 1824, Jan. 8, 15, 1825; *National Gazette*, March 15, 1825; *New York Evening Post*, March 8, 1824.

trespasses on State-Rights, a more speedy and adequate remedy was proposed, when, in April, 1822, Andrew Stevenson of Virginia introduced in the House a resolution for the repeal of the Twenty-Fifth Section of the Judiciary Act. While he said that it was offered "in a spirit of peace and forbearance, and from a sense of duty to himself and his State", his direct purpose was to nullify the decision of the Court in *Cohens* v. *Virginia* and to abolish appellate jurisdiction over the State Courts.[1] In the next Congress, in 1824, Charles A. Wickliffe of Kentucky offered a similar resolution to inquire into the expediency of either repealing entirely the obnoxious Twenty-Fifth Section or modifying it so that the writ of error "shall be awarded to either party, without reference to the manner in which the question shall have been decided by the Supreme Court of the State."[2] In the Senate, also, Isham Talbot of Kentucky proposed to avoid the use of writs of error to State Courts, by allowing parties in all suits involving a Federal or constitutional question to remove the suit to the Federal Court before trial in the State Court. But while these direct attacks received practically no support, and while no action was taken by Congress on them, the Court was assailed from a new angle by Senator Johnson of Kentucky, who, aroused by the second decision in *Green* v. *Biddle* (which was alleged to have been made by a minority of the full Court), proposed a bill, December 10, 1823, requiring concurrence of seven Judges in any opinion

---

[1] *17th Cong., 1st Sess.*, April 26, 1822; *18th Cong., 1st Sess.*, Jan. 2, 30, 1824.

[2] This resolution was undoubtedly due to the courageous action of the Kentucky Court of Appeals in holding unconstitutional various Kentucky statutes on authority of decision of the United States Supreme Court. The suggestion is interesting as embodying at that early date the exact amendment which was made to the Judiciary Act in 1914, at the suggestion of the American Bar Association, viz.: that appeals to the Supreme Court should lie on State Court decisions adverse to the constitutionality of a State law as well as on decisions in favor.

involving the validity of State statutes or Acts of
Congress. "Tremendous evils might result to the
country from the powers imparted to its Judiciary,
when a whole State might be convulsed to its very
center by a judicial decision," said Johnson. "Some
remedy must, ere long, be adopted to preserve the
purity of our political institutions." Since many
persons in the country believed that strong arguments
could be made in behalf of such a measure, a bill was
reported from the Committee on Judiciary by Senator
Martin Van Buren of New York, on March 11, 1824,
providing that no law of any of the States should be
rendered invalid without the concurrence of five of
the seven Judges. The bill, however, was laid upon
the table.[1] In the House, similar measures were proposed by Robert P. Letcher and Thomas Metcalfe,
both of Kentucky.[2] That this reform in the Judiciary
system seemed, superficially, to have much to commend
it is seen from the fact that Webster wrote to Judge
Story, informing him that Judge Todd had told him
it would give great satisfaction in the West, and asking
him if he saw any evil in such a provision. Later,
however, Webster decided to oppose the change, although he was willing to go so far as to offer a substitute
to provide that, in cases involving the validity of a
State statute or Constitution, "no judgment shall be
pronounced or rendered until a majority of all the
Justices of the said Court legally competent to sit in

[1] *18th Cong., 1st Sess.*, Dec. 10, 1823, March 11, 23, April 26, May 3, 4, 14, 17,
1824. The *New York Evening Post*, March 22, 1814, expressed the general sentiment of the Bar as to the proposition, when it said editorially: "If this . . . should
prevail, will it not be an amendment in the very teeth of one of our republican maxims that a majority should govern? Turn it as you will, it comes at least to this —
that the opinion of two Judges in the negative shall have more weight than five in
the affirmative. It is, in fact, an impotent attempt to grasp what is not tangible."
[2] John Forsyth of Georgia, in the House offered as a substitute a proposal that
a quorum of the Supreme Court should consist of such a number of Judges that a
majority of the quorum should always be a majority of the whole Court.

the cause shall concur in the opinion, either in favor of
or against the validity thereof, and until such concurrence such suit shall be continued." [1] There were
two very vital objections to this requirement of a
concurrence of five of the seven Judges, which seem to
have been entirely overlooked in the debate. In the
first place, it would have worked with singular injustice upon litigants in the Federal Circuit Courts;
for, while an appeal to the Supreme Court from a State
Court decision was only possible in a case where the
latter had held a State law constitutional, an appeal
from a Circuit Court decision was possible, even if
that Court held the State law invalid. An appellant
in the Supreme Court in the latter case would find
himself in this predicament: if five out of seven Judges
concurred in finding the State law invalid, he would
lose his appeal; and if only four concurred, the proposed statute would prohibit the Supreme Court
from finding the law invalid; hence the decision of
the Circuit Court as to invalidity would become final;
so that the appellant would lose in either case, and
the proposed statute would be of no avail to him.
But the fundamental objection to the proposition
was that it completely ignored the true function of a
judicial tribunal, which was, to hold the scales of
justice even and to decide impartially between the
parties, the appellant and the appellee both meeting
before it on even terms. The proposed statute entirely
lost sight of the fact that suits in the Supreme Court

[1] *Webster*, XVII, letter of April 10, 1824; on May 4, 1824, Webster wrote: "We
had the Supreme Court before us yesterday, rather unexpectedly, and a debate
arose which lasted all day. *Cohens* v. *Virginia*, *Green* v. *Biddle*, etc., were all
discussed. Most of the gentlemen were very temperate and guarded; there were,
however, some exceptions, especially Mr. Randolph, whose remarks were not a little
extraordinary. Mr. (P. P.) Barbour reargued *Cohens Case*. Mr. Letcher and Mr.
Wickliffe did the same for *Green* v. *Biddle*. I said some few things *eo instanti*, which
I thought the case called for. The proposition for the concurrence of five Judges
will not prevail."

involving the validity of State statutes were litigation between individuals and presented questions of the property or personal rights of individuals, and that each litigant was entitled to equal protection. These suits were not impersonal attempts to adjudicate between the Constitution, or the Federal Government, and the State; they were simply adjustment of the respective rights of two persons, one claiming a right under the Constitution, the other under the State law. A Federal statute, therefore, which required an appellant to persuade five out of seven Judges, in order to win, while the appellee in order to prevail had to persuade but three Judges, gave to the appellee in a law suit very heavy odds. The parties no longer came into the Court on an equal basis, but with the chances heavily weighted against an appellant — and this was not in consonance with any Anglo-Saxon system of justice. The debate over the proposed statute, however, was based little on general grounds of justice, but largely on the local political grievances which a few of the States felt might be cured by such legislation, and on the subjects of political controversy which might possibly be thus removed from the cognizance of the Court. In this connection, it is to be noted that the contingency of a decision on one dangerous political topic — Congressional power over slavery — was referred to during the debate on the Metcalfe resolution in a remarkably prophetic manner, by Daniel P. Cook, a Congressman from Illinois. In supporting the resolution, on the ground that the validity of the compact against introduction of slavery under which Illinois was admitted into the Union, would undoubtedly, at some time, be before the Supreme Court for decision, he said: "Should it happen, it will be a fearful question. It will involve nothing less, sir, than the balance of power between the slave and non-slaveholding States. Those who witnessed, as well as those who know of, the convulsive discussion in this House on the Missouri question cannot fail to appreciate the magnitude of this subject. In deciding that question, should it ever arise, if a majority of that Court shall be found to decide against the validity of the act of the State, but not a sufficient majority under the provision now under consideration, it could not fail to shake the Nation to its center. While this tribunal may be called on to decide questions of such momentous magnitude, it behooves the House to examine well the effects of the principle now proposed." [1]

None of these projected changes in the Judiciary system received any considerable support. Before Congress met in 1825, however, the decision by the Court of two more great cases holding State laws of New York, Ohio and Georgia unconstitutional — *Gibbons* v. *Ogden* on March 2, 1824, and *Osborn* v. *Bank of the United States* and *Planters Bank of Georgia* v. *Bank of the United States* on March 19, 1824, and the pendency of the noted case of *Ogden* v. *Saunders* which involved the constitutionality of many State bankruptcy laws and which had been argued for the first time, March 3–5, 1824, reinforced the determination of the advocates of State-Rights in Congress to curb the Court's power.[2] In the Senate, in the debate over the bill providing three new Circuits and three new Supreme Court Judges, February 10–16, 1825, Senator Talbot of Kentucky, while stating that he cast no "imputation on the purity of intention or the correctness of judgment" of the Judges, and while

[1] *18th Cong., 1st Sess.*, 2647.
[2] *18th Cong., 2d Sess.*, Feb. 10, 16, 17, 18, 21, 1825.

admitting that they possessed individually the power
to declare null and void the laws of every State, called
attention to the decisions of *Fairfax* v. *Hunter* and
Cohens v. *Virginia*, as "occurrences strongly calculated
to arouse the feelings and excite the apprehensions of
the patriotic statesmen anxious for the perpetuation
of our happy Union." He criticized also the decisions
of the Court upholding the Bank of the United States,
saying: "Maryland and Ohio in their turns have had
to encounter the power and influence of that great engine
of political power — the Bank; have been severely attacked, have been successively vanquished in the
contest." His colleague, Senator Johnson, of Kentucky, also returned to the attack, and, while admitting
the "moral worth, intellectual vigor, extensive acquirements and profound judicial experience" of the
Court, he complained that "according to the views
of the Judiciary, it is in the power of the tribunals
of the country to arraign, prostrate and annul not
only a single law . . . but laws sanctioned by experience, consecrated by all the departments of State
legislation, and acquiesced in by all good citizens. . . ."
On the other hand, Philip P. Barbour of Virginia,
although formerly counsel for the State in *Cohens* v.
Virginia and virulent in opposing the Court's exercise
of jurisdiction in that case, made light of the charge
that the Court, "in which was deposited the peace and
tranquillity of the Union", was destroying the rights or
prostrating the independence of the States, and said
that, if after forty years it had been found that the
power of the Court had not been abused, the people
"might reasonably expect that it would not be, hereafter."

At the next session, 1825–1826, when the bill for
three new Circuits was again under discussion in the

House, John Forsyth of Georgia presented an amendment that no final judgment should be pronounced affecting the rights, liberty or life of any citizen of the United States by less than a majority of the whole Court. Kentucky Congressmen supported a similar amendment, confined to judgments pronouncing a State law unconstitutional; and they with others again launched attacks on this power of the Court to declare the invalidity of State laws.[1] Richard A. Buckner of Kentucky said that "its restrictive powers over the States have set with a strong and bold current like the Gulf Stream sweeping every obstacle before them in an undeviating course to the Federal ocean." George Kremer of Pennsylvania said that he entered his "solemn protest against the whole doctrine that the Supreme Court has power to pronounce acts of this House to be unconstitutional. In vain did our armies shed their blood in the field and our sages toil in the cabinet to secure our liberty, if it is to be subjected to the arbitrary decision of these Judges."

On the other side, Webster magnificently defended the Court under the Constitution and its necessary place in the scheme of the Federal Government. Charles F. Mercer of Virginia also defended the Court, and contended that the dissatisfaction with it was greatly exaggerated: "This Court has encountered much discontent, but in patient fortitude; not by its numbers, nor by bending to circumstances, it has ultimately prevailed over prejudice and passion, as it will yet continue to do, if left to the impulse which has hitherto guided its judgment, — the principles of eternal truth. Sir, it is a gratifying source of reflection, and manifests

---

[1] *19th Cong., 1st Sess.*, Dec. 13, 14, 15, 22, 1825, Jan. 4–25, May 3, 4, 8, 12, 1826, especially Webster's speech, Jan. 25. Charles A. Wickliffe, Dec. 12, 1825, again offered a resolution for a bill repealing the 25th Section, and providing for removal of cases containing a Federal question from the State to the Federal Courts.

the durability of our political fabric, that amidst all
the shocks of this part of our Federal system, very
few States have at any one time been united in its
condemnation; and their successive efforts to shake
the public confidence in its decisions have found those
who were, at one time, its enemies, at another, its
steadfast friends."

In the Senate, Van Buren of New York delivered a
speech severely criticizing the powers of the Court,
and attacking especially its broad construction of the
phrase "impairment of obligations of contract", —
"a brief provision which," he said, "had given to the
jurisdiction of the Court a tremendous sweep. . . .
There are few States in the Union upon whose acts
the seal of condemnation has not from time to time
been placed by the Supreme Court. The sovereign
authorities of Vermont, New Hampshire, New York,
New Jersey, Pennsylvania, Maryland, Virginia, North
Carolina, Missouri, Kentucky, and Ohio, have in turn
been rebuked and silenced by the overruling authority
of the Court." He admitted, however, that under
the Constitution, its jurisdiction was justified; but
if the question of conferring this jurisdiction should
now arise for the first time, he would say that "the
people of the States might with safety be left to their
own Legislatures and the protection of their own
Courts." Of the Judges themselves, however, Van
Buren said that they possessed "talents of the highest
order and spotless integrity", and that the Chief Justice "is in all human probability, the ablest Judge now
sitting upon any Judicial Bench in the world." [1] To
this attack upon the Court's jurisdiction by a Senator
of New York, it was singular that the finest defense
of the Court should be made by a Senator of South

[1] *19th Cong., 1st Sess.*, debate in the Senate, April 7, 10, 11, 12, 13, 14, 1826.

Carolina, William Harper, who said: "The independence of the Judiciary is at the very basis of our institutions. . . . It is in times of faction, when party spirit runs high, that dissatisfaction is most likely to be occasioned by the decisions of the Supreme Court. I do not believe that the Supreme Court, or the Constitution itself, will ever be able to stand against the decided current of public opinion. It is a very different thing from the temporary opinion of a majority; for a majority acting unjustly and unconstitutionally, under the influence of excitement, a majority though it be, is nothing more than a faction, and it was the object of our Constitution to control it. The Constitution has laid down the fundamental and immutable laws of justice for our Government; and the majority that constitutes the Government should not violate these. The Constitution is made to control the Government; it has no other object; and though the Supreme Court cannot resist public opinion, it may resist a temporary majority and may change that majority. However high the tempest may blow, individuals may hear the calm and steady voice of the Judiciary warning them of their danger. They will shrink away; they will leave that majority a minority, and that is the security the Constitution intended by the Judiciary."

That none of all these various attempts to restrict the powers of the Court succeeded was an amazing tribute to the popular confidence in that tribunal; and that Jefferson and his followers in Virginia, Kentucky and Georgia failed so completely to convince the American people of the need of reform in the Judiciary system can only be explained by the assumption that the country at large was convinced of the Court's integrity, of its freedom from partisan bias, and of its infinite value in the maintenance of the

American Union. It was not until five years later, during President Jackson's Administration in 1831, that it was confronted with a real crisis in its history.

But while these attacks from 1821 to 1826 upon the fundamental powers of the Court had been unsuccessful, attempts which had been coincidentally pressed in Congress for relief of the Court and reform of the Judiciary system had unfortunately proved equally without avail. Ever since the year 1816, there had been a series of efforts made for legislation to abolish the performance of Circuit Court duties by the Judges of the Supreme Court, and for the creation of an additional number of Circuits, in order to provide for the growing business in the West and Southwest. The demand for this reform had become more and more urgent as the number of States admitted to the Union increased; for since the Western States, with a population equal to that of the entire Union in 1789, had only one Judge of the Supreme Court assigned to them, such a judicial system was naturally a constant source of dissatisfaction.[1] Bills to accomplish reform in this respect had been recommended by Presidents Madison and Monroe, and had been introduced into Congress in 1816, 1817, 1818 and 1819, but had failed of passage.[2] As Jeremiah Mason wrote: "There is repeated a saying of A. Burr, 'that every Legislature, in their treatment of the Judiciary, is a d—d Jacobin Club.' There is certainly nothing in a good Judiciary likely to attract the favorable regards of a Legislature in turbulent party times. The dominant party in such times can expect no aid in furtherance of some of their meas-

[1] Kentucky was admitted in 1792, Tennessee in 1796, Ohio in 1802 and Louisiana in 1812; Indiana became a State in 1816, Mississippi in 1817, Illinois in 1818, Alabama in 1819, Maine in 1820, Missouri in 1821.

[2] *14th Cong., 3d Sess.*, Dec. 23, 1816; *Madison*, VIII, letter of Dec. 9, 1817; *15th Cong., 1st Sess.*, Jan. 27, 1818, in the Senate, Dec. 9, in the House. *15th Cong., 2d Sess.*, Nov. 30, Dec. 2, 1818, in the Senate, Jan. 4, 1819, in the House.

ures from the Judiciary. Indeed, both parties, having unreasonable expectations of aid from the Judiciary are usually disappointed and are apt to view it with jealousy." [1] But while the defeat of the bills carrying the much-needed relief to the Court had been partly due to this indifference on the part of Congress, it had also been caused by the fear of increasing Executive patronage and the unwillingness of the Anti-Administration forces to allow the new offices to be filled by the President. "They fear," wrote Judge Story, "there is danger . . . that the new Judges will be exclusively selected from the Republican Party. Both these motives will probably induce the great bulk of the Federalists to vote against it, and among the Republicans, it is well known there are many hostile in the highest degree to any scheme which changes or gives more effect to the jurisdiction of the Courts of the United States; so that the bill will, between these opposing parties, fall to the ground." [2]

So far as the bills were opposed on their merits, the arguments were chiefly based on the fear lest the Judges, on being relieved of Circuit duty, would become "completely cloistered within the City of Washington, and their decisions, instead of emanating from enlarged and liberalized minds, would assume a severe and local character", or lest the Judges might

[1] *Mason*, letter of Jan. 15, 1818.

[2] *Story*, I, 327, letter of Feb. 17, 1819; see also letter of Webster to Story, Dec. 9, 1816. Rufus King wrote to Christopher Gore of Massachusetts, Jan. 20, 1819: "Whether the bill will pass the House, I am unable to foretell, but if it should, I fear that Monroe would be afraid to appoint (Jeremiah) Mason, (David) Daggett, or other Federalists. John Holmes would be a more likely candidate than Mason for the Eastern Circuit," and Gore replied, Jan. 29, 1819: "If your Judiciary Bill shall pass the House and Monroe shall have the baseness to put Holmes on the Bench instead of Mason, he will act worse than I have predicted, though I have never believed he would or could do as well as from various motives we are disposed to presume in this part of the country." *King*, VI. The same fear of Executive patronage had been largely responsible for the failure of President Madison's recommendation in 1816–17, see *Papers of Thomas Ruffin* (1918), I, by T. J. de R. Hamilton, letter of W. N. Edwards to Ruffin, Dec. 9, 1816.

become "another appendage to the Executive authority", subject to the "dazzling splendors of the palace and the drawing room", and the "flattery and soothing attention of a designing Executive", as a Senator from Pennsylvania, Truman Lacock, said.[1] The same Senator uttered the following extraordinary forebodings as to the undue influence and control which Washington lawyers would acquire over the Court, if, by locating the Judges in Washington, they should be subjected to the "dangerous influences and strong temptations that might bias their minds and pollute the stream of National justice":

You will have not only your Judges but your attorneys confined to the City of Washington. The Judges are to be old men when appointed, and the infirmities of old age will every day increase, and as the useful and vigorous faculties of their minds diminish, in the same proportion will their obstinacy and vanity increase. Old men are often impatient of contradiction, frequently vain and susceptible of flattery. These weaknesses incident to old age will be discovered and practised upon by the lawyer willing to make the most of his profession, and located in the same city, holding daily and familiar intercourse with the Judges. And thus, your Court may become subservient to the Washington Bar. The Judges, bowed down by the weight of years, will be willing to find a staff to lean upon; and the opinion of the Washington Bar is made the law of the land. A knot of attorneys at or near the seat of Government having gained the ear, and secured the confidence of the Court, will banish all competition from abroad. . . . With what painful reflections and awful forebodings would a Kentucky lawyer enter this Court? No man that had heard the cause argued at home — no man personally known to him, and on whom he can rely for official integrity, is seen on the Bench. Like a stranger in a strange land he feels his situation comfortless and gloomy. He takes his solitary seat at the Bar — he views the Court as belonging to the

[1] *15th Cong.*, *2d Sess.*, 131, Jan. 12, 1819.

same family, and almost identified with the great Crown lawyers that are to oppose him; and thus with fear and trembling, he approaches the cause of his client, doubting and half believing that the cause has already been prejudged by the Bench, or that the weight and influence of legal talents will stifle the calls of justice; and should an observation drop from the Bench during the discussion to confirm his doubts, he abandons, as desperately hopeless, the cause of his client, however just. This would be a deplorable state of things. But adopt this system (thus subject to abuse) and this state of things takes place sooner or later. The distributive justice of the Nation may be subjected to the control of a combination of Washington lawyers.

In 1823 and 1824, determined efforts were again made to effect the Judiciary reform, and President Monroe earnestly recommended it.[1] Judge Story wrote to Webster that while he was quite sure of the advantage to the Judges "in quickening their diligence and their learning, . . . it is scarcely possible that they can do the duties long, as business increases upon them." He favored a Supreme Court of nine members, so that the Judges might be numerous enough "to bring to the Court an extensive knowledge of local jurisprudence" in view of the "vast extent of our territory and the vast variety of local laws", and he felt that the West should have at least two out of the present seven Judges.[2] In

[1] Madison wrote to Jefferson, June 15, 1823, that it could not be denied that "there are advantages in uniting the local and general functions in the same persons, if permitted by the extent of the country, but if this were ever the case, our expanding settlements put an end to it. The organization of the Judiciary Department over the extent which a Federal system can reach involves peculiar difficulties. There is scarcely a limit to the distance which turnpikes and steamboats may, at the public expense, convey the members of the Government and distribute the laws. But the delay and expense of suits brought from the extremities of the Empire, must be a severe burden on individuals, and in proportion as this is diminished by giving to local tribunals a final jurisdiction, the evil is incurred of destroying the uniformity of the law." *Madison*, X; Eighth Annual Message of President Monroe to Congress, Dec. 7, 1824.

[2] *Story*, I, 435, letter of Jan. 4, 1824. Six days later, Story wrote that he did not wonder at the impatience of the West and he hoped for two additional Judges. "If we should be so fortunate as to have the gentlemen you name, in Judge W.

1824–1825, a bill was reported in the Senate from the Committee on the Judiciary by Martin Van Buren of New York, providing for ten Circuits, abolition of Circuit Court duty by the Supreme Court Judges, and two Terms of the Supreme Court. Over this bill and an amendment to provide for ten Supreme Court Judges to do Circuit Court duty, a hot debate arose — the merits of the question being complicated by many amendments seeking to curb the power of the Court to declare State Laws unconstitutional. But again Congress failed to act, fearing to trust the President with the new appointments. "I have as yet reported no bill on the Judiciary but incline to think we shall recommend a partial system of Circuit Judges," wrote Webster. "If we had more confidence as to the course the appointing power would take, we might act differently." [1] Finally, in 1826, the situation of the Court became such that some form of relief by legislation became imperative. The docket was heavily congested and the number of causes of high importance was constantly increasing. The Chief Justice was seventy-one years of age; Duval was seventy-four; Washington was sixty-four; Todd had been long ill, Thompson was new to the position; and the Court seemed unable to cope with the burden of its duties.[2] Accordingly a bill

and Judge B. I shall congratulate myself upon the favorable auspices under which we live." The identity of the men, thus suggested for the new positions, is not known.

[1] *18th Cong., 1st Sess.*, Dec. 10, 11, 1823, March 11, 23, April 26, 1824; *18th Cong., 2d Sess.*, Feb. 10, 16, 17, 18, 31, 1825; *Letters of Daniel Webster* (1902), ed. by C. H. Van Tyne, letter of Webster to Jeremiah Mason, Feb. 15, 1824.

[2] In 1825, the Court disposed of 38 out of 164 cases on the docket, hardly more than one a day. "This would seem," said *Niles Register*, XXVIII, March 26, 1825, "to be doing business fast enough, when we reflect on the importance of the decisions of the tribunal; but even now it has matters sufficient ahead to occupy all the spare time of the Judges for nearly five years to come." April 1, 1826, *Niles Register*, XXX, said: "After an incessant occupation of more than six weeks, out of 190 cases on the docket, the Court was able to dispose of only 49." A graphic complaint of the condition was made by Pearce of Rhode Island in the House of Representatives. *19th Cong., 1st Sess.*, Jan. 17, 1826.

was introduced in the Senate by Martin Van Buren, and in the House by Daniel Webster, providing for an increase in the number of Circuits to ten with three additional Supreme Court Judges and this measure actually passed the House.[1] One of the chief arguments in its favor had been the necessity for allaying the feeling of distrust of the Court which had been growing for many years in the West. "The most important consequence of this measure is its tendency to satisfy and conciliate the Western States. It will lessen, if not destroy, their antipathy to the Supreme Court," wrote Jeremiah Mason to Webster.[2] On the other hand, there was opposition even in the West itself. "The real truth is, the gentlemen in the Senate who are called the opposition do not wish the bill to pass," wrote Webster to Story. "Even those of them who are from the West have but a cool desire for it. I suppose the reason is, they do not wish to give so many important appointments to the President."

In the debate, the arguments in favor of and against the relief of the Judges from Circuit Court duty were again urged with considerable extravagance and often in picturesque language.[3] The necessity of having the

[1] Judge Story wrote March 15, 1826: "A bill has passed the House of Representatives to increase our number to ten, and it is very probable that it will receive the approbation of the Senate. It gave rise to one of the most vigorous and protracted debates which we have had this winter. Our friend, Webster, greatly distinguished himself on this occasion and in the estimation of all competent Judges, was *primus inter pares.*" *Story*, I, 493.

[2] *Life of Daniel Webster* (1870), by George T. Curtis, II, letter of Feb. 4, 1826. It is a singular fact that considerable doubt was expressed in the Eastern States, as to the existence of Western lawyers qualified to fill the new positions. This view, however, was not held by Webster, who favored the appointment of two of the new Judges from the West, and who wrote to Judge Story, Jan. 29, 1826: "There will be no difficulty in finding perfectly safe men for the new appointments. The contests on those constitutional questions in the West have made men fit to be Judges." On Dec. 26, 1826, Webster wrote "that the West should have two Judges on the Supreme Bench." *Webster*, XVII.

[3] For these debates in the House, see: *19th Cong., 1st Sess.*, Dec. 22, 1825, Jan. 4, 5, 6, 9, 10, 11, 12, 18, 19, 21, 23, 24, 25, April 17, 24, 28, May 7, 12, 1826, in the Senate, *ibid.*, Dec. 14, 15, 1825, Jan. 9, April 7, 10, 11, 12, 13, 14, 15, May 3, 8, 1826.

Judges keep in touch with local conditions, and with the peculiar statutes of the various States, especially with the Western land laws, was vigorously urged, as well as the danger that, by absenting themselves from jury trial and the active life of different parts of the country, the Judges might become mere "cabinet lawyers", "book-men." "The Supreme Court is, itself, in some measure, insulated," argued Webster, "it has not frequent occasions of contact with the community. The Bar that attends it is neither numerous nor regular in its attendance. . . . If the Judges of the Supreme Court, therefore, are wholly withdrawn from the Circuits, it appears to me there is danger of leaving them without the means of useful intercourse with other judicial characters, with the profession of which they are members, and with the public. . . . I think it useful that Judges should see in practice the operation and effect of their own decisions. This will prevent theory from running too far, or refining too much." James Buchanan also feared any policy which should confine the Judges to sitting at Washington, and said: "Next to doing justice, it is important to satisfy the people that justice has been done. This confidence on their part in the Judiciary of their country produces that contentment and tranquillity which is the best security against sudden and dangerous political excitements." If the Judges should become an Appellate Court only, sitting in Washington, he asked: "What will be the consequence when this tribunal shall be brought into collision with State laws and excited State authorities? Is there not great danger that it will become odious? . . . Is this atmosphere so pure that there would be no danger from such a residence? A large portion of the people of this country hold a different opinion. They think this atmosphere is more tainted than that of any other portion of the country. If the Supreme Court should ever become a political tribunal, it will not be until the Judges shall be settled in Washington, far removed from the People, and within the immediate influence of the power and patronage of the Executive." [1] Van Buren in the Senate held similar views, saying that he conscientiously believed "that to bring the Judges of the Supreme Court to the Seat of the General Government, and making them, as it were, a part of the Administration — for such, it is to be feared, would soon be its effect — would bode no good to the State Governments." Ralph J. Ingersoll of Connecticut, in the House, deplored a condition in which the Judges "should be always snuffing the atmosphere of Washington, and living, as it were, under the eaves of the Palace." John L. Kerr of Maryland, in the House, feared that if the Judges remained in Washington "where they would never be seen but by lawyers and idle spectators, they would in a few years become indolent, and lose their dignity and influence in the eyes of the nation. They will fall into a natural indulgence in the ordinary literary pursuits or other occupations . . . When the Judges shall have sunk in indolence, they will become objects of suspicion."

On the other side, Charles F. Mercer of Virginia in the House claimed that Circuit duty was "to send a Judge from this Court into a distant Circuit, popularity hunting. You send him to imbibe the taint of popular

---

[1] In 1830, in a debate on a similar bill for new Judges and Circuits, Buchanan arguing retention of Circuit duty stated that he feared the danger of bringing the Supreme Court Judges permanently to Washington "within the very vortex of Executive influence" and of converting them "into the minions of the Executive"; while he did not anticipate actual corruption "if you place them in a situation where they or their relatives would naturally become candidates for executive patronage, you place them in some degree under the control of Executive influence. . . . If they were to be confined in the exercise of their high and important duties "to the gloomy and vaulted apartment they now occupy, would they not be considered a distant and dangerous tribunal?" *21st Cong., 1st Sess.*, Jan. 14, 1830.

prejudice and then bring him back to innoculate the Court." [1] He treated with much sarcasm the charge as to the "infectious air of Washington."

Is it to escape, as gentlemen more than insinuate, the atmosphere of Washington — of the ten miles square? The Judges need not reside here. But is this atmosphere inconsistent with judicial purity? Is it really infected? . . . Its atmosphere! Do we not breathe it ourselves? and are we infected with the contagion? Our Chief Magistrate is compelled to inhale it, and with him, his Cabinet, the greater portion of every year; are we afraid to trust the Supreme Court within an influence which we ourselves encounter, it seems, without apprehension, for a longer period of every Congress, than the Judges themselves would be required to do? Is it of their encroachments upon our rights, that we are afraid? They sit at the other end of the Capitol, with open doors, guarded by a solitary officer; and we, the sentinels of the People, are here to watch them, with the power of impeaching and removing them from office. Do we apprehend that they will pronounce our acts unconstitutional? We have but to step a few hundred feet, to hear their reasons for so doing; to explore their motives if we please; and as *amici curiae*, to partake of the argument by which those acts are vindicated.

Do the Representatives of a particular State apprehend the subversion of their local laws, from misapprehension, or corruption, in the Supreme Court? Let them go forth to the Hall of Justice and enlighten, by their knowledge, the ignorance of the Bench; or detect, by their discernment, the evidences of its criminal intentions.

To the arguments that the Judges should "associate with the people" Tristram Burgess of Rhode Island, said in the House:

. . . They must, however, have the benefit of travel; and if so, in the common method, in coaches, wagons, solos, gigs, carryalls; in steam-boats, packet-boats, and

---

[1] *19th Cong., 1st Sess.*, speeches of Mercer and Burgess, Jan. 25, 1826.

ferry-boats; receiving the full benefit, in eating houses, taverns, boarding-houses and bar rooms, of the conversations of learned tapsters, stewards, and stage coach drivers. No man, I must own, who travels in the ordinary method — and Judges can hardly afford to travel in different style — will lose any portion of these several sorts of accommodation and instruction. Judges will, in serious truth it is said, by travel, mingle with the People, and often come in contact with them. Will they mingle with the poor, the ordinary? With mechanical men; with middling interest men; with the great community of toil, and sinew, and production? No, sir, they can do no such thing. Let them have the humility of Lazarus, and the versatile affability of Alcibiades, and they can do no such thing. There is to such men, as it was once said of a learned Judge — than whom no man ever bore his honors more meekly — there is, I say, to the feelings of such men, around a Judge, a kind of repulsive atmosphere. They stand aloof, and give him a large room. They bow not, indeed, with servility, but with profound respect; and they look towards him with a kind of hallowed reverence, as one set apart, and consecrated to the service, and surrounded by the ritual of justice. With all these men, the Judge can hold no tangible communion.

And he said that the "apprehended odiousness is but an apprehension. Such a Court cannot be suspected; it cannot be odious so long as it is filled with the Marshalls and the Storys of our country." Asher Robbins, Senator from Rhode Island, denied that a Court "stationed and stationary at the seat of Government" would become "dangerous to the Government, and the Government dangerous to the Court"; and John M. Berrien, Senator from Georgia, said that: "I have not myself been sensible of any peculiarly corrupting influence in the air of Washington. I do not believe that the integrity of a Judge would be sacrificed by a residence here, and it does not seem to me that the confidence which that department of the Government justly enjoys is to be ascribed to the semi-annual visits

of its members to the people of their respective Circuits.
On the contrary, I believe it is derived from their
personal integrity, from the intelligence and fidelity
with which they have discharged their duties, and
from the general correctness which has marked their
decisions."

The necessity of abolishing Circuit duty for the relief of the Judges from the tremendous labors imposed
upon them by the existing system was urged by many.
Wickliffe of Kentucky said: "By refusing to reduce
the labors of the Judge of the Seventh Circuit, by
requiring him to travel 3360 miles per annum, you have
prostrated his constitution, you have literally murdered
him." Mercer pointed out that the Spring Circuits
did not allow the Judges to remain in Washington later
than March 20, giving them there only sixty-five working days. To the charge made in the House that this
bill was an attempt by Kentucky, Ohio and other
States to facilitate the packing of the Court, in order
to reverse obnoxious decisions adverse to the constitutionality of laws of those States, and as an answer
to the fears that the selection of Judges would be made
from those States which were known heretofore to be
hostile to the decisions of that Court, John C. Wright
of Ohio said: "I have lived in the West many years,
and am entirely ignorant of any feeling of this character
there. How has it been manifested? Where is it?
It is true, Ohio was dissatisfied with a decision of the
Supreme Court, and she caused a case to be appealed
from the Circuit to the Supreme Court, and presented
certain points for decision requiring a reëxamination
of the cause she was dissatisfied with, having perfect
confidence in the Court. The examination was had
and the decision quietly acquiesced in, though leaving
unnoticed one of the principal points relied in. These

facts, instead of sustaining the gentleman's argument, prove the reverse of it true. I am also ignorant of any hostile feeling in the other Western States."

From a combination of many causes, the antagonism to President Adams, the jealousy of Virginia and the East against Kentucky and the West, the impossibility of arranging the States satisfactorily in the new Circuits, the opposition to the amendment requiring concurrence of seven Judges on any decision invalidating a State statute or Act of Congress, which had been adopted by the Senate — the bill was finally lost by a disagreement between the two branches of Congress. This unfortunate result seems to have been largely due to political maneuvering between Van Buren in the Senate and Webster in the House, the latter being desirous of having Ohio included in a separate Circuit from Kentucky, in order to facilitate the appointment as Judge of John McLean of Ohio, then Postmaster-General.[1]

[1] Webster wrote to Mason, May 2, 1826: "The Judiciary Bill is yet between the two Houses. It may possibly be lost but I think it will not be. If the Senate do not yield their amendment probably we shall agree to it. A pretty satisfactory arrangement will be made as to the Judge. The present Postmaster General (John McLean of Ohio) will be named in case Ohio be separated from Kentucky. Otherwise I conjecture the Judge in that quarter will be N. F. Pope, at present District Judge of Illinois." *Letters of Daniel Webster* (1902), ed. by C. H. Van Tyne.

Van Buren wrote to B. F. Butler, May 15, 1826 (*Van Buren Papers MSS*), that: "There has been a great deal of shuffling on the part of Webster & Co. to let the Bill die in conference. This plan we have defeated by a pretty strong course. With characteristic Yankee craft he has, though defeated in his main object, seized upon some clumsy expressions of Holmes (who reported the bill or rather amendment during my sickness) to hide the true ground of collision, the union of Kentucky and Ohio, by raising another question upon the form of the amendment. But the matter is perfectly understood here. Unless they can have a Judge in Kentucky (who is already appointed) and one in Ohio also, they wish to defeat the bill, in hopes of getting a better one next year. The great object is to get McLean out of the Post Office which can only be effected by his promotion, as they dare not displace him. It is also said that Ingham is to be P. M. G. and Webster, Speaker. There may be some mistake about this latter part although I am not certain that there is. The question will be taken in the House tomorrow and it is probable, though not absolutely certain, that the bill will fall. Webster has lost ground this winter and is not as happy as he expected to be."

Relief from the pressure of work on the Judges by abolition of Circuit duty being thus denied, it became necessary to apply some other remedy, and a bill was introduced and enacted, lengthening the term of session of the Court in Washington. Consequently, beginning in 1827 (12 Wheaton), the Court met on the second Monday of January in each year. President Adams had waited to ascertain whether the bill for additional Judges would pass during the 1826 Term, before filling the vacancy on the Bench caused by the death of Judge Todd; but on April 11, he finally decided to nominate Robert Trimble of Kentucky.[1] The new Judge was forty-nine years old, and had been for nine years United States District Judge. While holding that position, he had made himself obnoxious by reason of his insistence on the supremacy of Federal laws over State processes, in consequence of which his nomination was strongly opposed in the Senate by the Kentucky Senator, Rowan;[2] but after a motion of Senator Benton that it be referred to the Committee on the Judiciary "with instructions to report on the character of the rules adopted by said Trimble, while District Judge of Kentucky, relative to executions, and the authority,

[1] Henry Clay wrote to John J. Crittenden, March 10, 1826: "The President wishes not to appoint a Judge in place of our inestimable friend, poor Todd, until the Senate disposes of the bill to extend the Judiciary, though he may, by the delay to which that body seems now prone, be finally compelled to make the appointment without waiting for its passage or rejection. It is owing principally to Mr. Rowan that an amendment has been made in the Senate, throwing Kentucky and Ohio into the same Circuit, and his object was to prevent any Judge from being appointed in Kentucky. He told me that he wished the field of election enlarged for a Judge in our Circuit." *Life of John J. Crittenden* (1871), by Ann M. B. Coleman, I, 63, 65.

[2] Clay wrote to Crittenden, May 11: "Our Senator, Mr. R. made a violent opposition to Trimble's nomination and prevailed upon four other Senators to record their negatives with him. He is perfectly *impotent* in the Senate, and has fallen even below the standard of his talents, of which, I think, he has some for mischief, if *not* for good. The Judiciary bill will most probably be lost by the disagreement between the two Houses as to its arrangements. This day will decide."

under which the same were adopted ", had been lost, the nomination was finally confirmed, May 9, 1826, by a vote of twenty-seven to five.[1]

[1] Marshall wrote to Story, May 26: "I am glad our brother Trimble has passed the Senate *maugre* Mr. Rowan. . . . I hope the seven Judges will convene at our next Term, and that the constitutional questions pending before us may be argued and decided." *Story Papers MSS.*

CHAPTER EIGHTEEN

CONSTITUTIONAL LAW AND DANIEL WEBSTER

1827–1830

DURING the year 1827, the assaults upon the Court, which, for the past ten years, had been almost continuous both in Congress and in the press, temporarily ceased. Partisan controversy had become much less embittered. The financial conditions in the country were improving; the Bank of the United States was being less regarded as an engine of oppression to debtors and of prostration of State-Rights. The bitterest political opponents of the Court, Jefferson and Spencer Roane, were dead; and the dire predictions as to the effect of the Court's decisions on the scope of Federal power had thus far been unfulfilled. So that even *Niles Register*, which had long objected to the doctrines and jurisdiction of the Court, now confessed that "we have often thought that no person could behold this venerable body without profound respect for the virtue and talents concentrated on its bench, and with a degree of confidence that, as there must be some power in every government having final effect, it could hardly be vested anywhere more safely than in the Supreme Court, as at present filled." [1] As will be seen, however, this condition of affairs was but the calm before the storm which broke four years later. Meanwhile, the Court showed itself a potent factor in the development of the country, through its decisions in three great cases at the 1827 Term.

In the first of these, *Ogden* v. *Saunders*, 12 Wheat. 213, it settled the great question as to the respective

[1] *Niles Register*, XXXIII, Jan. 19, 1828.

powers of Congress and of the States over the subject of bankruptcy. Ever since the decision of the *Sturges Case* in 1819, the business community and the Bar had been left in doubt as to what the ultimate decision of the Court would be. The case had first come before it in 1824 and had presented questions not involved in the previous cases — a contract made in New York by a New York debtor with a citizen of another State, and made after the passage of the New York insolvent law.[1] "It will present a most interesting question for the decision of the Court," said a newspaper of that State, "and next to the Steamboat cause will be of more importance to the future welfare of the State than any other which will be agitated during the present Term. It is probable that Congress will soon pass a general bankrupt law — yet, if Congress declines passing any bankrupt law and the States are prohibited from adopting laws for themselves, the commercial state of the country will present a spectacle not found in history. The debtor, the merchant whose fortune has been swept away by events beyond his control, will be pursued by unrelenting creditors without cessation. New York has deep interest in the decision." Argument was begun on March 3, 1824, the day after the decision in *Gibbons* v. *Ogden*, and was continued for two days by Charles G. Haines, David B. Ogden and Henry Clay against Daniel Webster and Henry Wheaton. The Court, however, being greatly divided in opinion, adjourned without rendering a decision.[2] In 1825,

---

[1] See *New York Statesman*, Feb. 24, March 6, 9, 1824. Argument had been delayed in this case "until the state of the Chief Justice's health enabled him to be in Court." *Washington Gazette*, Feb. 23, 1824.

[2] "On many accounts," said the *New York Evening Post*, March 27, 1824, "we feel happy at the postponement — first, it shows that the Court has great doubt and difficulties and that the question is to be weighed and discussed with great caution and candor. Twelve months may produce able and luminous discussion on the subject."

owing to the absence of Judge Todd from illness, the
Court was evenly divided. The same condition prevailed
in 1826, as Judge Todd had died and his successor,
Judge Trimble, was not appointed until after the end of
the Term. It was finally argued (with several other cases
presenting similar points) before a full Court on January
18–20, 1827, Webster and Wheaton appearing in opposition to the validity of the laws, and William Wirt,
Edward Livingston, David B. Odgen, Walter Jones and
William Sampson in their support. While the case was
still under consideration by the Court, a vigorous debate
took place in the Senate over the passage of a Bankruptcy
bill then pending before it; and in a lengthy discussion
of the constitutional powers of the Federal Government
relative to such laws, the trend of the decisions was
again the subject of much criticism. Van Buren of New
York spoke of the "injurious extension of the patronage
of the Federal Government and an insupportable enlargement of the range of judicial power," contemplated by the
bill, and said that he "was aware of what, at the moment
he was speaking, was going on below; but he would not
for an instant anticipate further limitations upon the
rights of the States upon this subject. As yet, they had
not been restricted by the Supreme Court from passing
prospective insolvent laws." Tazewell of Virginia
denied the right of Congress to pass an insolvent
law authorizing voluntary petitions for discharge from
debt, saying that to permit such laws would be to prostrate the sovereignty of the States. Woodbury of
Maine held a similar view, stating that such power
in the Congress would bring "a vortex of disaster and
difficulty to State-Rights and State independence."
On the other hand, Hayne of South Carolina believed
that the Court was about to hold that the States had
no power to pass any insolvent law, whether before

or after the making of the contract; and he, therefore, advocated a National law. Berrien of Georgia agreed with Hayne. Reed of Mississippi opposed the bill, saying: "Let us vindicate the rights of the States in this respect, until that Department, intended to be coördinate, but, I fear, in practice supreme, shall have decided otherwise. Fortunately for the States, their power to pass prospective bankruptcy laws has not yet been paralyzed by the talisman of judicial authority. That right still remains unimpaired and, I have the fullest confidence, will escape unhurt through the ordeal of the Judiciary tribunals of the country." [1] Senator Reed's confidence thus expressed was justified when the Court, on February 18, 1827, four weeks after the argument of *Ogden* v. *Saunders*, rendered its decision, in which four Judges (three dissenting) concurred in upholding the validity of State insolvent laws enacted after the date of the contracts.[2] Judge Washington, though retaining his previous belief that the power of Congress over bankruptcy was exclusive, consented to uphold the New York statute, on the narrow ground that it formed a part of the contract when made and therefore did not impair its obligation; and he said, if he had any doubt, "a decent respect due to the wisdom, the integrity and the patriotism" of the Legislature made a presumption in favor of validity. "This has

[1] *19th Cong., 2d Sess.*, Jan. 18, 23, 24, 25, 26, 27, 1827. The bill was rejected Feb. 6, 1827.

[2] The close decision of the Court upon this important constitutional question was seized on by those Senators and Congressmen who, in this year and for several years past, had been pressing for the passage of a bill requiring the concurrence of all the Judges, or of five or seven, in any opinion rendered on such questions; and Wickliffe of Kentucky, on Jan. 22, 1827, had said in a vigorous speech urging a bill of such a nature: "What is at this very moment transpiring in another part of this Capitol? The validity of the New York insolvent laws, which have been enacted for thirty years in that State, which laws have received the highest judicial sanction in the Courts of that State, depends upon the opinion of a single Judge of the Supreme Court . . . the Court heretofore being equally divided upon the question."

always been the language of this Court . . . and I
know that it expresses the honest sentiments of each and
every member of this Bench." Judge Johnson, holding
the view that the power of Congress was not exclusive, said that most of the dangers feared in leaving
this power with the States are imaginary, "for the
interests of each community, its respect for the opinion
of mankind, and a remnant of moral feeling, which
will not cease to operate in the worst of times, will
always present important barriers against the gross
violation of principle"; and he upheld the right of
New York to enact insolvent laws applicable not only
to contracts made after but before its passage. Judge
Thompson, after stating that questions of the validity
of State laws were "always questions of great delicacy" and that he was impressed "with the sentiment
that this is the point upon which the harmony of our system is most exposed to interruption", upheld the law as
applied to subsequent contracts. Judge Trimble held
broadly that the law did not impair the obligation of
contract. Chief Justice Marshall and Judges Story
and Duval dissented, denying especially that an insolvent
law enacted prior to a contract entered into the contract
as a part of it, and stating that such a doctrine would
cause this important clause of the Constitution to "lie
prostrate and be construed into an inanimate, inoperative and an unmeaning clause." It is to be noted that
though the question of bankruptcy legislation had
become a heated political issue at this time, the Court
did not divide on partisan lines, two Judges with strongly
Federal tendencies joining with two strongly State-
Rights Republicans to compose the majority.

This decision disposed of several of the cases before the
Court, but not the case of *Ogden* v. *Saunders*, which presented the further question whether a State insolvent law

could discharge a contract of a citizen of another State. This point was argued on March 6, and one week later, the Court, in an opinion rendered by Judge Johnson and concurred in by the three Judges who had dissented upon the other point (Marshall, Duval and Story), decided that such a contract could not be discharged and that: "When the States pass beyond their own limits and the rights of their own citizens and act upon the rights of citizens of other States, there arises a conflict of sovereign power, and a collision with the judicial powers granted to the United States which render the exercise of such a power incompatible with the rights of other States and with the Constitution of the United States." To this decision, there was a dissent on the part of the three Judges (Washington, Thompson and Trimble) who had united with Johnson in the previous cases in upholding the statute. This close division of opinion among the Judges, and the limitation of the legal operation of a State bankruptcy law to citizens of the State, gave great dissatisfaction to the country at large; and a prominent Western lawyer, in a thoughtful review of the decision, expressed the general opinion that: "The decision partakes more of legislation than adjudication. . . . The Judges have run into some very mischievous errors. One is the deep admixture of political expediency which is infused into and pervades many of their decisions, especially in expounding the Constitution. . . . It is understood that three of the Judges — Marshall, Story and Duval, — considered them (the insolvent laws) wholly invalid, wherever they provided for discharging the contract. The subdivisions of opinion, by which they are made inoperative in some cases, and obligatory in others, existed among the other four Judges. Without admitting that the three Judges were right, it seems clear to me that the others must be wrong. And I hazard the opinion that, half a century hence, the decision now made will not be regarded as law." [1] Even as late as 1844, the *Western Law Journal* stated that these bankruptcy decisions "were most unfortunate cases for the people of this country and have had a most disastrous effect on multitudes of unfortunate debtors and have very much embarrassed Congress and the whole country." [2] Students of economic history will be inclined to agree with the views thus contemporaneously expressed and to believe that it would probably have been better for the country, had the Chief Justice's opinion prevailed and had the exclusiveness of the power of Congress over the subject been upheld. Certainly, the financial troubles which arose, during the next ten years, out of the over-speculation in public lands, canals and railroads, and out of disastrous banking methods, could have been alleviated by the exercise of Congressional power in the passage of a National Bankruptcy Act, when they could not be adequately dealt with by the insolvent laws of the separate States. The hard-pressed condition of the debtors, however, was somewhat relieved by a decision of the Court, in the year 1827, immediately after the decision in *Ogden* v. *Saunders*. For in *Mason* v. *Haile*, 12 Wheat. 370, it held that a Rhode Island statute abolishing

[1] *Liberty Hall and Cincinnati Gazette*, March 27, 1827.

[2] *Western Law Journal* (1843–44), I: "If the States are to be reasoned out of their sovereignty in this manner, they will soon have a narrow field to operate in. The Supreme Court will weave a web about them that will as effectually restrain their action as a strait jacket." And again in 1849, the same *Journal* criticizing Judge Johnson's opinion in *Ogden* v. *Saunders* said: "This was the first time that such a distinction had been heard of. That a law should be constitutional as to one set of creditors and unconstitutional as to another set was a striking novelty, but when the distinction was still further refined by making its constitutionality depend on the place where the contract was made or the parties resided, it appeared to be not only novel, but in direct conflict with the Fourth Article of the Constitution which requires 'full faith and credit' to be given in each State to the public acts and judicial proceedings of every other State." See also *Ogden* v. *Saunders Reviewed*, by Conrad Reno, *Amer. Law Reg.* (1888), XXXVI.

imprisonment for debt and passed after the date of a contract did not constitute an impairment of the obligation of the contract, since, as it stated: "This is a measure which must be regulated by the views of policy and expediency entertained by the State Legislatures. Such laws act merely upon the remedy, and that in part only." This decision, it will be noted, was in accord with the liberal sentiment of the times; for as James Kent wrote in his *Commentaries*, this very year: "The power of the imprisonment for debt, in cases free from fraud, seems to be fast going into annihilation in this country, and is considered as repugnant to humanity, policy and justice." Kentucky, in 1821, had been the first State to abolish such imprisonment as one of her series of laws for relief of debtors who had been injured by the specie-payment policy of the Bank of the United States. New York was soon to follow in 1831, and by the year 1857, practically all the States had enacted this form of relief for debtors.[1]

Three weeks after the decision in *Ogden* v. *Saunders*, the Court rendered an opinion in the second of the great cases at this Term, *Brown* v. *Maryland*, 12 Wheat. 419. This case was thenceforth to be noted as affording the occasion not only for one of the great fundamental decisions of American constitutional law, but for the first argument on that subject by a future Chief Justice of the United States, Roger B. Taney.[2]   As Robert

[1] On this subject, see *History of the American People*, by John B. McMaster, VI; *Kent's Commentaries* (5th ed. 184), II, 398 note; *Imprisonment for Debt* (1842), by Asa Kinne; *Personal Memoirs of J. T. Buckingham* (1837), I, 102; *Beers* v. *Haughton* (1835), 9 Pet. 329; *Vial* v. *Penniman* (1881), 103 U. S. 714; *Thirty Years' View* (1856), by Thomas H. Benton, 291.

[2] Taney's first appearance was in 1825 in *Manro* v. *Almeida*, 10 Wheat. 473.   In 1826, in *Etting* v. *Bank of the United States*, 11 Wheat. 59, involving the defalcation of the cashier, McCulloch (the *McCulloch* of *McCulloch* v. *Maryland*), Taney and Webster appeared against Wirt and Emmet; and Marshall in his opinion spoke of the "great efforts which have been bestowed upon the case", and the "elaborate arguments which have been made at the Bar." The Court being divided in its opinion, Taney and Webster lost their case. Story wrote of this

G. Harper had died in 1825, William Wirt alone remained to contest with Taney the leadership of the eminently talented Maryland Bar, and of these two competitors, who met in the argument of this great case, a contemporary gave the following vivid picture: "Between Mr. Taney and Mr. Wirt there was the greatest possible difference, in manner and appearance. Portly and erect, with what must have been a handsome figure before the assumed Aldermanic proportions, Mr. Wirt, when he arose to address a jury, impressed them with the idea of perfect health, whose only drawback was suggested by the pallor of his skin. His opening sentences were always accompanied by a pleasant smile, and it was apparent that he desired to establish in the beginning personal relations with those to whom he was speaking. His voice I have already described (the sweetness of his voice was only equalled by the charm of his smile). When Mr. Taney rose to speak you saw a tall, square-shouldered man, flat-breasted, in a degree to be remarked upon, with a stoop that made his shoulders even more prominent, a face without one good feature, a mouth unusually large, in which were discolored and irregular teeth, the gums of which were visible when he smiled, dressed always in black, his clothes sitting ill upon him, his hands spare with projecting veins, in a word, a gaunt, ungainly man. His voice, too, was hollow, as the voice of one who was con-

case (I, 492): "The Court has been engaged in its hard, dry duties with uninterrupted diligence. Hitherto, we have had but little of that refreshing eloquence which make the labors of the law light; but a case is just rising which bids fair to engage us all in the best manner. Webster, Wirt, Taney (a man of fine talents, whom you have probably not heard of) and Emmett are the combatants, and a bevy of ladies are the promised and brilliant distributors of the prize." Another case argued by Taney at the 1826 Term, in company with Wirt against Webster, "with great ability and care" and involving "a great variety of feudal and constitutional learning which the Court did not think it necessary to examine" was *Cassell* v. *Carroll*, 11 Wheat. 134. John Quincy Adams wrote of "Taney of whose talents, I had heard high encomium." *J. Q. Adams*, VI, Feb. 7, 1825.

sumptive. And yet, when he began to speak, you never thought of his personal appearance, so clear, so simple, so admirably arranged were his low-voiced words. He used no gestures. He used even emphasis but sparely. There was an air of so much sincerity in all he said, that it was next to impossible to believe he could be wrong. Not a redundant syllable, not a phrase repeated, and, to repeat, so exquisitely simple. . . . In connection with Mr. Taney's style of address, a story current at the Bar was, that Mr. Pinkney (Wirt?) had said when speaking of it, 'I can answer his argument, I am not afraid of his logic, but that infernal apostolic manner of his, there is no replying to.'" [1]

The arguments of *Brown* v. *Maryland* took place on February 28 and March 1, 1827, and the Court rendered a decision only eleven days later. It firmly declined to sustain Taney's contention and held that the Maryland statute involved, which imposed a license tax of fifty dollars on all importers and vendors of foreign commodities, was invalid as an interference with the Federal right to regulate foreign commerce and as a violation of the prohibition of import duties by a State. [2] "It may be doubted," said Marshall, "whether any of the evils proceeding from the feebleness of the Federal government contributed more to that great revolution which introduced the present system, than the deep and general conviction that commerce ought to be regulated by Congress. It is not, therefore,

---

[1] *Life and Times of John H. B. Latrobe* (1917), 202–203, by John E. Semmes.

[2] Taney, C. J., said as to this case in *Almy* v. *California* (1861), 24 How. 169: "It will be seen by the report of the case that it was elaborately argued on both sides, and the opinion of the Court delivered by Chief Justice Marshall, shows that it was carefully and fully considered by the Court." As this case first announced the "original package" doctrine, and first introduced the phrase "police power", see interesting historical discussion in *The Federal Power Over Carriers and Corporations* (1907), by E. Parmalee Prentice.

For early definitions of police power, see Taney, C. J., in *Pierce* v. *New Hampshire* (1846), 5 How. 583.

matter of surprise that the grant should be as extensive
as the mischief, and should comprehend all foreign
commerce and all commerce among the States.   To
construe the power so as to impair its efficacy would
tend to defeat an object, in the attainment of which
the American public took, and justly took, that strong
interest which arose from a full conviction of its necessity." "This cause has excited much interest," said a
Baltimore paper.   "The impolicy of such a law, in its
effects upon the commercial interests of Baltimore, was
so obvious as to induce a strenuous opposition to its
passage on the part of the merchants of that city.
That opposition, however, was fruitless.   Doubts were
also entertained of its constitutionality, and it was
at length determined to have that question finally
settled.   The result is that the law has been solemnly
pronounced, by the highest judicial tribunal of our
country, unconstitutional and void." [1]   And *Niles
Register*, in its editorial comment, described the law
as "one of that class which is perpetually planning
to tax Baltimore City for the benefit of the State of
Maryland, and nearly the whole of the imposition
would have been levied upon it.   It is well known
that we are not exceedingly anxious for the introduction
and sale of foreign merchandise; but to have admitted
the constitutionality of this law would have been to
commit the regulation of commerce to the individual
States, though expressly given to the United States." [2]

The third important case of the 1827 Term, *Bank
of the United States* v. *Dandridge*, 12 Wheat. 64, involved a vital question of corporation law — whether

---

[1] See *Baltimore Gazette*, quoted in *Niles Register*, XXXII, March 17, 1827.

[2] It may be noted that the State of New York had imposed a tax on all foreign
goods sold in New York at auction. This statute, making the other States buying
their foreign goods "tributary" to New York, was undoubtedly invalid under the
decision in *Brown* v. *Maryland*.   See *Baltimore Patriot*, April 3, 1827.

approval of acts of its agents by a corporation may be shown by presumptive testimony or only by written record and vote. Though Marshall had held on Circuit that such record and vote were necessary, an affirmance of this view by the Court would have retarded the commercial development of this country immeasurably, for it is to be noted that it was just at this time that American business corporations were beginning to "increase in a rapid manner and to a most astonishing extent" (as Kent then wrote).[1] Prior to 1827, owing to the tendency of State legislation to increase the personal responsibility of shareholders, business corporations had played a comparatively small part in commercial life; and practically the only corporations appearing as litigants in the Court, prior to 1830, were the banks and the insurance companies.[2] In this *Dandridge Case*, Webster and Wirt argued for the Bank of the United States against L. W. Tazewell.[3]

[1] See letter of Marshall to Story, July 2, 1823, describing his ruling and saying: "The case . . . goes to the Supreme Court and will probably be reversed. I suppose so, because I conjecture that the practice of banks has not conformed to my construction of the law. The Judge, however, who draws the opinion must have more ingenuity than I have if he draws a good one. . . . I shall bow with respect to the judgment of reversal, but till it is given, I shall retain the opinion I have expressed." *Mass. Hist. Soc. Proc., 2d Series*, XIV; *Kent*, II, 219.

[2] The Bank of the United States was involved in forty-four cases between 1815 and 1830, and other banks in about sixty cases.

[3] *Webster*, XVI; see letter to Biddle at the previous Term, March 21, 1826; "Dandridge's case was not reached until almost the last day of the Court, and until the Court had intimated that they should not take up another long or important cause. It was ready for argument, and printed cases are prepared for the use of the Court. In this case, according to your request, I engaged Mr. Wirt on the part of the Bank, as I have already advised you. I wish it to be understood in regard to this cause, that I consider myself as only filling Mr. Sergeant's place temporarily. If he should be here at the next Term, he will conduct the case, with Mr. Wirt."

An interesting illustration of the degree to which practice in the Supreme Court absorbed the time of eminent members of Congress the correspondent of the *Boston Courier*, March 3, 1827, wrote: "Mr. Webster, since I have been here, has been occupied almost every day in the Supreme Court. He is engaged in nearly all the important causes on the opposite side to Mr. Wirt. Mr. Wirt is a very able and powerful speaker. Mr. Webster is, therefore, now very little in the House, and had not made any speech there of much importance since my arrival." See also an interesting account of Webster in *Boston Courier*, March 5, 1830.

To the Bank's President, Nicholas Biddle, Webster wrote, February 24, of his confidence in winning the case:

When Mr. Sergeant went away and I was left in charge of the concerns of the Bank here, he told me that the Bank had at that time *not lost any cause in the Supreme Court.* If he should return at the next Term, I shall have the happiness, I trust, to tell him that it has lost none since. Dandridge's cause is not yet decided, but I have confidence the judgment below will be reversed, so that that will form no exception to our good fortune. I shall forward a little statement of my fees and Mr. Wirt's receipt tomorrow. In Dandridge's case, I shall take the liberty of charging somewhat *liberally.* I never gave more attention, either to the preparation or the discussion of a cause; and I am vain enough to think that my labours were not without some influence on the result.

And on February 20, after the argument, he had written: [1]

As to Dandridge, we hear nothing from the Court yet. The Ch. Jus. I fear will *die hard.* Yet I hope that, as to this question, he is *moribundus.* In everything else, I cheerfully give him the Spanish Benediction "may he live a thousand years." I feel a good deal of concern about this; first, because of the amount in this case; second, because of its bearing on other important questions, now pending or arising, as I have understood; and last, because I have some little spice of professional feeling in the case, having spoken somewhat more freely than usually befits the mouth of an humble attorney at law, like myself, of the "manifest errors" in the opinion of the Great Chief. I suppose we shall have a decision in a few days. You see what a fire the Judges have made on the question of State Bankrupt laws. No two of those who are *for* the validity of such laws agree in their reasons. Those who are *against* their validity, concur entirely. Is there not an old saying—if there be not, let it go for a new one—that truth is one, but error various?

---

[1] Webster wrote again on Feb. 25: "In my letter I have spoken of success in Dandridge's case only on the ground of general confidence, arising from the consciousness of a good case, etc., — but you may take it for granted that my expectation will not be disappointed."

The opinion of the Court, delivered by Judge Story on February 28, upheld Webster's cause and overruled the Chief Justice, the latter dissenting but also admitting that the Court's decision might be " perhaps to the advancement of public convenience." [1]

While a few lawyers feared lest the decision might increase the power of corporations and might "enable a vast engine of factitious wealth to crush communities", the principle laid down by the Court was welcomed by the business world.[2]

The Court, "after an arduous and important session" of ten weeks, adjourned on March 16, 1827, having decided and dismissed seventy-seven causes "some of them of deep and delicate interest and of high consequence", and leaving on the docket for the next Term one hundred and nine causes. "The industry and vigor of the Judges is worthy of all commendation and fit to be examples even to younger men," said the newspapers of the day. "Abstaining altogether from, or partaking very sparingly in, the hospitality and society of the city, they have given their days to the hearing, and their early mornings and evenings to the consideration, of the many important and interesting causes which have come before them from the different parts of the Union." [3]

With the year 1828, there came a great change in the character of the cases before the Court. Piracy,

---

[1] Of his victory, Webster wrote to Mason, April 10, 1827: "We got on with the Virginia cause famously. You will see, when you see the report, that our friend Judge Story laid out his whole strength and made a great opinion. The Attorney-General argued the cause with me. It was not one of his happiest efforts. By the aid of your brief, I got on tolerably well, and took the credit, modestly, of having made a good argument; at any rate, I got a good fee; and although I shall not send you your just part of it, I yet enclose a draft for the least sum which I can persuade myself you deserve to receive."

[2] See argument of Charles J. Ingersoll in *Bank of Augusta* v. *Earle*, 13 Pet. 576, in 1838.

[3] *Niles Register*, XXXIII, March 24, 1827; *Boston Courier*, March 22, 1827.

slave trade, prizes, war and violation of neutrality largely disappeared as subjects of litigation; and the growing commercial development of the country was signified by the decision, during the three years, 1828 to 1830, of nearly thirty cases involving banking questions and of numerous cases on notes, bills of exchange and insurance.[1] The chief case of historic importance at this 1828 Term was the noted *American Insurance Co. v. Canter*, 1 Pet. 511, involving the validity of the decrees of a Territorial Court of Florida, argued by David B. Ogden against Webster and Whipple. In this case, the Court affirmed the right of Congress to authorize such Courts, in the exercise of its power " to make all needful rules and regulations respecting the territory or other property belonging to the United States ", and unhampered by the provisions of the Constitution respecting the tenure of office of the Federal Judiciary. The decision became the foundation of much of the discussion, thirty years later, in the debates on the power of Congress over slavery in the Territories.

Judge Trimble died in September, after but two years' service on the Court; and a bitter political contest ensued over the appointment of his successor. President Adams was defeated by Jackson at the Presidential election in that autumn, and the Democrats very naturally believed that the appointment of Trimble's successor should be left to the newly elected President. The position was offered, however, by Adams to Charles Hammond,[2] the most distinguished lawyer

---

[1] Writing to Jeremiah Mason, March 20, 1828, Webster said: "The Court has had an interesting session and decided many cases. The Judge of our Circuit (Story) has drawn up an uncommon number of opinions and I think some of them with uncommon ability." *Letters of Daniel Webster* (1902), ed. by C. H. Van Tyne. Judge Story wrote to Jeremiah Mason, Feb. 27, 1828: "We have done a good deal of business, and shall not probably leave sixty causes behind us. This is a great victory over the old docket, and encourages me to hope much for the future course of the Court." *Mason.*

[2] *History of Ohio* (1912), by Emilius O. Randall and Daniel J. Ryan, III, 331.

in Ohio, and to Henry Clay, both of whom declined. Clay strongly urged upon Adams the appointment of the eminent lawyer and Whig statesman, ex-Senator John J. Crittenden of Kentucky, and Chief Justice Marshall was favorable to the latter, though stating to Clay that it would not be decorous for him to approach the President: [1]

I need not say how deeply I regret the loss of Judge Trimble. He was distinguished for sound sense, uprightness of intention and legal knowledge. His superior cannot be found. I wish we may find his equal. You are certainly correct in supposing that I feel a deep interest in the character of the person who may succeed him. His successor will, of course, be designated by Mr. Adams, because he will be required to perform the most important duties of his office, before a change of administration can take place. Mr. Crittenden is not personally known to me, but I am well acquainted with his general character. It stands very high. Were I myself to designate the successor of Mr. Trimble, I do not know the man I could prefer to him. Report, in which those in whom I confide concur, declares him to be sensible, honorable and a sound lawyer. I shall be happy to meet him at the Supreme Court as an associate. The objection I have to a direct communication of this opinion to the President arises from the delicacy of the case. I cannot venture, unasked, to recommend an Associate Justice to the President, especially a gentleman who is not personally known to me. It has the appearance of assuming more than I am willing to assume.

Many, including Crittenden himself, believed John Boyle, the distinguished Chief Justice of Kentucky, should be the nominee.[2] On December 17, 1828, Presi-

---

[1] *J. Q. Adams*, VIII, Dec. 2, 1828; *Works of Henry Clay* (1897), IV, letter of Marshall, Nov. 28, 1828.

[2] Crittenden wrote to Clay, Dec. 3, 1828: "As to the Federal Judgeship to which you say I have been recommended, I have only to remark that should it come to me, neither the giving or the receiving of it shall be soiled by any solicitation of mine on the subject. . . . Though I have never been guilty of the affectation of pretending that such an office would be unwelcome to me, I have certainly never asked anyone to recommend me. Indeed, I wrote to Judge Boyle that I would not

dent Adams sent Crittenden's name to the Senate. Within a few days, however, it became apparent that the Senate, which was Democratic in politics, did not propose to act on any nominations until after the inauguration of the new President. This policy aroused the bitterest feelings among the Whigs,[1] both because of the partisan nature of the action and because of the serious interference with the work of the Court, which was embarrassed by the vacancy and by the illness of the other Judges. "If there are no better reasons for neglecting to ratify or reject this

permit myself to be thrown into competition with him. He informed me that he would not accept the office, preferring the one he now holds." Later, he wrote to Clay, Dec. 27, 1828, when the question of his rejection by the Senate was pending: "I have felt great difficulty in acting on this subject. Though for many reasons, I would not solicit such an office, yet when the question may be whether my nomination shall be rejected by the Senate, I am warranted by a principle of self-defence in endeavoring to avert such a sentence. In this view of the subject, I have written letters to several of my old acquaintances in Congress, claiming the interposition of their liberality and justice in my behalf." *John J. Crittenden Papers MSS.*

[1] John Chambers, a Kentucky Congressman, wrote to Crittenden, Dec. 28, 1828: "What a set of corrupt scoundrels, and what an infernal precedent they are about to establish;" and again, Dec. 29: "But independent of their wish to reward their friends, there is, in the appointment to the Judiciary, a still more important ulterior object in view. Three of the present Judges of that Court are very old and becoming infirm. A party ascendancy in the Court is therefore hoped for and will be obtained if possible. . . . Whether the spirit of party is to triumph over the sense of constitutional obligation and imperious duty or not, will be tested by the disposition which may be made of your nomination. We still hope that there are a sufficient number of Jackson Senators to carry the nomination, who will rise above the disgraceful and degrading party feeling which would snatch from the present Executive the power of appointment." Charles A. Wickliffe of Kentucky wrote to Crittenden, Jan. 7, 1827, advising him to come to Washington and combat the "host in opposition to you." See also letter of Senator R. M. Johnson of Kentucky, Dec. 25, 1826. *John J. Crittenden Papers MSS.*

Timothy Pickering wrote to Marshall, Dec. 26, 1828: "When a vacancy occurs in the bench of the Supreme Court of the United States, I feel a deep solicitude that it may be filled, not merely with ability and learning, but with *Independence;* for without the latter, honesty in ordinary cases, involving no political consequences, is an essentially defective virtue. My solicitude for an able and independent Supreme Judiciary arises from my considering it as the guardian of public liberty, as holding the Moral Sceptre of the Union. In this regard, therefore I earnestly hope Mr. Adams may close his political course with an act distinguished for its high National importance, like that of his father's at the completion of *his* contracted cycle of four years. For himself it would be a redeeming act." *Pickering Papers MSS.*

nomination than party feelings or party politics," said a New York paper, "the majority of the Senate must be held responsible to the country for conduct which is unjustifiable in principle and most pernicious in practice. When the highest judicial tribunal in the Nation is made the tool of a party — when a Court, which has been established by the Constitution for the purpose of deciding questions of the highest importance, as it regards the welfare of the Union, the rights and independence of the several States, the interests of individuals and the character of the Nation, is selected for the express purpose of subserving the plans, and promoting the views of plotting, intriguing, selfish and ambitious politicians, the corner-stone of the government will be undermined, and the fabric left exposed to speedy destruction." To such attacks, a violent newspaper supporter of Jackson answered that the Whigs were equally playing politics, and that "it was nothing more or less than a movement of Mr. Clay to abuse the Senate for refusing to obey his dictation in placing one of his men on the Supreme Bench for life — a devoted partisan of Mr. Clay." [1] A few days later, it charged Clay with using the office to further his Presidential ambitions: [2] "If the proposition to reduce the number of Judges to six should prevail, it will follow, of course, that no nominations should be confirmed. If it does not succeed, the people have said that Messrs. Adams, Clay & Co., are not the persons to whom they would refer the important duty of nominating for office. . . . Mr. Clay, however, preferred to hold that office as a ' bait to catch gudgeons ' . . . under the hope that each aspirant would be stimulated to redoubled exertions in his behalf during the late canvass." On January 27,

[1] *New York Daily Advertiser*, Jan. 24, 1829; *United States Telegraph*, Jan. 22, 1829.
[2] *United States Telegraph*, Jan. 24, 1829.

Clay wrote to Crittenden: "Should your nomination be rejected, the decision would be entirely on party grounds, and ought, therefore, to occasion you no mortification. . . . Besides the general party grounds, there are two personal interests at work against you — one is that of Mr. [George M.] Bibb, the other that of Mr. [Hugh L.] White of Tennessee. If General Jackson has to make a nomination, I think it probable that the Tennessee man will get it. Cultivate a calmness of mind and prepare for the worst event." [1]

On February 12, 1829, the Democratic Senate, by a vote of twenty-three to seventeen, declared that it was inexpedient to act upon the nomination; and Crittenden wrote to Clay: "I can smile, though there may be some ire mixed with it, at the political game that is now playing." [2] The inauguration of President Jackson found the vacancy still unfilled and there was considerable doubt as to his probable choice. It was reported that John Rowan (Senator from Kentucky and a bitter opponent of the Court's constitutional doctrines) would be the nominee.[3] Rowan himself favored Judge Hugh Lawson White of Tennessee.[4] Jackson, however, was at first determined to appoint William T. Barry of Kentucky. Finally, he decided upon John McLean of Ohio, who had been a very able Postmaster-General under President Adams, but who was not in entire sympathy with Jackson's political policy as to removals,

[1] *Life of John J. Crittenden* (1871), I, 73, by Ann M. B. Coleman.
[2] Crittenden had written to Clay, Jan. 16, 1829: "Whatever may be the fate of my nomination in the Senate, I am prepared to bear it with becoming fortitude and resignation, though in rejection there is a taste of dishonor which my nature revolts at." *John J. Crittenden Papers MSS.*
[3] *National Gazette*, March 4, 1829, quoting Washington correspondent of *New York Commercial Advertiser*. Jackson was also considering John Pope, a former Senator from Kentucky. See *Jackson Papers MSS*, letter of Pope to Jackson, Feb. 19, 1829.
[4] See letter of James A. Hamilton to Martin Van Buren, Feb. 27, 1827. *Van Buren Papers MSS.*

and hence unsuitable for retention in his Cabinet.[1] Desiring first to assure himself that "McLean would not continue to be a candidate for the Presidency and make his official influence a means of promoting his success and thereby impairing the dignity of the office and the Court", Jackson consulted with his friend, James A. Hamilton, who advised the President to send for McLean, and to say that "he contemplated nominating him for Judge, but that he had, perhaps, peculiar views in regard to the course to be pursued by judicial officers; that he considered them as Ministers of the Temple of Justice, and that as such, they were necessarily separated from all party politics or feelings."[2] Jackson followed this advice, sent for McLean, and on March 6, 1829, nominated him as Judge. The appointment was a surprise to all, Democrats and Whigs alike. "It

---

[1] *Reminiscences of James A. Hamilton* (1869), 100. As early as 1827, it had been supposed that President Adams would appoint McLean to the Supreme Court, and Clay had written to Francis Brooke, Feb. 21, 1827, that speculation had it that "McLean is to continue as Postmaster General or to be put upon the Bench of the Supreme Court."

[2] James A. Hamilton wrote to Van Buren, March 6, 1829, an interesting account (not hitherto published) of the manner in which the appointment was made:

"The P. M. G. was also nominated for a Judge of the Supreme Court. It will be taken up tomorrow and passed. This new arrangement happened as follows. He suggested yesterday through a friend, Ingham, that he desired that place. It was well received and immediate measures taken to induce the Kentucky Delegation to acquiesce. The Gen'l gave Moore to me. I called upon him before breakfast (a man is less proud with an empty than a full belly). I talked the whole matter over and he sent a message to the General which was satisfactory. Bibb was in favor of it and the matter was immediately decided, McLean sent for, and the work done. Branch, Eaton and Berrien supposed not to have been in favor, because, as is said, they supposed it would weaken the Cabinet. My desire was: first to avoid Barry who was too much a partisan, a Relief man, and to whom there would have been much opposition; next to restore, instead of again wounding, the public confidence. This choice will have the first; the former would have had the latter effect, and lastly I wished to remove him from the Cabinet and from the contest. Calhoun is cut up by this measure as is very manifest. He begins to feel that there is an influence beyond, that he can hope to exercise. Barry will be P. M. G." *Van Buren Papers MSS.*

James M. Clayton wrote to Caleb S. Layton, March 9, 1829: "Barry was preferred to McLean of Ohio for P. M. G. because the latter declared he would not proscribe. McL., therefore, was transferred to the Bench to make way for a 'whole hog' man." *Clayton Papers MSS.*

came like a thunderclap upon the Senate," wrote Hamilton, "and was stunning to Calhoun, who hoped that, with the Postmaster-General in the person of McLean, . . . he could have some influence or perhaps constraint." There was, however, very general satisfaction; and even Whig papers spoke of McLean's "urbanity as well as his energy, his resistance of proscription, his sense of justice and his impartiality"; and said: "If Mr. McLean is such a man as we have been led to suppose, notwithstanding the great loss which will be experienced by his removal from his former office, the country will still gain by it. We presume he is too sound a man, both in principle and intellect, to countenance the deep-laid scheme of breaking down the Judiciary. If we form a just estimate of his character in this respect, his recent appointment is a measure of great importance to the safety of the government and the welfare of the Union."[1] Judge Story, whose relations with Jackson were not cordial and who might have been supposed to be antagonistic to the new appointee, wrote: "It is a good and satisfactory appointment, but was, in fact, produced by other causes than his fitness, or our advantage." "The truth is," Story continued, "a few days since, he (McLean) told the President that he would not form a part of the new Cabinet, or remain in office, if he was compelled to make removals upon political grounds. The President assented to the course, but the governing ultras were dissatisfied, and after much debate and discussion, Mr. McLean remaining firm to his purpose, they were obliged to remove him from the Cabinet, and to make the matter fair, to appoint him (not much to his will) a Judge."[2] The new appointee was forty-

[1] *National Intelligencer*, March 9, 1829; *New York Daily Advertiser*, March 11, 1829.
[2] *Story*, I, 564. See *J. Q. Adams*, VIII, March 14, 1829: "I told the Judge (McLean) that as the Senate had not thought proper to confirm the nomination

four years old; he had served as a Judge of the Ohio Supreme Court from 1816 to 1822, and as Postmaster-General under Presidents Monroe and Adams.

Meanwhile the Court, pending the filling of the vacancy, was having difficulty in performing its duties; for on the day for the convening of the 1829 Term (January 12) only Judges Todd and Washington were present; Duval and Thompson were detained by illness, and Johnson by accident due to the upsetting of a stagecoach in North Carolina.[1] Finally, after nearly three weeks' delay, six Judges appeared and arguments were begun, on February 28, by Robert Y. Hayne against Hugh Legaré and Cruger (all of South Carolina) in one of the most important of the Court's constitutional cases, *Weston* v. *City Council of Charleston*, 2 Pet. 449, involving the power of the city to tax stock of the United States.[2] Singularly, Hayne, whose

of J. J. Crittenden, made by me, I was much rejoiced at hearing of his appointment. He said it had not been agreeable to himself — which is well known. He was removed from the Post Office because he refused to be made the instrument of that sweeping proscription of postmasters which is to be one of the samples of the promised reform."

James A. Hamilton's version of the episode was as follows: "The day before the nomination was to be made, Ingham, at McLean's instance, called upon the President and told him that the Postmaster-General would like to take the office of Judge and urged again the peculiar delicacy of his situation as Postmaster-General in regard to removals. The President sent for me, told me of this intimation and asked my opinion. I immediately said of all things, it was best, and nothing should be left unattempted to accomplish it." See also a lively description of the episode in *Reminiscences of Sixty Years at the Metropolis* (1886), by Ben Perley Poore. The correspondent of the *Boston Courier*, Feb. 27, 1829, writing Feb. 21, said that it had been "a week of speculation" in Washington, and that "it is not only our concern to enquire 'Who is in the Cabinet today?' but 'What is to be done with Mr. McLean today?'"

[1] *National Intelligencer*, Jan. 13, 17, 1829. Congress was forced to pass a special act, providing that if less than four Judges were present at the sitting of the Court, they might adjourn from day to day for twenty days from the opening of the Term, and if a quorum were not then present the Court should adjourn for the year. *20th Cong., 3d Sess.*, Jan. 20, 21, 1829.

[2] The case had been argued at the previous Term by the same counsel. The *Baltimore Patriot*, quoted in *Charleston* (S. C.) *Courier*, March 5, 1829, said: "In the Supreme Court during the present Term, I have carefully noticed the many gentlemen at its Bar, and could not shut my eyes to the very great advantages of a liberal education and opportunities of study. In Mr. Legaré of Charleston, for

name, two years later, was to become widely known as
the defender of Nullification in the famous debate on
the Foote Resolution, argued in this case in behalf of
the National powers, while Legaré, who later became
Attorney-General of the United States, made an extreme
plea for State-Rights, saying: "The doctrine that interference with Federal powers will suffice, by implication, to neutralize or even annihilate State-Rights is
startling in itself, and most pernicious when carried out
to its legitimate results. The degree of interference
being unsettled and incapable of adjustment, however slight or shadowy it may be, the issue can never
be started but to a fatal issue." The Court, in an
opinion rendered on March 18 by Chief Justice Marshall (Johnson and Thompson strongly dissenting),
held the tax repugnant to the Constitution as an interference with the power of the United States to borrow:
"a power which is given by the whole American people
for their common good, which is to be exercised at
the most critical periods for the most important
purposes, on the free exercise of which the interests
certainly, perhaps the liberty of the whole may
depend."

While this decision was a further bulwark to the
Federal Government against encroachments by the
States, it also added more fuel to the flames of opposition to the Court's Nationalistic attitude in cases affecting the assumed rights of the States. That the Court,
however, was not inclined to push to an extreme its

example, there is an instance of a young gentleman on his first visit in this city
and first appearance in this Court, astonishing the enraptured audience, surprising
his seniors and eliciting smiles of approbation from the grave members on the Bench.
It was a genius, prepared by education, reaping a full harvest of reputation."

It is interesting to note that at this period, it was a frequent occurrence for the
argument of a case to be interrupted by other cases, and to be resumed at a later
day. In this case, in 1829, there was an interruption of ten days, Hayne opening
on Feb. 28, and Legaré closing on March 10. Decision was rendered only eight
days later March 18.

broad construction of the Constitution, in cases which did not involve conflict between the National and State supremacy was clearly shown in three other interesting cases decided at this Term. In *Wilson* v. *Blackbird Creek Marsh Co.*, 2 Pet. 245, argued by Richard S. Coxe against William Wirt, and involving a statute of Delaware authorizing a dam on a navigable river, Chief Justice Marshall held, that, inasmuch as Congress had passed no law in execution of its power to regulate commerce on such small navigable creeks (which abound throughout the lower country of the Middle and Southern States), the Delaware statute would not, "under all the circumstances of the case, be considered as repugnant to the power to regulate commerce in its dormant state, or as being in conflict with any law passed on the subject." To reconcile this expression as to the "dormant state" of Congressional power, with the broad lines of the decision in *Gibbons* v. *Ogden*, five years before, became a difficult task in later years; and for a long time produced great uncertainty in the whole law of interstate commerce.

In *Satterlee* v. *Matthewson*, 2 Pet. 380, a Pennsylvania statute had been attacked as impairing the obligation of contract. It was particularly for its decisions on this clause of the Constitution that Southern and Western Congressmen, and even Van Buren of New York and Holmes of Maine had assailed the Court in the Senate, three years before, and again this year. The Court now held the statute in question to be merely retrospective but not an impairment of any contract; and it stated that a Legislature had the power to create a contract between parties where none previously existed — even though such legislation might be censured as "an unwise and unjust exercise of legislative power." "To create a contract and to destroy or impair one," it said, do not "mean the same thing." [1] A similar decision was rendered in *Wilkinson* v. *Leland,* 2 Pet. 627, argued by Wirt against Webster, in which a retrospective law of Rhode Island was sustained as constitutional, Judge Story remarking that while such legislation presented "danger, inconvenience and mischief", yet its validity must be decided "not upon principles of public policy, but of power." [2]

One other case at this Term deserves note; for in view of the fact that the question of slavery and the status of the slave had been for years the subject of heated political discussion, it is singular that it had been involved in no case before the Court until it now arose in a peculiar fashion in *Boyce* v. *Anderson,* 2 Pet. 150. The question presented was, whether a slave drowned in an accident to a steamboat was a passenger or merchandise freight, for which the steamboat company was to be liable as a common carrier. "In the nature of things," said Marshall, "and in his character, he resembles a passenger, not a package of goods. It would seem reasonable, therefore, that the responsibility of the carrier should be measured by the law which is applicable to passengers, rather than that which is applicable to the carriage of common goods." This decision was not agreeable to the slave owners, who regarded slaves as property merely, and

[1] This case involved the famous Connecticut Settlers' claims which had been involved in *Van Horne* v. *Dorrance,* in 1795.

[2] Salmon P. Chase (then a student in Wirt's office) in his *Diary,* Feb. 14, 1829, gave a striking account of Webster's argument in this case: "He states his case with great clearness and draws his inferences with exceeding sagacity. His language is rich and copious; his manner, dignified and impressive; his voice, deep and sonorous; and his sentiments high and often sublime. He argues generally from general principles, seldom descending into minute analysis where intricacy is apt to embarrass and analogy to mislead. He is remarkable for strength, rather than dexterity, and would easier rend an oak than untie a knot. If I could carry my faith in the possibility of all things to labor — so far as to suppose that any degree of industry would enable me to reach his height, how day and night would testify of my toils!" *The Private Life and Public Services of Salmon Portland Chase* (1847), 165, by Robert B. Warden.

who had insisted that the absolute liability of carriers of property should be applied; but the Court said that the rule relating to conveyance of goods had been established "as commerce advanced, from motives of policy", and that it did not apply to the conveyance of slaves.

Before the opening of the 1830 Term, another vacancy on the Bench was caused through the death of Judge Bushrod Washington, after a long service of thirty-two years. To succeed him, three lawyers from Pennsylvania were considered by President Jackson: Horace Binney, who had the enthusiastic support of the Philadelphia Bar;[1] John Bannister Gibson, then Chief Justice of Pennsylvania, who was favored by Calhoun; and Henry Baldwin, who was indorsed by most of the Pennsylvania Bench and Bar outside of Philadelphia and by a large majority of the Legislature.[2] Baldwin was fifty years of age; he had served for six years in Congress with great distinction as Chairman of the Committee on Manufactures, his reports on the doctrine of protective tariffs being regarded as the standard authority;[3] and he had been Jackson's first

[1] Binney wrote: "My friend Baldwin got it, and I saw his letter to my friend Chauncey in which he did me the honor to say that I deserved it, but he *wanted* it more." William Wirt told Binney that President J. Q. Adams had intended to appoint Binney if Judge Washington had died during the Adams Administration. *Life of Horace Binney* (1903), by Charles C. Binney.

[2] As reported in the *Pittsburgh Statesman* "four out of five of the people of Kentucky, Ohio, Indiana and Pennsylvania are warmly and strongly in his favor."

[3] See interesting speech on Baldwin by Dudley Marvin of New York in the House, Dec. 19, 1848. *30th Cong., 2d Sess.*, and see *The Forum* (1856), by David Paul Brown, II, 76. For details as to the conflict over the appointment, see *New York Daily Advertiser*, Dec. 8, 1829, Jan. 9, 1830; *United States Telegraph*, March 28, Dec. 7, 12, 30, 1829. The Washington correspondent of the *Boston Courier*, Jan. 16, 1830, said: "A general topic of conversation is the blow which it is supposed has fallen upon Gen. (Duff) Green, the editor of the *Telegraph* in the appointment of Mr. Baldwin. It appears that Mr. Van Buren is lopping off some of the excrescences of the Administration party and is endeavoring to cultivate the vast estate to which he is heir-apparent. The nomination and appointment of Mr. Baldwin . . . so soon after the bitter denunciation in the *Telegraph* must convince the editorial General that his influence over the Executive General is on the wane."

choice for Secretary of the Treasury, but his close
friendship with Clay and the opposition of Calhoun
made his appointment inadvisable. Now, he was violently opposed again by the Calhoun Democrats;
but Jackson, determined not to yield a second time,
appointed him as a Judge, on January 4, 1830. "It
is a step which will create no inconsiderable sensation,"
wrote Van Buren. "Mr. Baldwin of Pittsburg is to
be the new Judge, *vice* Washington. This is another
escape," wrote Webster. "We had given up all hope
of anything but Chief Justice Gibson's nomination.
Mr. Baldwin is supposed to be, substantially, a sound
man, he is undoubtedly a man of some talents." [1]   The
Democrats were by no means satisfied, and were inclined to fight the appointment; but the fact that Calhoun was opposed to Baldwin, led to his speedy confirmation, the only votes cast against him being those
of the South Carolina Senators, Hayne and Smith.[2]
The whole episode was an eminent example of Jackson's independence of character; and the appointment
received general approbation even from his political
opponents. It is "both good and popular," said the
Whig *New York Daily Advertiser*. "It was quite satisfactory to those who wish well to the country and the
Court," wrote Judge Story. "Mr. Justice Baldwin
is thought to give promise of being a very good Judge,"
wrote Webster. Even John Quincy Adams, who
seldom could see any good in an act of Jackson,
wrote: "Judge Baldwin paid me a short visit. This
is another politician of equivocal morality, but I hope

[1] *Reminiscences of James A. Hamilton* (1869); *Webster*, XVI, letter of Jan. 6,
1830.
[2] *New York Daily Advertiser*, Jan. 11, 1830. In *The Chief Phases of Pennsylvania
Politics in the Jacksonian Period* (1919), by Marguerite G. Bartlett, an account
is given of Calhoun's efforts, aided by Ingham, Branch and Berrien, to control
Pennsylvania, in the interest of his nomination for the Presidency. Baldwin was
confirmed, Jan. 6, 1830, by a vote of 42 to 2.

will make a more impartial Judge. I told him I had been gratified by his appointment — which was true; because I had dreaded the appointment of Gibson, the Chief Justice of Pennsylvania, precisely the most unfit man for the office in the Union." [1] The opposition to Gibson, it may be noted, was partly due to the fact that at this time (though he later changed his views) he was strongly opposed to the right of the Judiciary to pass upon the constitutionality of statutes; and it was chiefly owing to his attitude on this question that he was supported by the extreme State-Rights and Nullification faction.[2]

The 1830 Term, at which the new Judge, Baldwin, first took his seat, may with justice be called Daniel Webster's Term. Not only did he appear as counsel on one side or the other of most of the cases of importance, but it was largely due to his unanswerable defense of the Court as an indispensable feature of the American system of Government, made in the famous reply to Hayne which he delivered in Congress at this Term, that the Court was placed in a more impregnable position in the confidence of the people than it had been during the past thirty years. While the cases decided at this Term involved questions of great magnitude and interests of immense monetary values, such as *Inglis* v. *Trustees of Sailors Snug Harbor*, 3 Pet. 99, on which Webster wrote: "I have made a greater exertion than

[1] *Story*, II, 35, letter of Jan. 31, 1830; *Webster*, XVII, letter to Jeremiah Mason, Feb. 27, 1830; *J. Q. Adams*, VIII, Jan. 17, 1830.

[2] Gibson was born in 1780, was Chief Justice of Pennsylvania from 1827 to 1851, and died in 1853; he delivered a dissenting opinion in *Eakin* v. *Raub*, 12 Serg. Rawle, 320, in 1825, opposing judicial power; but in 1845, in *Norris* v. *Clymer*, 2 Pa. St. 277, 281, he said: "I have changed my opinion for two reasons: the late Convention by their silence sanctioned the pretensions of the Courts to deal freely with the acts of its Legislature; and from experience of the necessity of the case." See *Law Reporter* (1855); *Life, Character and Writings of John B. Gibson* (1855), by William A. Porter; *Memoirs of John Bannister Gibson* (1890), by Thomas P. Roberts; *Gibson and Progressive Jurisprudence, Penn. Bar Ass.* (1909); *John Bannister Gibson*, by Samuel D. Matlack, *Great American Lawyers*, III.

in any other case since Dartmouth College or than it is
probable I shall ever make on another," [1] and such as
Carver v. *Johnson ex dem. Astor*, 4 Pet. 1, settling the
title to a valuable tract of 51,000 acres in the State of
New York claimed by John Jacob Astor, few of the
decisions had a permanent effect on the constitutional
history of the country. One case, however, is to be
noted as significant of the fact that the changed conditions, the new spirit of the times and the immense development of banking and other corporations during
the past decade had led the Court to consider with more
care the scope and effect of the views as to corporate
charters which it had first announced, in 1819, in the
Dartmouth College Case. In *Providence Bank* v.
Billings, 4 Pet. 514, it now showed that it was unwilling to enlarge the rights of corporations by any
further extension of the doctrine of the earlier case.
It upheld a Rhode Island statute taxing the capital stock of a bank; and it decided that, unless a
charter contained an express agreement on the part
of the State not to tax a corporation, none could be
implied; and that though the power to tax might be
abused so as to destroy the charter, the Constitution
"was not intended to furnish the corrective for every
abuse of power which may be committed by the State
governments. The interest, wisdom and justice of
the representative body and its relations with its constituents, furnish the only security, where there is no

---

[1] *Inglis* v. *Sailors Snug Harbor* may be noted as being (according to Wirt's
statement) the first case before the Court in which a reargument had been asked
for after the decision. It had been argued in 1829 by Webster and David B. Ogden
against Wirt and Samuel L. Talcott. Judges Trimble and Washington having died,
it was reargued in 1830, and decision was rendered against Webster, who then
asked for a rehearing and was denied. Of the *Astor Case* it may be noted, as a
sequel, that New York by an Act of the Legislature finally paid Astor $500,000
for a surrender of his claim; see *Niles Register*, XXXIV, 235. For other cases
involving the Astor title, see *Crane* v. *Lessee of Morris* (1831), 6 Pet. 598; *Kelly*
v. *Jackson ex dem. Morris*, 6 Pet. 622.

express contract, against unjust and excessive taxation, as well as against unwise legislation generally." This decision, said a prominent Whig paper, "has excited much attention, interest and approval. It is particularly opportune and of a sound constitutional purport." [1] Furthermore, as it was rendered in the midst of the criticisms of the Court in the debate on the Foote Resolution, and at a time when President Jackson was beginning his determined warfare on the Bank of the United States and allied banking interests, the decision was welcomed by the Democrats. It thus strengthened the Court with both parties.

It was exactly two months before the rendering of the decision in the *Providence Bank Case* that the famous debate arose in the Senate on the Foote Resolution relative to the disposition of public lands; and in its course, a violent attack was directed at the scope of the Court's judicial power — a topic which, as Senator Foote plaintively remarked, had been unnecessarily "spliced upon his Resolution." This attack grew out of an argument over the right of a State to refuse obedience to Federal laws, whose constitutionality should be upheld by the Court but denied by the State. As at the time of the Virginia-Kentucky Resolutions, so now, there was no alarm over decisions of the Court holding Acts of Congress invalid, nor were any doubts uttered as to the Court's right to exercise such power. But for the past decade, and especially during the last three years, constant apprehensions had been voiced by the Democrats at the encroachments by Congress on State sovereignty, supported by the broad construction of the Constitution by the Court. Of the criticisms on the Court in this connection, the following may be

[1] *National Gazette*, March 13, 1830. See articles on the case in *United States Intelligencer* (1830), II.

taken as typical. In the Bankruptcy bill debate, in 1827, Senator John McKinley of Alabama (destined to become a Judge of the Court, ten years later) said that while he held its decisions in the highest respect and considered the Chief Justice one of the ablest Judges in the world, "such appears to be the political bias of a majority of that Court and the great authority of its decisions upon constitutional law, that the powers of the Federal Government are, by mere construction, made to overshadow State powers and render them almost contemptible." [1] In 1826, in the debate on the Judicial Process bill, Senator Rowan of Kentucky made a furious attack on the Court, stating that the liberties of the people were being endangered by its decisions, and he "did not rate very highly that sanctity which was unceasingly employed in profaning the State laws and the State authorities." [2] In the debate, in 1828, on the Internal Improvements bill, Senator Smith of South Carolina said that should Congressional power construed by the Court continue to advance, it would soon be "more unlimited than any monarch in Europe and one which would shake the Government to the centre"; and Philip P. Barbour, a Virginia Congressman (who was appointed a member of the Court, nine years later) said: "This tribunal in construing the Constitution have enlarged the sphere of its action, in my estimation, to an indefinite extent beyond what was in the contemplation of those who formed it. . . . By construction, a breach may be made in the Constitution by which not only these powers may be let in, but a flood of others, strong enough to break down all the barriers erected to preserve the residuary rights of the States and the People. . . . The danger is that construction will find

[1] *19th Cong., 2d Sess.*, Jan. 27, 1827.
[2] *20th Cong., 1st Sess.*, Feb. 21, 1828

its way to the vitals of the Constitution."[1] In the debate on the Tariff bill, in 1828, Mark Alexander, a Virginia Congressman, said that now the Government under the Constitution, "so far from being a charter of delegated powers, ... was a monarchy in disguise; it was anything a majority of Congress might choose to make it", and that he "never expected to see the Supreme Court ever declaring a law of Congress unconstitutional which accumulates power in the Federal head."[2] In the Cumberland Road bill debate in 1829, James Buchanan said that "jealousy of Federal power is now the dictate of the soundest patriotism."[3] In the debate, in 1829, on his bill to require concurrence of five out of seven Judges in any decision involving a constitutional question, Philip P. Barbour said that it was necessary to allay popular discontent with the Court, and to produce "an increased degree of contentment and of confidence in the decisions of that dread tribunal", and to fence around with proper guards a power so tremendous as that of "nullifying" the legislation of the Union of the States.[4] In December, 1829, Worden Pope, a close friend of President Jackson in Kentucky, wrote to him that: "The Federal Courts should be limited to matters arising only out of the Constitution and the law merchant. . . . The lex loci of the States must in private rights govern

---

[1] *20th Cong., 1st Sess.*, April 11, 1828; Feb. 26, 1828. See on the other hand, speeches in the House of Charles F. Mercer of Virginia, Feb. 26, and of John Carter of South Carolina, Feb. 28, 1828, defending the Court from the charges of unduly enlarging the boundaries of Federal power and usurping the reserved powers of the States.

[2] *20th Cong., 1st Sess.*, April 29, 1828.

[3] *20th Cong., 2d Sess.*, Feb. 2, 9, 10, 1829; and see especially speeches of Stevenson of Virginia and Daniel of Kentucky.

[4] *20th Cong., 2d Sess.*, Jan. 2, 21, 1829; *App.*, Jan. 2, 1829. A Massachusetts Congressman opposed a motion to print this report on the ground that if the bill should not pass, "the public circulation of such a report was calculated to spread discontent in the public mind and shake the confidence of the people in the Judiciary."

the decisions of the Federal tribunals. . . . The present collisions and evils exist in the present jurisdiction of those tribunals; and the remedy will be found alone in its reduction to National principles and interests. The whole seven Judges should be unanimous in deciding against the validity of a State Constitution or law. Sooner or later the jurisdiction of the Federal Courts must be curtailed, and we had better at once cut off every graft or inoculation upon the roots or trunk of the constitutional judicial tree. It is a dangerous encroaching power and ought thus to be limited. . . . The District Judges and all Federal officers, to obey the State laws until decided against by the unanimous judgment or decree of the Supreme Court." [1] In 1830, at the very time when the debate over the Foote Resolutions was in course, Congress was considering again the proposition to create two additional Supreme Court Judges and two new Circuits; and James Buchanan of Pennsylvania in arguing for retention of Circuit Court duty by the Judges spoke of the fact that in many States the people had been taught to consider them "with jealousy and distrust." [2] In addition to this dissatisfaction with the Court's doctrines, the advent of the Jackson

---

[1] *Jackson Papers MSS*, letter of Dec. 25, 1829.

[2] *21st Cong., 1st Sess.*, Jan. 14, 19, Feb. 16, 17, March 10, 1830. The leading arguments in favor of the bill were made by James K. Polk of Tennessee, Charles A. Wickliffe of Kentucky and James Buchanan of Pennsylvania; those against the bill by Jabez W. Huntington of Connecticut. A curious amendment was suggested by James Strong of New York, to abolish the Circuit Courts entirely and to have the Supreme Court sit in Washington in January, and in Philadelphia in August. Political considerations affected this much-needed reform; for it was defeated by the North and East out of fear of allowing President Jackson to appoint the new Judges. John Quincy Adams in his *Memoirs*, VIII, March 22, 1830, says that he was opposed to the bill "considering upon whom the appointments would probably fall." On the other hand, James K. Polk of Tennessee in debate ridiculed these fears saying: "Some gentlemen seem to have great apprehension, if this is increased by the appointment of additional Judges from the West, that it will be innoculated with Western opinions and Western doctrines. Are gentlemen prepared to say that the opinions, the legal opinions . . . and the constitutional doctrines of the West are less authentic or more unsound than the opinions of other portions of the Union?"

Administration in 1829, the accompanying general up-
heaval of political conditions in the country and the
rise of bitter partisanship had imbued the leaders of
the Democratic Party with the idea that the Court,
in spite of the fact that five of its seven members had
been appointed by Democratic Presidents, was partisan
in its support of views obnoxious to the Democracy.
Its decisions were attributed to political causes. The
Chief Justice, whose scrupulous abstention from taking
part in any political movement had hitherto been un-
questioned, was now attacked as a politician, because
of a statement, falsely attributed to him but categori-
cally denied by him in the Jackson campaign, to the
effect that, should Jackson be elected, he would "look
upon the government as virtually dissolved." [1] "The
Judges are all ultra-Federalists but W. Johnson, and
he is a conceited man, and without talents," Dr. Thomas
Cooper, President of South Carolina College, had written to Mahlon Dickerson, Senator from New Jersey.
"If the power of the Judiciary be not curtailed, the
liberties of the people are gone. To make every class of
constitutional authorities subservient to a power under
Presidential bias, if not controul, placed far above and
aloof from the people . . . thus to construe the Constitution, is to make it whatever the Judges chose to make
it. . . . When you add to this influence, the sweeping
power under General Welfare and the United States
Bank, I am tempted to exclaim *c'en est fait de nous.*" [2]
Louis McLane, a former Senator from Delaware and recently appointed Minister to England, wrote to Martin
Van Buren, expressing his fears that the Court must be
preserved "from the taint of party." "You fear Judge
Marshall," he said. "I fear a thousand times more

[1] For full account of this episode, see *Marshall*, IV, 463–465.
[2] *Amer. Hist. Rev.* (1901), VI, 729, letter of Aug. 31, 1826.

Judge Story and a line of such miserably frivolous bookworms, destitute of solid understanding, which the effervescence of party and the course of things may throw upon the Bench. . . . I fear Judge Story is but the wretched tool of Mr. Webster." [1] McLane then proceeded to state that if there was "any one source of peculiar danger to the harmony and tranquillity of our Union, it is in my opinion, in the loss of public confidence in the Judiciary. I may be pardoned for adding that, with all Mr. Jefferson's claims to the admiration and gratitude of his country, he is on that score not free from blame. He did much to inspire a jealousy of that tribunal which will never be cured. The Court itself, by travelling out of the record to decide constitutional questions always in favor of the powers of the National Government, and in resisting unjust restraints upon its legitimate powers, usurping powers of the most dangerous scope, naturally encouraged this jealousy." Though he believed that the want of confidence in the Judiciary proceeded now, "not so much from any actual abuse or any crying usurpation, as from an apprehension of what may come, and a fear that with the extravagant powers now claimed, without a greater check and responsibility, it may materially enable Congress to change the Constitution", he believed it necessary to provide some check "which should give the people some better control over the tenure of the office." As a remedy, McLane said that he considered the power of impeachment to be "absolutely worthless"; and that a power of removal on address of Congress would be dangerous, as with the Court a creature of the majority in Congress, there would be no limit to the powers of the General Government or to the "danger of usurpation on the part of the forefoot." The cure which he advo-

---

[1] *Van Buren Papers MSS*, letter of July 20, 1830.

cated was original and unique, namely, to empower the President to remove Judges of the Court upon the address of the Legislatures of two thirds of the States of the Union. Such a change in the Judiciary system, he said, would be "more potent than any other means to preserve the Bench from the taint of party."

It was under such circumstances and amid such sentiments prevalent in the Democratic Party, that, on January 19 and 25, 1830, Robert Y. Hayne of South Carolina, in debating an innocuous resolution regarding public lands, advanced the theory of the right of State veto on laws deemed by a State to be palpably unconstitutional but which had been held valid by the Court; it was as a remedy or corrective for judicial support of Congress that he urged Calhoun's new doctrine of Nullification. While Webster's famous Reply to Hayne, delivered on January 26 and 27, has rung through the annals of American history as the keynote of American Union, it constituted at the same time an unanswerable defense of the functions of the American Judiciary.[1] And in this speech, and in the debate which ensued during the following three months, the fundamental principles of the American judicial system were discussed, both by its advocates and adversaries, with an illuminating thoroughness never equaled on the floor of Congress. The Court's alleged encroachments on the States, its support of unwarranted Congressional powers, and its alleged assumption of jurisdiction of political questions affecting State sovereignty became

[1] It is interesting to note that Webster made his famous Reply on Jan. 26, 27, during an interval in the argument of one of his most important cases in the Court, *Carver* v. *Johnson ex dem. Astor*, 4 Pet. 1, which was argued Jan. 20, 21, 22, 23, by Ogden and Bronson, and after a lapse of ten days on Feb. 3, 4, by Wirt, and on Feb. 4, 5, 8, by Webster. Moreover, on the day after his Reply to Hayne, Webster argued in *Bell* v. *Cunningham*, 3 Pet. 69, and on the next succeeding days, on Jan. 28, 29, in *Parsons* v. *Bedford*, 3 Pet. 433, on Feb. 1, in *Amer. Ins. Co.* v. *Canter*, 3 Pet. 307, and on Feb. 9, in *Harris* v. *Dennie*, 3 Pet. 292.

the subject of especially heated criticism by the following Senators.[1]   Thomas H. Benton of Missouri stated
that the "despotic power over the States" claimed by
Webster for the Court was "a judicial tyranny and
oppression", and that : "The range of Federal authority
is becoming unlimited under the assumption of implied
powers. . . .   It will annihilate the States and reduce
them to the abject condition of provinces of the Federal
empire." John Rowan of Kentucky said that Webster's view of the Court "will lead to the consolidation
of the Government" and that : "The State cannot submit its sovereignty to judicial control. . . .   When the
Court asserts its right to impose restraints upon the
sovereignty of the States, it should be treated as a
usurper, and driven back by the States within its appropriate judicial sphere"; and he concluded : "I view
the State sovereignty as the sheet-anchor of the Union.
I look to the States and not to the Supreme Court for
its strength and perpetuity. There is no danger of
the States flying off from the Union ; you may possibly
drive them off, by attempting to prostrate their
sovereignty and make them vassals of the Supreme
Court or provinces of the General Government." Levi
Woodbury of New Hampshire (who fifteen years later
became a member of the Court) said that he did not
fail in respect for the great personal worth of the Judges
but that since 1803, the Court had "evinced a manifest
and sleepless opposition, in all cases of a political bearing, to the strict construction of the Constitution
adopted by the democracy of the Union in the great
Revolution of 1801. I say nothing now against the
honesty or legal correctness of their views in adopting
such a construction. I speak only of the matter of

[1] *21st Cong., 1st Sess.*, speeches of Benton, Jan. 18, Feb. 2, Hayne, Jan. 19, 25,
27, Rowan, Feb. 8, Woodbury, Feb. 24, Smith of South Carolina, Feb. 26, Grundy,
March 1, 1830.

fact . . . of this sliding onward to consolidation, this giving a diseased enlargement to the powers of the General Government and throwing chains over State-Rights, chains never dreamed of at the formation of the General Government." Felix Grundy of Tennessee said that he respected the Judges, and would defend "their independence as final arbiter of individual rights, but not of the sovereign rights of the States." None of these critics appeared to comprehend the fact that the Court did not, in fact, act directly on the States or assume jurisdiction of mere political questions, but that in a case arising between individuals or in criminal prosecutions involving individual rights and liabilities, the Court was compelled to construe the Constitution and the law in order to determine such rights and liabilities, regardless of the fact that its construction might affect some question regarding which political controversy had arisen. It was this misunderstanding which impelled Hayne to say: "It is not my desire to excite prejudice against the Supreme Court. I not only entertain the highest respect for the individuals who compose that tribunal but I believe they have rendered important services to the country. . . . I object only to the assumption of political power by the Supreme Court, a power which belongs not to them and which they cannot safely exercise."

The replies made by the defenders of the Court were ardent and conclusive.[1] Webster's great argument was followed by David Barton of Missouri in an able speech, arraigning "the attacks of this debate upon the sheet-anchor of the vessel of State, the Supreme Court — the great, common tribunal of the States of this Union." He deplored "the ease with which it

[1] *20th Cong., 1st Sess.*, speeches of Webster, Jan. 20, 26, 27, 1830, Barton, Feb. 9, John Holmes of Maine, Feb. 19, Clayton, March 4, Livingston, March 15, Johnston, March 30, April 2, Robbins, May 20, 1830.

may be rendered odious, by making it a topic of party and electioneering discussion, and representing it to the people, who have the least means of judging it, as a despotic department of the Government, changing the relative powers of the States and the Union and harboring designs of consolidating the Government into one single empire. By depriving it of the confidence of the public it loses its great utility in quieting instead of inflaming the public mind, when it decides any of the important questions and principles of our yet young government of the Union. I enter my protest against making the Judiciary of the United States the topic of mere party denunciations and popular declamation." John M. Clayton of Delaware said that there was no other direct resource "to save us from the horrors of anarchy than the Supreme Court", and that while "it would seem that in their turn most of the sisters of this great Family have fretted for a time, sometimes threatening to break the connexion and form others, in the end nearly all have been restored, by the dignified and impartial conduct of our common umpire, to perfect good humor." Edward Livingston made a superbly able speech, supporting the Court and demolishing, with arguments fully as strong as Webster's, the theory of a State veto on Acts of Congress upheld by the Court. Johnston of Louisiana denounced the "deliberate attempt to undermine the power and destroy the confidence of the country in that great tribunal upon which this Union rests. . . . A Court created by the Constitution, without power or patronage, depending upon its virtues and talents to sustain itself in public opinion and which is essential and indispensable to the Union."

Before the end of this debate on May 22, 1830, and only six weeks after Webster's eloquent defense of the

Judiciary, the Court itself was forced to listen to arguments, bristling with truculent opposition to its authority over the State sovereignties, in the great case of *Craig* v. *Missouri*, 4 Pet. 410. This case, which had been pending in the Court for four years,[1] and had been previously argued in 1828, involved the question whether a Missouri statute authorizing a form of State loan-certificate was in contravention of the prohibition of the Constitution against issue of bills of credit by a State. The point at issue was of vital importance to those who opposed the financial operations of the United States Bank, and who favored currency issuable by the States or by State banks guaranteed by the States. The argument for the State, made on March 3, 1830, by its Senator, Thomas H. Benton, was replete with phrases of indignation at the exercise by the Court of jurisdiction under the 25th Section of the Judiciary Act, and of outrage that any State should be forced by legal process to appear before it. "The State of Missouri," he said, "has been 'summoned' by a writ from this Court under a 'penalty' to be and appear before this Court. In the language of the writ she is 'commanded' and 'enjoined' to appear. Language of this kind does not seem proper when addressed to a sovereign State, nor are the terms fitting, even if the only purpose of the process was to obtain the appearance of the State." The Court's decision, holding the State law invalid, was rendered on March 12, only nine days after the close of the argument, and while the debate on the Foote Resolution was still progressing in Congress. In his opinion, Chief Justice Marshall replied with lofty firm-

[1] See *United States Telegraph*, March 10, 1826, which said that on March 8, the Court ordered *Craig* v. *Missouri* and other similar cases "to be docketed, being of opinion that they were regularly before the Court and that the objections urged on the ground of want of jurisdiction were such as must be taken on the argument and not on motion to dismiss."

ness to Benton's charges, and incidentally to the similar criticisms which were being voiced in the Senate :

In the argument we have been reminded by one side of the dignity of a sovereign State; of the humiliation of her submitting herself to this tribunal; of the dangers which may result from inflicting a wound on that dignity : by the other of the still superior dignity of the people of the United States, who have spoken their will in terms which we cannot misunderstand.   To these admonitions, we can only answer that if the exercise of that jurisdiction which has been imposed upon us by the Constitution and laws of the United States shall be calculated to bring on those dangers which have been indicated, or if it shall be indispensable to the preservation of the Union, and consequently of the independence and liberty of these States, these are considerations which address themselves to those departments, which may with perfect propriety be influenced by them.   This department can listen only to the mandates of law, and can tread only that path which is marked out by duty.

The decision of the Court, holding the State law invalid, caused great excitement in Missouri, Kentucky and other States in which it was felt that financial distress and panic could only be averted by legislation of this kind placing some form of State guaranty behind the issue of currency.[1]   The decision came, moreover, as the climax of the accumulation of grievances which

[1] After the decision in *Craig* v. *Missouri*, Daniel Webster was asked for an opinion with regard to the validity of a law of Kentucky providing for the incorporation of a bank in which the State was the sole stockholder and which issued banknotes, having the security of the State behind them.   (See *Briscoe* v. *Bank of Kentucky*, 11 Pet. 257.)   He replied in an interesting letter, Feb. 23, 1831, stating that while he would not object to being retained in the case, "there are, however, I think good reasons why I should refrain from giving an opinion on this great question, as preliminary to judicial proceedings.   There would, probably indeed, be little value in such an opinion, since the clause of the Constitution, which must be the subject of argument, has been so recently considered and interpreted by the highest judicial authority in the Missouri case.   Indeed, sir, whatever my opinion might be, on a full consideration of the case, it seems to me that the respect due from me to the State of Kentucky and her law, and to the great interest she must feel in the question, may justly impose on me a forbearance from expressing such opinion, in advance of the regular forensic discussion."   *Letters of Daniel Webster* (1902), ed. by C. H. Van Tyne.

the States felt they were entitled to enter against the Court and its decisions — Virginia's over the exercise by the Court of appellate jurisdiction in her criminal prosecutions; Ohio's over the invalidation of her laws directed against the United States Bank; Kentucky's over her Bank legislation, and the overthrow of her land laws and of her laws protecting debtors; South Carolina's over the conflict between the Court's views as to interstate commerce and her slavery legislation and over the incompatibility of the Court's doctrine with her growing Nullification movement.

In view of these conditions, it was evident to all thinking men that the most critical period in the career of the National Supreme Judiciary had been reached. "The crisis of our Constitution is now upon us. A strong dispensation to prostrate the Judiciary has shown itself," wrote Marshall to Story; and a few months later he wrote that he had read the dissenting opinions of Judges Johnson, Thompson and McLean in the *Craig Case* "and think it requires no prophet to predict that the 25th Section is to be repealed or to use a more fashionable phrase, to be nullified by the Supreme Court of the United States. I hope the case in which this is to be accomplished will not occur in my time, but accomplished it will be at no very distant period." [1] And a leading Whig paper in New York summed up the situation by saying: "It is manifest that there is a settled determination in the minds of some of the warm and violent politicians of the country to circumscribe, if not destroy, the weight and influence of the National Judiciary. . . . So long as the Court maintains its talents, its integrity, and its independence, the great constitutional interests of the State

[1] *Story Papers MSS*, letter of Jan. 8, 1830; *Mass. Hist. Soc. Proc., 2d Series*, XIV, letter of Oct. 15, 1830.

are safe. If the Court should be broken down, and
the places on the Bench be filled with ignorant or unprincipled men, violent partisans and desperate politicians, the strength and security of the Republic will be
undermined, and the very first serious convulsion that
occurs will endanger the very existence of the Republic." [1]

Though these pessimistic predictions appeared, at the
time, to be justified, popular confidence in the integrity
of the Court sustained it through the two following
critical years. No one, however, can overestimate
the potent influence in maintaining such confidence
which is to be attributed to Webster's soul-stirring
appeal in behalf of the Union and judicial supremacy
at this particular juncture; and history has confirmed
the contemporary view of his great speech — that "if
his name were unwritten in the legislative and judicial
history of the country . . . he has now inscribed it
upon a monument, in letters so legible and so durable
that it will be read and remembered, as long as there
is an American to read and rejoice in the glory of his
country." [2]

---

[1] *New York Daily Advertiser*, March 19, 1830. See an article containing bitter
criticism of the Court, *The Tribunal of Dernier Resort* in *Southern Review* (1830),
VI.

[2] *New York Journal of Commerce*, Jan. 28, 1830; *National Gazette* (Phil.), Jan. 29,
1830; *New York Daily Advertiser*, Feb. 26, March 3, 19, 1830; the *National Intelligencer*, Jan. 26, 1830, said it had "never yet heard a speech in all respects equal
to that which Mr. Webster has produced." For the fullest and best account of the
speech, see the *National Journal*, the Whig paper in Washington, Jan. 27, 28, 29,
30, Feb. 1, 2, 3, 6, 9, March 8, 11, 24, 1830, quoting comments from other newspapers. J. Q. Adams wrote in his diary, Feb. 23, 1830: "It demolishes the whole
fabric of Hayne's speech, so that it leaves scarcely the wreck to be seen." On the
other hand, the *United States Telegraph*, and the *New York Courier*, both Jackson
papers, attacked the speech, terming it full of "dangerous doctrines", which, if successfully established, "would make the General Government an absolute autocracy,
lording it over the States and the people. Let Democracy look to it."

DANIEL WEBSTER

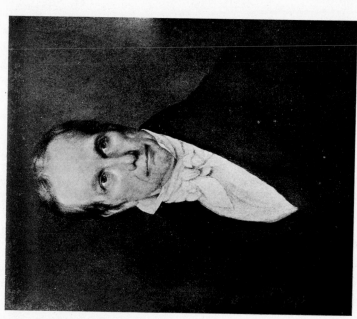

HENRY CLAY

CHAPTER NINETEEN

THE CHEROKEE CASES AND PRESIDENT JACKSON

1831 – 1833

THE case which was destined now to bring about the most serious crisis in the history of the Court arose in Georgia and had its roots in a treaty, made forty years prior, between the United States and the Cherokee Indians, a tribe which occupied a tract of country lying within the limits of Georgia, North Carolina, South Carolina, Tennessee and Alabama. In this Treaty, in 1791, the United States "solemnly guaranteed to the Cherokee Nation all their lands not therein ceded." Eleven years later, Georgia, in ceding to the United States all that portion of its territory now constituting the States of Alabama and Mississippi, did so upon the express condition that the United States should extinguish for the use of Georgia the Indian title to lands within the remaining limits of the State, "as soon as it could be done peaceably and on reasonable terms." Unfortunately, the United States failed to perform its agreement; and though, from 1805 to 1819, it purchased over eight million acres from the Cherokees in Alabama and Mississippi, it bought only about one million out of the five million acres owned by that tribe in Georgia. Moreover, it adopted a fostering and humanitarian policy towards the Georgia Cherokees which developed them into a civilized settlement, very little open to persuasion, and very little desirous to emigrate. The increasing permanency, however, of an Indian tribe within its borders, claiming and exercising a totally independent government, exempt in every respect from the jurisdiction of the State, was a political anomaly which was bound to meet later with fierce opposition from the people of Georgia. Moreover, an important decision of the Supreme Court of the United States, in 1823, in *Johnson* v. *McIntosh*, 8 Wheat. 543, had settled the question of the nature of the Indian title to the soil, and had held that the fee to lands in this country vested in the British Government, by discovery, according to the acknowledged law of civilized nations; that it passed to the United States by the Revolution; and that the Indian tribe had a right of occupancy only.[1] This decision confirmed the determination of Georgia to exercise full right of sovereignty over its soil and over those who lived within its borders. Accordingly, in 1824, it formally asserted its complete jurisdiction over the Indians, and declared that the Federal Government lacked the power to bind a State by a treaty made with Indian inhabitants. At the same time, the State asserted its sovereignty over lands within its borders owned by the Creek Indians, and almost came to actual military conflict with the United States, owing to the policy maintained by President Adams in upholding treaties with that tribe.[2]

[1] This case involved an immense tract of land in Illinois (upwards of 50,000,000 acres between the Illinois and Wabash Rivers). It was argued by R. G. Harper and Webster against W. H. Winder and Murray, the former losing the case. . . . Of the decision, the *Washington Republican* said: "The great importance of the subject matter in controversy seems to require rather a more detailed notice than is usual. . . . One of the most luminous and satisfactory opinions, we recollect ever to have listened to." See *Niles Register*, XXIV, March 8, 1823.

[2] See *State Documents on Federal Relations* (1911), by Herman V. Ames. An attempt to enforce a prosecution of Georgia surveyors who had entered the Creek Indian Territory in violation of the Act of Congress of March 30, 1802, "to regulate trade and intercourse with the Indian tribes and to preserve peace on the frontiers", is interestingly referred to by John Quincy Adams in his *Memoirs* (during his Presidency) as follows:

Feb. 9, 1827. Company to dine. The Judges and Bar of the Supreme Court. I spoke to Judge Johnson of this controversy with Georgia, which, I told him, would first be tried by him. He said he would laugh them out of it.

Additional complications also arose through the discovery of gold in the Cherokee lands. A crisis came, in 1828, when the Cherokees held a convention and adopted a Constitution for a permanent government, displaying their intention to remain on their lands. The Legislature of Georgia responded by passing, in 1829, a series of laws of the most cruel and stringent nature, invalidating all laws and ordinances adopted by the Indians, and providing for a division of their lands. As these laws were clearly in violation of the treaty with the United States, Congress was forced now to take cognizance of the situation, but its action was feeble; and the new President, Andrew Jackson, was in entire sympathy with the State of Georgia in its claim of right to legislate over all persons within its territory, regardless of the Federal treaty. To an application made by the Cherokees for protection by Federal troops against the efforts made by Georgia to remove the Indians by force, Jackson replied "that the President of the United States has no power to protect them against the laws of Georgia." The Cherokees, after obtaining a favorable legal opinion from Ex-Chancellor James Kent, retained John Sergeant of Philadelphia and William Wirt, ex-Attorney-General of the United States, as counsel to bring a case in the United States Supreme Court to test their rights as a sovereign Nation.[1] To

March 10, 1827. When Judge Johnson last dined with me, he promised to look into the Act of Congress . . . upon which the prosecution of the Georgia surveyors within the Indian Territory has been directed. The Judge now suggested that there might be a constitutional difficulty in the execution of the law. . . . The Judge appeared very desirous of being relieved from trying the cause, and said there could be no possible reliance upon a Georgia jury to try it. But he said he should take occasion as soon as possible to send it for trial to the Supreme Court, and he said he had decided many years ago the principle that Indian territory was not within the civil jurisdiction of the United States.

[1] This opinion was concurred in by Daniel Webster, Ambrose Spencer (formerly Chief Justice of New York), Horace Binney and other leaders of the Bar. It must be admitted, however, that the Cherokee Nation did not display great tact or any disposition to conciliate the President in their choice of counsel, inasmuch as both

a suggestion made by Wirt that the State should join
in this test case, the Governor of Georgia answered
by an indignant and sarcastic letter of refusal, in which
he claimed the absolute immunity of the State from
any suit in the Federal Courts and its right to decline
obedience to any Federal mandate. The leading
newspaper of Georgia voiced public sentiment in that
State by an editorial saying: "Has it come to this that
a sovereign and independent State is to be insulted, by
being asked to become a party before the Supreme
Court, with a few savages residing on her own territory!!! Unparalleled impudence!" On the other
hand, the view of those who denied Georgia's assertion
of a nullifying power was expressed by *Niles Register*.
"The people are not ripe for such a state of things —
and until they are, the authority of the Supreme Court
will be supported. . . . Without some high and common arbiter for the settlement of disputes of this character, the Union is not worth one cent. . . . There
must needs be some tribunal of a last resort; something
which the common sense of all men, for self-preservation,
shall accept, not as infallible, but as the nearest possible
approach to perfection." [1]

The form of action decided upon was an original
bill in equity, to be filed in the Supreme Court by the
Cherokee Nation as an independent state, against the
State of Georgia, seeking an injunction to restrain it
from executing the laws claimed to be illegal and unconstitutional. Before this suit was begun, however,
another case arose in the State of Georgia which pre-

men were bitter political opponents of the President, — Wirt as Attorney-Gen-
eral under Jackson's predecessor, and also as a rival for the Presidency — Sergeant
as chief counsel for the Bank of the United States, Jackson's *bête-noire*. That
Wirt appreciated his situation was shown in an eloquent and honorable letter to
James Madison, Oct. 5, 1830; see letter of Wirt to Judge Dabney Carr of Virginia,
June 21, 1830. *Wirt*, II, 253, 261.

[1] See *Niles Register*, XXXIX, Sept. 18, 1830.

sented the same issues. A Cherokee named Corn Tassel had murdered another Indian within the territory occupied by the tribe. He was arrested by the State authorities under one of the recent State laws, tried and sentenced to be hanged. Application was at once made to the United States Supreme Court for a writ of error to the State trial court, on the ground of the illegality of the State laws. The writ, which was issued on December 22, was treated by the Governor of Georgia, Gilmer, with utter disdain. He transmitted it to the Legislature, then sitting, with a message in which he referred to the subpoena as "a copy of a communication, received this day, purporting to be signed by the Chief Justice of the United States and to be a citation of the State of Georgia to appear before the Supreme Court, on the second Monday in January next, to answer to that tribunal for having caused a person who had committed murder within the limits of the State to be tried and convicted therefor." And he declared that any attempt to execute the writ would be resisted with all the force at his command, saying: "If the judicial power, thus attempted to be exercised by the Courts of the United States, is submitted to or sustained, it must eventuate in the utter annihilation of the State Governments or in other consequences not less fatal to the peace and prosperity of our present highly favored country."[1] The Legislature responded with a violent resolution bitterly denouncing the action of the Supreme Court; and it "requested and enjoined the Governor and every officer of the State to disregard any and every mandate and process

[1] *Niles Register*, XXXIX, Oct. 2, 1830, Jan. 8, 15, 1831. The name of the party suing out the writ in this case, is given in 5 Peters 1, 12, as "Corn Tassel", and I have used the name in this form. In the Resolutions of the Georgia Legislature of Dec. 22, 1830, and as given by some historians, the name appears as "George Tassels."

that should be served upon them." Two days later, on December 24, 1830, Tassel was executed. This absolute disregard of the process of the Court (characterized mildly by Judge Story as "intemperate and indecorous") was, in fact, practical Nullification. "It is idle to pretend to wink this question out of sight. The integrity and permanence of the Union are at stake," said a Boston Whig newspaper.[1] "If we continue in a false security, we shall find too late that the sheet-anchor of our National being is lost forever." And another paper said very truly that: "The plain question which the rashness of these intemperate politicians has forced on the country is whether the judicial arm of the General Government shall be amputated, or armed with additional vigor, and whether by the mere volition of one of the States of the Union, the structure of our government shall be at once and violently overthrown." To these views, on the other hand, the Administration paper in Washington, the *United States Telegraph*, replied editorially, that "the position in which the Supreme Court is placed by the proceedings of Georgia demonstrates the absurdity of the doctrine which contends that the Court is clothed with supreme and absolute control over the States." To the Whig paper, the *National Intelligencer*, which deplored the "awful consequences" of aiding Georgia, and the "extraordinary circumstance of the present conjuncture, that the Official Gazettes are engaged in a combination to weaken the Supreme Court of the United States in the confidence and esteem of the People", the *Telegraph* retorted by referring to "affected hysteria" and said: "No one is more desirous than we are to preserve for the Supreme Court that veneration and confidence upon which its

[1] *Boston Courier*, Jan. 21, 1831; *National Journal*, Jan. 4, 1831.

usefulness, if not its existence, depends; and for that purpose we would guard against all political collisions with public sentiment. A difference of opinion as to the extent of the powers vested in that Court has existed since its organization. . . . All who desire to perpetuate our institutions and look to our Courts as the arbiters of justice must regret the attempt to identify them with political aspirants." [1] Violent remarks in other Northern papers to the effect that resistance to the Court by Georgia might be treason, that the Supreme Court was not to be intimidated, and that President Jackson must enforce the laws, brought forth the countercharge that: "There is a determination on the part of some of the political managers to bring the Supreme Court in collision with the Executive of the Union as well as with the States . . . a determination to enlist the influence of the Court and the spirit of the Judiciary and Bar in opposition to the Administration. . . . Why else is it said that the Court will not be *intimidated?* Is it that the pride of the Court may be roused under the pretense of vindicating its authority? Every friend of the Court must condemn the effort to enlist it as a party to an angry political contest. The friends of Andrew Jackson know that *he* is not to be *intimidated.*" The *Richmond Enquirer,*

[1] *United States Telegraph,* Jan. 3, 7, 1831; *National Intelligencer,* Jan. 4, 7, 8, 1831. The *National Journal,* Jan. 4, said: "The people should have a watchful eye to the course which Gen. Jackson may pursue in this very extraordinary crisis of our affairs;" on Jan. 6, it said: "The Union is in danger. Gen. Jackson must sustain the Court process"; on Jan. 10, after noting the editorials in the *Telegraph* it said: "After this language sanctioned, perhaps suggested by the Administration, what hope is there of any action on the part of the President of the United States to sustain the Supreme Court in the execution of the laws?" The *New York Commercial Advertiser,* Jan. 12, said: "The authority of the Supreme Court is contemned, the Constitution of the United States is trampled in the dust, and all this Gen. Jackson will pronounce to be right." The *New York Daily Advertiser,* Jan. 4, 6, 1831, said that it would be interesting to see what course the President would take. "In case of resistance to the authority of the judicial tribunals and the process of the law, he must enforce obedience to the law at all hazards. A refusal will render him liable to impeachment."

noting that the Georgia and South Carolina papers
had expressed their "astonishment and resentment"
at the issuing of a summons to the State of Georgia,
stated that Georgia "is being dragged to the bar"
as Virginia was in the *Cohens Case;* and that in cases
like this, the two Governments, — the Federal and the
State — "ought to bear and forbear." [1]

The position taken by the State of Georgia and its
adherents was further indorsed by the determined effort
which was being made in Congress, early in 1831, to
repeal the much feared Twenty-Fifth Section. Before
Congress met in December, 1830, it had become known
that such an attack on the Court's appellate jurisdiction
was impending. The *National Intelligencer* warned
"the friends of the Union to awake from their dreamy
indolence. . . . Repeal the vital part of the Judiciary
Act and we would not give a fig for the Constitution.
It will have become a dead letter." "There is obviously a determination, on the part of the politicians
of a certain school, to curtail the constitutional jurisdiction and destroy the influence and independence
of the Supreme Court of the United States," said a
leading Whig paper in New York. [2] "This disposition
has existed in the minds of some persons from the early
history of the Government, but it has more recently
become the policy not only of individual politicians,
but of large numbers, and even of majorities in some of

[1] *United States Telegraph,* Jan. 8, 10, 26, 1831. See also *Washington Globe,* Jan.
5, 1831: "But it seems now there is to be a crusade carried on against the South
by the party of whom the Chief Justice has been always the uniform representative.
He has achieved for them infinitely more in the Court than all the rest of the party
have been able to effect elsewhere." The *New York Daily Advertiser,* Jan. 10, 1831,
quoted a correspondent of the *Charleston Mercury* applauding Georgia, and rejoicing that the "high-handed, and now at least palpable, usurpations" of the Federal
power "have been bravely met." The *National Intelligencer,* Jan. 11, 12, 15, 1831,
quoted the *New York Courier* and *Southern Times* (Columbia, S. C.) as approving
Georgia's course.

[2] *New York Daily Advertiser,* Jan. 13, 1831.

the States; and there now appears to be a regular organized system of measures and operations calculated to produce the result so long and so eagerly desired and sought after. At the present period of the world, no intelligent and honest man will call in question the necessity of the absolute independence of Courts of popular sentiment and party clamour. . . . Every attempt, therefore, to destroy their independence, from whatever source it proceeds, is a direct effort to violate the spirit of the Constitution in one of its vital principles. One mode of producing this effect is to impair the influence and reputation of the Court by calumny and slander, representing it as greedy of power, desirous of extending its jurisdiction, and, in the end, of consolidating the National Government by taking away the legitimate powers of the State governments, and rendering them mere cyphers in the construction of the confederation. . . . Accusations of this sort are calculated for effect. The object is to alarm the fears and excite the jealousies of the States. They are, however, wholly without foundation." All this outcry, it was urged, came from interested sources — the opposition of the Southern States to the tariff policy of the Government, the "licentious desires" to obtain Indian territory, the refusal of Georgia to allow Federal interference in her treatment of the Indians and to submit the validity of her acts "to this learned, able, upright and respectable tribunal." That the people of the country would "stand carelessly by and see this great branch of their government trampled under foot by interested, ambitious and unprincipled politicians", the New York paper said, was not to be believed. "When the Supreme Court are stripped of their constitutional powers and prerogatives, the government itself will be undermined, and its destruction cannot be avoided. . . . Once deprive the Court of the power of determining constitutional questions, and the Legislatures of the States will be let loose from all control, and as interest or passion may influence them, will reduce the National Government to a state of dependence and decrepitude, which would be more characteristic of the authority of a feeble colony than that of a large, powerful, independent nation. . . . If the people do not manifest a determination to support the Judiciary, they may make up their minds to part with the Government." [1]

Shortly after Congress convened, the House of Representatives instructed its Judiciary Committee to inquire into the expediency of a bill to repeal this Section; and it was under such "very peculiar and trying circumstances" that the Court assembled for its January, 1831, Term. " The Court has met, with a knowledge that it will be violently assailed in the House of Representatives, and that an attempt will be made to deprive it of its constitutional right to decide on the constitutionality of State laws," said a New York Whig paper. "A bill to that effect will be reported in a few days. If it shall become a law, the Government will be at an end. There is no law of the United States that may not be rendered wholly inoperative by any one of the States. The Supreme Court has been justly considered as the sheet-anchor of the Constitution; and while every other department of the Government has been contaminated within less than two years, our hopes have been placed on this anchor. . . . The appointment of Judges McLean and Baldwin by the present Administration was wholly fortuitous and produced by a combination of political causes beyond the control of the President. If their seats were now va-

[1] *New York Daily Advertiser*, Jan. 13, 14, 15, 1831.

cant, there is no doubt they would be filled with thorough-going nullifiers." On January 24, 1831, a repeal bill was reported favorably by a majority of the Judiciary Committee by Warren R. Davis of South Carolina.[1] A minority report, however, was made at the same time, which must be regarded as one of the great and signal documents in the history of American constitutional law. It was drafted by James Buchanan of Pennsylvania, and signed also by William W. Ellsworth of Connecticut (son of Chief Justice Ellsworth) and Edward D. White of Louisiana (father of Chief Justice White).[2] Though Thomas F. Foster of Georgia, one of the signers of the majority report, stated that the passage of the bill was necessary, since the powers of the Court were so "vast and alarming that the constantly increasing evil of interference of Federal with State authorities must be checked", the measure was, in fact, an offspring of the doctrine of Nullification then prevalent in the South. Such a connection between the two was admitted by John C. Calhoun, who, in writing that he thought the report would pass the House, said: "However strange it may seem, there are many who are violently opposed to what they call Nullification. The discussion of the report will doubtless strengthen our doctrines." [3]

---

[1] The *Boston Courier* said, Feb. 1, 1831: "The bill will be supported by the ultra-exclusive friends of State-Rights and probably meets the views of the Executive and the Cabinet, so that the country is in the singular position of being ruled by an Administration, opposed to the powers of the Federal Government and which recommends and adopts every measure calculated to break up the Union." How false a statement of Jackson's position this was, his course, two years later in the Nullification movement, showed conclusively. See also *National Journal*, Feb. 17, 1831.

[2] *21st Cong., 2d Sess.*, Jan. 24, 25, 29, 1831; see *House Report No. 43;* see also *Works of James Buchanan* (1908), II, 56–80; *22d Cong., 2d Sess.*, debate in the Senate on the Force Bill, speeches of Frelinghuysen of New Jersey, Feb. 2, 1833, Holmes of Maine, Feb. 5, 1833, in defense of the 25th Section of the Judiciary Act.

[3] *21st Cong., 2d Sess.*, Feb. 17, 1831; *Letters of J. C. Calhoun, Amer. Hist. Ass. Report* (1899), II; see *22d Cong., 1st Sess.*, June 11, 1832, speech of Foster of Georgia. In view of President Jackson's determined opposition to Nullification

Another great statesman, James Madison, saw equally
clearly at this time that to deprive the Court of its
power to construe the Constitution and to place this
power in the hands of the separate States were cor-
relative propositions, and he wrote: "The jurisdiction
claimed for the Federal Judiciary is truly the only
defensive armor of the Federal Government, or rather
for the Constitution and laws of the United States.
Strip it of that armor, and the door is wide open for
nullification, anarchy and convulsion, unless twenty-
four States, independent of the whole and of each other,
should exhibit the miracle of a voluntary and unanimous performance of every injunction of the parchment compact." [1]   And Judge Story wrote to George
Ticknor of Boston: "If the Twenty-Fifth Section is
repealed, the Constitution is practically gone.   It is an
extraordinary state of things, when the Government
of the country is laboring to tread down the power on
which its very existence depends.   You may depend that
many of our wisest friends look with great gloom to the
future.   Pray read, on the subject of the Twenty-Fifth
Section, the opinion of the Supreme Court, in *Hunter
v. Martin*, 1 *Wheaton's Reports*, it contains a full survey
of the judicial powers of the General Government, and
Chief Justice Marshall concurred in every word of it."
Writing more fully, six days later, Story termed the bill:
"A most important and alarming measure. . . .   If it
should prevail (of which I have not any expectation) it
would deprive the Supreme Court of the power to revise
the decisions of the State Courts and State Legislatures,
in all cases in which they were repugnant to the Con-

it is interesting to note that Daniel of Kentucky, speaking in the House on the Force
Bill, Feb. 28, 1833, said: "It was well known in the House that the President was
in favor of the repeal of the 25th Section, — this, you yourself well know" (addressing Polk of Tennessee who was then in the Chair).   *22d Cong., 2d Sess.*

[1] *Madison*, IV, 296, letter to Joseph C. Cabell, April 1, 1833.

stitution of the United States. So that all laws passed and all decisions made, however destructive to the National Government, would be utterly without redress . . . the measure would enervate the whole power of the United States. I have said that it will not probably succeed; indeed, the expectation is that it will fail by a very large vote; but the introduction of it shows the spirit of the times." [1] This prediction of the defeat of the bill was accurate; for on a motion to order to second reading it was rejected on January 29, practically without debate, and by a vote of 158 to 51, all but six of the minority votes coming from Southern and Western States.[2] "The House by a vote of more than 2 to 1 have rejected a bill the tendency of which was to shake our institutions to their very foundation," said the *United States Gazette*. "The audacious attempt of a few hot-headed demagogues to break up the Supreme Court has been foiled," said a Boston Whig paper,[3] and its Washington correspondent wrote that the reason for disposing of the bill by a motion to lay on the table was "the very solid one that the subject is one which it is sacrilegious to touch and which will be defiled by the rude handling of partisan soldiers. . . . Mr. Doddridge said in debate that he considered himself voting on the question whether the Union should be preserved or not, and though the language is strong, yet the declaration is correct and in common use." "This is a momentary respite for the

---

[1] *Story*, II, 48, 43, letters of Jan. 22, 28, 1831.

[2] See editorial in *National Intelligencer*, Jan. 31, 1831.

[3] *Boston Courier*, Feb. 1, 5, 1801. The Washington correspondent of the *United States Gazette*, wrote Jan. 29, 1831 : "I understand that a great many of the friends of the Judiciary are very much disconcerted with this motion for the previous question, as they were very desirous that the subject should be fully discussed, in order that the advocates and enemies of the Judiciary might have an opportunity to measure their strength. Many on the other side, equally confident, were desirous to bring on a debate; whether good or harm would have resulted from a fuller discussion of so delicate a matter it is bootless now to inquire."

Judiciary of the Union," wrote John Quincy Adams in his diary, "and to the Union itself, both of which are in imminent danger. . . . I had a short visit from Judge Thompson of the Supreme Court. He is alarmed for the fate of the Judiciary . . . and thinks, as I do, that the leading system of the present Administration is to resolve the Government of the Union into the National imbecility of the old Confederation." "We rejoice here (in Massachusetts) most heartily at the rejection by so large a majority," wrote one of Webster's correspondents. "That such a proposition ever could be made is, however, ominous of a bad spirit. The times are critical." [1]

The adherents to the bill were not discouraged by the vote, but showed the violence of their feelings in a subsequent heated debate, which took place over the motion to print 600 copies of the Report of the Judiciary Committee for wide public distribution. "The strides of Federal usurpation begin to alarm the most indolent. The spirit of indignation has already gone abroad in the land, and the people are now seeking a remedy for the evil. It cannot be stifled nor subdued," said Henry Daniel of Kentucky. "The exercise of power by virtue of the 25th Section strikes directly at the root of State sovereignty and levels it with the dust. . . . In some instances, the Federal Government, the harmony of the country, has been shaken to its very centre by these collisions. Nearly every State in the Union has had its sovereignty prostrated, has been brought to bend beneath the feet of the Federal tribunal. It is time that the States should prepare for the worst, and protect themselves against the assaults of this gigantic tribunal." And William F.

---

[1] *J. Q. Adams*, VIII, Jan. 29, 30, 1831; *Van Tyne Copies of Webster Papers*, in Library of Congress, letter of Stephen White to Daniel Webster, Feb. 5, 1831.

Gordon of Virginia urged that the repeal of the Section, more than anything else, would tend "to compose the present agitation of this country and allay the prevailing excitement." On the other hand, Philip Doddridge of Virginia said that he considered the proposition to repeal, "as equivalent to a motion to dissolve the Union." [1]

Though defeated on the question of repeal, another form of attack was at once devised by the extreme State-Rights men, and a resolution was introduced in the House, in 1831, by Joseph Lecompte of Kentucky, calling on the Judiciary Committee to inquire into the expediency of amending the Constitution so as to limit the term of office of Federal Judges. This resolution, however, was also lost by a vote of 115 to 61.[2]

Nevertheless, in spite of these defeats of Congressional measures to change the Judiciary system, the situation was extremely serious; and Judge Story wrote with much reason: "I have for a long time known that the present rulers and their friends were hostile to the Judiciary, and have been expecting some more decisive demonstrations than had yet been given out. The recent attacks in Georgia and the recent Nullification doctrine in South Carolina are but parts of the same general scheme, the object of which is to elevate an exclusive State sovereignty upon the ruins of the General Government. . . . The opinions upon this subject have been yearly gathering strength, and the

[1] *21st Cong., 2d Sess.*, Feb. 7, 9, 17, 25, 1831.
[2] *21st Cong., 2d Sess.*, Jan. 28, 1831. A similar resolution for a Constitutional Amendment was offered by Lecompte, Jan. 30, 1832, and was defeated by a vote of 144 to 27, *22d Cong., 1st Sess.* A similar resolution offered by Thomas L. Hamer of Ohio, Jan. 7, 1835, was defeated by a vote of 84 to 90, *23d Cong., 2d Sess.* See also similar resolutions offered by Benjamin Tappan of Ohio, in 1839, 1840, 1842 and 1844, all of which were defeated. See *Proposed Amendments to the Constitution*, by Herman V. Ames, *Amer. Hist. Ass. Rep.* (1896), II. See also *J. Q. Adams*, IX, 197; and *Niles Register*, Feb. 24, 1831, as to resolution of the Pennsylvania House of Representatives, upholding the 25th Section.

non-resistance and passive obedience to them exhibited
by the rest of the Union, have encouraged, and indeed
nourished them. If, when first uttered, they had been
met by a decided opposition from the Legislatures
of other States, they would have been obsolete before
now. But the indifference of some, the indolence of
others, and the easy good-natured credulity of others,
have given a strength to these doctrines, and familiar-
ized them to the people so much, that it will not hereafter be easy to put them down." [1]

That the Chief Justice and his Associates on the Court,
however, were not in any way intimidated by these
attacks, or to be deterred from following the path of
official duty, by any fear of legislation diminishing their
jurisdiction, was seen by a decision made very soon
after the Court assembled for its 1831 Term.[2] In
Fisher v. *Cockerell*, 5 Pet. 248, in which the occupying
claimant laws of Kentucky were again before the Court,
Marshall, in dismissing the case on a procedural point,
referred to the hostile attitude of the States and of
Congress as follows:

In the argument, we have been admonished of the jealousy
with which the States of the Union view the revising power
intrusted by the Constitution and laws of the United States
to this tribunal. To observations of this character, the
answer uniformly given has been that the course of the Judicial Department is marked out by law. We must tread the
direct and narrow path prescribed for us. As this Court
has never grasped at ungranted jurisdiction, so will it never,
we trust, shrink from the exercise of that which is conferred
upon it.

[1] *Story*, II, 47, letter of Jan. 30, 1831.
[2] The Washington correspondent of the *Boston Courier*, Feb. 2, 1831: "The
Supreme Court, during the repeated attempts to ascertain whether it would exist
after losing the principle of life, has gone on with its business in an almost forgotten
corner of the Capitol, with its usual dignity. Notwithstanding the necessity of
passing over all the cases in which Members of Congress were engaged as counsel,
the Court has disposed of an extraordinary number of cases."

Such was the situation when the bill had been filed by the Cherokee Nation in the Court for an injunction "to restrain the State of Georgia, the Governor, Attorney General, Judges, justices of the peace, sheriffs, deputy sheriffs, constables and others, the officers, agents and servants of that State, from executing and enforcing the laws of Georgia, or any of these laws, or serving process, or doing anything towards the execution or enforcement of those laws within the Cherokee territory, as designated by treaty between the United States and the Cherokee Nation."[1] A subpoena was served on the Governor of Georgia in this suit on December 27, 1830, just three days after the execution of Tassel and five days after the nullifying resolution of the Legislature. The Governor, in accordance with the Legislative instruction, and recognizing "no authoritative arbiter between the State and its Cherokee inhabitants" paid absolutely no attention to the subpoena.[2] No appearance was entered for the State in the Supreme Court at Washington, and the State preserved officially an "ominous and sullen silence"; although unofficially it was freely stated that, in case of an adverse decision by the Court, the State would refuse to abide by any of its mandates. Whig papers at the North furthermore asserted that "the President has very recently and vehemently declared that he would not lend any assistance to support the authority of the Court, in case Georgia should be, as no doubt she

[1] See The Cherokee Nation v. The State of Georgia, 5 Pet. 1. On March 12, 1831, a supplemental bill in equity was filed by the Cherokee Nation in the Supreme Court, describing the proceedings in the Tassel Case, the deliberate violation of the mandate of the Court, and the adverse legislation of December, 1830, in Georgia.

[2] The sympathy of other States holding extreme views of State-Rights and of the interference of the Supreme Court with such rights was shown at this time by a resolution offered in the House of Delegates of Maryland for an Amendment of the National Constitution, so as to provide for the decision of all cases in which the constitutionality of a State law should be brought in question, by a two thirds vote of the United States Senate. See Niles Register, XXXIX, Jan. 15, 1831.

will, in contempt." Though no official or authentic
statement by Jackson could be cited to this effect,
and though his supporters stated that the charge was
merely designed by his party foes to rouse a prejudice
against him, there was sufficient likelihood of its truth
to make the Court extremely reluctant to have the
issue raised between it and the Executive and the State
of Georgia. "The affair of Georgia, so far as Tassels
is concerned has probably passed by with his death,"
wrote Story on January 22. "But we are threatened
with the general question in another form. At this moment, it would have been desirable to have escaped
it, but, you know, it is not for Judges to choose times
and occasions. We must do our duty as we may." [1]

On March 5, 1831, Mr. Sergeant moved the Court
for an injunction. The argument was interrupted,
March 7–11, to allow another of Wirt's cases to be
argued (*Charles River Bridge* v. *Warren Bridge*). It
was renewed by Sergeant on March 12, in "a very
able and profoundly legal argument", and by Wirt,
who delivered "one of the most splendid discourses
ever pronounced in the Court, and as powerful in
argument, as it was beautiful in diction", the peroration being described by newspaper correspondents
as "sublime indeed", "of deep feeling and pathos." [2]

---

[1] *Boston Courier*, Feb. 16, 1831; *National Journal*, March 17, 1831; the Washington correspondent of the *New York Daily Advertiser* wrote in its issue of Jan. 15,
1831: "The Court has assembled under a very peculiar and trying circumstance.
Heretofore it has met with the certainty that its orders, judgments and decrees
would be carried into effect by the Executive branch of the Government, however
much they might conflict with the interests, prejudices, or prepossessions of the
parties or of the States. It has now met with a full knowledge that the Executive
will not enforce its decisions, if they are counter to his views of constitutional law."
Story, II, 48, letter of Jan. 22, 1831.

[2] *National Intelligencer*, March 7, 14, 16, 18, 1831; *Niles Register*, March 26,
1831, quoting *New York Journal of Commerce;* the *National Journal*, March 15,
1832, said: "The Court was considerably crowded throughout the day; some
of the Cherokee delegation were present, one of whom of very respectable and intelligent appearance, shed tears copiously." See *Story*, II, 51, letter of March 10,
1831.

A picturesque account was given by John Quincy Adams in his diary:

March 12, 1831: I walked to the Capitol and heard J. Sergeant for about three hours, before the Supreme Court, upon the injunction prayed by the Cherokee Nation. . . . Sergeant and Wirt are now arguing the question of jurisdiction without any counsel to oppose them; but the weight of the State will be too heavy for them. The old vice of confederacies is pressing upon us — anarchy in the members. . . . Mr. Sergeant's argument made it necessary for him to maintain that the Cherokee Nation are a foreign State, and this is the very point upon which the judgment of the Court may be against them. The argument was cold and dry. . . . There were however several ladies among the auditory who sat and heard him with exemplary patience.

March 14: Walked to the Capitol again to hear the conclusion of the argument on behalf of the Cherokee Indians by Mr. Wirt. . . . His health is much broken down, but his voice is strong and his manner animated beyond the condition of his strength. After finishing the argument upon the constitutional points and chiefly on the jurisdiction of the Court he concluded by a short appeal to the sympathies of the case in a low tone of voice and that accent of sensibility which becomes doubly impressive by being half subdued. The deep attention of the auditory was the indelible proof of its power. His argument was little more than a repetition of what has been said by Sergeant. His pathos was his own.

The closing words of Wirt's oration are particularly significant, in showing the grave fears that were popularly felt lest Georgia might continue to set the Supreme Court at defiance: [1]

Shall we be asked (the question has been asked elsewhere) how this Court will enforce its injunction, in case it shall be awarded? I answer, it will be time enough to meet that question when it shall arise. At present, the question is

[1] *Wirt*, II, 336–341.

whether the Court, by its constitution, possesses the jurisdiction to which we appeal. . . . In a land of laws, the presumption is that the decision of Courts will be respected; and, in case they should not, it is a poor government indeed in which there does not exist power to enforce respect.

What is the value of that government in which the decrees of its Courts can be mocked at and defied with impunity? Of that government did I say? It is no government at all, or at best a flimsy web of form, capable of holding only the feeblest insects, while the more powerful of wing break through at pleasure. If a strong State in this Union assert a claim against a weak one, which the latter denies, where is the arbiter between them? Our Constitution says that this Court shall be the arbiter. But, if the strong State refuses to submit to your arbitrament, — what then? Are you to consider whether you can of yourselves, and, by the mere power inherent in the Court, enforce your jurisdiction, before you will exercise it? Will you decline a jurisdiction clearly committed to you by the Constitution, from the fear that you cannot, by your own powers, give it effect, and thus test the extent of your jurisdiction, not by the Constitution, but by your own physical capacity to enforce it? . . .

But, if we have a government at all, there is no difficulty in either case. In pronouncing your decree you will have declared the law; and it is part of the sworn duty of the President of the United States to "take care that the laws be faithfully executed.". . . If he refuses to perform this duty, the Constitution has provided a remedy. But is this Court to anticipate that the President will not do his duty, and to decline a given jurisdiction in that anticipation. . . . Unless the Government be false to the trust which the people have confided to it, your authority will be sustained. I believe that if the injunction shall be awarded, there is a moral force in the public sentiment of the American community, which will, alone sustain it and constrain obedience.

On the last day of the Term, March 18, and only four days after the close of the argument, Chief Justice Marshall, after saying that "if Courts were permitted to indulge their sympathies, a case better calculated to excite them can scarcely be imagined", held that the Cherokee Nation was not a foreign nation and that the Court had no original jurisdiction of the cause. "If it be true," he said in closing, "that wrongs have been inflicted and that still greater are to be apprehended, this is not the tribunal which can redress the past or prevent the future." [1]

The decision of the Court was greeted with a singular and contradictory variety of opinion. Van Buren (probably representing Jackson's view) considered that Marshall's *dictum* at the end of his opinion stating that "the mere question of right to their lands might perhaps be decided by the Court in a proper case with proper parties" was a deliberate "design to operate upon the public mind adversely to Georgia and the President", and to affect the political situation.[2] Georgia, the Nullifiers and the extreme State-Rights papers were elated at the decision, and sought to give to the public the impression that the Court had decided in favor of Georgia's contentions and had given "sanction to the pretensions and conduct of that State with regard to the Indians." [3] The extreme Whigs of the North were correspondingly disconcerted. "The nullifying politicians of Georgia," said a Boston paper, "must be not a little astonished to find themselves accidentally on the side of the Union and receiving aid from its highest legal tribunal, when they have been laboring so hard to convince their constituents that they were traduced, abused

[1] The *National Intelligencer*, March 28, 1831, noted with regret the publication in the *New York Journal of Commerce* the fact that Story and Thompson dissented. "This fact, if true, made the decision that of a bare majority of the Court, as Duval was absent."

[2] *Autobiography of Martin Van Buren*, Amer. Hist. Ass. Rep. (1918), II, 291.

[3] *Richmond Enquirer*, March 22, 1831; see protests of *National Gazette* at this misrepresentation, March 22, 24, 26, 1831.

and oppressed by the Federal Government." [1] While it was greatly to the honor of a tribunal, which had been so often taxed with a spirit of usurpation, that it should have refused to decide the merits of the case on which it held very clear views, its refusal to do so, on the ground that it had no jurisdiction, subjected it now to severe criticism by those who had hitherto been its ardent supporters; for in the North and the East the treatment of the Cherokees was felt to be a moral issue almost equal to the slavery question. "It is certainly much to be regretted," said the *North American Review*, "that a case of this importance should have been decided, on any other principle than that of doing substantial justice between the parties." And Judge Story himself vehemently wrote to a friend: "The subject touches the moral sense of all New England. It comes home to the religious feelings of our people; it moves their sensibilities, and strikes to the very bottom of their sense of justice. Depend on it, there is a depth of degradation in our National conduct, which will irresistibly lead to better things. There will be, in God's Providence, a retribution for unholy deeds, first or last." [2] On the other hand, the *American Jurist* said in defense of the Chief Justice that: "Aspersed by a great statesman (now no more) as amplifying jurisdiction, this case shows he cannot do it, even to amplify justice; and together with

---

[1] *Boston Courier*, March 25, 1831.

[2] See *North Amer. Rev.*, XXXIII, 136; see also *Review of the Cherokee Case*, by Joseph Hopkinson, *Amer. Quar. Rev.*, X (March, 1832), *Story*, II, 46, letter of June 24, 1831, to Richard Peters. Writing to his wife, Jan. 13, 1832, Judge Story said: "At Philadelphia, I was introduced to two of the Chiefs of the Cherokee Nation so sadly dealt with by the State of Georgia. They are both educated men, and conversed with singular force and propriety of language upon their own case, the law of which they perfectly understood and reasoned upon. I never in my whole life was more affected by the consideration that they and all their race are destined to destruction. And I feel, as an American, disgraced by our gross violation of the public faith towards them. I fear, and greatly fear, that in the course of Providence, there will be dealt to us a heavy retributive justice." *Ibid.*, 79.

Burr's trials, the steamboat case, and the case of Marbury and Madison, abundantly evinces how, with equal solicitude and firmness, he can exercise whatever jurisdiction the Court has and renounce whatever of jurisdiction it has not." [1]

Since it was evident that this Cherokee question was not definitely settled and that it was likely to involve the Judiciary in a further struggle, Chief Justice Marshall, whose health had been feeble for some time and who was now in his seventy-fifth year, seriously considered resigning his office. [2] But in response to many protests, he finally decided to postpone such a step, although he wrote to Judge Story : "I am most earnestly attached to the character of the department, and to the wishes and convenience of those with whom it has been my pride and my happiness to be associated for so many years. I cannot be insensible to the gloom which lours over us. I have a repugnance to abandoning you under such circumstances which is almost invincible. But the solemn convictions of my judgment, sustained by some pride of character, admonish me not to hazard the disgrace of continuing in office a mere inefficient pageant." The feeling of the country in general, at the mere rumor of Marshall's resignation, had been voiced by a New York Whig paper, [3] which stated that it would be considered "as one of the greatest National calamities that could at this time befall the United States. In our estimation, he is, beyond question, the most important public character of which the Union can now boast. Probably much more that is interesting to the welfare of the country may depend upon the continuance of his

[1] *American Jurist* (Oct., 1831), VI.
[2] See letters to Judge Story, June 26, Oct. 12, 1831. *Mass. Hist. Soc. Proc.*, 2d *Sess.*, XIV.
[3] *New York Daily Advertiser*, March 28, 1831.

judicial life for some time to come, than upon that of any other individual in existence. The loose and heterodox sentiments, openly professed by men occupying important stations in the General Government, and, among them, by him who holds the highest office under that Government, renders it a dangerous thing to vacate so immensely important an office as that of Chief Justice. The safety of the very Union might be hazarded by the appointment of a successor. . . . The mischief which a nullifying Chief Justice might introduce into the execution of the laws and the administration of justice would be boundless and in the highest degree fatal to the peace and safety of the Union." [1] The Whig fear so expressed as to the character of Marshall's possible successor was made clear in a characteristically pungent comment of John Quincy Adams in his diary at this time: "Wirt spoke to me also in deep concern and alarm at the state of Chief Justice Marshall's health. He is seventy-five years of age and has until lately enjoyed fine health, exercised great bodily agility and sustained an immense mass of bodily labor. . . . His mind remains unimpaired, but his body is breaking down. He has been thirty years Chief Justice, and has done more to establish the Constitution of the United States on sound construction than any other man living. The terror is that, if he should be now withdrawn, some shallow-pated wild-cat like Philip P. Barbour, fit for nothing but to tear the Union to rags and tatters, would be appointed in his place. Mr. Wirt's anticipations are gloomy, and I see no reasonable prospect of improvement." [2] As seen in the calm

[1] This editorial closed by saying that it had learned that the rumor as to resignation was untrue, and it stated: "It is not improbable that the story was set on foot with the hope of inducing him by a broad hint to do that which some violent party politicians may be anxious he should do — leave his office to some thoroughgoing nullifier."

[2] *J. Q. Adams*, VIII, Feb. 13, 1831.

light of history, all these fears as to the fate of the Judiciary at Jackson's hands were unwarranted; and Adams's characterization of Barbour was of course unjust, for the latter, when appointed on the Supreme Court in 1836, made an excellent and broad-minded Judge; but they accurately picture the alarm felt by the more conservative of the community over the attacks on the integrity of the Union and on its Judiciary.

This alarm was now enhanced by the even more serious conflict between the Court and the State of Georgia which arose in the following year. Among the statutes passed by the Georgia Legislature, pending the excitement over the first Cherokee case in December, 1830, was one requiring all white persons living within the Cherokee country after March 11, 1831, to obtain a license and to take an oath of allegiance to the State. Two missionaries, Samuel A. Worcester and Elizur Butler, who refused to obtain a license or to leave the country when ordered by the State, were arrested, convicted in the Georgia State Court and sentenced to four years' imprisonment at hard labor. On an appeal to the United States Supreme Court, a writ of error was issued by that Court to the Superior Court of Georgia, October 27, 1831, and was duly served on the Governor and on the Attorney-General. On receipt of the writ, Governor Lumpkin transmitted it to the Georgia Legislature in a message inspired by the same spirit of defiance as the message of Governor Gilmer, the preceding year, and saying that: "Any attempt to infringe the evident right of a State to govern the entire population within its territorial limits, and to punish all offences committed against its laws within those limits (due regard being had to the cases expressly excepted by the Constitution

of the United States) would be the usurpation of a
power never granted by the States. Such an attempt,
whenever made, will challenge the most determined
resistance; and if persevered in, will inevitably eventuate in the annihilation of our beloved Union." [1] And
the Legislature, as in the prior case, responded by passing rebellious resolutions, stating that: "Any attempt
to reverse the decision of the Superior Court . . . by
the Supreme Court of the United States, will be held
by this State as an unconstitutional and arbitrary
interference in the administration of her criminal
laws and will be treated as such. That the State of
Georgia will not compromit her dignity as a sovereign
State, or so far yield her rights as a member of the Confederacy, as to appear in, answer to, or in any way become
a party to any proceedings before the Supreme Court,
having for their object a reversal or interference with the
decisions of the State Courts in criminal matters."
It also directed the Governor to pay no attention to
any subpoena or mandate of the Supreme Court
and required him, "with all the power and means
placed at his command, by the constitution and laws
of this State to resist and repel any and every invasion from whatever direction it may come, upon the
administration of the criminal laws of this State."

This second *Cherokee Case* was finally argued on
February 20, 1832, no counsel appearing for the State
of Georgia, but William Wirt and John Sergeant making eloquent pleas for the missionaries. "Sergeant's
speech was equally creditable to the soundness of his
head and the goodness of his heart," wrote a Washington correspondent. "The belief was, when he had
resumed his seat, that he had left little or no ground
for Mr. Wirt to occupy. Were I to judge from Mr.

[1] *Niles Register*, XLI, Dec. 24, 31, 1831.

Wirt's speech today, I should say the subject is inexhaustible. He spoke until after three o'clock, and was obliged, from fatigue, to ask the Court to adjourn. So interesting was the subject, so ably did he present it to the Court, that in addition to the number of gentlemen and ladies who attended from curiosity, so many of the Members of the House resorted to the Court-room that an adjournment was moved before two and after several unsuccessful attempts, it was carried before three o'clock. Several Cherokees, delegated by their Nation, were present; and the deep solicitude depicted in their countenances must have moved the sympathy of every one present whose heart was not as hard as adamant." [1] "Both of the speeches were very able and Mr. Wirt's in particular was unusually eloquent, forcible and finished," wrote Judge Story, February 26. "I confess that I blush for my country when I perceive that such legislation, destructive of all faith and honor towards the Indians, is suffered to pass with the silent approbation of the present Government of the United States."

Two weeks after the argument, Chief Justice Marshall, on March 3, 1832, rendered the opinion of the Court, holding the Georgia statute unconstitutional, on the ground that the jurisdiction of the Federal Government over the Cherokees was exclusive, and that the State had no power to pass laws affecting them or their territory. The judgment of the Georgia Superior Court convicting the prisoners was reversed, and a

---

[1] *New York Daily Advertiser*, Feb. 27, 1832. The *National Intelligencer* said Feb. 22, 1832: "The Supreme Court-room has attracted a numerous audience for the last two days. The writ of error in behalf of the missionaries tried and punished under the laws of Georgia, has been under argument, learned and eloquent." John Quincy Adams wrote in his diary, February 21: "This is a cause of deep interest and there were 50 or 60 members of the House who left their seats to hear him (Wirt)." See *Worcester* v. *Georgia*, 6 Pet. 515.

special mandate was ordered to issue to that Court, March 5, ordering their release. The Judges who delivered opinions showed that they were deeply impressed by the gravity of the issue presented to the Court. To the argument that the Supreme Court had no power to review final decisions of the State Courts, Chief Justice Marshall replied: "It is, then, we think, too clear for controversy, that the Act of Congress, by which this Court is constituted, has given it the power and of course imposed upon it the duty, of exercising jurisdiction in this case. This duty, however unpleasant, cannot be avoided. Those who fill the Judicial Department have no discretion in selecting the subjects to be brought before them."[1] The impression created upon the public was described by a newspaper correspondent as follows:[2] "The Chief Justice was an hour and a quarter in delivering the opinion. His voice was feeble, and so anxious were the audience to hear him that the space in the rear of the Justices, and in front of the bench, was crowded with Members of Congress, gentlemen of the Bar and visitors. . . . The original manuscript, in the handwriting of the Chief Justice, should be preserved; and the friends of the Union and of the Constitution will look upon it with veneration, when its author shall be removed from amongst us." And Judge Story wrote to his wife, March 4: "It was a very able opinion, in his best manner. Thanks be to God, the Court can wash their hands clean of the iniquity of oppressing the Indians and disregarding their rights." Writing four days later to George Ticknor, Story expressed the fear which prevailed in the minds of

[1] Judge Story said to his law students, Nov. 18, 1844, that "Judge Marshall was affected to tears by the eloquent peroration of Wirt. He then said 'I have not shed a tear before, since Webster delivered his speech in the Dartmouth College Case. I then did not expect ever to shed another upon such an occasion.'" See *Life of Rutherford Birchard Hayes* (1914), by Charles R. Williams, I.

[2] *New York Daily Advertiser*, March 7, 1832.

many men, lest the judgment of the Court should not be executed : "Georgia is full of anger and violence. What she will do, it is difficult to say. Probably she will resist the execution of our judgment, and if she does, I do not believe the President will interfere unless public opinion among the religious of the Eastern and Western and Middle States should be brought to bear strong upon him. The rumor is, that he has told the Georgians he will do nothing. I, for one, feel quite easy on this subject, be the event what it may. The Court has done its duty. Let the Nation now do theirs. If we have a Government, let its command be obeyed; if we have not, it is as well to know it at once, and to look to consequences." [1] These apprehensions as to the President's attitude were voiced by many newspapers. Jackson's bitterest antagonist, the *New York Daily Advertiser*, stated that : "The President has said within a few days past, that he had as good a right, being a co-ordinate branch of the Government, to order the Supreme Court as the Court have to require him to execute its decisions. . . . If he refuses to exercise the power vested in him to execute the laws, either he must be impeached and removed from office or the Union of the States will be dissolved. . . . Whatever General Jackson and Georgia may do, the great majority of the Union will support the Judiciary." [2] "We will not anticipate contumacy on the part of Georgia; nor, in that event, inertness in the Executive Department of the General Government," said the *National Gazette*. "But if both should prove delinquent, the question will then arise, is the Constitution indeed the supreme law of

[1] *Story*, II, 86, 83.

[2] *New York Daily Advertiser*, March 7, 8, 9, 13, 1832; see *New York Commercial Advertiser*, which also advocated impeachment; *National Gazette*, March 14, 1832; *National Intelligencer*, March 12, 1832, quoting *Richmond Whig*.

the land? . . . Was the Supreme Court intended
to be an efficient tribunal? Will Congress allow
any one of its rightful decisions to be treated as a mere
brutum fulmen?" "The prevalent opinion here," said
the *Richmond Whig*, "seems to be that the President
will do his duty and see that the laws be enforced;
but from the tone of the Court Journal, we have little
expectation of this. If it be asked, ought the judgment
of the Court to be carried into execution by arms,
we retort and ask what will be the consequence of
failing to execute it? Will not the Federal Government
be virtually dissolved? Is that, in truth, any longer
a Government which is too feeble to execute its laws?
We are brought at once to the point — is it better to
have recourse to the bayonet to attempt to keep the
Union together, or to permit a peaceable withdrawal of
its members, or lastly, to hobble on like the old Confederation, each State obeying such laws as she liked
and disobeying others?" "Will a final mandate
issue from the Supreme Court to deliver the missionaries during the present Term?" wrote a virulent
opponent of Jackson, ex-Chief-Justice Ambrose Spencer
of New York, to Daniel Webster. "If not, is it not
all important to collect and embody proof, if such
exists, that General Jackson declares he will not aid
in enforcing the judgment and mandate of the Court?
It seems to me very important, if he has made the
declarations imputed to him; but the proof of them
should be spread before the public, in an authentic
shape. The effect of fastening upon him such
declarations would be incalculably great." [1] "It

---

[1] *Webster MSS*, letter to Webster, March 14, 1832; Spencer wrote July 28, 1832,
as to the necessity of "inviting the whole strength of the State to rid the Nation
of the monster now holding the reins of Government"; and on Jan. 11, 1834, he
wrote of Jackson's "despotism" and his "unbalanced attempt to concentrate all
power in himself." *Clay*, IV, letter of Clay, March 17, 1832.

is rumored," wrote Henry Clay, "that the President has repeatedly said that he will not enforce it, and that he even went so far as to express his hope, to a Georgia member of Congress, that Georgia would support her rights." "Well, John Marshall has made his decision, now let him enforce it," was the President's commentary on the decision according to the recollection of a Massachusetts Congressman.[1] It is a matter of extreme doubt, however, whether Jackson ever uttered these words. He certainly did not, in fact, refuse to aid in enforcing the Court's decision; and the charge so frequently made in modern histories and legal articles that Jackson actually defied the Court's decree is clearly untrue; for the time never arrived when the exercise of Executive power to enforce the law was called for. Moreover, the debate in 1832 as to whether the President, at some time in the future, would or would not perform such limited functions as he possessed in aiding the Court to execute its decrees was largely hypocritical. Much of the criticism of his alleged attitude towards the Court arose, not so much from sympathy for the Judiciary, as from political hatred of Jackson and his financial policies; and it is certain that most of the attacks came from

[1] The first reference to such a remark is in *The American Conflict* (1864), by Horace Greeley, I, 106, as follows: "The attorneys for the missionaries sought to have this judgment enforced but could not. General Jackson was President and would do nothing of the sort. 'Well, John Marshall has made his decision, now let him enforce it,' was his commentary on the matter. (Note: I am indebted for this fact to the late Governor George N. Briggs of Massachusetts who was in Washington as a member of Congress when the decision was rendered.)"

No previous historian appears to have quoted the alleged remark, but it has been given currency by William G. Sumner in his *Life of Andrew Jackson* (1899) and by many later writers. John Spencer Bassett in his *Life of Andrew Jackson* (1910), II, 690–691, says with reference to it, that it is "a popular tradition, first printed, so far as I know, by Horace Greeley. It is not sure that the words were actually uttered, but it is certain, from Jackson's views and temperament, that they might have been spoken." Bassett further expresses his own view that Jackson "could hardly have known his own mind" on the question of whether there was power in the Government to enforce a Court decree in this case, and on this point Bassett cites two unpublished papers from the *Jackson Papers MSS.*

partisans of the Bank of the United States. "It is truly melancholy to see the mad, malignant fury with which certain opposition papers already urge on the President to enforce the decision of the Supreme Court . . . even before it is ascertained whether the State of Georgia will resist or not," said a New York Democratic paper, which reprobated the denunciation of Georgia, and stated that the safety of the Union lay "in forbearance and moderation, not in coercion. . . . We have no apprehension of any insurrection-ary movement, and consequently do not believe that it will become necessary for the President to interfere. The President is not the Executive Officer of the Court. . . . Bitter and unrelenting opposition to the Administration may be masked under an affectation of universal philanthropy. . . . The coalition against Jackson and the fanaticism of his opponents is the key to their affected sympathy with the Indians." [1] So too a Baltimore Democratic paper said: "Many of the opponents of General Jackson have illy disguised, while many of them have openly expressed, their delight at the decision of the Court, not impelled by any feeling of humanity towards the Indians or any admiration of even-handed justice, as they have pre-tended, but in the hope that it might work injury to the popularity of the President, that he might be brought into collision with the Supreme Court." The *United States Telegraph* (a Washington paper formerly pro-Jackson and then pro-Calhoun) warned the Court as to the effect of reports of impeachment of the President: "The bare suspicion that the Supreme Court participate, in any degree, in the contemplation of such a proceeding cannot fail to impair the high character which it has maintained, which is essential to

[1] *New York Courier*, March 20, May 7, 8, 1832.

an acquiescence in its decisions, and to the peace and harmony of society. It becomes every friend of the Court to mark with the most decided disapprobation all attempts to bring its character and influence within the infected sphere of party politics. We should all feel that that tribunal is sanctified to the cause of justice." [1]

As this Georgia controversy had occurred during the extremely passionate political debate in Congress and in the country which had been taking place, from January to June, 1832, over the bill to renew the charter of the Bank of the United States, the influence of partisan prejudice must be considered in testing the accuracy of statements made by the President's opponents, and particularly with reference to his alleged refusal to execute the law as laid down by the Supreme Court. It is probable that a misconception of Jackson's exact attitude towards the Court in the *Cherokee Case* arose from his known views as to Presidential authority, which he later set forth at length in his message to Congress vetoing the Bank charter, July 10, 1832. In this veto, he had replied to the point raised by the advocates of the bill to the effect that the Supreme Court had already decided the Bank's charter to be constitutional. Such a decision "ought not to control the co-ordinate authorities of this Government," said Jackson. "It is as much the duty of the House of Representatives, of the Senate and of the President, to decide upon the constitutionality of any bill or resolution which may be presented to them for passage or approval, as it is of the Supreme Judges when it may be brought .before them for judicial

[1] *Baltimore Republican*, March 23, 1832; *United States Telegraph*, April 5, 13, 1832; The *Washington Globe* (the Administration Organ) said, March 13, 1832, as to previous articles in the *Telegraph* that "it has at last boldly raised the flag of nullification."

decision. The opinion of the Judges has no more authority over Congress than the opinion of Congress has over the Judges; and on that point the President is independent of both. The authority of the Supreme Court must not, therefore, be permitted to control the Congress, or the Executive, when acting in their Legislative capacities, but to have only such influence as the force of their reasoning may deserve." This statement of the President was assailed by his political opponents, as being the assertion of the right of the Executive to refuse to respect and carry into effect the decisions of the Court; and it was undoubtedly on such a basis that the numerous charges were made against Jackson that he intended to disregard the Court's opinion in the *Cherokee Case*.[1] That the President's real meaning and intention was grossly misconceived at that time and in later years is now certain; and in a recently published letter of Roger B. Taney to Van Buren, the true interpretation of the President's doctrine has been made very clear.[2] Jackson never asserted a right to decline to carry out a Court decision, when acting in his Executive capacity. It was when exercising his part of the law-making function of the Nation, and when deciding upon signature or veto of a bill presented to him, that he claimed the privi-

[1] The *National Gazette* said March 10, 1831, referring to the report that President Jackson denied the constitutionality of the laws and treaties as to the Indians: "Such denial is the exercise of an ex-post-facto veto-power, unknown to the Constitution, and, indeed, places the authority of the Executive above all the laws and processes of legislation. Heretofore, it had been supposed that a law . . . was to be universally obeyed as constitutional until the Supreme Court declared it otherwise. . . . This new doctrine or practice of nullification is worse than that of South Carolina." The *National Gazette* of April 7, 1832, said that if the President's view was correct that he had a right to judge for himself of the constitutionality of laws and treaties "then with him, no branch of the government can be deemed co-ordinate in fact; the prerogative of nullifying laws and political decisions, by denying their conformity to the Constitution, makes him supreme — the final arbiter — the very Celestial Majesty."

[2] *Taney's Letters to Van Buren in 1860*, in *Maryland Hist. Mag.* (March, 1915), X, 23, letter of June 30, 1860.

lege of determining for himself the constitutionality
of the proposed measure.   As Taney wrote:

He has been charged with asserting that he, as an Executive officer, had a right to judge for himself whether an
act of Congress was constitutional or not, and was not
bound to carry it into execution if he believed it to
be unconstitutional, even if the Supreme Court decided
otherwise; and this misrepresentation has been kept alive
for particular purposes of personal ill-will, and has, I learn,
been repeated in the Senate during its late session.   Yet
no intelligent man who reads the message can misunderstand the meaning of the President.   He was speaking of his
rights and his duty, when acting as a part of the Legislative
power, and not of his right or duty as an Executive officer.
For when a bill is presented to him and he is to decide
whether, by his approval, it shall become a law or not, his
power or duty is as purely Legislative as that of a member
of Congress, when he is called on to vote for or against a
bill.   If he has firmly made up his mind that the proposed
law is not within the powers of the General Government, he
may and he ought to vote against it, notwithstanding an
opinion to the contrary has been pronounced by the Supreme Court.   It is true that he may very probably yield
up his preconceived opinions in deference to that of the
Court, because it is the tribunal especially constituted to
decide the questions in all cases wherein it may arise, and
from its organization and character is peculiarly fitted for
such inquiries.   But if a Member of Congress, or the President, when acting in his Legislative capacity, has, upon
mature consideration, made up his mind that the proposed
law is a violation of the Constitution he has sworn to support, and that the Supreme Court had in that respect fallen
into error, it is not only his right but his duty to refuse to
aid in the passage of the proposed law.   And this is all the
President has said, and there was nothing new in this.   For
that principle was asserted and acted upon in relation to the
memorable Sedition Law.   That Law had been held to be
constitutional by every Justice of the Supreme Court before
whom it had come at Circuit, and several persons had been
punished by fine and imprisonment for offending against

it. Yet a majority in Congress refused to continue the law, avowedly upon the ground that they believed it unconstitutional, notwithstanding the opinion previously pronounced by the judicial tribunals. *But General Jackson never expressed a doubt as to the duty and the obligation upon him in his Executive character to carry into execution any Act of Congress regularly passed, whatever his own opinion might be of the constitutional question.*

All this discussion in 1832 as to Jackson's intention was, however, as has been above pointed out, wholly premature. The Court had adjourned on March 17, without issuing any mandate in the case; nothing could be done in regular course of legal procedure until it reconvened in January, 1833, when, after issue of the mandate and in case of disobedience, it was supposed that the Court would issue a writ of habeas corpus in behalf of the prisoners, or would direct the United States marshal to summon a *posse comitatus* to execute its mandate, or would summon the State officials before it for contempt. Not until after such proceedings could the President be called upon to set in motion the military force of the Nation. It appears, however, that owing to a deficiency in the statute law at that time, there was no method by which the Court could enforce its mandate; for the habeas corpus law then only applied to prisoners in custody under Federal authority, and there was no provision for a writ of error in case a State Court refused to make any record of its action. Advice to this effect was given by William Wirt to a Congressman; and an unsuccessful attempt was made in Congress to secure additional legislation as to judicial process.[1] Wirt further stated

---

[1] See hitherto unpublished letter in *Wirt Papers MSS*, letter (12 folio pages) from Wirt to Lewis Williams, a Member of Congress, April 28, 1832. *22d Cong., 1st Sess.*, May 28, June 11, 1832, petition for legislation introduced in the House by Pendleton of New York, and debated.

John W. Burgess in *The Middle Period* (1897), 219–220, says: "It was certainly

that he believed that the only remedy was for the President to declare the State of Georgia to be in rebellion and to demand the submission of the State to the law by discharging the prisoners. "If this step cannot be taken, I see none that can. The authority of the Supreme Court is annihilated," he wrote. "Thus the State of Georgia is likely to be victorious at every point, and the President has the pleasure of seeing his will the law of the land. Be it so, I have endeavored to do my duty, in my humble sphere, to vindicate the Constitution, treaties and laws of the United States. If they are prostrated with impunity, the fault will not rest with me. But ought not a consultation to take place among their friends in Congress to see what measures can be devised for the restoration of the National authority?"

The Whigs, in general, believed that Jackson was determined to make a political issue of the case and their views were well represented by a letter written to Webster by Theodore Dwight.[1] "It will be but a very short time before the leading Jackson papers all over the country will come out in favour of Georgia against the Court. . . . As soon as that takes place, . . . it will be the duty of those who favour the Constitution and consider it as worth preservation, to make an effort for that purpose, and, it appears to me, if the necessary pains are taken and in the right manner, a sufficient number of our countrymen can be roused to the support of the Judiciary, and the discomfiture of the

the duty of the President of the United States to have executed this decision of the Court with all the power necessary for the purpose which the Constitution conferred upon him. He did not do it." This statement, like many similar statements by historians and law-writers as to Jackson's refusal to enforce the Court's decree, is erroneous; for the case never reached the stage when the exercise of the President's authority could have been properly called for, or employed.

[1] *Webster Papers MSS*, letter of April 5, 1832.

man and his myrmidons who are obviously bent on sacrificing both the Constitution and the Union. I cannot but believe that, when the point is ascertained that Georgia will resist the execution of the sentence of the Court and General Jackson refuses to enforce it, a majority of the people of this country will support the Constitution."

Such forebodings as to a general attack upon the Judiciary by the Jackson newspapers were not justified; for only a few assailed the correctness of the opinion of the Court, criticizing it as an infringement upon State-Rights;[1] and most of them simply deplored the heated charges made by the Whigs, and counseled exercise of patience, and moderation of language and action both on the part of Georgia and of the anti-Jacksonians. The *New York Courier*, speaking of the Court's opinion as "learned and temperate", said: "Let Georgia ask herself whether the game is worth the candle — whether these treaties with the Indians have not checked the action of the State authorities, — whether their miserable strip of land is worth quarreling about, and keeping alive the

[1] The *Boston Statesman* said: "Of all the attempts made at a 'Federal' consolidation, this last decree of the Supreme Court on the Georgia question is the boldest; though, of all the opinions heretofore given, this is the least creditable to the intellectual character of the Court. There is not a constitutional lawyer in the United States who will not be shocked by the heresies which it contains; there is not any man of any capacity who, after a full examination of it, will not pronounce it to be an open defiance of all common sense, as well as of law and precedent, and a total perversion of the facts of the case." The *Baltimore Republican*, March 21, 1832, said: "Frenzy or infatuation seems to have taken possession of the minds of many of the people of the North in relation to the Indian question. In indulging their sympathy for the Indians in Georgia, they seem to lose sight of all other considerations, and to forget that the State has rights and feelings equal to their own"; see also *ibid.*, March 19, 1832, quoting *Petersburg Intelligencer* (Va.). The *Onondaga Standard* (N. Y.) said: "In regard to the intimation of Judge McLean that upon the enforcement of this decision, depends the resolution of the Court ever to convene again, we have only to say that we trust in heaven they will adhere to their determination. We should rejoice in the event. A new Bench might be organized into which should enter some portion of the spirit of the age." *Niles Register*, XLII, April 14, 1832.

hopes of open and concealed traitors that this Union can be broken down. If Georgia is wise, tranquil, and patient, justice will be done her, and the fanatics will be discomfitted." [1] *Niles Register* said: "The feeling in Georgia, as shown in the remarks in the newspapers etc., is, to go on — let the consequences be what they may; and we notice some proceedings of the people which exhibit an uncalled-for spirit of violence, and speak great things about 'force' and 'judicial despotism', as though a child's play was only concerned in this matter. We are sick of such talks. If there is not power in the Constitution to preserve itself, it's not worth the keeping. But an awful responsibility rests somewhere, and history, too, may give up persons to the infamy of ages. Many, however, entertain a hope that Georgia, being allowed time to get cool, and content with executing her laws over the Indians and their lands, will quietly release Messrs. Worcester and Butler, and so remove the present cause of action — and cast future controversies on their own precarious issue." Some of the more moderate Whig papers joined in these sentiments, the *National Intelligencer* saying that it had "too much confidence in the love of country and the common sense of the Georgian to apprehend that the present collision between the judicial authorities of that State and of the United States will terminate tragically. Let all parties keep their temper as well as they can; let the friends of the

---

[1] *Washington Globe*, March 31, 1832; and as to this latter, see letter of Ambrose Spencer, to Henry Clay, Dec. 14, 1833, in *Works of Henry Clay* (1904); *Niles Register*, XLII, March 31; *ibid.*, June 23, 1832, reproduced an editorial from the *Cincinnati Gazette*, calling the attention of Georgia to the fact that when Pennsylvania in 1809, in the *Olmstead Case*, came into conflict with the Federal Court, the State of Georgia supported the Court, and that though since that time "both Georgia and Ohio have had their turn at dissatisfaction with the Supreme Court, . . . the Court nevertheless retains the confidence of the Nation, because that confidence is founded in the plain good sense of all, when uninfluenced by extrinsic circumstances." *National Intelligencer*, April 5, 1832.

Union stand firm by the sheet anchor; let no one doubt the safety of the gallant ship." [1]

Meanwhile, the State of Georgia was in process of ferment which was just short of open rebellion. As soon as the decision of the Court had been rendered, its Senator, George M. Troup, had issued an open letter saying: "The people of Georgia will receive with indignant feelings, as they ought, the recent decisions of the Supreme Court, so flagrantly violative of their sovereign rights. I hope the people will treat it, however, as becomes them, with moderation, dignity and firmness; and so treating it, Georgia will be unhurt by what will prove to be a *brutum fulmen*. The Judges know you will not yield obedience to mandates, and they may desire pretexts for enforcement of them which I trust you will not give." Protests, voiced in equally violent terms and of an insurrectionary nature, were made in the newspapers and at public meetings in the State. Finally, when the mandate of the Court was served on the Judge and upon the Clerk of the Georgia Superior Court, motions to reverse the judgment, and to place the mandate on the records of the Court were denied. The two prisoners remained in prison. And everything went on exactly as if the Court had rendered no decision. On November 6, 1832, Governor Lumpkin referred in his message to the Legislature to the decision as, "an attempt to prostrate the sovereignty of the State in the exercise of its constitutional criminal jurisdiction." To the American Board of Missionaries, President Jackson for the first

[1] *National Intelligencer*, April 3, 5, 1832; on March 14, 1832, it printed a copy of the mandate; on March 22, it said that it deplored " the infatuation under the influence of which this course will be pursued;" on March 24, it printed Gov. Troup's letter; on March 27, it quoted the *Newark Advertiser* as stating that it did not doubt that " every State in the Union would promptly furnish the Executive of the Nation its requisite portion of patriotic freemen to aid him in upholding the Judiciary and preserving the integrity of the Nation."

time personally announced his position: "The power invested in me has been placed in my hands for the purpose of seeing the laws of the United States justly and impartially administered, and not for the purpose of abusing them, as I most assuredly should do, were I to interpose my authority in the case brought before me in your memorial. The State of Georgia is governed by its own laws; and if injustice has been, or is committed, there are competent tribunals at which redress can be obtained." [1]

Such were the conditions of affairs in the fall of 1832, just prior to President Jackson's reëlection; and they had impressed themselves so seriously upon the mind of Chief Justice Marshall as to lead him to write to Judge Story, as follows: [2] "If the prospects of our country inspire you with gloom, how do you think a man must be affected who partakes of all your opinions and whose geographical position enables him to see a great deal that is concealed from you? I yield slowly and reluctantly to the conviction that our Constitution cannot last. I had supposed that North of the Potomack a firm and solid government competent to the security of rational liberty might be preserved. Even that now seems doubtful. The case of the South seems to me to be desperate. Our opinions are incompatible with a united government even among ourselves. The Union has been prolonged thus far by miracles. I fear they cannot continue."

[1] This letter appeared in the *St. Joseph Beacon*, of South Bend, Ind., Sept. 27, 1832, and is cited in *A History of Travel in America* (1915), by Seymour Dunbar, 596, as "apparently not included in biographies of Jackson or other historical reviews of the events or times under discussion." The letter concluded with a characteristically pungent comment by Jackson: "I do not wish to comment upon the causes of the imprisonment of the missionaries, alluded to in the memorial; but I cannot refrain from observing that here, as in most countries, they are, by their injudicious zeal (to give it no harder name), too apt to make themselves obnoxious to those among whom they are located."

[2] *Mass. Hist. Soc. Proc., 2d Series*, XIV, letter of Sept. 22, 1832.

The fears thus expressed as to the sentiment of the North had undoubtedly been enhanced by the fact that, in two other cases, involving Northern States pending before the Court in 1831 and 1832, there had appeared an opposition to its jurisdiction and an outcropping of much the same State-Rights sentiment as was rampant in Georgia and South Carolina. The first was a case which had involved a long conflict and much friction between New York and New Jersey.[1]   In a bill in equity brought in *New Jersey* v. *New York*, 3 Pet. 461, in 1829, on motion of William Wirt and Samuel L. Southard, counsel for New Jersey, a subpoena had been awarded by the Court, returnable in August; no appearance having been entered by the State of New York, an alias subpoena had been issued, returnable in January, 1830.   Meanwhile, the Attorney-General of New York had written to the Clerk of the Court, July 27, 1829, and to each of the Judges, January 8, 1830, alleging that the State considered such service of process on a State "as utterly void," since the Court could not exercise jurisdiction in controversies between States, without the authority of an Act of Congress carrying into execution that part of the judicial power of the United States.   On March 6, 1830, the Court, stating that "the precedent for granting the process has been established upon very grave and solemn argument", in the cases against Georgia and Virginia, forty years before, issued a further subpoena, returnable in August, 1830.   Again the State of New York failed to appear.   In this refractory attitude, the State Attorney-General was largely supported by the Democrats, but the Whigs assailed what they termed "the Nullification doctrines of the law officer of the State."   An

[1] See *Brief History of the Boundary Dispute between New Jersey and New York*, by Joel Parker, *New Jersey Hist. Soc. Proc.*, VIII.

attempt to procure an Act of Congress, said a New York paper, "would be considered by Georgia as a brilliant achievement — being nothing less than enlisting the State of New York under the banner of the State of Georgia in opposition to the legal and constitutional authority of the National Judiciary." [1] New Jersey having moved that this cause be proceeded with in the absence of the State of New York, the Court, after an argument from Wirt as to the existence of its authority to hear cases within the original jurisdiction of the Court without further legislation by Congress, decided that it possessed power to proceed, and it entered an order that, unless the State of New York appeared and answered before August, the Court would hear the cause at the next Term (*New Jersey* v. *New York*, 5 Pet. 284). "The Court has proceeded with great forbearance and moderation towards this State," said the New York paper. "Whatever the object may be, in those under whose influence the State has been placed in the predicament in which it now stands, the loss of jurisdiction over one half of the breadth of the Hudson will probably be the smallest of the evils which may be the consequence of the refusal to acknowledge the legitimate power of the Supreme Court." In 1832, Attorney-General Bronson filed a demurrer denying the Court's jurisdiction, which the Court ruled was to be treated as an appearance (6 Pet. 323); and the direct question of its jurisdiction was then presented for its final decision. The proceedings which followed were vividly described by a Washington correspondent of a Democratic paper, who expressed a belief that the Cherokee and the New York litigation had "some affinity to each other. No one will impute any wrong intention; but this ugly question has been

[1] *New York Daily Advertiser*, Feb. 25, 28, 1831.

put : Why hurry the decision of the *Cherokee Case* and delay that of the *New York Case?* Did the principles growing out of both come in conflict ? Some of your city journals have been blaming most erroneously Mr. Bronson, the able Attorney-General of New York for delay. . . . Nothing can be farther from the fact. It was the Court itself which very unceremoniously cut his argument in the middle (after three hours) and sent it over to the next Term. The New York case has been peculiar. It has brought the Supreme Court into a temper of reflection on the subject of State-Rights, more than any case ever before them. It is the first time in the history of our general legislation that a sovereign State ever consented to employ counsel to contest the jurisdiction of the Court. On the first day in which the case was begun, by Mr. Bronson, he entered into a long and learned argument showing the entire unconstitutionality of the jurisdiction assumed by the Court. I understand from good authority that the array of names and authorities in favor of the ground assumed by the Attorney-General of New York startled, in no small degree, the Supreme Bench, particularly the Chief Justice. Mr. Bronson occupied the Court several hours with the argument and yet he had scarcely concluded his first point — the ground of jurisdiction. On the morning of the next day, the Chief Justice, I believe it was, said that as the case had assumed a more important aspect than had been contemplated, the Court had agreed to postpone any further proceeding till next session." [1] The Court never rendered a decision on the delicate question of State sovereignty involved, inasmuch as Congress by the Act of June 28, 1834, consented to a com-

---

[1] *New York Courier*, March 21, 1832; United States *Telegraph*, March 8, 1832; *National Intelligencer*, March 16, 1832.

promise agreement voluntarily entered into by the States.

The other case which had awakened a feeling of State-Rights in the North was the famous *Charles River Bridge* v. *Warren Bridge*, as to which a bitter fight had been waged in Massachusetts for many years over the right to charter a free bridge in competition with a previously chartered toll bridge. When the case was first argued before the Court, March 7–11, 1831, a committee of the Massachusetts Democratic Convention reported that "in the *Warren Bridge Case* the Supreme Court at Washington has no more constitutional right to meddle with the question than the Court of King's Bench." [1] The case was not decided at this Term, and at the end of the 1832 Term, it was ordered continued, "one Judge before whom the case was argued at the last Term being absent and the Judges differing." [2]

[1] *United States Telegraph*, Jan. 27, 1831.

[2] *National Intelligencer*, March 14, 1832. Judge Story wrote as to this case, March 10, 1831: "We have been sadly obstructed of late in our business by very long and tedious arguments, as distressing to hear as to be nailed down to an old-fashioned homily. We are now upon the *Charlestown Bridge Case*, and have heard the opening counsel on each side in three days. Dutton, for the plaintiffs, made a capital argument in point and manner, lawyerlike, close, searching, and exact; Jones, on the other side, was ingenious, metaphysical, and occasionally strong and striking. Wirt goes on today, and Webster will follow tomorrow. Six Judges only are present, which I regret; Duvall having been called suddenly away by illness of his wife." To Mason, Story wrote, Nov. 19, 1831, that he had prepared his opinion and wished Mason to read it over, saying: "It is so important a constitutional question, that I am anxious that some other mind should see, what the writer rarely can in his zeal, whether there is any weak point which can be fortified or ought to be abandoned." On Dec. 23, 1831, he wrote that his opinion was prepared and that he had written it "in the hope of meeting the doubts of some of the brethren which are various and apply to different aspects of the case." On March 1, 1832, he wrote that the case was not yet decided, as Judge Johnson had been absent for the whole Term, and the Judges were "greatly divided in opinion and it is not certain what the finale will be." *Story*, II, 51, 91; *Mason*. It seems that, as the Court stood in 1832, Story, Marshall and Thompson were in favor of reversing the decree of Massachusetts Court, McLean was doubtful as to jurisdiction, Baldwin dissented, and Johnson and Duval had been absent. When the case was finally decided in 1837, seven Judges took the contrary view, and Story and Thompson dissented; see 11 Peters, 420, 583, App. 2, 134.

Before the Court met to hold its 1833 Term, the situation of the country had been miraculously altered, and the danger of a clash between the Federal and State authorities in the *Missionaries Case* had disappeared.   For President Jackson had stepped forward as the staunch and vigorous upholder and defender of the Union, and of the National authority.   Startling events had rapidly ensued after Chief Justice Marshall's despondent letter in September, 1832, above quoted.   On November 24, 1832, the Legislature of South Carolina had passed its Nullification Ordinance, one section of which constituted a serious attack upon the jurisdiction of the Supreme Court.   It provided that in no case in law or equity decided in the Courts of the State, involving the validity of the ordinance or of any Act of Congress, should any appeal be taken or allowed to the Supreme Court of the United States, nor should any copy of the record be permitted or allowed for that purpose ; and if any such appeal should be permitted to be taken, the Courts of the State should proceed to execute and enforce their judgments according to the laws and usages of the State, without reference to such attempted appeal, and the person or persons attempting to take such appeal should be dealt with as for contempt of court.[1]   This was flat rebellion or treason ; and so it was held by President Jackson.   He at once issued his celebrated Proclamation, December 10, 1832, and recommended the enactment by Congress of rigorous and radical legislation giving to the Federal Courts and officials adequate powers to deal with the situation.   A bill which became known as the Force Bill (or "Bloody Bill") was introduced amidst the hot opposition of the more extreme

[1] To the everlasting honor of the Supreme Court of South Carolina, it held unconstitutional, a year later, the legislation of which this bill was a part. *State v. McCreardy* (March, 1834), 2 Hill, 1–282.

State-Rights men. Many of Jackson's former supporters were unable to see any difference between
Georgia's refusal to recognize the mandate of the Court
in the *Cherokee Cases*, and South Carolina's announcement of a similar intention; and the Calhoun newspapers rang with abuse of Jackson's inconsistency and
tyranny. This bill, said the *Richmond Enquirer*, "constitutes Gen. Jackson Monarch of the American Empire, and must be resisted to the death." [1] "Is it not
very extraordinary," said the *United States Telegraph*, "no person but a Jackson or Van Buren man
can see any essential difference between the cases of
Georgia and South Carolina? This is really passing
strange. Georgia refuses to obey the decisions of the
Federal Judiciary. Not a word is said by the Executive or his minions, except that she is right in doing so.
South Carolina says that she will do so at a future
period. And the Palace is in arms. Denunciations
fall thick and heavy from its enraged occupant." [2]

The debate in Congress, during the months of January and February, 1833, over the passage of the Force
Bill evoked once more violent attacks upon the Court
and its functions in relation to the States. The trans-
formation, however, of Nullification from a mere theory,
as it was in 1830 during the Foote Resolution debate,
to an actuality had profoundly modified the views of
many of its former upholders; they now saw that it
meant either anarchy, subjugation of a State by force
or dissolution of the Union; they realized that Webster's great argument in behalf of National supremacy
had been fully justified, and that only by submission
to the settlement of constitutional questions through

[1] See *National Intelligencer*, Jan. 29, 1833.
[2] *United Stated Telegraph*, Dec. 19, 1832, Jan. 3, 1833; see an interesting letter
from Martin Van Buren to Roger B. Taney in 1833, *Maryland Hist. Mag.*, March,
1910, V, describing his attitude and that of Jackson towards Nullification.

judicial decision could peace and Federal unity be preserved; consequently the Court received a stronger and more widely distributed support throughout the debate than had been given to it in Congress for the past fifteen years.[1]

Even before the final passage of the Force Bill, the officials of the State of Georgia perceived that the President's insistence on the supremacy of the National authority in South Carolina would render it impossible for him to countenance disobedience to the mandates of the National Court in any other State; and early in January, a Washington correspondent of a New York paper predicted a settlement of the *Cherokee Case*, writing: "The President has said, since the Proclamation was promulgated, that he would carry any decision the Supreme Court should make in the imprisonment of the missionaries into effect. The Georgians have been restive under the Proclamation, and there is much to induce a belief that they will in some way avoid a direct collision with the General Government." This prophecy was soon fulfilled; for the Governor of Georgia, influenced by the President's determined stand and by political reasons relating to Presidential candidates, finally issued a pardon to the missionaries upon their withdrawal of their suit; and thus the crisis in the history of the Court was averted.[2]

[1] *22d Cong., 2d Sess.*, see speeches in the Senate in support of the Court: Wilkins of Pennsylvania, Jan. 28, 29, 1833, Grundy of Tennessee, Jan. 30, Frelinghuysen of New Jersey, Feb. 3, Holmes of Maine, Feb. 5, Clayton of Delaware; and see violent speeches in the Senate in opposition to the Court by Bibb of Kentucky, Jan. 30, 31, Feb. 1, Poindexter of Mississippi, Jan. 22, Brown of North Carolina, Feb. 4, Tyler of Virginia, Feb. 6, and speeches in the House of Daniel of Kentucky, Feb. 28.

[2] *New York Daily Advertiser*, Jan. 16, 1833; the *United States Telegraph* said, Jan. 4, 1833, that the Van Buren Administration had been "intriguing to get Georgia to release the missionaries. By so doing they will avoid the evident collision that would take place if the principles of the Proclamation are carried" — and it said that it was necessary to get Georgia in order not to have it lost to Van Buren; again it said, Jan. 18, that if Georgia were dis-

The settlement of this dangerous litigation, and the inflexible determination of the President to defend the principles of the Union against Nullification, revolutionized the sentiments which had hitherto been held towards him in many parts of the country. "The Proclamation, but more especially the Message, adopt all your principles," wrote Ambrose Spencer to Daniel Webster.[1] "Notwithstanding I am 'the most dangerous man in America', the President specially invited me to drink a glass of wine with him. But what is more remarkable, since his last Proclamation and Message, the Chief Justice and myself have become his warmest supporters, and shall continue so just as long as he maintains the principles contained in them. Who would have dreamed of such an occurrence?" so wrote

posed of, Jackson would "have full play with South Carolina." On Jan. 23 it said as to the issue of the pardon: "They say that they are induced to take this step from considerations of a public nature! What these considerations are does not admit of a doubt. It is that the whole force of the Administration and of the interest which controls the Board of Foreign Missions may be made to bear on South Carolina. It was necessary to keep the South divided, and therefore Georgia, who had been threatened with the bayonet, is to be paid for the desertion of her own principles and bribed into the coalition against South Carolina." See also *United States Telegraph*, Jan. 28, March 12, 1833. One of the missionaries, S. A. Worcester, wrote to their counsel John Sergeant, Jan. 22, 1833, inclosing a copy of a letter which they had sent to Governor Lumpkin, Jan. 8, notifying him of their instructions to counsel to discontinue prosecution of their case. "We beg leave respectfully to state to your Excellency that we have not been led to the adoption of this measure by any change of views in regard to the principles on which we have acted, or by any doubt of the justice of our cause, or of our perfect right to a legal discharge in accordance with the decision of the Supreme Court, in our favor already given, but by the apprehension that the further prosecution of the controversy under existing circumstances, might be attended with consequences injurious to our beloved country." Worcester continued: "We soon learned that the Governor was very much irritated by our assertion of our rights and considered the latter part of our communication as an indignity to the State"; and he said that they had written again to the Governor, Jan. 9, as follows: "We are sorry to be informed that some expressions in our communication of yesterday were regarded by your Excellency as an indignity offered to the State or its authorities. Nothing could be further from our design. In the course we have now taken it has been our intention simply to forbear the prosecution of our case and to leave the question of the continuance of our confinement to the magnanimity of the State." *Niles Register*, XLII, Feb. 16, 1833.

[1] *Webster Papers MSS*, letter of Feb. 21, 1833; *Story*, II, 117, letter of Jan. 27, 1833.

Judge Story of a dinner at the White House, January 27. And since no man gave to Jackson warmer support than his former opponent, Daniel Webster, it was even reported that Jackson was contemplating the appointment of Webster as Chief Justice, in case of Marshall's death.[1]

With this union of Andrew Jackson, Daniel Webster and John Marshall in support of the supremacy of the Nation, the Court, which had done so much to establish such supremacy, now found itself in a stronger position than it had been for the past fifteen years. The attacks directed against it from the moment of its vital decision in *McCulloch* v. *Maryland,* and the Legislative attempts to impair its functions now ceased; and it was not until nearly twenty years later that it became the subject of serious criticism or antagonism by either Congress or the people. In connection with this renewed respect for the Constitution and the renewed confidence in the Court, it should be noted that in this year, 1833, Judge Story published his famous *Commentaries on the Constitution of the United States.* Its appearance was acclaimed, by lawyers and laymen alike, as an important contribution to the defense of the principles on which the American Government had been founded and which had recently been subjected to assault. "Constitutional law, in our day, instead of being the calm occupation of the schools or the curious pursuit of the professional student, has become, as it

---

[1] James Louis Petigru wrote to Hugh Legaré, March 5, 1833: "But is it not very strange to think of Webster and Jackson? It has been hinted, and I think not improbable, that Webster will be Chief Justice." *Life, Letters and Speeches of James Louis Petigru* (1820), by James Petigru Carson. *Harper's Weekly,* Sept. 20, 1873, quoted Senator Foote of Mississippi, as stating in his reminiscences of R. Y. Hayne, that after development of the Nullification contest, "General Jackson became so great an admirer of the Senator of Massachusetts that he thought seriously of making him Chief Justice of the Supreme Court of the United States upon the decease of the venerable Marshall." See also *New York Courier,* Feb. 8, 1833; *United States Telegraph,* Feb. 8, 1833.

were, an element of real life. The Constitution has been obliged to leave its temple, and come down into the forum and traverse the streets," wrote Edward Everett; and a writer in the *American Jurist* said that the work appeared "very opportunely, since we have most strangely, now at this late day, been unexpectedly thrown back to the very threshold, to the agitation of the question whether we have, in fact, any constitution of government, or are entirely destitute of a supreme law; and which is, in effect, equivalent, whether we have any tribunal to interpret and apply, and an authority to enforce that law." And Marshall wrote to Story: " I greatly fear that south of the Potomack, where it is most wanted, it will be least used. It is a Mohammedan rule, I understand, 'never to dispute with the ignorant', and we of the true faith in the South abjure the contamination of infidel political works. It would give our orthodox nullifyer a fever to read the heresies of your Commentaries.[1] . . . Nothing in their view is to be feared but that bugbear, consolidation; and every exercise of legitimate power is construed into a breach of the Constitution. Your book, if read, will tend to remove these prejudices."

[1] *North Amer. Rev.* (1834), XXXVIII, 65; *Amer. Jurist* (April, 1833); *Mass. Hist. Soc. Proc.*, *2d Series*, XIV, letters of April 24, June 3, 1833.

CHAPTER TWENTY

THE LAST YEARS OF CHIEF JUSTICE MARSHALL

1833–1835

FOR the two years succeeding the subsidence of the Nullification movement, the Court ceased temporarily to be a center of sectional or political attack. Its time was chiefly occupied with cases involving great commercial questions and landed interests; but at the 1833 Term, it delivered the last of the series of vital decisions on constitutional law which had made the Chief Justiceship of John Marshall so memorable an era in American history. In *Barron* v. *Baltimore*, 7 Pet. 243, the Court finally determined the Amendments to the Constitution to be limitations only on Congressional action and not applicable to State legislation. "These Amendments demanded security against the apprehended encroachments of the General Government, not against those of the local governments," Marshall said. "The great revolution which established the Constitution of the United States was not effected without immense opposition. Serious fears were extensively entertained that those powers, which the patriot statesmen who then watched over the interests of our country deemed essential to Union, and to the attainment of those invaluable objects for which Union was sought, might be exercised in a manner dangerous to liberty." It is a striking fact that this last of Marshall's opinions on this branch of law should have been delivered in limitation of the operation of the Constitution, whose undue extension he had been so long charged with seeking.

At the 1834 Term the Court was confronted with an immense number of suits based on land claims arising out of the Spanish Treaty of 1819; and in *United States* v. *Clarke*, 8 Pet. 436, Chief Justice Marshall reaffirmed an opinion, delivered three years before, the doctrines laid down in which determined the whole future policy of the United States with respect to its public lands acquired by cession or compact. By its treaty with Spain of February 22, 1819, the United States had put an end to the serious controversies over alleged breaches of neutrality, spoliation claims and the boundaries of Florida and Louisiana. Under this treaty, while relinquishing all its claims to land in the ceded territories, Spain provided that all grants made therein by the King or his lawful authorities prior to January 24, 1818, should be "ratified and confirmed to the person in the possession of the lands to the same extent that the same grants would be valid", if the territory had remained in Spain's hands. During the long period while this treaty was pending, awaiting final ratification, a vast number of grants had been hurriedly made by Spanish officials in Florida and elsewhere, many of them without authority, many by fraud of subordinate officers, many with conditions attached which were never performed or expected to be performed by the grantees. Congress, confronted with this abnormal situation, provided a judicial machinery for establishment of these land claims; but so great a flood of claimants had appeared that it seemed as if no land would be left for the public in the newly acquired territory. Rarely did a claimant present the original document establishing his grant; nor were such originals to be found in the offices of the keepers of public archives; copies of Spanish documents, coupled with the flimsiest excuses for the non-production of original certificates from notoriously rascally Spanish officials, and papers bearing every earmark of fraud and forgery, constituted the chief evidence for many of the claims presented; and as John Quincy Adams, himself, said, a demand for production of the archives would result in little advantage, for "the chance was that the archives would follow from the grant, instead of the grant from the archives . . . the office of archivist was purchasable."[1] Similar conditions prevailed in Louisiana and Missouri under the Louisiana Treaty of Cession in 1803. Such was the situation when the case of *United States* v. *Arredondo*, 6 Pet. 691, involving a claim to about 300,000 acres in Florida, came before the Court in 1832. Its importance amply warranted the length of its argument (from March 2 to 7), and the array of notable counsel — Richard K. Call of Florida, William Wirt and Attorney-General Roger B. Taney against Joseph M. White of Florida, John M. Berrien of Georgia and Daniel Webster. Few decisions of the Court at this period had a more permanent effect upon the history of the country; for in this case the Court established the public land policy of the Government on the basis of the most scrupulous respect for treaties, preferring to preserve the honor, rather than the property of the government, and to run the risk of confirming possibly fraudulent claims rather than to impair the reputation of the Government with foreign nations. In a superb opinion by Judge Baldwin, the Court had laid down the broad principle that, if a grant was made by a public official purporting to be in accordance with the laws of the sovereign power for which he was acting, there was a

[1] *J. Q. Adams*, VIII, March 9, 1830.

legal presumption that it was a valid official act, and that the burden rested on the United States to prove lack of authority.[1] It was also held that the treaty was intended to protect all rights in land of any nature, and that in case of grants with conditions attached, the Court would consider the facts presented by the claimants in excuse of non-performance of conditions, and would construe liberally such excuses. These doctrines were again emphasized by Marshall in the *Clarke Case* in 1834. "He who would controvert a grant executed by the lawful authority, with all the solemnities required by law, takes upon himself the burden of showing that the officer has transcended the powers conferred upon him, or that the transaction is tainted with fraud." And they were consistently adhered to by the Court in the long series of cases (over ninety in number) which arose, in the succeeding twenty years, in Florida, Arkansas, Louisiana and Missouri. The fact that a large number of these Spanish claims had been assigned to and were being prosecuted by bankers, financiers and speculators in New York and London had given to President Jackson, in his fight with the financial interests, a vivid interest in the outcome of these cases. Consequently, the decisions of the Court upholding the claims were a great disappointment and gave grave offense to the President, so much so, that, as reported in the newspapers, "he sent for Judge Baldwin, who drew up the opinion of the Court, and gave him a lecture, and if he had been subject to Executive power, he would un-

[1] The Washington correspondent of the *New York Courier*, writing March 17, 1832, said: "Today Judge Baldwin of the Supreme Court gave a most able and interesting opinion on the great Florida land case. It was in favor of the claimants. The numerous local facts, the great knowledge displayed of the historical and other records of Florida bearing on the case were principally drawn from the able argument of Col. White, who has conducted the case with uncommon learning and research. In many respects, besides to the claimants, this opinion has deep and abiding interest, from the glimpses it gives of the opinions of the Court on questions *non coram judice*, as the learned lawyers say."

doubtedly have made him walk Spanish." [1]   As Baldwin was an appointee of Jackson, the episode forms
another striking illustration of the independence of
the Judiciary from Executive influence. In later
years, when the claims for land in California and New
Mexico under the Mexican Treaty of 1848 began to
flood the Courts, the doctrines laid down by the Court
were severely criticized by Government counsel, as
unwarrantably hampering the efforts to preserve the
public domain from fraudulent claimants; and it
is undeniable that the Court's decision resulted in the
unjust enrichment of many speculators whose claims
possessed no legal foundation.[2] On the other hand,
if the Court had held that the burden was on the claimant to prove, rather than on the Government to disprove, the authority of the public official making the
grant, such a decision would have been, as Judge Baldwin said, "an entire novelty in our jurisprudence",
and would have entailed consequences of the most
sweeping nature to all land titles theretofore established
in the older parts of the United States. While the
area of the public lands of the United States might
have been increased, had the Court construed the
treaty more strictly against private claimants, the
policy which the Court adopted gave to the world
conclusive proof of its devotion to the theory of the
sanctity of treaties; and as Judge Baldwin said:
"Nothing can tend so much to their interest, to preserve
their high position at home and abroad, as for the United

---

[1] *National Gazette*, Feb. 6, 1834; *New York Daily Advertiser* said, Feb. 4, 1834:
"It appears that the old hero has set his heart against the confirmation of all the
Spanish titles in Florida, and has the causes continued from year to year, to send
his agents all over the world to find out something on which to found his objections
and justify his deep-rooted prejudices."

[2] See this view of the law of the cases by a recent Socialist historian of the Court
in an able, but non-judicial and sometimes inaccurate, presentation of numerous
facts, many of which do not appear in the Court records. *History of the Supreme
Court of the United States* (1912), by Gustavus Myers.

States to consider this treaty to have consummated all the great objects which it was intended to effect. . . . The protection and maintenance of the rights of private property in the disputed territory may conduce more to the honor and interest of the United States than a contrary course, which, in my opinion, will cause injury to their fame and hazard to their power."[1]

Next in importance to the land cases, at this 1834 Term was the noted case of *Wheaton* v. *Peters*, 8 Pet. 591, a suit by the old Reporter of the Court against the present Reporter for alleged violation of copyright, argued by Webster against Charles J. Ingersoll and John Sergeant.[2] Wheaton, having failed to comply with the technical requirements of the Federal copyright law, attempted to maintain his copyright at common law; but the Court, through Judge McLean, decided against him, and reaffirmed its doctrine, laid down twenty years before, that: "It is clear there can be no common law of the United States. The Federal Government is composed of twenty-four sovereign and independent States, each of which may have its local usages, customs and common law. There is no principle which pervades the Union and has the authority of law that is not embodied in the Constitution or laws of the Union. The common law could be made a part of our Federal system only by legislative adoption." Of this decision, ex-Chancellor Kent wrote to Judge Story a letter full of pessimism as to existing conditions in American politics:[3]

---

[1] *Lessee of Pollard's Heirs* v. *Kibbe* (1840), 14 Pet. 353.

[2] Horace Binney wrote to John Sergeant, Jan. 15, 1834, inclosing a letter to Sergeant from the Reporter, Richard Peters, in which the latter said: "I will endeavor to give you as little trouble as possible in the case. . . . Mr. Wheaton is here and looks 'very mad.'" *John Sergeant Papers MSS.*

[3] *Mass. Hist. Soc. Proc.*, 2d Series, XIV, letter of April 11, 1834. See also curious note by Kent on Story's views and Commentaries, in *Amer. Law Rev.* (1870), V, 368.

I don't feel satisfied that you or the Ch. J. did not write an opinion on the copyright case, & discuss the grounds of the claim at criminal law. It would appear to me to have fairly presented itself as a new question for discussion in our American jurisprudence. I don't complain of the decision on the point. It is more than probable I should have been of the same opinion had I studied the case; but that imposing brief of Mr. Wheaton ought to have been met by one of the only two men who could have met it with a giant's force. . . . To deny the common law right and to construe the statute right with such severity is not palatable to us humble authors. However, when the case comes to be reported I shall be better able to judge of the merits of the two principal questions, and I should not have said anything but in entire confidence and with the utmost attachment to the Court and its reputation. In these wretched times I am for sustaining the Supreme Court with my utmost efforts. My despair is a little over. Light breaks in upon the gloom. The complete revolution in Connecticut; the immense changes (almost without effort) in the interior of this State, and the results of the awful and tremendous election in this city, animate me. I look upon Jackson as a detestable, ignorant, reckless, vain and malignant tyrant, and I think the country begin to open their eyes in astonishment and see things in the true light. This American elective monarchy frightens me. The experiment, with its foundation laid on universal suffrage and an unfettered and licentious press, is of too violent a nature for our excitable people. We have not in our large cities, if we have in our country, moral firmness enough to bear it. *It racks the machine too much.* . . .

To this Story replied:[1]

I am sorry for the controversy between Mr. Wheaton and Peters, and did all I could to prevent a public discussion of the delicate subject of copyright. . . . The strict construction of the statute of Congress we adopted with vast reluctance, but after turning it fully and freely to our minds, the majority of the Court did not see how they could give any other construction to it. I wish Congress would make some

---

[1] *Story*, II, 181, letter of May 17, 1834.

additional provision on the subject to protect authors, of whom I think no one more meritorious than Mr. Wheaton. You, as a Judge, have frequently had occasion to know how many bitter cups we are not at liberty to pass by. . . . Your views of politics and men run exactly in the same mould as mine.

The argument of another case at this Term, *Binney* v. *Chesapeake and Ohio Canal*, 8 Pet. 201, involving the navigation of the Potomac River at Little Falls above the city of Washington was amusingly described by an auditor in the Court-room, Charles Sumner: "Mr. F. S. Key is now speaking in the Supreme Court, where I write these lines. The case before the Court is an important one — Key, Walter Jones and Webster on one side and (Richard S.) Coxe and (Thomas) Swann on the other. Key has not prepared himself, and now speaks from his preparation on the trial below, relying upon a quickness and facility of language rather than upon research. Walter Jones — a man of acknowledged powers in the law, unsurpassed, if not unequalled, by any lawyer in the country — is in the same plight. He is now conning his papers and maturing his points — a labor which of course he should have gone through before he entered the Court room. And *our* Webster fills up the remiss triumvirate. He, like Jones, is doing the labor in Court which should have been done out of Court. In fact, politics have entirely swamped his whole time and talents. All here declare that he has neglected his cases this Term in a remarkable manner. It is now whispered in the room that he has not looked at the present case, though the amount at stake is estimated at half a million dollars." [1]

[1] *Sumner*, I, 135. Webster wrote to Jeremiah Mason, Feb. 6, 1835: "My habits, I must confess . . . render it more agreeable to me to attend to political than to professional subjects. But I have not lost all relish for the Bar. I can

In *Carrington* v. *Merchants Insurance Company*, 8 Pet. 495, argued by Horace Binney and John Sergeant against Daniel Webster and Franklin Dexter of Massachusetts, an American trader dealing in contraband goods with Peru was held to forfeit his ship to a Spanish captor, even after he had landed the contraband, owing to the fact that he sailed with false papers and a disguised destination. Judge Story insisted with the utmost vigor on the duty of neutrals to act without fraud themselves, if they desired to assert rights against a belligerent. This case gave rise to a striking criticism by Charles J. Ingersoll of the effect of Webster's arguments: "Mr. Webster's professional influence, much more signal than his political, has succeeded in corrupting American jurisprudence with some of the most extravagant and intolerable dogmas of the English code — nay, what would now be rejected by it. What may be deemed his first great effort in the Supreme Court was in the case of the Dartmouth College, when he induced that tribunal to carry the corporation privilege beyond all bounds, owing, as has been thought, to the absence of Pinkney who was opposed to him; and his latest labor there, in the case of a Boston Insurance Company, prevailed over a majority of the Bench to adopt one of the most unwarrantable aberrations of the English maritime policy from the law of nations; in the first mentioned case against the sound judgment of one dissentient Democrat on the Bench, and the law as taught from Locke to Hallam; in the last against the judgment of all the Democrats

still make something by the practice; and by remaining in the Senate, I am making sacrifices which my circumstances do not justify. . . . I find it inconvenient to push my practice in the Supreme Court, while a member of the Senate, and I am inclined under any view of the future to decline engagements hereafter in that Court, unless under special circumstance." *Webster Papers MSS.*

on the Bench and the law of all nations except modern Great Britain." [1]

In the midst of this case, "the Court, having been informed of the decease of Mr. Wirt, an exalted member of this Bar, in order to manifest the sense entertained by the Court of this deep loss immediately adjourned"; and on the next day, in response to a resolution of the Bar, moved by Attorney-General Benjamin F. Butler, the Chief Justice said: "We too, gentlemen, have sustained a loss it will be difficult, if not impossible to repair. In performing the arduous duties assigned to us, we have been long aided by the diligent research and lucid reasoning of him whose loss we unite with you in deploring. We, too, gentlemen, in common with you have lost the estimable friend in the powerful advocate." [2] Thereupon, the Court resolved "to wear the usual badge of mourning during the residue of this Term, in token of their respect and regard for the memory of the deceased, and of their deep sense of this afflicting event." This striking tribute has been paid by the Court to but few members of the Bar other than Pinkney and Wirt.

The transition stage, through which the Court was now passing was very clearly shown at this Term by the difficulty which the Court experienced in deciding several important cases which had been pending for some time. Of the older Judges, Johnson and Duval were incapacitated and absent much of the time; and the new Judges, Thompson, McLean and Baldwin,

---

[1] *Life of Charles J. Ingersoll* (1897), 192, by William M. Meigs, see Ingersoll's speech of July 4, 1835. Horace Binney wrote of the case, Feb. 18, 1834: "Resumed my argument in the Supreme Court with some freshness and pretty good effect. I went on till one, when the Court adjourned in consequence of the death of Mr. Wirt," and (later), "I thought I had satisfied the Court (I did satisfy Chief Justice Marshall) that England had wrested the old-established law of nations as to contraband in her favour. The continentals are much more impartial, and more disposed to favour the weak, the neutral, and the peaceable and so it ought to be."

[2] *National Intelligencer*, Feb. 19, 20, 1834.

differed frequently from Marshall and Story. Consequently the Chief Justice at the close of the Term announced that the three constitutional cases — *Charles River Bridge* v. *Warren Bridge*, *Briscoe* v. *Commonwealth Bank of Kentucky* and *New York* v. *Miln* — then pending, would be continued, and he said: "The practice of this Court is not (except in cases of absolute necessity) to deliver any judgment in cases where constitutional questions are involved unless four Judges concur in opinion, thus making the decision that of a majority of the whole Court." [1]

Of the Supreme Court, as it appeared in these closing years of Chief Justice Marshall's life, vivid pictures have been given by contemporary writers. Harriet Martineau wrote in 1835 : [2]

I have watched the assemblage while the Chief Justice was delivering a judgment, the three Judges on either hand gazing at him more like learners than associates; Webster standing firm as a rock, his large, deep-set eyes wide awake, his lips compressed, and his whole countenance in that intent stillness which easily fixes the gaze of the stranger. Clay leaning against the desk in an attitude whose grace contrasts strangely with the slovenly make of his dress, his snuff box for the moment unopened in his hand, his small grey eye,

[1] These cases were again continued in 1835, when Marshall said in answer to any inquiry whether the Court had come to a final decision as to reargument of the cases, that as the Court was then composed, it would not take them up (two of the Judges being absent, and only three of the remaining five concurring in opinion); see 9 Peters, 85, and argument of A. H. Garland in *Brenham* v. *Bank* (1892), 144 U. S. 549; *New York* v. *Miln* (1843), 8 Pet. 122. As late as 1824, a decision had been rendered by a minority of the Court — in *Renner* v. *Bank of Columbia*, 9 Wheat. 581. As already shown, the charge had been frequently made that in the important case of *Green* v. *Biddle* in 1823, involving the constitutionality of the Kentucky occupying claimant laws, the decision was that of less than a majority of the Judges, and bitter attacks had been made on the Court in Congress, in consequence. See also comments of Baldwin, J., on the decision of *Livingston* v. *Story* (1837), 11 Pet. 399, as to the decision of the prior case in 1835 (9 Pet. 632) by three out of five Judges present.

[2] *Retrospect of Western Travel* (1838), by Harriet Martineau, I, 143, 165. See also description of the manner of argument before the Court and especially of Webster in *Men and Manners in America* (1833), by Dana Hamilton.

and placid half-smile conveying an expression of pleasure, which redeems his face from its usual unaccountable commonness. The Attorney-General, his fingers playing among his papers, his quick black eye and thin tremulous lips for once fixed, his small face, pale with thought, contrasting remarkably with the other two; these men, absorbed in what they were listening to, thinking neither of themselves nor of each other, while they are watched by the groups of idlers and listeners around them; the newspaper corps, the dark Cherokee chiefs, the stragglers from the far West, the gay ladies in their waving plumes, and the members of either House that have stepped in to listen; all these I have seen at one moment constitute one silent assemblage, while the mild voice of the aged Chief Justice sounded through the Court. . . . There is no tolerable portrait of Judge Story, and there never will be . . . the quick smile, the glistening eye, the gleeful tone, with passing touches of sentiment; the innocent self-complacency, the confiding, devoted affections of the great American lawyer. . . . It was amusing to see how the Court would fill after the entrance of Webster, and empty when he had gone back to the Senate Chamber. The chief interest to me in Webster's pleading, and also in his speaking in the Senate, was from seeing one so dreamy and nonchalant, roused into strong excitement. Webster is a lover of ease and pleasure, and has an air of the most unaffected indolence and careless self-sufficiency. It is something to see him moved with anxiety, and the toil of intellectual conflict; to see his lips tremble, his nostrils expand, the perspiration start upon his brow; to hear his voice vary with emotion.

Charles Sumner, in 1834, thus depicted the personal life of the Judges of this time:[1]

[1] *Sumner*, I, 135, 136, two letters of March 3, 1834.

Ben Perley Poore in his *Reminiscences of Sixty Years at the Metropolis* (1886), 222, 295, referring to the Court about 1837 said: "Their Honors, the Justices, were rather a jovial set, especially Justice Story, who used to assert that every man should laugh at least an hour during each day, and who had himself a great fund of humorous anecdotes. . . . The best Madeira was that labelled 'The Supreme Court', as their Honors, the Justices, used to make a direct importation every year, and sip it as they consulted over the cases before them, every day after dinner, when the cloth had been removed." In 1831, Marshall appears to have been much disturbed at a proposal to change the lodgings of the Judges to

Every day's attendance in the political part of the Capitol shows me clearly that all speeches there are delivered to the people beyond, and not to Senators and Representatives present. In the Supreme Court, the object of speaking is to convince. The more I see of politics the more I learn to love law. . . . Since last I wrote, I have seen many great men and attended at the Capitol every day, making the Supreme Court (which is on the lower floor in a dark room, almost down cellar) my first object of attention. . . . All the Judges board together, having rooms in the same house and taking their meals from the same table, except Judge McLean whose wife is with him, and who consequently has a separate table, though in the same house. I dined with them yesterday; being Sunday, Judges Marshall, Story, Thompson and Duval were present who, with myself, made up the company, with two waiters in attendance. Sunday here is a much gayer day than with us. No conversation is forbidden, and nothing which goes to cause cheerfulness, if not hilarity. The world and all its things are talked of as much as on any other day. Judge Marshall is a model of simplicity — "in wit a man, simplicity a child." He is naturally taciturn, and yet ready to laugh; to joke and to be joked with. Judge Thompson is a kindhearted man, now somewhat depressed from the loss of his wife. Judge Duval is 82 years old and is so deaf as to be unable to participate in conversation.

And George Bancroft, in 1832, recorded his impressions of the Judges as follows: [1]

a house, situated "between the palace and Georgetown", which he feared would not be approved by all the Judges, and which might cause them to scatter; see letters to Story May 3, Oct. 12, Nov. 10, 1831; *Mass. Hist. Soc. Proc., 2d Ser.*, XIV. In 1845, the practice of rooming together was partially broken up; the Chief Justice with three of his Associates living in one boarding house, while three lived at a hotel, and the others in private houses. In 1850, the Judges entirely abandoned the practice — the "mess style" as it was called; and five lived in various boarding houses, and four in various hotels and private houses. *Pictures of the City of Washington in the Past* (1895), by Samuel C. Busey.

[1] *Life and Letters of George Bancroft* (1908), by Mark A. DeW. Howe, I, 202, letter of Jan. 23, 1832. A striking personal description of Chief Justice Marshall appeared in the *Norfolk Beacon*, in May, 1835: "He was tall and awkward in his movements. His eyes were black and remarkably fine. They told the tale of his genius, despite his careless dress and ungainly demeanour. The spectator was astonished at the smallness of his head; it was the smallest he had ever seen,

We went to call upon Judge Story, and we found there Judge Baldwin and Chief Justice Marshall. I drew my chair close up to the latter, nor can you readily conceive of the great suavity or rather calmness of manner by which he is distinguished. In conversation, he makes no display nor is he remarkable except for this venerable coolness of manner. There are about him no marks of genius, but in his entire collectedness, great precision and calm uniformity, you may discern the signs of an unerring judgment. He is by all acknowledged to stand foremost on the bench of the Supreme Court, a first rate *man* in the first class of greatness. He has travelled very little; has not been in New England since the War; has hardly seen New York, but has lived in the regular exercise of his judicial functions, unincumbered by other care than that of giving character and respectability to the Bench over which he presides. Judge Baldwin thinks more of tariff than he does of law, but he is an agreeable man, full of vivacity, and a thorough advocate of the protective system.

The less serious side of the Judge's life was touched upon by Story in a letter to his wife, in 1833 : [1]

The Court opened on Monday last, and all the Judges were present, except Judge Baldwin. They were in good health, and the Chief Justice looked more vigorous than usual. He seemed to revive and enjoy anew his green, old age. . . . We have had little to do this week in Court, for it is always difficult for some days to get business in a steady train. The lawyers are tardy and reluctant, and they move with unequal efforts at first. Having some leisure on our hands, the Chief Justice and myself have devoted some of it to attendance upon the theatre to hear Miss Fanny Kemble. . . . We attended on Monday night, and on the Chief Justice's entrance into the box, he was cheered in a marked

unless he had been fortunate enough to see John Randolph, and, as we are told, Lord Byron's." *National Intelligencer*, July 11, 1835.

[1] *Story*, II, 116, letter of Jan. 20, 1833. Writing Jan. 27, 1837, Story described a dinner attended by the Judges at the Secretary of State's (Edward Livingston) "being invited to dinner at half past five and actually sitting down to the table at half past seven; so that we have reached at Washington the fashionable hour of St. James'."

manner. He behaved as he always does, with extreme modesty, and seemed not to know that the compliment was designed for him. We have seen Miss Kemble as Julia in The Hunchback, and as Mrs. Haller in The Stranger. . . . In Mrs. Haller she threw the whole audience into tears. The Chief Justice shed them in common with younger eyes.

On August 4, 1834, Judge Johnson died, after a service of thirty years on the Bench marked by a high degree of independence and by a series of opinions noted for individuality and freedom of expressive phrase.[1] As this vacancy occurred at a time when the warfare between the President and the Senate over the removal of the Government deposits from the Bank of the United States was at its height, and only six weeks after the Senate had refused to confirm the appointment of Roger B. Taney as Secretary of the Treasury because of his participation in the removal, the Whigs gravely feared lest the President might seek now to appoint Taney to the Bench. It is not probable, however, that Jackson contemplated such a move, as the appointment would properly go to the South. After considering for some months the names

[1] See *National Gazette*, Jan. 10, 1835; the *New York Courier*, a supporter of the Bank of the United States, within a few days after Judge Johnson's death had said that Taney's nomination should be "rejected by an overwhelming majority", that the attention of the press and public must be awakened, and it said: "Let the Senate beware that they do not contribute to the promotion of a mere political driveller who would sell his birthright for a mess of pottage. Let them beware that they do not advise and consent to the foul pollution of the judicial ermine." To this violent and unjustified invective, the *Albany Argus*, Aug. 11, 1834, replied in an editorial, headed "Bank Insolence, Designs of the Bank upon the Judiciary", in which it deplored the indecent haste of the *Courier* in discussing a successor to Johnson before his remains were consigned to the grave; and the *Argus* praised Taney as incorruptible and well fitted for appointment; and attacked the "insolent and corrupt moneyed corporation" which was thus apparently through the press attempting to dictate to the President and Senate. Of this situation, Van Buren wrote to Jackson, Aug. 12, 1834: "The opposition papers are waxing warm upon the subject of the vacant seat on the Bench and swear, in substance, that it shall be filled by none but a friend of the Bank. I shall endeavor to obtain an article from the *Albany Argus*, showing the ground taken upon the subject here, and send it to you." *Van Buren Papers MSS.*

of James Louis Petigru,[1] Hugh Legaré and William Drayton, all of South Carolina, who were actively urged upon him, Jackson appointed on January 5, 1835, his close friend and supporter, James M. Wayne of Georgia. Wayne was forty-five years old; he had been for five years a Judge of the Supreme Court in Georgia, and later, as a Democratic member of Congress, had been an active Union man, advocating all measures directed against Nullification. For this reason, his appointment was generally acceptable both to the Whigs and to the Jackson Democrats. "Few Whigs would hesitate to acknowledge," said the Whig Bank paper in Philadelphia, "that Judge Wayne is preferable for the bench of the Supreme Court to some other candidate of the Jackson party." "The appointment seems to be acceptable generally," said a New York Whig paper. "He is a gentleman of great urbanity, a high-minded, honorable man. I know nothing of his legal talents, but in the present state of the country and of parties, I consider the selection judicious, and incomparably better than I anticipated." "No unworthy motives, I think, will ever influence his decision," said another New York paper. "Mr. Wayne's character as a Republican of talent, education, firmness and honesty is well known," said the Democratic *New York Evening Post*.[2] "Mr. Wayne has taken his seat on the Bench," said *Niles Register*, "of which lofty place all parties agree on considering him worthy, believing that he will not be a partisan Judge. This is a compliment to be proud of, in times like the present." Thus far, President Jackson had had three opportu-

---

[1] *Life, Letters and Speeches of James Louis Petigru* (1920), by James Petigru Carson, letter to Drayton, Aug. 12, 1834, letter to Legaré, Nov. 29, 1834.

[2] *New York Journal of Commerce*, Jan. 16, 1835; *New York Courier*, Jan. 10, 1835; *New York Evening Post*, Jan. 12, 1838; *Niles Register*, XLVII, Jan. 17, 1835.

nities to make appointments on the Supreme Bench, and in each case he had surprised his political opponents, who charged him with reckless, political motives, by appointing lawyers of high capacity; and the reputation of the Court, so far from suffering, had been established on a firm basis. "Its hall," said *Niles Register* (which had been out of sympathy with the Court for many years), "is 'the cave of Trophonius' or of oracles, as John Randolph called it in the asperity of his temper; but many of its formerly supposed errors have become acknowledged truths by the silent yet sure operations of Time; and if some of its decisions are still regarded wrong (though very few, if any, are generally so) it is accepted that they were the result of an honest and enlightened judgment. . . . For so it is that law-makers, as well as Judges, are not infallible, and that 'angels do not descend' to give us unerring Legislative, Executive or Judicial decision. Perfection is not hoped for; and all that can be expected is the honest judgment of independent and intelligent individuals, who, in the frailty of human nature, are liable to error, however zealously they may strive to avoid it."

In curious contrast to this optimistic attitude towards the Court, Ex-Chancellor Kent's account of an interview at this time with Judge Story is striking: "He says that Hamilton was the greatest and wisest man of this country. He saw fifty years ahead, and what he saw then is *fact now*. Next to him in wisdom and sense, intuitive rectitude and truth and judgment is Ch. J. Marshall. He says all sensible men at Washington, in private conversation, admit that the Government is deplorably weak, factious, and corrupt. That everything is sinking down into despotism, under the disguise of a democratic government. He says the

Sup. Court is sinking, and so is the judicial in every
State. We began with first-rate men for judicial
trusts, and we have now got down to the third-rate.
In twenty-five years there will not be a Judge in the
U. S. who will not be made elective, and for short
periods and on slender salaries. Our Constitutions
were all framed for man as he *should be* and not for
man *as he is and ever will be.*" [1]

Before the Court met for its 1835 Term, a further
vacancy on the Bench occurred through the resignation
of Judge Duval who was eighty-two years old, almost
totally deaf, and worn out from his service of twenty-
four years.[2] Duval's death or resignation had been
expected for nearly six years, and as early as 1829,
President Jackson had promised the position to Louis
McLane of Delaware. In August, 1831, McLane
hoped to receive appointment on the resignation of
Judge Baldwin, which was daily expected to occur.
Though Baldwin had then been on the Bench for only
two years, his dissatisfaction with the trend of the
Court's opinions was so great that he had determined
to retire.[3] At the 1831 Term, he had dissented in
seven cases, and in one he had expressed with much
heat his view of the extensions of jurisdiction which
he considered the Court had unwarrantably made.

[1] *Amer. Law Rev.* (1871), V, 368, report of interview, March 18, 1835.

[2] Tappan of Ohio said in the House, Jan. 16, 1843: "Judge Duval sat on the
Bench more than ten years after he had become so deaf that he could not hear a
word that was spoken in Court." *28th Cong., 1st Sess.* The *New York Evening
Post* (then a Democratic paper) said, Jan. 17, 1835, that the report of Duval's
resignation was "good news if true. . . . We have it on the testimony of a highly
respectable Member of Congress that Judge Duval 'has not heard an argument
for ten years past, though a person by no means above the necessity of such aids
to his judgment.' The Nation does not contain a man whose elevation to the vacant place would be so generally acceptable to the great body of the people as that
of Mr. Taney, the victim of the factious and malignant coalition of Bank aristo-
crats in the United States Senate."

[3] See *Ex parte Crane*, 5 Pet. 190. Van Buren wrote to McLane in August, 1831:
"Judge Baldwin is dissatisfied with his situation, for reasons which it is unnecessary to explain further than they grow out of opposition to what he regards as an

"Judges do not sit on cushions of down while administering the supreme law of the land in this Court," he had said. "Fully satisfied that on the discreet exercise of the powers of this Court, much of the strength and public usefulness of the Government depends, I have no fear that its judgments will ever cease to command the support and confidence of the country, while they are applied only to subjects clearly within the judicial power, according to the laws. . . . But I do most seriously apprehend consequences of the most alarming kind by the extensions of its powers." Pressure from the President induced Baldwin to remain on the Court. When the vacancy finally occurred, through Duval's resignation, McLane and the President were no longer on friendly terms; and on January 15, 1835, Jackson nominated to the position his former Attorney-General and Secretary of the Treasury, Roger B. Taney of Maryland. This act aroused intense political excitement. For the past two years, a storm of partisan passion had raged over the removal of the Government deposits from the United States Bank, ordered by Jackson and carried out by Taney. The Whigs, aided by Calhoun's adherents, had refused to confirm Taney as Secretary of the Treasury, and this appointment to the Bench, which they regarded as a reward for Taney's "servility," seemed to them an unbearable act of effrontery on the part of the President. Their wrath was unbounded, their denunciations of the nominee were violent in the extreme, and they thrust aside all consideration of his

unwarrantable extension of its powers by the Court, and has given the President notice of his intention to resign." *Amer. Hist. Ass. Rep.* (1918), II, 578; see also letter of Van Buren to Jackson, Aug. 3, 1831, hoping that McLane would be appointed if Duval should die; letter of McLane to Van Buren, Aug. 11, 1831, stating that Maj. Lewis (Jackson's secretary) "sent me a letter once upon the subject containing an express promise of the President"; letter of Maj. W. B. Lewis to Van Buren, April 22, 1859.

preëminent professional qualifications, in their desire
to punish him for his acts as an executive official.
"Will the Senate oppose the nomination? Can they
approve it, without contradicting virtually, by the act
of approval, the sentence they passed on Mr. Taney's
outrageous violation of the law and the Constitution,
while he was in the Cabinet? The President has no
expectation that the Senate will approve; he does not
even wait for their approbation, except inasmuch as
it would, in effect, reverse the former decision. If the
Senate approve, the President and his tools may boast
of their ingenuity in procuring a reversal of the sentence
of condemnation in this circuitous manner; if the
Senate object, the circumstances will furnish new topics
for the vituperative propensity of the President,"
said a Boston Whig paper. Another said: "We hope
that the Senate will not only apply the veto to the pretensions of this man, but that it will pass a decided
resolution to oppose the elevation of any man who is
not perfectly sound in regard to the fundamental
principles of the Constitution as expounded by Daniel
Webster." [1] A New York paper said, referring to the
previous rejection of Taney's appointment as Secretary of the Treasury: "Is it to be supposed that the
same Senate who had deservedly rejected him will
now approve his nomination as an expounder of the
Constitution? The idea is ridiculous. . . . Mr. Taney
will be rejected, and I should think promptly rejected.
It is true there is a kindly feeling in the Senate at this
moment and a desire on the part of the Whigs to avoid
collision, but not by a sacrifice of principle. . . . It
is full time that public men should be made to feel that
offices of honor and emolument are not in the gift solely

[1] *Columbian Centinel*, Jan. 22, 1835; *Washington Globe*, Feb. 11, 1835; *Boston
Courier*, Jan. 22, 1835; *New York Courier*, .Jan. 19, 1835.

of the Executive, and that subserviency to his will or truckling to his behests is not enough to secure to them the reward they anticipated." That these criticisms were due to the partisan spirit of the times and not to doubt of Taney's legal qualifications is clearly shown by the fact that Chief Justice Marshall himself, looking solely to the legal phase of the appointment, was favorable to Taney's confirmation.[1]

As it appeared that the vote in the Senate would be very close, Taney's opponents determined to evade the problem presented by the nomination, by an ingenious indirect method of shelving it.[2] There was pending in Congress at this time a bill to extend the Circuit Court system to the States of Louisiana, Alabama, Mississippi, Missouri, Illinois and Indiana, which States had long been unjustly deprived of any Circuit Court.[3] The resignation of Judge Duval now presented an opportunity to make this provision, without enlarging the number of Judges on the Court, through the device of combining the States in Judge Duval's

[1] Marshall wrote to Senator Leigh of Virginia: "If you have not made up your mind on the nomination of Mr. Taney, I have received some information in his favor which I would wish to communicate." *Taney*, 240.

[2] Webster wrote to Jeremiah Mason, Jan. 22, 1830: "I am busy in the Court. Mr. Taney is yet before us. Probably will not be confirmed; but that is not certain." *Webster Papers MSS*. On Feb. 1, 1835, he wrote to Mason: "Mr. Taney's case is not yet decided. A movement is contemplated to annex Delaware and Maryland to Judge Baldwin's Circuit and make a Circuit in the West for the Judge now to be appointed. If we could get rid of Mr. Taney on this ground, well and good; if not, it will be a close vote." *Letters of Daniel Webster* (1902), ed. by C. H. Van Tyne.

[3] Van Buren had written to Jackson, Aug. 7, 1834, suggesting that the appointment of a successor to Judge Johnson be postponed in order to see if Congress would not remodel the Circuit system so as to embrace the six Western and Southwestern States. "The wonder is that they have submitted to it so quietly," he said. "Neither party has hitherto been willing to incur the responsibility of increasing the Judges, or both are unwilling to leave to its adversary the appointment of new ones. It is to one or both of these causes that this unequal and unjust state of things has been allowed to continue." See also letter of Van Buren to Jackson, Nov. 5, 1834, again urging that the Circuit system be changed; that no new Judges be created, but that Maryland be thrown into the Virginia Circuit and Johnson's and Duval's Circuits be divided among the six Southwestern and Western States. *Van Buren Papers MSS*.

Circuit, Maryland and Delaware, with the Third Circuit which then consisted of New Jersey and Pennsylvania. As Judge Baldwin represented on the Court the proposed consolidated Circuit, the possibility of Taney's confirmation would be automatically disposed of. "The great and serious obstacle," said Senator Frelinghuysen, "which has stood in the way of the claims of the West has been the difficulties and dangers of enlarging the Court to the number that was desired. It was a well-founded apprehension that such enlargement would impair the energy and moral influence of the Court. A door is now opened by which all these dangers are avoided." President Jackson's friends in the Senate, particularly Benton of Missouri, Buchanan of Pennsylvania and Bibb of Kentucky, opposed the project, and advocated a bill providing for two new Judges and two new Western Circuits. A single Western Circuit composed of six States, said Benton, would be a "perfect monstrosity . . . which extended from the Gulf of Mexico to Lake Michigan, from the torrid to the frigid zone"; he said that he did not know "how the Judge was to be shot from one end of the Circuit to the other"; he thought that we ought to wait "till we have arrived at a greater art in aerial navigation" or "perhaps the Judge might in his journeys south be transported by one of those flights of wild geese which periodically emigrate from the North, if he could manage to have his car attached to them." The bill finally passed the Senate, abolishing the Fourth Circuit and providing one new Judge of the Supreme Court and two new Western Circuits. In the House, however, Jackson's friends rallied, and after arguing that the bill was simply intended "to destroy one of the worthy citizens of Maryland", "to relieve the Senate of a responsibility imposed upon them by the Constitution", "to affect injuriously the interests of Maryland and to crush one of her most valued citizens", they succeeded in defeating it.[1]

Taney's nomination being thus forced to a vote, it was taken up by the Senate on the last day of the session and was rejected.[2] "The Senate, which has been for the last four years but a council of war in which three disappointed Presidential aspirants have united their influence and abilities in devising schemes to break down the Administration, maintained its savage temper to the last," said the *Globe*. And so incensed was President Jackson at his defeat that, though he was in the Capitol at the time, he refused to make another nomination. It was even stated in a contemporary newspaper that when, on the night of March 3, the Clerk of the Senate "announced to the President the rejection of Mr. Taney, he replied that it was past twelve o'clock and he would receive no message from the damned scoundrels." [3]

At the 1835 Term of the Court, while Taney's nomination was pending, little business of importance was transacted, and Judge Story wrote, March 2: "We are approaching the close of the session of the

---

[1] See *23d Cong., 2d Sess.*, Jan. 15, Feb. 6, 11, 23, 24, 25, March 3, 1835. The *United States Telegraph* said, March 6, 1835: "This bill has been claimed as an act of justice to the West and Southwestern States. It was urged by Mr. Adams and then defeated only because the majority was unwilling to trust him with the nomination of Judges. It was again urged by General Jackson and again defeated for the same reason; and now an occasion having arisen whereby the system may be extended by merging the Fourth Circuit and adding another Judge, reluctant as the opponents of the Administration were to place the power of filling that body in the hands of the present President, they were induced to yield to the just demands of this long neglected section, and the Judiciary bill was passed by a vote of 31 to 5. It, too, was permitted to sleep the sleep of death. And why? Because the nomination of Roger B. Taney was superceded by it."

[2] The Senate voted indefinite postponement of the nomination, March 3, 1835, by the close vote of 24 to 21.

[3] *Washington Globe*, March 5, 1835; *National Intelligencer*, March 5, 10, 1835; *United States Telegraph*, Jan. 30, 1836, quoting letters from "The Spy in Washington" in the *New York Courier*, Jan. 16, 21, 1836.

Court and have not had any very interesting business before us, though the arguments have been long and intricate; but we have now a case from Florida, involving a claim for one million, two hundred and fifty thousand acres of land, which has been under argument eight days, and will probably occupy five more. Yet I firmly believe that it ought not to have occupied one third of the time, to have developed all the merits. . . . But this is the very region of words; and Americans, I fear, have a natural propensity to substitute them for things." [1]

This was the last Term at which Chief Justice Marshall was destined to preside. "He still possesses his intellectual powers in very high vigor," wrote Story, March 2, "but his physical strength is manifestly on the decline . . . what a gloom will be spread over the Nation when he is gone! His place will not, nay, it cannot be supplied." To the Reporter, Richard Peters, Story wrote, June 19, of the "very melancholy intelligence respecting the Chief Justice's health. . . . Great, good and excellent man! I perceive we must soon, very soon, part with him forever. . . . I shall never see his like again. His gentleness, his affectionateness, his glorious virtues, his unblemished life, his exalted talents, leave him without a rival or a peer." [2] Within a few months after the Court adjourned, it became evident that the Chief Justice was rapidly failing;

[1] The case to which Story referred was *Mitchel* v. *United States,* 9 Pet. 711, docketed in 1831 and argued at this Term by White and Berrien against Attorney-General Butler. It was extraordinary, not only for the immense tract of land in litigation, but also for the very dubious character of the land claim involved — being a purchase from the Seminole Indians in Florida by an English trading firm, claimed to have been authorized by Spanish officials in lieu of compensation for losses incurred for, and services rendered to the Spanish Crown. In this case again, the Court decided against the Government, solving all doubts in favor of the claimant, and again holding that the right of the Spanish officials to make or assent to the grant would be presumed.

[2] *Story,* II, 192, 199.

and a discussion arose in the newspapers as to his possible successor. For several years past, the name of Daniel Webster had been everywhere in the public mind as the fitting candidate for the place. In 1833, a Washington correspondent had written: "Rumor says that Daniel Webster, who, in my opinion, is decidedly the greatest man in the Nation, is considered somewhat in the way of the President's candidate for the succession, and that in consequence he is to be provided for. He will not stoop to ask for anything, and it is known that nothing but the most exalted station would be considered worthy his acceptance. Under these circumstances, Chief Justice Marshall has intimated his willingness to resign, provided he can be assured that Mr. Webster will succeed him. The President is willing to give such assurance, but Mr. Webster declines entering into any arrangement on the subject. He will no doubt accept, but he declines committing himself on a subject which might give his contemplated course the appearance of being the result of a bargain." [1] In the same year a close friend of Webster wrote to him:

I have no doubt you wish to render the greatest possible services to your country within your power, and might you not contribute more towards perpetuating our free institutions on the bench of the Supreme Court, than it would be possible for you to do in the Executive Chair? What President has done as much for his country as John Marshall has, in the station he has occupied? And who has secured for himself a more imperishable fame? So long as the Judiciary shall remain unpolluted, and shall possess intelligence, the citadel will be defended against the machinations of the Executive, or the sudden convulsions of the people.

[1] *New York Courier,* Feb. 8, 1833; the *United States Telegraph,* Feb. 8, 1833, quoted the *United States Gazette* as to the "whisper that Webster is to be Chief Justice." *Webster Papers MSS,* letter of E. Whittlesey, Sept. 14, 1833; *Van Buren Papers MSS,* letter of Benton, June 7, 1835.

It is to preserve the sheet-anchor of our hope, against the withering influence of New York politics that I am opposed to Mr. Van Buren. I do not wish to see Silas Wright or Lot Clark occupying Judge Marshall's seat, nor to see their nakedness covered by his gown. You may smile at my suggestion that Silas Wright or Lot Clark, by any possibility, would be placed by any person on the bench of the Supreme Court of the United States. If to sustain the party, the appointment of either should be necessary, it would be made; and so great is the power of the New York party discipline, that if the Executive should think proper to elevate either of the persons named, from personal considerations, or personal friendship, he would be justified by acclamation.

Early in the year 1835, Senator Thomas H. Benton began to be frequently mentioned as a probable nominee for the position; but Benton himself disclaimed his candidacy, and writing on June 7, to Van Buren, he said: "I see that Walsh and some others are tormenting themselves with a story of their own invention that I am to succeed Ch. Justice Marshall when death makes a vacancy. Now, my dear sir, these fellows are no more able to comprehend me than old hack lawyers, according to Burke, are able to comprehend the policy of an empire, and that was no more than a rabbit, which breeds twelve times a year, could comprehend the gestation of an elephant, which carries two years. So of these fellows and me. Dying for small offices themselves, they cannot understand that I can refuse all, even the Chief Justiceship of the Supreme Court; for, rest assured, that I should not take it, if it was offered to me. Taney is my favorite for that place, and P. P. Barbour next. . . . The Chief Justice ought to resign. The elevation of the station requires that a man should descend from it with grace and dignity, instead of hanging on until he tumbles off."

On July 6, 1835, the fears of the country were fatally realized, for on that day John Marshall died in Philadelphia, at the age of eighty and after thirty-four years' service on the Bench. The sorrow which spread throughout the land was almost universal, shared by lawyers and laymen alike, and the warm tributes which were paid to the dead Chief Justice were well depicted by a Philadelphia paper as follows: "As the intelligence of the death of the late Chief Justice extends throughout the Union, fresh testimonials are everywhere afforded of the almost universal veneration in which his illustrious character is held, as well as of the grief which is experienced at the loss sustained by the Nation in his decease. A nearly unanimous chorus of fervent eulogy and heartfelt regret is resounding on every side. The journals of all kinds, with but one or two exceptions, utter the same language of reverence; and meetings, without distinction of party, are everywhere assembled, breathing the same admirable spirit. All this speaks well for the country. It shows that however pernicious may have been the operation of faction and other causes upon the practice, it has not yet destroyed the knowledge of what is right in the land." [1]

Though the greatness of his work in the Court, and of its influence in building up a strong Union, had not at that time been as fully appreciated as it has in subsequent years, nevertheless, many of his contemporaries had already paid high tribute to his powers. His opinions on the construction of the Constitution, wrote Jeremiah Mason to Story in 1828, "constitute the stronghold for the Chief Justice's fame, and must sustain it while the Constitution of the country remains. . . . They have done vastly more for the stability

[1] *National Gazette*, July 25, 1835.

and permanency of our system of government than the present generation is aware of. The principles involved in those decisions are constantly developing themselves with increased importance. If our Constitutions ever get to definite and well-settled constructions, it must be chiefly effected by judicial tribunals. . . . Hence the vast importance that the early decisions of the Supreme Court should be rested on principles that can never be shaken." And in 1833, Mason had said: "If John Marshall had not been Chief Justice of the United States, the Union would have fallen to pieces before the General Government had got well under way. . . . John Marshall has saved the Union, if it is saved." [1]

Amidst the general tributes of respect, praise and grief which appeared in the newspapers of the country, Democratic and Whig alike, there were, however, a number of Democratic papers of the radical type which hailed the opportunity now presented for the appointment of a new Chief Justice.[2] The *New York Evening Post*, edited by the able journalist, William Leggett, in several long editorials expressed its relief at the removal of the Chief Justice from the Bench, stating its position to be that while "we lament the death of a good and exemplary man, we cannot grieve that the cause of aristocracy has lost one of its chief supporters." Its first editorial said :

Judge Marshall was a man of very considerable talents and acquirements and great amiableness of private character. His political doctrines unfortunately were of the ultra-federal or aristocratic kind. He was one of those, who, with Hamilton, distrusted the virtue and intelligence of the people, and was in favor of a strong and vigorous General Government

---

[1] *Mason*, 313, letters of Feb. 16, 1828; *ibid.*, 172–173. See also an account of Marshall's work in *North American Review* (Jan., 1836), XLII.

[2] *New York Evening Post*, July 8, 10, 13, 28, 1835; *Collection of the Political Writings of William Leggett* (1840), by Theodore Sedgwick, Jr.

at the expense of the rights of the States and of the people.
His judicial decisions of all questions involving political
principles have been uniformly on the side of implied powers
and a free construction of the Constitution. That he was
sincere in these views, we do not express a doubt, nor that
he truly loved his country; but that he has been, all his
life long, a stumbling block and impediment in the way of
democratick principles, no one can deny; and his situation,
therefore, at the head of an important tribunal, constituted
in utter defiance of the very first principles of democracy,
has always been to us, as we have before frankly stated, an
occasion of lively regret. That he is at length removed
from that station is a source of satisfaction, while at the
same time we trust we entertain a proper sentiment for the
death of a good and exemplary man."

Two days later, in answer to attacks, it further explained
its sentiments as follows:

That a man so aristocratick in his views on Government as
John Marshall should occupy a place where his opinions
could be, and were, exercised so prejudicially to the cause of
democratick principles, was necessarily an occasion of deep
regret to us. We should have been pleased had he been
removed long ago, and are pleased that he is removed at
last. But we never desired that he should be removed by
death; and now that he is taken away in ripe old age, we
regret his demise as that of an eminent and exemplary man;
at the same time we view the circumstance, politically, as
auspicious to the cause of those great principles of democratick government which furnish, in our judgment, the only
stable foundation for the equal rights of mankind.

The sentiments, so expressed, received violent condemnation, especially from the leading Whig papers. The
New York Courier said, July 17: "The brutality of
the *Evening Post* is meeting bitter rebuke from every
quarter of the Union where its infamous notice of the
death of Chief Justice Marshall has reached"; and
it spoke of the editor as in an "insulated position of
infamy", and termed the article "an atrocious out-

pouring of partisan venom", "the ravings of a mad man", "the gloating over the melancholy event as a most important and desirable democratic triumph." The *National Gazette* of July 11, replying to the arguments of the *Post*, asked: "What has democracy or federalism or any other party appellation to do with the tribunal of justice? What discrimination of the kind has the divinity ever been known to make among those who appear before her judgment seat? Nothing shows better the spirit by which the adversaries of the Chief Justice are actuated than this endeavor to breathe the polluted breath of party upon the spotless ermine."

In explanation of its position, the *Post* stated, in a long editorial on July 28, that its views had been misunderstood; that it joined in the expressions of general respect and regard and it noted with pleasure the public and spontaneous demonstrations of honor for Marshall's character and talent; nevertheless, it said:

We cannot so far lose sight of those great principles of government which we consider essential to the permanent prosperity of man as to neglect the occasion offered by the death of Judge Marshall to express our satisfaction that the enormous powers of the supreme tribunal of the country will no longer be exercised by one whose cardinal maxim in politics inculcated distrust of popular intelligence and virtue, and whose constant object in the decision of all constitutional questions was to strengthen government at the expense of the people's rights. The hackneyed phrase *de mortuis nil nisi bonum* must be of comprehensive meaning indeed, if it is intended that the grave shall effectually shelter the theoretic opinion and official conduct of men from animadversion as well as the foibles and offences of their private lives. . . . Paramount consideration seemed to us to demand that in recording the death of Judge Marshall and joining our voice to that of general eulogy on his clear and venerable name, we should at the same time record our rooted hostility to the political principles he maintained and for the advancement of which he was able to do so much in his great office. . . . The articles of his creed if carried into practice would prove destructive of the great principle of human liberty and compel the many to yield obedience to the few. . . . Of Judge Marshall's spotless purity of life, of his many estimable qualities of heart and of the powers of his mind, we record our hearty tribute of admiration. But sincerely believing that the principles of democracy are identical with the principles of human liberty, we cannot but experience joy that the chief place in the supreme tribunal of the Union will no longer be filled by a man whose political doctrines led him always to pronounce such decision of constitutional questions as was calculated to strengthen government at the expense of the people. We lament the death of a good and exemplary man but we cannot grieve that the cause of aristocracy has lost one of its chief supports.

In subsequent issues, the *Post* referred to the "floodgates of vulgar abuse" which had been opened upon it, the "bitterness and malignity" with which it had been answered, the terms which had been applied to it of "fiends", "hyenas", "vampires", "miserable maniac", "atrocious outpouring of partisan venom", "ruffianism rankling in his own ruffian breast." Finally, answering an article in the *New York American*, which had pointed out that when Marshall stood out against the monopoly in the steamboat case of *Gibbons* v. *Ogden*, he could hardly be termed "aristocratick", and which had asked for "the definition of aristocracy and democracy as applied to a tribunal of law", the *Post* stated its creed as follows: "That tribunal is aristocratick which in its decisions of constitutional questions seeks to give powers by implication to the General Government at the expense of the reserved rights of the people; and that tribunal is democratick which keeps constantly in mind that the powers not delegated to the United

States by the Constitution nor prohibited by it to the States are reserved to the States respectively or to the people." [1] Since the statement has been frequently made that the *Post* and the *Washington Globe* were the only papers which expressed unfavorable views of Marshall at the time of his death [2] it may be noted that these views were entertained by a number of other papers in States where Marshall's constitutional doctrines had long been obnoxious. Thus a leading Ohio paper said that although it respected his talents, his patriotism and purity of motives, and was willing to say "Peace to his ashes!" it wished to express its decided dissent from his doctrines on the Constitution; for "they were of the ultra-federal cast and have had a greater tendency to warp that great charter of our rights than the opinions of any other man, owing to the ability and consistency with which they were advanced." Another Ohio paper said that "with all his virtues, with all his learning and his patriotism . . . his elevation to and long continuance in the office of Chief Justice was an injury to our institutions . . . and it may safely be affirmed that the decisions of John Marshall on the Bench have done more to consolidate this government and destroy the rights of the States than all the wild legislation of Congress." A South Carolina paper said that while his memory was revered and cherished for his learning, ability and ardent attachment to his country, "yet a respectful difference of opinion upon the fundamental principles of government from those

[1] *New York Evening Post*, July 29, Aug. 3, 7, 1835.

[2] *Niles Register* said editorially, referring to the *Post* editorials, that it was "happy to say it is the only thing of the sort that we have seen." The *National Intelligencer*, Aug. 15, 22, 1835, spoke of the attack on Marshall in the *Washington Globe*, as a "single discordant note." The *New York Courier* said July 17: "We have not looked into a paper save the *Post* that has not done full justice to his high character and lamented his death as a public calamity — Whig or Tory, Van Buren paper, Webster paper or White paper, all parties and all shades of parties have spoken in unison."

expressed by him will be entertained by a great majority of the American people." A North Carolina paper said that Marshall had "a spirit of hostility and inflexible opposition to Democracy." A Maine paper said that Marshall's removal was "a source of satisfaction", as he was kept in place by those "opposed in every way to Democratick principles." [1]

As against these comparatively few instances of failure to lament the death of the Chief Justice, there may be set two remarkable tributes from opponents. "An old Democrat of '98 and one who had been opposed to the political views of Judge Marshall all his lifetime remarked that there had been but one solitary instance, during his whole term of thirty-four years judicial service, in which the impartiality of the Judge had been impugned — the Burr trial." [2] And Andrew Jackson, to whom the constitutional doctrines of the Chief Justice represented all that was abhorrent politically, wrote to a committee who had invited him to be present at an address to be delivered by Horace Binney in memory of Marshall : [3]

I acknowledge with much satisfaction the receipt of your note of the 15th inst.; inviting me to hear the eulogy which Mr. Binney, at the request of the Select and Common Councils of the city of Philadelphia, is to pronounce on the life and character of the late Chief Justice of the United States. Having set a high value upon the learning, talents and patriotism of Judge Marshall, and upon the good he has done his country in one of its most exalted and responsible offices, I have been gratified at seeing that sentiments equally favorable have been cherished generally by his fellow citizens, and that there has been no disposition, even with those who dissent from some of his expositions of our constitutional

[1] See *Ohio Patriot; Western Hemisphere* (Columbus, Ohio); *Columbia Sentinel* (S. C.); *Fayetteville Green Mountain Democrat* (N. C.); *Ellsworth Patriot* (Me.), quoted in *New York Evening Post*, July 22, 23, 24, Aug. 15, 18, 1835.

[2] *New York Courier*, July 9, 1835.

[3] *Jackson Papers MSS*, letter of Sept. 18, 1835.

law (of whom it is perhaps proper that I should say I am one), to withhold from his memory the highest tribute of respect.   In the revolutionary struggles for our National independence, and particularly in the subsequent discussions which established the forms and settled the practice of our system of Government, the opinions of John Marshall were expressed with the energy and clearness which were peculiar to his strong mind, and gave him a rank amongst the greatest men of his age which he fully sustained on the bench of the Supreme Court.   With these views of Judge Marshall's character, it is a source of regret that my public duties will not allow me to be one of Mr. Binney's auditors on the interesting occasion to which you have been pleased to invite me.

"Chief Justice Marshall was the growth of a century," said Story.   "Providence grants such men to the human family only on great occasions to accomplish its own great end.   Such men are found only when our need is the greatest." [1]   "His proudest epitaph may be written in a single line — 'Here lies the expounder of the Constitution.'" [2]   But while it is impossible to exaggerate Marshall's service to his country in vitalizing the Constitution and making it a stronger bond of Union, it must be admitted that the time had arrived when

[1] *Life of Rutherford Birchard Hayes* (1914), by Charles R. Williams, diary entry, Sept. 16, 1843.

[2] Between 1801 and 1835, there were sixty-two decisions involving constitutional questions in thirty-six of which Marshall wrote the opinion; in twenty-three of which cases, there was no dissent.   In the remaining twenty-six constitutional cases, Story wrote the opinion in eleven, Johnson six, Washington five, Paterson, Cushing, Baldwin and Thompson in one each.   Of a total of one thousand two hundred fifteen cases during that period, in ninety-four, no opinions were filed; in fifteen, the decision was by the Court; and in the remaining one thousand one hundred six cases, Marshall delivered the opinion in five hundred nineteen, and he filed a dissent in only nine cases.

In the same period there were one hundred ninety-five cases involving questions of international law or in some way affecting international relations.   In eighty of these, the opinion was delivered by Marshall, in thirty by Story; in twenty-eight by Johnson, in nineteen by Washington, in fourteen by Livingston, in five by Thompson, and one each by Baldwin, Cushing and Duval, and in eight "by the Court."   *Constitutional Development in the United States as Influenced by Chief Justice Marshall* (1889), by Henry Hitchcock; *Address* by John Bassett Moore, before the Delaware Bar Association, Feb. 5, 1901.

a change in the leadership of the Court was possibly desirable. For at least thirty-one out of his thirty-five years as Chief Justice, Marshall had been out of sympathy with the political views predominant among the people, and inspiring the statesmen at the head of the Government. Moreover, he had never been a profound lawyer deeply grounded in the common law; and he had possessed a highly conservative nature and mental attitude. In view of the changes and reforms which were now taking place in the economic and social conditions, and the liberalization of political sentiment and processes which was marking a new era in the country's development, he was clearly out of touch with the temper of the times and less fitted to deal with the new problems of the day than with the great constitutional questions of the past. This phase of the situation must be regarded, in any correct appraisal of the struggle which ensued over the appointment of Marshall's successor.[1]

[1] See especially *John Marshall* (1919), by Edward S. Corwin, presenting a clear-sighted and unconventional view of Marshall's character, work and opinions.

CHAPTER TWENTY-ONE

CHIEF JUSTICE TANEY AND WHIG PESSIMISM

1835-1837

The appointment of Marshall's successor was looked forward to with painful interest by the legal profession and by the country at large. The Democrats were hopeful of the appointment of a Chief Justice who would curb what they termed the policy of prostration of the States. "Nearly every State of the Union," said the *Democratic Review*, "had been brought up for sentence . . . passed through the Caudine Forks of a subjugation which has more than revived the suability of States. Beginning with Madison's case, there are near forty of these fulminations, from 1803 to 1834 . . . a great fabric of judicial architecture stupendous as the pyramids, and as inexplicable." [1] The Whigs gravely feared that President Jackson's choice would be a purely political one, and they were despondent of the future, "if the appointment be a party appointment — if the Chief Justiceship too is to be deemed one of the spoils which the ravenous clutches of party may seize and appropriate to its sordid purposes." "Well may the country look forward with absorbing interest to the choice of Judge Marshall's successor," said a prominent Whig paper, "for on it, we conscientiously believe depends the character, in a great degree, of its future destinies." Another Whig organ said: "The peculiar position of our public affairs and the crisis which is evidently approaching, involving the existence of our

[1] *Democratic Review* (Jan., 1838), I, 165.

institutions, renders this one of the most important and most to be regretted deaths which has occurred since the decease of Washington. His identity with the Supreme Court of the United States, and the disreputable assaults now making upon that sheet-anchor of our Government, for party purposes, create a new era in affairs which may result most calamitously for the country." Another said: "In reference to the party principles of the man who should be elevated to the Supreme Bench, all that need be remarked is, that the instant the question is asked and acted upon in the selection of an individual for that station — 'will his decisions be on the Democratic or on the Federal or on any other side?' instead of — 'Is he honest, is he capable?' that instant the majesty and utility of that great tribunal are destroyed; that instant, instead of being a safeguard of our rights and liberties, it becomes a party engine which may be wielded with tremendous irresistible power for their subversion. No one who could prefer to such a man as Judge Marshall . . . any other person, because he is a Democrat or a Federalist or an Administration or Opposition man, can be a sincere, or at least, a wise lover of the republic." [1]

John Quincy Adams wrote in his diary a characteristically pungent review of the situation of the Court: [2]

He has held this appointment thirty five years. It was the last act of my father's administration, and one of the most important services rendered by him to his country. All constitutional governments are flexible things; and as the Supreme Judicial Court is the tribunal of last resort for the construction of the Constitution and the laws, the

[1] *National Intelligencer*, July 16, 1835; *New York Courier*, July 8, 1835; *National Gazette*, July 13, 1835; *New York Daily Advertiser*, July 8, 25, 27, 1835.
[2] *J. Q. Adams*, IX, July 10, Aug. 10, 1835.

office of Chief Justice of that Court is a station of the highest trust, of the deepest responsibility, and of influence far more extensive than that of the President of the United States. The Associate Judges from the time of his appointment have generally been taken from the Democratic or Jeffersonian party. Not one of them, excepting Story, has been a man of great ability. Several of them have been men of strong prejudices, warm passions, and contracted minds; one of them, occasionally insane.[1] Marshall, by the ascendency of his genius, by the amenity of his deportment, and by the imperturbable command of his temper, has given a permanent and systematic character to the decisions of the Court, and settled many great constitutional questions favorably to the continuance of the Union. Marshall has cemented the Union which the crafty and quixotic democracy of Jefferson had a perpetual tendency to dissolve. Jefferson hated and dreaded him. . . . It is much to be feared that a successor will be appointed of a very different character. The President of the United States now in office, has already appointed three Judges of the Supreme Court; with the next appointment, he will have constituted the Chief Justice and a majority of the Court. He has not yet made one good appointment. His Chief Justice will be no better than the rest.

Some Whigs even went so far as to assert that the accession of a Democrat to the Chief Justiceship meant the destruction of the Constitution. "At no time," said a New York paper, "could such a melancholy event have been more unfortunate for this country, at a period when legal talent and acquirement are treated by the party in power with the utmost contempt, and ignorance not only considered a virtue, but a stepping to office and favour. The friends of constitutional liberty will look upon the decease of Judge Marshall as one of the greatest calamities that could

---

[1] Marshall wrote to Story, Dec. 25, 1832, referring to Baldwin's affliction; and Webster wrote, Dec. 27, that Baldwin had recently manifested an alienation of mind.

befall the Nation. He was one of the last pillars of the Constitution, which had withstood the ravages of the Goths and Vandals; and the event will be hailed by them secretly as a new triumph to their cause, while it will be a source of deep sorrow to every true friend of his country." Another New York paper even doubted the existence of any Democratic lawyer fit to succeed Marshall: "The liberties of a great people are put in peril by the departure of the most eminent of their conservators — the man who of all others was best calculated to fill the office, which, of all others, was most important, in its power of giving perpetuity to institutions threatened with subversion by other departments of the Government. We mourn not merely the loss of a great and good man, but we tremble in the contemplation of the risque we run in his successor. We know that the prerogative of nomination, possibly that of appointment, is in bad hands, and we have everything to apprehend from its weak or wicked exercise. We do not say that it would be impossible to find a successor capable of filling Judge Marshall's place among his surviving country men; but no unprejudiced American citizen will disagree with us when we say that it not only is not possible to find a suitable successor to that great man and upright Judge among those from which the present National Executive will make the selection; but the liveliest alarm must be felt lest the President shall so select as to endanger the very existence of our liberties. Heaven grant that our well-grounded apprehension may be disappointed!"[1] A Whig correspondent wrote from Washington: "The Executive and his Cabinet . . . consider the late Chief Justice as the most formidable obstacle which they were likely to encounter in the pursuit of

---

[1] *New York Daily Advertiser*, July 8, 27, 1835; *New York Courier*, July 9, 1835.

their great scheme of reform. . . . The conspirators now expect, from the reform to be worked in the Supreme Court, to carry on their future assaults on the Constitution under the cover of law. . . . Our Constitution is in imminent danger. It guarantees too securely the Legislative and Judicial checks on the Executive, to suit the temper and views of the present Administration."

Such apprehensions and such political bias were almost humorous; but the supercilious attitude toward the capacity of those lawyers who belonged to the Democratic Party was highly characteristic of the heated partisanship of the times. Fair or impartial consideration of anything which President Jackson might do was not to be expected. There had been nothing, however, in the record of Jackson's previous appointments to the Bench which warranted any such pessimistic apprehensions. McLean, Baldwin, Wayne and Barbour had all been men of high personal character and of eminent legal ability, and as jurists of standing they compared exceedingly favorably with the appointment of Associate Justices made by Washington or Adams. It was undoubtedly true that Jackson would consider only the appointment of a Democrat to fill the vacancy in the position of Chief Justice; and it was natural that he should desire a Democrat in sympathy with his constitutional views, just as President Adams had originally appointed Marshall as a strong Federalist. It by no means followed, as the Whigs seemed to assume, that no consideration should be given to the views of the appointee on the subject of politics, taking politics in its highest and philosophic sense as involving the theories of human rights and the principles of government. Political partisanship should of course be no qualification; but, as a leading paper in the South said:[1] "It would be indeed strange if, in selecting the members of so august a tribunal, no weight should be attached to the views entertained by its members of the Constitution, or their acquirements in the science of politics in its relations to the form of government under which we live. We can imagine the horror with which the annunciation would be received throughout the country of the elevation of a thorough Nullifier, however able and accomplished and learned, to the chief place in the interpretation of the Constitution. Yet the exclusion of a Nullifier would be the admission of a political, or it may in this sense be called, a party test, and it is one which the country will approve." The Democratic papers, in fact, demanded that a man should be selected "whose principles, profession and practice afford a sure guarantee that on all questions involving the power of the government, he will strictly adhere to the letter of the Constitution and faithfully abide by the stern dictates of popular opinion", — a man who would "keep pace with the steady progress of publick liberty and popular reform." They asserted that the Whig papers, in expressing a fear lest Marshall's successor should be "a party man", were indulging in "hypocritical cant." "There are none so base as to treat with disrespect the memory of the venerable Chief Justice; but when the Whigs, for party purposes, attempt to draw around his judicial decisions a sacredness not warranted, compare his acts with those of the administration of General Jackson, and represent him as frequently stepping between 'the bleeding Constitu-

[1] *Mobile Register*, quoted in *Washington Globe*, Aug. 13, 1835. The *New York Evening Post*, July 29, 1835, quoted the *Baltimore Republican* as saying that the Chief Justice was, throughout life, a party man, appointed as a Federalist by a Federalist: "Away then with the pretence that a man's belonging to a party, particularly when that party is in the majority, is a sound objection to his appointment to the Bench."

tion and usurpations of Jackson', mourn over his death because it will devolve upon General Jackson to nominate a successor, it becomes necessary that they should be met and their assertions canvassed." "The seat of Chief Justice ought to be filled by a man who has given evidence to the people of firmness and courage in the practice of Democratick principles." "We hope the President will justify the hopes of the country and give a sane jurist, an orthodox constitutional lawyer and an eminent citizen." "There is no doubt that as yet the Democratick tendencies of the Nation have never yet been fairly represented in that tribunal. It has been the stronghold of the antiquated, strong-government, Federal ideas, which, in every other branch of the Government, have been long since discarded." [1]

No one of the Judges on the Supreme Bench seemed to be a possible choice. Judge Story (whom most lawyers considered the logical successor of Marshall) would certainly be unacceptable to the President; and Story himself realized this, for he wrote to friends: "As to the Chief Justice's successor, I do not even venture to hazard an opinion, or even a conjecture. I shall await events. Whoever succeeds him will have a most painful and discouraging duty. He will follow a man who cannot be equalled, and all the public will see, or think they see, the difference. A situation which provokes a comparison so constant and so discouraging is not enviable. Let me only add, for your eye, lest there be some idle conjecture elsewhere, that I have never for a moment imagined that I should be thought of. So that I am equally beyond hope or anxiety.". . . "I take it for granted that all of us who are on the Bench

---

[1] See *Fayettesville Green Mountain Democrat; Columbus Centinel; Mobile Register; Baltimore Republican,* quoted in *New York Evening Post,* July, August, 1835, *passim,* Nov. 10, 1835.

are *hors du combat.*" [1]   Judge McLean also, while originally appointed by Jackson, seemed to the Democrats
to share too largely in Marshall's views of the Constitution, though some papers strongly urged his appointment. The names of many distinguished lawyers were mentioned in the newspapers as possible
appointees : [2] Henry St. George Tucker (President of
the Court of Appeals of Virginia) ; Philip P. Barbour
of Virginia ; William Gaston (Chief Justice of the Supreme Court of North Carolina) ; [3] Edward Livingston
and Benjamin F. Butler of New York ; Horace Binney
of Pennsylvania ; Thomas H. Benton of Missouri [4] and
Louis McLane of Delaware.[5] Many papers, not only
in the North but in the South, strongly advocated the

[1] *Story*, II, 200, 208, letter to Peters, July 24, 1835; to McLean, Oct. 12, 1835.
See also *Andrew Jackson and His Collision with Judges and Lawyers*, by Seymour
D. Thompson, *Amer. Law Rev.*, XXI. Judge Story was regarded with considerable
bitterness by Democratic Party leaders, and a newspaper at this time (*Fayettesville
Green Mountain Democrat*) termed him "the contemptible apostate, Story, arrogant
and supercilious."

[2] *Niles Register*, XLIX, Nov. 7, 1835; *New York Evening Post*, Aug. 15, 1835,
quoting the *Baltimore Republican* as copying from the *Mobile Register*, "what
we consider the very best article on Marshall's successor", and saying that
Livingston, McLane, Taney, Benton and Webster were suggested; see also
Washington Globe, Aug. 13, 1835.

[3] The *New York Courier*, July 22, 1835, said as to Gaston : "No possible chance
for the country under its present misrule to be blessed with such a man upon the
Supreme Bench. He is too pure a patriot and too good a man, and possesses too
much fitness for the station, to be thought of for a moment at the White House. . . .
He has never cursed his old acquaintances, and truckled to the caprices of the poor
old man who thinks he is President of the United States, but who is really the mere
puppet of Amos Kendall and Mr. Van Buren."

[4] The *Trenton True American* said, July 11, 1835 : "Col. Benton having been
spoken of as the probable successor of the late Chief Justice, Marshall, the *Globe*
asserts positively that the Col. would not accept, should the office be tendered him.
The people cannot spare Benton from the Senate so long as the Bank is in the field,
but Livingston for Chief Justice would be highly acceptable"; and, July 18,
it said that the suggestion of Livingston "meets with general approbation from
Democratic Journals."

[5] See *Richmond Enquirer*, July 14, 1835, quoting various papers. An interesting story is told in James A. Hamilton's *Reminiscences* (1869), 130, to the
effect that in 1829 Jackson promised to appoint Louis McLane to any vacancy
caused by Duval's retirement; McLane was Minister to England in 1835,
and was aggrieved at Jackson's failure to appoint him Chief Justice. This is
fully substantiated in *Autobiography of Martin Van Buren*, *Amer. Hist. Ass. Rep.*
(1918), II.

appointment of Daniel Webster,[1] but the Democrats as a rule opposed Webster because of his ultra-Federal principles. "These are too much in unison with the decisions of the Supreme Court itself, to command the support of the Republican party," said the *Richmond Enquirer.* "The Court has done more to change the character of that instrument and to shape, as it were, a new Constitution for us, than all the other departments of the Government put together. The President will nominate a Democratic Chief Justice, and thus, we hope, give some opportunity for the good old State-Rights doctrines of Virginia of '98–'99 to be heard and weighed on the Federal Bench. The very profound and brilliant abilities, with which they have been hitherto opposed in the Supreme Court, have only contributed to make us more anxious to bring back the ship to the Republican tack. We believe that Taney is a strong State-Rights man."[2] While President Jackson gave no definite intimation as to his choice, it became very generally understood that

---

[1] See *Alexandria Gazette* (Va.); *Charleston Courier* (S. C.); *Georgia Journal* referred to in *Richmond Enquirer,* July 14, 24, 28, Aug. 14, 1835; *Nashville Banner* (Tenn.), referred to in *New York Evening Post,* Aug. 22, 1835.

[2] The *Richmond Enquirer,* July 28, 1835, commented on the fact that while some Whig editors opposed Taney as a Roman Catholic, other Whig editors favored William Gaston who was also a Roman Catholic.

In the diary of John Quincy Adams, Jan. 29, 1829, there is a curious entry as to a suggestion that he might have appointed Daniel Webster as Marshall's successor, if Marshall had resigned during Adams' term: "Mr. Burnet, Senator from the State of Ohio, said he came to me on an unpleasant subject. He had a letter from Charles Hammond stating that Mr. Doddridge of Virginia had written to me that he (Mr. Burnet) had said that the elder Adams, by the appointment of John Marshall as Chief Justice, had entailed a curse upon the country, and that if I should have the opportunity to appoint Daniel Webster as Marshall's successor, it would be a still greater curse. He said there were not two men in the world for whom he had a greater veneration than for Chief Justice Marshall and Mr. Webster. I said Mr. Hammond had been misinformed. Mr. Doddridge, whom I scarcely knew, had written to me that he had heard Mr. Burnet had expressed disapprobation of the decisions of the Supreme Court of the United States with reference to questions involving the State authorities. He had not named Mr. Webster. Mr. Burnet said he had expressed the opinion that perhaps the decisions of the Supreme Court had sometimes encroached upon the State-Rights."

Roger Brooke Taney of Maryland was to be appointed.[1] No official announcement was made until December 28, 1835, when Jackson sent in to the Senate the name of Taney for Chief Justice, and at the same time appointed Philip P. Barbour of Virginia to fill the vacancy among the Associate Judges caused by Duval's resignation.[2] The Taney appointment was received with gloom and pessimism by the Whigs. "Judge Story thinks the Supreme Court is *gone*, and I think so too," wrote Webster.[3] The attack upon

[1] As early as July 11, 13, 1835, Taney's name was announced in the *Norfolk Herald;* see *New York Evening Post,* July 14, 15, 16, 1835, and *National Intelligencer,* July 15, 1835. As early as Dec. 12, 1835, the *National Gazette* said that: "It is stated from Washington, that Mr. Taney will certainly be nominated as Chief Justice to the Senate and Judge Tucker, Judge Barbour or Mr. Daniel in place of Judge Duval." The *New York Daily Advertiser,* Dec. 15, 1835, published the following bitter invective from its Washington correspondent, writing Dec. 11:

"The rumor that the famous Roger Brooke Taney will be nominated to fill the chair of Chief Justice vacated by the death of the lamented Marshall, gains strength every hour. If it is the will of the President, and who of his, or the partisans' of Van Buren, dare raise a finger against it — not one I am sure who are in power or dependent upon the party clan. No! not even that vandal horde who from the housetop at daybreak and at sunset proclaimed against the Federalism of Chief Justice Marshall. They can swallow Taney's Federalism, Jacksonism, Van Burenism, Johnsonism, and every ism which feeds them upon the loaves and fishes of office. The great and good Marshall was a Federalist, say they, and we could not support him. The notorious Taney is a Federalist, and this is recommendation to office — the purity of his past life, especially his political life, is the great lever which is to raise him to this exalted station — shame upon such inconsistency."

[2] As to the urgent demand in Virginia for Barbour's appointment, see letter of Dabney Carr to Martin Van Buren, Dec. 21, 1835. *Van Buren Papers MSS.*

[3] *Letters of Daniel Webster* (1902), ed. by C. H. Van Tyne; see other letters as follows: Dec. 23, 1835. ". . . No Chief Justice is yet nominated but it is expected Mr. Taney will be the man. The President has a party tomorrow eve — viz. card enclosed. . . . I have not been out — have invited no company — and occupy myself with common Congress matters or with some preparation for the Court — though in the Court, I have not a great deal to do this year and wish I had less." Dec. 28, 1835. "The President's party I forgot to mention. I was not present, but understand it was something quite new, and *went off* — as you New Yorkers say, very brilliantly. There was dancing in the East Room, a sumptuous supper in the dining room and so on." Jan. 10, 1836. "Judge Story arrived last evening in good health, but bad spirits. He thinks the Supreme Court is *gone* and I think so too; and almost everything is gone or seems rapidly going. We are in a state of some excitement about the French business. The President is warm and warlike. Mr. Van Buren more pacific. . . . Congress is not at all prepared for war, but no one knows what might be done if Gen'l. Jackson should sound a loud war note."

the appointment, however, was entirely political. The Whigs in general, and the adherents of the Bank of the United States in particular, could never forget or forgive Taney's action when Secretary of the Treasury in complying with Jackson's directions to remove the Government deposits from the Bank; and in Whig eyes anything which Jackson did was condemnable.[1] Taney is "unworthy of public confidence, a supple, cringing tool of power", said a New York paper.[2] Taney owes his appointment "to his latitudinarian doctrines as to the extent of the Executive power and to his vindication of the President's pet measure", said another New York paper, in a violent attack upon the appointment.[3] To these attacks, the Democrats replied, with equal political bias, that "all the venom of the Bank cabal, and the ambitious, electioneering rancor and influence of Whig Senators and the vile machinations" of the incongruous, Federal, Whig Party would be impotent to defeat the appointment; that the only objection which the Whigs could bring against Taney was "his proud honesty and independence and his want of subserviency to the United States Bank and other ' monied monsters '; but this is, in fact, one of his principal recommendations. Law-learning and superior talents may also be found among the prominent men of the Federal Whig party, but where is there one who can be safely trusted to hold the scales of Justice, when all the wealth of the country concentrated in the United States Bank and the Whig

[1] The *Washington Globe* said, Dec. 9, 1835 : "No man, we believe, ever had more falsehoods invented and propagated against him in a short space of time, than Mr. Taney has since he removed the deposits."

[2] *New York Courier*, Jan. 23, 1836; *New York American*, Jan. 14, 1836.

[3] To this, the *New York Evening Post*, July 16, 1835, said : "If Mr. Taney owes his appointment to his manly and patriotick conduct in seconding the great measures of the Executive in relation to the United States Bank, he owes it to a cause of which he may be justly proud."

party is placed on one scale and right and justice and the good of the country are its only opposing weight?" "He has shown by his firmness, independence, and disregard of his own personal benefit, by his sound judgment and pure patriotism, by his incorruptible integrity and purity of character, that he is eminently qualified, including his admitted great talents and legal knowledge, for the exalted station." "Mr. Taney is as sincere and thorough a Democrat as any in the country. He is not merely a Democrat according to party usages, he is not a loaf and fish Democrat, a *tutissimus ibis* Democrat; he is a sound, anti-monopoly Democrat. As a lawyer, even the *American* will hardly question his fitness for the office of Chief Justice, so far as legal talents and acquirements are concerned." [1]

In the calm light of history, it is now seen that the attacks upon Taney on political grounds had little reasonable basis; and as Judge Wayne said, after Taney's death, "the party contests of that day have passed away, with the admission of those who were engaged in them that his course was sincere and sustained with ability."

While a few Whig papers admitted that "as a lawyer, so far as regards his juridical abilities and acquirement, there could be no objection", and that he was "an able lawyer and profound civilian", [2] the Bar throughout the North, being largely Whig, entirely ignored Taney's eminent legal qualifications, and his brilliant legal career, during which he had shared with William Wirt the leadership of the Maryland Bar and had attained high rank at the Supreme Court Bar, both before and after his service as Attorney-General of the United States. "I believe it was

---

[1] *Boston Post*, Dec. 1, 15, 1835; *New York Evening Post*, July 16, 21, Aug. 12, 1835.

[2] *Columbian Centinel*, quoted in *Boston Post*, Dec. 1, 15, 1835.

then a general impression, in this part of the country, that he was neither a learned nor a profound lawyer," said ex-Judge Benjamin R. Curtis, at a meeting of the Boston Bar on Taney's death in 1864. "This was certainly a mistake. His mind was thoroughly imbued with the rules of the common law and of equity law; and when I first knew him, he was master of all that peculiar jurisprudence which it is the special province of the Courts of the United States to administer and apply. His skill in applying it was of the highest order. His power of subtle analysis exceeded that of any man I ever knew . . . in his case balanced and checked by excellent common sense and by great experience in practical business, both public and private. . . . It is certainly true, and I am happy to be able to bear direct testimony to it, that the surpassing ability of the Chief Justice, and all his great qualities of character and mind, were more fully and constantly exhibited in the consultation room, while presiding over and assisting the deliberation of his brethren, than the public knew or can ever justly estimate. There, his dignity, his love of order, his gentleness, his caution, his accuracy, his discrimination, were of incalculable importance. The real intrinsic character of the tribunal was greatly influenced by them, and always for the better."

For over two months and a half, the Senate struggled with the nomination, the Whig opposition being violently supported by the party organs.[1] "The nomination of Taney is made for the sole purpose of insulting and degrading the Senate," said a New York paper. "Should Mr. Taney now become Chief Justice 'by and with the advice of the Senate', the myrmidons of power will make the welkin ring with

[1] *New York Courier*, Jan. 21, 1836; *Boston Courier*, Jan. 4, 1836.

shouts of triumph that the President had now prostrated at his feet that branch of the Government which represented the States as States, that the Senate was no longer a refractory member of the Government, that General Jackson's will and pleasure was weal and woe to the individual or State that should dare to moot that point with him." And a leading Boston Whig paper said: "But if Mr. Barbour's appointment is extremely objectionable, what can be said of the appointment of Mr. Taney? The ready and most obsequious agent of the severest and most dangerous blow which has been given to our Constitution and law; before, rejected by the Senate for a trust far less critical and important, on account of his partisan servility; now, nominated as the Judicial High Priest of the nation! Will the Senate bow to such an insult? If they do, *then* no one can pity. But above all will they permit themselves and the Supreme Court of the United States to be prostrated at the same blow, in the depths of political pollution? To confirm this nomination would be, and would be considered, the general signal for defeat, dismay and despair. . . . If Mr. Taney be now confirmed, all will be lost."

It was stated on February 2, 1836, that the Senate was divided into twenty-two Administration and twenty-four Anti-Administration men, with two Senators doubtful. Shortly after this, John Tyler of Virginia resigned because of his unwillingness to support the Administration's Expunging Resolution; and his place was taken by William L. Rives who was favorable to Jackson's policies.[1] Finally, on March 15, Taney

[1] *National Gazette*, Feb. 2, 1836; on March 14, it said: "In consequence of Mr. Tyler's retiring, the Administration will probably be able to carry all its measures. If Roger B. Taney should now be appointed Chief Justice of the Supreme Court, who should be held responsible for the disgrace that would thereupon fall upon the Nation? Who, but John Tyler of Virginia? The man whc

was confirmed by a vote of twenty-nine to fifteen; but Calhoun, and Clay, Crittenden, Ewing, Southard, White and Webster[1] held out to the end against Jackson's nominee. The fight had, in fact, been led throughout by Webster and Clay. "There was hardly an opprobrious epithet which, as he told me himself, afterwards, Clay failed to use against the nomination," said Reverdy Johnson,[2] "and from a conviction that the nominee was unfit and would prove to be unfit for the discharge of the duties of the judicial station." How deeply his political bias colored Clay's views was interestingly shown by the fact that, within a few years, he frankly admitted his regret for his action. As described by Johnson: "After Taney had been upon the Bench for some four or five years, and Mr. Clay had been the witness, from having practiced before him and read his decisions, of the manner in which his duties had been discharged, he, as he told me himself, after hearing an opinion delivered by the presiding Judge, went to his quarters to see him, and found him alone; he said he felt the embarrassment necessarily incident to the object of his visit, and after exchanging salutations suited to the occasion, and being about

meanly shrunk from the performance of his duty to gratify one of the most ridiculous and affected whims that ever disturbed the weak head of a weak and silly politician."

[1] It appears that Webster was consistent in his action as it is said that he voted against all previous nominees to the Supreme Court Bench; for George F. Hoar in his *Autobiography* (1903), states that Judge Rockwood F. Hoar related the following incident of a visit to Washington in 1836: "Webster received him with great kindness, showed him about the Capitol and took him to the Supreme Court where he argued a case. Mr. Webster began by alluding very impressively to the great change which had taken place in that Tribunal since he first appeared as counsel before them. He said: 'No one of the Judges who were here then, remains. It has been my duty to pass upon the confirmation of every member of the Bench; and I may say that I treated your honors with entire impartiality, for I voted against every one of you.'" If Hoar was correct as to the date, Webster's remark was not strictly true as to Judge Story or Judge Thompson who were appointed on the Bench in 1811 and in 1823, before Webster became Senator in 1826.

[2] *38th Cong., 1st Sess.*, 1363, speech of Senator Reverdy Johnson, March 31, 1864.

to leave him, he took him by the hand and said:
'Mr. Chief Justice, there was no man in the land
who regretted your appointment to the place you
now hold more than I did; there was no member of
the Senate who opposed it more than I did; but I
have come to say to you, and I say it now in parting,
perhaps for the last time, — I have witnessed your
judicial career, and it is due to myself and due to you
that I should say what has been the result; that I
am satisfied now that no man in the United States
could have been selected, more abundantly able to
wear the ermine which Chief Justice Marshall honored.'
And with the tears trickling down the cheeks of both —
I speak the words of Henry Clay — they parted; and
that opinion he continued to hold, up to the last moment,
that his life was a blessing to the country."

The Whigs accepted the confirmation of Taney
with very bad grace.[1] "The pure ermine of the Supreme
Court is sullied by the appointment of that political
hack, Roger B. Taney," said one of their New York
papers. Another said: "Roger B. Taney of Maryland,
has been paid the price for removing the deposits. . . .
And today, we see a man elevated to the Chief Justiceship for violating the laws of the land "; and another
said: "General Jackson has at length succeeded in
his attempts to subdue the independent spirit of the
Senate and has brought that branch of the Government
under his feet. The consequence of this triumph
over public spirit and patriotism, over talents, integrity
and virtue, has been to place Roger B. Taney at the
head of the Judiciary. . . . The feelings of the new
Chief Justice, when he takes his place at the head of
the Court, will not be envied by any highminded and

---

[1] *New York American*, March 17, 1836; *Boston Courier*, March 22, 1836; *New
York Daily Advertiser*, March 21, 1836; *National Gazette*, March 19, 1836.

honourable person. Inferior in talents and learning, and especially in legal reputation, to most, at least, of his associates in the Court, he cannot but experience a sense of inferiority, a most humiliating frame of mind for any person to endure when placed in so elevated and responsible a situation. Mr. Taney cannot but know that he does not enjoy the confidence of a very large portion of the community." The *National Gazette* (which was the organ of the adherents of the United States Bank) said: "The Senate has indeed given *confirmation* strong of the character of the influence which now presides over its acts. . . . How much changed alas! from that assemblage which stood so nobly and efficiently between Executive passion and favoritism, and the interests of the Nation. The individual who was raised to a lofty post for the special purpose of trampling the Constitution under foot, and who was cast from it, in consequence, with patriotic indignation, is now invested with the amplest power of passing judgment on that Constitution."

On the other hand, the Democrats were unrestrained in their rejoicing. "The talents and integrity of Mr. Taney will add lustre to the station for which he is selected," said the *New York Evening Post.* "The accomplished Taney has succeeded against the vengeance of his foes and is now Chief Justice of the United States," said the *Richmond Enquirer.* The *Pennsylvanian* referred to Taney's "proud triumph" and stated that no one presumed to entertain a doubt as to his fitness for the position. "His surpassing abilities, his extensive acquirements, his firmness, moral courage, and his courteous, urbane deportment are generally acknowledged. . . . Even his vindictive enemies of 1834, who stigmatized him, when at the head of the

Treasury Department, with every epithet that party malevolence could devise, are now so far cooled by disappointment and popular rebuke that they either recant their hasty judgments or silently submit." "Mr. Taney has an excellent reputation as a lawyer and jurist. . . . Justice has been awarded to him and to those factious Senators who attempted his immolation," said the *Hartford Times.* The *Boston Post* said that Taney having been "the object of aristocratic hatred", in proportion to the ability and fidelity with which he had supported democratic principles, his confirmation now showed "the verdict of high approval which has been awarded to his sterling worth by the American people." [1]

Immediately after receiving news of his confirmation, the new Chief Justice sent to President Jackson an interesting expression of the close and warm personal friendship which had existed between the two men. "I feel that the first letter I write after the receipt of this intelligence," he wrote, "should be addressed to you to express the deep sense I shall ever retain of the constant kindness with which you have supported me, until you have finally placed me in the high station which I now fill, and which is the only one under the Government that I ever wished to attain. There are indeed circumstances connected with my appointment which render it even more gratifying than it would have been in ordinary times. In the first place, I owe this honor to you, to whom I had rather owe it than any other man in the world, and I esteem it the higher because it is a token of your confidence in me. In the second place, I have been confirmed by the strength

[1] *Pennsylvanian,* March 18, 1836; *New York Evening Post,* March 17, 1836; *Richmond Enquirer,* March 19, 1836; *Hartford Times,* March 19, 1836; *Boston Post,* March 22, 1836.

of my own friends, and go into office not by the leave, but in spite of the opposition of the men who have so long and so perseveringly sought to destroy me, and I am glad to feel that I do not owe my confirmation to any forbearance on their part." [1]

Coincident with its action on Taney, the Senate confirmed the nomination of Philip P. Barbour to succeed Duval. Barbour, about fifty-three years of age, was six years younger than the Chief Justice; he had served long in Congress, and had been a Judge of the General Court of Virginia, and a District Judge of the United States — "eminently fitted to adorn the Bench with his talents and enlighten it with his inflexible and uncompromising State-Rights principles." [2]

Owing to the delay in the Senate, the Court had sat through the 1836 Term with no Chief Justice and with one vacancy among the Associate Judges, Story acting as "President" of the Court. Few matters of importance were decided and the session was largely occupied with land claim cases from Florida and from Missouri. It is interesting to note that in this first year after Marshall's death, the first instance of a conflict between State and Federal authorities which had arisen for many years was decided by the Court in favor of the State. In *Hagan* v. *Lucas*, 10 Pet. 400, it was held that property seized by a State sheriff could not be taken by the United States marshal. "A most injurious conflict of jurisdiction," said Judge McLean, "would be likely, often, to arise between the Federal and the State Courts, if the final process of the one could be levied on property which had been taken by the process of the other."

[1] *Jackson Papers MSS*, letter of March 17, 1836.
[2] *Richmond Enquirer*, March 19, 1836. Barbour was confirmed by the Senate, March 15, 1836, by a vote of 30 to 11.

At the opening of the 1837 Term, the new Associate Judge, and the new Chief Justice (then in his sixty-first year) took their seats on the Bench for the first time; and two months later, the Chief Justice had the satisfaction of completing the triumph of his appointment, by administering the oath of office to the new President, his own former associate in Jackson's Cabinet, Martin Van Buren. In his letter to Jackson after his confirmation as Chief Justice, in March, 1836, Taney had said that it would be a gratification to him, if it should "be the lot of one of the rejected of the panic Senate, as the highest judicial officer of the country, to administer in your presence and in the view of the whole Nation, the oath of office to another rejected of the same Senate. . . . The spectacle will be a lesson which neither the people nor politicians should ever forget." This hope was now fulfilled, on March 4, 1837, when, as was said, "the oath was administered by the man whose pure, unsullied life, inflexible firmness, powerful intellect, and profound legal learning had unfitted him, in the eyes of the Senate, both for the office of Secretary of the Treasury, and for the Bench of the Supreme Court which he now adorns as its head." To Jackson himself, the event was also a culmination of all his hopes, and he attended the ceremony, in order to witness what he termed his vindication, in the spectacle of one of his rejected nominees sworn into office by another. "He declared," so a contemporary account stated, "that nothing should detain him from witnessing the august spectacle at the Capitol . . . and he wanted to see the great moral phenomenon of one citizen, who had been proscribed as a Minister to London, elevated to the Presidency, now sworn in by another citizen, who, after he had been twice rejected by the Senate, was now made Chief Justice of the

United States — and both changes effected by the force of public opinion in a free country." [1]

Within ten days after the opening of the Term, the Court heard the final rearguments in the three celebrated constitutional cases which had been pending, one for six years and the others for three years — awaiting the existence of a full Court. The first of these, *Charles River Bridge* v. *Warren Bridge*, 11 Pet. 420, had been argued at the 1831 Term (as Judge Story said) "with great learning, research, and ability, and renewed with equal learning, research and ability, at the present Term"; and it was now reargued on January 19, 21, 23, 24, 26, 1837, by Daniel Webster and Warren Dutton against Simon Greenleaf and John Davis (all of Massachusetts). The important question involved was, whether the obligation of contract contained in a charter to a corporation authorizing the construction of a toll bridge was impaired by a charter, subsequently granted to another corporation, authorizing the construction of a free bridge paralleling the toll bridge. In view of the economic conditions of the times and of the increasing construction of railroads paralleling previously chartered canals, the decision was likely to be of vast consequence to the development of the country; and the active interest shown in the case was illustrated by the vivid descriptions of the arguments of counsel which appeared in contemporary newspapers and letters.[2] A Washington press correspondent wrote, January 24:

Today the Supreme Court was the great scene of attraction at the Capitol. Mr. Webster was expected to speak, and at an early hour all the seats within and without the bar,

---

[1] *Richmond Enquirer*, March 9, 1837; *Washington Globe*, March 13, 1837; *Pennsylvanian*, Feb. 27, 1837.

[2] *Boston Daily Advertiser*, Jan. 30, 1837, quoting *New York Commercial Advertiser; History of the American Bar* (1911), by Charles Warren, 423, 424.

except those occupied by the counsel engaged in the cause,
were filled with ladies, whose beauty and splendid attire
and waving plumes gave to the Court-room an animated and
brilliant appearance such as it seldom wears. By the bye,
this chamber presents just now, in itself, a better look than
it ever did before. A great deal of the furniture is new, the
carpets are rich and beautiful; the desks and chairs of the
Judges of a pattern unsurpassed for beauty and convenience, and the whole appointments of the room, in short, in
excellent taste. The whole Court was present. . . . Mr.
Davis made a very powerful argument in behalf of the defendants in error. Mr. Webster followed him in a speech
which is generally spoken of as a most masterly effort of
argument and ingenuity. I only heard a portion of it. He
was describing the localities of the bridges. I never heard
or read any description more clear or accurate. Painting
could not have conveyed a better idea of the places to the
mind of the spectator than his picturesque description did
to the auditors. I envied the dashing young belles of the
metropolis their privilege of hearing Mr. Webster throughout; though I doubt not their looks distracted the attention
of many a man who went to listen to him.

On the same day, Simon Greenleaf wrote to Charles
Sumner:

For a week, I have had scarcely a thought that was not
upon Warren Bridge. The argument was begun Thursday
by Mr. Dutton, who concluded Saturday morning. I spoke
about two hours on Saturday and nearly three on Monday,
and yet merely went straight over my brief, answering, by
the way, a few objections on the other side. Mr. Davis
followed me yesterday and concluded in three hours today,
in a most cogent, close, clear and convincing argument.
Peters, the Supreme Court Reporter, says the cause was not
nearly as well argued before as now; and in proof of it says
that his own opinion is changed by it and that he now goes
for the Def'ts! Mr. Webster spoke about an hour this after-
noon on general and miscellaneous topics in the cause, and
will probably occupy all day tomorrow, as he said he should
consume considerable time. He told us he should "tear our

arguments to pieces", and abuse me. The former will puzzle him; the latter I doubt he will do, as he was observed to be very uneasy and moody during the whole defense. Both Mr. Davis and I avoided everything "peoplish" in our remarks, confining ourselves closely to legal views alone. But we expect a great effort from Mr. W. to-morrow.

Judge Story wrote to Sumner, January 25, 1837:

Every argument was very good, above and beyond expectation, and that is truly no slight praise, considering all circumstances. Our friend Greenleaf's argument was excellent — full of ability, point, learning, condensed thought, and strong illustration — delivered with great presence of mind, modestly, calmly and resolutely. It was every way worthy of him and the cause. It has given him a high character with the Bench and with the Bar. . . . At the same time, I do not say he will win the cause. That is uncertain yet, will not probably be decided under weeks to come. I say so the more resolutely, because on some points he did not convince me; but I felt the force of his argument. Governor Davis made a sound argument, exhibiting a great deal of acuteness and power of thinking. Dutton's argument was strong, clear, pointed, and replete with learning. Webster's closing reply was in his best manner,[1] but with a little too much of *fierté* here and there. He had manifestly studied it with great care and sobriety of spirit. On the whole, it was a glorious exhibition for old Massachusetts; four of her leading men brought out in the same cause, and none of them inferior to those who are accustomed to the lead here. The audience was very large, especially as the cause advanced; — a large circle of ladies, of the highest fashion, and taste, and intelligence, numerous lawyers, and gentlemen of both houses of Congress, and towards the close, the foreign ministers, or at least some two or three of them.

Within three weeks after the close of the argument, Chief Justice Taney delivered the opinion of the Court,

[1] Webster evidently expected to lose his case, his son, D. Fletcher Webster writing to him Feb. 24, 1837: "I regret that you will lose the Bridge case— perhaps you may be mistaken. I cannot but hope so, more especially as it may be, as you say, your last case." *Letters of Daniel Webster* (1902), ed. by C. H. Van Tyne; *Story*, II, 205.

upholding the validity of the statute, and establishing the doctrine that in the absence of express words granting exclusive privileges in a corporate charter, no such grant can be inferred as against the State. "No opinion of the Court," said one of its Judges, fifteen years later, "more fully satisfied the legal judgment of the country, and consequently none has exerted more influence upon its legislation." The rigid principle of the *Dartmouth College Case* which heretofore "had acted like a band of iron on legislative action" was modified by this decision in favor of the public interests.[1]

Except among the irreconcilable opponents of Jackson, the case was very soon recognized as a bulwark to the people in general, as well as to all business men who contemplated investments of capital in new corporate enterprises and who were relieved against claims of monopoly concealed in ambiguous clauses of old charters. Coming, as it did, just at the period when the new systems of transportation by railroads and canals were first developing, the decision was an immense factor in their successful competition; for as Taney pointed out, if contracts of monopoly were to be implied by the mere grant of a charter for trans-

[1] See Campbell, J., dissenting in *Piqua Branch of the State Bank of Ohio* v. *Knoop* (1854), 16 How. 409; and see Taney, C. J., in *Ohio Life Insurance Co.* v. *Debolt* (1854), 16 How. 435: "Nor does the rule rest merely on the authority of adjudged cases. It is founded in principles of justice, and necessary for the safety and well-being of every State in the Union. For it is a matter of public history, which this Court cannot refuse to notice, that almost every bill for the incorporation of banking companies, insurance and trust companies, railroad companies or other corporations, is drawn originally by the parties who are personally interested in obtaining the charter; and that they are often passed by the Legislature in the last days of its session when, from the nature of our political institutions, the business is unavoidably transacted in a hurried manner, and it is impossible that every member can deliberately examine every provision in every bill upon which he is called on to act." See especially the principles of the *Charles River Bridge Case* applied in an extreme case of competing railroads in *Richmond, Fredericksburg and Potomac R. R.* v. *The Louisa R. R. Co.* (1851), 13 How. 71; see also *Legislative Control over Railway Charters*, in *Amer. Law Rev.* (1867), I; *Private Turnpikes and Bridges* by Clinton T. Evans, *ibid.* (1916), L.

portation facilities, "the millions of property which
have been invested in railroads and canals, upon lines
of travel which had been before occupied by turnpike
corporations, will be put in jeopardy. We shall be
thrown back to the improvements of the last century,
and obliged to stand still, until the claims of the old
turnpike corporations shall be satisfied, and they shall
consent to permit these States to avail themselves of
the lights of modern science, and to partake of the
benefit of those improvements which are now adding to
the wealth and prosperity, and the convenience and
comfort, of every other part of the civilized world."
Nevertheless, while a decision to the contrary would
unquestionably have had a disastrous effect upon
the development of the country, there were many men
who took the view presented in Judge Story's dissenting opinion, saying: "I can conceive of no surer
plan to arrest all public improvements founded on
private capital and enterprise, than to make the out-
lay of that capital uncertain and questionable, both as
to security and as to productiveness. . . . The very
agitation of a question of this sort is sufficient to alarm
every stockholder in every public enterprise of this
sort throughout the whole country." The conservative lawyers and the corporate interests also regarded
the decision as radical, revolutionary and calamitous.[1]
"The vested-rights class cry out bloody murder, and
your friend, John Davis, has had the credit of maintaining radical and revolutionary doctrines," wrote a
Washington correspondent of a Boston paper.

On the day after the argument in the *Bridge Case*,
the *Mayor of the City of New York* v. *Miln*, 11 Pet. 102,

[1] Story wrote to his wife, Feb. 14, 1837: "A case of grosser injustice or more
oppressive legislation never existed." Webster wrote: "The decision of the
Court will have completely overturned, in my judgment, a great provision of
the Constitution." *Story*, II, 268; *Boston Courier*, Feb. 22, 1837.

was argued, January 27, 28, by D. B. Ogden and Blount against Walter Jones and Joseph M. White of Florida. The case involved a New York statute passed to protect the State from the influx of foreign paupers, requiring all masters of vessels arriving at the port of New York to report lists of passengers. It was argued for the State that this was no interference with the Federal power to regulate foreign commerce but a mere police regulation. "Such a condition," it was said, "produces no inconvenience, but, on the contrary, promotes a public good. It vests power where there is an inducement to exercise it. In Congress, there is no such inducement. The West seeks to encourage emigration, and it is but of little importance to them how many of the crowd are left as a burden upon the city of New York." Ogden referred to the dangers to the Constitution from an arousal of State feeling, saying: "To suffer State Legislatures to disregard the Constitution of the Union, which all their members are sworn to support, would soon leave the Constitution a dead letter, destroy the efficiency and put an end to every hope of benefit to be derived from it. On the other hand, to take from the Legislatures of the different States the powers legitimately vested in them, by a forced construction of the Constitution, would be equally fatal to it, by exciting State pride and State feelings against it; and thus driving it from that place in the good opinion, feelings and affection of the people without which it cannot long exist." The Court sustained the view that the statute was a mere exercise of police power to enforce the poor laws of the State, and that it was not a regulation of commerce, or at least not such an interference with the dominant power of Congress to regulate commerce as would come within the doctrine of *Gibbons* v. *Ogden*.

As soon as argument closed in the *Miln Case*, the third great long-pending constitutional case was begun, *Briscoe* v. *Bank of the Commonwealth of Kentucky*, 11 Pet. 257. It was argued by Joseph M. White and Samuel L. Southard against Henry Clay and Benjamin Hardin, January 28, February 1, 1837, and involved a Kentucky statute which authorized the issue of notes by a chartered bank, all of whose stock was owned by the State. Within ten days, on February 11, the Court reached a conclusion sustaining the State statute, and holding that these notes were not bills of credit, the issue of which by a State was prohibited by the Constitution.

In all three of these cases, Judge Story dissented, and stated that Marshall before his death concurred with his (Story's) views.

It has frequently been charged that in these three decisions the Court reversed the broad lines of construction on which Marshall and his Court had been proceeding. But this criticism can hardly be sustained in full. The *Miln Case* turned on a very narrow point, and the Court did not challenge in any way Marshall's opinion in *Gibbons* v. *Ogden*. In fact, it did not depart from Marshall's broad doctrines on interstate commerce as far as Marshall himself had gone in *Wilson* v. *Blackbird Creek Marsh Company*. Moreover, as Judge Baldwin explained (11 Pet., App. 2), the Court would have decided the case in the same way, even if Marshall had been alive. The *Briscoe Case* turned on an historical question of what constituted a bill of credit at the date of the Constitution. Marshall had only carried a bare majority of the Court with him in *Craig* v. *Missouri*, in 1830; and Baldwin now pointed out that, if the facts in the *Craig Case* had been similar to those in the *Briscoe Case*, Marshall would have been

in the minority.[1] In the *Bridge Case*, the Court did
not derogate from the doctrine of the *Dartmouth College
Case* that a charter was a contract, but merely decided that such a contract was to be construed strictly
and in favor of the State, and that nothing was to
pass by implication; in this case, however, Marshall's
Court would have undoubtedly reached the opposite
conclusion, for Baldwin stated that at the first argument, in 1831, he stood alone.

That the decisions met with great disapproval in
many quarters at the time is evident. So great was
Judge Story's despondency that he wrote to Judge
McLean : "The opinion delivered by the Chief Justice
in the *Bridge Case* has not been deemed satisfactory;
and indeed, I think I may say that a great majority of
our ablest lawyers are against the decision of the Court;
and those who think otherwise are not content with the
views taken by the Chief Justice. . . .   There will not,
I fear, ever in our day, be any case in which a law
of a State or of Congress will be declared unconstitutional; for the old constitutional doctrines are fast
fading away, and a change has come over the public
mind from which I augur little good." [2]   Kent wrote

---

[1] A curious situation arose as to this Kentucky statute. A suit was brought in
Missouri and the Kentucky statute was held unconstitutional by the Missouri
State Court on the strength of *Craig* v. *Missouri*. Later on, in 1840, in view of
the *Briscoe Case* decision, an attempt was made to take the case to the United States
Supreme Court, but the latter Court held it had no jurisdiction under the 25th
Section of the Judiciary Act which only applied where decisions of State Courts
were in favor of constitutionality — *Commonwealth Bank of Kentucky* v. *Griffith*
(1840), 14 Pet. 56.

[2] *Story*, II, 272, 270, letter to McLean, May 10, 1837, letter of Kent, June 23, 1837;
Sumner wrote to Story, March 25, 1837 : "As I read Taney's before I read yours,
I felt agreeably surprised by the clearness and distinctness with which he had
expressed himself, and the analysis by which he appeared to have been able to avoid
the consideration of many of the topics introduced into the argument. But on
reverting to his opinion again, after a thorough study of yours, it seemed meagre
indeed. Your richness of learning and argument was wanting. I thought of Wilkes'
exclamation on hearing the opinion of Lord Mansfield and his associates in his
famous case — that listening to the latter after the former, was taking hog-wash
after champagne." *Mass. Hist. Soc. Proc., 2d Series*, XV.

to Story: "I have re-perused the *Charles River Bridge Case*, and with increased disgust. It abandons, or overthrows, a great principle of constitutional morality, and I think goes to destroy the security and value of legislative franchises. It injures the moral sense of the community, and destroys the sanctity of contracts. If the Legislature can quibble away, or whittle away its contracts with impunity, the people will be sure to follow. *Quidquid delirant reges plectuntur Achivi.* I abhor the doctrine that the Legislature is not bound by everything that is necessarily implied in a contract in order to give it effect and value, and by nothing that is not expressed *in haec verba;* that one rule of interpretation is to be applied to their engagements, and another rule to the contracts of individuals. . . . But I had the consolation, in reading the case, to know that you have vindicated the principles and authority of the old settled law, with your accustomed learning, vigor, and warmth, and force. But the decision in *Briscoe* v. *The Bank of Kentucky* is quite as alarming and distressing. . . . It is in collision with the case of *Craig* v. *The State of Missouri.* . . . I have lost my confidence and hopes in the constitutional guardianship and protection of the Supreme Court." Other prominent Whigs expressed their apprehensions that the Legislatures of the States were hereafter to be free and unrestrained, "that they may pass ex post facto laws or such as impair the obligation of contracts, or issue bills of credit, without let or hindrance of the Supreme Court. A new era is begun and new lights have arisen. The provisions of the Constitution have been misunderstood by Judge Marshall and his Associates and new interpretations are to be given. Any clear manifestation of the popular will, in opposition to the powers of the Constitution as hitherto expounded by the Court, will be regarded with all due deference and embodied in the new code. That same popular will will be looked to as the leading star of the new dynasty and as the only exponent of the Constitution. Those among your friends who have already invested, or propose to invest their property, upon the faith of charters will do well to remember that this kind of property is no longer under the protection of law, but is held at the good pleasure of the Legislature." [1] Equally doleful prophecies were uttered by a writer in a prominent Whig review, who stated that it was undeniable that "the tone and character of the decision chime in with doctrines which tend or may be urged, deplorably, to the subversion of the principles of law and property. . . . Within a brief space, we have seen the highest judicial corps of the Union wheel about in almost solid column, and retread some of its most important steps. It is quite obvious that old things are passing away. The authority of former decisions, which had long been set as landmarks in the law, is assailed and overthrown, by a steady, destructive aim from the summit of that stronghold, within which they had been entrenched and established. It is very remarkable, also, that all the principles yielded by these decisions, either have relation to the sovereign powers of the Union, or to the very essence of social obligation. . . . We can hardly avoid the reluctant impression that it (the Judiciary) has already capitulated to the spirit of the old confederation; and that we are fast returning,

[1] See a letter from Washington to the *Boston Daily Advertiser*, Feb. 21, 1837; it continued: "Those who are satisfied of the good faith, equity and justice of that body will go on with the great work of internal improvement, but such as, from past experience, have doubts may well be excused. It is not improbable that in the downward course of things, this popular will, expressed in its accustomed forms, and which is hereafter to dictate to all the departments of Government, may demand a different tenure of judicial office; and I confess, for one, that I shall not be very anxious to retain the form when the substance is gone. The Lord Chancellor always goes out with the Minister."

among other things, to an old continental currency, and to what were once denominated, moreover, anti-federal doctrines. Under the progressive genius of this new judicial administration, we can see the whole fair system of the Constitution beginning to dissolve like the baseless fabric of a vision." [1] Another leading Whig magazine evinced even more solemn despair. After lauding the Court as "the balance wheel in the machinery of the Constitution. The people of the United States have confided to it the transcendent trust of preserving the Constitution, unimpaired and vigorous in all its parts, equally to be protected from the encroachments of the National departments, and from the more popular and more dangerous assaults of the State governments. It is looked up to as the last asylum of persecuted justice. There is no other tribunal on earth, so august in its functions, so vast in influence and so fearful in its responsibilities"; it stated that "under the new dynasty", it perceived "an altered tone and a narrower spirit, not only in Chief Justice Taney, but even in some of the old Associates of Chief Justice Marshall, when they handle constitutional questions. The change is so great and ominous that a gathering gloom is cast over the future." Commenting on the *Charles River Bridge Case*, it termed "the most alarming and the most heretical" part of the opinion, "the new fangled doctrine that the contracts of the State are to be construed strictly as against the grantee, and that nothing can be raised by implication. . . . Such a cold-blooded commentary on the contract, such a desolating doctrine coming from the head of the highest tribunal of the Nation . . . merits the severest animadversion that wounded justice and indignant patriotism can bestow." The

[1] *North Amer. Rev.* (1838), LVI, 153; *New York Rev.* (1838), II, 372–404.

Miln Case it called: "a fatal breach made in the Constitution. . . . The Court has yielded up the exclusive nature of the grant, and let loose upon us the old Confederation claim of the States to interfere, and perplex, and burden and alter the Congressional regulation of commerce with foreign nations, under pretexts (never wanting) that they were exercising only police authority for their own local interest and convenience." And it concluded with gloomy predictions as to the future of the Republic, because of the "revolution in opinion, in policy and in numbers that has recently changed the character of the Supreme Court. . . . The asylum of the Nation's safety from the violence of faction and the horrors of disunion was fondly confided to the firm tenure and powers and all pervading influence of the Supreme Court, and to the noble and elevated virtues which such confidence ought to inspire. And if the Constitution be destined prematurely to perish, and the last refuge of justice, and the last hopes of temperate and civilized freedom be destroyed, the expiring struggle will be witnessed in the decisions of that Court. Is it not possible to bring intelligent and enlightened public opinion to bear upon the Supreme Court and to endeavor to inspire it with a larger infusion of the spirit of moderation and forbearance?"

To this Whig pessimism, the *Democratic Review* replied that "the most ultra radical in this country never wrote a severer article against the Supreme Court"; but since at the date of the article, "the whole country was under furious excitement, we ought perhaps to make allowance for the influence of such a state of feeling." It added that while it revered Marshall's name, it was "sickened by the attempt to connect his name with a particular party of the present day, and make it the representative of all the ultra notions of those who, for a splendid government, would reason away the Constitution and all its checks and balances; who would, with one breath, make corporations override all individual and public interests, hold in check the power of the States, and defy that of the General Government — and at another moment would prostrate them all, to gratify some new whim or in advocating some new extreme of policy." [1]

All of these Whig forebodings were unjustified; and equally unfulfilled were the Democratic hopes that Taney's appointment would mean a reversal of the Court's constitutional doctrines. "His republican notions, together with those of his democratick associates, will produce a revolution in some important particulars in the doctrines heretofore advanced by the tribunal, over which he is called to preside, highly favorable to the independence of the States, and the substantial freedom of the people " had been the sentiment expressed by his strongest newspaper advocates.[2] There was, however, no real relaxation in the determination of the Court to uphold the National dignity and sovereignty, in any case where it was really attacked; and in fact, in the succeeding years, Chief Justice Taney went even further than Marshall had been willing to go in extending the jurisdiction of the Federal Courts in admiralty and corporation cases and in many other directions. If any real change in the course of the Court in cases affecting the National powers can be detected, between the thirty years after 1836 and the years prior, it may be said to amount only to this : that in doubtful cases, the Court possibly tended to give the benefit of the doubt to the State

[1] *Democratic Review* (June, 1840), VII, 497–515.
[2] *New York Evening Post*, March 17, 1836.

more than in Marshall's time, and even this statement
cannot be made without qualification. But Taney differed from Marshall in one respect very fundamentally,
and this difference was clearly shown in the decisions
of the Court. Marshall's interests were largely in
the constitutional aspects of the cases before him;
Taney's were largely economic and social. Marshall
was, as his latest biographer has said, "the Supreme
Conservative;" Taney was a Democrat in the broadest
sense, in his beliefs and sympathies. Under Marshall,
"the leading doctrine of constitutional law during the
first generation of our National history was the doctrine
of vested rights." Like his contemporary in England,
Sir Robert Peel, he believed that "the whole duty of
government is to prevent crime and to preserve contracts." Under Taney, however, there took place a
rapid development of the doctrine of the police power,
"the right of the State Legislature to take such action
as it saw fit, in the furtherance of the security, morality
and general welfare of the community, save only as
it was prevented from exercising its discretion by very
specific restrictions in the written Constitution." [1]
"The object and end of all government," Taney had
said with great emphasis in the *Charles River Bridge
Case*, "is to promote the happiness and prosperity of
the community by which it is established, and it can
never be assumed that the Government intended to
diminish the power of accomplishing the end for which
it was created. . . . We cannot deal thus with the
rights reserved to the States, and by legal intendments
and mere technical reasoning take away from them any
portion of that power over their own internal police and
improvement, which is so necessary to their well being

[1] *National Supremacy* (1913), by Edward S. Corwin, 113–115; see also Andrew
C. McLaughlin's review of Beveridge's *Marshall*, in *Amer. Bar Ass. Journ.* (1921),
VII, 231–233.

and prosperity." It was this change of emphasis from vested, individual property rights to the personal rights and welfare of the general community which characterized Chief Justice Taney's Court. And this change was but a recognition of the general change in the social and economic conditions and in the political atmosphere of that period, brought about by the adoption of universal manhood suffrage, by the revolution in methods of business and industry and in means of transportation, and by the expansion of the Nation and its activities. The period from 1830 to 1860 was an era of liberal legislation — the emancipation of married women, the abolition of imprisonment for debt, the treatment of bankruptcy as a misfortune and not a crime, prison reform, homestead laws, abolition of property and religious qualifications for the electorate, recognition of labor unions, liberalizing of rules of evidence and criminal penalties. It was but natural that the Courts amid such progressive conditions should acquire a new outlook responsive thereto. As has been well said, at the very moment when the election of Jackson meant the supremacy of the doctrine of strict construction, there arrived an era in the National life "when the demand went forth for a large governmental programme; for the public construction of canals and railroads, for free schools, for laws regulating the professions, for anti-liquor legislation, for universal suffrage." Taney came to the Bench with the view that the States must possess the sovereign and complete power to carry out this programme and to enact useful legislation for their respective populations. To Taney, the paramountcy of National power within the sphere of its competence was of equal but no greater importance than complete maintenance of the reserved sovereignty of the

States. Neither must be unduly favored or promoted.[1] The difference between the point of Marshall and that of Taney can be best understood by a study of the long series of letters of warm personal friendship which Taney sent to Jackson, between 1836 and 1844; for in them the former's sympathies with the broad rights of the people, as opposed to the individual rights of any monied or privileged class, are strongly set forth. Marshall's services to the Nation as a political organism can never be overvalued; but his whole temperament would have made it impossible for him to write as Taney wrote to Jackson, in 1838:[2] "In large commercial cities, the money power is, I fear irresistible. It is not by open corruption that it always, or even most generally operates. But when men, who have families to support who depend for bread on their exertions, are aware that on the one side they will be employed and enriched by those who have the power to distribute wealth, and that, if they take the other, they must struggle with many difficulties that can be thrown in their way, they are very apt to persuade themselves that that path is the best one in which they meet fewest difficulties and most favour, and surrender the lasting blessings of freedom and manly independence for temporary pecuniary advantages. They

[1] *Doctrine of Due Process of Law before the Civil War*, by Edward S. Corwin, *Harv. Law Rev.* (1911), XXIV.

"It is his (Taney's) glory that, with a sane mind, untroubled by the criticism of partisans, sincere and otherwise, he so interpreted the Constitution, or lent the weight of his influence to its interpretation, as to preserve unimpaired to the States the rights reserved to them, and at the same time, to give full effect to all the powers granted by the States to the Federal Government." *Roger Brooke Taney*, by William E. Mikell, *Great American Lawyers* (1908), IV, 128.

[2] See *Jackson Papers MSS*, letter of Sept. 12, 1838, letter of Oct. 15, 1836, in which Taney wrote that the freemen of the States "will never barter their liberties for money, nor shrink before the frowns of the money aristocracy. The same spirit will, I doubt not, be found to prevail in the great majority of the people of the United States." See also *ibid.*, letters of Aug. 31, 1839, April 24, 1841, Sept. 30, 1841, Oct. 24, 1842, Oct. 18, 1843.

forget the grinding oppression that awaits them from the power they are contributing to establish, as soon as it is firmly seated in the saddle and no longer needs their support. These attempts to destroy the spirit of freedom and manly independence in the working classes of society are new in this country. Ten years ago, such an attempt would have destroyed any party that countenanced such a principle. It is not so now. It appears to be daily more and more openly announced and acted upon; and it has been successful too, to a great extent. How far it will be able to go, it is difficult to foresee. I trust there is a saving spirit yet in the people of this country which will induce the honest of all parties, before long, to frown upon it and put it down. But one thing is clear, that if the effort to render the laboring classes of this country servile and corrupt and to destroy their independent spirit and self-respect shall be successful, that class of society who are striving to produce it, will be the first and most terrible victims of their own policy. The lessons of history upon this point are too plain to mislead us. But I confidently believe that, before long, public sentiment will put down these attempts to debase the character of our own people, and that honest men of all parties will refuse to purchase temporary success by inflicting a lasting and irreparable injury upon their own country."

Again, he wrote in 1843 to Jackson: "I remember your unshaken confidence in the virtue and intelligence of the people, and I trust they will yet, in due time, bring matters right   Nevertheless, I cannot conceal from myself that paper money and its necessary consequences — that is, speculation and the desire of growing rich suddenly and without labor, have made fearful inroads upon the patriotism and public spirit of what are called the higher classes; and if, in our divisions, they get that root of all evil, another Bank, it is not easy to foresee how far its powers of corruption may extend." Holding views like these, it is evident that Taney would approach a case from the human rather than the juristic standpoint, and that he would regard, as of the higher importance, the State power, which touched the individual and the community more closely than the National power.

CHAPTER TWENTY-TWO

CORPORATIONS AND SLAVERY

1838–1841

WHEN the Court met for the 1838 Term, two new and additional Judges sat upon the Bench, as a result of legislation which had been enacted on the last day of President Jackson's term of office — the Act of March 3, 1837. With the passage of this statute increasing the number of Associate Judges of the Supreme Court from six to eight, establishing two new Circuits in the West and Southwest, and abolishing Circuit Court jurisdiction of the District Courts, the long contest which had been waged for twenty years came to an end.[1] Hitherto (as has been described in previous chapters) propositions to increase the number of Judges and of Circuits, though recommended at various times by Presidents Madison, Monroe, Adams and Jackson, had failed to receive the approval of Congress, owing to its unwillingness to allow the new appointments to be made by the existing President.[2] Meanwhile, the

---

[1] Jackson, in his first Annual Message to Congress, Dec. 8, 1829, had said that the benefit of the judicial system should be given to all the States equally. In his Message, Dec. 6, 1831, he pointed out that one quarter of the States of the Union did not participate in the benefit of Circuit Courts, and that all should be on the same footing. "I trust that Congress will not adjourn, leaving this anomaly in our system." In his Message, Dec. 4, 1832, he hoped that "this duty will be neglected no longer." In his Messages of Dec. 6, 1834, and Dec. 7, 1835, he spoke of the "great injustice" of the present system of Circuits. The bill passed the Senate Jan. 6, 1836, and the House, March 3, 1837. *24th Cong., 2d Sess.* By an Act of Feb. 19, 1831, partial relief had been given by extending Circuit Court jurisdiction to certain District Courts in New York, Pennsylvania, Indiana, Illinois, Missouri, Mississippi and Alabama.

[2] See *National Intelligencer,* March 9, 1837.

crowded conditions of the inferior Federal Courts in the States of the West and the Southwest had become such as to make relief absolutely necessary, and its refusal a scandalous denial of justice to those parts of the country.

Jackson filled the new positions on March 3, 1837, before he went out of office, by appointing John Catron of Tennessee and William Smith of Alabama. Catron, fifty-one years old, was Chief Justice of the Supreme Court of Tennessee; he also had the further qualification of being a master of the law of real property, a subject as to which there was much litigation in the Federal Courts. As a Southerner who had been a vigorous Union man throughout the Nullification movement and a warm supporter of Jackson's policy of maintenance of Federal supremacy, he was a valuable addition to the strength of the Court.[1] Smith, who had been a United States Senator from South Carolina, and who was also an active Jackson supporter though a more radical State-Rights man than Catron, declined the position and issued a public statement of refreshing frankness. "It has become a matter of considerable inquiry, as well as of some speculation, why I would decline a very dignified office of light labors, and a permanent salary of $5000 a year," he wrote, and he explained that it was not due to bodily infirmity or "to any doubt of my legal learning" nor "to cold indifference to the honor", but rather to his desire to retain his freedom to take part in political discussion in support of Jackson's policies. For, he continued, "although I have always believed a Judge was not bound by any moral principle to abstain from the polit-

[1] See interesting letter from Catron to Jackson, Jan. 2, 1833, setting forth his views as to energetic form of action which should be employed to put down Nullification in South Carolina. *Jackson Papers MSS.* The nominations were confirmed, March 8, 1837.

ical discussions that so much agitate our country, I have, nevertheless, believed him under the strongest prudential motives to do so; as he might, with perfect innocence, in discussing a political subject elsewhere, express an opinion which might afterwards cross his judicial path whilst on the Bench, place him in a delicate situation, and in public estimation cast a blot upon the sacred ermine."[1] In place of Smith, President Van Buren appointed, April 22, 1837, John McKinley of Alabama, a former United States Senator, then fifty-seven years of age.[2] The Bar in general considered the appointments to be entirely adequate; but the Whig politicians harshly criticized the choice of Southern men and of Democrats, in spite of the fact that, since the new Circuits were in the Southwest, it had been necessary to appoint lawyers from that region, and the further fact that there were then but two Judges on the Court (Wayne and McLean) from west of the Alleghanies or south of Virginia. The Whig fear that, since all the Judges (with the exception of Story and Thompson) had been appointed by Jackson and Van Buren, the decisions of the Court would respond to its politics seems to have been equally the Democratic hope; for the *Democratic Review*, newly established in Washington, said in February, 1838: "The late renovation in the constitution of this august body, by the creation of seven of the nine members under the auspices of the present Democratic ascendancy, may be regarded as the closing of an old and the

---

[1] *Niles Register*, LII, May 20, 1837. Chief Justice Taney wrote to Jackson, Sept. 12, 1838, that the more he saw of Catron the more he had been impressed "with the strength of his judgment, legal knowledge and high integrity of character. He is a most valuable acquisition . . . and will, I am confident, continue to rise in public estimation, as he was a stranger at the time of his appointment." *Jackson Papers MSS*. Henry Clay, on the other hand, remarked sarcastically in a letter of March 7, 1837: "And what Judges they will make!" *Clay*, IV.

[2] McKinley's nomination was sent to the Senate, Sept. 18, 1837, and was confirmed, Sept. 25.

opening of a new era in its history." [1] But, as in every other instance in the history of the Court when it has been either feared or hoped that it would divide on party lines, the expectations of the politicians were unfulfilled. The Court continued to decide its cases without regard to party, and pursued its calm and majestic course, protecting the National sovereignty, the rights of the States, the rights of individuals and the rights of property, uncontrolled by the political views of its members or by the desires of officials at whose hands the individual Judges had received their appointments.

That the enlargement of the Court in numbers did not have the effect of adding to its efficiency may be inferred from a letter by Judge Story, at the end of the 1838 Term : "You may ask how the Judges got along together? We made very slow progress, and did less in the same time than I ever knew. The addition to our number has most sensibly affected our facility as well as rapidity of doing business. 'Many men of many minds' require a great deal of discussion to compel them to come to definite results; and we found ourselves often involved in long and very tedious debates. I verily believe, if there were twelve Judges, we should do no business at all, or at least very little." [2]

At this 1838 Term, two cases of historic importance were presented. In *Rhode Island* v. *Massachusetts*, 12 Pet. 657, the Court was called upon for the first time to decide whether it possessed jurisdiction under the Constitution to decide a conflict between two

---

[1] To this remark, the *National Gazette* replied, Jan. 25, 1838 : "That is, the Supreme Court has been renovated, since seven party men, including the apostate Federalist, Judge Taney gained access to it. Such opinions may suit an electioneering official like the *Globe*, but they ill befit anything pretending to the dignity of a review." See also bitter Whig attack on the *Democratic Review* and its articles on the Supreme Court, in *Amer. Monthly Mag.* (March, 1838), XI.

[2] *Story*, II, 296, letter of March 15, 1838.

States of the Union, involving a disputed boundary line and the sovereignty over disputed territory. On a motion to dismiss, argued by Daniel Webster and James T. Austin, Attorney-General of Massachusetts, the Court (Chief Justice Taney strongly dissenting) held that it had jurisdiction. That adherence to the doctrine of State-Rights was not peculiar to the Southern States was interestingly shown in this case by the argument of Austin, who questioned the Court's power to execute its judgment against the State. To this, Daniel Hazard, counsel for Rhode Island, very properly answered: "I could not help feeling great surprise when I heard the Attorney-General of Massachusetts so solemnly and portentously warning this Court of consequences, and expressing his anxious hopes that if it should decide against Massachusetts it will, for the honor of the Court and for the honor of the country, be sure to find some way to execute its decree. What! Does Massachusetts threaten? Is Massachusetts ready to become a nullifying State, and to set up her own will in defiance of the decrees of this Court and of the Constitution itself?" And the Court, through Judge Baldwin, took occasion to notice Austin's unfortunate argument, by saying at the conclusion of its opinion: "In the case of Olmstead, this Court expressed its opinion that if State Legislatures may annul the judgments of the Courts of the United States, and the rights thereby acquired, the Constitution becomes a solemn mockery, and the Nation is deprived of the means of enforcing its laws, by its own tribunal. So fatal a result must be deprecated by all; and the people of every State must feel a deep interest in resisting principles so destructive of the Union, and in averting consequences so fatal to themselves."

In *Kendall* v. *United States*, 12 Pet. 524, the Court

settled a serious controversy between the Executive
and the Judiciary, and established the power of the
Circuit Court of the District of Columbia to issue writ
of mandamus to Government officers — a power previously held not to be possessed by the Circuit Courts
of the United States.[1]   The case had given rise to much
political feeling, which was plainly shown in the argument by Richard S. Coxe and Reverdy Johnson
against Francis Scott Key and Attorney-General Butler.   Kendall, Jackson's Postmaster-General, had re-
voked the settlement of certain claims of postal con-
tractors made by his predecessors; thereupon, Congress had referred the claims to be adjusted and settled
by the Solicitor of the Treasury; the latter official
having allowed them, Kendall still refused to recognize
the claims (by President Jackson's order, so it was
said); whereupon, the Circuit Court of the District
issued a mandamus to the Postmaster-General.   The
case took on the aspect of a struggle between the Court
and the President.   It was argued by Key that this
was an attempt by the Court to control the Executive, or one of his officials, in the performance of an
Executive duty.   Coxe retorted that the mandate of
the Judiciary had been disregarded in language "highly
menacing in its character" by an "insubordinate inferior who still hangs out the flag of defiance."   Butler replied, deprecating the "very brilliant vituperative eloquence" of opposing counsel, and said that the
hall of the Supreme Court had hitherto "been regarded
as holy ground . . . one spot where questions of constitutional law could be discussed with calmness of
mind and liberality of temper . . . where it was usually deemed repugnant to good taste to offer as argument the outpourings of excited feeling or the creations

[1] *McIntyre* v. *Wood*, 7 Cranch, 504; *McClung* v. *Silliman*, 6 Wheat. 598.

of an inflamed imagination, and where vehement invective and passionate appeals, even though facts existed which in some other forum might justify their use, were regarded as sounds unmeet for the judicial ear." The Court, through Judge Thompson, stated in a striking and dignified opinion that it did not think that the proceedings in the case interfered "in any respect whatever with the rights or duties of the Executive, or that it involves any conflict of powers between the Executive and Judicial departments of the Government." It held that the mandamus was properly issued to the Postmaster-General "to enforce the performance of a mere ministerial act, which neither he nor the President had any authority to deny or control"; that while "there are certain political duties imposed upon many officers in the Executive department, the discharge of which is under the direction of the President . . . it would be an alarming doctrine that Congress cannot impose upon any Executive officer any duty they may think proper, which is not repugnant to any rights secured and protected by the Constitution; and in such cases the duty and responsibility grow out of and are subject to the control of the law, and not to the direction of the President." The *National Intelligencer*, in reviewing this decision, congratulated its readers "upon the spirit of independence and of resistance to the insidious encroachments of despotism which are embodied in it. . . . This opinion confirms and fixes our respect for the character of the Supreme Court and our reverence for the principle of judicial independence, so intimately blended in our mind with those of judicial integrity and consistency. It will stand as a beacon to mark to demagogues in office, for all future time, the point at which their presumption and tyrannous disposition

will be rebuked and effectively stayed." [1]   One episode connected with the opinion in this case does not
appear in the official report, but is of striking interest,
in view of the general belief among the Whigs that
President Jackson considered that the Executive was
not bound by the decisions of the Court and that he
was an independent and coördinate branch of the
Government, with a right to execute the laws and
Constitution as he understood them.   From a newspaper article which appeared years afterward,[2] it seems
that the Court in the case of *Kendall* v. *Stokes* originally intended to controvert this doctrine of Jackson's,
and that Judge Thompson had inserted in his opinion
a very strong paragraph, which was read when the opinion was delivered in open Court, but which does not
appear in the printed report except as follows :

It was urged at the bar that the Postmaster-General was
alone subject to the direction and control of the President
with respect to the execution of the duties imposed upon
him by this law; and the right of the President is claimed as
growing out of the obligation imposed upon him by the Constitution to take care that the laws be faithfully executed.
This is a doctrine that cannot receive the sanction of this
Court.   It would be vesting in the President a dispensing
power which has no countenance for its support in any part
of the Constitution, and is asserting a principle which, if
carried out in its results to all cases falling within it, would
be clothing the President with a power entirely to control
the legislation of Congress and paralyze the administration
of justice.

When the opinion containing the above paragraph
was read, Attorney-General Butler rose, and said that :
" in that opinion, it had been stated that the obligation imposed on the President to see the laws faith-

[1] *National Intelligencer*, March 13, 1838.
[2] *National Intelligencer*, Oct. 14, 1854.   See also *Public Men and Events* (1875),
by Nathan Sargent.

fully executed implied a power to forbid their execution. For himself, he disclaimed such a doctrine . . . but he felt it to be a duty he owed to himself and the station he occupied to repudiate such a doctrine as contrary to his long-established opinions, and he hoped that the Court would either expunge that part of the opinion or so modify it as to exonerate him from the imputation of having asserted such a principle." Judge Thompson said he had "endeavored faithfully and impartially to state the arguments of counsel, but if he had fallen into error, in this respect, he was always willing to rectify it. In this case, the opinion as delivered had been submitted to all the Judges in conference, and no one had intimated that the argument had been misapprehended." Judges Baldwin, McKinley and Wayne stated that they had also understood counsel to make the assertion, now controverted; and Judge Wayne said that: "There was neither mistake nor misapprehension in the matter. He had heard the doctrine, as stated in the opinion, advanced by counsel, with equal astonishment and indignation. He had not supposed there was any intelligent man in the country so ignorant of the principles of our Government and institutions as to entertain such a principle; much less could he have anticipated that it would ever be advanced before that tribunal by distinguished professional gentlemen. He was, however, in favor of granting the application to modify the opinion of the Court in the matter adverted to; but he wished to be distinctly understood that it was upon one ground, and but one; which was, that no memorial should go down to posterity which would state that such a dangerous and unfounded doctrine had ever been addressed to and heard by the Supreme Court." Though the opinion was modified in conformity with Mr. Butler's request, it was stated by the *National Intelligencer*, in 1854, that the original opinion, as read, would be found in the handwriting of Mr. Justice Thompson, among the archives of the Court, and that it still showed how it stood before the alteration. "Thus," said the editor, "in the Tribunal of the highest resort under the Constitution were the prerogative claims and arbitrary constructions of his own power by President Jackson stamped with the seal of condemnation, decisively, irreversibly, now and forever." [1]

Both the majority and the dissenting opinions became the subject of political attack.[2] President Van Buren took the very unusual step of criticizing the decision in his Annual Message to Congress, December 3, 1838, — a "decision which has resulted," he said, "in the judgment of money out of the National Treasury, for the first time since the establishment of the Government, by judicial compulsion exercised by the common law writ of mandamus . . . a decision founded upon a process of reasoning which, in my judgment, renders further legislative provision indispensable to the public interest and the equal administration of justice." The extraordinary result of the decision was, as he pointed out, that "the officers of the United States stationed in different parts of the United States are, in respect to the performance of their official duties, subject to different laws and to a different supervision. . . . In the District, their official conduct is subject to a judicial control from which in the States they are exempt, and a very different one. . . . Disparaging discrepancies in the law and in the administration of

---

[1] *National Intelligencer*, Oct. 14, 1854, which states that "the circumstances which we shall now relate have never before, that we know of, found their way into print, but which can be corroborated by the testimony of all who were present to witness them."

[2] *Taney*, 306, 317, letter to Richard Peters, March 27, 1838, declining to reply to attacks.

justice ought not to be permitted to continue." Congress paid no attention to this recommendation, and the power to issue writs of mandamus directed to Federal officials still rests in the Court of the District of Columbia.[1]

At this Term, a curious episode occurred, in the refusal of the Judges (with the exception of Baldwin) to attend the funeral of Congressman Jonathan Cilley of New Hampshire to which, in accordance with the custom, the Court had been invited. Cilley had been killed in a duel with Congressman William J. Graves of Kentucky — "the natural fruit of the ferocious spirit manifested in Congressional debates during the past few years", said the *National Gazette*.[2] The Judges, in declining, passed a resolution which they ordered recorded on the minutes of the Court, that "with every desire to manifest their respect for the House of Representatives and the Committee of the House by whom they have been invited, the Justices of the Supreme Court cannot, consistently with the duties they owe to the public, attend in their official character the funeral of one who has fallen in a duel." "Whether they will be sustained by public opinion in taking this stand," wrote Story, "is more than I can pretend to conjecture. But we shall in any event be satisfied with having done our duty, and our appropriate duty."[3]

---

[1] A bill to repeal the power of the Courts of the District of Columbia to issue writs of mandamus passed the Senate in 1839. That neither the Chief Justice, nor the Court, however, were inclined to interfere with Executive officials unless the official duty as to which mandamus was asked was clearly ministerial was made perfectly plain when, two years later, it unanimously refused to grant a mandamus against Van Buren's Secretary of the Navy, in *Decatur* v. *Paulding,* 14 Pet. 497, on the ground that the duty involved was executive and not ministerial. "The interference of the Courts with the performance of the ordinary duties of the Executive departments of the government," said Taney, "would be productive of nothing but mischief; and we are quite satisfied that such a power was never intended to be given to them." See also *Federal Judges and Quasi Judges,* by Edward B. Whitridge, *Yale Law Journ.* (1896), VI.

[2] *National Gazette,* March 1, 3, 1838.   [3] *Story,* II, 289, letter of March 5, 1838.

At the 1839 Term, the Court was confronted with a question of immense consequence to the commercial development of the country — the power of a corporation to make a contract outside of the State in which it was chartered. It was presented in three cases argued together — *Bank of Augusta* v. *Earle, Bank of the United States* v. *Primrose* and *New Orleans and Carrollton R. R.* v. *Earle*, 13 Pet. 519. The three plaintiff banking corporations, one chartered in Georgia, one in Pennsylvania and one in Louisiana, having through agents in Alabama purchased or discounted bills of exchange in that State, the makers of the bills refused to pay them on the ground of want of power in the banking corporations to do any business in Alabama and outside their home States. This contention had been upheld by Judge McKinley, in the United States Circuit Court in Alabama, by a decision which produced surprise and consternation throughout the business world, and which was graphically commented upon by Judge Story in a letter to Charles Sumner. "My brother, McKinley, has recently made a most sweeping decision in the Circuit Court in Alabama which has frightened half the lawyers and all the corporations of the country out of their proprieties. He has held that a corporation created in one State has no power to contract (or, it would seem, even to act) in any other State, either directly or by an agent. So banks, insurance companies, manufacturing companies, etc., have no capacity to take or discount notes in another State, or to underwrite policies or to buy or sell goods. The cases in which he has made these decisions have gone to the Supreme Court. What say you to all this? So we go!" [1] As the Bank of the United

---

[1] *Sumner Papers MSS*, letter of June 17, 1838. A dispatch from Mobile in the *National Intelligencer*, April 28, 1838, said: "The decision produced great excite-

States (which, on the expiration of its Federal charter in 1836, had been incorporated by the State of Pennsylvania) and other moneyed corporations had, for many years, been in the habit of discounting bills in States throughout the country, the decision opened the door to widespread repudiation of their obligations by debtors. They at once took advantage of the defense thus offered to them. Manufacturing and trading corporations hesitated to continue to do business in outside States. Fire and life insurance companies, which were just beginning their development in the country, curtailed the writing of policies. General commercial confusion ensued; and the result of the decision was likely to be the more disastrous because of the fact that it came at a time when the effects of the great financial panic of 1837 were still being severely felt. The opinion of the Bar was almost unanimous against the decision, ex-Chancellor Kent giving a very strong adverse opinion.[1] On the other hand, the decision was hailed with enthusiasm by large sections of the Democratic, or Locofoco, Party who were anti-corporation men, and especially by the radical Jackson and Van Buren antagonists of the Bank of the United States who felt the decision to be "an aftermath of Jackson's mortal combat with the Bank." [2]

ment here and is the subject of general conversations and alarm. Its ruinous consequences, if it be sustained, can scarcely be imagined." The *Mobile Commercial Register* on the other hand, May 8, 1838, spoke of the decision on the rights of foreign corporations and said as to Judge McKinley: "The new Judge by his promptness, ability and urbanity has received an abiding popularity with the Bar and the suitors in the Court."

[1] See opinion of Kent in *Law Reporter* (July, 1838), I, 57; see also *Remarks on Chancellor Kent's Opinion*, by J. R., *ibid.*, 185.

[2] See *The Position of Foreign Corporations in American Constitutional Law* (1918), by Gerard C. Henderson, 42 *et seq.* The Bank's newspaper organ, the *National Gazette* in Philadelphia, even went so far as to intimate that the decision was intended as an attack on the Bank, and said, May 2, 1835: "The importance of this case does not appear to be duly estimated. . . . If this is a covert attack on the dead monster, we suspect that it proceeds from that infusion of Democracy into the Judiciary of which Mr. Dallas boasted."

The supporters of State banks also welcomed the chance that the lucrative business of the Bank of the United States might now be monopolized by them, as a result of the decision.

The case was argued in the Supreme Court on January 30, 31, February 1, 2, 9, 1839, by David B. Ogden, John Sergeant and Daniel Webster for the banks, against Charles J. Ingersoll, William H. Crawford of Georgia and Van de Gruff of Alabama. "We consider it," said a leading Whig paper, "one of the most important questions to the Union of the States, affecting the commercial intercourse which binds them together, that can arise." [1] Another Whig paper, in New York, describing the argument, said that the Court-room was "thronged to overflowing with as brilliant and intelligent an audience as ever met within the walls of a single room. A case of immense importance, not to the parties concerned, but to the whole country, was to be argued. . . . The importance attached to this decision is that upon it rests the business of a large class of commercial men and the practice of numerous corporations. . . . Mr. Webster has gone to the foundation of the question and discussed it constitutionally, legally and socially. The most interesting and eloquent part of his argument, the peroration excepted which was singularly striking and effective with the Court, was a statement of the constitutional and social relationship of the States and the Union one to another. . . . There were also some fine passages of eloquence conceived and spoken in the peculiar vein of this great-minded pleader." And the *National Intelligencer* said: "When we say that the argument which we have heard was profoundly learned,

[1] *Madisonian* (Wash., D. C.), Feb. 2, 1839; *New York Express*, Feb. 15, 1839; *National Intelligencer*, Feb. 11, 1839.

as well as original and luminously illustrated, we express no more than everyone has a right to expect from the great New England jurist and legislator." The arguments took a very wide range over the financial, economic and social conditions of the United States. "A learned gentleman on the other side said, the other day, that he thought he might regard himself in this cause as having the country for his client," said Webster. "I agree with the learned gentleman, and I go indeed far beyond him, in my estimate of the importance of this case to the country. . . . For myself, I see neither limit nor end to the calamitous consequences of such a decision. I do not know where it would not reach, what interests it would not disturb, or how any part of the commercial system of the country would be free from its influences, direct or remote. . . . The decision, now under revision by this Court is, in its principle, anti-commercial and anti-social, new and unheard of in our system, and calculated to break up the harmony which has so long prevailed among the States and people of this Union. . . . But it is for you, Mr. Chief Justice and Judges, on this, as on other occasions of high importance, to speak and to decide for the country. The guardianship of her commercial interests; the preservation of the harmonious intercourse of all her citizens; the fulfilling, in this respect, of the great object of the Constitution, are in your hands; and I am not in doubt that the trust will be so performed as to sustain at once the high National objects and the character of this tribunal." And Ogden portrayed in his argument the commercial complications which would ensue. "The proposition in the Circuit Court," he said, "is that a corporation of one State can do no commercial business, can make no contract and can do nothing in any State of the Union

but in that in which by the law of the State it has been
created. This proposition is the more injurious, as
in the United States associated capital is essentially
necessary to the operations of commerce and the creation and improvement of the facilities of intercourse,
which can only be accomplished by large means. . . .
One of the most important objects and interests for the
preservation of the Union is the establishment of railroads. Cannot the railroad corporations of New York,
Pennsylvania or Maryland make a contract out of the
State for materials for the construction of a railroad?
Cannot these companies procure machinery to use on
their railroads, in another State?" On the other side,
Charles J. Ingersoll delivered a vigorous anti-corporation argument, pointing out the danger of increasing
the power of corporations in this country, and insist-
ing that a State ought not to be forced, by any doctrine
of comity or otherwise, to allow a corporation of another
State to do business within its borders: "It is confidently submitted to this Court that it will best ful-
fill its duties by holding the States united by sovereign
ties; by the State remaining sovereign and the corporations subject; not by sovereign corporations and
subject States. . . . If Courts are bound by common
law to restrict corporations to the specific purposes of
their creation, they are bound by the same common
law to prevent their wandering out of place, as much
as out of purpose. . . . As to the ruinous consequences denounced . . . such have always been au-
gured, and always will be, of measures offensive to
certain political prejudices. They are abundantly
disproved by the improvement and prosperity of the
country. The Court, instead of being alarmed from
its duty, by such appeals, should feel encouraged to
support the laws of State sovereignty, which, well

understood, were the broad foundations of the general welfare. Neither man nor State can stand erect without these self-preserving rights, against which the pleas of comity and cries of politics are equally futile and unavailing in this Court as now constituted."

A vivid picture of the political aspect of the case from the Democratic standpoint was given by the *Washington Globe*, which stated that after Judge McKinley's "strikingly just and proper" decision in the lower Court, "the Bank press forthwith opened its batteries of abuse, not only against the judgment, but the character and purity of the Judge who gave it. Wall Street was conspicuous in these calumnies, stimulated by which, a great corporation had the audacity to procure and publish the opinion of an old Federal lawyer of New York, of course condemning Judge McKinley's opinion out and out, in order to forestall that of the Supreme Court here." After describing Ingersoll's argument in the Court demolishing Ogden's "tissue of arrogant technicality", it stated that "Judge McKinley fortunately arrived and took his seat on the Bench, just in time to hear a complete vindication of his position, and a conclusive argument against the right of these money-mongering monsters to stray from their spheres and invade the quiet regions of distant States, there to ravage, monopolize and *destroy*. Messrs. Clay, Webster and Sergeant were all in attendance, the two latter busily taking notes of Mr. Ingersoll's thorough exposition of legal, political and economical principles, which, if we are not mistaken, have inflicted the *coup de grace* on, at any rate, *wandering* corporations. Vagabond banks are in a fair way to be chained up, to bite and bark only at their own houses. The Court-room was crowded with a brilliant audience of both sexes and from all parts, many

of whose countenances seemed to respond to Mr. Ingersoll's argument, of many hours' duration, in favor
of a recurrence to first principles, and upholding them
against the speculations of upstart combinations and
their advocates. What a blessing it would be if the
Judiciary should interpose to administer law upon the
wrongdoers whose rapacity has so deeply encroached
on the best interests and institutions of the country !"

This highly improper animadversion on the Court
was noticed by Webster in his argument; and the
National Intelligencer stated that: "With the solemnity which well became the magnitude of the questions at issue, Mr. Webster alluded in an impressive
manner to the indignity offered to the Court by a publication in a newspaper of this city, since the opening
of the argument in this very case; and repelled with
a proper indignation the attempt from that quarter to
dictate to the Court, and almost to command what
judgment it should render in the premises." [1]

Within two weeks, Chief Justice Taney rendered
an opinion, in which it was held that while no corporation could make a contract in a State outside of its
home State, without the sanction express or implied
of the outside State, nevertheless, under the law of
comity among nations which prevailed among the
several sovereignties of the Union, power to make
such contract was to be presumed in the absence of
any prohibition by the outside State. In other words,
while recognizing the right of a State to exclude foreign
corporations, the Court would not assume that such
right had been exercised, unless its exercise were clearly
shown. A singular misunderstanding as to the exact

---

[1] *Washington Globe*, Feb. 1, 1839; *Ohio Statesman*, Feb. 8, 1839; *National Intelligencer*, Feb. 11, 1839; the *National Gazette*, April 6, 1839, referred to the "terms
of vilest insolence" in the *Globe's* article, which, it stated, emanated from Postmaster-General Amos Kendall.

scope of the opinion of the Court prevailed for some time in the press. The Whig newspapers hailed it as a just rebuke to Democratic doctrines and to Democratic politicians, and were delighted that it had been rendered by a Court composed of appointees of two Democratic Presidents.[1] Thus, the *National Gazette* said: "The result of this decision by the Supreme Court, which so utterly disregarded the Kitchen's decree, shows that its revolutionary doctrines are repudiated in that high place, and that patriotism may still find a tribunal high above the destructive and depraving influence of party." The *National Intelligencer* considered that the anti-corporation feeling in the country was merely a symbol of Locofocoism, which it defined as "the levelling or pulling down principle" — "the enmity to the established order of things", "the disposition to set the poor against the rich, the idle against the industrious, the unruly against the law-abiding and finally the State government against the government of the Union." Misinterpreting the decision of the Court to mean that a State could not exclude a foreign corporation, it hailed the decision as a check and a signal rebuke to Locofocoism "in its most towering and ambitious flight", and "in its first attempt to wrest the judicial authority to its aid"; and it exulted "that there is in our political system a barrier, which power cannot break down nor party undermine. This decision, following that in the mandamus case at the preceding Term of the Court, has given increased confidence to our glorious institutions, and doubled the security of the tenure by which every individual in the community holds his life, his liberty and his property. . . . It has shown to us, by one bright example more, the inappreciable

[1] *National Gazette*, April 6, 1839; *New York Express*, March 12, 1839.

value of an independent Judiciary." A New York Whig paper said: "The reversal is one of the happiest and best omens of the signs of the times. Important as is every election, and of the gravest importance as are sometimes the appeals to the Ballot Box, yet they all dwindle into comparative insignificance, when contrasted with some great principle now and then brought before that High Tribunal, the Supreme Court, upon a proper and just settlement of which hang both the Constitution and the Union of the States. Such a principle was this, in substance, whether a corporation of a State can maintain a suit or a contract, or collect a debt, in the Courts of another State or in the Courts of the United States. If such debts and contracts were not binding, it is certain the Union would be of little value for any of the purposes of commerce; and if an individual could thus nullify a contract, the States would hardly be as well off, the one to the other, as any State and a foreign Government." And this prominent Whig representative actually admitted that Taney was not to be as greatly feared as the Whigs had apprehended: "The progress of Locofocoism, as it took its strides from the Palace to the Capitol, we feared had reached the Supreme Court. Mr. Justice McKinley, the country saw, was infected by it. The course of Mr. Taney as Secretary of the Treasury naturally created a great deal of apprehension as to the course of Mr. Chief Justice Taney; and it was feared, and greatly feared, that the fabric of constitutional law which the great Marshall had so long been rearing would be demolished at once by a new impression of Locofocoism upon the Supreme Bench. In the words of Mr. Webster then, 'we breathe freer and deeper' upon the discovery that such is not the fact. The Supreme Court is yet sound; and much as we cherish

Whig victories, yet we cherish this Conservative victory much more; it is the triumph of the Constitution and the Union again." "We are rejoiced that the march of agrarianism which had reached the ermine, has been stayed by the Supreme Court," said another Whig paper, "in the reversals, by that tribunal, of Judge McKinley, who is of the *Globe* and C. J. Ingersoll School, in his hostility to banks. The decisions of Judge McKinley struck at the root of all commercial intercourse between the States, and if they had not been reversed must have utterly annihilated it." "The decision will give great satisfaction to the business community at large. It will increase the confidence of the people in the purity and independence of the Court. The insolent organ of the Executive has found its attempts at dictation in this instance repelled," said a leading commercial paper.[1] "Your opinion in the corporation cases," wrote Judge Story to Taney, "has given very general satisfaction to the public, and I hope you will allow me to say that I think it does great honor to yourself, as well as to the Court."[2] "It is a most consolatory reflection," wrote Joseph R. Ingersoll to Charles Sumner, "that while the Executive Department is likely to be imbued with too popular a hue, the fears of Judicial radicalism have not been realized. Your professional feelings will be gratified at the combined judgment in the Ala-

---

[1] *National Gazette*, April 16, 1839; *Madisonian*, March 13, 1839; *Boston Daily Advertiser*, March 13, 1839, quoting *New York Commercial Advertiser;* see also *New York Courier*, March 12, 1839: "The opinion read by Chief Justice Taney is as far from Loco-Foco doctrine as Alexander Hamilton himself could have desired." The *Mobile Commercial Register*, March 19, 1839, pointed out that the report of the decision in the *National Intelligencer* was not to be trusted, inasmuch as all Whig political papers were inclined to color their reports. "Anything which aims a blow at the sovereignty of the States, or goes to justify Mr. Jefferson's apprehensions of the Supreme Court that it tended to federal consolidation, chimes with their wishes and accords with the public lives of its editors."

[2] *Taney*, 288, letter from Story, April 19, 1839.

bama case. If the Judiciary remain strong in principle and conduct, and no recall shall take place of the reign of Jacksonism, the necessity for *dent operam consules* will not arise." [1]

On the other hand, the Democratic, or Locofoco, papers equally misconceiving the scope of the decision, attacked the Court for the "deadly blow to the rights of the States" in the sanction given "by this august tribunal, of the vandal overrunning by these paper corporations of the policy and laws and Constitutions of the sovereign States." An Alabama paper said that it was unwilling to believe that the Court had announced a doctrine "subversive of the dearest rights of the States" and that it was confident that the Court would "protect States-rights and personal rights from being swallowed up by the encroachments of chartered companies." A radical Pennsylvania paper stated that : "We are not prepared to submit to this doctrine. We are prepared to take our stand, now and forever, against it. We are ready to battle for the rights, the inalienable rights of the People; and the first blow that we strike is against the *Life Judiciary of the United States* — the judicial noblemen of America." Little support was given through the country to such revolutionary talk; and it was well said, in reply, in the *National Intelligencer* that "this is war against the Constitution", and that without the safeguard of an independent Judiciary "all the reservations to the States and to the People contained in the Constitution, would be no more worth than the strip of parchment on which they are engrossed, and our Government would become one vast, illimitable and unfathomable despotism." [2] It is interesting to note

<hr />

[1] *Sumner Papers MSS*, letter of April 22, 1839.

[2] *Mobile Commercial Register*, March 11, 19, 1839; on May 14, it said that it was "agreeably disappointed" and that the decision "leaves us in the enjoyment

that this Democratic diatribe, leveled against a Democratic Court and a Chief Justice appointed by Jackson, is of almost exactly the same tenor as that previously made against a Federalist Court and Chief Justice appointed by Adams. The incident affords again a striking proof that contentment with the Court's decisions did not depend upon the political composition of the Court.

The fact is that the decision did not wholly satisfy the extremists of either party.[1] On the one hand, the Chief Justice denied Webster's contention that a corporation of one State was entitled to the constitutional rights and privileges of a citizen of another State; on the other hand, he refused to adopt the defendant's contention that a foreign corporation had no power whatever to do business outside of its own State. By his rejection of the extreme Nationalistic views, he saved to the States the vital right to say what corporations should do business within their boundaries, and on what terms.[2] In emphatically proclaiming the power of a State by express action to repudiate the principle of comity and to refuse recognition to a foreign corporation, he gave sanction to the immense mass of State legislation regulating foreign corporations which followed in later years. The views held by the Court, however, as to the status of a corporation outside the boundaries of its home State produced con-

of much of our constitutional right which we had been led to apprehend had been entirely swept away." *National Intelligencer*, April 18, 1839, quoting a *Harrisburg Reporter* editorial, which, it said, was "in the true Locofoco spirit, upon the decision of the Supreme Court, showing the exasperation of that party at being foiled by the firmness of the Judges of the Supreme Court in their attempt to obtain its sanction to their levelling and demoralizing doctrines."

[1] Bitter criticisms of the opinion were made by the leading anti-bank counsel, Charles J. Ingersoll, to which, however, a prominent Pennsylvania colleague at the Bar, Henry D. Gilpin, retorted that "he should not be worried at his inability to defeat a corporation, when the whole country had to bear them, as Sinbad had his burden." *Life of Charles J. Ingersoll* (1897), by William M. Meigs.

[2] *Roger B. Taney*, by William W. Mikell, *Great American Lawyers* (1908), IV.

siderable confusion in the law, and the invention of legal fictions as to implied consent to extraterritorial service in case of suits against foreign corporations actually doing business in outside States.[1]

Two other cases connected with the commercial development of the country may be briefly noted. In *Stokes* v. *Saltonstall*, 13 Pet. 181, there appeared for the first time a subject which has later filled the reports — negligence of a common carrier (in this case, a stage-coach owner).[2] In *Smith* v. *Richards*, 13 Pet. 26, there occurred the first case connected with mining, and involving alleged fraud in the sale of a Virginia gold mine. The arguments on January 23, 24, by Webster and John J. Crittenden (the Senator from Kentucky), were interestingly described in the press as follows: "The Supreme Court has been the scene of attraction today. . . . Mr. Crittenden is a volume of pungent satyre, and whether the Senator or the Lawyer, he wields his satyrical weapons in a manner the most effective. He has eloquence, too, of a high order; he is as well read in law as politics, and always looks 'quite through the deeds of men.' Mr. Webster drew a great crowd to hear him and will fill the Supreme Court-room tomorrow. He is more of a giant at the bar than in the forum, and never appears so well as when discussing great principles of law and equity. No one becomes tired of hearing him, and the dullest plodder listens to him with interest and attention. · . . Webster concluded his argument. He was Dan-

[1] See *The Position of Foreign Corporations in American Constitutional Law* (1918), by Gerard C. Henderson; see also *State Control of Foreign Corporations*, by G. W. Wickersham, in *Kentucky State Bar Ass. Report* (1909). See also for résumé of the effect of the decision, *Runyon* v. *Coster* (1840), 14 Pet. 122. It is to be noted that the decision had no practical effect in behalf of foreign corporations in Alabama, for that State immediately passed a statute forbidding transaction of business by agents of foreign banks.

[2] The first case on the docket of the Court in which a railroad was a party was a patent case in 1840 — *Philadelphia & Trenton R. R.* v. *Stimpson*, 14 Pet. 448.

iel Webster to the last, clear, logical, powerful, with all the simplicity of a child and backed by the strength of a giant. The Court-room was thronged to hear him." [1]

In *Ex Parte Hennen*, 13 Pet. 230, a topic on which much political controversy has raged in this country was involved — the power of removal from office. The Court, having been asked to issue a mandamus to the District Court to restore the Clerk of the Court to office, held that in the absence of constitutional or statutory regulation, "it would seem to be a sound and necessary rule to consider the power of removal as incident to the power of appointment" and that "it was very early adopted as the practical construction of the Constitution that the power was vested in the President alone" with reference to all Presidential appointees. It refused the mandamus, saying that "if the Judge is chargeable with any abuse of his power, this is not the tribunal to which he is amenable." [2]

The 1840 Term, in the closing years of Van Buren's Administration, was not marked by notable cases, but there were two which exercised an important influence on the country's history. [3]

---

[1] *New York Express*, Jan. 25, 28, 1839. In his dissenting opinion (concurred in by Judges McLean and Baldwin) Judge Story used the following picturesque language: "In my opinion the appellant stands acquitted of fraud, the victim, if you please, of a heated and deluded imagination, indulging in golden dreams; but in this respect, he is in the same predicament with the appellee."

[2] Two matters relating to the practice of the Court may be noted. For the first time, by Rule 46, all motions were required to be reduced to writing and to contain a brief statement of the facts and objects of the motion. Theretofore it had been one of the duties of the Associate Justice for the Fourth Circuit to attend in Washington on the first Monday of August annually "to make orders respecting the business of the Supreme Court." This duty was now abolished by the Act of Feb. 28, 1839, c. 36. "For many years past, the business of the Court had been entirely *pro forma* requiring neither attendance of counsel nor decision by the Court, and the attendance of the Judge has not always been deemed necessary." *Niles Register*, LIV, Aug. 4, 1838.

[3] *Story*, II, 327-328, Judge Story wrote, Feb. 6, 9, 1840: "We are going on steadily in the Supreme Court with our business. None of it is of very great public interest, but there have been a few questions of a commercial nature of considerable

In *United States* v. *Gratiot*, 14 Pet. 526, the plenary power of the United States over its public lands, even when situated in the States, was firmly upheld, and the power of Congress to lease lead mines on public lands in the State of Illinois (and the Territory of Wisconsin) and formerly in the Territory of Indiana was sustained. Thomas H. Benton had contended that the original States would never have ceded to the United States the lands in this territory, "if Congress were to have the power to establish a tenantry to the United States upon them. The State-Rights principles would have resisted this: no lands would have been ceded." Under the Constitution, he said, the lands are "to be disposed of" by Congress, not "held by the United States." The Court held that "there can be no apprehensions of any encroachments upon State-Rights by the creation of a numerous tenantry within their borders, as has been so strenuously urged in the argument"; and that the right to dispose of the lands meant disposal at the discretion of Congress and included a lease as well as a sale. The importance of this decision upon the future control and conservation of public lands is evident.

Following this case upholding the power of the Federal Government came another of importance, *Holmes* v. *Jennison*, 14 Pet. 540. In this, though the suit was dismissed for want of jurisdiction, a superbly able opinion was given by Chief Justice Taney (concurred in by Judges Story, McLean and Wayne), asserting

importance. . . . The nomination of Harrison runs like wild-fire on the prairies. It astonishes all persons, friends and foes. The general impression here is that he will certainly be chosen President. Mr. Webster told me last evening that there was not the slightest doubt of it. The Administration party are evidently in great alarm, and some are preparing to leap overboard before the ship sinks. In the meantime, the farmers of the West are beginning to feel the public pressure most severely. All their produce is at a very low price, money is exceedingly scarce and business at a dead stand. . . . What I most anxiously desire is, to see a President who shall act as President of the country, and not as a mere puppet of party."

the exclusive authority of the Federal Government to control the foreign relations of the United States, and denying the power of a State to surrender to a foreign nation a fugitive criminal found within the State. The case involved the right of the Governor of Vermont to order the delivery to the Canadian authorities of a Canadian murderer, no extradition treaty with Great Britain being then in existence, and the Vermont State Court having sustained the Governor in his order to send the fugitive back to Canada.[1] "This involves an inquiry into the relative powers of the Federal and State governments, upon a subject which is sometimes one of great delicacy," said Taney, the principle to be decided in which "in times of war and of great public excitement may reach cases where great public interests are concerned and where the surrender may materially affect the peace of the Union. . . . It was one of the main objects of the Constitution to make us, so far as regarded our foreign relations, one people and one nation; and to cut off all communications between foreign governments and the several State Governments." In using this prophetic language, Taney undoubtedly had in mind the somewhat strained relations already existing between the United States and Canada and Great Britain; for, two years before, an expedition from Canada had invaded New York in December, 1837, and had burned the steamer *Caroline*, and killed an American citizen. There had been vigorous diplomatic negotiations over the episode. Within one year after the decision in the *Holmes Case*, the

---

[1] The *Pennsylvanian*, March 14, 1839, quoted the *Burlington Sentinel* (Vt.) : "We understand that the President (Van Buren) has declined acting upon the application for surrender of Dr. Holmes and referred the subject to Gov. Jennison. We understand the position taken at Washington to be that, inasmuch as neither the Constitution nor the laws of Congress provide for the case at all, it must rest on the ground of mere comity between the British provinces and the adjoining States, and therefore the decision should be left to the State authorities."

indictment and trial in New York of McLeod for murder in connection with this expedition, and the refusal of the State of New York to yield her rights even at the request of the United States Government, had brought the United States and Great Britain to the verge of war. The most striking feature, however, of Taney's notable opinion was the fact that it sustained the supremacy of the powers of the Federal Government, with a breadth and completeness which had been excelled by no one of Marshall's opinions. While, therefore, it was naturally received with enthusiasm by men like Judge Story, who wrote that it "is a masterly one and does his sound judgment and discrimination very great credit. . . . I entirely concurred in that opinion with all my heart; and was surprised that it was not unanimously adopted", the opinion was criticized by Democrats. And James Buchanan stated in the Senate that he had "always entertained the highest respect for the present Chief Justice of the United States; but I must say, and I am sorry in my very heart to say it, that some portions of his opinion in the case are latitudinous and centralizing beyond anything I have ever read in any other judicial opinion." [1]

The next Term, beginning in January, 1841, was held at an exciting period in American history. The twelve years of the Democratic Administrations of Jackson and Van Buren, with their long contests against banking and corporate monopolies, had come to an end. New problems and new conditions appeared likely to confront the country under the leadership of the Whig President, Harrison; and control of Congress by the Whigs rendered it probable that the

---

[1] *Taney*, 290, letter of Story to Richard Peters, May, 1840; *27th Cong.*, *2d Sess.*, *App.*, speeches in the Senate of Buchanan, May 9, 1842, Robert J. Walker of Mississippi, June 21, 1842.

virulent attacks on Jacksonian policies would moderate. It is interesting to note, however, that so fully had Jackson's appointees on the Court satisfied the country, that political criticism of its decisions had already almost entirely disappeared. It was, therefore, with expectations on all sides of a period of comparative political calm in all branches of the Government that the Court convened. "I hope that the Court will have a harmonious session," wrote Story, "and I am sure that the Chief Justice and a majority of my brethren will do all that is proper to accomplish the purpose. The change in the Administration will produce no change in my own conduct. I mean to stand by the Court, and do all I can to sustain its dignity and the public confidence in it. Indeed, I should think myself utterly inexcusable, if I could be brought to act otherwise." [1] The most important case decided at this Term, however, brought the Court into contact with a dangerous political issue, when, in *Groves* v. *Slaughter*, 15 Pet. 449, for the first time opinions were elicited from the Judges on the subject of the respective powers of the States and of the Federal Government over the introduction of slaves within State borders. Though it was this case on which, after the Mexican War, the slavery men in Congress rested their arguments in behalf of Squatter Sovereignty and Territorial and State control of slavery, the actual decision of the Court, nevertheless, was rendered on a point distinct from the slavery issue.[2] The Constitution of

---

[1] *Story*, II, 341, letter to Richard Peters, Jr., Dec. 4, 1840.

[2] For interesting citations and discussions of *Groves* v. *Slaughter* in Congress, see *29th Cong., 2d Sess.*, speeches of Burt of South Carolina, Jan. 14, 1847, and Bowdon of Alabama, Jan. 16, 1847; *30th Cong., 1st Sess.*, speech of Bayly of Virginia, Aug. 3, 1848, saying: "In that case was discussed the extent of the power of Congress over what is familiarly called the internal slavetrade . . . it went to the Supreme Court; it was there decided; and the decision has tended greatly to put an end to the agitation growing out of it." See also speeches of Hunter and Clay, in the House, Aug. 23, 1850. *31st Cong., 1st Sess.*

Mississippi of 1832 had declared that "the introduction of slaves into this State as merchandise or for sale shall be prohibited from and after the first day of May, 1833." [1] The question before the Court was whether a note given for the purchase of such slaves after that date was void, and, if so, whether the State Constitution itself was invalid, as conflicting with the power of Congress over interstate commerce. The presence of the latter question in the case was the cause of the splendid array of counsel — United States Attorney-General Henry D. Gilpin and Robert J. Walker of Mississippi appearing for the State against Henry Clay and Daniel Webster "the Ajax and Achilles of the Bar" (as their associate counsel, Walter Jones, termed them). The argument was elaborate, lasting for seven days, from February 12 to 19, 1841. "Very many of the distinguished counsellors of the country were present and scores of men eminent in other professions; the ladies occupied all the vacant seats of the Court-room and crowded everyone but the Judges and counsel out of the bar," said a newspaper account. "Mr. Clay spoke for some three hours, and with a patient audience to the end. With a jury, he would be irresistible. With grave Judges to address, of course he is less successful; but many who heard him today pronounced his argument to be a very able one. Mr. Webster followed. The Senate Chamber has

[1] It may be noted, as a curious sidelight upon this Mississippi case, that the State prohibition of the introduction of slaves for sale was a financial rather than a slavery measure. Owing to the great financial difficulties into which that State had been plunged, its Governor had recommended such prohibition in order to check the drain of capital away from the State, through withdrawal to other States of the purchase price of slaves so introduced. The decision of *Groves* v. *Slaughter* in the lower Court, declaring that the note was void, it was said by a Natchez paper, "will have an important bearing on Northern negro debts to the amount of at least $2,000,000." See *Law Reporter* (Feb., 1840), II; and see *Washington Globe*, May 16, 1838, March 28, 1839; also see *History of the People of the United States*, by John Bach McMaster, VI, 398, for vivid pictures of the conditions of financial distress, bankruptcy and repudiation in Mississippi.

presented a beggarly account of empty boxes through
this week thus far, in consequence of the interesting
trial going on in the Court-room. . . . Many come
to mark the contrast between Mr. Clay's and Mr. Webster's mode of address. . . . As usual, Mr. Webster
wasted not a word. He spoke about two hours, with
a closeness of logic no other man in the country can
equal. There was not the least attempt at display,
and a child of ten years could have kept the run of the
whole case. It is a curious case under our complex
Government. Mr. Clay says that two or three million
dollars depend on it. Among the auditors was John
Quincy Adams, intent throughout, who, for a wonder,
deserted the Representative wing of the Capitol in
business hours, for once." [1] Many contemporaries
believed that Walter Jones, who appeared as the associate of Clay and Webster, was fully their equal in legal ability. "A small, spare man of insignificant appearance, with plain features, except his eyes, which
for piercing intelligence and shrewdness of expression
I have never seen surpassed, his mental activity spoke
in them. His voice was a thin, high pitched one, and
he was without any pretension to grace of manner.
Few men who occupied prominent places in the pro-

[1] *New York Express*, Feb. 19, 23, 1841. The *Southern Patriot* (Charleston, S. C.),
March 4, 1841, said that the Court-room was crowded "in consequence of the
great display of argument and eloquence. Mr. Clay made a splendid argument.
He connected it a little with the popular topic of abolition, intimating that his
view of the question was the anti-abolition view." Adams wrote in his diary,
Feb. 19, 1841: "I left the House, and went into the Supreme Court, and heard the
argument of Mr. Webster on the second Mississippi Slavery case, and the closing
argument of Mr. Walker, the Senator from Mississippi, in reply. The question is
whether a State of this Union can constitutionally prohibit the importation within
her borders of slaves as merchandise. Mr. Walker threatened tremendous consequences if this right should be denied to the State — all of which consequences
sounded to me like argument for the constitutional authority to prohibit it in all
the States, and for the exercise of it." Senator Westcott of Florida, July 25, 1848,
described Robert J. Walker's argument as "in my judgment never excelled by any
made in that Court for masterly ability, profound learning and accomplished eloquence." *30th Cong., 1st Sess.*

fession were ever listened to with more interest than
Mr. Jones," wrote a fellow member of the Federal Bar.
"His fluency was only equalled by the choiceness of
his language. He was so deliberate, so quiet that perhaps fluency does not accurately describe his oratory.
He was one of the closest reasoners. He never spoke
at random. His style was simplicity itself." [1]

The case appeared to present questions of a most
explosive nature, and to require the Court to decide
whether, if negro slaves were articles of commerce, the
State Constitution was repugnant to the Commerce
Clause of the Federal Constitution; or, if slaves were
persons, whether they were citizens of the United States
whose constitutional rights had been infringed by the
State Constitution. A decision on the latter question
would have caused the Court to confront, in 1841, the
same mighty problem which was to come before it,
fifteen years later, in the *Dred Scott Case*. When,
however, on March 10, 1841, three weeks after the argument, the Court gave its decision, it found itself
fortunately able to avoid the slavery issue, since a ma-

---

[1] *Life and Times of John H. B. Latrobe* (1917), by John E. Semmes; see also,
for a picturesque description of Walter Jones, *The Black Book or a Continuation of
Travels in the United States* (1828), by Mrs. Anne Royall, 127. A correspondent
of the *Boston Post*, Jan. 30, 1839, wrote: "He is a great lawyer, as eccentric in his
dress as John Randolph. The other day he appeared in Court in gray, and a
stranger would sooner have taken him for a Georgia cracker than the eminently
great lawyer." A correspondent of the *New York Tribune* wrote, Feb. 4, 1850, of
him: "The rival of Pinkney and Wirt and Webster and other leading counsel in past
days. As a common law counsellor, he excelled them all in depth and variety of
learning. He has received enormous fees in former times, and has had several
large legacies; but is now without fortune, and still engaged in practice, though
he must be more than seventy years old. He speaks slowly and in a low tone, but
with great purity of diction and clearness of thought. There is, however, a great
want of force in his manner, and few listen to him. Some years ago, a citizen of
Ohio, after being in Court during an argument of General Jones, said to one of his
acquaintances that he had witnessed that day the greatest curiosity which had
ever met his observation; he had heard a man talk for two hours in his sleep! The
appearance and dress of this distinguished and worthy gentleman are most peculiar, and it would be hardly fair to describe them. He is universally respected, and,
by those who know him, warmly beloved." See also *Gen. Walter Jones*, by Joseph
Packard, *Virg. Law Reg.* (1901), VII.

jority of the Judges, Thompson, Taney, Baldwin and Wayne (two Northern and two Southern men), agreed in holding that, on a proper construction of the language of the State Constitution, statutory legislation was contemplated and necessary before it could take effect, and that hence, as no such legislation had been enacted, the decision of the Circuit Court in favor of the validity of the notes in question was correct. Judge Thompson in delivering the opinion stated that as the Court had reached the above conclusion, it became unnecessary to inquire if the State Constitution was repugnant to the Federal Constitution.[1] Judge McLean, an ardent anti-slavery man, however, felt that it was his duty to express his views on the slavery question. "As one view of this case," he said, "involves the construction of the Constitution of the United States in a most important part, and in regard to its bearing upon a momentous and most delicate subject, I will state in a few words my own views on that branch of the case . . . and although the question I am to consider is not necessary to a decision of the case, yet it is so intimately connected with it, and has been so elaborately argued, that under existing circumstances, I deem it fit and proper to express my opinion upon it." [2] He, thereupon, entered into a defense of the

[1] Judge Catron was ill and did not sit; Judge Barbour was present at the argument, but died before the decision. Baldwin, alone of all the Judges, was of opinion that the power to regulate introduction of slaves was vested solely in Congress. Judge Story and Judge McKinley dissented, holding the notes void, but were of the opinion that the Federal Constitution did not interfere with the provisions of the State Constitution.

[2] From the diary entry by John Quincy Adams in his *Memoirs*, X, March 10, 1841, the decisions were rendered in a different way from that in which they are reported in 15 Peters, and it would appear that Taney (instead of Thompson) read the opinion of the Court. Adams' account is as follows: "The Chief Justice read an opinion upon the Mississippi Slavery Case, whereupon Judge McLean took from his pocket and read a counter-opinion, unexpectedly to the other Judges, to which the Judges, Thompson, Baldwin, and McKinley severally replied, each differing from all the others. About one, the Court adjourned without delay."

right of his native State of Ohio to exclude slaves, saying that : "Each State has a right to protect itself against
the avarice and intrusion of the slave dealer; to guard
its citizens against the inconveniences and dangers
of a slave population. The right to exercise this
power by a State is higher and deeper than the Constitution. The evil involves the prosperity and may
endanger the existence of a State. Its power to guard
against, or to remedy the evil, rests upon the law of
self-preservation; a law vital to every community,
and especially to a sovereign State." These were
the plainest and boldest words on the slavery question which had yet been uttered by a Judge of the
Court, and while gratifying the anti-slavery men of the
North as an indorsement of their efforts to prevent the
spread of slavery, Judge McLean's dictum was equally
satisfactory to the slavery party and to the South, who
regarded it as a confirmation of their contention that
they had exclusive power to regulate all questions affecting slavery within their borders. "All the abolitionists who respect the unanimous opinion of the
Supreme Court will now abandon so much of their petitions as call on Congress to regulate or prohibit transportation of slaves," said a Mississippi paper. "One
point of the abolition controversy (and that the most
important) is solemnly settled in favor of the South."[1]
McLean's dictum, furthermore, was regarded as as-
suring the validity of the laws of South Carolina, Georgia and Louisiana, forbidding the entrance of free negroes. While these laws had produced much friction
with these States of the North, who considered such
free negroes to be citizens, the South had long argued
that the quarantine principle justified all laws which
provided for the safety of the people in relation to their

[1] *Columbus Democrat* (Miss.), May 8, 1841.

slaves, and that such laws were an absolute necessity, "when in the very bosom of the Northern States, the fell abolitionists are to be found whose fanaticism would provoke every species of excess against our laws and institutions." [1]

On the day after the argument of this great case closed, the Court entered upon another involving the slavery issue, *United States* v. *Schooner Amistad*, 15 Pet. 518. It was of interest, not only in its singular facts, but owing to the appearance at the Bar, for the first time in thirty-two years, of Ex-President John Quincy Adams, then seventy-four years of age. With Adams, there appeared Roger S. Baldwin of Connecticut and against him the Attorney-General, Henry D. Gilpin, and eight days were devoted to the arguments. [2] The question presented was the right to freedom of certain negroes who, while being brought to this country illegally by slave traders, had gained mastery of the vessel and murdered the officers. On being carried here by a United States war vessel, they were claimed as slaves by their alleged Spanish owners. As Baldwin said in opening his argument, the case "involves considerations deeply affecting our National character in the eyes of the whole civilized world, as well as questions of power on the part of the Government of the United States, which are regarded with anxiety and alarm by a large portion of our citizens. It presents, for the first time, the question whether that Government . . . can, consistently with the genius of our in-

---

[1] *Georgia Journal*, Jan. 26, 1841.

[2] "The *Amistad Case* will create much feeling for itself, and for the reason that Mr. Adams will take the prominent part as counsel for the prisoners." *New York Express*, Feb. 25, 1841; the *National Intelligencer* said that the "Supreme Court was yesterday the theater of great interest and attracted a crowded audience, the occasion being the argument of Ex-President Adams as an attorney at the Bar of that Court." The last previous professional appearance by John Quincy Adams was in 1809, in *Hope Insurance Co.* v. *Boardman*, 5 Cranch, 56.

stitutions, become a party to proceedings for the enslavement of human beings cast upon our shores, and found in the condition of freemen within the territorial limits of a free and sovereign State." Much political feeling had been aroused by the case; and as Adams was then the most vigorous of all the anti-slavery advocates in Congress, and consequently, of all statesmen, the most obnoxious to the South, his argument was awaited with great interest by the public. Of its preparation and delivery Adams himself has written a vivid depiction: [1]

February 22. I walked to the Capitol with a thoroughly bewildered mind — so bewildered as to leave me nothing but fervent prayer that presence of mind may not utterly fail me at the trial I am about to go through. At the opening of the Court, Judge Thompson read a decision of the Court on a certain case. . . . The Attorney-General Henry D. Gilpin then delivered his argument in the case of the Amistad Captives. It occupied two hours. . . . Mr. Baldwin followed, in a sound and eloquent but exceedingly mild and moderate argument in behalf of the captives, till half past three, when the Court adjourned.

February 23. With increasing agitation of mind, now little short of agony, I rode in a hack to the Capitol. . . . The very skeleton of my argument is not yet put together. When the Court met, Judge Wayne and Judge Story read in succession two decisions of the Court, and Mr. Baldwin occupied the remainder of the day, four hours, in closing

[1] *J. Q. Adams*, X. Of his retainer, he wrote, Nov. 27, 1839: "Mr. Ellis Gray Loring of Boston and Mr. Lewis Tappan of New York, called on me this morning, and earnestly entreated of me to assume, as assistant counsel to Mr. Baldwin of Connecticut, the defence of the Africans before the Supreme Court of the United States, at their next January Term. I endeavored to excuse myself, upon the plea of my age and inefficiency, of the oppressive burdens of my duties as a member of the House of Representatives, and of my inexperience, after a lapse of more than thirty years, in the forms and technicals of argument before judicial tribunals, — but they urged me so much, and represented the case of those unfortunate men as so critical, it being a case of life and death, that I yielded."

The *Madisonian*, Feb. 16, 1842, said that Mr. Adams was responsible for much of the disorder in Congress on the slavery question, and that it had no desire "to shield that venomous old man from public reprobation."

his argument. . . . The point upon which he dwelt with most emphatic earnestness was the motion to dismiss the appeal of the United States on the contest of their right to appear as parties in the cause, they having no interest therein. His reasoning therein was powerful and perhaps conclusive. But I am apprehensive there are precedents and an Executive influence operating upon the Court which will turn the balance against us on that point. . . . He closed at half past three and left the day open for me to-morrow.

February 24. . . . The Court-room was full but not crowded and there were not many ladies. I had been deeply distressed and agitated till the moment when I rose; and then my spirit did not sink within me. With grateful heart for aid from above, though in humiliation for the weakness incident to the limits of my powers, I spoke four hours and a half, with sufficient method and order to witness little flagging of attention by the Judges or the auditory — till half past three o'clock. . . . The structure of my argument, so far as I have yet proceeded, is perfectly simple and comprehensive, needing no artificial division into distinct points but admitting the steady and undeviating pursuit of one fundamental principle — the ministration of *justice*. I then assigned my reason for inviting *justice* specially, aware that this was *always* the duty of the Court, but because an immense array of power — the Executive Administration, instigated by the Ministers of a foreign nation — has been brought to bear, in this case, on the side of injustice. . . . I did not, I could not, answer public expectation; but I have not yet utterly failed. God speed me to the end!

February 25. The agitation of mind under which I have been laboring for weeks had yesterday gradually subsided, in a continuous extemporaneous discourse of four hours and a half, through which I was enabled to pass, but the exhaustion consequent upon the effort, and the remnant of mental solicitude still heavily weighing upon my spirits, I had an uneasy, restless night, and short, not undisturbed repose. I rose however, with much encouraged and cheerful feeling. . . .

March 1. I went to the Supreme Court and concluded my argument. . . . I spoke about four hours and then closed somewhat abruptly. . . . I was unwilling to encroach upon the time of the Court for half of a third day . . . and finished with a very short personal address to the Court.

March 2. The Attorney-General then closed the argument on the part of the United States in about three hours, reviewing with great moderation of manner chiefly Mr. Baldwin's argument and very slightly noticing mine.

Judge Story, writing to his wife, February 28, 1841, described the old man as full of accustomed virility and belligerency and spoke of the "extraordinary" argument made by him. "Extraordinary, I say, for its power and its bitter sarcasm, and its dealing with topics far beyond the record and points of discussion." [1] Within one week after the close of the argument, the Court, on March 9, through Judge Story decided the case, holding that the negroes should be freed and sent back to Africa, and thus adjudging in favor of Adams' clients. [2]

On the day after this decision, the Court, through Chief Justice Taney, took a further step in the great case which had been long pending between the two sovereign States — *Rhode Island* v. *Massachusetts*, 15 Pet. 233, — by overruling the demurrer of the latter State and ordering her to file an answer. [3] That the

---

[1] *Story,* II, 348.

[2] Adams, writing to Richard Peters, Jr., May 19, 1841, with reference to the report of his argument in *Peters Reports* said (*Peters Papers MSS*): "If you leave out my flagellation of the later Secretary of State and of the man of Kinderhook for his *lettre de cachet,* because the Court took no notice of them — no more than of the bright intellect of the South, or of the *Globe* of 7 Jan., 1841 — you may put in what you please for my speech. The best epigram upon the *lettre de cachet* was the decree of the Court pronouncing the negroes *free.* The rest is 'leather and prunella.' "

Writing in his diary, a year later, Feb. 17, 1842, Adams referred to his victory, with striking modesty for an old man of seventy-six: "I went into the room where the Supreme Court of the United States were in session. This room I re-entered with a silent thrill of delight, for the first time since I was there at this time last year, under such a heavy pressure of responsibility and with so glorious a result. I dare not trust myself with the exultation of my own heart on this occasion, so fearful am I of incurring the guilt of presumptuous vanity, for the feeling of deep humility." *J. Q. Adams,* X.

[3] It is interesting to note that Daniel Webster argued this case for Massachusetts, March 8, 1841, after his appointment as Secretary of State under President Harrison.

members of the Court, though appointed by Democratic Presidents, were obtaining the confidence even of the Whig Bar of the North is seen from a comment on this case which appeared in a highly conservative magazine edited by Boston Whigs: "Although we are certainly disappointed with the reasoning of the Court on the demurrer, still we have entire confidence in the intelligence and fidelity of that dignified tribunal. There is, we are sorry to perceive, a disposition sometimes apparent to undervalue its high and commanding character. Because its decisions on some questions are not in unison with our general opinions, and because some principles are adopted which are not in harmony with the doctrines of our schools, and possibly because a majority of the members are of a political party in opposition to the one to which we belong, we are in danger of losing our respect for its learning, its authority and its power. But the members of this high Court have, as a body, no superiors in all the great qualities of mind and heart, in honor, integrity, ability and learning, which are the ornaments of the Bench and the security of its people. We should encourage this belief." [1]

It is to be noted that there was a break in the argument of the *Amistad Case*, from February 25 to March 1. This was due to the death of Judge Barbour, which occurred with great suddenness on February 25.[2] He "had been daily with us in the hall, listening to the animated and earnest discussions which the great subjects in controversy here naturally produce," said Taney at the meeting of the Court held in his memory,

[1] *Law Reporter* (May, 1841), IV.
[2] Adams wrote in his diary: "At eleven o'clock the surviving Judges came in. Excepting Judge McKinley, all in their robes, and in procession. They took their seats and Chief Justice Taney said: 'One of the Judges of the Court — Brother Barbour — is dead. The Court will adjourn till Monday.'"

"and he had been with us also in the calmer scenes of the conference room, taking a full share in the deliberations of the Court, and always listened to with the most respectful attention. It was from one of these meetings, which had been protracted to a late hour of the night, that we all parted from him apparently in the usual health; and in the morning we found that the Associate whom we so highly respected and the friend we so greatly esteemed had been called away from us." In view of the Whig criticisms which had been leveled against President Jackson for the appointment of Barbour, it is interesting to note that Judge Story now wrote of him: "He was a man of great integrity, of a very solid and acute understanding, of considerable legal attainments (in which he was daily improving) and altogether a very conscientious, upright and laborious Judge, whom we respected for his talents and virtues, and his high sense of duty." [1]

This death occasioned a contest in Congress over a bill to reorganize the judicial Circuits which had been long needed. While there were then six Circuits for the Eastern and Southern States, the whole West and Southwest had only three Circuits, in which the traveling distances for the Judges were immense, and the amount of litigation, due to complicated land titles, the deranged state of the currency and the rage for speculation, was unbearably heavy. It was proposed to abolish the present Fourth Circuit (consisting of Virginia and North Carolina), and to throw Virginia into the Circuit with Maryland, and North Carolina into the Circuit with South Carolina and Georgia, thus eliminating one Eastern Circuit and giving it to the Southwest. As Barbour had come from Virginia, it

---

[1] Judge Story wrote, Feb. 28, 1841: "He dined heartily, and remained with the Judges in conference until after ten o'clock in the evening, and then in a most cheerful humor." *Story*, II, 348–350.

was felt that it was a peculiarly fortunate time to make
the change, there now being no Supreme Court Judge
from the Fourth Circuit. The proposition, however,
touching Virginia's State pride, was bitterly resented
by her Senators, and the bill after passing the Senate
was finally lost in the House, on its adjournment.[1] It
may be noted that Senator Benton of Missouri opposed
the bill, on the ground that the real remedy for the increase of business in the West was the increase of the
number of Judges on the Supreme Court to twelve,
since "to determine these weighty matters, there should
be an ample number and they should be brought from
every great section of the country."   Senator Buchanan
of Pennsylvania, on the other hand, thought that "the
present number of Judges was already greater than
he could have desired. Nine was too large a number
if it could have been avoided." As soon as it was
seen that the Circuits were not to be altered, President
Van Buren, in the last moments of his Administration,
on February 26, nominated to fill the vacancy Peter
V. Daniel of Virginia. Daniel was fifty-six years old
and was serving as United States District Judge in
Virginia, having succeeded Barbour in that position;
he had also been tendered the position of Attorney-
General on Taney's resignation of that post, but had
declined. Of the new Judge, a leading Democratic
paper said: "With talent, both natural and acquired,
equal to all the duties of the office, he combines the

---

[1] *26th Cong., 2d Sess.*, Feb. 27, 1841. The bill proposed to make three Circuits
in the Southwest — Alabama and Louisiana in one; Mississippi and Tennessee in
another; and Arkansas, Missouri and Kentucky in the third. One object sought to
be accomplished was, to eliminate Judge McKinley from the Mississippi Circuit;
for owing to the fact that he had been bodily assaulted in the street in Jackson,
Miss., by a deputy marshal, he had declined to hold a Circuit Court in that State
in 1840 and 1841, and for this action he had been the subject of severe criticism in
a debate in Congress, on a proposal to deduct $500 from the salary of any Judge
who failed to hold his Circuit Court. *27th Cong., 2d Sess.*, April 6, 1842.

moral qualifications, that are not only valuable in themselves but indispensable to our security; a steadiness and firmness which no strategies can overcome, which all the arts of sophistry and the seduction of power and acumen cannot overreach or deceive"; and another said that "the selection has afforded general satisfaction; he is one of the strict construction, State-Rights school."[1] The Whig Senators, however, were indignant at this appointment, made so soon before the inauguration of the new President, Harrison. They denounced Daniel as a political partisan, though admitting his purity of character and legal ability; and, with the exception of Smith of Indiana, they all left the Senate Chamber before the final vote was taken on confirmation. The appointment was confirmed, on March 2, by a vote of twenty-two to five —less than a majority of the Senators. The action was criticized with true party acridity by the Whig papers, one of which gave the following vivid description of this episode of another "Midnight Judge." "It appears that the Senate, by an unexampled majority, had passed a bill abolishing the Circuit which the late Justice Barbour was attached to, and whilst that bill was pending before the House of Representatives, a majority of the Senate took up the nomination of Mr. Daniel as a Judge of the Supreme Court of the United States, on Tuesday night. It was in vain that the Whigs protested against filling an office, which had been suspended so far as the Senate could act; it was in vain that they plead for time, by laying the nomination on the table or referring it until it was known whether the House would reject or agree to the bill of the Senate. All postponement was refused, and about 12

---

[1] *Richmond Enquirer*, March 5, 1841; *Charleston Courier*, Feb. 27, 1841; *Daily Georgian*, March 6, 1841.

o'clock at night, after all the Whigs but one had retired, the nomination of Mr. Daniel was confirmed by a small majority, several of his own political friends voting against him.   The nomination of Mr. J. Y. Mason to the office of District Judge of Virginia which had been filled by Mr. Daniel was also confirmed.   The public cannot fail to contrast the conduct of the party, fortunately now no longer dominant, when Mr. Adams was going out of power, with what it is when Mr. Van Buren is retiring.   Then, the nomination of Mr. Crittenden, whose great merits are now so generally recognized for a seat on the bench of the Supreme Court, was laid on the table.   Now, that of Mr. Daniel is refused to be laid on the table, taken up in the very Senate which had passed a bill dispensing with it, and the nomination confirmed, whilst that bill is actually pending before the House of Representatives.   True to the spoils principles in these last moments of their expiring power, a gentleman who had signalized himself as a partisan in an inferior judicial station is elevated to the exalted office of a Judge of the Supreme Court of the United States."

Other Whig papers denounced the President's action as "another flagitious act.   The breath was hardly out of Judge Barbour's body before Van Buren hurries a successor into the Senate Chamber; and an approval of him is insisted upon, and carried at midnight by dragging Senators out of their bed.   It is not an easy thing, one would think, to find a Judge fit for the Supreme Bench in 24 hours, but Mr. Van Buren found no difficulty in it. . . .   Thus, in shame, and dishonor, injustice and disgrace ends the career of Mr. Van Buren."[1]   In thus assailing a Democratic President,

---

[1] *National Intelligencer*, March 4, 5, 1841; *New York Express*, March 9, 1841; *Richmond Enquirer*, March 9, 11, 1841.

however, the Whigs conveniently forgot that he was but following the precedent set by President Adams, a Federalist, in appointing John Marshall during the closing days of his Administration; and in view of the extremely harsh and violent campaign of invective waged by Harrison and Tyler against Van Buren in the preceding fall, the expectation that he would defer to his successor in the matter of appointments was hardly reasonable.[1]

[1] It is interesting to note that another Whig opportunity to make an appointment on the Court during this year was lost when Judge McLean declined to resign from the Bench to take a position in the Cabinet. The expectation, never fulfilled, had been that John J. Crittenden of Kentucky would receive the appointment; but again, as in 1829, Crittenden's chance to go upon the Bench escaped him. *Crittenden Papers MSS*, letter of Reverdy Johnson to Crittenden, Sept. 5, 1841.

CHAPTER TWENTY-THREE

FEDERAL POWERS, TYLER, AND THE GIRARD WILL CASE

1842–1844

Two phases of the delicate issue of slavery having been passed upon at its session in the first year of the new Whig Administration of Harrison and Tyler, still another phase of this question was presented at the 1842 Term. Now for the first time in its history the Court's attitude in this connection became the subject of attack, after its decision in *Prigg* v. *Pennsylvania*, 16 Pet. 539, in which the constitutionality of the Pennsylvania statute relative to fugitive slaves was involved.[1] The increasing tension in the community over the issue of the respective powers of the States and of Congress as to such slaves was clearly shown at the argument. A denial of the right of the State to legislate on this subject, said the Attorney-General of Pennsylvania, will "arouse a spirit of discord and resistance that will neither shrink nor slumber till the obligation itself be cancelled or the Union which creates it be dissolved"; and another of the State's counsel said that of all solemn questions ever argued before this

---

[1] Owing to the illness of the Chief Justice, Judge Story presided during most of the 1842 Term. His situation, Story amusingly described in a talk with one of his classes at the Harvard Law School, as follows: " Was Tyler President or Acting President at the demise of Gen. Harrison? A nice question, gentlemen, and hard to solve. The question was debated in cabinet meeting, and on Mr. Webster's opinion, Tyler was addressed as President. On one occasion, when Chief Justice Taney was ill, I took his place as Chief Justice and was thus addressed. At first, I felt nervous, but soon becoming used to it, found it, like public money to new members of Congress, '*not bad to take.*' And this was probably the feeling with Mr. Tyler." *Western Law Journ.* (1846), II, 432; *Story*, II, 506.

Court "no one has arisen of more commanding import, or wider scope in its influence, or on which hung mightier results for good or ill to the Nation"; and he stated that it involved "a subject which is even now heaving the political tides of the country, which has caused enthusiasm to throw her lighted torch into the temples of religion, and the halls of science and learning, while the forum of justice, and the village barroom have equally resounded with the discussion. . . . Whilst it has become 'sore as gangrene' in one region, it is the football of the enthusiast in another." That the Court itself fully realized the seriousness of the situation was shown in the opening words of its opinion, delivered by Judge Story: "Few questions which have ever come before this Court involve more delicate and important considerations, and few upon which the public at large may be presumed to feel a more profound and pervading interest." Fortunately, the Court found itself able to deliver a unanimous opinion, holding that the power of Congress over the subject of fugitive slaves was exclusive, and that the State statute, being in conflict with the Federal Fugitive Slave Law, was consequently unconstitutional. But while all agreed that a State statute could not interfere with the provisions of the Federal law, there was a sharp dissent by Chief Justice Taney and Judges Thompson and Daniel from the further proposition laid down by Judge Story (and concurred in by the majority of the Court, including the Southern Judge, Wayne) to the effect that the power of Congress was so exclusive as to render invalid every State statute on the subject, whether in aid of, or in conflict with, the Federal law. The decision was equally unsatisfactory to both pro-slavery and anti-slavery men. The former regarded it as a severe blow to State-

Rights, even though it sustained their views on the slavery question.[1] Among the latter, the decision was regarded as a complete surrender to the South. John Quincy Adams wrote in his diary, March 10, that he had spent much of the day in reading the various opinions delivered by the seven Judges, " everyone of them dissenting from the reasoning of all the rest, and everyone of them coming to the same conclusion, the transcendent omnipotence of slavery in these United States, riveted by a clause in the Constitution." For his part in the "ignoble compliance with the slaveholders' will", Judge Story was hotly assailed at the North; but such criticism could not perturb a Judge who had penned to a friend the following noble words: "I shall never hesitate to do my duty as a Judge under the Constitution and laws of the United States, be the consequences what they may. That Constitution I have sworn to support, and I cannot forget or repudiate my solemn obligations at pleasure. You know full well that I have ever been opposed to slavery. But I take my standard of duty as a Judge from the Constitution." [2] To the State of New York, the *Prigg Case* decision gave particular offense; for it completely nullified a law of that State which, by granting jury trials in case of the arrest of fugitive slaves, had heretofore resulted in rendering utterly nugatory the provisions of the Federal Fugitive Slave Law, and which had very naturally caused great friction between New York and Southern States. "Thus ends the controversy between New York and Virginia, and between New York

[1] In a strongly adverse review of Judge Story's life in the *New York Evening Post*, Jan. 27, 1852, it was said: "The Supreme Court has never struck a more decisive and fatal blow at State-Rights than in this decision, and there is no one of Judge Story's honors of which he has less reason to be proud than that of being selected to deliver the opinion of the Bench."

[2] *Story*, II, 430, letter of Story to E. Bacon, relating to the case of *La Belle Eugénie*.

and Georgia," said a leading New York paper. "The conclusion to which the Court have arrived involves consequences which can by no means be satisfactory to this part of the country. A freeman now may be arrested and carried into slavery, after but a slight investigation before a magistrate and without the intervention of a jury. The (Federal) Law of 1793, the practice under which New York and Pennsylvania endeavored to correct, is now pronounced to be supreme law." [1]

Since, however, public attention, at this date was absorbed in the bitter contests over the Sub-Treasury, the Banks, the Texas and the Oregon questions and the struggle between President Tyler and the Whigs, the slavery issue, for the time being, became subordinate; the excitement over the *Prigg Case* died away; and the *North American Review*, the very next year, in speaking of "the beneficial action of the Judiciary in quieting public contests and maintaining unruffled the majesty of the law", referred to the effect of the *Prigg Case* as follows: "At this majestic bar, the matter was argued with as much dignity and calmness as if it has never set the country in a flame; and the judgment was received by the public with the quiet submission which they usually manifest when ordinary judicial decisions are announced. Some murmurs were heard from both parties about the insufficiency or hardship of certain provisions in the Constitution. We hardly heard a whisper against the fidelity and even-handed justice with which that judgment had been expounded by the Court." [2]

---

[1] *New York Daily Express*, March 8, 1842.

[2] *The Independence of the Judiciary*, in *North Amer. Rev.* (Oct. 1843), LVII; and see Crawford, J., *In re Booth* (1859), 3 Wisc. 79, for the view taken of the *Prigg Case* by contemporaneous opinion; see also article in *New York American*, quoted in *New York Express*, March 5, 1842. The case was discussed on many occasions in Congress during the next seven years. See especially *30th Cong., 1st Sess.*, speeches of Ashmun of Massachusetts, April 10, 1848, Bayly of Virginia and McLane

Undoubtedly, the chief reason for the equanimity with which the decision was finally accepted was the rapid realization by the Northern States of the effective weapon which had been placed in their hands. Those portions of Judge Story's opinion which declared that the States were prohibited not only from passing laws in violation of the fugitive slave provision of the Constitution, but from enacting legislation in furtherance of it, and that the States were not bound and could not be obliged to enforce this provision of the Constitution through State officers, were seized upon by anti-slavery States as a justification for legislative measures refusing the assistance of their officials to enforce the Federal Fugitive Slave Law.[1] Relying on this theory, Massachusetts, as early as 1843, passed a statute which made it a penal offense for any State officer or constable to aid in any way in carrying the Federal Law into effect. Other States soon followed with similar legislation;[2] and the difficulty of reclaiming a fugitive slave became so great as to force Congress to enact new and more stringent Federal legislation, in 1850, and thus to precipitate the great conflict between State and Federal authority which finally led to war.[3]

of Maryland, April 11, 1848; *30th Cong., 2d Sess.*, speech of Baldwin of Connecticut, Jan. 22, 1849, Crisfield of Maryland, Feb. 17, 1849.

[1] Story himself believed that "a great point had been gained for liberty — so great a point, indeed, that on his return from Washington," wrote his son: "He repeatedly and earnestly spoke of it to his family and his intimate friends as being 'a triumph of freedom.'" *Story*, II, 392, 394.

[2] Personal Liberty Laws (so called) similar to that of Massachusetts, were enacted in Vermont in 1843, Connecticut in 1844, New Hampshire in 1846, Pennsylvania in 1847, Rhode Island in 1848, Wisconsin in 1857. On the other hand, South Carolina, Mississippi and Missouri passed laws prohibiting free negroes from entering their boundaries. For one of the best summaries of the Personal Liberty Laws, see *National Intelligencer*, Dec. 11, 12, 1860.

[3] Slavery was further involved at this 1842 Term in a singular case, *Gordon* v. *Longest*, 16 Pet. 97. In this suit, argued by John J. Crittenden against Thomas H. Benton, and involving a Kentucky statute forbidding steamboats to take on board slaves from the Ohio shore, Judge McLean in his opinion said: " This is the first instance known to us in which a State Court has refused to a party a right to remove his cause to the Circuit Court of the United States."

While the Court, composed of a majority of State-Rights Democrats, had thus upheld the exclusiveness of Federal power in relation to the limited subject of fugitive slaves, it took an even greater step at this Term in expanding the domain of Federal power with relation to a great variety of subjects. For in *Swift* v. *Tyson*, 16 Pet. 1, it announced for the first time that the Federal Courts had the authority to lay down principles of general law, without regard to the decision of State Courts, even where no question of the Federal Constitution or laws was involved. Marshall himself had never asserted such power for the Court; and theretofore it had been commonly assumed (and there had been loose expressions of the Court to the effect) that the Thirty-Fourth Section of the Judiciary Act which provided "that the laws of the several States . . . shall be regarded as rules of decision in trials at common law" in the Federal Courts, included within the scope of the meaning of the word "laws", the decisions of the local State Courts as well as statutory laws.[1]   Now, in 1842, in this case of *Swift* v. *Tyson* the question arose whether the Court would hold itself bound to follow the doctrine laid down by the Courts of New York relative to the law of bills of exchange. The case had been previously argued, in 1840, by Daniel Webster against Richard H. Dana of Massachusetts, and was now submitted on briefs by William P. Fessenden of Maine and by Dana. Judge Story held (without noticing any expression to the contrary in previous decisions of the Court) that this Section of the Judiciary Act did not apply to "questions of a more general nature not at all dependent upon local statutes or usages of a fixed and per-

---

[1] In *Bank of Kentucky* v. *Wister*, 2 Pet. 318, 324, however, as late as 1829, the Court had said that it was "unnecessary at this time to enter into the inquiry how far its decisions and those of other States upon a question of a general, not a local case or character, are to be controlled by those of any particular State."

manent operation"; that as to such questions, the
Federal Courts were not to be bound by the law of the
States as laid down by the State Courts; that the interpretation and effect of contracts and other instruments of a commercial nature, were to be sought "in
the general principles and doctrines of commercial
jurisprudence"; and that in this case, the Court would
not follow the law as to negotiable instruments laid
down by the New York Courts, but would ascertain
the law for itself. This decision, which, as the newspapers said, "settled an important commercial question which ought to be soon and generally known",
introduced a novel and original doctrine into Federal
law — that there existed in the United States a general
commercial law independent of the decisions of a
State.[1] Probably no decision of the Court has ever
given rise to more uncertainty as to legal rights; and
though doubtless intended to promote uniformity in
the operation of business transactions, its chief effect
has been to render it difficult for business men to know
in advance to what particular topic the Court would
apply the doctrine; and the adverse criticisms by
Judges and jurists, which have continued to the present day, have had much justification.[2] In another
famous case at this Term, *Martin* v. *Waddell's Lessee*,

---

[1] In the *Western Law Journ.* (April, 1844), the editor expressed a hope that
Judge Story would prepare a bill "founded on the power of Congress to regulate
commerce, which might have the effect of rendering the law of commerce as well
as of navigation uniform throughout this country. Think, for example, of the
evils arising from the conflicting doctrines as held in different States on the subject
of negotiable paper and insurance." See also review in *Law Reporter* (1842), V.

[2] *Is there a General Commercial Law*, by Robert G. Street, *Amer. Law Reg.*
(1873), XXI; *Federal Common Law*, by Hunsdon Cary, *Virg. Law Reg.* (1904), X;
Common Law Jurisdiction of the United States, by Alton B. Parker, *Yale Law Journ.*
(1904), XVII; *The Non-Federal Law Administered in Federal Courts*, by W.
Trickett, *Amer. Law Rev.* (1906), XLI. See also comments on Judge Story and his
decision in this case by John C. Gray in *The Nature and Sources of the Law* (1909);
see also especially Field, J., in *Baltimore & Ohio R. R.* v. *Baugh* (1892), 149 U. S.
368, 401.

16 Pet. 367, the Court still further limited its obligation
to follow the law of the State under the Thirty-Fourth
Section of the Judiciary Act. This case involved the
right of the State of New Jersey to grant exclusive oys-
ter-bed rights in flats under its tide-waters, a question
which had "created much ill-blood in the past twenty
years." The Court was called upon to construe certain
royal charters and deeds of surrender by the Colonial
Proprietors, which had already been construed and the
legal question presented by which had been decided by
the New Jersey Supreme Court, as early as 1818. While
deciding in favor of the State, the Court, through Judge
Taney, held that as the question did not depend "upon
the meaning of instruments framed by the people of
New Jersey or by their authority", the State Court
ruling did not bind the Federal Court, though it was
"unquestionably entitled to great weight." "The
very learned and lucid opinion of Taney will give as
much satisfaction to the lovers of law as the decision
gives to the people of New Jersey," said a New York
paper. "It will increase the general confidence in the
uprightness and legal capability of this truly august
tribunal." [1] .One other instance of the scrupulous zeal
with which this Democratic Court adhered to its determination to protect the functions of the Federal
Government against encroachment by the States was
seen in *Dobbins* v. *Erie County*, 16 Pet. 435. In this
case, a statute of Pennsylvania imposing a tax on the
income of a Federal revenue officer was held unconstitutional as an "interference with the constitutional
means which have been legislated by the government
of the United States to carry into effect its powers to
lay and collect taxes, duties, imports, etc., and to regulate commerce", and as diminishing the recompense

---

[1] *New York Journal of Commerce*, quoted in *Boston Daily Advertiser*, Feb. 14, 1842.

secured to the Federal officer by Federal laws. The decision, rendered through a Southern Judge, Wayne, reaffirming and applying the doctrines of *McCulloch* v. *Maryland*, met with criticism from State-Rights Democrats. "This appears to be a carrying of the doctrine of National Sovereignty very far," said the *Pennsylvanian*. "When the tax is laid on all persons indiscriminately who receive official salaries, on State officers as well as National, there appears no danger of the action of the National Government being impeded by the tax. . . . It is a natural weakness of the human mind for the officers of every government and every branch of government to be prone to stretch the powers of their own government or department and to abridge those of others. Hence, there has been generally a disposition in the Courts of the United States to encroach somewhat on the rights of the States as understood by the Democratic party. We do not undertake to pronounce that the decision is erroneous, but we should have been well pleased, had the Constitution been framed or the Judges so construed it, that no such decision should have been made."[1]

The stand taken by the Court, composed chiefly of Democratic Judges, in support of the powers of the Federal Government was the more marked, by reason of the fact that during the past two years, 1841 and 1842, the Democratic Party in Congress and throughout the country had been peculiarly violent in assailing the extension of Federal power contained in the Whig legislation of these years. The Whig Congress, as soon as it convened after the death of President Harrison and the accession of John Tyler to the Presidency, had passed a series of statutes, each of which had been charged by the Democrats to be violative of the sovereignty

[1] *Pennsylvanian*, April 21, 1842.

of the States—the Fiscal Bank Acts, the National Bankruptcy Act, the Habeas Corpus Act and the Congressional District Election Act. As the debates on these measures produced the first criticisms which had been made upon the Court and its functions since the year 1833, and as the discussion of the effect of the Court's position in constitutional Government was conducted with masterful ability, these debates deserve the attention of all students of American legal history.

As to the Fiscal Bank Acts, the discussion naturally centered about the power of Congress to charter a National Bank; and this much-argued question, which had been the source of party conflict since 1789 and which had been supposed to have been settled by the decisions of the Court in *McCulloch* v. *Maryland* and *Osborn* v. *Bank of the United States*, twenty-two and seventeen years before, was now reargued with increased fervor. The views which Jefferson, Jackson and Calhoun had advanced, as to the non-binding force of Court decisions upon the President or the Congress, when acting in Executive or Legislative capacity, were now reasserted by the Democrats with great vigor. "A Senator must exercise his own judgment as a legislator on the question of the constitutional power of Congress to charter a Bank," said James Buchanan of Pennsylvania: "I respect judicial decisions within their appropriate sphere, as much as any Senator. They put at rest forever the controversy immediately before the Court; and as a general rule they govern all future cases of the same character; but even these decisions, like all other human things, are modified and changed by the experience of time and the lights of knowledge. The law is not now what it was fifty years ago, nor what it will be fifty years hereafter. . . . But even if the Judiciary had settled the question, I should never hold myself bound by their decision, whilst acting in a legislative character. . . . I cannot agree that 'its judicial expositions are of equal authority with the text of the Constitution.' This is an infallibility which was never before claimed for any human tribunal. . . . No man holds in higher estimation than I do the memory of Chief Justice Marshall; but I should never have consented to make even him the final arbiter between the Government and people of this country on questions of constitutional liberty. . . . It is notorious that the Court, during the whole period which he presided over it, embracing so many years of its existence, has inclined towards the highest assertion of Federal power. That this has been done honestly and conscientiously I entertain not a doubt." [1] Similar views were expressed in the House by John T. Mason of Maryland, who, though the youngest Congressman, voiced the old fears of Federalism: "The Court is not authorized to interfere with the free exercise by Congress of its constitutional functions. While I have the highest veneration for the ability and purity of the late Chief Justice, yet I would be unwilling that upon this question his opinions should govern my judgment, for the plain reason that his prejudices, his partialities, his interests and his education, all contributed to the formation of an opinion which should be entirely free from the bias of either."

On the other hand, the binding force of the decision of the Court in *McCulloch* v. *Maryland*, even upon Congress, was supported by many strong lawyers, both Democratic and Whig — such as Senator John M.

[1] *27th Cong., 1st Sess.*, and *App.*, 161, 298, speeches of Buchanan, July 7, 1841, Israel Smith of Connecticut, July 20, 1841, Levi Woodbury of New Hampshire, July 10, 1841; speeches in the House, of John T. Mason of Maryland, Aug. 3, 1841, Ezra Dean of Ohio, Aug. 5, 1841, John Hastings of Ohio, Aug. 9, 1841, Henry A. Wise of Virginia, Aug. 5, 1841.

Berrien of Georgia (who had been Attorney-General under President Jackson), and Henry Clay of Kentucky, Jabez W. Huntington of Connecticut and James Simmons of Rhode Island. " The Supreme Court have repeatedly and unanimously decided that Congress have the constitutional power to establish a National Bank and this is the only constitutional mode of determining the question," said Simmons. " The decisions have been uniform, always recognized and submitted to by every State Court, by every State Government, and by the whole people. If after this, men will contend that it is an open question, a doubtful question, they by it insist that no question can be settled under our Constitution." [1] And Berrien eloquently protested against " that political heresy of the most alarming character . . . that the interpretation of the Constitution by its own appointed arbiter is not obligatory on any man who is called, in the discharge of his official duty, to interpret that instrument, but that he is at liberty to follow out implicitly the dictates of his own understanding uncontrolled by that decision. . . . To the judicial power belongs, by the express provisions of the Constitution itself, in all cases properly brought before it, the right to interpret that instrument, to decide what it permits and what it forbids : in fine, to determine what it is. Each judicial decision, so made under the authority of the Constitution, becomes incorporated in, and is part and parcel of, the instrument itself, enlarging, restraining or modifying the original text, according to the legal import and effect of such decision. He who disregards it, whether he be legislator or executive officer, disregards

[1] *27th Cong., 1st Sess.*, and *App.*, 358, speeches of Berrien, Sept. 1, 1841, Archer of Virginia, Sept. 2, Huntington, July 3 ; speeches in the House of Clay, July 1, Simmons, July 2 ; *27th Cong., 2d Sess.*, speech of Berrien, Jan. 26, 1842 ; see, however, vigorous denial of Berrien's doctrine by Israel Smith of Connecticut, Jan. 23, 1842.

the Constitution itself, of which it is a part and confessedly of higher authority than the original text, since in all cases of supposed conflict it controls that text." [1] While thus maintaining that in their legislative capacity, they were not bound by Court decisions, the Democratic Senators advanced further a view of the effect of the decision in the *McCulloch Case*, which was more tenable, and consideration of which has been sometimes lost sight of by Judges and jurists. "That decision," said Buchanan, "amounted only to this, that the Court would not rejudge the discretion of Congress, but it necessarily referred the constitutional question back to the conscience of each member about to vote for or against a new Bank, untrammelled by any judicial exposition." [2] All that the Court decided was that Congress, in 1816, in determining that a National Bank was a necessary and proper means of executing certain express powers of the Constitution, was acting then within its powers; but the question whether a Bank was such a necessary and proper means was for the exclusive determination of Congress in the first instance; hence, each successive Congress had full and untrammeled power so to determine. And as Senator Levi Woodbury of New Hampshire said: "The decision of the Supreme

[1] Berrien also urged further an interesting argument to the effect that the State-Rights advocates ought not to reject this principle for they were insistent that the Supreme Court, in adhering to its doctrine of following the laws of the States, should follow that law as construed by the State Courts. "It is upon the very principle for which I am contending that our State laws receive the interpretation, which those who framed them designed they should have, that the intention of our State Legislatures is carried out when these laws are brought into controversy in the Federal tribunals. The decisions of State Judges are considered in these tribunals as part and parcel of the laws which they are called to interpret, the principle which I maintained being equally applicable to acts of ordinary legislation and to the fundamental law. When a question arises there upon the construction of a State law, the Judges of these tribunals do not undertake to interpret it according to their own understanding. The immediate inquiry is, what construction has been given to this law by the State Judiciary; and that construction is the rule of interpretation in the Federal tribunal."

[2] *27th Cong., 1st Sess.*, and *App.*, 161, 341, 180, 201, speeches of Buchanan, July 7, Sept. 2, Woodbury, July 10, Benton, July 27, 1841.

Court that a National Bank is constitutional, however much urged on the other side as binding and final, has been merely a decision contingent on certain facts. It is, that any existing institution, first agreed by Congress to be necessary and proper, is by them [the Court] considered in that event constitutional, but not so in any other event. . . . Such a judicial opinion covers the legality of only that special charter granted under those special facts, and decides nothing as to any other period or any other proposed charter." And, as Benton said: "It decides that the constitutionality of the institution depends upon its necessity to the Government, and that of this necessity Congress is the sole judge."

This debate on the Fiscal Bank bill also produced severe criticisms of the Court's decision in the *Dartmouth College Case*. "I think it is not law and could not be recognized as law, were the question again brought before that Court," said Benjamin Tappan of Ohio. "It is, in truth, an instance of judicial Constitution-making, not very uncommon formerly with the Court who gave the decision . . . an ægis manufactured by judicial charlatans for preservation of bank charters." Denying that a charter was a contract, or ever intended to be included within the term "impairment of obligation of contract," he continued: "Nothing proves more clearly the great influence of corporations in a society than the prevailing opinion that it would be unsafe to trust Legislatures with the power of repealing charters. Why unsafe? . . . Even if your Legislative Assembly is composed of the most intelligent, pure and upright men, they cannot foresee the effect of their legislation in all cases. They may incorporate companies which to their judgment can only be used beneficially for the public, and yet they may be mistaken; the chartered powers which they have conferred may prove to be powers of mischief and destruction, instead of being used to promote the public interest and welfare; guided by a private cupidity, they may be used to corrupt the morals of the people and sap the foundations of our government, and yet upon this theory of vested rights, there is no remedy—the enslaved people must submit." [1]

The second extension of Federal power denounced by the Democrats was the enactment of the Whig National Bankruptcy Act of August 12, 1841. This measure, which extended the privilege of voluntary bankruptcy to all classes of persons, had been passed as a result of earnest pressure from debtors ruined by the banking and currency troubles and the land speculations of the past decade. The fact that imprisonment for debt still existed in many of the States rendered the condition of many debtors utterly desperate. The number of insolvents was estimated by some as high as five hundred thousand. At the South, the situation was particularly distressing. [2] In spite of the economic pressure for this legislation, however, there was a vigorous political opposition to the Act from the Democrats, based chiefly on two grounds: first, its unconstitutionality, as being in fact an insolvency law and not a bankruptcy law within the meaning of the Constitution;

---

[1] *27th Cong., 1st Sess.*, and *App.*, 195, speeches in the Senate of Benjamin Tappan of Ohio, July 14, Thomas H. Benton of Missouri, July 27, 1841.

[2] John J. Crittenden wrote Dec. 9, 1842, as to the Bankruptcy Act: "It was one of a series of measures urgently sought for by the Whigs of New York, Louisiana, etc. and rather conceded to them than desired by those of the Kentucky Whigs who supported it. It has to a great extent accomplished its object, and though there may have been abuses, it has relieved from imprisonment (for in many of the States that remedy is continued) and a hopeless mass of debt, many an honest man whose fortunes had been wrecked in the disastrous times through which we have passed." *Life of John J. Crittenden* (1871), by Ann M. B. Coleman, I.

It should be noted that the need of national bankruptcy legislation had been recently emphasized by the decision of the Court in 1840 in *Suydam* v. *Broadnax*, 14 Pet. 67, reaffirming the doctrine that a State insolvent law could not operate to bar contracts made in another State.

second, its invasion of the sovereignty of the States. "It is much more glaringly unconstitutional, much more immoral than the Alien and Sedition Laws," said Senator Benton. "The most daring attack on the State laws and the rights of property and on public morals which the history of Europe or America has exhibited. . . . It broke down the line between the jurisdiction of the Federal Courts and the State Courts in the whole department of debtors and creditors . . . bringing all local debts and dealings into the Federal Courts at the will of the debtors." [1] Senator Woodbury said that it brought the States "into the whirlpool of the Federal Courts, and is an alarming encroachment on State-Rights, because such an act, coupled with a like usurping power . . . to transfer from the States the trial of all burnings and murders like those of McLeod to the same Federal Courts, . . . tends most rapidly to prostrate all State independence, as well as to build up a frightful, monopolizing, overshadowing despotism at the centre, which neither our fathers contemplated, nor we should tolerate." A leading Democratic paper, after describing the bill as "working a regular process of encroachment on State jurisdiction," said that: "The whole latitudinarian school will go for it, because it invades State jurisdiction, extends Federal power, destroys contracts and brings the persons and property of the people under the sceptre of the Federal Judges." [2]

The third extension of Federal power was the Act of August 29, 1842, conferring upon the Federal Courts authority to issue writs of habeas corpus in certain cases of persons confined by the States. This legislation had

---

[1] *Thirty Years' View* (1856), by Thomas H. Benton, II, 464, 233; *27th Cong., 3d Sess.*, speech of Woodbury, Feb. 25, 1843.

[2] *Washington Globe*, March 8, 1842; see *ibid.*, May 5, 1842; and for description of the political factors in bankruptcy legislation see *New York Evening Post*, Feb. 26, 1840; *Story*, II, 404, 405, letters to Berrien, April 29, July 23, 1842; *J. Q. Adams*, X, 529.

originated in the dangerous complications which had arisen out of the trial in the New York State Court of Alexander McLeod, a British citizen, indicted for murder, in connection with the steamer *Caroline* episode in 1838. Though McLeod's defense was founded on international law, and though Great Britain denied the right of the State of New York to insist on trial under the international circumstances, the Federal Government had been powerless to prevent the trial. To obviate such a condition and to enable the Federal Courts to take jurisdiction, a bill was introduced providing for the issue of a writ of habeas corpus by such Courts, in case a foreign citizen should be imprisoned by any State for "any act done or committed under any alleged right, title, authority, privilege, protection or exemption set up or claimed under the commission, order or sanction of any foreign state or sovereignty, the validity and effect whereof depend upon the law of nations or under color thereof." This measure, favored by Webster and the Whigs generally, encountered heated opposition from the Democrats. "It is one of the most high-handed, daring invasions of State-Rights which Federalism has ever yet attempted," said the *Washington Globe*. "Truly between the bankrupt law, which invades and captures nearly all the civil jurisdiction of the State Courts, and this habeas corpus against the States, which may oust them of all their criminal jurisdiction, the poor States stand a good chance to be stripped of nearly all their judicial authority." [1] Senator Buchanan termed it "a dangerous and untried experiment, calculated to bring the sovereign States into collision with the Fed-

---

[1] *Washington Globe*, April 27, 1842, further said: "The friends of the reserved rights of the States will not be frightened into a surrender of their rights upon any cry, real or sham, of war with an arrogant power which seized the present brief period when Federalism is in power to bear down upon us. This bill is a British bill and is properly brought forward now."

eral Government, and thus to endanger the peace and harmony of the Union . . . an extension of the jurisdiction of the Federal Courts over criminal cases arising in the sovereign States under their own laws, which, from its very nature, cannot fail to wound their sensibility and arouse their jealousy." "It will produce dangerous collision between the Federal and State authorities," he said, "and you will have to enforce the mandates of the District Judge by the armed power of the Executive. There are cases in which the States will not patiently submit to be stripped of their inherent jurisdiction over criminals." [1] This bill is "one of those silent encroachments in the march to power, not likely to attract the attention of the great body of the people;" said Arthur P. Bagby of Alabama, but "the idea of State sovereignty is lost, if this colossal power can be exercised constitutionally by the Government." Senator Benton termed it "the infamous act . . . polluting our code of law." [2]

The bill requiring the States to elect their Congressmen by districts was the last of the extensions of Federal control, and was equally attacked as unconstitutional and unjustifiable. [3] "All the dangerous collisions which have ever existed between the State and Federal authorities have arisen from the exercise of doubtful

[1] *27th Cong.*, *2d Sess.*, and *App.*, 382, 355, speeches in the Senate, of Buchanan, May 9, Arthur P. Bagby of Virginia and Calhoun, July 8, Robert J. Walker of Mississippi, June 21, Aug. 3, 1842; speeches in the House of John G. Floyd of New York, Samuel Gordon of New York, William Smith of Virginia, Aug. 15, 1842. See also especially speeches in Senate of Berrien of Georgia, April 26, Huntington of Connecticut, May 10, 11, Choate of Massachusetts, July 8, 1842, supporting the bill. The bill passed by a strict party vote, and see speech of John McKean of New York in the House, Jan. 12, 1843. *27th Cong., 3d Sess.*

[2] *Thirty Years' View* (1856), by Thomas H. Benton, II, 276–304, 437.

[3] *27th Cong., 2d Sess.*, speeches of Buchanan and Woodbury, June 2, 4, 1842. It was stated in the House, April 6, 1846, that New Hampshire, Mississippi and Missouri had failed to comply with the Congressional Districting Act, and were electing their members by general ticket. "This is rank, practical Nullification." *29th Cong., 1st Sess.*

and dangerous powers by Congress," said Buchanan. "This is an attempt to interfere with what immediately concerns the dearest domestic institutions of the States, their discretion as to the mode in which they will elect their Representatives to Congress." Senator Woodbury said that there had been more alarming encroachment by the General Government on the sacred rights of the States in the last twelve months than in the previous half century — "the bankrupt law, in a form voluntary, novel, unconstitutional, and absorbing within the vortex of the General Government the jurisdiction over almost the whole system of contracts as well as liens and of the action of the State Courts over them — the distribution bill by which all the States were to come and feed from the public crib of the General Government and be subjected, in return for it, to unconstitutional taxation. . . . Next, close at the heels of the others, was the attempt to strip the States of all criminal jurisdiction for burnings and murders committed within their limits, if defenses were set up like those of McLeod. . . . Last of all, a bill unprecedented in our annals, a bill dictating to the States as to their system of elections, and no less encroaching in its principle and overshadowing in its influence on State independence than the numerous other measures that have, in such rapid succession, characterized the policy, so fatal towards the States, of those now in power in the General Government."

That these reiterated attacks by the Democrats in Congress upon the alleged encroachments on the sovereignty of the States met with little response in the Court was interestingly shown at its next session, in 1843, when, in the only decision of historic importance rendered by it, the doctrine of the *Dartmouth College Case* was applied with great strictness, and a State statute seriously affecting commercial relations in the States was held unconstitutional. The case of *Bronson* v. *Kinzie*, 1 How. 311, in which this decision was rendered, had involved a recent statute of Illinois providing that a mortgagor's equity should not be lost for twelve months after foreclosure sale and that no sale should occur unless two thirds of the appraised value should be bid for the property. This was one of the many statutes which had been the outcome of the frightful state of business and finance then prevalent. The country had just passed through the panic of 1837; it was in the midst of the era of State bank failures and of State debt repudiations; scarcity of hard money had destroyed the inflated value of property; men who had debts to pay were forced to dispose of their property at ruinous prices to the few who had money to buy. As a consequence of these conditions, State after State had enacted statutes for the relief of debtors, stay-laws postponing collection of debts, relief-laws modifying remedies on contracts, laws granting exemption from execution and postponing sales on execution and foreclosure of mortgages.[1] So far as these statutes applied to contracts made prior to their enactment, they were everywhere attacked by creditors as mere attempts to enable debtors to escape payment of their just debts. And newspapers in the commercial centers, criticizing "the unconstitutionality as well as the impolicy of the dishonest and knavish legislation which, more than all the defalcations of individual swindlers though multiplied a thousand-fold, attests the almost hopeless depravity and corruption of the age", expressed the confident hope that the Court would "determine the paramount law of the land to

---

[1] See laws of Pennsylvania, Virginia, Ohio, Indiana, Illinois, Michigan, Mississippi, New York, Georgia, Kentucky, Tennessee, Michigan, Missouri. *History of the People of the United States*, by John Bach McMaster, VII, 44–48.

be in strict accordance with the immutable principles of honesty and justice. Meanwhile, we congratulate the whole business community that the vexed question will soon be put at rest, and in a way, we trust, that will command their hearty acquiescence." [1] The hope so expressed was made a reality by the Court; for in its decision, speedily rendered, it held that statutes of this nature, changing the mortgage laws of the State, affected the rights, and not merely the remedies, of a mortgagee, and were, therefore, in violation of the clause of the Constitution forbidding the impairment of obligation of a contract. "It would be unjust to the memory of the distinguished men who framed the Constitution," said Taney, " to suppose that it was designed to protect a mere barren and abstract right, without any practical operation upon the business of life. It was undoubtedly adopted as a part of the Constitution for a great and useful purpose. It was to maintain the integrity of contracts and to secure their faithful execution throughout this Union by placing them under the protection of the Constitution." [2] Those who, in 1837, had feared that in his decision in the *Charles River Bridge Case* Taney had departed from Marshall's doctrines, now witnessed him announcing a decision which carried Marshall's view of obligation of contract even further than Marshall had himself. "I read the opinion," wrote Story to Taney, "with the highest satisfaction, and entirely concur in it. I think your opinion is drawn up with great ability, and in my judgment is entirely conclusive," and after regretting Judge

---

[1] *New York Journal of Commerce*, Feb. 8, 1843.

[2] In view of the widespread and important interests involved, it was singular that the case was not argued orally; and as Taney said in delivering the opinion: " On the part of the complainant, a printed argument has been filed (by Isaac N. Arold), but none has been offered on behalf of the defendant. As the case involves a constitutional question of great importance, we should have preferred a full argument at the bar."

McLean's dissent, Story added: "There are times in which the Court is called upon to support every sound constitutional doctrine in support of the rights of property and of creditors." [1]

Unquestionably, the country owes much of its prosperity to the unflinching courage with which, in the face of attack, the Court has maintained its firm stand in behalf of high standards of business morale, requiring honest payment of debts and strict performance of contracts; and its rigid construction of the Constitution to this end has been one of the glories of the Judiciary. That its decisions should, at times, have met with disfavor among the debtor class was, however, entirely natural; and while, ultimately, these debtor-relief-laws have always proved to be injurious to the very class they were designed to relieve and to increase the financial distress, fraud and extortion, temporarily, debtors have always believed such laws to be their salvation and have resented judicial decisions holding them invalid. Consequently, this opinion of the Court in the *Bronson Case* aroused great antagonism in the Western States. In Illinois, a mass meeting was held which resolved that the decision ought not to be heeded, called on Illinois officials to withstand the findings of the Court or resign and declared that they would resist peaceably or forcibly as might be necessary.[2] Judge McLean (who had warmly dissented) stated, in holding Circuit Court in Illinois, that he should hold the law invalid in that Court, not because he believed it so, but only because of the controlling power of the Supreme tribunal; but he refused to hold invalid a stay-law relative to sales on execution, although containing similar provisions to the mortgage

---

[1] *Taney*, 289, letter of Story, March 25, 1843.

[2] See *Sangamon Journal* (Springfield, Ill.), March 16, 1843; *Missouri Republican*, March 6, 1843; *Niles Register*, LXIV, June 17, 1843.

law.[1]   An Ohio law magazine termed the Bronson decision "a wide departure," and spoke of the "uncertainties in title to real estate already produced in Indiana and Illinois, and the consequent sacrifice of prosperity."[2]   Later, deference to the antagonism aroused against the Court by this decision was made when the Senator from Illinois, James Semple, introduced in the Senate in 1846, a joint resolution proposing a Constitutional Amendment to prohibit the Supreme Court from declaring void "any Act of Congress or any State regulation on the ground that it is contrary to the Constitution of the United States or contrary to the Constitution of any particular State."[3]   The effect of the Bronson decision upon the financial conditions of the country was rendered the more severe by reason of the fact that, almost coincident with that decision, came the repeal of the National Bankruptcy Act by Congress, on March 3, 1843; and thus, at the same moment, relief was denied to debtors under both State and Federal laws.

At the end of this 1843 Term, it became evident that a considerable change in the membership of the Court was impending.   The death of Judge Baldwin, whose mental powers had been impaired, was expected at any moment; Judge Thompson was seriously ill; and Judge Story was considering his resignation, for his relations with his Associates had been unpleasantly affected by an episode occurring during the Term — the appoint-

[1] A similar stay-law of Illinois as to executions was held invalid in 1844, in *McCracken* v. *Hayward*, 2 How. 608; and a similar law in Indiana in 1845, *Gantly* v. *Ewing*, 3 How. 707; see also *Law Reporter* (1843), VI, 46.

[2] *Western Law Journ.* (1846–47), IV, 254; V, 173; "Who can foresee the amount of litigation, who can foretell the evils to flow from this unhappy confusion of obligation, and remedy, of contract and judgment?"   Chief Justice Gibson in *Chadwick* v. *Moore* (1844), 8 Watts & Serg. 49, refused to follow the decisions of the Supreme Court of the United States as to this form of statute.

[3] *29th Cong., 2d Sess.*   John M. Berrien, Senator from Georgia, introduced a bill to regulate the appellate jurisdiction of the Court, on Jan. 19, 1847.   Both of these measures died, however, in the Committee on the Judiciary.

ment of Gen. Benjamin C. Howard of Maryland as
Reporter of the Court in place of Richard Peters.
Though Peters had served since 1828, personal friction
had long existed between him and Judges Baldwin and
Catron; there had been complaint also as to delays in
publication of his reports;[1] and the newspaper press
had resented difficulties put in its way by the Reporter
relative to the furnishing of copies of opinions.[2] His
removal, while possibly justifiable, had been made in so
extraordinarily summary a manner as to arouse considerable sympathy; for no advance intimation of such
a step had been given by members of the Court, and it
was taken at a time when neither Judge Story nor Judge
McKinley had reached Washington and when the vote
of the other Judges was divided — Baldwin, Wayne,
Catron and Daniel favoring Howard, and Chief Justice
Taney and Judges McLean and Thompson voting for
Peters.[3]   Of this action, Judge Story wrote to McLean
that he had "seldom been more pained", and that the
removal was wholly unexpected and beyond anything

[1] See *Sumner Papers MSS*, letter of Peters to Sumner, Aug. 23, 1843, as to "a
most unexpected and unmerited attack by the publication of what he (Catron) calls
Errata spread out into three pages in the volume of Mr. Howard." See also
McLean Papers MSS, letter of Peters to McLean, Jan. 23, 1843 (five days before
Peters' removal), explaining that delays were frequently due to withholding of
opinions from the Reporter by the Judges, and stating that publication of Vol. 16
of *Peters Reports* "was delayed five weeks for want of your own opinion in the
Prigg Case."

[2] *National Intelligencer*, March 3, 1842; March 12, 1844.   The *National Intelligencer*, March 17, 1835, published a correspondence between Richard S. Coxe,
Richard Peters and Chief Justice Marshall relative to publication to Supreme Court
opinions by Duff Green, the editor of the *United States Telegraph*, as interfering
with the official reports.   To Peters, Marshall had written, March 14, 1835:
"Your gentlemanly deportment and the accuracy and fidelity with which your
official duties have been performed, have secured the lasting esteem of, dear Sir,
your obedient servant, J. M."

[3] The appointment of Howard was made under the recent Act of Aug. 26, 1842;
see also comments on this appointment in *United States Gazette*, Jan. 29, Feb. 1,
1843; *National Intelligencer*, Jan. 30, 1843; *Western Law Journ.*, I, 83.   Peters himself wrote an indignant letter to Charles Sumner, Feb. 11, denouncing the "coarse,
rude, and ungentlemanly mode" in which the removal was made without any intimation of it to him in advance, and attributed it largely to the "malignant hostility" of Judge Baldwin, *Sumner Papers MSS*.

he could have dreamed of; that Peters had always been most courteous and deferential to the Court and "ought not to have been subjected to the mortification of an ejection from office without notice and without enquiry." He also wrote that he felt personally "the full force of this neglect and want of courtesy", of the other Judges in making the appointment in his absence, "an occurrence which never before took place during the absence of a Judge, accidental or otherwise, since I have belonged to the Court, in matters that equally concerned all of them. But let it pass, I no longer ever expect to see revived the kind and frank courtesy of the old Court, and I am content to take things as they are." [1]

On December 18, 1843, Judge Smith Thompson died, after twenty years of service on the Bench. "He was not only their honored and respected Associate in the discharge of their official duties, but he was beloved as their friend and endeared to everyone by his frankness, his kindness and his unstained honor," said the Court in response to the resolutions of the Bar. The vacancy caused by his death (which left Judge Story the only survivor of the old Marshall Court) gave rise to a prolonged contest between the Executive and Senate. The bitter political feud between President Tyler and the Whigs was now at its height. Tyler had determined to become a candidate for the Democratic nomination for President; and any nomination for the Bench which he might make was certain to be subjected to searching scrutiny by the Senate. No one, however, anticipated the extraordinary move which Tyler now made. Mar-

---

[1] *McLean Papers MSS*, letter of Story to McLean, Feb. 9, 1843. Charles Sumner wrote to McLean, Feb. 2, 1843, *ibid.*: "I think that nothing has occurred at Washington which has affected his (Story's) spirits so deeply. His sleep was destroyed the night after he received your letter." (Incidentally, Sumner added that if Peters had resigned, he himself would have liked to be a candidate for the position, as suggested by Story and McLean.)

tin Van Buren, seemingly at the height of his popularity, was the leading candidate of the Democracy for the Presidency; and it was to this political opponent and rival that Tyler ingenuously made the offer of the vacant position on the Court. The episode was described by Silas Wright, Senator from New York and leader of the Van Buren Democracy (then becoming known as the Locofocos), in an extraordinary, vivid letter to Van Buren, as follows : [1]

Our day yesterday was beautiful and the consequence was a very great press at the President's house. I was there about one o'clock and never saw more people, and never so few whom I knew. It is said that very few of the prominent Whig members or their families presented themselves. Still, I doubt not that the Captain is delighted this morning, and is now more than ever satisfied that the *masses* are clearly for him, and that he is even more personally popular with them than even Gen. Jackson was. The fact that the Clay-Whigs staid away will increase his confidence and his joy. Is it not happy to be so constituted? . . . I never knew the city so entirely destitute of strangers at this season of the year or the hotels appearing so desolate. You will ask where our crowd have come from? I suppose mostly from the City, and from Georgetown, Alexandria and Baltimore. I never saw so few carriages at the levee by quite the half, and yet I doubt whether there were ever more people. So that you will see I shall agree with the Capt. that it was a *democratic* turnout. Indeed I never knew half so many of the dignitaries and their ladies walk.

But enough of this, as you have a more direct interest now discussing here, of which it is my object to speak and not of the proceedings at Court, on New Year's Day. You have been made a candidate for the vacancy upon the bench of the Supreme Court, for a week past, and for a portion of this time your prospects have been said to be decidedly promising — better even than those of our friend Spencer. You

[1] *Van Buren Papers MSS;* letter of Wright to Van Buren, Jan. 2, 1844 ; see *History of the People of the United States*, by John Bach McMaster, VII, 345, quoting part of this letter.

must not suppose me as attempting to hoax you or to play off a joke upon you. I am telling you the mere truth, and for the last week and a half, I expected your nomination to us as an Associate Justice of the S. C. of the U. S. The first intimation of this sort which came to me was from General Mason of Michigan, the father of the late Gov. Mason, whom you doubtless know very well. He called upon me very diplomatically and broke the subject to me in the most solemn and formal manner. I can usually keep my face when I try hard to do so and have any warning that the effort will be required, but this took me too much by surprise and I did not succeed at all, but met the suggestion by a most immediate fit of laughter. Seeing that this annoyed the General more than I could suppose it ought, the idea at once occurred to me that he had been sent to me from a high quarter. I at once changed my manner and left him at liberty to talk on — I discovered too that he had a carriage at the door, and apologized for detaining him and leaving his driver exposed to the storm, for I think he had sat an hour and it rained and blew most violently. He said that was of no consequence and remained, I think, for full another hour. I told him very gravely that I was sure you would not seek, or accept, the place, if your name had not been and was not to be connected with the Presidential election at all, and so believing I must suppose you would be compelled respectfully to decline the offer, if made, situated as you was, but really treated the matter decorously. This seemed to please him, and he talked very freely, professed to be strongly your friend, but was perfectly convinced you could not be elected President, if nominated; and what was more sagacious, entertained quite as deep a conviction that the consequence of your appointment as Judge would be *my* nomination for President with the certainty of an election. I asked him very gravely if Mr. Tyler thought as he did upon that point, and then he said he had not seen, or conversed, with Mr. Tyler upon either subject, but he *knew* that your name had been presented to him, as a proper one to be used in his nomination of Judge, and that too by some of your best friends.

In the course of the conversation, he often asked me if I thought either you, or your friends, could look upon your nomination by the President as an act of hostility to you or

as an attempt to degrade you, and whether, if you were nominated, your friends in the Senate and even I *could* vote
against you, and he seemed anxious to have my answers
upon those points. I finally told him that to propose a man
for a place upon that elevated Bench, and thus proclaim to
the country his fitness and that by a political opponent, could
not be tortured into an act of hostility; that no man in this
Country was so high as to be authorized to feel himself
degraded by the offer of such a position, and that I certainly
could not vote to *reject* your nomination for such an office.
These replies seemed to delight him, and his answer was quick
and triumphant with deep laughter: "You are right, you are
right, you *can't* vote against him." At length, rising to go,
he asked me what, upon the whole, I thought of the proposition. I replied, very steadily looking him in the face: "Tell
Mr. Tyler from me that if he desires to give the whole country
a broader, deeper, heartier laugh than it ever had, and at his
own expense, he can effect it by making that nomination."
This did not seem to please him, and he left at once. I
laughed myself almost sick, not entertaining a doubt, as I
do not now, that the Capt. had sent him to me. Still, I kept
the communication wholly to myself, only getting my wife
to help me keep it and to help me laugh, and did not hear
another word upon the subject for two or three days, when
all at once the matter became one of public notoriety, and
conversation and laugh; and since that time I have it from
Davies, who gets his news from Parmelee, that the President
has been, upon various occasions, determined to send your
name, and has considered the movement one of the most
happy which ever occurred to a statesman, and that his
friends had had great trouble to keep him from doing it.
My information of yesterday, however, is that your prospects are at an end and that Spencer's name will be given
to us tomorrow.

Wright's discouragement of Tyler's project to appoint Van Buren had its effect; and on January 8, 1844,
the President sent to the Senate the name of John C.
Spencer of New York, a lawyer of great talent, but a
man whose varying course in politics had brought upon

him the violent enmity of a portion of the Whig Party. Though an ardent Whig in politics, a strong former opponent of Tyler, his opposition to Henry Clay as a Presidential candidate had led him to accept from President Tyler appointments, first as Secretary of War, and next as Secretary of the Treasury. He had administered the latter office "with an ability, assiduity, integrity and faithfulness seldom equalled since the days of Hamilton", wrote a contemporary, "a man of great abilities, industry and endurance, curt manners and irascible temper." [1] The appointment was highly obnoxious to the Clay Whigs.[2] "I have no confidence in the political integrity of Mr. Spencer," wrote Erastus Root of New York to Senator John J. Crittenden. "He was always first to foist himself into any political party which could give him hopes of preferment. . . . There is but one consideration in this instance to recommend him to Whig favor; that is, to place him in a situation where he can inflict but little political injury." Henry Clay wrote to Crittenden that "if Spencer be confirmed he will have run a short career of more profligate conduct and good luck than any man I recollect." Francis Granger of New York wrote that Spencer's recreant course at Washington had "developed a character that should not be approved by an appointment to one of the most dignified positions in the world"; that ninety out of one hundred Whigs in New York were opposed to

[1] *Public Men and Events* (1875), by Nathan Sargent. "Before being tendered a position in Mr. Tyler's Cabinet, he had written an address upon his (Tyler's) treachery to the Whig party, more severe than anything that appeared from any other quarter. He fairly flayed the President, lashing him as with a whip of scorpions."

[2] *John J. Crittenden Papers MSS*, letters of Erastus Root, Jan. 1, 1844, Henry Clay, Jan. 24, 1844, Francis Granger, Feb. 3, 1844. Stephen Van Rensselaer wrote to Crittenden from Albany, Jan. 20, 1844, that it would be a great injury to the Whig cause to confirm "one who has been and always will be bitterly opposed to the elevation of Mr. Clay to the Presidency", and that in politics "he is the most finished scoundrel I know." The *New York Herald*, Feb. 9, 14, 1844, stated that the opposition to Spencer was headed by Webster.

Spencer's confirmation, that the universal sentiment was: "Well, if such treachery is to be rewarded by the votes of those who have been betrayed, we do not see any necessity for political integrity." In view of the nominee's unpopularity, and of the Whig bitterness towards him, it became evident that he could not be confirmed, although, wrote a Washington correspondent, "all acknowledge his legal ability to fill with honor the office." [1] On January 31, 1844, the Senate rejected the nomination by a vote of twenty-one to twenty-six. "Spencer has terrible but just punishment," wrote Thurlow Weed. "But it was hard, killing him. He made a tremendous struggle for confirmation." "The Senators felt," said the *New York Herald*, " that our Supreme Court is our last bulwark, our fortress, our rock and tower of defence when all else fails and the vacancy must be filled with a man of diamond purity, and adamantine integrity." "I consider the rejection of Spencer as one of the very best acts of the Senate," wrote Senator Crittenden to Granger. "His confirmation would have been a plain violation of all public political morality and would have been to make the Supreme Court an asylum for broken down, disgraced and guilty politicians. As far as I can hear, the people everywhere approve his rejection." [2] While the rejection was thus

[1] *New York Herald*, Jan. 6, Feb. 2, 1844. On Jan. 16, 1844, the correspondent wrote that there was considerable feeling in Washington that the appointment ought to be confirmed, out of justice to the President and respect to the Supreme Court, in order that the Bench might be filled before the argument of so great cases as those of the *Girard Will* and of *Myra Gaines* then pending.

[2] *Francis Granger–Thurlow Weed Papers MSS;* letter of Weed to Granger, March 11, 1844, letter of Crittenden to Granger, Feb. 10, 1844. Crittenden continued in this letter: "I congratulate you on the bright and heightening prospects of the Whigs. Unless all human reasonings and appearances are vain, there can be no doubt of the success of their cause, and the election of Clay to the Presidency."

Eliphalet Nott wrote to Chesselden Ellis (Congressman from New York), Feb. 4, 1844: "I perceive that the die is cast and that our friend Spencer is rejected. So be it, I only hope that a worse man may not be forced, through party animosity, upon the country." *Mass. Hist. Soc. Proc.*, LIII. The *Madisonian*, the Tyler Administration paper in Washington, hotly criticized "the sanguinary proceedings

JOHN SERGEANT

HORACE BINNEY

REVERDY JOHNSON

JOHN J. CRITTENDEN

placed upon high moral grounds, the fact was that it was due solely to Whig politics.

After this rejection of an eminently qualified lawyer from New York in the Second Circuit, President Tyler next made the unusual move of offering the position to two of the great leaders of the Supreme Court Bar, coming from another Circuit (the Third) — John Sergeant and Horace Binney of Philadelphia. These two lawyers were then engaged in arguing the *Girard Will Case* before the Court, and their ability had strongly impressed the President. The curious manner in which the offers of appointment were received has been told by Henry A. Wise of Virginia, through whom they were made, as follows:[1] "The evening after Mr. Binney had concluded his great argument . . . Mr. Sergeant was visited by us, at his hotel, to deliver the message of Mr. Tyler. Mr. Binney was in the next room. Mr. Sergeant received the compliment with graciousness and evident pleasure; but he hesitated not to decline the tender of a place upon the Supreme Bench. Before he assigned his reason, he enjoined secrecy during his life, and especially it was not to be disclosed to Mr. Binney. It was that he was past sixty years of age, and that he ought not to accept, but he regarded Mr. Binney as being much more robust than himself, considered that Mr. Binney might accept, and did not wish him to know that he had declined because he considered himself too old, and requested that the President would make the tender of the place to him. It was tendered to Mr. Binney at once, and, behold, he declined it for the same

of the Senate", "the private pique and party considerations" which had led to Spencer's rejection, and stated that it was principally due to Senator Thomas H. Benton; see issues of Jan. 24, 31, Feb. 10, 12, 13, 1844.

[1] *Seven Decades of the Union* (1876), by Henry A. Wise. In the *Life of Horace Binney* (1903), by Charles C. Binney, a doubt is intimated as to the accuracy of the details given by Wise, but, in the main, Wise's account seems to be accurate.

reason, but begged that Mr. Sergeant should not be informed of his reason, and that the place might be tendered to him.   Neither, we believe, ever knew the reason of the other for declining." Failing to secure the acceptance of either of these Philadelphia lawyers, the President again turned to the Second Circuit; and several lawyers of distinction were considered for the position.   At one time, the newspapers stated that the nomination of Henry Wheaton of New York, the former distinguished Reporter of the Court and recently Minister to Prussia, had been absolutely determined upon.   William L. Marcy, Governor of New York, who had resigned from Tyler's Cabinet, had strong friends "who knew and appreciated his worth and peculiar fitness", and his chances for appointment were considered favorable.[1]   Hiram Ketchum of New York was said to be backed by Tyler's Secretary of State, Daniel Webster; and Ralph J. Ingersoll of Connecticut, and Cornelius Peter Van Ness of New York were considered as possibilities.   In March, Tyler twice offered the position to the Democratic leader of the Senate, Silas Wright who, though urged by Judge Daniel to accept, twice declined the position, probably wisely, as his

---

[1] *New York Journal of Commerce*, Feb. 17, 21, March 9, 1844; *Boston Post*, Feb. 19, 1844; *New York Tribune*, Feb. 13, 17, 1844.   Marcy's chances of appointment apparently disappeared when his warm supporter, Thomas W. Gilmer of Virginia, Secretary of the Navy, was killed Feb. 28, 1844, in the shocking explosion on the gunboat *Princeton*, on the Potomac River below Mt. Vernon, of which Silas Wright wrote to Van Buren, March 1, 1844 (*Van Buren Papers MSS*): "We are at this moment as much in the dark about the Judgeship as you can be.   Two weeks ago, I thought the Chancellor had some prospect, and one week ago, I supposed the same thing of Marcy, but the delay has induced me to suppose that neither nomination is now probable.   I relied upon Gov. Gilmer for Marcy's prospect and the awful calamity which we have witnessed here has deprived us of his support further.   I cannot write of that shocking affair.   The papers will tell you all I know and it is too horrible to think of.   It was rumored, a few days since, that the Whigs were making another effort at conciliation, so as to secure the Judge, and I think the fact was so; and you can see, if it was so then, and for that single office, how much more likely such an attempt will be now vigorously made when the two Cabinet places fall in to be struggled for."

confirmation by the Senate would have been doubt-ful.[1] "No one can conjecture what we shall have as a Judge for the Second Circuit. What the President will do, we cannot determine," wrote Judge Story. "I have my own wishes on the subject, strong and warm, but I have no hope that they will be gratified. I want an associate of the highest integrity, with youth and ambition enough to make him become a deep student in all the law, and with a spirit of love for the Constitution, and an independence to proclaim it, which shall make him superior to all popular clamors — and these to be united with courtesy of manners and kindness of heart. These, I admit, are high qualities; but I think I could find them, and so could you, if either of us had the appointment." [2]

Finally, on March 13, 1844, Tyler sent to the Senate the name of Reuben H. Walworth, then Chancellor of the State of New York. The new appointee, though unquestionably of the highest legal ability, was not only personally unpopular but politically disliked by the Whigs; and Thurlow Weed of New York wrote at once to Senator Crittenden: [3] "He is recommended by many distinguished Members of the Bar of the State *merely because they are anxious to get rid of a querulous, disagreeable, unpopular Chancellor.* Indeed so odious is he that our Senate, when a majority of his own political friends were members, voted to abolish the office of Chancellor. Those who recommended him admit and avow that they did so to get him out of his present

---

[1] *New York Tribune,* Feb. 16, 1844; *New York Journal of Commerce,* March 9, 14, 1844; *Life and Times of Silas Wright* (1874), by Ransom H. Gillet.

[2] *Story,* II, 480, letter to Kent, March 2, 1844; and on April 25, he wrote to Kent: "O! that I had your excellent son (William Kent) as my colleague on the Bench; then should I feel ready to depart in peace. I have even thought that he and Mr. (Daniel) Lord were the only candidates that, as to age, qualifications and character, a President ought to select for the office."

[3] *John J. Crittenden Papers MSS,* letter of Weed to Crittenden, March 17, 1844.

office. Should this nomination be confirmed, we shall have a Loco Foco appointed to the office of Chancellor. If suffered to remain 'unfinished business', we may expect to see the Nation profit by the appointment of a better Judge of the Supreme Court, and when Walworth reaches the age of sixty, we may *hope* to get a better Chancellor."

While this nomination was pending, Judge Baldwin died, April 21, 1844, after serving thirteen years on the Court. "Poor Baldwin is gone. Another vacancy on the Bench. How nobly it might be filled! But we are doomed to disappointment," wrote Judge Story to Ex-Chancellor Kent. "What can we hope from such a head of an Administration as we now have but a total disregard of all elevated principles and objects? I dare not trust my pen to speak of him as I think. Do you know (for I was so informed at Washington) that Tyler said he never would appoint a Judge 'of the school of Kent'?"[1] To fill this second vacancy, President Tyler first tendered the position to James Buchanan who declined;[2] he then nominated Judge Edward King, a distinguished lawyer of Philadelphia, June 5, 1844.

The heated contest which had long prevailed between the President and the Whig Senate made it unlikely that his appointments would be confirmed. Moreover, Congress was again considering a rearrangement of the Circuits; and the Presidential election was approaching. And furthermore, John J. Crittenden, who had failed of confirmation in 1829 in the closing days of the Adams Administration, still had his eye on the Supreme Court; for, should Henry Clay, the Whig candidate for the President against James K. Polk, be elected, Crittenden no doubt would receive the appointment, if the filling

[1] Letter of Story to Kent, April 25, 1844, *Mass. Hist. Soc. Proc.*, 2d Series, XIV.
[2] *New York Journal of Commerce*, June 20, 1844; *National Intelligencer*, June 19, 1844.

of the vacancy could be delayed until after the election.[1] Although influenced solely by personal prejudice, the Senate was sustained by the Whig newspapers, one of their leaders saying that it deprecated the evils of an incompetent, complying or corrupt Judiciary, and that it looked with entire confidence to the Senate.   "Better the Bench should be vacant for a year, than filled for half a century by corrupt or feeble men, or partisans committed in advance to particular beliefs."[2]   This statement, entirely unwarranted by the facts or by the character of the eminent lawyers nominated, illustrated the bitterness of the hostility to the President.   Accordingly, on June 15, on the last day of the session, the Senate ordered the nominations to lie on the table — an act which brought upon the Whigs the bitter condemnation of the Democrats.[3]   Five months later, Whig hopes were crushed by the election of Polk as President; and there was no longer the slightest excuse for a failure to confirm Tyler's appointees.   A striking view of the situation was given in a letter from the former Reporter of the Court, Richard Peters, himself a Whig, to Judge McLean :[4]

I look forward with growing apprehension to the condition of the Supreme Court within the next four years.   May heaven in its tenderest mercy preserve the life of our good Chief Justice.   Catron will succeed him, if he should, while Polk is President, be called to a better world. . . .   The nominations of Judge King and Chancellor Walworth, now

[1] New York Journal of Commerce, March 19, 1844.

[2] National Intelligencer, April 26, 1844.

[3] See editorial of the New York Evening Post, quoted in the Washington Post Globe, June 27, 1844, speaking of the "pitiful, canting defense of the Whig Senators." See also National Intelligencer, June 17, 1844, and ibid., June 18, which describes a curious maneuver of Tyler's, who withdrew the nomination of Walworth and substituted Spencer's name; objection being made to its consideration, he withdrew Spencer's name and again reinstated the Walworth nomination.   The vote on June 15 to lay on the table the nomination of Walworth was 27 to 20; as to King, 29 to 18.

[4] John McLean Papers MSS, letter of Peters to McLean, Dec. 6, 1844.

before the Senate, present an opportunity, by the confirmation of the first, to put on the Bench a man of sound opinions on all the great questions which have come before that Court. I was not the advocate of the confirmation of Judge King, when hopes were entertained that we should elect Mr. Clay. The question is now presented in very different aspects, and I most earnestly desire that he shall be confirmed. He is a man of very strong mind, with extraordinary judicial faculties. His opinions are all that you can desire. (See *Ashmead's Reports*.) For yourself, Judge Story, and such of the Court with whom you agree and associate, he has the highest respect. Altho' he has not the manner in private intercourse as polished as you justly appreciate, yet he has a strong sense of decorum and propriety. He and I have never belonged to the same political school, but I have always regarded him as possessed of perfect probity of character, and his judicial duties have always been performed with perfect impartiality. . . . If King is rejected the next nominee will be John M. Read, as suited for a Judge as I am for an admiral.

And a view of the King nomination from the opposite political standpoint is found in a letter written by John C. Calhoun to Francis Wharton, of Philadelphia, after the election of Polk, in November :[1]

I must say that your letter places his character in a light, which I have not heretofore regarded it. I had taken the impression, that although a man of talents, his political association connected him with a set of politicians of a very objectionable character which subjected his to doubt. Under this impression, I was disinclined to his nomination, without, however, taking any part against it while before the Senate. It is due to the occasion to say that the impression made on my mind, has, I am inclined to think, been made on that of many others; so much so, that his nomination will be in great danger, unless it should be well sustained from the respectable portion of your Bar and the City, especially if your two Senators should be opposed to him. I take it, that the wing of the party, usually opposed to the nomi-

[1] *Amer. Hist. Ass. Rep.* (1899), II, letter of Calhoun to Wharton, Nov. 20, 1844.

nations of the President, will be against him, which would certainly cause his defeat, unless he should receive the support of the better portion of the Whig party. If, however, your two Senators will support him, I should think his prospects would be fair. . . . I regard the defeat of Clay and the election of Polk, under all circumstances as a great political revolution. Great events may grow out of it, if the victory be used with prudence and moderation. There is much to be done to bring things right, and save the Government; but in order to be successfully done, it must be done gradually and systematically. I say, save the Government; for to my mind it is clear, that it cannot go on much longer as it has for the last 15 or 20 years, and especially the last 8.

In the closing days of his Administration, Tyler made a last attempt to fill the two vacancies on the Bench by withdrawing King's nomination[1] and sending in the name of John Meredith Read of Philadelphia, a former United States District Attorney, and by withdrawing Walworth's name and nominating Samuel Nelson of New York. Nelson was a lawyer of conspicuous ability, fifty-two years old, a Judge of the Supreme Court of New York for fourteen years and for seven years its Chief Justice. The choice was so preëminently a wise one that the Senate at once confirmed it, February 14, 1845, and on March 5, 1845, Nelson took his seat on the Bench, where he served for twenty-seven years. As to Tyler's other appointment, there was more difference of opinion. Richard Peters wrote to Judge McLean that Read was "as suited for a Judge as I am for an admiral." On the other hand, an equally strong Philadelphia Whig wrote to W. P. Mangum, the Whig Senator from North Carolina, that Read was "one of the very best appointments Mr. Tyler ever made"; that "a more correct gentlemanly man I never knew" and that the Whigs

---

[1] Tyler renominated King, Dec. 4, 1844, and withdrew the nomination, Feb. 7, 1845. Nelson was nominated, Feb. 4, and Read, Feb. 7.

wanted his confirmation rather than risk an appointment by President Polk. The Democratic papers stated him to be "a sound and able lawyer and a firm, true man", and they rejoiced that the Senate must either confirm him or leave the appointment to Polk; "and in either case the Democracy of the country now have a reasonable assurance that this fearful tribunal, the Federal Court, will be more in harmony than heretofore with the Democratic principles and doctrines of the apostle of republicanism." And James Buchanan wrote of Read that "there are few lawyers, if any, in Philadelphia his superior, a man of firmness, energy, and industry. . . . He holds a ready and powerful political pen and is a gentleman of the strictest honour and integrity." [1] The Senate, however, adjourned without acting on Read's nomination.

By a decision rendered at this 1844 Term, the future business of the Federal Courts was enormously augmented and the growth of corporations in the country was undoubtedly stimulated when the Court decided, in *Louisville etc. R. R.* v. *Letson*, 2 How. 497, that for the purposes of a suit in a Federal Court brought on the ground of diverse citizenship, a corporation was presumed to be a citizen of the State in which it was chartered. For over thirty-five years, the Federal Courts had held that they had no jurisdiction, on the ground of diverse citizenship, in a case in which a corporation was a party, unless all the individual stockholders were citizens of a State other than the State of the opposing party to the suit.[2]

---

[1] *John McLean Papers MSS; Willie P. Mangum Papers MSS*, letter of William G. Cochran to Mangum, Feb. 8, 1845; *New York Herald*, Feb. 8, 1845; *Boston Post*, Feb. 15, 1845; *Works of James Buchanan*, VI, letter to Gov. Shunk, Dec. 18, 1844. A letter to Judge McLean from B. W. Richards of Philadelphia, Feb. 10, 1845, termed Read a man of "great energy, very considerable talents, and irreproachable habits — a man of political zeal", who held Jacksonian beliefs but " whose political aspirations would terminate when he took a seat on the Bench."

[2] See *Strawbridge* v. *Curtiss*, 3 Cranch, 267, *Hope Ins. Co.* v. *Boardman*, 5 Cranch, 57, and *Bank of the United States* v. *Deveaux*, 5 Cranch, 61.

There had been strong protests made and good reasons advanced against this doctrine. Thus, John Quincy Adams, arguing in 1809, had well said that : "The reason of giving jurisdiction to the Courts of the United States in cases between citizens of different States, applies with the greatest force to the case of a powerful moneyed corporation erected within and under the laws of a particular State. If there was a probability that an individual citizen of a State could influence State Courts in his favor, how much stronger is the probability that they could be influenced in favor of a powerful moneyed institution which might be composed of the most influential characters in the State. What chance for justice could a plaintiff have against such a powerful association in the Courts of a small State whose Judges perhaps were annually elected, or held their office at the will of the Legislature?" And Robert G. Harper had argued at the same time : "One great object in allowing citizens of different States to sue in the Federal Court was to obtain a uniformity of decision in cases of a commercial nature. The most numerous and important class of those cases, and the class in which it is most important to have uniform rules and principles, is that of insurance cases. They are almost wholly confined to corporations, though most frequently, in fact, between citizens of different States." Judge Wayne now, in deciding the *Letson Case*, said that the old cases had "never been satisfactory to the Bar" nor "entirely satisfactory to the Court that made them"; and he practically overruled them. Of this decision, Story wrote to Kent that he rejoiced that the Supreme Court " has at last come to the conclusion that a corporation is a citizen, an artificial citizen, I agree, but still a citizen. It gets rid of a great anomaly in our jurisprudence. This was always Judge Washington's opinion. I have held

the same opinion for very many years, and Mr. Chief
Justice Marshall had, before his death, arrived at the
conclusion, that our early decisions were wrong." [1]
Though several later decisions of the Court firmly established this jurisdiction of the Federal Courts in corporation cases, there were strong dissenting opinions
which met the approval of many persons who feared the
establishment of any doctrine favorable to the corporations of the day, so rapidly growing in power and corrupt influence.   This fear was expressed later by Judge
Campbell: "Nor can we tell when the mischief will
end.   It may be safely assumed that no offering could
be made to the wealthy, powerful and ambitious corporations of the populous and commercial States of the
Union so valuable, and none which would so serve to
enlarge the influence of those States, as the adoption, to
its full import, of the conclusion, 'that to all intents and
purposes, for the objects of their incorporation, these
artificial persons are capable of being treated as a citizen
as much as a natural person.' . . . The litigation before this Court, during this Term, suffices to disclose the
complication, difficulty and danger of the controversies
that must arise. . . .   I am not willing to strengthen or
to enlarge the connections between the Courts of the
United States and these litigants." [2]   On the other
hand, as Judge Catron later pointed out: "If the
United States Courts could be ousted of jurisdiction,
and citizens of other States and subjects of foreign countries be forced into the State Courts, without the power
of election, they would often be deprived, in great cases,
of all benefit contemplated by the Constitution; and in

[1] *Story*, II, 469, letter of Aug. 31, 1844.
[2] Campbell, J., diss. in *Marshall* v. *B. & O. R. R.* (1853), 16 How. 314, 353; see
also Daniel, J., diss. in *Rundle* v. *Delaware & Raritan Canal Co.* (1852), 14 How. 80,
95, and in *Northern Indiana R. R.* v. *Michigan Central R. R.* (1853), 15 How. 233,
249, and in *Marshall* v. *B. & O. R. R.* (1853), 16 How. 314, 339.

many cases, be compelled to submit their rights to Judges and juries who are inhabitants of the cities where the suit must be tried, and to contend with powerful corporations in local Courts, where the chances of impartial justice would be greatly against them, and where no prudent man would engage with such an antagonist, if he could help it." [1]

Fifty years after the *Letson Case*, Judge Taft (now Chief Justice of the Court) warmly defended the decision, on the ground that "the ruling was directly in the interest of the new States, who were thirsting for foreign capital, because it removed one of the hindrances to its coming. . . . While the provision of the Constitution was of course intended to avoid actual injustice from local prejudice, its more especial purpose was to allay the fears of such injustice in the minds of those whose material aid was necessary in developing the commercial intercourse between the States, and thus to induce such intercourse and the investment of capital owned in one State in another." [2] An opponent of the doctrine, on the other hand, pointed out that the decision was rendered at the beginning of the era of railroad building, "when public opinion ran strongly in favor of railroad enterprise", and that at that time, as most corporations were chartered by special acts, and as there was no such thing as a "tramp corporation", the evil possibilities in the doctrine were obscured. In view of the vast amount of litigation in modern times which would have been eliminated from the Federal Courts, and in view of the popular hostility towards them which has risen from the extensive resort to these Courts by cor-

[1] *Rundle* v. *Delaware & Raritan Canal Co.* (1852), 14 How. 80, 95; Taney, C. J., in *Covington Drawbridge Co.* v. *Shephard* (1857), 20 How. 227.

[2] *Criticism of the Federal Judiciary*, by William H. Taft, *Amer. Law Rev.* (1895), XXIX; *Federal Jurisdiction in Case of Corporations*, by Seymour D. Thompson, *ibid.*; see also *John Archibald Campbell* (1920), by Henry G. Connor, 30.

porations challenging the validity of State legislation, it may well be doubted whether the Court would not have acted more wisely, if it had adopted Judge Campbell's views.[1]

A second case at this 1844 Term, *Vidal et al.* v. *Philadelphia*, 2 How. 127, had an important connection with the history of the country and of the Court; for its argument by one of the counsel, Daniel Webster, was utilized as a factor in his campaign for the Presidency; the arguments of two of the other counsel, Horace Binney and John Sergeant, resulted in the offer to them by President Tyler of appointment on the Court; and owing to the very peculiar facts of the case, and to the extraordinarily vivid and picturesque description of the arguments by contemporary newspapers, few cases ever more keenly interested the general public or brought it more closely in contact with the Court. Under the will of Stephen Girard, a bequest of several million dollars had been left to the City of Philadelphia to found a College for the benefit of poor white orphans, but subject to the unusual condition that all ecclesiastics, missionaries and ministers of any sort were to be excluded from holding or exercising any station or duty in the College or even visiting the same. Three questions were presented in the case: whether a city was capable of acting as trustee of such a trust; whether the trust was too indefinite to be enforced in a Court of Chancery; and whether the trust by reason of its ex-

[1] Simeon E. Baldwin in *A Legal Fiction with its Wings Clipped, Amer. Law Rev.* (1907), XLI, said that legal fictions are of service "because they make bridges between several epochs, useful while travel goes that way, easily burned or shifted to new positions when it may be forwarded to some new goal." See also *Abrogation of Federal Jurisdiction Over State Corporations*, by Alfred W. Russell, *Harv. Law Rev.* (1893), VII, in which it was said "the welfare of the Federal Courts demands the non-existence of jurisdiction over State corporations." The first legislative recognition of Federal jurisdiction over corporations in suits based on diverse citizenship was in the Judiciary Act of March 3, 1887, which, for the first time, used the word "corporation."

clusion of ecclesiastics was contrary to public policy, as
being opposed to the Christian religion.   The case was
argued for ten days; by Walter Jones on February 2, 3,
5, 1844; by Horace Binney, February 5, 6, 7, 8; by John
Sergeant, February 8, 9; and by Daniel Webster (who
had just resigned as Secretary of State under Tyler),
February 10, 12, 13, — Jones and Webster undertaking
the task of breaking down the will.[1]   Of the opening
arguments by Jones, an interesting description has been
given by a prominent Member of Congress, who was
present in the Court-room, Henry A. Wise of Virginia:[2]

In his quaint insinuating, lisping tones, he said: "Mr.
Girard had devised more nourishment for the mind, without
care of moral instruction, and the trustees had expended an
immense sum in erecting a temple to the 'unknown God.'
The testator had not meant to make the College religiously
free, but to make it free of all religion.   The orphans needed
a fish, but they were given a serpent; bread, and they had
gotten a stone!"   All this was taken to be personal to Mr.
Sergeant who was one of the chief counsellors of the city of
Philadelphia in administering the charity; and the point of
Mr. Jones was a poniard to him — the more so, because he
had always admired and respected Mr. Jones as one of the
first forensic men of his day.   Jones did not seem to be con-
scious of where or whom his point touched, but whilst he was
speaking in front of the Judge's seat, Mr. Sergeant was boil-
ing with indignation and wrath in the Court lobby, and the
moment Mr. Jones was done, he took him to the lobby and
called him to severe account.   Jones was astonished, disclaimed all personality, and calmly remonstrated against

[1] The *National Intelligencer*, Feb. 13, 1844, said: "The interest excited by
the nature and magnitude of the great suit growing out of the will of the late Stephen
Girard and the fame of the eminent counsel engaged in the cause — Messrs. Jones,
Sergeant, Binney and Webster — have for some days past made the hall of the
Supreme Court, the centre of attraction.   On Saturday, and yesterday especially,
the multitudes of both sexes which crowded into the hall and filled every nook of it,
even with the sanction of the Bench itself, exceeded anything which we have for a
long time seen in the way of packing a room."

[2] *Seven Decades of the Union* (1876), by Henry A. Wise; see also *Public Men
and Events* (1875), by Nathan Sargent; *Life of Horace Binney* (1903), by
Charles C. Binney, 215 *et seq.*

Mr. Sergeant's wrath; but the latter was not appeased, and it was feared that some one would have to interpose to prevent serious collision between these two, giants of intellect and champions of argument, but both small in stature. They were finally reconciled, however, though the one was sore under the figure of speech, and the other was sore from the scolding he got for it. . . . Again there was another scene — When Mr. Binney rose to deliver his argument, Mr. Webster having the conclusion, was obliged, by rule, to furnish him with all his points and all his authorities. This he did with great urbanity, just as Mr. Binney was about to open his address to the Court. . . . Mr. Binney had taken a moment to retire to the anteroom of the Court to adjust his personal attire and presence. He was particular about that, and came into the Court refreshed by water and smooth from the comb and brush. He was always very serene in his aspect, and without a forward look, expressed a composed self-reliance. He had just begun, when Mr. Webster rose and apologized for not having obeyed the rule before, and then cited his points and references. Mr. Binney paused to hear him, with his arms folded, and when he was done, smiled a sweet smile of indifference, and gently said, with a slight wave of his hand, that he "fully excused his brother for his delay of citation, for he would have no occasion to touch a single point or anything cited by him"; . . . Mr. Webster was taken back and staggered. Mr. Binney was no better lawyer than Mr. Sergeant, but was a far better speaker, and his style was as rich and pure as that of any other orator or writer of English in his days. . . . His forte was lucid order, perfectly expressed by the clearest logic and the richest but most chaste figure. Mr. Sergeant's forte was solid terseness, direct to the truth, but didactically dry. Neither was superior to Mr. Jones as a forensic debater.

The personalities, by-plays and clashes of counsel were most picturesquely described from day to day by the correspondents of the *New York Herald:* [1]

February 5: The highest judicial officers of the Nation, each robed in a black silk gown, and sitting in a large arm-

[1] *New York Herald,* Feb. 7, 8, 10, 12, 13, 14, 1844.

chair, before his separate table, Justice Story presiding, as Chief Justice Taney is confined to his room by sickness. In front, and some distance off, are four mahogany tables; seated at one of these is a small old gentleman, that is the celebrated Gen. Walter Jones; next is Daniel Webster with beetled brow and dark eyes, poring over the papers, books or printed statements of facts in the case; behind him sits John Calwalader, Esq., of Philadelphia and, in this cause, the principal grubber after facts and documents. He is Horace Binney's son-in-law. At the table parallel to Mr. Webster you behold Horace Binney, white hair, a large head and frame, wearing spectacles, and with strongly marked features. Next to him is John Sergeant. . . . Mr. Jones' argument, probably owing to his ill health, was a rather dull affair, and he spoke so low and with so much hesitancy as to keep the Court on nettles all the time. Mr. Binney appears to have a very ample brief, and to have every link in his chain of argument in its place. The best evidence of this is the fact that Webster and the Judges are kept busy with their pens, noting his points and positions. The argument is very close, searching and logical; and every now and then Webster stops, takes a long breath and goes at his pen again. Daniel evidently has woke up, he is not taking up notes for nothing. . . . It is going to be a tall fight and no mistake, and as the clear voice of the speaker sounds through the arches, you can see the people stretching their necks round the pillars and over the screens, wondering at the transition from Gen. Jones' soporifics. Tomorrow the grand fight begins, and I have no doubt the cars will bring a fresh stock of lawyers.

February 6: The Court-room was densely crowded this morning with ladies and gentlemen at a very early hour. Distinguished members of the legal profession were in diligent and earnest attendance from every part of the United States, intently eager to hear the arguments of these mighty and gigantic intellects. . . . Mr. Webster evidently enjoys his opponent's argument very much, although now and then I think Mr. Binney took the Court and the rest of the counsel into deeper waters than they commonly swim in. . . . Mr. Binney is a pleasant speaker, with a good voice, and evidently a belles lettres scholar. . . . Today in quoting from one of Mr. Webster's own arguments in 13 Peters, he begged him to answer his own authorities. Webster answered: "That was a *bad* case and I had to make my arguments to suit my case." This raised quite a laugh. Throughout the Court-room there is a great silence, save now and then when a bevy of ladies come in. In fact, it looks more like a ballroom sometimes; and if old Lord Eldon and the defunct Judges of Westminster would walk in from their graves, each particular whalebone in their wigs would stand on end at this mixture of men and women, law and politeness, ogling and flirtation, bowing and curtesying, going on in the highest tribunal in America.

February 7: Mr. Binney is still evolving his mighty argument; Mr. Webster looks on with undisguised dismay. It seems he has hitherto regarded the moderate sized octavo brief, which Mr. Binney has been using, as the mighty engine with which he had to contend. But the direful fact has been revealed today that it is but one of seven thunders, and that there are six more yet to come. The Court was astounded at the discovery. There is but one opinion among all those who have listened to this masterly argument; that it has been like a huge screw, slowly turning round on its threads. . . . It has pulverized Mr. Jones' argument. . . . It remains to be seen what Mr. Webster will do; that he will be more powerful as a speaker and more effective with his audience is very probable; but that he can pull Mr. Binney's argument to pieces and build up a better one in its place may well be doubted.

February 10: Daniel Webster is speaking. . . . There is a tremendous squeeze, you can scarcely get a case knife in edgeways. . . . Hundreds and hundreds went away, unable to obtain admittance. There never were so many persons in the Court-room since it was built. Over 200 ladies were there; crowded, squeezed and almost jammed in that little room; in front of the Judges and behind the Judges; in front of Mr. Webster and behind him and on each side of him were rows and rows of beautiful women dressed "to the highest." Senators, Members of the House, Whigs and Locos, foreign Ministers, Cabinet officers, old and young — all kinds of people were there. Both the President's sons, with a cluster of handsome girls, were present. John Quincy Adams sat through the whole of it, listening attentively to every word. Mr. Crittenden sat on Webster's left side, and Horace Binney on his right.   The body of the room, the sides, the aisles, the entrances, all were blocked up with people.   And it was curious to see on the bench a row of beautiful women, seated and filling up the spaces between the chairs of the Judges, so as to look like a second and a female Bench of beautiful Judges.[1]

February 13:   All of the seats of the members of the Bar and half the area behind the Judges were occupied.   The audience trespassed hard upon the Judge once.   But few persons of the great multitude who desired to be present could get within hearing distance.   The opening of the argument was remarkable for all the impressiveness of manner, clearness of expression and power of analysis for which Mr. Webster is so distinguished.   The closing part of his address for the day produced a thrilling effect upon those who heard him, and many at times were shedding tears, from his eloquent defence of the power and influences of the Christian religion.   The Court adjourned at three o'clock.   Mr. Webster finished his argument nobly.   Some evil minded persons, as I have no doubt they might be proved to be, have delicately insinuated that Mr. Webster made rather a failure. If it were a failure, they say it must have been either because he was on the wrong side of the case, or else because he had not allowed himself sufficient time to prepare his brief. Others think that Mr. Binney's arguments were so double-and-twisted and tied-up together that Mr. Webster was somewhat bothered to disentangle and tear them to pieces.

" The curious part of the case is that the whole discussion has assumed a semi-theological character," wrote Judge Story to his wife.   "Mr. Girard excluded ministers of all sects from being admitted into his college as instructors or visitors; but he required the scholars to be taught the love of truth, morality, and benevolence

---

[1] Judge Story wrote to his wife, Feb. 10: "The Court room was crowded to suffocation, with ladies and gentlemen to hear him.   Even the space behind the Judges, close home to their chairs . . . all presented a dense mass of listeners." *Story,* II, 467.

to their fellow-men.　Mr. Jones and Mr. Webster contended that these restrictions were anti-Christian, and illegal, Mr. Binney and Mr. Sergeant contended that they were valid, and Christian, founded upon the great difficulty of making ministers cease to be controversialists, and forbearing to teach the doctrines of their sect. I was not a little amused with the manner in which, on each side, the language of the Scriptures and the doctrines of Christianity were brought in to point the argument; and to find the Court engaged in hearing homilies of faith and exposition of Christianity, with almost the formality of lectures from the pulpit."　"To escape an hour or two of soporifics," wrote Adams in his diary, "left the Hall (of Representatives) and went into that where the Supreme Court were in session to see what had become of Stephen Girard's will, and the scramble of lawyers and collaterals for the fragments of his colossal and misshapen endowment of an infidel charity school for orphan boys.　Webster had just before closed his argument, for which, it is said, if he succeeds, he is to have fifty thousand dollars for his share of the plunder."[1]　And another Member of Congress, John Wentworth of Illinois, wrote regarding the remarkable effect of Webster's argument upon his auditors: "One day, a member came into the House and exclaimed that 'Preaching was played out.　There was no use for ministers now.　Daniel Webster is down in the Supreme Court-room, eclipsing them all by a defense of the Christian religion.　Hereafter we are to have the Gospel according to Webster.'　. . .　As I entered the Court-room, here are his first words: 'And these words which I command thee this day, shall be in thy heart.'. . . Then again: 'Suffer little *children* to come unto me',

---

[1] *J. Q. Adams*, XI, entries of Feb. 9, 10, 13, 1844; *Congressional Reminiscences* (1882), by John Wentworth, 36.

accenting the word, children.   He repeated it, accenting
the word, little.   Then rolling his eyes heavenward and
extending his arm, he repeated it thus: ' Suffer little
children to come unto *Me*, unto *Me*, unto *Me*, suffer
little children to come.'   So he went on for three days.
And it was the only three days' meeting that I ever attended where one man did all the preaching, and there
was neither praying nor singing.   I have heard such
stalwarts in the American pulpit as Lyman Beecher,
Robert J. Breckinridge, Hosea Ballou, William Ellery
Channing, and Alexander Campbell, but Webster over-
shadowed them all in his commendation of doctrines
which they held in common.   One could best be reminded of Paul at Mars Hill. . . .   There was the
closest attention and the most profound silence except
when, assuming an air of indignation with all the force
with which he was capable, he exclaimed: 'To even
argue upon the merits of such a will is an insult to the
understanding of every man.   It opposes all that is in
heaven and all on earth that is worth being on earth.'
Here the audience, with one accord, broke out in the
most enthusiastic applause.   This is the only time that
I ever heard applause in the Supreme Court-room.
The first day, I easily obtained a seat.   With difficulty,
the next.   But on the third, I scarcely found standing
room."   How widespread was the interest of the public
in Webster's argument was illustrated by an editorial
remark of the *New York Herald*, which was opposed to
Webster, but stated that the demand for its paper,
"yesterday among all the religious circles of the city
was truly extraordinary.   Parsons, clergymen, saints,
the elect of all sects, including sinners, seemed to make
a general rush for the only paper that contained the
wonderful argument of that wonderful man."   That
Webster, in making his eloquent plea in behalf of the

Christian religion, was influenced by the thought of its possible effect on his position as a Presidential candidate seems to have been generally believed, and one of his friends apparently had this in mind in writing to him : "It is a noble argument, and I think unanswerable; if you are not the man for the clergy and all the clergy of the country, I greatly err in judgment."[1] With a view to minimizing this political effect of the argument, the Washington correspondents of the Democratic papers evinced a disposition to ridicule it. One wrote that : "Mr. Webster's sermon has created no small amusement here among the members of the Bar. It is not known when he will 'take orders.'" Another wrote of the Court-room "crowded almost to suffocation to witness the greatest novelty of the season — Mr. Webster as the peculiar advocate of religion, . . . working himself up into such a fervor of piety as to shed tears while contemplating the malign influence which the bequest would exercise upon the destinies of the rising generation." And another wrote : "The prevailing expectation is that the Supreme Court will sustain Girard's will. Binney's rather lengthy *argument* was a most powerful position of professional cannons. Webster's reply today was only a *speech*, at which ladies wept, and reporters cried Amen, but only a speech after all. . . . *His* eulogium of religion! *His* description of the blessings of a holy Sabbath! Mercy upon us! What will this world come to? But the ladies were delighted, the reporters much edified and most of all who crammed the Court to surfeit thought it very fine indeed."[2]

Two weeks after the close of the arguments, the Court,

[1] *Webster Papers MSS, Van Tyne copies*, letter of Ketchum to Webster, Feb. 21, 1844; see also *Works of Daniel Webster* (1866), VI, 133.

[2] *Pennsylvanian*, Feb. 14, 1844; *Boston Post*, Feb. 16, 1844; *New York Herald*, Feb. 15, 18, 1844.

through Judge Story, on February 27, 1844, decided in favor of the will, sustaining the trusts created by it and rejecting Webster's contentions as to its invalidity. "The great *Girard Case* has been decided against the argument of Mr. Webster, by the unanimous opinion of all the Judges; a circumstance somewhat unexpected, as upon the former argument there was a considerable diversity of opinion among the Judges," wrote Judge Story to his wife; and to Kent, he wrote of the opinion delivered by him: "Not a single sentence was altered by my brothers as I originally drew it. . . . Mr. Webster did his best for the other side, but it seemed to me, altogether, an address to the prejudices of the clergy." [1] The loss of this famous case by Webster was followed only four months later, by the loss of the Presidential nomination, when, in May, Henry Clay was chosen as the Whig candidate for President.

[1] *Story*, II, 473, 469, letters of March 3, Aug. 31, 1844. It is interesting to note that in order to sustain the will, the Court was obliged practically to overrule a decision of Chief Justice Marshall made in 1819; it was, however, aided in so doing by the great development of information as to the old common law which had taken place in England in the twenty-five years since that date, for Binney in his brief had gleaned from the Calendars of the Proceedings in Chancery in the reign of Elizabeth and prior reigns (published first in 1827), more than fifty instances of an exercise of a chancery jurisdiction of which Marshall had stated there was no trace whatever.

CHAPTER TWENTY-FOUR

STATE POWERS, COMMERCE AND BOUNDARIES

1845–1848

WITH the year 1845 and the beginning of the Administration of President Polk, the country had entered upon a period of commercial and economic development in the trend of which the decisions of the Court were destined to play a considerable part. Hitherto, questions of law arising under the Commerce Clause of the Constitution had been few, and (with the exception of that in *Gibbons* v. *Ogden*) had aroused little general attention. Now, however, the interest of the country in a Nationalistic interpretation of that Clause was becoming increasingly evident. The new methods of interstate and foreign communication were rapidly expanding; in 1831, the first railroads were successfully operated by steam; in 1834, the first through railroad between New York and Philadelphia was opened; in 1846, a bill was reported in Congress to set aside public land for the construction of a railroad from Lake Michigan to Oregon on the Pacific Ocean;[1] by 1848, monopolistic conditions with reference to rail-

---

[1] *29th Cong., 1st Sess.*, see debate in the Senate, July 31, 1846. Senator Sidney Breese of Illinois said that the proposition though novel was "a subject of great importance to the whole Nation and to the world. If the work accomplished by this bill should be accomplished it must revolutionize the commerce of the world." Senator William Woodbridge of Michigan said that it was of consequence to tie the remote States together, to furnish facilities for commercial intercourse. Senator Benton of Missouri said in opposition that "the idea of granting 90,000,000 acres of land to individuals, for the purpose of constructing a road three or four thousand miles through a wilderness and over a range of mountains double the height of the Alleghenies, was one of the most absurd that could be presented to Congress." See also *30th Cong., 1st Sess.*, July 29, 1848.

roads in New Jersey had become so great a grievance
to New York merchants as to result in petitions for
Congressional action; [1] by 1851, Chicago had been
connected with the East by rail, and by 1854, the railroad first reached the Mississippi from the East. The
effect of this development upon the Union of the States
was marked; and as early as 1830, a South Carolina
railroad in asking the Senate for Federal aid had
pointed out that: "It will, under the fostering care of
the Government, be made to constitute a link of Union
with the rising States of the West, attaching them more
strongly, through the powerful influences of interest,
to their Atlantic brethren." The first law book on
railroads, *Angell on Carriers*, in 1849, spoke of their
instrumental effect "in cementing in this connection
and dependence sections of the country far removed
from each other." Foreign commerce was also rapidly
developing, since the arrival of the first ocean steamship in 1838. The express business originated in 1838,
and the telegraph in 1844. [2] A cheaper postage law

[1] *30th Cong., 1st Sess.*, June 10, 1848, see petition of merchants of New York,
presented by Tallmadge of New York in the House, asking for Federal relief
against the monopolies granted by New Jersey to the Camden & Amboy R. R.
and the Delaware and Raritan Canal Co.

[2] The electro-magnetic telegraph patent was first upheld in 1854 in *O'Reilly* v.
Morse, 15 How. 62. The first public Morse telegraph instrument was located in
a room adjoining the Supreme Court-room in the Capitol, and it was from that
room in May, 1844, that the famous dispatches from the Democratic convention
in Baltimore announcing the nomination of Polk were read to the large crowd assembled around the window outside, who received them with "speechless amaze-
ment." *National Intelligencer*, May 22, 28, 30, 1844; *Samuel F. B. Morse, His
Letters and Journals* (1914), II, 221. Senator Willie P. Mangum, the Whig Senator
from North Carolina, wrote, May 29, 1844: "The telegraph is in a room in the
north end of the Capitol and under my room. Every new turn at Baltimore comes
here in less than a twentieth part of a second — absolutely a miraculous triumph
of science. Yesterday evening from 4 to 7 o'clock, more than a thousand people
were in attendance at the window, at which placards in large letters were exhibited
upon the receipt of each item of news. Today, from 700 to 900 were attending when
the news came that Polk was unanimously nominated. I was out of my seat at
a window above, observing and ready to enquire. Some one cried out 'Three
Cheers for Clay.' The air resounded with the outpourings of 500 pairs of strong
lungs in three hearty cheers. A call was made for three cheers for Polk, and the
feeblest wail of some 20 or 30 voices were heard in modest, subdued and conquered

was enacted in 1846, and postage stamps were provided for in 1847.[1] In 1842, the tide of immigration rose above the 100,000 mark, and from Great Britain and Germany there began to arrive that large influx of new population which became such a factor in the development of the cities and of the new West. The first broad general business corporation laws were enacted in 1848 and 1849, in New York and Pennsylvania. Gold was discovered in California in 1848. All these factors contributed to the importance of the interpretation which the Court should give to the Commerce Clause of the Constitution; and the potency of this Clause in its relation to the respective powers of the Federal and State Governments was recognized with apprehension by the advocates of State-Rights. These fears were interestingly expressed, as early as 1847, in a debate over a seemingly harmless proposition made in Congress to separate the House Committee on Commerce into two committees, one on interstate and one on foreign commerce — desirable, as Samuel F. Vinton of Ohio explained, because of the "vast extent of the Union, the great amount of its commerce and the growing importance of our commercial relations not only between the several States of the Union but with foreign nations." The change was vigorously opposed by Southern Congressmen;

strains, and they were in literal truth, a majority of them, boys who had with equal zeal joined for Clay." *Willie P. Mangum Papers MSS.*

The *National Intelligencer* of June 19, 1844, said that: "The Magnetic Telegraph continues to work wonders. Among the reports of its marvels in the *Patriot* of June 17, is that at 12 o'clock, Chief Justice Taney being at the Electric Register in Baltimore sent his respects to the President (then at the Capitol) with the hope that he was well. The President (Tyler) returned his compliments immediately, stating that he enjoyed good health, and *felt much better since Congress had finally adjourned.*"

[1] In 1846, the rate of postage was fixed at 3 cents up to 300 miles and 10 cents over 300 miles; in 1851, the rate was 3 cents up to 3000 miles and 10 cents over 3000 miles. Adhesive postage stamps were first authorized by the Act of March 3, 1847, and made compulsory by the Act of June 1, 1856.

Robert B. Rhett of South Carolina and Henry Bedinger of Virginia, who said that "the covert" and "the
greatest danger to the institutions and freedom of this
country is to be apprehended from the constant encroachments, or efforts at encroachment, of the confederated Government upon the rights and sovereignty of
the individual States"; and that they feared "the
black cloud on the horizon", and the possibility that
the proposed Committee might interfere with the subject of slavery.[1] Similarly, a proposition for a new
Department of the Interior, or "Home Department",
was opposed as a measure to increase the power of the
Federal Government over the internal commerce and
internal improvements of the States, "to bring the
industrial pursuits of our people within the vortex of
Federal action", "to overshadow by the influence of
this great Federal power the interests of the States",
"another of the pernicious experiments which have
been made with a view to bring the people of the country
under the supervision of the Federal power." "There
is something ominous in the expression 'The Secretary
of the Interior'," said Senator Calhoun. "This Government was made to take charge of the exterior relations of the States. . . . This monstrous bill will
turn over the whole interior affairs of the country to
this Department, and it is one of the greatest steps that
ever has been made in my time to absorb all the remaining power of the States." To all these fears, and
to this "strange confusion of ideas which identified
creation of a new Department with extension of Fed-

[1] *30th Cong., 1st Sess.*, speeches in the House of Vinton and Rhett, Dec. 9, 1847,
of Rhett and Bedinger, Dec. 15, 1847; *30th Cong., 2d Sess.*, debate in the Senate
on the Home Department Act of March 3, 1849, speeches of Robert H. T. Hunter
of Virginia, James M. Mason of Virginia, John M. Niles of Connecticut, John C.
Calhoun of South Carolina opposing, and Daniel Webster of Massachusetts, George
E. Badger of North Carolina favoring, March 3.

eral powers", Webster made a remarkably sane and patriotic reply, declaring: "I always feel respect for a voice which is raised against encroachment of the Federal Government, and always feel ready to co-operate with those who declare a purpose to restrain it to its constitutional limits. But to restrain, is not to cripple or to destroy. Within their sphere, the powers of the General Government are supreme, entitled to the respect and support of all, and to be maintained and defended with the same zeal with which encroachments upon the reserved rights of a State should be resisted."

It was at this striking period in the country's economic development that the Court entered upon its 1845 Term. Owing to the fact of the two vacancies on the Court caused by the deaths of Judges Thompson and Baldwin and the refusal of the Senate to confirm Tyler's appointees, few cases of moment were decided. The question as to the extent of the power of the States over interstate commerce, in the absence of Congressional legislation, arose in *Thurlow* v. *Massachusetts*, involving the temperance laws of several of the Eastern States; but after an able argument by Rufus Choate against Daniel Webster, a reargument was ordered and decision was postponed, awaiting completion of the full Court.[1] A decision in *Searight* v. *Stokes*, 3 How. 151, involving two subjects rapidly becoming obsolete — turnpikes and mail coaches — marked the growing tendency of the Court to sustain the powers of the Federal Government, as it held in-

---

[1] Webster's appearance "drew a crowded audience of both sexes to hear him speak; the first overflow of the Court-room that has occurred during the present Term." *National Intelligencer*, Feb. 1, 1845. The Washington correspondent of the *Boston Post*, Jan. 30, 1845, wrote: "Mr. Attorney Huntington arrived here and took his lodgings with all the big wigs at Coleman's National Hotel. The case under the license laws of your State, involving their constitutionality, will be argued about the first of next month, and will be regarded as a great moral phenomenon in the Capital, where if a man does not get absolutely drunk, he is considered pretty temperate."

valid an attempt on the part of the State of Pennsylvania to tax vehicles carrying the United States mail on the old Cumberland Road.[1]

At the end of this Term, Judge Story finally decided to resign from the Bench, and to devote his entire time to his law professorship at the Harvard Law School. For some few years past, he had become greatly depressed over the trend of the Court and its decisions, as well as over the political conditions of the times.[2] The fact is that, though not an old man, he was prematurely worn by his long term of judicial service and by his labors on his great Commentaries on the law. Moreover, he was by nature and by association a conservative, to whom the progressive views of Taney and of other recent members of the Court did not appeal. "Although my personal position and intercourse with my brethren on the Bench has always been pleasant," he wrote to his long-time friend, Ezekiel Bacon, "yet I have been long convinced that the doctrines and opinions of the 'Old Court' were daily losing ground, and especially those on great constitutional questions. New men and new opinions have succeeded. The doctrines of the Constitution, so vital to the country, which in former times received the support of the whole Court, no longer maintain their ascendency. I am the last member now living of the old Court, and I cannot

[1] See also *Neil, Moore & Co.* v. *Ohio* (1845), 3 How. 720; and *Achison* v. *Huddleson* (1851), 12 How. 293, on this same subject.

[2] Story had written to Judge McLean, Aug. 16, 1844: "My heart sickens at the profligacy of public men, the low state of public morals, and the utter indifference of the people to all elevated virtue and even self respect. They are not only the willing victims but the devotees of Demagogues. I had a letter a few days ago from Chancellor Kent, in which he utters language of entire despondency. Is not the *theory* of our Government a total failure?" So again he wrote to Judge McLean, Nov. 23, 1844, after the election of Polk: "You will know that I have for a long time desponded as to the future fate of our country. I now believe that we are too corrupt, imbecile and slavish, in our dependence upon and under the auspices of Demagogues, to maintain any free Constitution, and we shall sink lower and lower in National degradation." *John McLean Papers MSS.*

consent to remain where I can no longer hope to see those doctrines recognized and enforced. For the future, I must be in a dead minority of the Court, with the painful alternative of either expressing an open dissent from the opinions of the Court, or by my silence, seeming to acquiesce in them. . . . I am persuaded that by remaining on the Bench, I could accomplish no good, either for myself or for my country." [1] This was but a repetition of a sentiment which he had voiced in almsot each year since Chief Justice Marshall's death. "I am the last of the Judges who were on the Bench when I first took my seat there," he wrote to Richard Peters in 1836; and the next year: "I am the last of the old race of Judges. I stand their solitary representative with a pained heart and a subdued confidence;" and in 1838: "To me an attendance here is but a melancholy renewal of the memory of departed days and pleasures never to return."

Nothing is more strikingly illustrative of the extreme and bitter partisanship of the politics of the times than the manner in which the news of Story's proposed resignation was received by the Whigs. Loud in their lamentations, they professed the belief that no Judge of any fitness was left on the Bench, since most of the remaining Judges had been appointed by non-Whig Presidents. "I am not surprised at his (Story's) disgust with his service and the bench of the Supreme Court. Among the causes of regret on account of our recent defeat scarcely any is greater than that which arises out of the consequence that the Whigs cannot fill the two vacancies on the Supreme Court," wrote Clay to Crittenden. [2] "The Supreme Court has 'fallen

[1] *Story*, II, 527, 226, 275, 296, letter of April 12, 1845; and see letters of Feb. 8, 1836, April 7, 1837, March 15, 1838.

[2] *Life of John J. Crittenden* (1871), by Ann M. B. Coleman, I, 225, letter to Crittenden, Jan. 9, 1845.

from its high estate.' It will never rise again," said
Richard Peters, and again he wrote: "The Bench is
no longer fit for him. The glory of the Supreme Court
as *he* now leaves it will be for *history*. His retrospects
of his judicial life will be most gratifying. His days
in that tribunal were those of Marshall, Livingston,
Washington, Todd, and Trimble. McLean alone remains of that school — what a contrast! Taney is
an eminent and a good man, but he will never cease to
feel the influence of Jacksonism. . . . The presence
of Judge Story was very important, but I did not desire he should sacrifice himself to stay the progress of
evil. He could but have delayed it. The Court is
now composed of third-rate men, the Chief Justice and
McLean excepted. I suppose we shall have as small
a successor to Baldwin as any of the *Puny* Judges." [1]
Ex-Chancellor Kent (who died two years later) wrote
to Story one of his characteristically pessimistic and
conservative letters: "I have for some time from various reports and observations anticipated the sad event
of your retirement from the Bench. The loss will be
immense and altogether, and in any genial times, wholly
irreparable. But you have done your duty most successfully and most nobly, and your decisions and writings will ' delight and instruct the most distant posterity.' What a succession of great and estimable men
have you witnessed as Associates since you ascended
the Bench. Now what a 'melancholy mass' it presents!
I would not sit on that Bench for all the world! I do
not regard their decisions (yours always excepted) with
much reverence; and for a number of the Associates
I feel habitual scorn and contempt. I can never think
well of a man who consented to do what his predeces-

[1] *Sumner Papers MSS;* letters of Peters to Charles Sumner, Jan. 23, Sept. 11,
1845.

sor thought dishonest to do, that is, to remove the U. S.
Bank deposits to gratify the malignant persecutions
of a savage despot, and in palpable violation of contract. Indeed, the prospect of the country appears
to me to be deplorable. I am very apprehensive our
weak and wicked Administration of unprincipled
demagogues will involve us in war, misery, disgrace.
Considering such characters as Tyler and Polk,
the idea of a great people electing their chief magistrate by popular vote, and with discretion, judgment and honesty, appears to me to be a complete
humbug." [1]

On September 10, 1845, Judge Story died. His
death came as a great blow to the Bar and to the public
and as a genuine grief to the members of the Court.
There was a general and universal mourning throughout the country, regardless of party or section. "What
a loss the Court has sustained," wrote Chief Justice
Taney. "It is irreparable, utterly irreparable in this
generation; for there is nobody equal to him," [2] and
in his reply to the address of the Supreme Court Bar, in
December, he uttered these noble words: "It is here
on this Bench that his real worth was best understood,
and it is here that his loss is most severely and pain-
fully felt. For we have not only known him as a learned
and able Associate in the labors of the Court, but he
was also endeared to us, as a man, by his kindness of
heart, his frankness and high and pure integrity."
But though the affection and esteem felt for the personal character of the deceased Judge were widespread,
for some years there had been a feeling, especially
among the Democrats, that his exaggerated conservatism was to be deplored; and a few of the more radical

[1] *Mass. Hist. Soc. Proc.*, *2d Sess.*, XIV, letter of June 17, 1845.
[2] *Taney*, 290, letter to Richard Peters, Nov., 1845.

papers now indulged in criticisms, which, while not generally indorsed, were nevertheless symptomatic of an increasing desire for a more modern attitude towards the laws in those who sat upon the Bench. "While we would pay the profoundest tribute of respect to his memory as a great lawyer, and to his preëminent social virtues as a man," said the *Boston Post*, "we are not among those who regard his action as a Judge or his authority as a commentator, on the whole favorable to our institutions, or his decisions in questions between general right and exclusive privilege, as sufficiently republican to form the code of laws by which the highest constitutional tribunal should hereafter be governed." It stated that the tendencies of the Court had always been "to a high toned conservatism," and "to sustain privilege and monopoly," which must be counteracted "by placing on the Bench, American Judges instead of British lawyers or learned civilians — men so thoroughly imbued with the spirit of our democratic institution that they cannot be swerved from the right, by the possession of uncontrolled power, or the precedents of English Judges, however profound, but which are drawn from and go to sustain monarchical and privileged institutions, and whose utmost merit is that they protect the strictly legal rights of the poor man, but take care never to extend those rights by construction, while they always favor vested privileges of exclusive classes, even beyond the letter and spirit of the written law." This paper rejoiced that President Polk now had a chance to make an appointment of a Judge who should have moral courage, as well as learning, and who should look to the American people, rather than to British precedents, "for the sanction and approval of the doctrines of popular rights and constitutional construction that ought to govern the

decision of this tribunal." [1] Such form of criticism
had of course been prevalent from the earliest days,
since the Judges of the Court were oftentimes required
to oppose themselves, in excited periods of financial or
economic stress, to temporary popular demands for
legislation which would overthrow the cardinal principles of honesty and good faith in the observance of
contracts. The charge, however, that Story lacked
anything of Americanism in his principles was of course
ridiculous, and arose only from ignorance on the part
of his critics. Nevertheless, since law writers have
usually indulged in indiscriminate praise of Story's
judicial career, it is important, in considering the relations of the Court to the development of the country
and the effect of its decisions upon contemporary
thought and action, to bear in mind the fact that the
views and decisions of both Story and Marshall were
disliked and distrusted by a considerable section of
the American people, in many cases affecting the social
and political conditions. Yet, in spite of these temporary adverse comments, Story well earned the place
of honor in American legal history to which he was assigned by the Bar; and his decisions will always be
one of the great glories of the American Judiciary. [2]

To succeed Judge Story, the names of three strong

[1] *Boston Post,* Sept. 13, 1845. Seven years after Story's death, a writer in the
New York Evening Post, Jan. 29, Feb. 4, 1852, which was violently opposed to his
political and economic views, sharply criticized his judicial decisions: "The truth
is Judge Story had an insatiable appetite for admiration; for he was never con-
tented with any position in which that appetite was not indulged, and he preferred
lecturing awe-stricken boys at Cambridge, where everybody sneezed when he
took snuff, to sitting upon the bench of the Supreme Court at Washington by the
side of men of more influence and the objects of more public attention than himself. . . . The fame which he left behind him as a Judge, we think, will not last
long. He has been author of a great deal of bad law, some of which he himself
lived long enough to regret. His opinions are unnecessarily lengthy and display
a vast amount of unprofitable learning which contributes neither to his clearness
as a writer nor to the education of his readers."

[2] See *Judge Story in the Making of American Law,* by Roscoe Pound, *Amer. Law
Rev.* (1914), XLVIII.

Democratic Judges were urged upon President Polk, — Ether Shepley, Chief Justice of the Supreme Court of Maine; Marcus Morton, former Governor, and Judge of the Supreme Court of Massachusetts; and Levi Woodbury of New Hampshire. On September 20, 1845, Polk finally appointed the latter during the recess of the Senate (recommissioning him on January 3, 1846). Woodbury was fifty-six years of age; he had been a Judge of the State Supreme Court, Governor and Senator of his State, Secretary of the Navy under Jackson, Secretary of the Treasury under Van Buren, and, when appointed on the Court, was again serving in the Senate. "A thorough American statesman and jurist, and a sagacious, sound, and always republican expounder of the Constitution," said a leading Democratic paper, "possessing also every personal quality, urbanity, courtesy, dignity, and every moral requisite of firmness, fidelity and discretion which would render him an ornament to the Bench, and above all a faithful and fearless guardian there of the constitutional rights of the States and the people. Taking the whole Union, no man can be named who would carry to the Bench higher qualifications." [1] Woodbury's term of judicial service unfortunately was a short five years, as he died in 1851.

Polk had still one vacancy to fill, that caused by Judge Baldwin's death in 1844, for which his predecessor, Tyler, had in vain sent in several nominations. The situation was difficult and complicated, owing to the rivalries of Pennsylvania politics. He would have been glad to appoint his Secretary of State, James Buchanan; but the latter, after announcing in Septem-

[1] *Boston Post*, Sept. 13, 1845. It appears from a letter of John Fairfield, of Saco, Maine, to Martin Van Buren, May 16, 1845, that the Woodbury appointment was not approved in Maine, the Bar of which wished the appointment of Shepley. *Van Buren Papers MSS.*

ber his desire for the position, decided in November to remain in the Cabinet, and indorsed Tyler's appointee, John Meredith Read of Pennsylvania.[1] The claims of Peter D. Vroom, Governor of New Jersey, and of Charles J. Ingersoll and Robert C. Grier of Pennsylvania were also urged upon the President with much pertinacity.[2] Finally, on the recommendation of George M. Dallas, his Secretary of the Treasury, Polk nominated, December 23, 1845, George W. Woodward, a Judge of a Pennsylvania inferior Court.[3]

[1] See *Diary of James K. Polk* (1910), pub. by the *Chicago Hist. Soc.*, entries of Sept. 23, Sept. 29, Nov. 19, Dec. 24, 1845. Buchanan wrote to Louis McLane, Feb. 26, 1846: "I have for years been anxious to obtain a seat on the bench of the Supreme Court. This has been several times within my power, but circumstances have always prevented me from accepting the offered boon. I cannot desert the President, at the present moment, against his protestation. If the Oregon question should not be speedily settled, the vacancy must be filled; and then farewell to my wishes." *Works of James Buchanan* (1908–1911), VII.

George Bancroft wrote to Louis McLane, June 23, 1846: "He (Buchanan) goes upon the Bench, to fill the vacancy in the Pennsylvania and New Jersey Circuit. But of this, the public is as yet uninformed." *Life and Letters of George Bancroft* (1908), by Mark A. E. W. Howe.

[2] *New York Herald*, March 8, 1845.

[3] Thomas Corwin wrote, Jan. 14, 1846: "The Cabinet is perfectly mosaic in its lines. Buchanan is treated as no gentleman would treat a sensible hireling. For instance, Woodward from Pa. is nominated by the President for the vacant seat on the Bench of the Supreme Court, and Buch. does not know of this till a friend drops him a note (in pencil) saying 'it has been done yesterday.' Thus Dallas and Walker prevail over Pennsylvania's favorite son, yet the ass bears his burden and still shakes his ears and is Secy. of State!!" *Quart. Pub. of Hist. and Phil. Soc. of Ohio* (1918).

Richard Peters wrote to Judge McLean, Dec. 25, 1845: "You have a nomination for a Judge for this Circuit. The gentleman who is before the Senate has high talents and much private worth. In both of these respects, he is certainly superior to either of those who have been presented to Mr. Polk. He was a member of the Convention which altered the Constitution of Pennsylvania and there manifested very considerable ability. But he was *radical* in all his views. In favor of a limited term of the judicial office — of the election of Justices of the Peace, and of all such errors. No doubt, when made a Judge of the Supreme Court, he will think a *life* tenure of his office *most* safe and *most* proper. King would have made a better Judge, and he was *sound* on all constitutional questions. Those who prevented his appointment last winter have now their reward! We hear that the Secretary of State was not advised of the nomination of Woodward until after it was sent to the Senate! Modern politicians are like spaniels; the more they are beaten, the more they love their masters." *John McLean Papers MSS.*

The *New York Herald*, Jan. 3, 9, 15, 18, 26, 1846, gave an entertaining account of the opposition to Woodward by the Irish-Americans, whom he had offended by certain "Native American" expressions contained in a speech by him; and it

Woodward was a man of high talents and sterling ability, but without any extended reputation and somewhat radical in his views. He had become obnoxious, however, to certain elements of the party owing to alleged "native American sentiments"; and for this reason and owing to the opposition of Senator Cameron of Pennsylvania, the Senate rejected the nomination, January 22, 1846, by a vote of twenty to twenty-nine. Polk then again turned to Buchanan, who, it was generally understood, would now accept. "The country would unquestionably hail with universal approval the acquisition of the learning and ability of James Buchanan to the highest judicial tribunal in the land," said the *Boston Post*. In June, Polk informed Buchanan that he had again decided to nominate him, and Buchanan accepted, but in August changed his mind for a second time and favored William Bradford Reed, a former Attorney-General of Pennsylvania. Thereupon, the President nominated Robert Cooper Grier, of Pennsylvania who was confirmed, August 4, 1846.[1] Grier was fifty-two years of age, and had been Judge of the District Court of Allegheny County for eight years. He served on the Bench twenty-four years, resigning in 1870.

The Supreme Court met in December, 1845, for the first time under the recent statute lengthening its Term and providing for its convening on the second Monday

stated that in the Senate every Whig voted against him and that he had only nineteen Democratic votes and these were given to him out of compliment to the President; it also stated that the Virginia Democrats opposed Woodward as "scene shifters in this interesting drama of decapitation, to get Buchanan into the Court and Stevenson of Virginia into the Cabinet"; see also *Boston Post*, Sept. 13, 1846. In *The Forum* (1856), by David Paul Brown, II, 734, there is an interesting sketch of Judge Woodward.

[1] As early as Jan. 29, 1846, the *New York Herald* stated that Grier would be appointed, though George M. Dallas was also a strong candidate. See also as to Grier, *The Forum*; *Green Bag* (1904), XVI. Hampton L. Carson in his *History of the Supreme Court of the United States*, 343, states erroneously that Grier was commissioned by President Tyler, Aug. 4, 1844.

of December in each year.[1] The most important case
decided at this Term was that involving the great conflict between two sovereign States, *Rhode Island* v.
Massachusetts, 4 How. 591, a bill in equity brought
by Rhode Island alleging a mistake in the original lo-
cation of the boundary line between the two States,
and demanding its establishment by judgment of the
Court and the restoration and confirmation of Rhode
Island in the sovereignty and jurisdiction over the disputed territory. The case had been pending in the
Court for ten years, pursuing the long road of an ordinary equity suit, although it involved the sovereign
rights over territory claimed by two States. Counsel
of the highest ability had presented every point of
which legal skill and strategy were capable, and rulings had been made at successive Terms on many
points of pleading, in all of which Massachusetts had
been heretofore defeated.[2] In 1838, Webster had argued
against Benjamin Hazard that the Court had no jurisdiction in such a controversy. The Court, however,
settled this question of supreme importance, by holding that it possessed jurisdiction in cases involving
disputes as to boundary lines between States (Taney
dissenting on the ground that Rhode Island was suing
for merely political rights). In February, 1844, Rufus
Choate, one of the counsel for Massachusetts, wrote
to Charles Sumner, in the following lively fashion, as
to the enforced continuance of the case due to the two
vacancies on the Bench: "The cause is assigned for
the 20th, and being, as Mr. Justice Catron expressly

---

[1] Act of June 17, 1844. By this statute, the Judges of the Supreme Court were
relieved of holding more than one Term of the Circuit Court within any District
of such Circuit, in any one year. The result of this provision was to enable the
Court to sit later each Spring in Washington; and in alternate years thereafter
it made a practice of sitting through March, adjourning through April, and sitting
again in May.

[2] See 12 Pet. 657, 755; 13 Pet. 23; 14 Pet. 210; 15 Pet. 233.

declared, a case of 'Sovereign States' it has, before this
tribunal of strict constructionists, a terrified and implicit
precedence. Great swelling words of prescription ought
to be spoken. For the rest, I see no great fertility or heights in it." And on February 17, he wrote :
"To my horror and annoyance, the Court has continued our cause to the next Term! The counsel of
Rhode Island moved it yesterday, assigning for cause
that the Court was not full; that the Chief Justice
could not sit, by reason of ill-health; Mr. Justice Story
did not sit; and there was a vacancy on the Bench.
The Court was, therefore, reduced to six Judges. We
opposed the motion. Today Judge McLean said, that
on interchanging views they found that three of the
six who would try it have formally, on the argument
or the plea, come to an opinion in favor of Massachusetts, and that therefore they thought it not proper
to proceed. If Rhode Island should fail, he suggested,
she might have cause of dissatisfaction. I regret this
result, on all accounts, and especially that the constant preparatory labors of a month are, for the present, wholly lost. I had actually withdrawn from the
Senate Chamber to make up this argument, which
may now never be of any use to anybody." The case
was finally argued on the merits, in February, 1846,
by Richard K. Randolph and John Whipple against
Webster and Choate; and Massachusetts won a complete and signal victory, in an opinion in her favor.
The brilliancy and power of Rufus Choate's oratory
made a strong impression on the Court; and it is said
that Judge Catron was so charmed by it that at future
sessions of the Court it became a standing inquiry with
him whether Choate was coming on to argue any case.[1]

---

[1] *Life of Rufus Choate* (1878) by Samuel G. Brown, 103. The *New York Express*, Feb. 7, 1846, said that Choate's argument was "adorned with all that was

"I have heard the most eminent advocates," he said, "but he surpasses them all." Of Webster's argument, a newspaper correspondent wrote that "it was of solid masonry and apparently impregnable" and that "Mr. Choate, with his remarkable diction, with his clear and searching analysis and his subtle logic, went far utterly to destroy the work of the preceding three days. Everyone who heard that argument must have felt that there was something new under the sun, and that such a man as Mr. Choate had never been heard in that Court before."

This case set a precedent of most solemn and serious import in the subsequent relations of the States of the Union, and was of high consequence in inspiring a respect for the position of the Court as an arbitrator between sovereignties. Its immediate effect was seen, the next year, in the filing of a similar bill to settle a boundary dispute between two States in the West which had almost led to armed conflict. On December 10, 1847, an original bill was filed in the Court by Missouri against Iowa to determine the rights to a valuable strip of territory, two thousand square miles on the northern and southern boundaries respectively of the two States. The controversy had been in existence for ten years (during which time Iowa had been a Territory). At one time, fifteen thousand troops had been called for by the Governor of Missouri and fifteen hundred had marched to the line to protect the State's alleged rights, while the Governor of Iowa had called out eleven hundred men under arms to retain possession.[1] Missouri had finally abandoned forcible action and appealed to the Court, where the case

able in logic and beautiful in imagery. The Court-room was crowded and all hearers must have been delighted with its power and brilliancy."

[1] See *National Politics and the Admission of Iowa into the Union*, in *Amer. Hist. Ass. Ann. Report* (1897); *The Southern Boundary of Iowa*, by Charles Negus, in *Annals of Iowa — State Hist. Soc.* (Oct., 1866–Jan., 1867); *Iowa Journ. of Hist. and Econ.*, IX, 245 (1909).

was finally decided against her and in favor of Iowa.[1]
The long line of boundary disputes between the States
which have been determined by the Court since 1846,
and with complete acquiescence on the part of the
States in the results, is evidence of the success of the
exercise of its jurisdiction in this class of cases; and
no more eloquent tribute to the influence of such jurisdiction has ever been paid than that which was uttered
by Lewis Cass in the Senate, in 1855.[2] "It is an impressive spectacle, almost a sublime one, to see nine
men, all of them of mature age and some of them in the
extremity of human life, sitting here in the Supreme
Court, establishing great principles, essential to private and to public prosperity, and to the duration of
the Government, whose influence is felt through the
whole Union and whose decrees are implicity obeyed.
It is the triumph of moral force. It is not the influence
of the sword. . . . I repeat, it is a great moral spectacle to see the decrees of the Judges of our Supreme
Court on the most vital questions obeyed in such a
country as this. They determine questions of boundaries between independent States, proud of their character and position, and tenacious of their rights, but
who yet submit. They have stopped armed men in
our country. Iowa and Missouri had almost got to
arms about their boundary line, but they were stopped
by the intervention of the Court. In Europe, armies
run lines, and they run them with bayonets and cannon. They are marked with ruin and devastation.
In our country they are run by an order of the Court.
They are run by an unarmed surveyor with his chain and
his compass, and the monuments which he puts down are
not monuments of devastation but peaceable ones."

[1] *Missouri* v. *Iowa* (1849), 7 How. 660.
[2] *33d Cong., 2d Sess.*, Jan. 17, 1855, 298.

Though the Term beginning in December, 1846, was held in the midst of the War with Mexico, no question connected with the War came before the Court, but the Term was notable for the number of cases in which the question of State-Rights was involved and decided from many different angles.

The problem of the extent to which the States might go in regulating commerce was once more involved in the *License Cases, Thurlow* v. *Massachusetts*, 5 How. 504. In these cases, the Northern States were urging upon the Court the strictest possible construction of the Constitution, in defense of their State laws, and were adopting the extreme Southern State-Rights point of view. "The fact is," said a Democratic Boston newspaper, "Massachusetts by her narrow legislation has sought to nullify the laws of Congress in liquors, while she denounced South Carolina for doing the like in woolens and cottons. She has undertaken in the same way to defraud a constitutional power of the General Government. She dare not pass a law to prohibit commerce direct in this article, but she has evasively empowered her agents, the county commissioners, to do what she had no power to do herself. . . . It is now in a way to be exploded by a tribunal that will not suffer a plain power in the Constitution to be annulled for one purpose, under pretence of arriving at another purpose." [1] At the first hearing of the case, in 1845, the Court had paid great attention to the arguments of Daniel Webster and Rufus Choate attacking the validity of the statutes. "Mr. Choate as usual held his audience during his whole speech which was very able, ingenious and beautiful," wrote a Washington correspondent. "He took the ground that a law of Congress authorizing importation on payment of

[1] *Boston Post*, Feb. 15, 1845.

duties was a license to the importer to enjoy the *consuming ability* of the country, and that any law breaking any link in the chain of traffic from the importer to the final consumer was unconstitutional. The grave consideration the Court gave to the argument against the validity of these laws, which was pressed with the highest vigor by Mr. Webster, should have shamed the Courts, lawyers and juries of Massachusetts who have treated it so flippantly. . . . The impression here is very strong that the Court will decide against their validity." Owing to the two vacancies on the Bench in 1845, the Court had reached no decision, but had ordered a reargument.[1] In 1846, the case was again continued owing to illness of two Judges; but it was finally argued in 1847 (with two cases from New Hampshire and Rhode Island) by the following array of counsel — Daniel Webster against John Davis of Massachusetts, Samuel Ames and John Whipple against Richard W. Greene of Rhode Island, and John P. Hale against Edmund Burke of New Hampshire. "One would have wished to have been today, as Mrs. Malaprop would say, 'like Cerberus', three gentlemen at once," wrote a newspaper correspondent, "that he might have heard Webster in the Supreme Court, Calhoun in the Senate, and the debate on the Wilmot Proviso in the House. Mr. Webster made in the Supreme Court an argument with his usual ability." [2] Of these arguments, those of Webster, Davis and Hale were of particular weight; and it is interesting to note that Hale, who only five years later, as one of the leading abolitionist Senators in Congress, devoted most of his time to attacking the Court and its authority, now, as counsel, concluded his arguments

---

[1] *Boston Post*, Feb. 15, 1845, March 6, 1846.
[2] *New York Tribune*, Feb. 11, 1847.

with this eloquent tribute to the Court: "My clients rely with confidence upon that protection to commerce which this Court on divers occasions have extended, though in so doing they have been under the necessity of pronouncing the legislation of more than one State invalid and unconstitutional. It was to protect commerce that this Union was established. Take away that power from the General Government, and the Union cannot long last. . . . I leave this case, in the confidence that my clients, in common with all the other citizens of this whole country, will ever find (as they ever have in times past) in this Court, a full and ample protection for their constitutional rights, against which the waves of fanaticism, as well as of faction, may beat harmlessly." The Court rendered a decision, upholding the State statute in each case, but differing greatly among themselves as to the grounds of decision — six Judges rendering separate opinions upon the much vexed points as to the exclusiveness of the power of Congress to regulate commerce, and as to the definition of the word "regulate." That partisan politics did not enter into the result may be seen, however, from the fact that the newspapers of both parties praised the decision.[1] The *New York Tribune* said editorially: "The decision is so manifestly right that we never for a moment dreamed or feared that any other could be given. Overwhelming as is the power of the leading counsel on the beaten side, it was morally impossible that he should prevail in this case, without subverting the powers of the State to regulate the sale of poisons or gunpowder and all dangerous substances whatever. Regarding this decision as in-

[1] *New York Tribune,* March 13, 1847; *Boston Post,* March 10, 1847. The *Western Law Journ.* (1847), IV, 525, said that since the decision of the *License Cases,* "there seems to be increased excitement upon that subject. This is especially the case in Massachusetts."

evitable from the outset, we have regretted the delay
in pronouncing it, only as giving a sort of countenance
to a state of anarchy and pernicious license which
could not fail to prove injurious to public morals and
that salutary reverence for law which should be cherished in every community." The *Boston Post* said
that the decision "will happily put the question of
power at rest and settle beyond successful legal controversy the power of the States over the retail trade
in ardent spirits." While the decision was naturally
of intense interest to the supporters of the Temperance
Movement, it was unsatisfactory to the Bar, because
of the diversity of reasoning by which the Judges
reached their conclusions; and it was not until five
years later, when the case of *Cooley* v. *Port Wardens*
was decided in 1852, that a lawyer could advise a client
with any degree of safety as to the validity of a State
law having any connection with commerce between the
States.

The relation of the States to the slavery question
was presented again in *Jones* v. *Van Zandt*, 5 How.
215, a case argued by William H. Seward of New York
and Salmon P. Chase of Ohio against Senator James
T. Morehead, and involving the constitutionality of
the Federal Fugitive Slave Law of 1793.[1] The Court,
through Judge Woodbury, once more upheld the full
power of the Nation over this subject, asserting that:
"While the compromises of the Constitution exist, it
is impossible to do justice to their requirement, or ful-

---

[1] *Western Law Journ.* (1846–47), IV, 286, said as to Chase's argument: "We do
not know where, within the same compass, can be found so complete and yet so dis-
passionate a view of the bearing of the great question of slavery upon the relations
of the States, so far as fugitives are concerned." See for account of this case *Life
of William H. Seward* (1900), by Frederick Bancroft; *Life and Public Services of
Salmon P. Chase* (1849), by J. W. Shuckers; see also the other fugitive slave cases
of *Norris* v. *Crocker* (1851), 13 How. 429, and *Moore* v. *Illinois* (1852), 14 How.
13; and the *First Fugitive Slave Case of Record in Ohio, Amer. Hist. Ass. Rep.* (1893).

fill the duty incumbent on us towards all the members of the Union, under its provisions, without sustaining such enactments as those of the statute of 1793." To the argument urging the Court to disregard the Constitution and the Act of Congress, on account of the supposed inexpediency and invalidity of all laws recognizing slavery or any right of property in man, Judge Woodbury very properly replied: "That is a political question, settled by each State for itself; and the Federal power over it is limited and regulated by the people of the States in the Constitution itself, as one of its sacred compromises, and which we possess no authority as a judicial body to modify or overrule. Whatever may be the theoretical opinions of any as to the expediency of some of those compromises, or of the right of property in persons which they recognize, this Court has no alternative, while they exist, but to stand by the Constitution and laws with fidelity to their duties and their oaths. Their path is a straight and narrow one, to go where the Constitution and laws lead, and not to break both, by travelling without or beyond them." The utterance of such views, and the fact that Judges like Story and Woodbury, though strongly opposed to slavery, should have given the opinion of the Court in the *Prigg Case* and the *Van Zandt Case*, ought, it would seem, to have preserved the Court from attack by the abolitionists. But the latter now began an incessant war on the Court, charging it with prejudice, partisanship and even corrupt control by the slavery interest. So extreme were their views that Judge McLean himself, the strongest anti-slavery man on the Court, felt called upon now to address a public letter to one of the abolitionist editors, deploring such accusations and saying:[1]

[1] *John McLean Papers MSS,* undated letter to a Mr. Mathews in 1847.

It is an easy matter to denounce the action of any Court who may differ from our own views, and thereby endeavor to lessen the public confidence in such Court. But denunciation is not argument, and however well it may be calculated to create prejudice and mislead ignorant minds and thereby promote party purposes, it is not the best mode of attaining a high and honorable object. Had you examined the facts of the cases referred to, I am quite sure you would have been restrained from saying, in effect, that the Court was corrupt and that its decisions were always in favor of slavery. . . . Mr. Justice Story wrote the opinion of the Court in the case of *Prigg* which you also refer to. That great Judge has gone to his account, and he has not left behind him in the country or in England a lawyer or Judge of greater learning or purity. All who knew him knew well how strongly he was opposed to slavery. No man had a deeper conviction of its impolicy and injustice than he had. But this could not influence his judgment when he was called upon, under the highest sanctions, to give construction to the Constitution. . . . Differences of opinion may exist as to this judgment of the Court, but no man acquainted with Judge Story could suppose that any motive except that of a conscientious discharge of duty could have influenced his judgment. His reputation is safe. It is above reproach. In Europe and America, he is considered as an honor to his country. I speak of him, as he wrote the opinion. A charge of corruption against such a man, and against Judges Thompson and Baldwin who have also gone to their account, and who were opposed to slavery, to say nothing of the Judges who still live and who agreed with Judge Story, should not be lightly made. . . . It is known to every one that Judges are sworn to support the Constitution and laws. They cannot consider slavery in the abstract. If they disregard what they conscientiously believe to be the written law in any case, they act corruptly and are traitors to their country. The Constitution and Act of Congress give to the master of a slave a right to reclaim him in a free State. So plain are the provisions on this subject that no one can mistake them. How is it expected or desired that a Judge shall substitute his own notions for positive law? While this shall become the rule of judicial action, there will be no security for character, property or life.

In one other case at this Term, the Court showed its freedom from sectional or partisan bias in relation to the slavery issue, and its determination not to adopt the extreme State-Rights point of view in its decisions. In *Rowan* v. *Runnels*, 5 How. 134, it was argued that the decision in *Groves* v. *Slaughter*, relating to contracts for the sale of slaves in Mississippi, should be reversed, because of the fact that since that case the Mississippi Court had adopted a contrary view. Chief Justice Taney held, however, that although the Court would always feel bound to respect State Court decisions, yet, since the State Court had not given any opinion before *Groves* v. *Slaughter*, this Court was not required now to reverse itself; and he stated that if the comity due to State decisions were "pushed to this extent, it is evident that the provision in the Constitution of the United States which secures to the citizens of another State the right to sue in the Courts of the United States might become utterly useless and nugatory." [1] This decision met with severe criticism in Mississippi where it was regarded as an extreme attack upon the dignity of the State, the importance of which could not be exaggerated. It was even charged that the Judiciary department of the government was "silently absorbing the rights of the States, and destroying those of the people, without attracting that attention which the magnitude of the interests require. . . . What, in this state of things it becomes the State of Mississippi to do, in order to vindicate its sovereign dignity and protect the rights of its citizens, is a subject for the profoundest reflection of her wisest men. Tamely to ac-

[1] See an article on *Constitutional Law* severely criticizing this case, in *Western Law Journ.* (1847–48), V.

quiesce is voluntarily to assume a position subordinate to that of every other State in the Union," and it was urged that Mississippi should call to the attention of the other States "the invidious discrimination, which in an unguarded hour, has been made against her institutions and people by the Supreme Court." [1]

But while it jealously guarded its right to construe State laws for itself, in the absence of previous decisions by the State Courts, the Court made it plain in several cases that it was not inclined to press unduly the Federal authority in this respect. Thus in *Commercial Bank of Cincinnati* v. *Buckingham's Exors.*, 5 How. 317, it held that no question was presented under the Judiciary Act, inasmuch as "it was the peculiar province and privilege of the State Courts to construe their own statutes and it is no part of the functions of this Court to review their decisions or assume jurisdiction over them on the pretense that their judgments have impaired the obligation of contracts. The power delegated to us is for the restraint of unconstitutional legislation by the States, and not for the correction of alleged errors committed by their Judiciary." And in *Walker* v. *Tailor*, 5 How. 64, it stated that the power of reviewing State Court decisions "has been, in some instances, looked upon with jealousy. Our decisions may fail to command respect, unless we carefully confine ourselves within the bounds prescribed for us by the Constitution and laws." [2]

Three decisions at the Term beginning in Decem-

---

[1] See *Mississippian* (Jackson, Miss.), March 5, 1847; March 30, 1849.

[2] In this connection, the case of *Scott* v. *Jones*, 5 How. 343, is especially interesting. The dry facts in the report of the case do not reveal the historic episode out of which it arose — "the Toledo War", in which the States of Ohio and Michigan had been arrayed in arms against each other in 1836, prior to the admission of Michigan to the Union. See especially *Ohio-Michigan Boundary Line Dispute*, by Todd B. Galloway, *Ohio State Archaeological and Historical Society Reports*, IV; *History of the People of the United States*, by John Bach McMaster, VI, 243, 249, 303, 307; *History of Ohio* (1912), by Emilius O. Randall and Daniel J. Ryan, II, 438, 446.

ber, 1847, profoundly affected the commercial development of the country. The first of these was rendered in *New Jersey Steam Navigation Company* v. *Merchants' Bank*, 6 How. 344, arising out of the loss of the steamer *Lexington* with most of her passengers, crew and freight, through fire caused by gross negligence. Suit had been brought by the Bank for loss of specie shipped on board through an expressman, the latter having contracted with the steamboat company that goods shipped were to be at his risk. Because of the alarming increase in steamboat explosions and conflagrations during the past five years, and in view of the rapid development of the express business and that of other common carriers, a decision by the Court as to a carrier's right by contract to restrict his liability for loss was of utmost consequence to the business community. The case had been argued at the previous Term, and was now reargued by Samuel Ames and John Whipple of Rhode Island, against Webster and Richard W. Greene of Rhode Island. "We have the same Judges here as last year, and no more," wrote Webster. "The second argument, therefore, appears to me a very useless labor. Yet it is ordered, and must be had; and if the case is to be again argued at all, it must be thoroughly argued. I shall be obliged to listen to other counsel, and take notes for five days at least, before time for closing the argument will arrive. Mr. Greene thinks that the opinions of the Judges last session in a collision case on the Mississippi, or some of them, give him new hopes of success in the *Lexington Case*, on the question of jurisdiction. I hope it may be so; but I look for much division and diversity. The Court wants a strong and leading mind." [1] Ten days later,

---

[1] The case referred to was *Waring* v. *Clarke*, 5 How. 441; *Correspondence of Daniel Webster* (1857), letters to Franklin Haven, Dec. 28, 1847, Jan. 8, 1848; see also letter of March 18, 1848.

Webster wrote: "We finished the argument of the *Lexington* about the middle of this week, after a discussion of some eight days. I am glad the cause was re-argued; I think we gained by it; and now begin to feel a good deal of hope about the result. I think it now probable, that the Court, by a majority, greater or less, will decide that it is a case of Admiralty jurisdiction; that the owners of the Boat are common carriers, and so answerable, at all events, for the loss, without going into any proof of actual negligence; that the Bank has a right to call on the owners of the Boat, directly; and cannot be turned over to Harnden, by virtue of his notice, etc. These three great propositions of course give us the case; and at this moment I have confidence they will all be sustained. I wish you, however, to keep this communication to yourself, or regard it as confidential for the present. Mr. Greene is going home, but I shall keep all necessary look out." Webster's predictions as to the final decision were exceedingly accurate. The Court sustained the jurisdiction of the lower Court in Admiralty over maritime freight contracts, and made the important finding of substantive law that a common carrier could not by contract relieve itself from liability for want of care, and that, even if it could restrict its liability for gross negligence or absolute insurance, it could only do so by express agreement, brought home to the shipper.[1]

The second decision of importance to the business interests of the country was that in *Planters' Bank of Mississippi* v. *Sharp*, 6 How. 301, a case which had

---

[1] In *Morewood* v. *Enequist* (1860), 23 How. 491. Judge Grier said that the Court would not review the *Lexington Case* as "the whole subject was most thoroughly investigated by counsel and the Court," and "everything which the industry, learning and research of most able counsel could discover was brought to our attention."

been very elaborately argued by Francis Wharton and John Sergeant of Philadelphia, against Daniel Webster, and Henry D. Gilpin, January 31 and February 1, 2, 3, 4, 1848. It presented the following facts: the State of Mississippi, after chartering the plaintiff bank with power to discount bills and notes and to grant and dispose of property, subsequently enacted statutes making it unlawful for a bank to transfer any bill or note; this was designed to enforce another statute requiring banks to receive their own bank-notes in payment of debts due to them, for, because of the fact of the bank-notes being below par, it had been found that the banks, to evade this statutory form of payment of bills and notes held by them, would transfer such bills and notes to a third person. The statute involved was illustrative of the unsettled conditions of State banking and of the extreme hostility felt at this time towards banking corporations —"giant monsters in a mad career of speculation and fraud", "long and iniquitous violators of every line and letter of their charters, as well as of the general laws of the land" (as they were termed by a Mississippi paper).[1] The Court held that the statute impaired the obligation both of the contract contained in the bank's charter, and of the contract between the maker of the note and the bank.[2] At the same time, the Court, through Judge

---

[1] *Mississippian* (Jackson, Miss.), March 19, 25, 1846; see also *Mississippi Free Trader* (Natchez, Miss.), Feb. 23, 1848, speaking of the "utter disregard to the rights of the people always exhibited by bank corporations."

[2] A similar case arising out of the disorganization of State banking was *Woodruff* v. *Trapnall* (1851), 10 How. 190, in which an Arkansas statute repealing a provision in a State bank charter that the notes of the bank should be received in payment of debts due to the State was held to be an impairment of the obligation of the contract made by the State with the holder of the bank's notes. "A State can no more impair, by legislation, the obligation of its own contracts," said Judge McLean, "than it can impair the obligation of contracts of individuals. We naturally look to the action of a sovereign State, to be characterized by a more scrupulous regard to justice, and a higher morality, than belong to the ordinary transactions of individuals."

Woodbury, again expressed its views that the most favorable and least hypercritical construction must be given to acts of State Legislatures in passing upon their validity. "Those public bodies must be presumed to act from public consideration, being in a high public trust; and when their measures relate to matters of general interest, and can be vindicated under express or justly implied powers, and more especially when they appear intended for improvements, made in the true spirit of the age, or for statutory reforms in abuses, the disposition in the Judiciary should be strong to uphold them." The decision was an example of the influence which the Judiciary exerted upon the financial conditions of the country by its insistence upon the rigid observance of contracts.[1]

That the Court, however, was not inclined to allow the doctrine of impairment of the obligations of contracts to limit the State police power or its power of eminent domain was seen by its decision in *West River Bridge Company* v. *Dix*, 6 How. 507. This case was argued by Webster and Jacob Collamer against Samuel S. Phelps of Vermont on January 5, 6, 7, 1848, and presented the question of the constitutional validity of a State law passed under the exercise of the right of eminent domain and condemning a toll bridge operated under a previous State charter. Webster in his argument stated that: "This power, the eminent domain, which only within a few years was first recognized and naturalized in this country, is unknown to our Constitution or that of the States. It has been adopted from writers on other and arbitrary governments. . . . But being now recognized in Court, our only security is to be found in this tribunal, to keep it within some safe

---

[1] The decision caused some consternation in Mississippi. See *Mississippi Free Trader* (Natchez, Miss.), March 21, 1848.

and well-defined limits, or our State Governments will be but unlimited despotisms over the private citizens." "If the Legislature," he said, "or their agents are to be the sole judges of what is to be taken, and to what public use it is to be appropriated, the most levelling ultraisms of Anti-rentism or Agrarianism or Abolitionism may be successfully advanced." [1] It is notable that as late as 1848, the doctrine of eminent domain (now so axiomatic in our law) should have been regarded as novel. That fears should have been expressed as to its employment to further radical doctrines was less singular. The Court held the statute constitutional, saying that all contracts are made in subordination to certain conditions "superinduced by the pre-existing and higher authority of the laws of nature, of nations, or of the community to which the parties belong . . . conditions inherent and paramount, wherever a necessity for their execution shall occur." It is difficult to conceive how disastrously a decision to the contrary would have affected the development of the country and of its commerce, the improvement of means of communication by railroad, and the abolition of toll-roads and bridges; and the decision was hailed with enthusiasm by the many who regarded the Courts as having hitherto gone to an extreme to protect corporate rights. "It is one of the most important decisions ever given," said the *Boston Post*. "Thus has a new era appeared upon the power of monopolies by a broad decision in favor of popular rights, in the high tribunal which, under the guidance of Judge Story, seems to have been constituted for no purpose but to secure exclusive privileges to corporations and monopolies. It is a great blow at monopoly, and will

[1] "Mr. Webster argued this as a new case and as one of much importance, and it is unquestionably one of great importance as a precedent." *Boston Post*, Jan. 10, 1848.

hold up a wholesome rod over the railroad corporations. . . . Under this decision, any State has the
power to check the assumption of these corporations,
while, at the same time, all the necessary privileges
of corporations are as well secured as ever, and their
real value and utility enhanced by thus harmonizing
them with popular sentiment. The Supreme Court
has done a great act, and posterity will honor and
thank them for it. The motto now is in corporations,
as in civil institutions: 'The present is not the slave
of the past.'" [1] One Southern paper commended the
decision "to the particular notice of those who consider corporations too sacred to be made amenable to
the laws"; while another termed it "a very important decision which reverses some of the humbuggery
which has hereto been considered law. . . . In its
decision, the Court has triumphantly sustained the
republican doctrine that a corporation can have no
more rights than individuals, and has declared that the
franchise of a corporation is as much property as the
materials it owns, and, as such, may be appropriated
for public use, on reasonable compensation, by the
power of eminent domain in the State. This is a great
triumph of progress over the absurd and venerable
dogmas that have hitherto made charters too holy to
be repealed or legislated on." [2]

This Term was made further notable by reason of
an argument from two veterans of the Bar, who now,
in 1848, opposed each other practically for the last time
before the Court — Henry Clay and John Sergeant.
Though the case, *Houston* v. *City Bank of New Orleans*,
6 How. 486, presented an uninteresting question arising under the defunct Bankrupt Law, nevertheless, as

[1] *Boston Post*, Feb. 4, 1848.
[2] *Mississippi Free Trader*, Feb. 27, 1848; *Mississippian*, Feb. 25, 1848.

was usual whenever Clay appeared in Washington, public interest was intense. "At an early hour, the avenues leading to the Capitol were thronged with crowds of the aged and young, the beautiful and gay, all anxious to hear, perhaps for the last time, the voice of the sage of Ashland," wrote a newspaper correspondent. "On no former occasion was the Supreme Court so densely packed — every inch of space was occupied, even to the lobbies leading to the Senate. Mr. Clay rose a few minutes after eleven o'clock, the hour at which the Court is organized. It has been often said, and truly, that he never was and never could be, reported successfully. His magic manner, the captivating tones of his voice, and a natural grace, singular in its influence, and peculiarly his own, can never be transferred to paper." [1] Another correspondent wrote: "The Supreme Court this morning was at an early hour, inundated by ladies. They not only filled all and every seat appropriated for the usual audience, but got within the bar and crowded the Judges in their seats — almost pushed them from their stools. The *liberty of the press* never carried to a more dangerous extent. Mr. Clay has always been a great favorite with the ladies. Justly so. The gallantry of his bearing, the dignity of his gestures, the warmth of his manners, his sonorous voice, and the many graces with which he is ideally associated in the general imagination make him the proper favorite of the more discriminating portion of Creation. It is a barren case in which he is interested. It carries no general interest save as it is connected with the constitutionality of

[1] *Works of Henry Clay* (1897), III, 79; *New York Tribune*, Feb. 12, 15, 1848; *Philadelphia North American*, Feb. 14, 1848; *Baltimore Republican*, Feb. 9, 1848; the *National Intelligencer* stated, Feb. 12, 1848: "The Supreme Court-room was, as we had anticipated, crowded almost to suffocation yesterday to see and hear Mr. Clay. . . . Very many were unable to get into the room."

the Bankrupt Law. . . . It mattered not to the audience, however, how dry or intrinsically uninteresting the subject. It was Mr. Clay they wished to hear.
. . . They hung upon his words as if each was an
inspiration. He looks well. Three score years and
ten have passed over him without diminishing the
brilliancy of his eye or his towering form. He is every
inch a man." Another correspondent wrote that, by
the common consent of the Court and the Bar, "Mr.
Clay exhibited as much vigor of intellect, clearness of
elucidation, power of logic and legal analysis, as he
ever did in his palmiest day." In opening his argument, Clay recalled to the Judges that not a face was
on that Bench which was seen when he first had the
honor of appearing there; [1] and he stated that "it was
a grateful reflection that amidst all the political shocks
to which the country had been subject, the Court had
maintained its elevated name, its dignity and its purity, untouched and unsuspected"; he alluded to "his
high gratification at the manifestations of respect he
had now met with from old friends of the Bar and
Members of Congress, as well as from private citizens,
on his reluctant return to scenes of former action; it
was usual, he said, for the Court to extend peculiar
leniency to young practitioners, and though not of
that class, he might have need of indulgence with those
not having familiarity with the practice of the Bar." [2]

[1] Clay was seventy-one years old; he had first appeared before the Court in 1807
in *Marshall* v. *Currie*, 4 Cranch, 172. An interesting contemporary account of
his early days in Washington is given in the diary of William Plumer.

[2] *New York Times*, Feb. 12, 1848. While Clay remained in Washington to await
the decision of the case (which he finally won) his former friend, the aged Ex-President, John Quincy Adams, was stricken ill, while in his seat in the hall of the House
of Representatives, and died two days later, February 23, 1848; and in the Supreme
Court, the next day in the midst of an argument by Thomas Ewing, of Ohio, the
Chief Justice said: "Gentlemen of the Bar, in consequence of the death of Mr.
Adams, the Court will not proceed with the case under argument. From the long
public service of Mr. Adams, and the distinguished station he has held in the Government, the Court thinks it their duty to show their respect to his memory by

The Term beginning in December, 1848, was marked by the elaborate argument and opinions rendered in the long pending *Passenger Cases, Smith* v. *Turner* and *Norris* v. *Boston*, 7 How. 283. For ten years, the increasing tide of immigration, particularly of paupers and petty criminals from Great Britain, had alarmed the seaboard States; legislation had been enacted to guard against this evil by the imposition of taxes upon alien passengers, and by the requirement of bonds from masters of vessels carrying immigrants; and it was laws of this nature in the States of Massachusetts and of New York whose constitutionality was now challenged, on the ground that Congress had exclusive power over this form of commerce. But while the validity of these laws was the ostensible issue, there was, in reality, a far greater interest at stake, since it was believed by the South that much of its slavery legislation depended on the position which the Court should finally take relative to the scope of the Commerce Clause. Once more it was clearly shown that the opposition of Southern statesmen to the expansion of the power of Congress over commerce was based but slightly on abstract political doctrines relative to strict or broad constructions of the Constitution, and very greatly on the concrete fear as to its effect on the power of the Southern States over slavery.

The relation of the slavery issue to the question of interstate commerce had arisen first in connection with the refusal of two Northern States to extradite persons charged with kidnaping slaves in the South. In 1837 and again in 1838, the Governor of Maine had declined to surrender such persons indicted for violation of criminal statutes of Georgia; and in 1839,

adjourning today without transacting any business." *National Intelligencer*, Feb. 28, 1848.

Governor Seward of New York took a similar action with regard to persons indicted in Virginia. These acts had aroused great indignation in the Southern States, which was further enhanced by the passage of a law in New York granting jury trial in fugitive slave cases.[1] As a retaliation for what they termed "the incendiary dogmas and unconstitutional legislation of New York", the States of South Carolina and Virginia passed laws, in 1840 and 1841, directed against the departure of slaves on vessels and specifically restricting New York-owned vessels; and their newspapers said that "it will not be long before every State in the South . . . will array itself under the example of Virginia against the encroachments of New York on the Constitution and the dangers of these encroachments." [2] That these retaliatory laws were unquestionably in violation of the Commerce Clause and other provisions of the Constitution cannot now be doubted. And that they would be so held, if brought before the Court, was anticipated as early as 1841, when a leading Southern newspaper thus voiced its alarm: "There have hitherto been said to be two 'sweeping clauses' in the Constitution, threatening to sweep off the rights of the States and the People; first the 'necessary and proper' clause; second the 'general welfare' clause. But a third sweeping clause has been

[1] *The Rise and Fall of the Slave Power in America* (1874), by Henry Wilson, I, 474–475; *Law Reporter* (Jan., 1846); *American Jurist* (July, 1840); *26th Cong., 1st Sess.*, speech of John H. Lumpkin of Georgia, in the Senate, March 11, 1840; *30th Cong., 2d Sess.*, speech of Joseph Mullin of New York in the House, Feb. 26, 1849. In *Van Zandt* v. *Jones*, 2 McLean, 596, 671, laws of Kentucky punishing kidnaping of slaves, etc., were upheld at a trial in 1840, and later in *Jones* v. *Van Zandt*, 5 How. 215, in 1846.

[2] *Washington Globe*, Feb. 17, 1842. The statute passed by South Carolina in 1841 provided that any vessel owned or commanded or navigated by a citizen or resident of New York or owned by any citizen other than of South Carolina and departing from any port in New York should not sail with any slaves on board, and if arriving and owned as above by citizens of New York, the vessel should be held and bond for $1000 given to pay all judgments for runaway slaves.

sprung, which threatens to do us as much mischief
as its two predecessors. This is the power over commerce." After speaking of the "dangerous excesses
to which the Federalists are prepared to carry this
power", it said: "In the name of Heaven, what power
would the States have of protecting the lives and property of their own citizens, if this sweeping power of
Commerce were admitted? What becomes of our
quarantine laws, inspection laws, pilot laws — laws
which would prevent the seeds of yellow fever from
being imported from New Orleans? What becomes
of the power to keep the citizens of New York from
stealing our property and refusing to give it up or
those who stole it, if we cannot pass such a bill as may
authorize us to search their vessels, or to demand bond
and security for the indemnity of masters, whose
slaves may be stolen, by every kidnapper?" [1]   In opposition to this extreme assertion of State supremacy,
the *National Intelligencer* expressed the view taken by
the more conservative men in all sections of the country that: "If every State may take the laws into its
own hands, in regard to questions involving the regulation of commerce among the several States, and if
the States are to be allowed to do what Congress cannot do, that is, to give preference by regulation of
commerce to the vessels of one State over those of
another, or to vessels of all other States over those of
any one State — then has the Constitution failed in
one among the most important of the purposes for
which it was established. These attempts of the
State to usurp authority belonging to the Government of the United States are becoming more and
more frequent. The success of such an attempt in
New York lately brought us to the verge of a war with

[1] *Richmond Enquirer*, March 4, 1841; *National Intelligencer*, Feb. 17, 1842.

a foreign power, as the attempt itself on the part of another State did with the same power, three years ago; and now two or three States are about having a war of commercial interdicts among themselves, which, unless ended by judicial interposition, may be attended with consequences ever to be lamented."

Owing to the decision of the Court in the *Prigg Case* in 1842, and a decision of the New York Supreme Court based upon it, holding the New York jury trial law invalid, the dangerous question as to the scope of the Commerce Clause of the Constitution and its effect upon these retaliatory laws of South Carolina and Virginia was not presented to the Court. Between 1842 and 1848, however, the question arose in connection with other slavery legislation. For many years, South Carolina had been enforcing its statute against the entry of free negroes into its ports, disregarding entirely the fact that it had been held unconstitutional by Judge Johnson in the United States Circuit Court, in 1823. Louisiana had enacted similar legislation, in 1842; and the Territory of Florida, seeking admission as a State, in 1845, had embodied in its Constitution express power to its Legislature to pass laws for the exclusion of free negroes. The constitutionality of such laws had been the subject of frequent debate in Congress, the anti-slavery men of the North contending that they were in clear violation of the Commerce Clause and of Section Two of Article Four of the Constitution guaranteeing the privileges and immunities of citizens of the several States. The Southerners, on the other hand, claimed that the laws were a valid exercise of the State police power, and like quarantine laws, necessary as a "protection against what is infinitely more dangerous than physical contagion — the introduction of free persons of color into a community where slavery exists, with the means of practicing upon the ignorance of these people, of deluding them into insurrection and of placing in jeopardy the lives of the people of the States." "On the very same principle by which a State may prevent the introduction of infected persons or goods and articles dangerous to the person and property of its citizens, it may exclude paupers, incendiaries, vicious, dishonest and corrupt persons such as may endanger the morals, health or property of the people. The whole subject is necessarily connected with the internal police of a State, no item of which has to any extent been delegated to Congress," argued Senator Lumpkin of Georgia in 1840.[1] In the debate in 1845, on the admission of Florida as a State, the question was discussed with much warmth, on a motion by George Evans of Maine for a proviso withholding from Florida the power to prevent the entrance of free negroes. The proposal was attacked by Robert J. Walker of Mississippi, and by John M. Berrien of Georgia who said: "Each State has the power to protect

---

[1] See *supra*, II, 83–87; and see *26th Cong., 1st Sess.*, speech of Lumpkin in the Senate, March 11, 1840, on a bill to require the United States District Judge to require the surrender of persons found in any State charged with crime committed in another State; *28th Cong., 1st Sess.*, speeches of John Quincy Adams in the House, Dec. 22, 1843, pointing out that South Carolina had officially declared that she preferred both dissolution of the Union and war with Great Britain to repeal of her laws against the introduction of free negroes; *28th Cong., 2d Sess.*, speeches of George Evans of Maine, Robert J. Walker of Mississippi, John M. Berrien of Georgia, Rufus Choate of Massachusetts, William S. Archer of Virginia, in the Senate, March 1, 1845; *30th Cong., 1st Sess.*, speeches of Thomas H. Bayly of Virginia, and George Ashmun of Massachusetts, in the House, April 10, 11, 1848; *30th Cong., 2d Sess.*, speeches of Charles Hudson of Massachusetts, Robert B. Rhett of South Carolina, Isaac E. Holmes of South Carolina, George Ashmun of Massachusetts, in the House, Jan. 31, 1849; *31st Cong., 1st Sess.*, speeches of Jefferson Davis of Mississippi and Berrien, and *passim* in the debate on the Fugitive Slave Law, in the Senate (pp. 1581–1630), Aug. 19–23, 1850, speech of Roger S. Baldwin of Connecticut in the Senate, March 28, 1850. See also *The Rise and Fall of the Slave Power in America* (1874), by Henry Wilson, I, 576–586, II, 1–6; and see *New York Evening Post*, Jan. 24, 31, Feb. 7, 25, 1851, on the official correspondence with England as to these South Carolina statutes in their effect on English subjects.

itself — a power which never would be surrendered. It is, therefore, useless for the other States to attempt to deprive any one of them of the right . . . to suppress a moral pestilence within her borders. I shall rejoice to see this question carried to the Supreme Court for its decision. I have not the slightest doubt that the power of the States to pass police laws for their own protection will be recognized." Rufus Choate of Massachusetts replied that his State would also welcome a decision of the Court; and he pointed out that Massachusetts had, in 1844, appointed an agent, Samuel Hoar, to go to South Carolina to protect the rights of her free colored citizens, and that South Carolina had by statute penalized any attempt by Hoar to litigate the question.[1] William S. Archer of Virginia replied that: "Though Massachusetts is the most enlightened State in the Union, this position has not restrained her from being the instrument of throwing distraction into the Federal councils of the Union by her action on this slavery subject. . . . If we believe that the vessels of New England and Maine are about to bring firebrands to cast into the midst of our cities, we will take precautions to keep off and keep out such an element of mischief. . . . We cannot allow shiploads of persons calling themselves sailors from Massachusetts to come into these ports . . . for the purpose of stirring up the latent embers of the worst forms of civil combustion. . . . Are we going to let the fire break out and conflagrate our cities and towns, in deference to what they call their constitutional rights?"

Under such circumstances, and with so inflammable a political question involved, it is not surprising that

[1] See long article in *Boston Post*, Feb. 12, 1845, on South Carolina and Massachusetts and the Hoar mission, written from the Democratic standpoint.

the Judges of the Court should have made every effort to confine their decisions relating to the scope of
the Commerce Clause of the Constitution to the particular statute presented in each case, rather than to
enounce any broad interpretation or definition of the
language of the Clause. Since 1845, however, there
had been pending on the docket cases involving the
validity of the New York and of the Massachusetts
immigrant laws, the decision of which apparently
would require a consideration of the questions presented by the free-negro legislation of the South, for
the Massachusetts laws appeared to be similarly repugnant to the Constitution. "Everything may be
said of them," wrote Daniel Webster, "that Massachusetts says against South Carolina"; and one of
the Democratic Party organs also remarked: "Massachusetts is getting a terribly bad reputation abroad
for her ultraism, mock-morals, false philanthropy
and illiberal laws infringing trade and commercial
intercourse." [1] These laws, however, were warmly
defended by the Whigs of the North, who, equally
with the Democrats of the South, sought to uphold
a strict construction of the Constitution, whenever
legislation which touched their particular social or
economic interest was involved. Owing to the importance of the issue, and to the fact that for three
Terms there had been vacancies on the Bench, the
Court had reached no final decision before the December Term of 1848. The case involving the New York
immigrant law had been the first to be argued, Decem-

---

[1] *Boston Post,* Feb. 10, 12, 1847. "The passenger law is a barbaric law in its
operation. . . . Add this illiberality in her laws to her constant assaults upon
the Union through her extreme anti-slavery doctrines . . . and you may well
suppose that in the broad theatre of the country the conduct of the Whig Legislature of Massachusetts is giving in the nostrils of the people the very opposite
savor to anything like National odor."

ber 10, 11, 15, 1845, by David B. Ogden and Daniel
Webster against John Van Buren (then Attorney-General of New York), and Willis Hall (ex-Attorney-General of New York); the Massachusetts case was first
argued by Webster and Rufus Choate against John
Davis of Massachusetts, February 5, 8, 9, 1847; both
cases were reargued in December, 1847, and again in
December, 1848. Of Webster's argument in 1847, a
Washington correspondent wrote: "The Court-room
was crowded, the ladies occupying most of the seats
assigned to the audience. The argument was eminently Websterian, close, compact, powerful. I know
not when I have heard Mr. Webster with more pleasure of instruction. His reply to Mr. Van Buren was
distinguished for point, force and great playfulness,
particularly in answering the argument that it was
New York which poured of her abundance into the
lap of the National Treasury. . . . Mr. Webster
spoke powerfully of the sanctity of the decisions of
the Supreme Court, in reply to a remark of the opposite counsel that people were beginning to forget the
life-tenure of the Judges, in consequence of the infusion of popular sentiment into the decisions of the
Court. He considered this as a very left-handed
compliment at best, and it was one he certainly should
not pay the Court. The early decisions of the Court
were, in some measure inherent to the Constitution
itself. They were, indeed, a part of the Constitution,
and he could not be so disrespectful to the memory
of Jay, Ellsworth, Marshall, Thompson, Baldwin,
Iredell, and others, as to reflect upon decisions made
by them and interwoven as they were with the Constitution of the Government. Mr. Webster early
came to the argument of the case, and spoke with a
power and force which cannot be surpassed, if equalled

by any counsel or jurist in the land." [1] A lively description of Webster's young and able opponent from New York, John Van Buren, was given by another newspaper correspondent, who termed him "one of the ablest, most logical and graceful debaters of the day" in whom "the old constitutional expounder finds a competitor that taxes severely his great powers of mind and acknowledged legal acumen. It was amusing to see with what attention and apparent eagerness Webster listened to the young debater"; and Van Buren's noted wit was illustrated by the request to the Court with which he closed, urging upon it the importance of an early decision as desirable in every point of view, "but especially in reference to the poor devils who are now at Quarantine. The cholera is raging among them with fearful mortality, and it would be a consolation to their friends to know that they are dying constitutionally." [2] Webster's own views of the case and a singularly accurate prophecy as to the final outcome were vividly presented in a series of letters written by him to his son, Fletcher Webster, and to his friend, Peter Harvey.[3] Writing, February 7, 1847, after the first argument of the Massachusetts case, he said:

The Massachusetts law laying a tax on passengers is now under discussion in the Supreme Court. It is strange to me how any Legislature of Massachusetts could pass such a law. In the days of Marshall and Story, it could not have stood one moment. The present Judges, I fear, are quite too much inclined to find apologies for irregular

[1] *Baltimore American*, Dec. 24, 1847. The *National Intelligencer*, Dec. 27, 1848, described Webster's argument as "a surpassing example of the highest power of reasoning and eloquence."

[2] Letter to *Cleveland Plain Dealer*, quoted in *Mississippi Free Trader*, Jan. 20, 1848; *Savannah Republican*, March 7, 1849.

[3] *Webster*, XVI, XVIII; *Letters of Daniel Webster*, edited by C. H. Van Tyne (1902); see also *Life of Daniel Webster* (1870), by George T. Curtis, II, 374; also *Law Reporter*, XI, 478.

and dangerous acts of State Legislatures; but whether the law of Massachusetts can stand, even with the advantages of all these predispositions, is doubtful. There is just about an even chance, I think, that it will be pronounced unconstitutional. Mr. Choate examined the subject, on Friday, in an argument of great strength and clearness. Mr. Davis is on the other side, and I shall reply.

Nobody can tell what will be done with the License Law, so great is the difference of opinion on all these subjects on the Bench. My own opinion is that the License Law will be sustained; that the Passenger Law of Massachusetts will not be sustained. This, however, is opinion merely.

After the second argument, he wrote, December 29, 1847: "At present I am engaged in those old causes now on second argument. I am tired of these constitutional questions. This is no Court for them." After the third argument, he wrote, December 26, 1848:

Saving and excepting a stiff back, I am quite well. I suppose I took cold in the Court room on Friday; when I finished, the heat was suffocating, the thermometer being at 90. The Court immediately adjourned — all the doors and windows were opened, and the damp air rushed in. I did all I could to protect myself. It was just such an exposure which caused Mr. Pinkney's death. He had been arguing against me, the cause arising on Gov. Dudley's will, the first case in 10 or 11 Wheaton. He came into Court the next morning, pale as a ghost; spoke to me, went to his lodgings at Brown's, and never again went out alive. I argued my cause well enough, and if I were not always unlucky nowadays in such cases, I should think I saw a glimmering of success. But tho' we shall get 4 Judges, I fear we may not a 5th.

Just before the final decision, he wrote, February 3, 1849:

There is a great interest here to hear the opinions of the Judges on Tuesday. . . . Several opinions will be read, drawn with the best abilities of the writers. In my poor judgment, the decision will be more important to the country than any decision since that in the steamboat cause. That was one of my earliest arguments of a constitutional question. This will probably be — and I am content it should be — my last. I am willing to confess to the vanity of thinking that my efforts in these two cases have done something towards explaining and upholding the just powers of the government of the United States on the great subject of Commerce. The last, though by far the most laborious and persevering, has been made under great discouragements and evil auspices. Whatever I may think of the ability of my argument — and I do think highly of it — I yet feel pleasure in reflecting that I have held on and held out to the end. But no more of self-praise.

The decision holding the laws of both States unconstitutional was rendered on February 7, 1849, each of the Judges reading an opinion, so that seven hours were thus occupied.[1] Judges McLean, Wayne, Catron, McKinley and Grier held that the laws were a regulation of commerce and conflicted with Congressional legislation, the first two Judges (one from the North and the other from the South) viewing the Federal power over commerce as exclusive, the other three ruling that it was unnecessary to decide the point. Chief Justice Taney, and Judges Nelson, Daniel and Woodbury, dissented, either on the ground that regulation of passengers was not regulation of commerce, or that the tax did not conflict with any Federal statute. As illustrating the freedom from political bias in the decision of this case, it was stated by one of the Washington correspondents that the deciding vote against the State laws was given by the most ardent State-Rights Judge, Judge McKinley.[2]

[1] *Boston Courier*, Feb. 13, 1849.

[2] The Washington correspondent of the *New York Commercial Advertiser*, quoted in the *Boston Post*, Jan. 25, 1849, wrote: "The New York case was once about to be decided on the opinion of four to three. It was then concluded to postpone judgment, until after another argument before a full Bench. Since then, the

The diversity, however, of the views of the Judges, as expressed in their various separate opinions, was so great that the Reporter himself, in perplexity, very frankly declared that there was no opinion of the Court as a Court. Equally perplexed were the members of the Bar and the newspapers. A Baltimore paper said: "Sailors say, in a very hard blow, point no point is the only one you can safely make. In the present gale of judicial wind, that is about the only point discernible. Seriously, the excess of words on the Bench is a great grievance. These seven or eight long opinions will greatly obscure the points really decided, and impair the force of the decision." [1] A New York paper stated that the Judges "have put the whole question of the constitutionality of such laws in doubt and mist. A slight change in the composition of the Court of nine Judges will upset the decision"; and it wisely said: "These separate opinions are to be deprecated as a great nuisance. It is of more consequence to society that the law should be settled, than that it should be wise. We can alter a bad law — we can even change the Constitution — but uncertain law is tyranny." Another New York paper stated that the questions raised "were the highest which ever have been or can be raised in Court", and that the decision "may be regarded as perhaps the most important which has ever received the sanction of this highest Court"; but it deplored the fact that "the Court have, by a meager majority of one, reversed the laws of so many States.

Judges have stood four to four, and upon the arrival of Judge McKinley, it was found that his opinion was adverse to the claims of the States." The *Washington Union*, Feb. 14, 1849, said that few cases were of more importance, and it termed the opinion of Chief Justice Taney "one of the ablest which ever emanated from that distinguished Bench."

[1] *Baltimore Sun*, Feb. 10, 1849; *New York Journal of Commerce*, Feb. 12, 1849; *Boston Daily Advertiser*, Feb. 12, 1849, quoting the *New York Express*.

At one fell swoop the taxing powers of many of the
States, New York, Massachusetts, Maryland, Louisiana, go by the board — and one branch of the New
York law, that imposing a tax upon passengers from
the States of the Union, the Court unanimously condemn. This domestic question has not, however,
been before the Court, but being a part of the law of
New York, and apprehensive that silence might be
deemed acquiescence, the Chief Justice spoke of it as
unconstitutional. . . . In listening to the opinions
of the eminent men who were heard in Court today,
it was impossible not to be more impressed with what
are sometimes called 'the glorious uncertainties of
the law' than with the stability of the wisest of human
judgments. The Chief Justice remarked more than
once, and I thought conclusively proved, that the
opinion of today was practically a reversion of the
previous judgment of the Court."

The decision of the Court, overturning the State
laws, was regarded as a disastrous judgment by the
dissenting Judges who held strict State-Rights views.
Judge Daniel termed it a "trampling on some of the
strongest defences of the safety and independence of
the States of the Confederacy. . . . I am unable to
suppress my alarm at the approach of power claimed
to be uncontrollable and unlimited"; and Judge
Woodbury said that: "A course of prohibitions and
nullifications as to their domestic policies in doubtful cases, and this by mere implied power is a violation
of sound principle and will alienate and justly offend,
and tend ultimately, no less than disastrously, to dissolve the bands of that Union so useful and glorious
to all concerned." These expressions of apprehension
were undoubtedly due to the fact that the Judges
feared the application of the doctrines of the majority

to the slavery legislation of the South. At the argument of the case, warning of this had been explicitly given by counsel for the States. Davis, for Massachusetts had asked, if Massachusetts cannot exclude immigrants likely to be paupers, "on what principle can the laws expelling or forbidding the introduction of free negroes be sustained?" Van Buren, for New York, cited laws forbidding or regulating the admission of free persons of color in fifteen States, non-slaveholding as well as slaveholding. Taney, in dissenting, stated that it must "rest with the State to determine whether any particular class or description of persons are likely to produce discontent or insurrection in its territory or to taint the morals of its citizens, or to bring among them contagious diseases, or the evils and burdens of a numerous pauper population . . . and to remove from among their people and to prevent from entering the State, any person or class or description of persons, whom it may deem dangerous or injurious to the interests and welfare of its citizens." Judge Woodbury in his dissent expressed the same view, and Judge Wayne, of the majority of the Court, stated that "the States where slaves are have a constitutional right to exclude all such as are, from a common ancestry and country, of the same class of men;"[1] the other four Judges of the majority, while failing to rule specifically on this phase of the question, announced views affecting it, which Taney evidently believed to be opposed to his own. The result of the decision was to give great alarm to the South.[2] Thus, the *Charleston Mercury*

[1] 7 Howard, 467, 543–544, 426.

[2] *Richmond Enquirer*, March 4, 1841. Thomas J. Turner of Ohio said in the House, Feb. 22, 1849: "The Supreme Court in the celebrated case which has lately been adjudicated within the Capitol says, in effect, that the law of South Carolina is unconstitutional." *30th Cong., 2d Sess.*

said of it: "The intellectual, as well as judicial, weight of the Court is clearly against the decision, but numbers prevailed. If we correctly understand the points decided, they sweep away our inspection laws enacted to prevent the abduction of our slaves in Northern vessels. They sweep away also all our laws enacted to prevent free colored persons — citizens of Massachusetts — or whatever abolition region, from entering our ports and cities. Thus it seems as if the Union is to be so administered as to strip the South of all power of self-protection and to make submission to its rule equivalent to ruin and degradation." [1] A leading Southern Quarterly stated with truculence that: "We have little doubt that the decision will be repudiated by the sober judgment of public opinion, as so many other decisions of the Supreme Court on constitutional questions have been before, and that, if ever the Court should be again filled with such men as formerly occupied its seats, this and other crudities of the present majority of little men would be swept away like chaff before the wind. In the meantime, we hope that the States of New York and Massachusetts will continue to collect their taxes, notwithstanding the adverse decision of the Supreme Court. There are some States in the confederacy, which, if we are not mistaken, would exercise their sovereign rights, in spite of Mr. Justice Wayne and his Associates."

That the dogma of State-Rights was not confined to the South, was strikingly illustrated by the case of *Peck* v. *Jenness*, 7 How. 612, the decision in which at this Term ended a seven years' controversy between the State of New Hampshire and the inferior

[1] *Charleston Mercury*, Feb. 14, 1849, quoted in *Boston Courier*, Feb. 21, 1849, and in *Richmond Enquirer*, Feb. 22, 1849; *Southern Quart. Rev.* (Charleston, S. C., Jan., 1850), XVI, 444.

Federal Courts. In 1842, Judge Story in the Circuit Court had held that the clause of the Federal Bankruptcy Act of 1841 preserving "all liens, mortgages or other securities on property, real or personal, which may be valid by the laws of the States respectively", did not apply to attachments on mesne process, and that property so attached in the State Courts should be turned over to the Federal assignee in bankruptcy, and that the Federal Courts had the power to restrain the State Courts by injunction from giving effect to such attachments.[1] This decision was immediately regarded by the Democrats as a confirmation of their fears of the National Bankruptcy Act, and of their claim that the Act was but a step in a general "process of encroachment on State jurisdiction." [2] In January, 1844, in another case, arising in the Supreme Court of New Hampshire, the Chief Justice of that State, Joel Parker, strenuously denied the correctness of Story's doctrine; but in July, 1844, Story reaffirmed his decision, saying that it would be his duty to enjoin a creditor or the State sheriff from proceeding to levy on property of a bankrupt attached in the State Court and that the laws and Courts of the United States were paramount to those of the State. To this, Judge Parker retorted, in another case in 1844, that Story's opinion "may well astonish, if it does not alarm us. . . . There is no principle, or pretence of a principle, of which we are aware, in which we can admit the right of the Circuit or District Court in any manner to interfere and stop the execution of the final process of the Courts of this State. It is an assumption of power that cannot be tolerated for a

[1] See *Ex parte Foster*, 2 Story, 131; *Kittredge* v. *Warren*, 14 N. H. 509; *Bellows* v. *Peck*, 3 Story, 428; *Kittredge* v. *Emerson*, 15 N. H. 227; *Peck* v. *Jenness*, 16 N. H. 516. See also *Amer. Law Rev.* (1876), X, 235.

[2] *Washington Globe*, May 5, 1842.

single instant," and he added that a resort to "coercive measures" by the Federal officers "might possibly not be entirely safe." [1]   In June, 1844, the Governor of New Hampshire called the attention of the Legislature to the controversy, and to the perils that must flow from it; and that body passed a joint resolution sustaining "the firm and decided stand of the Court" in opposition to "the unwarrantable and dangerous assumption of the Circuit Court of the United States." In taking this stand, the State of New Hampshire used almost precisely the same arguments in behalf of State Sovereignty which South Carolina and other Southern States had so long been maintaining. On December 31, 1844, Judge Story, in an opinion in *Ex parte Christy*, 3 How. 292, attempted to settle the question; [2] but as the case did not call for the decision of the point (the Court holding that it had no jurisdiction), Judge Parker, in a case arising in the State Court, the next year (1845), absolutely disregarded Story's opinion. It was this latter case, *Jenness* v. *Peck*, which now came before the Court for final decision. Jenness had attached goods of Peck; later Peck had gone into bankruptcy, and the United States District Court had decreed that the attachment was not a lien, and had ordered the State sheriff to deliver

[1] The *New York Evening Post*, Dec. 10, 1856, said editorially: "This remarkable controversy between the Federal and State jurisdiction produced a deep excitement in New Hampshire. Judge Story, who with all his blandness and bonhommie, was inclined to an arbitrary exercise of his prerogatives, did not brook pleasantly the resistance of a Judge who, though his superior in ability, was, as he thought, subordinate in judicial rank. Judge Parker, however, as Chief Justice of a Sovereign State, was equally indisposed to submit, and quite electrified his opponent by the declaration from the bench, that he should enforce the judgment of his Court against Federal usurpation with all the power the State would put at his command — an exploit reminding one of the threat of Ethan Allen, of retiring to the Green Mountains and waging war against human nature at large. The Chief Justice had fairly got his back up, and would doubtless have been sustained by the Legislature of his State, even to the point of armed collision with the General Government."

[2] See letter of Story, Jan. 1, 1845, *Story*, II, 509.

the property to the bankruptcy assignee. The case was argued by Charles B. Goodrich for the creditor against Webster. The Court, in its decision, sustained fully the contention of the State, disregarded Judge Story's *dictum*, and held, through Judge Grier, that the District Court had no authority to restrain proceedings in the State Court, or "much less to take property out of its custody or possession with a strong hand." It stated that: "An attempt to enforce the decree would probably have met with resistance, and resulted in a collision of jurisdictions much to be deprecated. . . . We can find no precedent for the proceeding, . . . and no grant of power to make such decree, or to execute it, either in direct terms or by necessary implication, from any provisions of the Bankrupt Act; and we are not at liberty to interpolate it on any supposed ground of policy or expediency." That the Court, however, was not blindly adhering to any extreme view of State powers was to be seen from *United States* v. *City of Chicago*, 7 How. 185, in which it held that the city had no right to open streets through property belonging to the United States. "Though this Court," said Judge Woodbury, "possesses a strong disposition to sustain the right of the States, and local authorities claiming under them, when clearly not ceded, or when clearly reserved, yet it is equally our duty to support the General Government in the exercise of all which is plainly granted to it and is necessary for the efficient discharge of the great powers entrusted to it by the people and the States."

Of all the cases decided at this December, 1848, Term, none had aroused so great an interest politically as that which involved the legality of the new and liberal People's Government and Constitution in

Rhode Island, out of which had grown the so-called Dorr's Rebellion, in 1841–1842. By its decision in this case, *Luther* v. *Borden*, 7 How. 1, which had been pending for five years, and which was now decided in January, 1849, the Court completely disproved the dark forebodings and the mischievously false predictions as to its partisan bias, made by Clay, Kent, Peters and other Whigs, upon the retirement of Judge Story. No case had ever come before it in which the possibility of division on political lines was greater; and yet the Court rendered an opinion (with but one dissenting voice), in opposition to the views of the political party from whose ranks most of the Judges had been appointed. Thomas W. Dorr, the head of the alleged State Government, the valid existence of which was questioned in the case, represented the popular cause — the right of the people to change, in its own way, its form of government. He had secured the support of a considerable portion of the Locofoco, or Democratic, Party in States outside of Rhode Island; and after the failure of his movement to establish his Government, and upon his conviction in 1844 and imprisonment for treason, he had received the sympathy of the Democratic press.[1] His cause, therefore, became distinctly a party issue. In 1845, he had tried to elicit the Court's opinion on the legality of his contentions, by means of an original petition for a writ of habeas corpus; but in *Ex parte Dorr*, 3 How. 103, the Court had unanimously held that it had no jurisdiction to issue an original writ for any prisoner held in custody under the sentence or execution of a State Court.[2] The legality of the

[1] See *Tammany Hall and the Dorr Rebellion*, by Arthur May Mowry, *Amer. Hist. Rev.* (1898), III.

[2] See especially *Niles Register*, LXVII, 242, 257, 289, Dec. 21, 1844. Richard Peters wrote to Judge McLean, Dec. 6, 1844, a prediction that if President Tyler's

Dorr Government, however, came before the Court in another case in 1845, *Luther* v. *Borden*, a suit in trespass brought against members of the Rhode Island militia, acting under martial law declared by the State Legislature, the plaintiff claiming that the act of the Legislature was void, inasmuch as the Dorr Government was the legal authority of the State elected by the people.[1] "This cause," said a leading Democratic paper, "will command the profound deliberation of this high Court, and the people look to the result with the deepest interest. It is, so far as this Court goes, to settle or overthrow the whole doctrines of the Declaration of Independence;" and again it stated that the decision of the case "will determine whether the American doctrine proclaimed in the Declaration of Independence or the doctrine of the divine right of rulers avowed in the manifests of the holy allies of Europe is the real theory of our institutions. A vast responsibility to the country and to all times rests upon the Supreme Court in this weighty cause." Since there were then pending two vacancies in the Supreme Court to be filled, either by President Tyler or President Polk, the *Boston Post* stated its belief that under this aspect "Governor Dorr's cause thus brightens"; and it predicted "that the day of triumph will come, when the great doctrine of popular sovereignty now pending before this high tribunal, and for which he is suffering in the accursed dungeons of reprobate Rhode Island will be reaffirmed

---

appointees, Walworth and Read, should be confirmed, a majority of the Court, Walworth, Catron, Daniel and Read and Taney would issue a writ of habeas corpus for Dorr and discharge him. The falseness of the prediction is seen from the fact that when the petition was actually presented, within a month, Catron, Daniel and Taney concurred in McLean's decision adverse to the writ. *John McLean Papers MSS.*

[1] See *Life and Times of Thomas W. Dorr* (1859), by D. King; *History of the Dorr War* (1901), by Arthur May Mowry.

as the supreme law of the land." The counsel for the plaintiff, Robert J. Walker of Mississippi and Benjamin F. Hallett of Massachusetts, representing the Dorr faction, and John Whipple of Rhode Island for the defendant, were prepared to argue the case in the spring of each of the years, 1845, 1846 and 1847; but owing to still pending vacancies and illness of Judges, the Court postponed the argument, being unwilling, without full numbers, to decide a case involving so critical issues and as to which so great political excitement had been aroused.[1] It was not until January 22, 1848, therefore, that it was finally argued, at a time when the Mexican War, the Wilmot Proviso and President Polk's policies were causing the sharpest of political divisions throughout the country. Hallett and Nathan Clifford appeared in behalf of the Dorr party, and Webster and Whipple in opposition. The warmth of partisan feeling developed by the argument (which lasted six days) may be seen in a comparison of the accounts by the Washington correspondents of the Whig and Democratic newspapers. One of the former wrote that Hallett had occupied three days, and that: "Mr. Webster's speech on Dorrism will be worth hearing. The Attorney-General of the United States (Nathan Clifford) will close the case in favor of the Dorr movement. Pretty work for the law adviser of the President!" Two days later, it said: "Mr. Webster demolished what was left of Dorrism. His argument was alike brilliant and profound. . . . The report of his speech will be read with eagerness, as it is, perhaps, the best exposition of constitutional liberty ever made. It is a subject that interests everyone. . . . He used up the last remnant of Dorrism. The Court-room was crowded

[1] *Boston Post*, Feb. 5, 15, 1845, Jan. 16, 1846, Feb. 12, 17, 26, 1847.

with ladies and distinguished gentlemen to listen to
the great effort." And on the next day: "Mr. Attorney-General Clifford undertook to defend Dorrism.
If he was no more successful in making the Court
understand it than he seemed to comprehend it himself, the defence must have recoiled upon its author." [1]
This paper rejoiced that, " as Locofocoism made some
capital out of this question in the contest of 1844, . . .
our tribunal of highest resort, which is about to settle
the law of the matter authoritatively, is almost entirely Loco-Foco, the only Whig on the Bench being
John McLean of Ohio, and he a very moderate partisan. The case comes up as an appeal of the Dorr-
ites from the District Court, and the first of their
seven points is as follows: 1. 'That the sovereignty
of the People is supreme and may act in forming a
government without the assent of the existing Government. . . . We can't believe they really think their
case has a leg to stand upon. At all events, we rejoice that the decision rests with Judges of their own
party, appointed by Presidents of their own choice;
and we trust these Judges will meet it manfully, deciding the question on its merits, and not evading it
by a decision based on some incident or technicality.
Let us have Dorrism fairly weighed and measured in
the Supreme Court of the Union." After Webster's
argument, another leading Whig paper wrote that:
"If anything was left of Dorrism and all its abomi-
nable Jacobin doctrines, it has, this day, been swept
from the face of existence. . . . In the whole range
of political controversy, there was no one subject better calculated to call forth all the powers of that giant
intellect than this, involving as it did an investiga-

[1] *New York Tribune*, Jan. 25, 26, 27, 28, 29, 31, Feb. 23, March 2, 1848; see also
National Intelligencer, Jan. 26, 1848.

tion of the whole character of the Constitution, the relations between the Federal and State Governments, and a philosophical analysis of what really constituted government at all. The occasion and the man were worthy of each other. The argument was one mass of lucid reasoning and conviction, that left not a vestige of the miserable pretexts and demagogism which had been piled up by the opposite counsel."[1] The Democratic press, on the other hand, regarded the case as involving a fundamental principle — the right of the people to change its form of government; and they hotly assailed Webster's argument that a new Constitution could be adopted by the people of the States only in the manner prescribed by statute or previous practice. The *Boston Post* wrote of it as "worthy of a monarchist and a despiser of everything democratic or republican. It is in the very face and eyes of the institutions of this country. . . . If it was made in consideration of a fee, it reflects discredit and dishonor on the man who can be hired to embrace and enforce dogmas that are only calculated to oppress, debase and enslave a free people. If it embraces the real opinion of the man, they are entitled, with their author, to popular execration. The sentiments breathed in that comment are infamous." Another paper spoke of the case as the greatest ever before the Court, involving "a question of the greatest moment to the people of any that ever will or can be passed upon by any power on earth. It is the question; are the people or are their rulers or servants, the sovereign power?" Of Clifford's

---

[1] *Philadelphia North American*, Jan. 29, 1848; the *New York Courier* said that Webster's argument was the "event of the day, one of his finest and most admirable efforts"; and that the whole argument "had a degree of public importance from its connection with great questions of government not often possessed by argument on legal points before our Courts." See also *Savannah Daily Republican*, Feb. 3, 1848.

argument, which the Whig papers derided, the *Boston Post* said that it had been termed "by lawyers of the highest eminence who were present, to have been one of the most powerful efforts ever made at that forum upon any great constitutional question. The broad platform on which Mr. Clifford stood . . . was that the right of the people to remodel their Constitution is an absolute, unqualified right, inherent in themselves, and may be exercised independently of the existing government, or without any request or recommendation of the same. . . . The triumphant manner in which Mr. Clifford maintained the proposition met with a hearty response from the large audience who listened to his arguments, and frequently could be seen the interchange of approving smiles, when the Federal doctrines of Mr. Webster and the Federalist *himself* received from the speaker the severe lesson of stern and sometimes indignant rebuke. Mr. Webster remained but a short time in the Court-room during Mr. Clifford's argument. . . . It was natural for the opposer of such doctrines to place himself beyond the sound of the eloquent and impressive censure which followed the enumeration of those anti-republican principles which had just before been the theme of his logic and praise. At the close of Mr. Clifford's speech, many learned members of the Supreme Court Bar stepped forward to congratulate him. Amongst the number was Henry Clay, who expressed himself warmly upon the eloquent and able manner in which the cause had been concluded and submitted to the Court." [1] Another representative

[1] It is interesting to note that the rivalry between Henry Clay and Webster at this time for the Presidential nomination was so keen as to lead to a coolness between them, and several newspapers commented on the fact that Clay should so pointedly compliment Webster's opponents in this case. *Baltimore Sun,* Jan. 31, 1848; *Boston Post,* Feb. 10, 1848.

Democratic paper rejoiced "that such a discussion as this has been commenced, under the solemn auspices of a contest before the Supreme Court of our great Nation; and we are content that Mr. Webster should be the exponent of the conservatives or Federalists in avowing the doctrines contained in his speech before that grave body. He is a profound lawyer and has a great name as a statesman. He is, moreover, the very embodiment of Federalism in this country. . . . The question shortly to be decided by the Supreme Court is one that lies at the very foundation of our free institutions . . . and that is so clearly an attribute of popular governments as to be the very breath of their nostrils. It is the question whether the people in this country have the right in themselves to alter or abolish the governments under which they exist. It is this which Mr. Webster has undertaken to disprove and to deny! It is this which the Supreme Court will be called upon to decide. . . . We need not repeat that the whole country will await the decision of the question with intense anxiety."[1]

Three weeks later, after the argument in February, 1848, it was reported in Washington that the Court had decided against Dorr, and the *Tribune* correspondent wrote: "The Dorr case, it is said, is decided in favor of Law and Order. . . . There will probably be some delay in the delivery of the decision,

[1] The *Pennsylvanian* (Phil.), Feb. 1, 3, 1848, quoted the *New York Evening Post* as follows: "It is nothing unusual that Mr. Webster and the Whigs generally should undertake to convince the public that the institutions of government, with all their offices and honors and emoluments and the distinction that attaches to its ministers, is far above and supreme over the plain, simple and humble mass of the people. . . . Are the people sovereign?" The *Boston Post*, Feb. 2, 1848, said: "The bringing up of these causes has been highly useful, whatever may be the result, in making the true issue of the Rhode Island question understood; and since the argument in the Supreme Court, and the deep attention given to them by the learned Judges, no man who respects himself will be found to speak lightly of the issues involved."

but Dorrism has been pronounced a 'miserable stain' by the Supreme Court of the United States, composed of eight Loco-Foco and only one Whig. Judge Taney, the friend and disciple of Jackson, is to be, it is said, its Executor. What *will* Loco-Focoism say to that? It is said that sometime since three of the Judges — Grier, Catron and Woodbury — were in favor of sustaining Dorrism. I wonder whether they will dissent." [1] Owing to the illness of the Chief Justice, no decision in the case was announced until the next Term, when in January, 1849, Taney delivered a magnificent opinion in which the firm position was taken that the question involved in the case, viz., which of the two opposing Governments in Rhode Island was the legitimate one, was purely a question of political power; that the political department of the State had determined it and the State Courts had recognized and acted upon this determination; and that this Court must, consequently, decline to pass upon the question. By this decision, the Court removed itself from the realm of purely political subjects, and proved its determination to withstand appeals to any partisan views which it might be supposed to hold. The fact that both political parties professed to be satisfied with the decision was a singular feature in this disposition of the case. A Whig paper in New York said: "Dorrism has at length received its quietus and in a form from which it can never hope to recover." Another said editorially: "The decision is unanimous against Dorrism. That this humbug should die out we all know; but that the last breath should be knocked out of it by the Chief Justice who was appointed by the great idol of Loco-Focoism was 'the unkindest cut of all.' If there

[1] *New York Tribune*, Feb. 23, 1848.

were any principles which B. F. Hallett & Co. loved, they were Cass and Dorr; and both are defunct. 'Green be the turf above them.'" Another said that the Court had "driven the last nail in the coffin of Dorrism." On the other hand, the Washington correspondent of the leading Democratic paper in Boston wrote that the decision recognized "Dorrism and Dorrism alone to be the fundamental principle of the political institutions of the country", and it continued this curiously erroneous view, by stating that the Court had sustained the right of the majority of the people "to modify or change their constitutional form, without the concurrence or consent of the existing holders of political power." The Administration paper in Washington, however, while recognizing that the Court had not decided in favor of "Dorrism", correctly stated that the Whig papers were wrong in contending that the Court "had denounced Dorrism and overruled all its principles and claims." And the leading Democratic paper in Pennsylvania also correctly said that, while the Court fully sanctioned the right of a majority to determine upon a Constitution, "they regard it to be a cardinal political principle which does not belong to the jurisdiction of the Judiciary. . . . No judicial tribunal can prescribe the rules under which the sense of the majority is to be ascertained. . . . It is therefore, purely a political question, and must be determined by such public agents as are clothed with political authority." [1] La-

---

[1] *New York Courier*, Jan. 4, 1849; *New York Tribune*, Feb. 5, 1849; the *Philadelphia North American*, Jan. 5, 1849; *Washington Union*, Jan. 12, 1849; *Boston Post*, Jan. 5, 1849; *Pennsylvanian*, Jan. 27, 1849.

It is interesting to note that Judge Woodbury, who dissented on a subordinate question as to the right of a State to declare martial law, agreed with his Democratic colleague, the Chief Justice, on the ruling that the case presented a political and not a judicial question; the three other Democratic Judges, Catron, Daniel and McKinley, owing to illness and other causes, did not sit.

ter, however, it was generally regarded by the Bar and the public that the failure of the Court to sustain the Dorr Government by an explicit ruling constituted a defeat for the Democracy; and the decision did much to establish confidence in the minds of the American people in the integrity and freedom from partisan bias of the Court as then established.[1] In the excited debates which ensued in Congress, a few years later, in 1856, 1858 and 1859, over the admission of Kansas as a State and over the validity of the Lecompton and Topeka Constitutions adopted respectively by the pro-slavery and anti-slavery factions in that State, *Luther* v. *Borden* was frequently cited with approval, on both sides, as showing that the question as to which Constitution was the legal one was not for the Court but for Congress to decide.[2]

One further case decided at this Term should be mentioned — *Lewis* v. *Lewis*, 7 How. 776 — not because of any important point involved, but because it was the first case argued before the Court by Abraham Lincoln (then a member of Congress from Illinois). It was decided against him, March 7, 1849.

As the number of cases on its docket continued to increase in number and importance, the Court now found itself unable to give proper attention to its Circuit duties, and a bill was introduced in the House in February, 1848, to relieve the Judges of all such duties for one year.[3] This project was hotly opposed,

[1] "The fundamental doctrines thus so lucidly and cogently announced . . . have never been doubted or questioned since, and have afforded the light, guiding the orderly development of our constitutional system from the day of the deliverance of that decision up to the present time." White, C. J., in *Pacific States Tel. & Tel. Co.* v. *Oregon* (1912), 223 U. S. 118, 148.

[2] See speeches in the House of Henry W. Davis of Maryland, March 12, 1856, *34th Cong., 1st Sess.*

[3] *30th Cong., 1st Sess.*, and *App.*, Feb. 29, March 6, April 7, 17, 18, 1848. On Jan. 29, 1846, *29th Cong., 1st Sess.*, Senator Johnson had introduced a resolution to modify the Judiciary system, relieve the Judges of Circuit duty, and to form a

as it was felt to be the opening wedge for the permanent abolition of Circuit Court duty; and accordingly the old battle of 1825–26 was refought. James B. Bowlin of Missouri argued in the House: "Make your Supreme Court a fixture here, with no associations but the corrupt and the corrupting influences of the metropolis; make them the drones of the great hive of American industry and American enterprise, and you will destroy (what is as essential in a Judge as legal learning) good old-fashioned common sense. . . . Let gentlemen of the distant States look to it, before they bind themselves to the car of centralism and consolidation. . . . Alienate the Judges from the States, consolidate the Court in the metropolis, and the day is not far distant, when the sovereign rights of the free States of this Confederacy will be swallowed up in this mighty vortex of power." He feared the effect upon the character of judicial appointments and that "the Supreme Court would be the place for the retirement of antiquated politicians, who might desire to spend the remnant of their days at the metropolis." In the Senate, William Allen of North Carolina voiced the curious fear that the Supreme Court permanently established in Washington would absorb the whole Government; would connect itself with the Executive and would have a large influence over the deliberation of Congress. George E. Badger, Senator from North Carolina, said: "We shall have these gentlemen as Judges of the Supreme Court of appeals, not mingling with the ordinary transactions of busi-

new Circuit of Louisiana and Texas. He stated that at the end of the last Term in 1845, there were 109 cases on the docket left undecided; that two new Circuits were necessary, one of Louisiana and Texas, and another of Iowa and Wisconsin; that the Court ought not to be enlarged to eleven by the addition of two new members but that it should be reduced to seven, the vacancy then existing (by the death of Judge Baldwin) should not be filled, and the Court should be relieved of Circuit duty.

ness, not accustomed to the 'forensic *strepitus*' in the Courts below, not seeing the rules of evidence practically applied to the cases before them, not enlightened upon the laws of the several States, which they have finally to administer here, by the discussion of able and learned counsel in the Courts below, not seen by the people of the United States, not known and recognized by them, not touching them, as it were, in the administration of their high office, not felt, and understood, and realized as part and parcel of this great popular Government; but sitting here alone, becoming philosophical and speculative in their inquiries as to law, becoming necessarily more and more dim as to the nature of the law of the various States from want of familiar and daily connection with them, unseen, final arbiters of justice, issuing their decrees as it were from a secret chamber, moving invisibly amongst us as far as the whole community is concerned; and, in my judgment, losing in fact the ability to discharge their duties as well as that responsive confidence of the people which adds so essentially to the sanction of all the acts of the officers of Government."

The bill passed the House, but was defeated in the Senate, April 18, 1848. A new bill to abolish Circuit Court duty for the next two Terms and to compel the Court to sit in Washington until the first Monday in July passed the Senate, but was rejected in the House, August 8, 1848. Out of the debate on this bill, however, there grew a Rule of Court which substantially relieved the pressure on the Court by imposing for the first time a limitation on the length of counsel's argument. In the debate, Congressman Bowlin objected to the argument being made a form of spectacle: he objected to the public being invited by the press to attend, and particularly to the attendance of ladies "to witness the displays of elocution; and that too, in a case which, if rightly argued upon the plain, stern principles of the law, could afford no kind of amusement — no kind of interest to the idle spectator." Senators Crittenden, Allen and Badger also objected to the latitude of talk allowed by the Court and the length of arguments, the latter saying: "Has the Court been careful to prevent discussion of questions which might be regarded as axiomatic in this country — dissertations or scholastic essays, like those delivered to young men prosecuting their studies in a lawyer's office, in the expectation of obtaining a license? It is quite familiar to us all, that in a case which attracted some attention, one of the learned counsel occupied an entire day for the purpose of demonstrating this very difficult proposition in America, that the people are sovereign; and then pursued his argument on the second day by endeavoring to make out the extremely difficult conclusion from the first proposition, that being sovereign they had a right to frame their own constitution! Well, now, if the Court sit quietly while gentlemen, from whatever motive, either to gain distinction from an exhibition of their polemical powers, capacity for didactic discussion, or any other reason, occupy the attention of the Court with such discussions, what hope, what expectation can be entertained, that this bill will supply any remedy for the evil of a surcharged docket?" Senator Reverdy Johnson of Maryland, while agreeing that the arguments were often too long, said that it was dangerous to suppress them; and that the people would term such an attempt an interference with freedom of speech: "There was a case in the Supreme Court at the last Term, which involved the constitutionality of the famous Dorr government in Rhode Island. I heard pamphlet after pamphlet, Fourth of July speech after Fourth of July speech, written and delivered years ago, read before that tribunal, to prove that a free people have the right to establish that form of government they think best. Sir, I imagine that if the Chief Justice, speaking for himself and his Associates, had said that no such authority should be cited, the press of the country would have run mad, particularly if the result had been, as in all probability it will be, that on the unanimous judgment of that tribunal, the Dorr revolution was nothing but naked and inexcusable rebellion. Besides, sir, as to stopping counsel in their argument, which of the Judges is to take it upon himself to do so? Is it to be left to any one of them, to the Chief Justice, to say what point is to be argued, and what not? Is he to arrest counsel? My life for it, before such a rule is practised for one Term, the Chief Justice would be told by some one of his Associates, on either side of him, that it was a point on which he wished to be enlightened." Johnson also described the daily work of the Judges, saying that they met at eleven in the morning, heard arguments until four (sometimes five), dined at five, went into consultation almost every day at seven and sat until nine, ten, eleven, or twelve at night. This was labor, he said, which could not be added to. "They are all, and should be all, comparatively old men. I do not wish to see young men placed upon the bench of such a tribunal. There is many a crude thought in the mind of a young man which the reflection of riper years enables him to see the folly of. They ought to have arrived at the period when man is found to possess the greatest vigor of mind and a matured experience."

That the Court itself evidently paid attention to this criticism of its laxness towards counsel may be gathered from the fact that on March 12, 1849, it adopted a new Rule of Court to the effect that no counsel would be permitted to argue more than two hours, without special leave granted before the argument began.[1]

Of the appearance of the Court-room and of the personal characteristics of the Judges at this era, interesting accounts were written in the journals.[2] "Let us to that scene repair, if we can, amid the winding corridors of the basement of the Capitol, succeed in finding it," wrote one correspondent. "Beyond the railing are the Judges' seats, upon pretty nearly

[1] On February 1, 1844, Judge Story (in the absence of the Chief Justice who was ill) had issued a formal address to the Bar, asking them to submit on brief, and to condense their argument, saying: "He was directed by the Court to call the attention of the Bar to the present state of the docket and in the spirit, not of complaint, but of the most entire courtesy and kindness, to make some few suggestions for their consideration. It must be apparent to all persons connected with the Court that the present docket was so large (arising from the great increase of the business of the country and the magnitude and importance of the interests involved in it) that the Court could accomplish little of themselves without the cordial coöperation of the Bar in the endeavor to dispose of the causes before it. The Court felt a deep anxiety, in which there could be no doubt that the Bar equally participated, to make a sensible impression upon the docket, and thus to give repose to suitors and satisfaction to their fellow citizens at large. Indeed, upon such a subject, it was obvious that the Court and Bar had a common interest with the public; and it had occurred to the Court that the suggestions which he was about to make might, therefore, be favorably received. In the first place, under the rule of the Court, the parties were entitled, if they chose, to lay before the Court printed arguments on both sides when a speedy decision was desired; and in such cases, the Court would have ample opportunity to come to a final decision by devoting the intervals of their leisure, not occupied in hearing arguments in Court, to that purpose. In the next place, although the Court was aware that, in many cases of great importance and difficulty, prolonged arguments must necessarily occur, in order to present their full merits, yet the condensation of these arguments, as far as it could be made by the Bar, consistently with their duty to their clients, would be of great utility and aid to the Court. And in the next place, where there were two counsel, one of whom was immediately to follow the other in argument, much time would be saved in cases embracing different points, if the counsel would divide those points, and each should argue when practicable the points not occupied by the other." See *National Intelligencer*, Feb. 2, 1844.

[2] *The Supreme Court of the United States in 1853–54*, by George N. Searle, *Amer. Law Reg.* (1854), II; *New York Tribune*, Feb. 4, 1850.

a level with the floor of the room, not elevated. . . .
By the side of the railing are nine neat desks, and behind them as many comfortable, high-backed chairs
for the use of the Judges. . . . In an alcove back
of the seat of the Chief Justice and nearly up to the
ceiling is a small portrait of Chief Justice Marshall —
the only ornament . . . except a representation of
the scales of justice, worked in marble, on the opposite
side of the room." Another correspondent wrote :
"The Court-room is in the northern wing of the Capitol on the ground floor. It is broken by pillars and
arched walls, and is badly lighted. It is handsomely
furnished with rich Wilton carpets, silken drapery,
etc. The light is admitted from the rear windows
alone, and the Judges sit with their backs to the light ;
the counsel who address them can scarcely see their
faces. At 11 o'clock they enter deliberately, all
dressed in black and with gowns. After they are
seated, the crier proclaims 'Oyez, oyez, oyez ! The
Supreme Court of the United States is now in session ; all persons having business therein are admonished to draw near and give their attendance (*sic*).
God save the United States and these honorable
Judges !' " The Chief Justice, he described as "tall,
sallow, thin, hard-featured, and careless in dress. . . .
His opinions are terse, pointed and luminous, not
incumbered with unnecessary learning, but exceedingly logical and convincing. He has great tenacity
of purpose and strength of will, and I may add stub-
born prejudices. The sincerity of his convictions
no one doubts. There is about him an unmistak-
able air of intellect and authority, and he is a not unworthy successor of John Marshall. He is a devout
Roman Catholic, and rigid in his observance of religious forms and duties." On the right hand of the

Chief Justice sat McLean. "He is a well-dressed, dignified person, about six feet in height, exceedingly well-formed, with fine teeth, a clear gray eye, lofty brow and forehead, thin hair but not gray, and in the general outline of his features the breadth of the lower part of his face, and the general carriage of his head, exceedingly like the statue of Washington by Houdon in the Capitol at Richmond. He is an upright and sensible man, with unquestionable, administrative talents, but not an accurate or profound lawyer. It is believed by some that he is not satisfied with his present position but is desirous of obtaining a higher position. He is a member of the Methodist Church, and is in high favor with that denomination." Next to McLean was Catron — "a stout, healthy man, respectable and solid in appearance, with a face and head more indicative of urbanity and benevolence than of intellect; with good sense, moderate learning, great benevolence of feeling, and kindness of demeanor, he is universally regarded as a useful, unpretending, respectable Judge." Next sat Daniel — "tall, bony, angular, with high cheek bones and dark complexion, and looks as if he had some Indian blood in his veins. His mind is narrow in its conceptions, and limited in its investigations, and his style is crude and confused; but his learning is accurate and his deductions sound and clear. He often dissents from the majority of the Court, and not unfrequently in favor of State-Rights. His amiability and honesty are universally conceded." Next to Daniel was Woodbury — "nearly six feet in height, of round and compact form, well-moulded features, a prominent and bright eye that at a distance appears dark but in nearer view is seen to be a blueish gray. He is strictly temperate in his habits, drinks nothing but cold water and a great deal of that, and works with surpassing rapidity and earnestness. He has great talent for research, and his opinions are crowded with its results. As a reasoner, he is cogent and accurate but not concise, and is apt to spend too much labor in proving what ought to be assumed as settled. His decisions would be the better for pruning and thinning, but the growth is deep-rooted and vigorous." On the Chief Justice's left was Wayne — "an exceedingly handsome man, about 5 feet 10 inches high, of stout but graceful figure, ruddy complexion, fine teeth and clustering wavy hair now mingled with gray; very courteous in manner and with a tone of refinement in his elocution and address that are very pleasing. He has cultivated the graces and has aimed (it is said not without success) to be in favor with ladies. He has an ingenious, copious mind, is fluent and rapid in expression, but lacks conciseness, lucid arrangement and vigor. He is, however, by no means deficient in learning, even of a technical character." Next to Wayne sat Nelson (McKinley being absent) — "a man of handsome features, bland and gentleman-like in expression, very courteous in manner, and dignified yet easy in deportment. He possesses much good sense, and is an excellent lawyer. His apprehension is not rapid, but he thinks clearly and reasons strongly. He is probably the best commercial lawyer on the Bench, thanks to his New York education. Since his elevation to his present place, he has shown an unusual degree of energy and industry, and is evidently working for a reputation. He is not suspected of ulterior political views, and his integrity and independence are not doubted." Next sat Grier — "He has a large, broad form, an expansive angular brow, blue eyes and looks like a strong minded, sagacious

German — such, I believe, is his descent (more probably Scotch — Ed. *Tribune*). His voice is very curious; he reads in a low, rapid, monotonous tone for some seconds, and then he will catch on a word, to spin round it as on a pivot, and start off to renew the same course. His opinions are unpretending and sensible, well expressed, and concise. His position as a Judge is hardly yet defined." [1] The manner of the deliberations of the Court at this period, in conference, "their most responsible and arduous duty" was interestingly described later by Judge Campbell: [2] "The Chief Justice presided, the deliberations were usually frank and candid. It was a rare

---

[1] The *American Law Register* (Oct., 1854), II, gave the following personal description of some of these Judges: "Mr. Justice Daniel, an older man in his prim wig and spectacles; next to him is Mr. Justice Wayne with his cheerful and ruddy face and hair slightly gray, decidedly the best looking man upon the Bench. By his side is the Chief Justice, Taney, broken in health and unattractive in personal appearance, but unquestionably the strongest man upon the Bench. Next is Mr. Justice McLean of Ohio, a large noble-looking man, bold and fearless, looking the personation of the upright Judge. By him is Judge Nelson of New York, short and slender built, looking kindly upon all."

"The two strong men are Chief Justice Taney and Judge McLean," wrote Oliver H. Smith, Senator from Indiana, about this time. "Nature so declared. Their powers of mind were stamped upon their faces, and their high judicial character distinctly marked upon the whole external man. . . . The Chief Justice was tall and slender, considerably bent with years, his face deeply furrowed, his hair hanging carelessly over his high forehead, which he frequently wiped away. His arms and fingers were long and bony and hairy, not unlike those of John Randolph. His countenance was marked by the study of many years. His dress, plain black. He sat, pen in hand, attentively listening to Mr. Cushing addressing the Court, frequently taking notes, as the arguments progressed." *Early Indiana Trials and Sketches* (1858), by Oliver H. Smith.

[2] See Meeting of the Bar on the death of Benjamin R. Curtis, October 12, 1874, 20 Wallace, ix. The *Boston Post's* Washington correspondent, March 18, 1847, wrote of the "remarkable degree of decorum and propriety" in the Court proceedings, and of the fact that "the feelings of the practitioner are never wounded or his pride offended by harsh and unkind treatment." He wrote again, Jan. 27, 1848: "The Supreme Court, with the dignity and uniform suavity that marks that elevated tribunal, are trying the elaborate causes before them. Their intercourse with the Bar is of the most agreeable character, becoming to them, and most grateful to those who have business before them." See also *How the Judges of the United States Supreme Court Consult*, Amer. Law Rev. (1896), XXX, 903; *Working of the United States Supreme Court*, ibid. (1900), XXXIV, 77; *Three Courts*, by Seymour D. Thompson, *ibid.* (1900), XXXIV; *How a Justice is Installed*, ibid. (1888), XXII, 276; *A Day in the United States Supreme Court*, by Fred Harper, *Virg. Law Reg.* (1901), VII, 239.

incident in the whole of this period, the slightest disturbance from irritation, excitement, passion or impatience. There was habitually courtesy, good breeding, self-control, mutual deference — in Judge Curtis, invariably so. There was nothing of cabal, combination or exorbitant desire to carry questions or cases. . . . The venerable age of the Chief Justice, his gentleness, refinement, and feminine sense of propriety, were felt and realized in the privacy and confidence of these consultations. . . . The Chief Justice usually called the case. He stated the pleadings and facts that they presented, the arguments and his conclusions in regard to them, and invited discussion. The discussion was free and open among the Justices till all were satisfied. The question was put, whether the judgment or decree should be reversed, and each Justice according to his precedence, commencing with the junior Judge, was required to give his judgment and his reasons for his conclusion. The concurring opinions of the majority decided the cause and signified the matter of the opinion to be given. The Chief Justice designated the Judge to prepare it."

CHAPTER TWENTY-FIVE

SLAVERY AND STATE DEFIANCE

1848–1855

IN the years 1848–49, the Court may be said to have reached its height in the confidence of the people of the country. While there were extremists and radicals in both parties, in the North as in the South, who inveighed against it and its decisions, yet the general mass of the public and the Bar had faith in its impartiality and its ability. The old partisan bitterness towards Chief Justice Taney had largely passed away, and even an ardent anti-slavery Senator, like William H. Seward, wrote to Taney of "the high regard which, in common with the whole American people, I entertain for you as the head of the Judicial Department." [1] Congressional attacks upon the Court had almost entirely ceased, and the serious attempts to destroy its most vital jurisdiction, which had been made during the last twenty years of Marshall's Chief Justiceship, seemed now to be forgotten and abandoned.

Only one subject — slavery — seemed likely to involve the Court once more in partisan controversy. Thus far, no serious complications had arisen in connection with this subject; and Martin Van Buren, writing his autobiography about this time, said, with keen perception, that since the Bank of the United States had "happily ceased to exist, we have not only been exempted from any such overwhelming convulsions as

---

[1] *Taney*, 317, letter of June 30, 1851; see eulogy of Taney by Reverdy Johnson, *30th Cong., 1st Sess., App.*, 588, April 18, 1848.

THE SENATE CHAMBER IN 1850

those caused by it, but the Supreme Court has occupied itself with its legitimate duties — the administration of justice between man and man — without being, as formerly, constantly assailed by applications for latitudinarian construction of the Constitution, in support of enormous corporate pretensions. We might, perhaps, have expected that in such a calm, even Mr. Jefferson's alarm, if he had lived to see, would, at least in some degree, have subsided; but this state of things can only be expected to last until a similar or equally strong interest is brought under discussion, of a character to excite the whole country and to enlist the sympathies of a majority of the Court, and requiring the intervention of that high tribunal to sustain its unconstitutional assumptions, by unauthorized and unrestrained construction. Whether the institution of domestic slavery is destined to be such an interest, remains to be seen." [1] The question thus presented by Van Buren was soon answered. For in the summer of 1848, the Court was thrown into the midst of the seething political issue, when a Whig Senator, John M. Clayton of Delaware, conceived the idea that the question of the power of Congress over slavery in the Territories and in the States annexed from Mexico might properly be settled by the Court. By the introduction of a bill for this purpose, he set in motion a train of circumstances which led directly to the crash of the Court's reputation, nine years later, in the Dred Scott decision. For many years after the Missouri Compromise in 1820, the question of Congressional authority over slavery in the Territories had lapsed as a serious issue in politics, or as a cause of serious division among statesmen. With the close of the Mexican War, however, the status of slavery in the newly acquired territory became a flaming

[1] See *Amer. Hist. Ass. Rep.* (1918), II, 184.

question; and on February 19, 1848, Calhoun introduced in the Senate a resolution announcing the dogma that Congress had no power to prohibit slavery in the Territories. The next year, when the bill to admit Oregon as a State was debated, he advanced the further contention that the Constitution itself, upon its extension to the Territories, carried with it the institution of slavery — "the doctrine of the self-extension of slavery into all the Territories by the self-expansion of the Constitution over them." [1] But while this issue was not acute in relation to Oregon, which lay north of the Missouri Compromise line, it had become exceedingly grave in connection with the bills which were proposed for the admission of California as a State and of New Mexico as a Territory (New Mexico then embracing the present States of Arizona, Utah, Nevada and parts of Colorado, Wyoming and the present New Mexico). Hot debate ensued over the question of the respective rights of Congress and of the Territorial and State Legislatures to establish or prohibit slavery. In the summer of 1848, Senator Clayton brought forward his unfortunate proposal for a compromise, in a bill providing: first, for the admission of Oregon with its existing laws against slavery so far as not incompatible with the Constitution; second, for the admission of California and New Mexico, with a prohibition against the passage of laws by their Territorial Legislatures either establishing or prohibiting slavery; third, for the right of an appeal to the Supreme Court of the United States from the Territorial Courts. By this plan, Clayton argued, the whole question as to the power of Congress over slavery in the Territories would be referred to the Supreme Court for its decision.

[1] See *Thirty Years' View* (1856), by Thomas H. Benton, II, 696, 713, 729; see also *30th Cong., 1st Sess.*, June 1, July 8, 10, 1848, speeches of Calhoun, Berrien, Reverdy Johnson in the Senate.

"The bill leaves the entire question in dispute to the Judiciary," he said. "Any man who desires discord will oppose the bill. But he who does not desire to distract the country by a question merely political, will be able, by voting for this bill, to refer the whole matter to the Judiciary. In any case, in which it may be deemed important, any lawyer can carry the question to the Supreme Court. . . . The people being law-abiding, will submit to the decision of that Court which occupies the highest place in their confidence. . . . In this dark and gloomy hour, that is the dial-plate which glitters through and which will, I trust, guide us to a safe and harmonious result." [1] Opinions varied greatly in the Senate, however, as to the wisdom of implicating the Court in so delicate and so explosive a question. [2] Democrats from the South and Free-soil Whigs from the North, alike, opposed the measure. Southerners argued that the Court, as then composed, was certain to decide against slavery. Northerners were equally confident that it would decide in favor of slavery — a difference of view which constituted a marked tribute to the freedom from sectional bias of the prior decisions of the Court. John P. Hale of New Hampshire, the most violent abolitionist in the Senate, attacked the Court with vigor, stating that he had no confidence in that tribunal as then constituted and was unwilling that it should decide the question. Thomas Corwin of Ohio, a Whig, asserted his belief that the Senators from the South would not vote for the bill unless they believed the decision of the Court would be in their favor. Henry S. Foote of Mississippi, an ardent pro-slavery Democrat, on the other hand, stated that he feared that the decision of the Court, as then con-

[1] *30th Cong., 1st Sess.*, 988, 1031, *App.*, 1140, July 22, Aug. 3, 1848.
[2] *30th Cong., 1st Sess.*, July 22, 24, 25, 26, 1848, and *App.*, 993, 1000, 1145, 1155, 1170.

stituted, would be against the South. George E. Badger of North Carolina, a Whig, thought the bill surrendered all the rights of the South. On the other hand, Samuel S. Phelps of Vermont, a Whig, said that he was "greatly surprised to find Whigs of the North disowning or distrusting the constitutional authority of the Supreme Court. I have yet to learn, either from political friends or political opponents, that that Court has in any degree forfeited the confidence of the country. In the integrity and capacity of that Court, I have equal confidence. Who doubts the integrity or the learning of the distinguished Chief Justice? And who is prepared to say that that Court has become so degenerate and is filled with such unworthy men, that it is not to be trusted with the power conferred upon it by the Constitution? I can preach no such heresy, and I am perfectly willing to leave this constitutional question to that Court. If the Court decide against me, I will submit. If we cannot trust the power there, where, in Heaven's name, shall we repose it?" Reverdy Johnson of Maryland, a Democrat, said that the appeal to the Court was "the only amicable mode of adjusting a question which threatened the honor and integrity of the South. . . . From the character of the Supreme Court, I am sure the compromise in this particular, will be acquiesced in by the country. . . . The members of the Supreme Court are not politicians. They are born in a different atmosphere, and address themselves to different hearers. . . . It ought not to be expected that the South shall surrender all that is dear to her and do the bidding of the North. They are willing to adopt the appeal to the Supreme Court, and if the decision of that Court be against them, they will be satisfied. . . . The question whether a slave owner is entitled to carry his slaves into the Territory will be decided on the first appeal, and that will decide the matter in every future case which can arise." Hannibal Hamlin of Maine, a Democrat, assailed; "this shuffling off, this skulking from, shrinking behind a political question which it is our duty to meet, and throwing it upon the Supreme Court to decide"; and he asserted that, since appeals to the Supreme Court under existing law could only be taken in cases involving a certain money value, the question of the rights and liberties of a slave could not be the subject of an appeal. Answering this latter objection, Sidney Breese of Illinois made a suggestion which was of singular interest, inasmuch as it set forth the exact method by which the famous *Dred Scott Case* was taken up to the Supreme Court, six years later. "Could not the question of servitude," he asked, "be brought before the Supreme Court very readily, by an action by the slave of assault and battery and false imprisonment? The master pleads that, true it is he holds the plaintiff in his custody, as he has a right to do, for he is his slave; the slave replies, setting forth the fact that California, on its cession to the United States, was free, that slavery did not exist there, and that it is not recognized by the Constitution, or any Act of Congress, and that by virtue of that Constitution he is free; the defendant demurs; and the question of law arising thereon is decided by the Court."

To meet this objection as to lack of remedy, Clayton amended his bill, and for the first time in the history of the country introduced the question of slavery into Federal judicial process and procedure, by providing specifically, that in all cases involving title to slaves writs of error or appeals should be allowed, without regard to the value of the matter in controversy, and that an appeal should be allowed to the Supreme Court from the decision of Territorial Courts and Judges upon any writ of habeas corpus "involving the question of personal freedom"— both provisions being new to Federal law. With such an amendment the compromise measure passed the Senate, July 26, 1848, by a vote of thirty-three to twenty-two, Democrats and Whigs, both of the South and North, voting on each side of the question.

When the bill was debated in the House of Representatives, both Southern and Northern Congressmen, with few exceptions, opposed it, showing clearer comprehension, than had the Senators, of the evils of dragging the Court into the dangerous whirlpool of politics.[1] The Whigs strongly attacked the proposition, one of them, George P. Marsh of Vermont, portraying in vivid colors the inevitable effect upon the Court as follows:

Is that Court a fit tribunal for the determination of a great political question like this? I am far from desiring to disparage the impartiality or the ability of a tribunal, distinguished for the possession of every judicial excellence, and which I hold in the highest reverence as the great bulwark of our constitutional liberties. Its pre-eminent ability is recognized by the universal voice of the legal profession; and its stern impartiality has been attested by decisions in the great cases of the *Amistad* negroes and *Prigg* v. *Pennsylvania*. But it is precisely because of my reverence for that Court, and my exalted estimate of its value as a conservative element in our system that I would not impose upon it the painful and dangerous obligation . . . of determining so weighty and so delicate a question as this. We should hazard not its impartiality and its high moral influence only, but its constitution and even its existence. During the long period of the pendency of this question, it would be incessantly exposed to every adverse influence. Local sympathies, long-cherished prejudices, the predilections of party, the known wishes of the Administration and of the National Legislature, would all conspire to bias the decision; intervening vacancies

---

[1] *30th Cong., 1st Sess.*, July 29, 31, Aug. 3, 7, 8, 1848, and *App.*, 1072–1076.

would be filled with reference to the supposed, perhaps even pledged, opinion of the candidate upon this one question, and when, finally, the decision should be promulgated, the Court itself would become, with the defeated party, the object of a hostility, as deep-rooted, as persevering, as widely diffused, and as rancorous as are at this moment the feelings and prejudices of the parties now arrayed against each other upon this great issue. Could a tribunal which relies for its support upon moral force and public opinion alone, awes not by lictor and fasces, enforces its decrees by no armed satellites, dispenses no patronage, and is sustained by no Executive power, long withstand the malignant influence which would thus be brought to bear?

Every word of this was prophetic of the storm of odium which the Court brought upon its own head when it attempted, in the *Dred Scott Case*, nine years later, to make a decision of the very question which the statute now under debate sought to obtain from it. A Democratic Congressman from North Carolina, John R. T. Daniell, took the same view, saying that if the bill should pass, a political struggle would inevitably result, and "the moral influence of the Court must be forever destroyed in one section or the other of the Union." Another Democrat from Tennessee, John H. Crozier, said — once more prophetically: "If the decision should be against the North, the North would not abide by it. They would agitate the country a great deal more than they do now on the subject. They would insist that the decision had been made by a Court, a majority of whose members were from the South and slaveholders; that their decision was either corrupt, or their judgment had been warped by prejudice and interest." This was, in fact, the precise attitude which was adopted by the North nine years later when it refused to accept the decision in the *Dred Scott Case*.

While the Whigs were absolutely right in their disapproval of dragging the Court into a political contest, the fact that many of them expressed a distrust of the Court, and even a refusal to abide by any judicial decision, showed how far they had drifted from their old position as the staunch defenders of the Judiciary, against Democratic attack; and for this change, they were taunted (with much reason) by many of the Southern Democrats. "It is a new position with the Whig party," said Thomas H. Bayly of Virginia, "that the Supreme Court is an unfit tribunal to decide such a question as this. In the memorable contest which preceded the political revolution of 1800, their predecessors, the old Federalists, maintained that even in contests as to the reserved rights of the States, the Federal Judiciary was the ultimate arbiter. Even in a controversy between the States and the General Government about State-Rights, the Federalists insisted that one of the departments of the latter was the exclusive judge, and again in the days of Nullification, the Whig party took the same ground," yet now in a question, not of a State, but simply of the right of an individual citizen slaveholder, the Whigs are unwilling to trust to the Court. And an eloquent expression of the public confidence in the Court was voiced by Franklin W. Bowdon of Alabama (who, though he believed the Court would decide against the South, was willing to accept its opinion as impartial). "The Supreme Court is elevated above the influence of popular clamor," he said. "That high tribunal is responsible to no local constituency, and would be swayed in the discharge of its great duties by none of the sectional prejudices which here prevail, or the political interests which exert upon our deliberations so baleful an influence. A decision from this elevated source would exercise a commanding influence upon public opinion, and go very far to restore harmony to the country. Should the decision of the much-mooted question be in accordance with either Southern or Northern opinion, it would command both respect and acquiescence. . . . The Supreme Court would act under a high sense of duty, free from any immediate influences to give direction to their action; its members come from the East, the West, the North, and the South; they have the confidence of the country; they have no party schemes to subserve, and their settlement of this question of constitutional law would appeal with irresistible force to the great body of the people, North and South." In spite of this optimistic view of the situation, the bill was defeated in the House; and the project to solve the slavery issue by a Court decision was temporarily abandoned.[1] The whole tenor of the debate had shown, however, the dangers which might threaten the Court's position in the confidence of the people, should the duty of attempting such a solution be imposed upon it. On the other hand, the conservative wing of the Whig Party continued to believe in this form of settlement. "Your project for settling the slavery question strikes me very favorably," wrote Crittenden to Clayton, "and seems to be quite practicable. You cannot render a greater service than by endeavoring to keep all our friends, and especially our tropical friends of the South, cool and temperate on that subject. They must see that numbers are against them, and that they must be beaten on the question of the extension of slavery. To be beaten in the least offensive and injurious form is the best that I can anticipate for them. And the very necessity of the case ought to teach them to look at it with com-

---

[1] See interesting letter from Alexander H. Stephens of Georgia, to the editor of the *Federal Union* (Milledgeville, Ga.), Aug. 30, 1848, explaining why he, as a Southern Democrat, opposed the compromise bill in the House. *Amer. Hist. Ass. Rep.* (1911), I, 120.

posure. The right to carry slaves to New Mexico or California is no very great matter, whether granted or denied. And the more especially when it seems to be agreed that no sensible man would carry his slaves there if he could. For the North or the South to talk about dissolving the Union for such a question, decided the one way or the other, sounds to my ears like nonsense, or something worse." [1]

At the session of Congress in 1849, it became increasingly evident that the Free-soilers were preparing to enter upon a deliberate campaign to undermine popular confidence in the Court, and in its impartiality of decision in any case involving even remotely the slavery issue. On the other hand, the Democrats, both of the North and South, reaffirmed on every occasion their belief in the Court's freedom from bias. "If the Constitution does not guarantee our rights as we contend, the Court would certainly so decide," said Senator Herschell V. Johnson of Georgia. "The Supreme Court has been established for the very purpose of giving it authoritative interpretation, and as a lover of the Union, I am willing to abide its solemn decision." [2] Richard W. Thompson of Indiana said in the House: "Nothing can be more dangerous to our peace and prosperity as a Nation than these repeated attempts to appeal from the decision of our highest Courts to the tribunal of party and of faction. . . . We have seen, more than once in the last ten years, both the Constitution and the law trodden under the feet of party. We have seen Dorrism, and other isms not less odious, ready to spring up upon their shattered fragments. . . . I hold that man to be an enemy to the public welfare and the public peace, who, for political party purposes,

[1] *John M. Clayton Papers MSS*, letters of Crittenden to Clayton, Dec. 19, 1848, Feb. 2, 1849.
[2] *30th Cong., 2d Sess.*, Feb. 27, 28, 1849, *App.*, 187, Jan. 25, 1849.

seeks to array popular prejudice against that Constitution and law, thus settled and fixed." Samuel F.
Vinton of Ohio proposed to settle the dangerous dispute
as to the boundary between Texas and New Mexico
(which involved the possible extension of slave territory)
by leaving it to be decided by a suit in the Supreme
Court where "it would receive the solemn, serious,
calm consideration which belonged to such a tribunal."
All propositions of this kind were hotly opposed by the
Free-soilers, who, realizing that the decision of the Court
in favor of the claim of Texas would carry slavery into
a territory much larger than the whole of New England,
were unwilling to commit such a question to that tribunal. Some of the Free-soilers could not refrain from
attacking the Court, even on a measure utterly disconnected with slavery, such as a bill to authorize the appointment of a clerk to relieve the Judges of the labor of
transcribing their own opinions; and their sneers elicited
warm defense of the Court. "The people of this great
Union," said Thomas Ewing of Ohio, in the House,
"revere it as one of the institutions of our forefathers,
illustrated and adorned by the genius and erudition of
a Marshall and a Story, and even now upheld and sustained by men scarcely inferior to those mighty masters
of their profession. I shall, in the darkest hour of our
Republic, look to the Supreme Court as the palladium
of our institutions and as one of the brightest and purest
ornaments of our system." [1]

With the cloud of slavery thus hanging over its head,
and during the years when the fateful Compromise
Acts of 1850 were debated and enacted by Congress,
the Court held two Terms, at neither of which were
many cases of signal consequence decided. Its most
important decision was rendered in the first case which

[1] *31st Cong., 1st Sess.,* Feb. 13, 14, 1850.

had arisen out of the War with Mexico, and which involved the legality of the collection of tariff duties on goods imported into Philadelphia from Tampico, during March and April, 1847, *Fleming* v. *Page*, 9 How. 603. The case presented for the first time the question of the status under the Constitution of territory conquered and held in possession by the United States. The Mexican War had begun in May, 1846; the battles of Palo Alto and Monterey had been fought in May and September; Tampico had been occupied in December; President Polk had suggested to Mexico negotiations for peace in January, 1847; Buena Vista was fought in February; Nicholas P. Trist, the President's Peace Commissioner, had arrived in Mexico in May, and had discussed peace terms until October; in November he had been recalled, but had finally signed a treaty, February 3, 1848. During all this period, from December, 1846, to February, 1848, the legal status of the occupied territory had been as unsettled as the peace negotiations. "What a state our Mexican affairs are in!" wrote Francis Lieber, in October, 1847. "Verily 'the next dreadful thing to a defeat is a victory', as Wellington is reported to have said. We conquer, beat and occupy; and peace, like a shadow, recedes. The fact is, I believe Mr. Polk cannot make a peace." [1] This *Tampico Duties Case* was elaborately argued by Daniel Webster and Peter McCall against the Attorney-General, Reverdy Johnson. Its decision, rendered by the Court on May 31, 1850, established a most important doctrine in American law and history, and one which was to constitute a potent factor in the great *Insular Cases*, fifty-one years later, that conquered territory remained foreign for the purpose of collection of duties until Congress should take action. "The genius and

---

[1] *Francis Lieber Papers MSS*, letter to Samuel B. Ruggles, Oct. 23, 1847.

character of our institutions," said Taney, "are peaceful, and the power to declare war was not conferred upon Congress for the purposes of aggression or aggrandizement, but to enable the General Government to vindicate by arms, if it should become necessary, its own rights and the rights of its citizens. A war, therefore, declared by Congress, can never be presumed to be waged for the purpose of conquest or the acquisition of territory. . . . The United States, it is true, may extend its boundaries by conquest or treaty. . . . But this can be done only by the treaty-making power or the legislative authority." [1] Three cases, in 1850, arising from the then recently admitted State of Texas had a certain historical interest. In *League* v. *Texas*, 11 How. 185, it was held that a statute of Texas, enacted before its admission into the Union in 1845, "however unjust or tyrannical," could not be interfered with by the Court under its Judiciary Act jurisdiction. In *Randon* v. *Toby*, 11 How. 493, and in *Bennett* v. *Butterworth*, 11 How. 669, the confused condition of legal procedure in the new

[1] On the other hand, the Court at this Term decided that a treaty is binding from the date of its execution, so that the nation ceding territory thereby may not exercise the power of making grants in such territory after that date. See *United States* v. *Reynes*, 9 How. 127. The same point was involved in *Davis* v. *Police Jury of the Parish of Concordia*, 9 How. 280, in which the opinion by Judge Wayne is of great historical interest, giving, as it does, a very lively account of the influences which led Napoleon to agree to the Louisiana Treaty of 1803. The Mexican War gave rise to very few cases in the Court; but the following may be noted as of interest; in *United States* v. *Guillem*, 11 How. 47, argued in 1850 by Attorney-General Crittenden against Pierre Soulé, it was held that a French citizen residing in Mexico was entitled to leave with his property to return to France, even though the French vessel on which he embarked was forfeited for breach of the blockade of Vera Cruz; in *Mitchell* v. *Harmony*, 13 How. 115, argued in 1852 by Attorney-General Crittenden against Cutting and Vinton, it was decided that a military officer sued for trespass for seizure of goods in Mexico was liable, unless his act of seizure was in a case of "immediate and impending danger" or "urgent necessity not admitting of delay"; in *Jecker* v. *Montgomery*, 13 How. 498, a question of prize law was involved for the first time since the long series of such cases between 1800 and 1825; *Cross* v. *Harrison*, 16 How. 164, decided in 1853, involved the question of the legality of the imposition of duties in California between the date of its military conquest in 1846 and the date when the Collector of Customs appointed under Act of Congress assumed his position, Nov. 13, 1849, the treaty of peace having been proclaimed, July 4, 1848, and notice having reached California, Aug. 7, 1848.

State was severely commented upon. One other earlier Texas case may be mentioned in this connection because of its curious facts — *Brashear* v. *Mason*, 6 How. 92, argued by George M. Bibb and Walter Jones against Attorney-General Clifford; the Joint Resolution of 1845, annexing Texas and admitting it as a State, provided that Texas should cede to the United States her navy; the plaintiff, who was commander-in-chief of the Texas Navy consisting of four vessels, claimed that he was a part of the navy ceded and therefore passed into the Naval Service of the United States and became entitled to pay as an officer of the Navy; the Court held that the word "navy" did not comprise persons, and also that even if the plaintiff were entitled to pay, a mandamus would not lie to the Secretary of the Navy to enforce payment.

During these Terms of the Court of December, 1849, and December, 1850, the rancor of the radical Freesoilers became increasingly violent, in the course of the long debate over the Compromise Acts proposed by Henry Clay for the settlement of all pending slavery questions.[1] They foresaw that the Court would inevitably be called upon to decide the question of the existence and extent of the power of Congress over slavery in the Territories; for these Compromise Acts expressly remitted this issue to the Court, writs of error or appeals from the Territorial Courts being allowed, without any monetary limitation, in all cases involving slavery, and also in all habeas corpus cases involving questions of personal freedom. One of the bills also proposed to settle the Texas-New Mexico boundary by

[1] These Compromise Acts provided for the admission of California as a State with its existing laws against slavery; the amendment of the Fugitive Slave Law; the organization of the Territory of New Mexico, without any condition as to slavery; and for the organization of the Territory of Utah, with a condition that when admitted as a State it should be received into the Union, with or without slavery, as its Constitution should then prescribe.

a suit in the Supreme Court; but this disposition was defeated.[1] In all the debates over these measures, lasting from January to September, 1850, Clay himself and the Southerners were, as a rule, willing to trust the Court as "the proper arbiter of this agitated and perplexed question between the two sections of the Union." Several Senators and Congressmen from the North, however, expressed vigorously their lack of confidence, chief among whom were Senator Salmon P. Chase of Ohio, John P. Hale of New Hampshire and Roger S. Baldwin of Connecticut. While, said Chase, no one would more cordially and respectfully acknowledge the probity, learning and ability of the distinguished Judges, yet "eminent and upright as they are, they are not more than other men, exempt from the bias of education, sympathy and interests," and the slaveholders have taken care to see that a majority of their number were placed on the Bench. Chase further assailed the decision of the Court in *Prigg* v. *Pennsylvania;* and, adopting the exact language of Jefferson and Jackson in their views of the power of the Court to construe the Constitution, denied that Congress was bound in any way to accept the Court's decision.[2] Hale charged that the opinions of the Court were "tinted and colored by geographical position", that its decisions had tended all in one direction, and that he had no doubt that it would decide in favor of slavery any case brought under the proposed bills. For this accusation, he was called to order by Henry S. Foote of Mississippi, who said that

[1] The right of the United States to sue a State for the determination of the boundary line between a Territory and a State was not determined until 1892, in *United States* v. *Texas,* 143 U. S. 621; see also *The State as Defendant under the Federal Constitution,* by William C. Coleman, *Harv. Law Rev.* (1917), XXXI.

[2] See *31st Cong., 1st Sess., App.,* speeches in the Senate of Yulee of Florida (p. 95), Phelps of Vermont (p. 96), Clay of Kentucky (p. 916), Butler of South Carolina (p. 926), Davis of Mississippi (p. 154), Turney of Tennessee (p. 297), Hunter of Virginia (p. 379), — all in favor of a Court decision; *ibid., App.,* 473 *et seq.,* 447 *et seq.* March 26, 1850.

Hale's language implied a charge of corruption on one of the coördinate branches of the Government. William L. Dayton of New Jersey also repelled Hale's charges with indignation, and said that however the Court was constituted, it had his unbounded confidence. "I look on them," he said, "as the sole and safe arbiter, and upon them I am willing to trust everything I have, and everything I feel, of interest in this country and its Constitution." It was important, he continued, that the Senate should sustain the Court "in the high confidence that it has heretofore held in the minds of the American people." Andrew P. Butler of South Carolina uttered a protest against the thought that Judges, "sworn to observe the Constitution, men who have the landmarks of precedent and law, and who have public opinion, the opinion of the whole Bar and of the world, to guide and control, could disregard those influences, would yield to the miserable and low suggestion of geographical lines." Thomas Ewing of Ohio said that he had practiced long before the Court, and that he had never known a case in which he thought he " had any right to impeach the motives, feelings or bias of a single Judge. . . . I look upon that Bench as above all political influence, above influence of every kind except the main object — right, justice and truth." Augustus C. Dodge of Iowa protested against Hale's general bill of indictment against the Court and cited, as a conclusive proof of the lack of sectional feeling, the Court's decision only a year previous, in 1849, in the boundary dispute between Missouri and his own State of Iowa — a case where feeling had run so high that troops of each State had been called out to enforce the State's contention. "If Iowa gained the suit, 2616 square miles became free territory; if Missouri gained, slavery would be extended over an area nearly twice the extent of Rhode Island. The Supreme Court, with whatever geographical bias the Senator from New Hampshire may ascribe to it, decided the long pending and angry dispute, and decided in favor of the free State of Iowa and against the slave State of Missouri." To all this, Hale retorted that he had nothing to retract, and that while " it is considered here as a sort of patriotic effort to express great confidence in the Supreme Court," he had no confidence in it, since the course of the Court on slavery questions had not been such "as to commend it to the friends of National freedom."

At the next session of Congress, in 1851, Hale returned to the attack with even more vituperative force.[1] " There is a tribunal which sits beneath this Senate Chamber which is the very citadel of American slavery. . . . Upon its decision rest the final hopes of slavery," he charged. For this, he was called to order by the President of the Senate, and Senators, Whigs and Democrats alike scored his language. Robert F. Stockton of New Jersey, Joseph R. Underwood of Kentucky, Lewis Cass of Michigan, and Butler of South Carolina challenged Hale to cite any decision where division of the Court had been on purely geographical lines. They noted that in the *Prigg Case*, settling the rights of the States and of Congress over fugitive slaves, "one of the most unfortunate decisions in its effect upon the South of any that has ever been made by that Bench ", Judge Wayne of Georgia had concurred with Judge Story of Massachusetts. Stephen A. Douglas of Illinois said that the Court had protected equally the rights of the North and the South, and that, while there

[1] *32d Cong., 1st Sess.*, Dec. 15, 17, 1851. The matter under debate was a resolution introduced into the Senate that "the Compromise Acts are, in the judgment of this body, entitled to be recognized as a definitive adjustment and settlement of the distracting questions growing out of the system of domestic slavery, and, as such, that said measures should be acquiesced in and faithfully observed by all good citizens."

had been much diversity of opinion on the Bench, both Southern and Northern Judges had divided amongst themselves. "If you examine the decisions on this question, you will see an entire absence of this supposed bias or impression on the minds of the Judges, growing out of locality of interest, or association, or both. . . . I believe the Court is above all such impression." The abolitionists were determined, however, to refuse to recognize the decisions of the Court on slavery; and at this same session, in 1852, Charles Sumner renewed Hale's attack, and in a debate on the repeal of the Fugitive Slave Law he stated that while he had respect for the Court, he declined to acknowledge its authority as binding on Congress. "It cannot control our duty as to legislation," he said, "and here I adopt the language of President Jackson in his memorable veto in 1832." The spectacle of a Massachusetts Free-soiler indorsing Jackson's view as to the Court's powers was a sign of the marked change towards that tribunal which was being effected in the North.[1]

Meanwhile, in the year 1851, the Court had become involved with the fugitive slave issue in three ways: first, through one of its decisions; second, through the filling of a vacancy upon the Bench; and third, through decisions of the Judges sitting on Circuit. In *Strader* v. *Graham*, 10 How. 82, which arose on a writ of error to the Kentucky Court of Appeals, the question was presented whether slaves, owned by a citizen of Kentucky, who had been allowed to go into Ohio to work, retained their status as slaves on their return to Kentucky, or whether by virtue of the laws of Ohio or of the Northwest Ordinance, they had acquired the status of freemen. The Court held unanimously that the ques-

---

[1] *32d Cong., 1st Sess., App.*, 1102 *et seq.*, Aug. 26, 1852. *The Constitutionality of the Fugitive Slave Acts*, by Allen Johnson, *Yale Law Journ.* (1921), XXXI

tion of their status depended entirely on the laws of Kentucky, and that "it was exclusively in the power of Kentucky to determine for itself whether their employment in another State should not make them free on their return"; hence, the Court decided that it had no jurisdiction over the case, since it presented no Federal question but only a matter of State law, already determined by the State Court. Had the Court adhered to its wise decision in this case, when the *Dred Scott Case* involving almost identical facts arose, six years later, the whole history of the country might have been changed. It is "a very clear, concise, and able opinion and will probably give general satisfaction to the Bar and the country," said the Democratic newspapers. "It settles the law on two very important questions, and *maugre* the grumbling of the abolitionists, will meet the general approbation of the country." [1] To the anti-slavery faction, this decision, so eminently reasonable and supported by well settled doctrines of the Court, was as objectionable as the *Prigg Case* had been; and the *New York Evening Post* said: "This has an important bearing on the Fugitive Slave Law. It shows that this Court will hold all men of color in slave States to be slaves, and will not look with favor upon their manumission. This serves to show what security a person transported from a free State on the charge of being a fugitive has for obtaining a trial by jury in the place to which he is conveyed. Looking at this decision in the view of common sense, it must be pronounced, in the language of Mr. Webster, 'not a respectable decision.' The Court needs reorganizing; instead of the four members allotted to the free States they should have six. . . . The history of this particular case illustrates the stupidity and danger of leaving to

---

[1] *Washington Union*, Jan. 7, 9, 12, 1851.

this tribunal the arbitration of issues that belong to the legislature or to the forum of popular discussion." [1] Such language might well have warned the Court that decisions on this subject of fugitive slaves must be rendered with extreme care. Further warning of its delicate position was given by the criticism which arose on the appointment of a successor to Judge Levi Woodbury, who died on September 4, 1851, after a brief but distinguished service on the Bench of only six years.[2] Within a week after his death, President Fillmore wrote to Webster, stating that he desired to "obtain as long a lease, and as much moral and judicial power as possible, from the new appointment" to be made by him, and that he "would therefore like to combine a vigorous constitution with high moral and intellectual qualifications, a good judicial mind, and such age as gives prospect of long service"; he added that he had formed a very high opinion of Benjamin Robbins Curtis of Boston, and he asked: "Does he fill the measure of my wishes?" This letter crossed in the mail a letter written by Webster to the President, in which Webster stated that the place should properly be offered to the famous Rufus Choate, a lawyer more extensively known and distinguished in public life; but that, as it was supposed

[1] *New York Evening Post*, Jan. 13, 1857.

[2] The *Boston Post* said, Feb. 3, 1846, in a letter from its Washington correspondent: "Judge Woodbury is taking a commanding position on the Bench which he dignifies and adorns, and the duties and details of which seem as familiar to him as if he had devoted his whole life to them. He has delivered several opinions, this Term, distinguished for ability, clearness and sound law which have elicited warm commendations from all quarters. In Judge Woodbury, I have great confidence that the country will find, what it rarely meets with, a Judge on the Bench, unchanged by his elevated position of irresponsibility to the people, and holding fast to the integrity of his original principles. It is hard to find a Judge who does not bury the fundamental rights of the people and the groundwork of democracy beneath his ermine, the moment he puts it on. But if ever the people had good cause to hope to find a true man in that position, Mr. Woodbury is the man." The *Washington Union* said of Woodbury, Jan. 12, 1851: "No man is more thoroughly known to the country as the firm and unwavering supporter of the Union, the Constitution and the laws." See *ibid.*, July 25, Sept. 6, 8, 13, 1851.

that Choate would not accept, he believed the general, perhaps the universal, sentiment, was that the place should be filled by the appointment of Curtis — a man "of very suitable age, forty-one, good health, excellent habits, sufficient industry and love of labor, and in point of legal attainment and general character in every way fit." [1]   Choate, as was expected, stated that he did not desire the place; [2] and accordingly the President appointed Curtis, September 22, 1851, giving him the place in preference to two able and experienced Judges of the United States District Court, who had been strongly urged for the vacancy, Judge Peleg Sprague of Massachusetts, and Judge John Pitman of Rhode Island. Of the appointment, a friend of Curtis wrote that President Fillmore, on his visit to Boston in the summer of 1851, had "assured himself that his intention of appointing a young man, provided he was the best man, could be best carried out by the appointment of Mr. B. R. Curtis; and he offered him the vacant seat solely because he thought it his duty to do so. . . . If there ever was a magistrate guided in every action by a stern sense of duty, that magistrate was Millard Fillmore. And I have reason to know that there was no act of his Administration in which he felt more pride and satisfaction than in this single appointment." [3] The Administration organ in Washington said that, though Curtis was a young man, "such is his profes-

---

[1] *Curtis*, I, 154 *et seq.*

[2] *Reminiscences of Rufus Choate* (1860), by Edward G. Parker, 299: "I wanted to know if he contemplated going on to the United States Supreme Court bench. He said he had received an intimation that he could have it, and had no doubt he could have the post, if he desired it; but that he would not on any account, spend a minute in Washington, absorbed as he should have to be in his evenings in labors and consultations, and in his days in court. 'Here,' said he, 'I can do just as I please; I can earn in three months as much as their whole salary; and I can work, more or less, as I please.' These views, expressed in 1857, were also held in 1851."

[3] *Curtis*, I, 166, 170, letter of March 22, 1879, from John O. Sargent to G. T. Curtis, remarks of Causten Browne.

sional reputation that there can be but one opinion among the members of the Bar as to the propriety of his selection. He has taken no very active part in political affairs, but has been always a decided and consistent Whig." While the appointment was generally commended by Democrats and Whigs alike, it was denounced by the radical anti-slavery men of the North, who charged that Curtis was a tool of Webster, a supporter of the doctrine of Webster's Seventh of March speech, and a believer in the constitutionality of the Fugitive Slave Law.[1] Over this statute and the cases arising out of it, a storm of partisan rage was now sweeping in the Northern States; and the anti-slavery men saw their worst fears realized, when the new Judge, before his confirmation by the Senate, proceeded to rule upon the constitutionality of the obnoxious statute and to sustain it, in *United States* v. *Robert Morris*, 1 Curtis C. C. 23. This noted case in the United States Circuit Court in Boston, involving the indictment of a young colored lawyer and his associates for the rescue of the fugitive slave Shadrach from the hands of the United States marshal, had been argued by the abolitionist lawyer and Senator, John P. Hale of New Hampshire, who had contended that the jury were the rightful judges of the law as well as the facts, and that if they conscientiously believed the law to be unconstitutional, they were bound by their oaths to disregard any instruction the Court might give. Among the extreme anti-slavery men of the North this was a legal doctrine which was finding high favor; and its controversion by the new Judge, whose personal friends and associates were largely imbued with this idea, was an act requiring

---

[1] *The Republic*, Sept. 23, 1851. The *New York Tribune* said, Jan. 29, 1856, that Curtis had been given his position on the Bench, as a reward for a "heartless and unscrupulous piece of sophistry" — an opinion in favor of the constitutionality of the Fugitive Slave Law.

firmness of character of a high order.   Judge Curtis, however, met the test without flinching and held:

This power and corresponding duty of the Court authoritatively to declare the law is one of the highest safeguards of the citizen.   The sole end of Courts of justice is to enforce the laws uniformly and impartially, without respect of persons or times, or the opinions of men.   To enforce popular laws is easy.   But when an unpopular cause is a just cause, when a law, unpopular in some locality, is to be enforced there, then comes the strain upon the administration of justice; and few unprejudiced men would hesitate as to where that strain would be most firmly borne. . . .   Finding that no Judge of any Court of the United States had in any published opinion examined it upon such grounds that I could feel I had a right to repose on his decision without more, I knew not how to avoid the duty which was then thrown upon me. My firm conviction is that under the Constitution of the United States, juries in criminal trials have not the right to decide any question of law; and that if they render a general verdict, their duty and their oath require them to apply to the facts, as they may find them, the law given to them by the Court.

Similar charges supporting the constitutionality of the Fugitive Slave Law, made by Judges Nelson, Woodbury and Grier, enhanced the growing feeling of hostility at the North towards the Judges of the United States Courts.   The anti-slavery sentiment was still more aroused by the action of President Fillmore and of the Federal law officers and Courts, in connection with an alarming riot and murder which occurred at Christiana, Pennsylvania, arising out of the rescue of a fugitive slave and which resulted from inflammatory speeches counseling disobedience to the Fugitive Slave Law.   The Administration, forced to the conclusion that stringent measures must be taken to suppress the increasing disloyalty of the abolitionists, resolved on indictments for

treason.[1] " An example should be made of some of
these pestilent agitators who excite the ignorant and
restless to treasonable violence," said the Whig organ
in Washington. Whig papers in New York and elsewhere said that "those who counsel resistance to law
should be regarded in their true light. They are virtually rebels, and practically public enemies; " and
another said that "an alarming tendency to anarchy"
was manifested in the North, and that "treason which
has been long preached from pulpits and the press begins to manifest itself in overt acts." Accordingly,
indictments for treason were pressed in the District
Court for the Eastern District of Pennsylvania, and the
law of treason was stated on very broad lines by District Judge Kane in a charge to the grand jury and later
confirmed by Judge Grier in a charge made at the trial
of the indicted men. In these charges, forcible resistance to a Federal law was held to be treasonable if
"with intent to overthrow the Government or to nullify
some law of the United States and totally to hinder its
execution or to compel its repeal." [2] Though the trial
resulted in an acquittal owing to insufficient evidence,
the action of the Federal Judges in sustaining the
application of the law of treason to cases of resistance to
the Fugitive Slave Law evoked bitter criticism from the
anti-slavery press. The *New York Evening Post* de-

[1] For full accounts of the Christiana riot and trials, see the Administration organ,
The Republic, Sept. 15, 19, 20, 24, 1851, quoting also *New York Courier, Albany
State Register* and *New York Times;* and the Democratic organ, the *Washington
Union*, Sept. 14, 16, 17, 18, 19, 21, Dec. 3, 10, 16, 17, 1851.

[2] Federal Cases No. 18276, 2 Wall. Jr. 134, charge of Judge Kane to grand jury,
Sept. 12, 1851; *United States* v. *Hanway*, Federal Cases No. 15299, 2 Wall. Jr. 139,
charge of Judge Grier, Oct. Term, 1854 ; see also charges of Judge Sprague and Judge
Curtis as to treason in the Shadrach rescue cases, Federal Cases No. 18263, March,
1851; Federal Cases No. 18269, 2 Curtis, 630, Oct. 15, 1851; and charge of Judge
Curtis as to obstruction of Federal process in the *Anthony Burns Case, United States*
v. *Stowell*, Federal Cases No. 16409, Oct. Term, 1854, 2 Curtis, 153; Federal Cases
No. 18250, June 7, 1854. See also *Law of Treason*, by Simon Greenleaf, *Law Reporter* (1851), XIV.

nounced "this monstrous doctrine", saying: "This strained doctrine of treason has slept till now, when it is revived by Mr. Fillmore and Mr. Webster." Again it said: "It is the constitutional duty, no less than the true policy of our Courts, as seldom as possible to recognize the existence of that disaffection to the Government which the crime of treason implies; and we are also clear that, if the law of treason had been defined by a bench of Democratic Judges, it would now be their recorded judgment that there has never been more than one case of treason proper, prosecuted in this country since the constitution was established." After the acquittal of the Pennsylvania rioters on the treason charge, this newspaper said: "Great pains were taken to prepare the people to accept this doctrine. Not only was the support of the Fugitive Slave Law to be made a test of political orthodoxy, but it was a law so sacred in its character that the violation of it was a higher crime than the violation of any other. . . . The Whig journals did their best to persuade their readers that treason had been committed. . . . Everybody seemed persuaded, but the people; and the question was, whether the people were ready to accept the view of the law taken by Fillmore and Webster. The trial was had, the prisoners were acquitted of treason, and the Administration sustained another mortifying defeat." [1]

It was at a time of such hostility to the enforcement of the law, that the Court met on December 1, 1851, the

[1] *New York Evening Post*, Oct. 25, Dec. 26, 1851, Oct. 11, 1853. The same paper noted Oct. 15, 16, 1853, that five hundred men had been engaged in rescuing a slave at Syracuse, N. Y., and said that the Administration journals were "clamorous for condemnation for treason."

The *Washington Union*, Dec. 16, 1851, said that the result of the treason trial was such as every one expected. "It is conclusive of one thing only, not that treason was not committed, but that it is and will be a very difficult thing to convict anyone of treason for resisting the Fugitive Slave Law, unless more vigilance and activity are exercised on the part of both Federal and State authorities."

new Judge Curtis taking his seat on the Bench, though his appointment was not sent in to the Senate until December 11, nor confirmed until December 20. Of his first impressions of Washington and of this December, 1851, Term, Curtis wrote: "I have now been here four weeks, — long enough to be settled both in my abode and occupations. I live at Brown's new hotel, where I have a comfortable and pleasant, though small room, and there are some pleasant people in the house. Judge and Mrs. McLean, and Judge and Mrs. Catron, live here, and probably Judge Wayne will come here on his return from New York, where he now is. The Bench is full, with the exception of Judge McKinley, and we have made uncommon good progress in our work. But it is already so great as to be beyond the ability of the Court to despatch it; and when the Texas and California land-titles get here, Congress will probably see that the judicial system of the country, fitted for fourteen States, with no Circuit Court west of the mountains, is not adequate to do the business of the United States now, when there are thirty-one States, and about four times as many people, and more than five times the wealth. In the days when Chief Justice Marshall used to deliver those great opinions, the calendar had about thirty causes on it; now it has two hundred and sixteen. I think there can be no question that, when the next Administration comes in, the Judges of the Supreme Court will be relieved from all duty out of that Court, and two sessions a year will be held; in which event, I shall live and keep house here a part of the year. I find rent, and all the necessary expenses of living, are less than in Boston, — I said to Mr. Appleton about twenty per cent less. . . . I do not hear much of politics, for there is a real and true separation of the Bench from politicians here, with perhaps one exception, — and

I do not know that there is any exception. But I think, from all I see and hear, Mr. Webster's chance for a nomination is very small. If the Democratic Party should nominate General Cass, or some other civilian from the North, the Whig party may possibly nominate Mr. Webster; but I doubt if the nomination would be of any value, for I think the Democrats will surely carry the next election. My brethren here have received me very kindly, and there are some pleasant gentlemen among them. I find my duties require constant labor; but there is no more than a fair day's work to be done in each day, and I have really more leisure than I have known for ten years. The great difference between my professional labors at the Bar and on the Bench consists in the entire freedom of the latter from anxiety and burdensome responsibility, and the certainty when I rise in the morning that no one can force me to do anything which I am not equal to; and, accordingly, my health has been better during the last month than any time for a year past. We have, argued and now under advisement, the case of the Wheeling Bridge, built across the Ohio under the authority of the State of Virginia. This is the first case since I have been here which involved constitutional questions on which the Court are likely to divide, though I have been obliged in one case to dissent from the majority. In general, we have thus far been very harmonious in our opinions." Of the impression made upon Washington by Judge Curtis, a friend wrote in his diary, January 29, 1852: "Judge Curtis impresses everybody most favorably by his modest demeanour and his agreeable conversation. He changes but little — he is of the same well-knit frame, with fine, expressive eyes, and white teeth, which you notice when he smiles, — not handsome, but his face lights up wonderfully. Crittenden who does not like or dislike by halves is perfectly charmed with him."[1]

At this Term, the ever present conflict between State sovereignty and Congressional power over commerce came to the front again in a new aspect, in *Pennsylvania v. Wheeling and Belmont Bridge Co.*, 13 How. 518, in which Pennsylvania, charging that a bridge over the Ohio River, construction of which had been authorized by a statute of Virginia, was a nuisance and an obstruction to interstate commerce on a navigable river, sought to have it enjoined. This case, which had been before the Court twice before, and was now eloquently argued, December 18, 22, 1851, by Edwin M. Stanton against Reverdy Johnson, was unique, inasmuch as the State sued, not in the exercise of its sovereignty, but by virtue of ownership of property seeking protection.[2] For many years past, Pennsylvania had been engaged in making extensive improvements by canals, railroads and turnpikes for the facilitation of the transportation of goods and passengers; and it was claimed that any obstruction of the Ohio River to the free passage of steamboats to Pittsburg would injuriously affect and divert this transportation, diminish the trade and lessen the revenue of the States, and occasion an injury to the State as the principal proprietor of the lines of transpor-

[1] *Curtis*, I, 163, 167, letter of Dec. 27, 1851; diary entry of Jan. 29, 1852, by John O. Sargent.

An article in the *American Law Register* (1854), II, by George N. Searle of Boston, describing the Judges, said of Curtis' appointment: "The professional judgment of New England turned to but one man for the place, and the doubt was not, whether he would have the offer, but whether he would accept it. The promotion was doubly flattering to him, as it was a tribute solely to his professional ability, he having rendered little of mere political service. The good opinion, thus formed of him, has been more than fulfilled. We speak from report, but have reason to believe we speak truly, when we say that, during the first Term after his appointment, he took rank with the first of the Bench for sureness of judgment, keenness of analysis and accuracy of legal research."

[2] See 9 Howard, 647; 11 Howard, 528; see also *Life of Reverdy Johnson* (1914), by Bernard C. Steiner; *Life and Public Services of Edwin M. Stanton* (1899), by George C. Gorham.

tation. Fundamentally, the case presented one phase of the great contest between the railroads and the steamboats in their struggle for supremacy and the development of modern means of transportation. "Few cases have ever excited greater interest or seemed to affect more extensively the internal commerce of the country than this celebrated controversy," said the *Western Law Journal*.[1] The Court held, February 6, 1852, that the State was entitled to maintain its bill in equity on the ground of nuisance, and that, inasmuch as Congress had power to regulate navigation on the Ohio River and had exercised its power in various statutes, interference with such Congressional exercise of authority by the State of Virginia was void. The Court, accordingly, ordered an abatement of the nuisance, through a modification in the construction of the bridge. Chief Justice Taney and Judge Daniel vigorously dissented — the latter saying that there never had been, " there perhaps never can be brought before the tribunal, for its decision, a case of higher importance or of deeper interest than the present." While the decision caused much excitement at the time, it had little practical effect upon the law; for later cases very greatly narrowed its compass.[2] Even the operation of the decree upon the particular bridge involved was nullified by Congress, which within six months passed a statute declaring the

[1] *Western Law Journ.*, IX (Sept., 1852). "The stupendous structure that spans the Ohio at Wheeling connecting the State of Virginia and Ohio strikes the eye of the traveller passing beneath it, as it looms above him in the darkness, as one of the great architectural wonders of the age. To many, the controversy for a time seemed to owe its origin to a spirit of contemptible rivalry between Pittsburg and Wheeling, and to have no other aim than the selfish obstruction of a great national enterprise. A long, careful, deliberate, conscientious, judicial investigation has shown it to be a question deeply interesting to the people of the United States, in its actual and immediate bearing on a trade embracing the transportation annually, of merchandise of over $40,000,000 and 80,000 passengers; and in the principles which it involved, affecting more than one half of the whole trade of the nation."

[2] *Gilman* v. *Philadelphia* (1866), 3 Wall. 713; *Willamette Iron Bridge Co.* v. *Hatch* (1888), 125 U. S. 1, 15.

bridge to be a lawful structure and not an obstruction to navigation.[1] This statute came before the Court, in 1856, and was upheld as constitutionally within the power of Congress to regulate the navigation of the river. "This was the first instance in the whole history of the Government," said the *New York Tribune*, "where Congress ever interposed or attempted to arrest a decree of the Supreme Court. The precedent may lead hereafter to serious embarrassments between the judicial and legislative departments; for if the law settled by the highest judicial tribunal be not accepted law of the land, and is liable to review by demagogues in Congress of their own motion, or by the usurpation of worse ones out of doors, the Court of last resort becomes but a mockery — *stat nominis umbra*." [2] Later, however, it admitted that the question had been properly settled "in conformity with the progressive spirit of the times. . . . The invention of railroads has quite changed the state of facts. . . . There are very few navigable rivers that, all things considered, can, as a medium of communication, taking passengers as well as goods into account, stand an advantageous comparison with a well built and well equipped railroad. . . . Under this new state of facts, it is evident that the old common law doctrine as to navigable waters must undergo a certain modification. . . . The public convenience will require that the uninterrupted freedom of passing up and down a river should give way, in cases of conflict, to facilities for crossing it."

Three days after the decision of this *Wheeling Bridge*

[1] See especially the debate over this measure, *32d Cong., 1st Sess., App.*, Aug. 13, 14, 16, 17, 18, 1852; see 18 How. 421.

[2] *New York Tribune*, Feb. 19, 1856, April 23, 1856. It is interesting to note that only one year from the above criticism, the *Tribune* itself was clamoring to have Congress set aside the decision of the Court in the *Dred Scott Case*. In *The Clinton Bridge* (1871), 10 Wall. 454, Congress again legalized a bridge, while a suit was pending.

Case in 1852, the Court heard an argument, February 9, 10, 11, by Job Tyson and Phineas Morris against James Campbell and George M. Dallas (all of Pennsylvania) in the important case of *Cooley* v. *Board of Wardens of the Port of Philadelphia*, 12 How. 299. The validity of the State pilotage fee statute was involved, and again the Court was called upon to consider the question how far the power of Congress under the Commerce Clause of the Constitution was exclusive. For years, the Judges had given hopelessly differing opinions on this subject. The law now received considerable clarification and fixity, through an opinion of the Court rendered by the new Judge, Curtis. Writing to George Ticknor, Curtis said: "I expect my opinion will excite surprise, because it is adverse to the exclusive authority of Congress, and not in accordance with the opinions of McLean and Wayne, who are the most high-toned Federalists on the Bench. But it rests on grounds perfectly satisfactory to myself, and it has received the assent of five Judges out of eight, although for twenty years no majority has ever rested their decision on either view of this question, nor was it ever directly decided before." [1] The doctrine thus finally adopted by the Court was evidently in the nature of a compromise between the previously conflicting views of the Judges; but it carried the Federal power to a greater height than it had hitherto attained. It pointed out that: "The power to regulate commerce embraces a vast field, containing not only many, but exceedingly various subjects, quite unlike in their nature; some imperatively demanding a single uniform rule, operating equally on the commerce of the United States in every port; and some, like the subject now in question, imperatively demanding that diversity which alone can meet the local necessities of

[1] *Curtis*, I, letter of Feb. 29, 1852.

navigation. Either absolutely to affirm, or deny, that the nature of this power requires exclusive legislation by Congress, is to lose sight of the nature of the subjects of this power, and to assert, concerning all of them, what is really applicable but to a part. Whatever subjects of this power are in their nature National, or admit only of one uniform system, or plan of regulation, may justly be said to be of such a nature as to require exclusive legislation by Congress." But it held that the pilotage law in question did not come within this class of subjects, and hence was a constitutional exercise of power by the State. The doctrine, so laid down for the control of commerce was really the adoption of a rule first stated by a strong Democrat, Judge Woodbury, in the *Passenger Cases*.[1] Even this compromise was not satisfactory to three of the Court, Judges McLean and Wayne still considering the power of Congress to be exclusive,[2] and Judge Daniel taking the extreme view that enactment of pilotage laws was an original and inherent power of the States not possessed by the Federal Government.

While this *Pilot Case* presented a distinct advance by the Court towards a broader view of Federal powers than had hitherto prevailed, another case decided at

[1] Woodbury stated that; "So far as reasons exist to make the exercise of the commercial power exclusive, as on the matters of exterior, general, and uniform cognizance, the construction may be proper to render it exclusive, but no further, as the exclusiveness depends, in this case wholly on the reasons, and not on any express prohibition, and hence cannot extend beyond the reasons themselves. Where they disappear, the exclusiveness should halt," 7 How. 559; and see *Cases on Constitutional Law*, by James B. Thayer, 219. The rule, in the broadened form given to it in *State Freight Tax Cases* (1873), 15 Wall. 232, 280, is the law today.

[2] Judge McLean in dissenting said (p. 325): "From this race of legislation between Congress and the States, and between the States, if this principle be maintained, will arise a conflict similar to that which existed before the adoption of the Constitution." To this prediction, Judge Wayne made answer in *Gilman* v. *Philadelphia* (1866), 3 Wall. 713, fourteen years later: "In the Pilot case, the dissenting Judge drew an alarming picture of the evils to rush in at the break made, as he alleged, in the Constitution. None have appeared. The stream of events has since flowed on without a ripple due to the influence of that adjudication."

this Term marked an even greater enlargement of the domain of power of the Federal Government. In fact, few decisions had ever produced so revolutionary a change in Federal jurisdiction as that of *The Propeller Genesee Chief* v. *Fitzhugh*, 12 How. 443, in which the Court, in a remarkable opinion by Chief Justice Taney, held for the first time that the admiralty Courts of the United States had jurisdiction over the public navigable lakes and rive s of the country, regardless of the question of tidewater. The question decided arose as follows: By an Act of February 26, 1845, Congress had extended the jurisdiction of the Federal District Courts to certain cases upon the Great Lakes and inland navigation connecting them. Previous cases decided by Marshall and Story had held that the admiralty powers of the Constitution only extended over navigable water within the ebb and flow of the tide. During the last few years, a change of view on the part of the Court had been foreshadowed in *dicta* of various Judges in two cases, the facts of which, however, did not necessitate a ruling on the precise question.[1] "The conviction that this definition of admiralty powers was narrower than the Constitution contemplated," now said Chief Justice Taney, "has been growing stronger every day with the growing commerce on the lakes and navigable rivers of the Western States." Taney met the problem boldly. "There is certainly nothing in the ebb and flow of the tide that makes the waters peculiarly suitable for admiralty jurisdiction, nor anything in the absence of the tide that renders it unfit. If it is a public navigable water, on which commerce is carried on between different States or nations, the reason for the jurisdiction is

---

[1] *Waring* v. *Clarke* (1847), 5 How. 441, argued by Reverdy Johnson against John J. Crittenden; *New Jersey Steam Navigation Co.* v. *Merchants' Bank* (1848), 6 How. 544.

precisely the same," he said. He then, in a masterly exposition, pointed out that in England the measure of admiralty jurisdiction by the extent of tide and water was sound and reasonable, because there was in that country no navigable stream beyond the ebb and flow of the tide, and therefore in England "tidewater and navigable water are synonymous terms", and "they took the ebb and flow of the tide as the test, because it was a convenient one and more easily determined the character of the river. . . . The description of a public navigable river was substituted in the place of the thing intended to be described." It was natural, he pointed out, for the Courts of the United States in early times to adopt the restricted English definition of admiralty jurisdiction as limited by the tide, inasmuch as in the early days in this country "every public river was tidewater to the head of navigation"; and indeed "until the discovery of steamboats there could be nothing like foreign commerce upon waters with an unchanging current resisting the upward passage"; and he further pointed out that when the decision was made in a former case, *The Steamboat Thomas Jefferson*, 10 Wheat. 28, in 1825, "the commerce on the rivers of the West and on the lakes was in its infancy and of little importance, and but little regarded compared with that of the present day." Since there could be no reason for admiralty power over a public tidewater which did not apply with equal force to any other public water used for commercial purposes and foreign trade, Taney reached the conclusion, and the Court so held, that admiralty jurisdiction must extend to all such navigable waters. Judge Daniel, in a vigorous dissenting opinion, said that the Court had construed the Constitution by geographical considerations, and that though his opinion might be regarded as "contracted and antiquated, unsuited to the day in which we live", he had "the consolation of the support of Marshall, Kent and Story." While this decision established the jurisdiction of the admiralty Courts over the Great Lakes, the principle was extended in *Steamboat New World* v. *King*, 16 How. 469, to a river beyond the tidal flow, in the case of a libel by a passenger for injury due to negligence on a boat on the Sacramento River.[1]

Before the opening of the Term in December, 1852, Judge McKinley died on July 19, after fifteen years of service, during much of which he had been prevented by illness from sitting on the Bench.[2] The session of the Court which was held on December 8, 1852, to receive the resolutions of the Bar as to the Judge's death was memorable by reason of the fact that the Court mourned the loss, not only of its deceased Associate, but also of the three great leaders of the Federal Bar — Henry Clay, Daniel Webster and John Sergeant, all of whom had died since the end of the last Term.[3] "In a few short

[1] Judge Daniel in his dissenting opinion presenting a somewhat humorous hypothetical case, reminding one that in those days a stream called the Tiber flowed through Washington across Pennsylvania Avenue: "In the small estuary which traverses the avenue leading to this Court-room, the tides of the Potomac regularly ebb and flow. Although upon the receding of the tide this watercourse can be stepped over, upon the return of the tide, there may be seen on this water numerous boys battling or angling or passing in canoes. Should a conflict arise amongst these urchins, originating either in collision of canoes or an entanglement of fishing lines or from any similar cause, this would present a case of admiralty jurisdiction fully as legitimate as that which is made by the libel in the case before us."

[2] On April 14, 1852, a fire occurred at two A.M. in the Clerk's office. "We are happy, however, to be able to state," said the *National Intelligencer*, "that the valuable archives of the Court were very little if any defaced or injured." Regarding another fire, Judge Curtis wrote, Dec. 27, 1851: "The Court was not disturbed by the fire and sat as usual while the building was burning. We were not aware that we were showing any peculiar coolness by doing so; for having made all necessary arrangements to have the records, etc., removed in case of need, we saw no reason why the business of the day should not proceed. But I understand people thought it was like the Senate sitting when the Gauls came." *Curtis*, I, 165; *National Intelligencer*, April 15, 1852; *New York Tribune*, April 16, 1852.

[3] Clay died, June 29, 1852; Webster, Oct. 23; Sergeant, Nov. 23. It may be noted that while the Bar resolved to wear the usual badge of mourning, this action was not taken by the Court, the custom of former years in that respect apparently having fallen into disuse. See articles in *Amer. Law Reg.* (1853), I, 58, 193, on the deaths of Webster and Sergeant.

months, the Bar has been bereaved of its brightest and greatest monuments," said Attorney-General Crittenden in presenting the Bar Resolutions to McKinley. "Clay, Webster and Sergeant have gone to their immortal rest in quick succession. . . . Like bright stars they have sunk below the horizon and have left the land in widespread gloom. . . . This hall itself seems as though it were sensible of its loss, and even these marble pillars seem to sympathize, as they stand around us like so many majestic mourners." To this, Chief Justice Taney made response, speaking of the "deep sense which the Court entertained of the loss sustained at the Bar as well as on the Bench."

To succeed McKinley, President Fillmore nominated on August 16, 1852, Edward A. Bradford, a leading lawyer of Louisiana, but the Senate failed to act affirmatively upon the nomination before its adjournment.[1] Fillmore then turned his attention to candidates living outside of McKinley's Circuit. His personal preference was for the appointment of John J. Crittenden of Kentucky, but Senatorial complications seemed likely to render confirmation impossible. Humphrey Marshall of Kentucky and Thomas Ruffin, Chief Justice of North Carolina, had many supporters.[2] The choice finally fell upon George E. Badger of North Carolina, whose name Fillmore sent in to the Senate, January 10, 1853. Badger, a man of fifty-eight years of age, had been Secretary of the Navy under Presidents Harrison and Tyler, and United States Senator since 1846; he was an able and eloquent lawyer, well fitted

---

[1] A Washington dispatch to the *New York Tribune*, Aug. 27, 1852, stated that Bradford's nomination was certain to be rejected.

[2] *New York Tribune*, Dec. 30, 1852; *Washington Union*, Jan. 28, 1853; *Thomas Ruffin Papers*, letter of Edward Stanley to David Outlaw, Jan. 26, 1853, stating that the President had said that he would not appoint Ruffin, since if he should go out of the Circuit at all, he must nominate either Crittenden or Badger.

for the position, and a strongly conservative Whig. Though it had been expected that the appointment of one of its members would commend itself to the Senate (then composed of thirty-six Democrats, twenty Whigs and two Free-soilers), it soon became evident that there was little chance of Badger's confirmation. The Democrats felt that Badger was too strong a partisan to warrant his confirmation, on the very eve of the retirement of a Whig and the accession of a Democratic President. The Democratic papers of the South were particularly vigorous in opposition. One said that "old Timothy Pickering himself was not a more thorough and incorrigible Federalist" and that his extreme Federalism would "lead him always to interpret the Constitution so as to derogate from the rights of the States and to augment the power of the General Government"; another termed him "a green-gilled Federalist." Another stated that: "It is no time to appoint men whose principles lead them to strengthen the powers of the Federal Government at the expense of the reserved rights of the States. On the question of slavery, Mr. Badger is worse than a Northern Abolitionist because, though a Southern Senator, he held that the accursed Wilmot Proviso was a constitutional measure." [1] The South also severely criticized the appointment of any man residing outside the Circuit in which the vacancy occurred; and the Free-soilers opposed Badger as too favorable to the slavery cause. Even the Northern Whigs were unenthusiastic in their support. The *New York Tribune*, while expressing the hope that Badger's nomination would be confirmed, and

---

[1] *Washington Union*, Jan. 28, Feb. 1, 2, 3, 1853, and *Petersburg Democrat, Mississippian, Mobile Register, Raleigh Standard, New Orleans Delta*, quoted in *ibid*. The Mobile newspapers and Bar protested the appointment as "a corrupt effort to seduce the independence of the Senate by the kindly sentiments that exist in that body for one of its members." *New York Times*, Jan. 14, 1853.

saying that he was "a lawyer of surpassing abilities"
whom Judge McLean had once termed " the ablest lawyer practicing before the Court", had at the same time
characterized Badger as "an iron-heeled old fogy . . .
a genuine and spotless example of the breed-hunker",
"wrongheaded, crabbed, intolerant, dogmatical, inveterate in his prejudices, dictatorial and unman-
nerly in his deportment . . . reserved, aristocratic
and exclusive", and it had stated that "as a statesman,
he is of no account, and as a politician detestable. He
lacks breadth and comprehensiveness of view and a
catholic roundabout sense essential to a man of affairs.
. . . His nature is gnarled and stubbed and refuses
to bend to new forms; it lacks flexibility. . . . Mr.
Badger is by no means a great man. . . . Mr. Badger's
qualifications are a tough, hard, wiry, mental organization, great clearness and distinctness of perception,
method, exactness and strong grasp of mind. . . . He
is a trained polemic, and plunges into a controversy with
as good a will as a Newfoundland dog plunges into the
water." [1]   On February 11, the Senate by a vote of
twenty-six to twenty-five postponed consideration of
the nomination until March 4.   "This is one of those
purely party operations which the country will not sustain," said the *New York Times*.   "There was no
possible objection . . . except that he is a Whig.   No
man dared utter a word against his private character;
no breath of suspicion has tarnished his fame as a
jurist; and there are none to be found to dispute that
he would have carried to the position . . . distinguished abilities, great caution, brilliant intellect, profound attainments, and true, most scrupulous regard
for the blind goddess. . . .   But the deed is done.   All

---

[1] *New York Tribune*, Jan. 8, 1853; *The Republic* in Washington was Badger's
chief active Whig supporter, Jan. 27, 1853.

JOHN McLEAN

BENJAMIN R. CURTIS

JOHN A. CAMPBELL

JEREMIAH S. BLACK

considerations of justice and the public good have been sacrificed to partisan zeal." [1] President Fillmore, rightly regarding the action of the Senate as a rejection of Badger, decided to make one more attempt. Taking cognizance now of the sentiment demanding a candidate resident in the Circuit, but being unwilling to appoint either George Eustis of Louisiana or Solomon W. Downs, the Senator from that State, both of whom, as Unionist Whigs, had received strong indorsement, he offered the position to Judah P. Benjamin, and on the latter's declination owing to his recent election as Senator from Louisiana, he nominated Benjamin's law partner, William C. Micou, on February 24, 1853.[2] The Democratic Senate, however, was determined not to confirm any Whig appointee, at so late a date in the session. Accordingly, when the new President, Franklin Pierce, was inaugurated, he found the vacancy still existing, and, on March 21, he nominated John Archibald Campbell, the leading lawyer of Alabama, who was confirmed by the Senate, four days later. The new Judge was but forty-one years of age; he had had no former judicial experience, but his reputation as a lawyer was of the highest, and his appointment had been urged upon Pierce by the Judges of the Court, acting through Catron and Curtis.[3] Even the Whig papers admitted his

---

[1] *New York Times*, Feb. 16, 1853. Thomas Ruffin wrote to J. B. G. Roulhac, Feb. 7, 1853: "I have been blaming the Senate for rejecting, or attempting to reject, the President's nomination to the Judiciary, on party grounds. It is not a fit ground for refusing a proper man, one who would make a Judge. But I am sorry to find that the President also wishes a partisan Court and refuses to listen to representations of persons not of 'his party.' Now a nomination made on that principle, and for that reason, may reasonably be rejected. A party nomination may be justly met by party opposition, and the Senate it seems understood the President better than I did."

[2] See *New York Times*, Feb. 12, 14, 1853; *Judah P. Benjamin*, in *Great American Lawyers* (1908), VI.

[3] See 20 Wall. viii; *John Archibald Campbell* (1920), by Henry G. Connor. The Court had had an opportunity to observe Campbell, for he had argued in six cases at the December, 1851, Term, including the famous *Gaines* v. *Relf*, 12 How. 472.

full qualifications.[1] "His professional learning is said to be vast, and his industry very great. Outside his profession he is most liberally cultivated, and in this respect ranks beside Story. . . . His mind is singularly analytical. Added to all and crowning all, his perfect character is of the best stamp, modest, amiable, gentle, strictly temperate and inflexibly just," said one paper in New York, and even a strong anti-slavery paper like the *New York Tribune* termed Campbell "about the ablest man connected with the ultra State-Rights organization anywhere. That is, he is chock full of talent, genius, industry, and energy. . . . For the last ten years, he has been deservedly at the head of the Alabama Bar . . . exceedingly popular, and as a jurist and a man commands the respect and confidence of everyone." While the well-known fact that Campbell was extremely radical in his pro-Southern views alarmed some Northern papers, nevertheless, as the *New York Times* very truly pointed out, though "he is said to be a 'fire-eater', meaning thereby an extremist on the sectional question of North and South, or in other words a nullifier, there is reason to suppose that his fame on this score is more the result of warm personal and party devotion to the fortunes of Mr. Calhoun . . . than to his own settled convictions on the right of secession. He will, doubtless, in his new

[1] *New York Times*, March 22, 23, 1853. A correspondent in the *New York Tribune*, March 24, 1853, wrote that Campbell was "a gentleman of shining and profound talents, vast legal attainments and withal is irreproachable in character; but he is a fire-eater of the blazing school. He is a secessionist *per sole*, while two of his competitors, Senator Downs and Judge Eustis of Louisiana, are strong National Union or Compromise men, and pronounce the doctrine of secession a vile heresy." The *American Law Register* (Oct., 1854), II, said that Campbell was "an exceedingly able man of whom the largest expectation will not be disappointed." The *New York Tribune*, May 4, 1856, termed Judge Campbell "a man who, though pure and unexceptionable in private life, is filled with all the dogmas and mad metaphysics of Mr. Calhoun, and whose best conception of the Constitution is that it is the *aegis* of slavery." The *Washington Union* said that "as a statesman and jurist his elevation is justly an occasion of congratulation to the country." *New York Evening Post*, March 25, 1853.

estate, prove true to the Constitution and to the Union
of States established by it . . . Past experience has
shown that, once in this exalted post and for life, the
professions of the partisan soon give place to the convictions and sense of high responsibilities of the jurist.
. . . It was so with the present Chief Justice, and so
with Justices Catron and Daniel, both, the nominees
of President Jackson on the score of warm party service
or devotion. . . . The highest-toned Federalists on the
Bench have been taken from the Democratic ranks, and
it will be strange if the views of a gentleman of first-rate
legal talent, like Mr. Campbell should prove less conservative." [1] The conservative Whig sentiment as to
the appointment was generously and favorably expressed by the unsuccessful candidate for Campbell's
position, George E. Badger, who, in a Senate debate,
two years later, speaking in advocacy of an increase of
salary for the Judges, praised "the two Juniors of the
Court, from the extreme points of the Union, North and
South, men of the highest character for learning, for integrity, for talent, for judicial propriety and decorum:
men who have been placed upon the Bench with the prospect of having a long career of usefulness to their country,
and of honor for themselves, men led by a natural and
honorable ambition, by a just professional pride, ele-
vating them above sordid consideration to accept a
position, the compensation of which does not exceed
the fourth of what their profession would have produced
and would have continued for many years to have
produced for them."

At this December, 1852, Term of the Court, two cases

---

[1] Compare this with Henry Adams' comment on judicial appointments at an
earlier period: "Jefferson and his party raised one Republican lawyer after
another to the Bench, only to find that, when their professions of political opinion
were tested in legal form, the Republican Judges rivalled Marshall in the Federalist
and English tendencies of his law." *History of the United States* (1898), II, 195.

may be noted as of historic interest. Negligence of a railroad — that topic in the law which later became so productive of litigation — was involved for the first time, in *Philadelphia and Reading R. R. Co.* v. *Derby*, 14 How. 468, in which case the Court spoke of the "powerful but dangerous agency of steam" and held that carriers must be held to the greatest possible care and diligence even in the transportation of gratuitous passengers, whose personal safety "should not be left to the sport of chance or the negligence of careless agents." Neutrality Laws were involved in *Kennett* v. *Chambers*, 14 How. 38, — a case of particular significance, owing to the fact that during this decade illegal military expeditions organized in this country in aid of revolutionary movements in Cuba and Nicaragua had frequently engaged the Government's attention. The Court held that a contract, made in 1836 after the independence of Texas but before it had been recognized by the United States, to furnish money to a Texas General for a military expedition from the United States, was invalid and unenforceable. When the contract was made, said Taney, "the constituted authorities were endeavoring to maintain untarnished the honor of the country, and to place it above the suspicion of taking any part in the conflict. . . . It was made in direct opposition to the policy of the government, to which it was the duty of every citizen to conform. . . . Every citizen . . . is bound to commit no act of hostility against a nation with which the government is in amity and friendship. This principle is universally acknowledged by the law of nations. It lies at the foundation of all government, as there could be no order or peaceful relations between the citizens of different countries without it." [1]

---

[1] Of this decision, the *National Intelligencer* said, Jan. 17, 1853: "Not to speak of its immediate effect upon existing contracts, bonds, and obligations which have been made, sold and bought in the prosecution of enterprises of the character,

The third case of note at the December, 1852, Term brought the Court again into contact with the dangerous question of the Fugitive Slave Law. The general defiance of this Law at the North during the past year, the refusal of State officials and others to aid in its enforcement, the State legislative impediments, the rescue of slaves from the lawful custody of Federal officials, had rightly and naturally alarmed and enraged the Southern States, and had resulted in many indictments under their laws punishing the harboring or secretion of fugitive slaves. In *Moore* v. *Illinois*, 14 How. 13, the validity of one of these laws was now upheld by the Court. Though this decision added to the anger of the anti-slavery forces, sanely thinking men could not deny that conditions justified, and even required, such legislation. "Experience has shown," said Judge Grier in his opinion, "that the results of such conduct as that prohibited by the statute in question are not only to demoralize their citizens who live in daily and open disregard of the duties imposed upon them by the Constitution and laws, but to destroy the harmony and kind feelings which should exist between citizens of this Union, to create border feuds and bitter animosities, and to cause breaches of the peace, violent assaults, riots and murder. No one can deny or doubt the right of a State to defend itself against evils of such magnitude, and punish those who perversely persist in conduct which promotes them."

At the next Term, in the spring of 1854, the Court

justly reprobated by this decision, it is easy to foresee how extensive will be its influence in the future, not only upon the action of individuals, but upon the habits of thinking of no inconsiderable portion of our fellow citizens, in regard to the duties of individuals to respect and obey the neutral obligations of their country." See also charges of Judge Campbell to the grand jury in the Circuit Court in Louisiana in 1854, *John Archibald Campbell* (1920), by Henry G. Connor; *Philadelphia North American*, Feb. 11, 1860; see also charges to the Grand Jury in the Circuit Court in Indiana, May 1851, Federal Cases No. 18266, 5 McLean, 249; in Ohio, Oct. 1858, Federal Cases No. 8267, 5 McLean, 306; in 1859, Federal Cases No. 18268.

was confronted with another delicate political issue —
the anti-corporation movement — in several cases involving the right of banking corporations to exemption
from taxation.   It was an unfortunate chance that this
question now arose in Ohio — a State in which the anti-
slavery sentiment was the strongest, and in which hostility to the Federal Courts on that issue was already
most pronounced; for a decision rendered against the
State in reference to these corporations was certain to
be met with enhanced opposition.   Privileges granted
to banks, railroads and other corporations had long been
a point of attack by the Democratic Party.   The numerous exemptions from taxation granted in corporate
charters by State Legislatures during the past fifteen
years had been a source of complaint and scandal.   The
right of a Legislature so to bind its successor had been
hotly denied.   A case brought to test this right, *Piqua
Branch of the State Bank of Ohio* v. *Knoop*, 16 How. 369,
was now argued on April 19–21, 1854, by Henry Stan-
bery against Rufus P. Spalding and George E. Pugh.
The Bank, holding a charter containing a provision for
exemption from certain taxation, claimed that a later
statute, which imposed a tax, was an impairment of the
obligation of the State's contract.   The State claimed
that no Legislature had the power, by a tax exemption,
to relinquish part of the sovereign authority of the
State.   Immense financial interests all over the country
depended on the decision of the Court.   On May 24,
1854, the Court, through Judge McLean, rendered its
decision declaring the law unconstitutional and holding
that: "A State, in granting privileges to a bank with
a view of affording a sound currency, or of advancing
any policy connected with a public interest, exercises
its sovereignty, and for a public purpose, of which it is
exclusive judge;" and that those privileges, proffered

by the State, accepted by the stockholders and in consideration of which funds were invested in the Bank, constituted a contract, " founded upon considerations of policy required by the general interests of the community" and which must be protected.   In closing, Judge McLean stated that he would not discuss general theories of Government, which were "an unsafe rule for judicial action.   Our prosperity, individually and Nationally, depends upon a close adherence to the settled rules of law and especially to the great fundamental law of the Union."   The four Democratic Judges, the Chief Justice, Catron, Daniel and Campbell, filed a strong dissenting opinion, largely directed at the dangers of protecting the growth of corporate power; they held that the Courts of Ohio had already decided that the statute granting the charter did not constitute a contract for the tax exemption claimed by the Bank, and that no Legislature could legally place a portion of the sovereign political power beyond the reach of subsequent Legislatures, unless so authorized by the State Constitution.   Judge Campbell further pointed out that : " The discussions before this Court in the Indiana Railroad and the Baltimore Railroad cases exposed to us the sly and stealthy arts to which State Legislatures are exposed, and the greedy appetites of adventurers for monopolies and immunities from the State right of Government.   We cannot close our eyes to their insidious efforts to ignore the fundamental laws and institutions of the States, and to subject the highest popular interests to their central boards of control and directors' management." [1]

[1] At the December, 1853, Term, the growth of the lobby evil in the country had been strikingly shown in *Marshall* v. *Baltimore & Ohio R. R.*, 16 How. 314, in which the Court refused its aid to enforce a contract for a railroad agent's services before a Virginia Legislature.   Judge Grier, after adverting to logrolling and other lobby methods, said that "legislators should act with a single eye to 'the true interest of.

The decision upholding the corporate exemption from taxation produced a great sensation, not only in Ohio, but in many States whose Legislature had granted similar exemptions to State banks. "An important and extraordinary decision," said the *Cincinnati Enquirer*. " The Supreme Court has always leaned strongly to the Federal idea of a strong National Government, and has been very conservative in maintaining and carrying out the old English common law principle of the sacredness of corporations and their immunity from legislation." In a later issue, it referred to " this outrageous decision by the truly Federal Court. The sober mind may begin to wonder how this unrighteousness can possibly be imposed upon a community in a democratic or, if you please, in a republican form of Government." It attacked the Court as a "silk-gowned fogydom, a goodly portion of it imbecile with age, a portion anti-republican in notions, a portion wedded to the antiquated doctrine of established precedents, no matter whether truth or fallacy." It contended, against the decision, that a Legislature could not give or barter away the sovereignty of the people; and it exclaimed: "People of Ohio, you see where you stand! . . . A crisis is here now, if it had not already been reached, and as this is the 'year of storms', look out for the greatest one yet to come." Again it said that the decision was clearly "an invasion of State sovereignty and a great outrage upon State-Rights —

the whole people, and Courts of Justice can give no countenance to the use of means which may subject them to be misled by the pertinacious importunity and indirect influences of interested and unscrupulous agents of solicitors. . . . The use of such means and such agents will have the effect to subject the State Governments to the combined capital of wealthy corporations and produce universal corruption, commencing with the representative and ending with the elector;" and the *New York Evening Post* referring to the decision said, Jan. 11, 1855, that it was "a melancholy thing to observe to what an extent the practice of corrupting and cajoling legislative bodies is carried on in this country by men who still preserve what is regarded as a respectable standing in society."

yet how is it to be met? It is the Court of last resort, and a large class of people have reluctance to being placed in any position that would cause any resistance to its judgment." [1] That the Court itself, however, realized the strength of the anti-corporation sentiment then prevailing in the country, as well as the grounds for its existence, and that it was not inclined to uphold corporate privilege in any case where such privilege was not clearly shown to be guaranteed by a State contract was shown in another Ohio bank case decided at this Term, *Ohio Life Insurance Company* v. *Debolt*, 16 How. 416. In this case, it held that the charter, properly construed, contained no such contract of tax exemption, and it pointed out in great detail many of the corporate evils of that day. Chief Justice Taney, referring to the doctrine that a charter carried nothing by implication, sagely said that the rule was "founded in principles of justice, and necessary for the safety and well-being of every State in the Union. For it is a matter of public history which this Court cannot refuse to notice, that almost every bill for the incorporation of banking companies, insurance and trust companies, railroad companies and other corporations, is drawn originally by the parties who are personally interested in obtaining the charter; and that they are often passed by the Legislature in the last days of its session, when, from the nature of our political institutions, the business is unavoidably transacted in a hurried manner, and it is impossible that every member can deliberately examine every provision in every bill upon which he is called to act. On the other hand, those who accept the charter have abundant time to examine and consider its provisions, before they invest their money. If they mean to claim under it any peculiar privileges, or any ex-

[1] *Cincinnati Enquirer*, May 26, 30, June 2, 1854.

emption from the burden of taxation, it is their duty to see that the right or exemption they intend to claim is granted in clear and unambiguous language." Judge Catron also spoke of " the unparalleled increase of corporations throughout the Union within the last few years; the ease with which charters containing exclusive privileges and exemptions are obtained; the vast amount of property, power and exclusive benefits, prejudicial to other classes of society, that are vested in and held by these bodies of associated wealth."

Two years later, however, the antagonism of the people of Ohio towards the Court was still further excited by a decision which carried the doctrine of the *Piqua Branch Case* to an even greater extreme; for in *Dodge* v. *Woolsey*, 18 How. 331, in 1856, the Court was confronted with the question whether a State Constitution containing a repeal of a prior statutory tax exemption was valid. After the Piqua Branch suit had been brought, involving the validity of a statute repealing a tax exemption, the people of Ohio amended their Constitution and inserted in it such a repeal clause. Suit to test this action had been instituted in a Federal Circuit Court by a stockholder, alleging that the directors of his bank were about to pay the tax, in spite of their belief in its invalidity. Thus confronted for the first time with the solemn question of its power to hold a Constitution of a sovereign State to be invalid, the Court did not flinch in its determination to hold a State to strict compliance with honesty in contracts; and accordingly it rendered its decision that the people of a State could no more impair the obligation of contracts by means of a Constitution than by a statute, and that the tax was consequently still invalid. "The moral obligations never die," it said. "If broken by States and Nations, though the terms of reproach are not the same

with which we are accustomed to designate the faith-
lessness of individuals, the violation of justice is not the
less." [1] A strong dissent was again filed by Judges
Campbell, Catron and Daniel, the former denouncing
"these extraordinary pretensions of corporations. . . .
They display a love of power, a preference for corporate
interests to moral or political principles or public duties,
and an antagonism to individual freedom, which have
marked them as objects of jealousy in every epoch of their
history." And he said that the consequence of establishing this "caste" would be "a new element of alienation and discord between the different classes of society,
and the introduction of a fresh cause of disturbance in
our distracted political and social system. In the end,
the doctrine of this decision may lead to a violent over-
turn of the whole system of corporate combinations."
The Ohio newspapers followed the dissenting Judges, in
prophesying future trouble from corporate wealth and
combination, and deplored the alleged tendency of the
Court to decide against the State, when "corporate
pretensions come in conflict with the sovereignty of the
people." "Whatever may be the excellencies of the
Supreme Court, and we are not disposed to deny that
they are many," said a leading paper, "a disposition
to curtail and limit corporation privileges, and to regard them with a jealous eye in their judicial action,
was never among them." And this paper earnestly
advised the banks, "having vanquished the State, to
waive voluntarily their obnoxious privilege. . . . We
are confident that it would be for their interest so to do,
as it would allay a well-founded public disgust at an

[1] The *New York Tribune*, April 9, 1856, said of the decision : "The case involved
the whole power of taxation and therefore was treated as one of the most important
ever considered." In *Sandusky City Bank* v. *Weber*, 7 Ohio State Rep. 48, the Ohio
Court held that the decision in *Dodge* v. *Woolsey* was not binding upon it, since
that case arose in the Federal Circuit Court.

odious distinction that cannot be sustained upon any principle of justice or equality." [1]

The gravity of the situation which was produced in Ohio by these decisions is seen from the fact that, for over two years from the date of the Piqua Branch decision, the Supreme Court of Ohio refused to enter the mandate of the Supreme Court of the United States. Finally, late in 1856, three Judges of the State Supreme Court decided to conform to the mandate which had been issued to it, stating that they were "not prepared to adopt the theory" on which a denial of the jurisdiction of the Supreme Court under the Judiciary Act was based. The State Chief Justice, dissenting, however, said that the doctrine of the decision in its "enormities and alarming import . . . wholly prostrates the municipal sovereignty of the people with the State." [2] Meanwhile, the same Chief Justice, sitting in the State District Court, in another case,[3] rendered a decision wholly denying the validity of the appellate jurisdiction of the United States Supreme Court under the Twenty-Fifth Section of the Judiciary Act, and overruling a motion to perfect the record of the State Court, so that the case might be taken up on writ of error.

While this serious attempt to derogate from the power

[1] *Cincinnati Daily Enquirer*, April 11, 1856. See also *Ohio Statesman*, Jan. 16, 1857.

[2] See for the Ohio decisions, *Ohio* v. *Commercial Bank*, 7 Ohio, Part I, 125; *Bank* v. *Knoop*, 1 Ohio State, 603; 6 Ohio State, 343; and *The Supreme Court and State Repudiation*, by John N. Pomeroy, *Amer. Law Rev.* (1883), XVII.

The seriousness of the situation may be seen from a description of Ohio conditions given in a California case, a few years later, *Warner* v. *Steamship Uncle Sam* (1858), 9 Calif. 697: "That State, for several years past, has been arrayed in hostility to the General Government; that this hostility has exhibited itself in the Legislative, the Judicial and the Executive departments of that State; that actual resistance to Federal authority on the part of the people is of common occurrence and is sanctioned and encouraged by legislative enactment, and justified by judicial decision — a part of a general system of resistance to the Constitution and laws of the United States, which has already led to the verge of civil war."

[3] *Stunt* v. *The Ohio* (1855), 3 Ohio Decisions Reprints, 362.

of the Court was taking place in the Central West, an
actual judicial decision denying the Court's jurisdiction
was made in the new and distant State of California.
In 1854, the Supreme Court of that State in *Johnson* v.
Gordon, 4 Calif. 368, refused to allow a writ of error to
the Supreme Court of the United States to a party
desiring to appeal from the decision of the State Court.
It held that acquiescence by other States in the exercise by that Court of jurisdiction over State Court
decisions did not constitute a sufficient reason for "the
surrender of a power which belongs to the sovereignty
we represent, involving an assumption of that power by
another jurisdiction in derogation of that sovereignty.
We think, too, that the acquiescence in this usurpation of the Federal Tribunal, under an Act of Congress
not warranted by the Constitution, is not so much owing
to a conviction of its propriety, as it is to the high character of the Court, and the general correctness of its
decisions." This hostile attitude towards the Court in
California was probably due to the peculiar isolated
situation of litigation in that State, at that period, when
there was absence of railroad communication, and little
contact with the rest of the Union ; and the inhabitants
felt, as counsel argued in the *Johnson Case*, that the
jurisdiction of the State Courts over these matters was
particularly important :   " The delays and expense of
the Federal Courts, especially where great monopolies
are concerned, able to carry cases to the Supreme Court,
make litigation in these forums almost a denial of justice." Such an attack upon the supremacy of the
United States Supreme Court, however, was not long
tolerated in California ; for, the next year, on April 9,
1855, the Legislature, by a nearly unanimous vote of
both branches, passed a law to enforce compliance with
the sections of the Federal Judiciary Act by Judges and

Clerks of Courts; and in 1858, the Supreme Court of California reversed its ruling — Judges Joseph V. Baldwin and Stephen J. Field (later a Judge of the United States Supreme Court) recognizing the validity of the Twenty-Fifth Section of the Judiciary Act,[1] and stating that : " A long course of adjudication by Courts of the highest authority, State and National, commencing almost from the foundation of the Government, and the acquiescence of nearly all the State Governments in all of their departments, have given to this doctrine a recognition so strong and authentic that we feel no disposition to deny it at this late day, even if the reasons for such denial were more cogent than they seem to us to be." [2]

While Ohio and California, in 1854, were thus placed by their Courts in open opposition to the Supreme Court of the United States, they were joined by the State of Wisconsin. The case which led to this unfortunate condition arose out of the rescue of a fugitive slave from Missouri by an abolitionist editor named Booth and

[1] *Ferris* v. *Coover* (1858), 11 Calif. 175; see also *Warner* v. *Steamship Uncle Sam* (1858), 9 Calif. 697.

[2] The opposite view, however, was maintained by the Chief Justice of the Court — David S. Terry, who used the following quite unjustifiable language : "It has never been admitted in Virginia, has always been repudiated by Georgia, and has lately been questioned in several other States. The decisions of the United States Supreme Court on this question embody the political principles of a party which has passed away. . . . The force and authority of the opinions of the Supreme Court of the United States upon the question of jurisdiction, as well as all others of a political nature, is much weakened, by the consideration that the political sentiments of the Judges in such cases necessarily gave direction to the decisions of the Courts. The Legislative and Executive power of the Government had passed, or was rapidly passing into the hands of men entertaining opposite principles. Regarding the Judicial as the conservative department; believing the possession by the General Government of greater powers than those expressly granted by the Constitution to be absolutely necessary to its stability, they sought, by a latitudinarian construction of its provisions, to remedy the defects in that instrument, and by a course of judicial decisions to give direction to the future policy of the Union. Hoary usurpations of power and jurisdiction on the part of the Federal Judiciary, or time-honored encroachments on the reserved rights of the sovereign States, are entitled to no additional respect on account of their antiquity, and should be as little regarded by the State tribunals as if they were but things of yesterday."

various other citizens of Wisconsin.[1] Booth, having
been arrested on a warrant issued by a United States Commissioner for violation of the Federal Fugitive Slave Law,
and having been taken into custody by a United States
marshal, had been discharged on a writ of habeas corpus
issued by a Judge of the Wisconsin Supreme Court, on
the ground that the Federal statute was unconstitutional. This extraordinary interference of a State
Judge with a Federal marshal's custody having been
sustained by the full bench of the State Supreme Court,
the marshal, Ableman, at once sued out a writ of error
to the United States Supreme Court, returnable in
December, 1854, and the record was duly certified by
State Court Clerk. In January, 1855, Booth was indicted, tried, convicted and sentenced in the United
States District Court for violation of the Fugitive Slave
Law; but he was at once released, on another writ of
habeas corpus issued by the State Supreme Court. And
this Court proceeded to hold that the Federal Court
had been without jurisdiction, the Law being invalid.[2]
This direct collision between State and Federal authority raised once more the old issue of Nullification. The
doctrines formerly advocated by South Carolina were
now maintained by the anti-slavery party in the North,
and its newspapers now openly counseled disobedience
to the Federal Courts and to the Federal laws.[3] "The

[1] The New York Evening Post, April 8, 1854, said that Booth, when arrested and
brought before the magistrate, stated that "rather than have the great constitutional rights and safeguards of the people, the writ of habeas corpus and the right
of trial by jury stricken down by the Fugitive law, I would prefer to see every
Federal officer in Wisconsin hanged on a gallows fifty cubits higher than Haman."

[2] In re Booth, 3 Wisc. 1, 49, the case was ably argued by Byron Paine for Booth
against Edward G. Ryan for Ableman (both Paine and Ryan becoming later Judges
of the Wisconsin Supreme Court); see A Historic Judicial Controversy, by Stephen
S. Gregory, Michigan Law Rev. (1913), I; Story of a Great Court (1912), by J. B.
Winslow; The Fugitive Slave Law in Wisconsin, by Vroman Mason, State Hist. Soc.
Proc. (1895); and see also authorities cited in State Documents on Federal Relations
(1911), by Herman V. Ames, 304.

[3] New York Tribune, Feb. 2, 7, 8, 26, Aug. 1, 10, 1855. Charles Sumner wrote,

North is just now taking lessons in Southern jurisprudence," said the *New York Tribune*. "South Carolina, Georgia and little Florida have, at one time and another, displayed a glorious independence of Federal legislation, whenever it suited their purposes. We trust that, under the influence of such illustrious examples, the States of the North may be excused for an occasional assertion of their notion of their own rights. We doubt not that it is the opinion of a large majority of the people of the free States that the existing Fugitive Slave Law is unconstitutional, and their present aim is to make their State Court so declare it and adhere to the declaration. We are a law abiding people. But we purpose to have laws fit to abide by, and Courts fit to be obeyed. The difficulty has always been, and now is, that our Northern Courts derive their inspirations from a Federal slavery-upholding Court. Our local Judiciary has been poisoned by the virus of a National Bench, whereon sits a majority in the interest of the peculiar institution. But happily a most refreshing example of the independence of this influence is to be seen in the late action of the Supreme Court of Wisconsin. The Judges of that State have won a lasting title to regard and admiration by their late decision in the case of Booth and Ryecroft, and this Congress will have to legislate fast and long in order to deprive them of it. The example which Wisconsin has set will be as rapidly followed as circumstances admit. By another year, we expect to see Ohio holding the same noble course. After that, we anticipate a race among the other Free States in the same direction, till all have reached the goal of

Aug. 5, 1854, to Byron Paine: "God grant that Wisconsin may not fail to protect her own right and the rights of her citizens in the emergency now before it. To her belongs the lead which Massachusetts should have taken." See *New York Evening Post*, May 10, 1854, for conflict between Federal and State authorities in a habeas corpus case in Pennsylvania involving fugitive slaves; *U. S. ex rel. Crossman* v. *Allen; ibid.*, April 9, 1855, as to a similar conflict in Ohio.

State independence. By that time, we expect to see the United States Court so constituted that all pre-existing conflicts will have been ended. Improper decisions will have been reserved, and truth and justice commence their sway. . . . Let the North but maintain its high purpose, its unflinching resolve that it will not submit to slave-driving dictation, whether coming through Courts pledged to the support of that institution, or in whatever way it may show itself; and the usurpations enacted by Congress will be torn to ribbons and its impudently unconstitutional laws defied. All that is wanting to this end is independent State Courts, fearless Legislatures, Governors with backbones and a determined people behind them." Again, in urging that active measures be taken " against the usurpation of the slave power ", it preached still more boldly a policy of Nullification, saying: "The North must learn to act as well as talk. . . . Wisconsin has taken one step in the true path. . . . It has always been the doctrine of the State-Rights or old Democratic party that the States had the right to judge of infraction of the Constitution, and in a case of importance to decide upon the mode and measure of redress. . . . The Free States may rightfully retaliate . . . by the overthrow and destruction of slavery itself. They are rightfully entitled to exercise this power under the Constitution, as expounded by its great authors." And again it said that " the Republican Party naturally stand on the State-Rights doctrine of Jefferson." [1]

Similar attempts by State Courts and State officials to interfere with the operation of the Federal Courts in Ohio and in Pennsylvania, about this time, were defeated by the firm action of the Federal Judges.

[1] See also editorial in *New York Tribune*, Jan. 29, 1856, entitled "A Star in the West."

In the former State, Judge McLean himself was called upon to sustain the supremacy of the Fugitive Slave Law over State action. In *Ex parte Robinson*, 6 McLean, 355, in April, 1855, a United States marshal had been imprisoned by a State Court, for re-arresting a fugitive slave whom the State Court, by a writ of habeas corpus, had taken from the marshal's lawful custody; the marshal sued out a writ of habeas corpus in the United States Circuit Court, under a Federal statute enacted in 1833 giving to the Federal Court the power to issue such a writ in cases of persons confined by State officials for an act done under authority of Federal law. Judge McLean, in spite of his anti-slavery views, granted the writ, and ordered the marshal's release by the State Court. The statute authorizing the writ, he said "was enacted to meet the Nullification doctrines proclaimed by South Carolina, but which in this respect, it is believed, were never acted upon by that State. Little was it supposed that the principle could ever have a necessary application to the Northern or Western States, whose Members of Congress advocated and voted for the law." Interference by a State Court with a case in a Federal Court before it was terminated was, he said, "unprecedented in judicial proceedings;" and he continued with this warning to the States: "There need be no apprehensions of the public peace being disturbed for any want of respect by the Federal authorities to the State Courts. State-Rights are invoked by the counsel. If these Rights are construed to mean a subversion of the Federal authorities, they may be somewhat in danger." [1]

Another case of assertion of Federal supremacy, which

[1] See denunciatory editorial in *New York Tribune*, April 18, 1855, entitled "Judge McLean's Jail Delivery."

arose in Pennsylvania in the summer of 1855 and which caused intense excitement, presented the following singular facts. While John H. Wheeler, the United States Minister to Nicaragua, was proceeding with his slaves from Washington to New York in order to embark for his post, certain abolitionists headed by Passmore Williamson deliberately took the slaves from his possession; Wheeler sued out a writ of habeas corpus against Williamson whom he alleged to be in control, of the rescued slaves. Williamson, denying having such control, declined to comply with the writ; and for this action he was sentenced to imprisonment for contempt of Court by United States District Judge Kane. Application was made by Williamson to the Supreme Court of Pennsylvania for a writ of habeas corpus to release him from the Federal sentence. Insistent demands were made by the abolitionist press that the State Court should assert its authority. That Court, however, declined thus to interfere with the Federal Judiciary. In a powerful opinion by Judge Jeremiah S. Black, it said that the District Court had power and jurisdiction to decide what actions constituted a contempt against it, and that:

Such conviction for contempt must be final, otherwise Courts totally unconnected with each other would be coming in constant collision. . . . There may be cases in which we ought to check usurpation of power by the Federal Courts. . . . But what we would not permit them to do against us, we will not do against them. We must maintain the rights of the State and its Courts, for to them alone can the people look for a competent administration of their domestic concerns; but we will do nothing to impair the constitutional vigour of the General Government, which is the "sheet-anchor of our peace at home and our safety abroad."

Judge Lowry also delivered an opinion in the case saying: "In the name of the order which we represent and enforce, I decline any and every usurpation of power or control over the United States, it being a system collateral to ours, as complete and efficient in its organization, and as legitimate and final authority as any other." [1]

The decisions of Judge Kane and of Judge Black were bitterly assailed by the *New York Tribune* and other similar papers, and the impeachment of Kane was insistently demanded. "A system of insolent and alarming usurpation" must be terminated, it was said: "It is high time that the insolence and tyranny of our Federal Judges should be rebuked and punished."

With such views prevalent in many of the Northern States, it now became evident that, if the supremacy of the Federal Government and of its officials was to be preserved, additional legislation was necessary for the enforcement of this supremacy. Accordingly, early in 1855, Senator Toucey of Connecticut introduced a bill in Congress to provide for the removal into the Federal Courts of any suit against a Federal officer, instituted in a State Court, for any act done under a Federal law or authority or color thereof. Although, twenty years later, this precise law was enacted by the Republican Party when it desired to enforce against the South the unpopular Reconstruction Acts, nevertheless, in 1855 it was denounced by Republican statesmen, as an instrument designed to enforce the monstrous Fugitive Slave Law. In opposition to its passage, the Virginia and Kentucky Resolutions of 1798–1799 were cited with approval, and all the State-Rights doctrines, against which the Whig Party had fought from 1800 to 1840, were now adopted by the anti-slavery men with ardor.

[1] See *United States* v. *Williamson*, Federal Cases Nos. 16725, 16726, July 27, Oct. 15, 1855; *Passmore Williamson's Case* (1855), 26 Penn. State, 9; *New York Tribune*, July 28, Aug. 28, 29, Nov. 5, 1855, and *passim* through July, August and September, 1855.

The bill was termed "a dangerous and preposterous usurpation of authority" by the Federal Government, an attempt "to abrogate the functions and jurisdiction of the State tribunals not for a moment to be tolerated", a bill to "bring the Judiciary of every State bound in chains to the foot of Federal power, and which ought to be spurned by the most vigorous assertion of the reserved powers of the States." [1]   Salmon P. Chase of Ohio called it "a bill to establish a great, central, consolidated Federal Government. It is a step — a stride rather — towards despotism"; and William H. Seward of New York, William P. Fessenden of Maine and Charles Sumner of Massachusetts argued similarly against the usurpation of the Federal Government and its Judiciary. "It will promote collisions between Federal and State jurisdiction — conflicts in which the States will never yield," said Benjamin F. Wade of Ohio. "Wisconsin has taught you a lesson, and it is only an incipient step. . . .   State after State will fall in the wake of noble Wisconsin. . . .   This is a most unfortunate time further to irritate a people, almost driven to desperation by what they consider your Federal usurpations. . . .   I am no advocate for Nullification," he continued, "but in the nature of things, according to the true interpretation of our institutions, a State, in the last resort, crowded to the wall by the General Government seeking by the strong arm of its power to take away the rights of the State, is to judge of whether she shall stand on her reserved rights. . . . Wisconsin has availed herself of those great principles that Virginia asserted in times of danger."

Such sentiments were, of course, those of Nullifica-

[1] *33d Cong., 2d Sess., App.,* 210 *et seq.,* Feb. 23, 1855. *Philadelphia North American,* Feb. 26, 1855. The *New York Tribune,* Feb. 19, 27, 1855, termed the bill "The New Outrage", and a bill "under a very innocent title . . . for the better protection of negro-hunters."

tion, pure and simple. "The Senator from Ohio has raised in the Senate Chamber the standard of rebellion again against the Court," said Stephen A. Douglas of Illinois; and Judah P. Benjamin of Louisiana asked: "Who would ever have expected, a few years ago, to have heard it said in the Senate of the United States by Senators from the North, that State tribunals were vested with jurisdiction in the last resort to determine upon the constitutionality of laws enacted by the Congress of the United States, that their decisions were of greater weight and entitled to higher respect than the decision of the Supreme Court of the United States?" The bill passed the Senate, but was not acted upon in the House.

Antagonism to the Court cropped out at this session of Congress, in 1855, in connection with two other measures. A bill to increase the Judges' salaries was defeated, as Senator Badger said, simply because the Judges of the Supreme Court on Circuit "had done their duty in enforcing a law obnoxious to public opinion", — the Fugitive Slave Law.[1] The subject of slavery was also responsible for the defeat of a renewed attempt (similar to those made in 1826, in 1835 and in 1844) to reform the Judiciary system by establishing additional Circuits. The urgent need of this reform, owing to the great expansion in territory and the enormous increase of the Court's business, had become so clear that President Pierce, in his messages to Congress in 1853 and 1854, had urged immediate legislation. While the bill,

---

[1] *33d Cong., 2d Sess.*, Jan. 11, 1855. In showing the need for increase of salary, Senator Badger pointed out the fact that, in the six years beginning in 1809 and ending in 1815, the Court sat 206 days and decided 235 cases — an average of 30 days and 39 cases a year; in the six years between 1822 and 1827, the Court sat 263 days and decided 194 cases, an average of 44 days and 32 cases a year; but in the six years from 1848 to 1853 the Court had sat 664 days and decided 448 cases — an average of 110 days and 74 cases a year. See also *National Intelligencer*, Dec. 20, 1854.

so advocated, establishing eleven (instead of nine) Circuits, and relieving the Judges of Circuit Court duty, met with opposition based on the old argument that "if you shut the Judges up here, they become a centralized metropolitan Court, almost as shut out from public view as the Veiled Prophet was," and that the Judges should mingle with the local Bars and not remain in Washington to become "mere paper Judges, losing weight of authority and knowledge of local legislation and practice", nevertheless, in spite of these oft-repeated arguments, the bill would probably have passed, had it not now encountered another element of opposition — the fear of the anti-slavery men lest President Pierce should make the two new appointments in the interests of slavery.[1] It is interesting to note, however, that an opening wedge for the abolition of Circuit duty by the Supreme Court Judges was effected by the passage of a singular Act at this session of Congress, establishing a Circuit Court of the United States for California and Oregon with a separate Circuit Judge who should not be a member of the Supreme Court. This anomaly in the Federal Judicial system was made necessary by the fact that, as there was then no railroad communication between the Pacific Coast and the East, no Supreme Court Judge sitting in the Circuit could perform his duties in Washington.[2]

At the next sessions of Congress during the spring and winter of 1856, the abolitionist campaign against

---

[1] *33d Cong., 2d Sess.*, Jan. 5, 17, 18, 1855. The *New York Evening Post*, Jan. 12, 1855, said that the relief of the Supreme Court Judges from Circuit duty and their reduction in number from nine to six was generally favored. "There are, however, a few Senators who oppose any change in the present system until a more thorough reform can be effected — to secure, for instance, the substitution of a term of years for that of good behavior. They think that decisions infringing the inherent personal and political rights of the people would not come from a Bench, liable to a rejection every eight years."

[2] *33d Cong., 2d Sess.*, Feb. 6, 7, 12, 1855.

the Court was continued with increasing fervor throughout the debate on the admission of Kansas as a State.[1]
Again and again, Hale used his favorite characterization
of it as "the citadel of slavery"; Seward in the Senate
and Bennett in the House reiterated the charge that the
majority of the Judges were appointed in the slavery
interests; Giddings asserted the doctrine of the right,
both of Congressmen and of individuals, to refrain from
executing, and to disregard and disobey, a law deemed
unconstitutional. On the other side, the Democrats
reaffirmed their entire willingness to leave the question
of the power of Congress over slavery in the Territories
to the Court, and to abide by its decision, and stated
that it was the duty of Congress not to forestall by legislation a judicial decision, and "not to coerce and dra-
goon that Court in the decision of a constitutional
question which is purely judicial."[2] Hale's diatribes
were warmly refuted. "For purity, integrity, virtue,
honor, and all that ennobles and dignifies, it stands un-
impeached and unimpeachable," said James C. Jones
of Tennessee. "The Judges are the sentinels and defenders of the Constitution; they do not decide by the
'higher law' of discretion and prejudice," said Andrew
P. Butler of South Carolina, Chairman of the Senate
Judiciary Committee. "I have never known a body
of men more honestly disposed to do their duty. . . .
I would rather regard that high tribunal as one which
could look abroad upon the vast and beautiful horizon
of truth and justice. I should not wish to see them
governed by that popular agitation which is threatening

[1] *34th Cong., 1st Sess.*, and *App.; 34th Cong., 3d Sess.*, and *App.;* see speeches
in 1856 of Hale, Feb. 26, May 2, Dec. 11, Seward, May 2, Trumbull, Dec. 2, Wade,
Dec. 4, in the Senate; Henry Bennett of New York, June 30, J. A. Bingham of Ohio,
Jan. 13, 15, and many others in the House.

[2] See speeches of Benjamin, May 2, Douglas, June 9, Geyer, April 7, Cass, May
12, Dec. 11, Jones, Feb. 25, Butler, March 5, Rusk, Dec. 4, Jones, Dec. 18, in the
Senate; David Ritchie, April 24, in the House.

to undermine the institutions of the country. . . . I wish it to stand firm, at least, as the type of the duration of the institutions of this country, and as an emblem of eternal justice." The falseness of the charge that the Court was controlled by the slavery interests was palpable. For, since the year 1840, when the slavery question first became a heated issue, the only appointments to the Bench had been those of Judges Grier, Nelson, Curtis and Campbell, of whom only one — Campbell — was from the South or of pro-slavery views, and that one simply succeeded Judge McKinley, who held like opinions on the subject. All the other Judges had been appointed to the Bench before the slavery question had become a vivid political and sectional issue. Moreover, the Judges had on numerous occasions proved their impartiality and lack of sectional bias in cases involving slavery decided by them since 1840 — the *Prigg Case*, a decision held by both South and North to be opposed to the respective interests of each — *Groves* v. *Slaughter* upholding the exclusive right of each State to deal with slavery within its borders, the *Passenger Cases* affecting laws both of the South and North, the *Missouri-Iowa Boundary Line Cases*. So far as the charge that Judges were appointed or were acting for political reasons was concerned, the South had more just reason to complain than the North; for the only Judge who had taken an active part in politics, or who had openly expressed his views on crucial political questions was a Northern Judge — John McLean of Ohio. In practically every campaign since his appointment to the Bench, Judge McLean had been, either actively or passively, a candidate for the Presidency; his name had been balloted for at several conventions; and he entertained and publicly expressed positive, though somewhat unusual, views as to the entire propriety of

a Judge being a candidate for that office.[1]   Moreover,
Judge McLean had not hesitated to write for publication
in the newspapers his views on burning political questions of the day.   Such a letter written in 1847, containing an attack upon the Mexican War, had given rise to
a criticism of the bitterest kind from men and newspapers of both political parties, who deprecated activities of this nature on the part of a member of the Judiciary.[2]   In 1848, McLean had committed a more
serious breach of judicial propriety, by writing a letter,
which was published, expressing his views as to the
power of Congress over slavery in the territories — a
question which the Clayton Compromise Bill, in that
very year, proposed should be submitted to the Court

[1] See letter of McLean to Gen. Duff Green, Sept. 16, 1829 (*John McLean Papers
MSS*): "I did not suppose that you or any other person who had reflected upon
the subject could entertain the least apprehension of any improper influence being
used by a Judge who comes before the people in a popular election, and especially
that it could lend to corrupt the Bench.   This has not been realized in the election
of Judges to the offices of Governor and Senator in Congress. . . .   By what
process of reasoning you could come to such a result, I cannot imagine.   Sure I am
that facts cannot aid you, however much might be gained by popular prejudice.
So far from a Judge occupying a position which gives him a commanding influence
in a popular election, it is without exception the most unfavorable post a candidate
can occupy.   He has no patronage to dispense.   In every decision he gives,
he disappoints one party and his counsel, who, though restrained in their
expressions of resentment against him as Judge, would gladly in the exercise of their
right of suffrage show their disapprobation.   And if the Judge can be supposed to
be influenced in any decision by popular consideration, his popularity is at once
destroyed.   A Judge can do nothing to advance his prospects which will not certainly destroy him.   For the reasons stated he would be the last person to unite the
Bar in his support.   In the event of his being before the people, he would necessarily act with the utmost circumspection and not only avoid the least ground for
an unfavorable imputation, but even the appearance of impropriety."

[2] See McLean's letter to the *National Intelligencer*, Dec. 28, 1847, quoted in speech
of Dickinson, Aug. 1, 1848; *30th Cong., 1st Sess.*   See among numerous criticisms,
the *National Intelligencer*, Jan. 31, 1848, which said that the Judge was "dragging
the ermine in the mire of politics"; the *Pennsylvanian*, Feb. 1, said that the letter
was entitled to "indignant censure"; the *Mississippian*, Feb. 18, said it was written
by a man "bereft of patriotism . . . unfit for the exalted station he holds"; the
Mississippi Free Trader, Feb. 8, said he had "stained his ermine with the bitter
waters of party"; the *Boston Post*, Feb. 7, said it was a "most melancholy exhibition of a partisan Judge . . . a display of party violence on the bench"; the
Washington Union, Feb. 3, said: "He deserves impeachment at the bar of
public opinion"; the *Trenton True American*, Feb. 4, termed him "a judicial
politician."

for decision. For this action, the Judge was justly, though savagely, attacked in Congress by Senator Foote of Mississippi, as having been "guilty of high offense against public decency"; [1] and while the Judge was defended by Senator Corwin and Senator Reverdy Johnson, the latter was forced to say that: "The judgment of the public, in its almost universal censure of the step, will effectually guard against its repetition. A Judge should be separated, not only while he is upon the Bench, but forever, from all the agitating political topics of the day. Once a Judge, he should ever be a Judge. The ermine should never be polluted, not suspected of pollution; it should be the very type of Justice herself — pure, spotless, faultless." And a representative of a Democratic paper in Philadelphia said that: "The good sense of the whole country condemns this offensive intermingling in politics . . . and the moral sense of the country revolts at the solemn prejudgment of questions, which, in all probability, must at last be decided by the Supreme Court of which he is a member. They justly respect the high responsibilities of their position and the notorious feelings of the people, by keeping themselves aloof from the altercations and animosities, the differences and the difficulties of party strife. Justice McLean is an exception." Unfortunately, McLean did not take warning by these merited censures; and a public expression of his views on the slavery issue in 1856 again elicited strong Congressional disapprobation for "an extrajudicial opinion which has excited much surprise and

[1] *30th Cong., 2d Sess.*, Jan. 17, 23, 1849. The *Philadelphia North American*, a Whig paper and an ardent admirer of Judge McLean, referred, Jan. 19, 25, 1849, to Senator Foote's attack as "wanton and gross"; "a wanton and libellous assault, as destitute of truth as it was vile in expression", and stated that it called out " a general expression of derision from the chamber." Other papers, however, greatly deplored Judge McLean's action; see *National Intelligencer*, Jan. 22, 23, 1849; *Pennsylvanian*, Jan. 20, 22, 25, 1849.

regret." "In exciting times like these," it was said, "when all earthly tribunals, in order to command respect, must be firm, unswerving, and above raving, popular clamor; when, too, the merits of the question were much involved in a case to come before him as one of the Judges of the last resort — to have made a parade of his opinion, thus intermingling with the partisan debates of a passing hour — cannot certainly commend him to the approval of an intelligent public." [1]

While it thus appears that the South had more cause than the North to complain of political bias shown by a Judge of the Court, the charge that the Court was constituted for the sole purpose of upholding slavery continued to be reiterated by the abolitionists, not only in the Senate but in their newspapers. "The people had been changing the Senate on the slavery issue," they said, but the slavery men had "quietly and without any excitement, with no word of remonstrance on the part of the North, in a strictly constitutional way, obtained the nomination and approval of a majority of Southerners upon the bench of the Supreme Court." [2] Violent personal attacks upon the Judges themselves became frequent in the press. Of Curtis, the *New York Tribune* wrote: "He is not a Massachusetts Judge. He is a slave-catching Judge, appointed to office as a reward for his professional support given to the Fugitive Slave bill. . . . Having had so many exhibitions of the ingenuity and adroitness of Mr.

---

[1] *34th Cong., 1st Sess., App.*, 982 *et seq.*, speech of James A. Stewart of Maryland, in the House, July 23, 1856.

[2] *Independent*, Jan. 1, March 12, 1857; see also *New York Tribune*, May 14, 1856; *New York Courier*, Dec. 23, 1856.

As an example of the extreme language used by the Abolitionists, the *Washington Union*, Jan. 14, 1851, quoted from an article in the *Boston Chronotype*, twenty thousand copies of which were circulated among the lawyers of the country, in which Judge Story and other Judges of the Court were spoken of "as if they were a set of ignorant and corrupt knaves, wilfully perverting the Constitution, disregarding its mandates and pandering to the prejudices and interests of the South."

Curtis on the side of tyranny and injustice, they would like, for once at least, and just for a change, if nothing else, to see him employ his abilities on behalf of justice and freedom." Judge Grier was attacked by the same paper in a diatribe against the Judges from Pennsylvania: "What other member of the Federal Union has, in its most violent fermentation, ever thrown to the surface such a judicial trio as Baldwin, Grier, and (District Judge) Kane?" Judge Nelson was equally obnoxious; and even Judge McLean was referred to as having given "frequent instance of his ready subserviency to the slaveholders." [1] Of Chief Justice Taney, at this time, much milder views were expressed by the abolitionist press than of some of the other Judges; and in view of the onslaught on Taney, only two years later, the following letter from the *Tribune's* Washington correspondent, in December, 1855 is of singular interest: [2]

As the Court is now constituted, consisting of nine Judges, he has held and exercised a moral balance of power of vast advantage in the interpretation of large constitutional questions, while it served as an effective check upon the latitudinarian dogmas of some of his colleagues. The importance of this restraint may not be sufficiently estimated by the country at large. . . .   But the value of such service is appreciated by the Bar, as it must be by members of the Court who sympathize and aid in the effort to protect the Court from the invasion of wild theories and nullifying notions wholly inconsistent with its spirit and letter. The loss of Judge Taney at any time would be a public calamity; but it would be peculiarly so now, when political considerations are pressed with so much pertinacity as almost to deprive the Executive of the exercise of that

[1] *New York Tribune*, April 9, 1855, referring to the indictment of Theodore Parker and Wendell Phillips, in the United States Circuit Court in Massachusetts, before Judge Curtis; *id.*, April 18, Oct. 16, 1855. See also *ibid.*, April 20, May 24, 1855, for editorials on "Judicial Infallibility" and "Judge Worshippers."

[2] *New York Tribune*, Dec. 18, 1855, letter from "Index" of Dec. 16.

discretion which he might otherwise be inclined to apply. If a vacancy should occur now, reasons enough would be trumped up for conferring that honor upon some faithful adherent, whose party claims would be allowed to overshadow the merit and integrity of the man upon whom the eye of the country would naturally rest.

While the anti-slavery men of the North thus expressed their distrust of the Court, there was also a section of the Southern Democrats — the secessionists or "fire-eaters" — led by William L. Yancey of Alabama, who contended that the Court had no power to pass on the rights of the States over slavery,[1] and in a radical speech directed against the Know-Nothing platform, in 1855, Yancey said that the proposition to submit the difficulty to the Court "is a monstrous doctrine, simply a revival of the federalism of John Adams' day. It was assailed by Jefferson in the revolution of 1798 and was successfully put down, and has never found a party at the South to urge it, until it was taken up by the Know-Nothings. There is no warrant for it in the Constitution. In the Constitution, a Judiciary is provided for to determine questions of property arising under the granted powers. Yet Know-Nothingism proposes to refer to the Supreme Court questions involving the reserved rights of the States, proposes to place the existence or non-existence of State sovereignty in the opinion of that Court. When or where, in what clause of the Constitution, did the Sovereign States who framed this government propose that any other but their own judgment should determine whether their reserved rights had been in-

---

[1] *Life and Times of William Lowndes Yancey* (1892), by John W. DuBose, 295, 307. Yancey wrote to William H. Northington, June 23, 1855: "I must think the revival of this long-repudiated and dangerous doctrine (that in all doubtful and disputed points of Federal law, the Constitution may be legally ascertained and expounded only by the judicial power of the United States) by so vigorous a party as that of the Know-Nothings portends evil to the country."

vaded and the mode and manner of redress for the grievance? . . . Imagine the great question of the right of a State to secede to be brought before such a Court for adjudication and the rendering of a decision adverse to the right.   What then?"

With such a campaign maintained by the anti-slavery men in the Senate and in the press for the express purpose of undermining popular confidence in the Judges, and with such radical views as to judicial power expressed by many in the South, it was small wonder that the status of the Court was seriously weakened.   Its members themselves felt their position keenly, and Judge Curtis wrote: "It cannot be doubted that the position of the Judges of the Supreme Court, at this time, is in a high degree onerous; and that while it exposes them to attack, such as no honest Judiciary, in any country within my knowledge have been subject to, they have not the consideration and support to which they are entitled.   Their salaries are so poor that not one Judge on the bench can live upon what the Government pays him, and the legislative branch of the Government are not friendly to them.   The people, though retaining some of the respect which, in the formation of the government, made the judicial element predominant over everything but the reserved power of the people, yet are ready to listen without indignation to the grossest charges against those who administer the judicial power." [1]   The attacks upon the Court in Ohio, California and Wisconsin for the exercise of its jurisdiction with reference to the State Courts also gravely impaired its supremacy; and the country was, with much reason, earnestly called upon by a leading law magazine to rally to the defense of the Judiciary. [2]

[1] *Curtis*, I, 174, letter of Dec. 20, 1854.
[2] *Appellate Jurisdiction of the Federal over the States Courts, Amer. Law Reg.* (Jan., 1856), IV, 129.

"Every disorganizing agency in the country appears to be at work. . . . There are those, we know, in some portions of the country, who profess to deride systematically all warnings of danger to the Union. This is the security of ignorance. Those who stand, as it were, upon the line which divides the sections, now so unhappily at variance, and can survey without prejudice the movements on either side see and know too well the imminence of the peril. There is such exasperation on one side and determination on the other, as was never known before; and it will need the greatest caution and good sense, to prevent an explosion which would rend the Union into fragments. . . . In such a crisis, it is the duty of all honest, thinking men to join in an endeavor to remove all those causes of controversy which are rankling and festering in the heart of the Nation, by submitting them to the peaceful arbitration of the Supreme Court. . . . To leave them, in the present temper of local politics, in the hands of State Courts could only tend to organize passion by giving it the sanction of law, and to convert party quarrels into the conflicts of States. Admit that the Federal Judiciary may in its time have been guilty of errors, that it has occasionally sought to wield more power than was safe, that it is as fallible as every other human institution. Yet it has been and is a vast agency for good; it has averted many a storm which threatened our peace, and has lent its powerful aid in uniting us together in the bonds of law and justice. Its very existence has proved a beacon of safety. And now, when the black cloud is again on the horizon, when the trembling of the earth and the stillness of the air are prophetic to our fears, and we turn to it instinctively for protection, — let us ask ourselves, with all its imagined faults, what is there that can replace it? Strip it of its power, and what shall we get in exchange?

Discord and confusion, statutes without obedience, Courts without authority, an anarchy of principles, and a chaos of decisions, till all law at last shall be extinguished by an appeal to arms."